11th International Conference on Parsing Technologies 2009

(IWPT 09)

Paris, France
7-9 October 2009

ISBN: 978-1-61738-572-8

Printed from e-media with permission by:

Curran Associates, Inc.
57 Morehouse Lane
Red Hook, NY 12571

Some format issues inherent in the e-media version may also appear in this print version.

Printed by Curran Associates, Inc. (2010)

For permission requests, please contact the Association for Computational Linguistics at the address below.

Association for Computational Linguistics
209 N. Eighth Street
Stroudsburg, Pennsylvania 18360

Phone: 1-570-476-8006
Fax: 1-570-476-0860

acl@aclweb.org

Additional copies of this publication are available from:

Curran Associates, Inc.
57 Morehouse Lane
Red Hook, NY 12571 USA
Phone: 845-758-0400
Fax: 845-758-2634
Email: curran@proceedings.com
Web: www.proceedings.com

Preface

Welcome to the Eleventh International Conference on Parsing Technologies, IWPT'09, in the splendid city of Paris.

IWPT'09 continues the tradition of biennial conferences on parsing technology organized by SIGPARSE, the Special Interest Group on Parsing of the Association for Computational Linguistics (ACL). The first conference, in 1989, took place in Pittsburgh and Hidden Valley, Pennsylvania. Subsequently, IWPT conferences were held in Cancun (Mexico) in 1991; Tilburg (Netherlands) and Durbuy (Belgium) in 1993; Prague and Karlovy Vary (Czech Republic) in 1995; Boston/Cambridge (Massachusetts) in 1997; Trento (Italy) in 2000; Beijing (China) in 2001; Nancy (France) in 2003; Vancouver (Canada) in 2005; and Prague (Czech Republic) in 2007.

Over the years the IWPT Workshops have become the major forum for researchers in natural language parsing. They have lead to the publication of four books on parsing technologies; a fifth one about to be published.

Where the IWPT conferences from 1989 through 2003 were standalone conferences, the last two IWPTs were organised as co-satellite event of large conferences: IWPT 2005 was co-loated with the HLT-EMNLP conference in Vancouver, and IWPT 2007 with the main ACL conference in Prague. This worked well from a logistic point of view, thanks to the support from ACL, but it was felt to lead to somewhat less interesting events than in the past, sitting in the shadow of the larger conference and competing with other satellite events. It was therefore decided to return to the standalone format in 2009, with INRIA Rocquencourt and the University of Paris 7 volunteering to take charge of the organisation. We would like to thank Eric de la Clergerie, Laurence Danlos, Benoit Sagot and the support staff at INRIA and University of Paris 7 for their efforts to realize IWPT'09.

IWPT'09 is fortunate to have three very distinguished invited speakers: John Carroll from the university of Sussex, Mark Johnson from Brown University, and Joakim Nivre from the University of Uppsala.

I would like to thank all the programme committee members for their careful and timely work, especially those that took up extra rewiewing obligations at very short notice and those who participated in discussions on diverging reviews. Special thanks go to Eric de la Clergerie, the programme chair, for organising the reviewing, designing the workshop programme and producing the proceedings. The scientific programme includes 14 accepted full papers and 27 accepted short papers (the latter being an all-time high for IWPT), covering virtually all currently hot topics in parsing technology. Together with the three invited talks by top experts in parsing, these papers provide a fascinating picture of the state of the art in parsing natural language, that I hope you will enjoy and will find inspiring.

Harry Bunt
IWPT'09 General Chair

Sponsored by

ACL/SIGParse

université PARIS DIDEROT PARIS 7

INSTITUT NATIONAL DE RECHERCHE EN INFORMATIQUE ET EN AUTOMATIQUE

INRIA

Springer

the language of science

ATALA

Association pour le Traitement Automatique des Langues

ANR Passage

Organizers

General Chair:

Harry Bunt (Tilburg University, Netherlands)

Programme Chair:

Éric Villemonte de la Clergerie (INRIA, France)

Logistic Arrangements Chair:

Laurence Danlos (University Paris Diderot, France)

Programme Committee:

Philippe Blache (CNRS/Provence University, Aix-en-Provence, France)
Harry Bunt (TiCC, Tilburg University, Netherlands)
David Chiang(USC/ISI, Marina del Rey, USA)
John Carroll (University of Sussex, Brighton, UK)
Stephen Clark (University of Cambridge, UK)
Éric Villemonte de la Clergerie (INRIA, Rocquencourt, France) (chair)
Jason Eisner (Johns Hopkins University, Baltimore, USA)
James Henderson (University of Edinburgh,UK)
Julia Hockenmaier (University of Pennsylvania, Philadelphia, USA)
Aravind Joshi (University of Pennsylvania, Philadelphia, USA)
Ronald Kaplan (Xerox Palo Alto Research Center, USA)
Martin Kay (Xerox Palo Alto Research Center, USA)
Sadao Kurohashi (University of Kyoto, Japan)
Alon Lavie (Carnegie-Mellon University, Pittsburgh, USA)
Rob Malouf (San Diego State University, USA)
Yuji Matsumoto (Nara Institute of Science and Technology, Japan)
Paola Merlo (University of Geneva, Switzerland)
Bob Moore (Microsoft, Redmond, USA)
Mark-Jan Nederhof (University of St. Andrews, Scotland)
Joakim Nivre (University of Uppsala, Sweden)
Gertjan van Noord (University of Groningen, Netherlands)
Stephan Oepen (University of Oslo, Norway)
Stefan Riezler (Xerox Palo Alto Research Center, USA)
Giorgio Satta (University of Padua, Italy)
Kenji Sagae (Institute for Creative Technologies, Marina del Rey, USA)
Khalil Sima'an (University of Amsterdam, Netherlands)
Hozumi Tanaka (Chukyo University, Japan)
K. Vijay-Shanker (University of Delaware, USA)
Éric Wehrli (LATL, University of Geneva, Switzerland)
David Weir (University of Sussex, Brighton, UK)
Shuly Wintner (University of Haifa, Israel)
Dekai Wu (Hong Kong University of Science and Technology, China)

Additional Reviewers:

Tejaswini Deoskar (ILLC, University of Amsterdam, Netherlands)
Sylvain Schmitz (ENS Cachan, France)

Invited Speakers:

John Carroll (University of Sussex, Brighton, UK)
Mark Johnson (Brown University, USA)
Joakim Nivre (University of Uppsala, Sweden)

Panel Chair:

Josef van Genabith (DCU, Dublin, Ireland)

Table of Contents

Conference Program

Wednesday, October 7, 2009

9:00–9:15 Opening Remarks

9:15–10:15 Invited Talk by John Carroll

Coffee Break and Poster Display

10:45–11:15 *Parsing Algorithms based on Tree Automata*
Andreas Maletti and Giorgio Satta

11:15–11:45 *Weighted parsing of trees*
Mark-Jan Nederhof

11:45–12:20 **Short Paper Session I**

Automatic Adaptation of Annotation Standards for Dependency Parsing ? Using Projected Treebank as Source Corpus
Wenbin Jiang and Qun Liu

Learning Stochastic Bracketing Inversion Transduction Grammars with a Cubic Time Biparsing Algorithm
Markus Saers, Joakim Nivre and Dekai Wu

Empirical lower bounds on translation unit error rate for the full class of inversion transduction grammars
Anders Søgaard and Dekai Wu

Lunch

14:00–14:30 *Predictive Text Entry using Syntax and Semantics*
Sebastian Ganslandt, Jakob Jörwall and Pierre Nugues

14:30–15:00 *Parsing Formal Languages using Natural Language Parsing Techniques*
Jens Nilsson, Welf Löwe, Johan Hall and Joakim Nivre

15:00–16:00 **Short Paper Session II**

An Incremental Earley Parser for Simple Range Concatenation Grammar
Laura Kallmeyer and Wolfgang Maier

Deductive Parsing in Interaction Grammars
Joseph Le Roux

Synchronous Rewriting in Treebanks
Laura Kallmeyer, Wolfgang Maier and Giorgio Satta

Wednesday, October 7, 2009 (continued)

An Improved Oracle for Dependency Parsing with Online Reordering
Joakim Nivre, Marco Kuhlmann and Johan Hall

Two stage constraint based hybrid approach to free word order language dependency parsing
Akshar Bharati, Samar Husain, Dipti Misra and Rajeev Sangal

Coffee Break and Poster Display

16:35–17:00 **Short Paper Session III**

Analysis of Discourse Structure with Syntactic Dependencies and Data-Driven Shift-Reduce Parsing
Kenji Sagae

Evaluating Contribution of Deep Syntactic Information to Shallow Semantic Analysis
Sumire Uematsu and Jun'ichi Tsujii

17:00–17:30 *Weight Pushing and Binarization for Fixed-Grammar Parsing*
Matt Post and Daniel Gildea

17:30–18:00 *Co-Parsing with Competitive Models*
Lidia Khmylko, Kilian A. Foth and Wolfgang Menzel

Thursday, October 8, 2009

9:00–10:00 Invited Talk by Mark Johnson

Coffee Break and Poster Display

10:30–11:00 *Capturing Consistency between Intra-clause and Inter-clause Relations in Knowledge-rich Dependency and Case Structure Analysis*
Daisuke Kawahara and Sadao Kurohashi

11:00–11:30 *Constructing parse forests that include exactly the n-best PCFG trees*
Pierre Boullier, Alexis Nasr and Benoît Sagot

11:30–12:30 **Short Paper Session IV**

Hebrew Dependency Parsing: Initial Results
Yoav Goldberg and Michael Elhadad

Scalable Discriminative Parsing for German
Yannick Versley and Ines Rehbein

Improving generative statistical parsing with semi-supervised word clustering
Marie Candito and Benoît Crabbé

Thursday, October 8, 2009 (continued)

Application of feature propagation to dependency parsing
Kepa Bengoetxea and Koldo Gojenola

Guessing the Grammatical Function of a Non-Root F-Structure in LFG
Anton Bryl, Josef Van Genabith and Yvette Graham

Lunch

14:00–14:30 *Cross parser evaluation : a French Treebanks study*
Djamé Seddah, Marie Candito and Benoît Crabbé

14:30–15:00 *Transition-Based Parsing of the Chinese Treebank using a Global Discriminative Model*
Yue Zhang and Stephen Clark

15:00–15:25 **Short Paper Session V**

Grammar Error Detection with Best Approximated Parse
Jean-Philippe Prost

The effect of correcting grammatical errors on parse probabilities
Joachim Wagner and Jennifer Foster

Coffee Break and Poster Display

16:00–18:15 Panel: Statistical Parsing for Morphologically-rich Languages

Friday, October 9, 2009

9:00-10:00 Invited Talk by Joakim Nivre

10:00–10:30 *Effective Analysis of Causes and Inter-dependencies of Parsing Errors*
Tadayoshi Hara, Yusuke Miyao and Jun'ichi Tsujii

10:30–11:00 *Clustering Words by Syntactic Similarity improves Dependency Parsing of Predicate-argument Structures*
Kenji Sagae and Andrew S. Gordon

Coffee Break and Poster Display

11:30–12:30 **Short Paper Session VI**

The chunk as the period of the functions length and frequency of words on the syntagmatic axis
Jacques Vergne

Using a maximum entropy-based tagger to improve a very fast vine parser
Anders Søgaard and Jonas Kuhn

Friday, October 9, 2009 (continued)

HPSG Supertagging: A Sequence Labeling View
Yao-zhong Zhang, Takuya Matsuzaki and Jun'ichi Tsujii

Smoothing fine-grained PCFG lexicons
Tejaswini Deoskar, Mats Rooth and Khalil Sima'an

Wide-coverage parsing of speech transcripts
Jeroen Geertzen

Lunch

13:45–14:15 ACL/SIGParse Business Meeting

14:15–15:15 **Short Paper Session VII**

Interactive Predictive Parsing
Ricardo Sánchez-Sáez, Joan-Andreu Sánchez and José-Miguel Benedí

Using Treebanking Discriminants as Parse Disambiguation Features
Md. Faisal Mahbub Chowdhury, Yi Zhang and Valia Kordoni

Heuristic search in a cognitive model of human parsing
John Hale

Dependency Parsing with Energy-based Reinforcement Learning
Lidan Zhang and Kwok Ping Chan

A generative re-ranking model for dependency parsing
Federico Sangati, Willem Zuidema and Rens Bod

Coffee Break and Poster Display

15:45–16:15 *Dependency Constraints for Lexical Disambiguation*
Guillaume Bonfante, Bruno Guillaume and Mathieu Morey

16:15–16:45 *Parsing Directed Acyclic Graphs with Range Concatenation Grammars*
Pierre Boullier and Benoît Sagot

16:45–17:00 Closing Remarks

Invited Talks

Moving Parsing into the Real World: Noisy Text, Grammatical Representations and Applications

John Carroll
University of Sussex, Brighton, UK
J.A.Carroll@sussex.ac.uk

Much recent research in natural language parsing takes as input carefully crafted, edited text, often from newspapers. However, many real-world applications involve processing text which is not written carefully by a native speaker, is produced for an eventual audience of only one, and is in essence ephemeral. In this talk I will present a number of research and commercial applications of this type which I and collaborators are developing, in which we parse text as diverse as mobile phone text messages, non-native language learner essays, internet chat, and primary care medical notes. I will discuss the problems these types of text pose for a parser, and outline how we integrate information from parsing into applications.

Learning Rules with Adaptor Grammars

Mark Johnson
Brown University, USA
Mark_Johnson@Brown.edu

Nonparametric Bayesian methods are interesting because they may provide a way of learning the appropriate units of generalization (i.e., the "rules" of a grammar) as well as the generalization's probability or weight (i.e., the rule's probability). Adaptor Grammars are a framework for stating a variety of hierarchical nonparametric Bayesian models, where the units of generalization can be viewed as kinds of PCFG rules. This talk describes the mathematical and computational properties of Adaptor Grammars and linguistic applications such as word segmentation, syllabification and named entity recognition. The later part of the talk reviews MCMC inference and describes the MCMC algorithms we use to sample adaptor grammars.

Joint work with Sharon Goldwater and Tom Griffiths.

Discontinuous Dependency Parsing

Joakim Nivre
University of Uppsala, Sweden
joakim.nivre@lingfil.uu.se

There is a strong tendency in natural language syntax such that elements that have a direct syntactic relation are also adjacent in the surface realization of a sentence. Nevertheless, notable exceptions to this generalization exist in practically all languages and are especially common in languages with free or flexible word order. Syntactic theorists, on the one hand, have developed a variety of representational devices for dealing with these exceptions, including phonetically null elements, gap threading, and non-projective dependency trees. Syntactic parsers, on the other hand, use these devices very restrictively since they add to the complexity of an already daunting task. This is especially true of data-driven parsers, where discontinuity is often simply ignored. In this talk, I will review techniques for dealing with discontinuous structures in the framework of dependency parsing, focusing on parsing algorithms that build structures from non-adjacent elements and in particular transition-based algorithms that use online reordering.

Parsing Algorithms based on Tree Automata

Andreas Maletti
Departament de Filologies Romàniques
Universitat Rovira i Virgili, Tarragona, Spain
andreas.maletti@urv.cat

Giorgio Satta
Department of Information Engineering
University of Padua, Italy
satta@dei.unipd.it

Abstract

We investigate several algorithms related to the parsing problem for weighted automata, under the assumption that the input is a string rather than a tree. This assumption is motivated by several natural language processing applications. We provide algorithms for the computation of parse-forests, best tree probability, inside probability (called partition function), and prefix probability. Our algorithms are obtained by extending to weighted tree automata the Bar-Hillel technique, as defined for context-free grammars.

1 Introduction

Tree automata are finite-state devices that recognize tree languages, that is, sets of trees. There is a growing interest nowadays in the natural language parsing community, and especially in the area of syntax-based machine translation, for probabilistic tree automata (PTA) viewed as suitable representations of grammar models. In fact, probabilistic tree automata are generatively more powerful than probabilistic context-free grammars (PCFGs), when we consider the latter as devices that generate tree languages. This difference can be intuitively understood if we consider that a computation by a PTA uses hidden states, drawn from a finite set, that can be used to transfer information within the tree structure being recognized.

As an example, in written English we can empirically observe different distributions in the expansion of so-called noun phrase (NP) nodes, in the contexts of subject and direct-object positions, respectively. This can be easily captured using some states of a PTA that keep a record of the different contexts. In contrast, PCFGs are unable to model these effects, because NP node expansion should be independent of the context in the derivation. This problem for PCFGs is usually solved by resorting to so-called parental annotations (Johnson, 1998), but this, of course, results in a different tree language, since these annotations will appear in the derived tree.

Most of the theoretical work on parsing and estimation based on PTA has assumed that the input is a tree (Graehl et al., 2008), in accordance with the very definition of these devices. However, both in parsing as well as in machine translation, the input is most often represented as a string rather than a tree. When the input is a string, some trick is applied to map the problem back to the case of an input tree. As an example in the context of machine translation, assume a probabilistic tree transducer T as a translation model, and an input string w to be translated. One can then intermediately construct a tree automaton M_w that recognizes the set of all possible trees that have w as yield, with internal nodes from the input alphabet of T. This automaton M_w is further transformed into a tree transducer implementing a partial identity translation, and such a transducer is composed with T (relation composition). This is usually called the 'cascaded' approach. Such an approach can be easily applied also to parsing problems.

In contrast with the cascaded approach above, which may be rather inefficient, in this paper we investigate a more direct technique for parsing strings based on weighted and probabilistic tree automata. We do this by extending to weighted tree automata the well-known Bar-Hillel construction defined for context-free grammars (Bar-Hillel et al., 1964) and for weighted context-free grammars (Nederhof and Satta, 2003). This provides an abstract framework under which several parsing algorithms can be directly derived, based on weighted tree automata. We discuss several applications of our results, including algorithms for the computation of parse-forests, best tree probability, inside probability (called partition function), and prefix probability.

Proceedings of the 11th International Conference on Parsing Technologies (IWPT), pages 1–12,
Paris, October 2009.

2 Preliminary definitions

Let S be a nonempty set and $\cdot$ be an associative binary operation on S. If S contains an element 1 such that $1 \cdot s = s = s \cdot 1$ for every $s \in S$, then $(S, \cdot, 1)$ is a monoid. A monoid $(S, \cdot, 1)$ is commutative if the equation $s_1 \cdot s_2 = s_2 \cdot s_1$ holds for every $s_1, s_2 \in S$. A **commutative semiring** $(S, +, \cdot, 0, 1)$ is a nonempty set S on which a binary addition $+$ and a binary multiplication $\cdot$ have been defined such that the following conditions are satisfied:

- $(S, +, 0)$ and $(S, \cdot, 1)$ are commutative monoids,
- $\cdot$ distributes over $+$ from both sides, and
- $s \cdot 0 = 0 = 0 \cdot s$ for every $s \in S$.

A **weighted string automaton**, abbreviated WSA, (Schützenberger, 1961; Eilenberg, 1974) is a system $M = (Q, \Sigma, \mathcal{S}, I, \nu, F)$ where

- Q is a finite alphabet of states,
- Σ is a finite alphabet of input symbols,
- $\mathcal{S} = (S, +, \cdot, 0, 1)$ is a semiring,
- $I \colon Q \to S$ assigns initial weights,
- $\nu \colon Q \times \Sigma \times Q \to S$ assigns a weight to each transition, and
- $F \colon Q \to S$ assigns final weights.

We now proceed with the semantics of M. Let $w \in \Sigma^*$ be an input string of length n. For each integer i with $1 \le i \le n$, we write $w(i)$ to denote the i-th character of w. The set $\mathrm{Pos}(w)$ of **positions** of w is $\{i \mid 0 \le i \le n\}$. A **run** of M on w is a mapping $r \colon \mathrm{Pos}(w) \to Q$. We denote the set of all such runs by $\mathrm{Run}_M(w)$. The weight of a run $r \in \mathrm{Run}_M(w)$ is

$$\mathrm{wt}_M(r) = \prod_{i=1}^{n} \nu(r(i-1), w(i), r(i)) \ .$$

We assume the right-hand side of the above equation evaluates to 1 in case $n = 0$. The WSA M recognizes the mapping $M \colon \Sigma^* \to S$, which is defined for every $w \in \Sigma^*$ of length n by[1]

$$M(w) = \sum_{r \in \mathrm{Run}_M(w)} I(r(0)) \cdot \mathrm{wt}_M(r) \cdot F(r(n)) \ .$$

In order to define weighted tree automata (Berstel and Reutenauer, 1982; Ésik and Kuich, 2003; Borchardt, 2005), we need to introduce some additional notation. Let Σ be a **ranked alphabet**, that is, an alphabet whose symbols have an associated arity. We write Σ_k to denote the set of all k-ary symbols in Σ. We use a special symbol $e \in \Sigma_0$ to syntactically represent the empty string ε. The set of **Σ-trees**, denoted by T_Σ, is the smallest set satisfying both of the following conditions

- for every $\alpha \in \Sigma_0$, the single node labeled α, written $\alpha()$, is a tree of T_Σ,
- for every $\sigma \in \Sigma_k$ with $k \ge 1$ and for every $t_1, \ldots, t_k \in T_\Sigma$, the tree with a root node labeled σ and trees $t_1, \ldots, t_k$ as its k children, written $\sigma(t_1, \ldots, t_k)$, belongs to T_Σ.

As a convention, throughout this paper we assume that $\sigma(t_1, \ldots, t_k)$ denotes $\sigma()$ if $k = 0$. The size of the tree $t \in T_\Sigma$, written $|t|$, is defined as the number of occurrences of symbols from Σ in t.

Let $t = \sigma(t_1, \ldots, t_k)$. The yield of t is recursively defined by

$$\mathrm{yd}(t) = \begin{cases} \sigma & \text{if } \sigma \in \Sigma_0 \setminus \{e\} \\ \varepsilon & \text{if } \sigma = e \\ \mathrm{yd}(t_1) \cdots \mathrm{yd}(t_k) & \text{otherwise.} \end{cases}$$

The set of **positions** of t, denoted by $\mathrm{Pos}(t)$, is recursively defined by

$$\mathrm{Pos}(\sigma(t_1, \ldots, t_k)) = \{\varepsilon\} \cup \{iw \mid 1 \le i \le k, w \in \mathrm{Pos}(t_i)\} \ .$$

Note that $|t| = |\mathrm{Pos}(t)|$ and, according to our convention, when $k = 0$ the above definition provides $\mathrm{Pos}(\sigma()) = \{\varepsilon\}$. We denote the symbol of t at position w by $t(w)$ and its rank by $\mathrm{rk}_t(w)$.

A **weighted tree automaton** (WTA) is a system $M = (Q, \Sigma, \mathcal{S}, \mu, F)$ where

- Q is a finite alphabet of states,
- Σ is a finite ranked alphabet of input symbols,
- $\mathcal{S} = (S, +, \cdot, 0, 1)$ is a semiring,
- μ is an indexed family $(\mu_k)_{k \in \mathbb{N}}$ of mappings $\mu_k : \Sigma_k \to S^{Q \times Q^k}$, and
- $F \colon Q \to S$ assigns final weights.

In the above definition, Q^k is the set of all strings over Q having length k, with $Q^0 = \{\varepsilon\}$. Further note that $S^{Q \times Q^k}$ is the set of all matrices with elements in S, row index set Q, and column index set Q^k. Correspondingly, we will use the common matrix notation and write instances of μ in the form $\mu_k(\sigma)_{q_0, q_1 \cdots q_k}$. Finally, we assume $q_1 \cdots q_k = \varepsilon$ if $k = 0$.

We define the semantics also in terms of runs. Let $t \in T_\Sigma$. A **run** of M on t is a mapping $r \colon \mathrm{Pos}(t) \to Q$. We denote the set of all such runs

[1] We overload the symbol M to denote both an automaton and its recognized mapping. However, the intended meaning will always be clear from the context.

by $\mathrm{Run}_M(t)$. The weight of a run $r \in \mathrm{Run}_M(t)$ is

$$\mathrm{wt}_M(r) = \prod_{\substack{w \in \mathrm{Pos}(t) \\ \mathrm{rk}_t(w)=k}} \mu_k(t(w))_{r(w),r(w1)\cdots r(wk)} \cdot$$

Note that, according to our convention, the string $r(w1)\cdots r(wk)$ denotes ε when $k = 0$. The WTA M recognizes the mapping $M\colon T_\Sigma \to S$, which is defined by

$$M(t) = \sum_{r \in \mathrm{Run}_M(t)} \mathrm{wt}_M(r) \cdot F(r(\varepsilon))$$

for every $t \in T_\Sigma$. We say that t is **recognized** by M if $M(t) \neq 0$.

In our complexity analyses, we use the following measures. The size of a transition (p, α, q) in (the domain of ν in) a WSA is $|p\alpha q| = 3$. The size of a transition in a WTA, viewed as an instance $(\sigma, q_0, q_1 \cdots q_k)$ of some mapping μ_k, is defined as $|\sigma q_0 \cdots q_k|$, that is, the rank of the input symbol occurring in the transition plus two. Finally, the size $|M|$ of an automaton M (WSA or WTA) is defined as the sum of the sizes of its nonzero transitions. Note that this does not take into account the size of the representation of the weights.

3 Binarization

We introduce in this section a specific transformation of WTA, called **binarization**, that reduces the transitions of the automaton to some normal form in which no more than three states are involved. This transformation maps the set of recognized trees into a special binary form, in such a way that the yields of corresponding trees and their weights are both preserved. We use this transformation in the next section in order to guarantee the computational efficiency of the parsing algorithm we develop. The standard 'first-child, next-sibling' binary encoding for trees (Knuth, 1997) would eventually result in a transformed WTA of quadratic size. To obtain instead a linear size transformation, we introduce a slightly modified encoding (Högberg et al., 2009, Section 4), which is inspired by (Carme et al., 2004) and the classical currying operation.

Let Σ be a ranked alphabet and assume a fresh symbol $@ \notin \Sigma$ (corresponding to the basic list concatenation operator). Moreover, let $\Delta = \Delta_2 \cup \Delta_1 \cup \Delta_0$ be the ranked alphabet such that $\Delta_2 = \{@\}$, $\Delta_1 = \bigcup_{k \geq 1} \Sigma_k$, and $\Delta_0 = \Sigma_0$. In

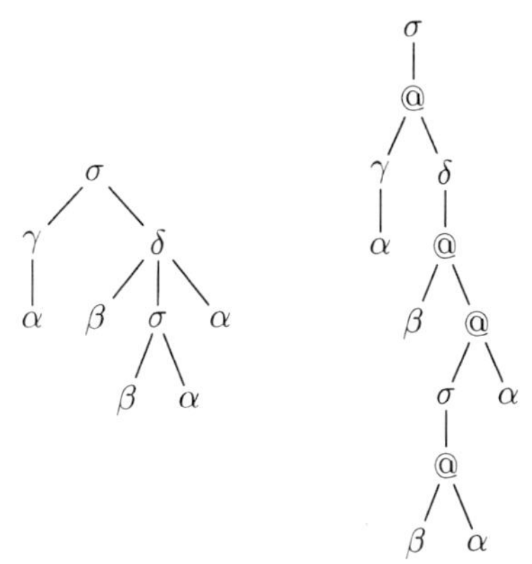

Figure 1: Input tree t and encoded tree $\mathrm{enc}(t)$.

words, all the original non-nullary symbols from Σ are now unary, $@$ is binary, and the original nullary symbols from Σ have their rank preserved. We encode each tree of T_Σ as a tree of T_Δ as follows:

- $\mathrm{enc}(\alpha) = \alpha()$ for every $\alpha \in \Sigma_0$,
- $\mathrm{enc}(\gamma(t)) = \gamma(\mathrm{enc}(t))$ for every $\gamma \in \Sigma_1$ and $t \in T_\Sigma$, and
- for $k \geq 2$, $\sigma \in \Sigma_k$, and $t_1, \ldots, t_k \in T_\Sigma$

$$\mathrm{enc}(\sigma(t_1, \ldots, t_k)) = \sigma(@(\mathrm{enc}(t_1), \ldots @(\mathrm{enc}(t_{k-1}), \mathrm{enc}(t_k)) \cdots)).$$

An example of the above encoding is illustrated in Figure 1. Note that $|\mathrm{enc}(t)| \in \mathcal{O}(|t|)$ for every $t \in T_\Sigma$. Furthermore, t can be easily reconstructed from $\mathrm{enc}(t)$ in linear time.

Definition 1 Let $M = (Q, \Sigma, \mathcal{S}, \mu, F)$ be a WTA. The encoded WTA $\mathrm{enc}(M)$ is $(P, \Delta, \mathcal{S}, \mu', F')$ where

$$P = \{[q] \mid q \in Q\} \cup \\ \cup \{[w] \mid \mu_k(\sigma)_{q,uw} \neq 0, u \in Q^*,\ w \in Q^+\},$$

$F'([q]) = F(q)$ for every $q \in Q$, and the transitions are constructed as follows:

(i) $\mu'_0(\alpha)_{[q],\varepsilon} = \mu_0(\alpha)_{q,\varepsilon}$ for every $\alpha \in \Sigma_0$,
(ii) $\mu'_1(\sigma)_{[q],[w]} = \mu_k(\sigma)_{q,w}$ for every $\sigma \in \Sigma_k$, $k \geq 1$, $q \in Q$, and $w \in Q^k$, and
(iii) $\mu'_2(@)_{[qw],[q][w]} = 1$ for every $[qw] \in P$ with $|w| \geq 1$ and $q \in Q$.

All remaining entries in F' and μ' are 0. □

Notice that each transition of $\mathrm{enc}(M)$ involves no more than three states from P. Furthermore, we have $|\mathrm{enc}(M)| \in \mathcal{O}(|M|)$. The following result is rather intuitive (Högberg et al., 2009, Lemma 4.2); its proof is therefore omitted.

Theorem 1 *Let $M = (Q, \Sigma, \mathcal{S}, \mu, F)$ be a* WTA, *and let $M' = \mathrm{enc}(M)$. Then $M(t) = M'(\mathrm{enc}(t))$ for every $t \in T_\Sigma$.* □

4 Bar-Hillel construction

The so-called Bar-Hillel construction was proposed in (Bar-Hillel et al., 1964) to show that the intersection of a context-free language and a regular language is still a context-free language. The proof of the result consisted in an effective construction of a context-free grammar $\mathrm{Prod}(G, N)$ from a context-free grammar G and a finite automaton N, such that $\mathrm{Prod}(G, N)$ generates the intersection of the languages generated by G and N.

It was later recognized that the Bar-Hillel construction constitutes one of the foundations of the theory of tabular parsing based on context-free grammars. More precisely, by taking the finite automaton N to be of some special kind, accepting only a single string, the Bar-Hillel construction provides a framework under which several well-known tabular parsing algorithms can easily be derived, that were proposed much later in the literature.

In this section we extend the Bar-Hillel construction to WTA, with a similar purpose of establishing an abstract framework under which one could easily derive parsing algorithms based on these devices. In order to guarantee computational efficiency, we avoid here stating the Bar-Hillel construction for WTA with alphabets of arbitrary rank. The next result therefore refers to WTA with alphabet symbols of rank at most 2. These may, but need not, be automata obtained through the binary encoding discussed in Section 3.

Definition 2 Let $M = (Q, \Sigma, \mathcal{S}, \mu, F)$ be a WTA such that the maximum rank of a symbol in Σ is 2, and let $N = (P, \Sigma_0 \setminus \{e\}, \mathcal{S}, I, \nu, G)$ be a WSA over the same semiring. We construct the WTA

$$\mathrm{Prod}(M, N) = (P \times Q \times P, \Sigma, \mathcal{S}, \mu', F')$$

as follows:

(i) For every $\sigma \in \Sigma_2$, states $p_0, p_1, p_2 \in P$, and states $q_0, q_1, q_2 \in Q$ let

$$\mu_2'(\sigma)_{(p_0,q_0,p_2),(p_0,q_1,p_1)(p_1,q_2,p_2)} = \mu_2(\sigma)_{q_0,q_1q_2} \ .$$

(ii) For every symbol $\gamma \in \Sigma_1$, states $p_0, p_1 \in P$, and states $q_0, q_1 \in Q$ let

$$\mu_1'(\gamma)_{(p_0,q_0,p_1),(p_0,q_1,p_1)} = \mu_1(\gamma)_{q_0,q_1} \ .$$

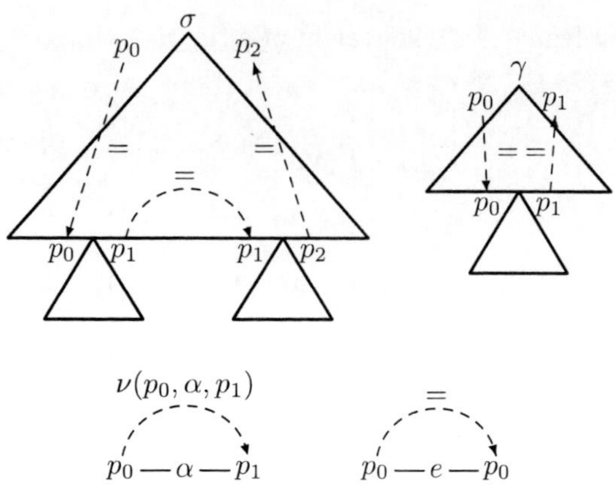

Figure 2: Information transport in the first and third components of the states in our Bar-Hillel construction.

(iii) For every symbol $\alpha \in \Sigma_0$, states $p_0, p_1 \in P$, and $q \in Q$ let

$$\mu_0'(\alpha)_{(p_0,q,p_1),\varepsilon} = \mu_0(\alpha)_{q,\varepsilon} \cdot s$$

where

$$s = \begin{cases} \nu(p_0, \alpha, p_1) & \text{if } \alpha \neq e \\ 1 & \text{if } \alpha = e \text{ and } p_0 = p_1 \ . \end{cases}$$

(iv) $F'(p_0, q, p_1) = I(p_0) \cdot F(q) \cdot G(p_1)$ for every $p_0, p_1 \in P$ and $q \in Q$.

All remaining entries in μ' are 0. □

Theorem 2 *Let M and N be as in Definition 2, and let $M' = \mathrm{Prod}(M, N)$. If $\mathcal{S}$ is commutative, then $M'(t) = M(t) \cdot N(\mathrm{yd}(t))$ for every $t \in T_\Sigma$.* □

PROOF For a state $q \in P \times Q \times P$, we write q_i to denote its i-th component with $i \in \{1, 2, 3\}$. Let $t \in T_\Sigma$ and $r \in \mathrm{Run}_{M'}(t)$ be a run of M' on t. We call the run r **well-formed** if for every $w \in \mathrm{Pos}(t)$:

(i) if $t(w) = e$, then $r(w)_1 = r(w)_3$,

(ii) if $t(w) \notin \Sigma_0$, then:

(a) $r(w)_1 = r(w1)_1$,

(b) $r(w\,\mathrm{rk}_t(w))_3 = r(w)_3$, and

(c) if $\mathrm{rk}_t(w) = 2$, then $r(w1)_3 = r(w2)_1$.

Note that no conditions are placed on the second components of the states in r. We try to illustrate the conditions in Figure 2.

A standard proof shows that $\mathrm{wt}_{M'}(r) = 0$ for all runs $r \in \mathrm{Run}_{M'}(t)$ that are not well-formed. We now need to map runs of M' back into 'corresponding' runs for M and N. Let us fix some $t \in T_\Sigma$ and some well-formed run $r \in \mathrm{Run}_{M'}(t)$.

We define the run $\pi_M(r) \in \text{Run}_M(t)$ by letting

$$\pi_M(r)(w) = r(w)_2,$$

for every $w \in \text{Pos}(t)$. Let $\{w_1, \ldots, w_n\} = \{w' \mid w' \in \text{Pos}(t),\ t(w') \in \Sigma_0 \setminus \{e\}\}$, with $w_1 < \cdots < w_n$ according to the lexicographic order on $\text{Pos}(t)$. We also define the run $\pi_N(r) \in \text{Run}_N(\text{yd}(t))$ by letting

$$\pi_N(r)(i-1) = r(w_i)_1,$$

for every $1 \leq i < n$, and

$$\pi_N(r)(n) = r(w_n)_3 \ .$$

Note that conversely every run of M on t and every run of N on $\text{yd}(t)$ yield a unique run of M' on t.

Now, we claim that

$$\text{wt}_{M'}(r) = \text{wt}_M(\pi_M(r)) \cdot \text{wt}_N(\pi_N(r))$$

for every well-formed run $r \in \text{Run}_{M'}(t)$. To prove the claim, let $t = \sigma(t_1, \ldots, t_k)$ for some $\sigma \in \Sigma_k$, $k \leq 2$, and $t_1, \ldots, t_k \in T_\Sigma$. Moreover, for every $1 \leq i \leq k$ let $r_i(w) = r(iw)$ for every $w \in \text{Pos}(t_i)$. Note that $r_i \in \text{Run}_{M'}(t_i)$ and that r_i is well-formed for every $1 \leq i \leq k$.

For the induction base, let $\sigma \in \Sigma_0$; we can write

$$\begin{aligned}
&\text{wt}_{M'}(r) \\
&= \mu'_0(\sigma)_{r(\varepsilon),\varepsilon} \\
&= \begin{cases} \mu_0(\sigma)_{r(\varepsilon)_2,\varepsilon} \cdot \nu(r(\varepsilon)_1, \sigma, r(\varepsilon)_3) & \text{if } \sigma \neq e \\ \mu_0(\sigma)_{r(\varepsilon)_2,\varepsilon} & \text{if } \sigma = e \end{cases} \\
&= \text{wt}_M(\pi_M(r)) \cdot \text{wt}_N(\pi_N(r)) \ .
\end{aligned}$$

In the induction step (i.e., $k > 0$) we have

$$\begin{aligned}
&\text{wt}_{M'}(r) \\
&= \prod_{\substack{w \in \text{Pos}(t) \\ \text{rk}_t(w) = n}} \mu'_n(t(w))_{r(w), r(w1)\cdots r(wn)} \\
&= \mu'_k(\sigma)_{r(\varepsilon), r(1)\cdots r(k)} \cdot \prod_{i=1}^{k} \text{wt}_{M'}(r_i) \ .
\end{aligned}$$

Using the fact that r is well-formed, commutativity, and the induction hypothesis, we obtain

$$\begin{aligned}
&= \mu_k(\sigma)_{r(\varepsilon)_2, r(1)_2 \cdots r(k)_2} \cdot \\
&\quad \cdot \prod_{i=1}^{k} \Big(\text{wt}_M(\pi_M(r_i)) \cdot \text{wt}_N(\pi_N(r_i)) \Big) \\
&= \text{wt}_M(\pi_2(r)) \cdot \text{wt}_N(\pi_N(r)) \ ,
\end{aligned}$$

where in the last step we have again used the fact that r is well-formed. Using the auxiliary statement $\text{wt}_{M'}(r) = \text{wt}_M(\pi_M(r)) \cdot \text{wt}_N(\pi_N(r))$, the main proof now is easy.

$$\begin{aligned}
&M'(t) \\
&= \sum_{r \in \text{Run}_{M'}(t)} \text{wt}_{M'}(r) \cdot F'(r(\varepsilon)) \\
&= \sum_{\substack{r \in \text{Run}_{M'}(t) \\ r \text{ well-formed}}} \text{wt}_M(\pi_M(r)) \cdot \text{wt}_N(\pi_N(r)) \cdot \\
&\qquad \cdot I(r(\varepsilon)_1) \cdot F(r(\varepsilon)_2) \cdot G(r(\varepsilon)_3) \\
&= \Big(\sum_{r \in \text{Run}_M(t)} \text{wt}_M(r) \cdot F(r(\varepsilon)) \Big) \cdot \\
&\qquad \cdot \Big(\sum_{\substack{w = \text{yd}(t) \\ r \in \text{Run}_N(w)}} I(r(0)) \cdot \text{wt}_N(r) \cdot G(r(|w|)) \Big) \\
&= M(t) \cdot N(\text{yd}(t))
\end{aligned}$$

■

Let us analyze now the computational complexity of a possible implementation of the construction in Definition 2. In step (i), we could restrict the computation by considering only those transitions in M satisfying $\mu_2(\sigma)_{q_0, q_1 q_2} \neq 0$, which provides a number of choices in $\mathcal{O}(|M|)$. Combined with the choices for the states p_0, p_1, p_2 of N, this provides $\mathcal{O}(|M| \cdot |P|^3)$ non-zero transitions in $\text{Prod}(M, N)$. This is also a bound on the overall running time of step (i). Since we additionally assume that weights can be multiplied in constant time, it is not difficult to see that all of the remaining steps can be accommodated within such a time bound. We thus conclude that the construction in Definition 2 can be implemented to run in time and space $\mathcal{O}(|M| \cdot |P|^3)$.

5 Parsing applications

In this section we discuss several applications of the construction presented in Definition 2 that are relevant for parsing based on WTA models.

5.1 Parse forest

Parsing is usually defined as the problem of constructing a suitable representation for the set of all possible parse trees that are assigned to a given input string w by some grammar model. The set of all such parse trees is called **parse forest**. The extension of the Bar-Hillel construction that we have presented in Section 4 can be easily adapted to obtain a parsing algorithm for WTA models. This is described in what follows.

First, we should represent the input string w in a WSA that recognizes the language $\{w\}$. Such an automaton has a state set $P = \{p_0, \ldots, p_{|w|}\}$ and transition weights $\nu(p_{i-1}, w(i), p_i) = 1$ for each i with $1 \leq i \leq |w|$. We also set $I(p_0) = 1$ and $F(p_{|w|}) = 1$. Setting all the weights to 1 for a WSA N amounts to ignoring the weights, i.e., those weights will not contribute in any way when applying the Bar-Hillel construction.

Assume now that M is our grammar model, represented as a WTA. The WTA $\text{Prod}(M, N)$ constructed as in Definition 2 is not necessarily **trim**, meaning that it might contain transitions with non-zero weight that are never used in the recognition. Techniques for eliminating such useless transitions are well-known, see for instance (Gécseg and Steinby, 1984, Section II.6), and can be easily implemented to run in linear time. Once $\text{Prod}(M, N)$ is trim, we have a device that recognizes all and only those trees that are assigned by M to the input string w, and the weights of those trees are preserved, as seen in Theorem 2. The WTA $\text{Prod}(M, N)$ can then be seen as a representation of a parse forest for the input string w, and we conclude that the construction in Definition 2, combined with some WTA reduction algorithm, represents a parsing algorithm for WTA models working in cubic time on the length of the input string and in linear time on the size of the grammar model.

More interestingly, from the framework developed in Section 4, one can also design more efficient parsing algorithms based on WTA. Borrowing from standard ideas developed in the literature for parsing based on context-free grammars, one can specialize the construction in Definition 2 in such a way that the number of useless transitions generated for $\text{Prod}(M, N)$ is considerably reduced, resulting in a more efficient construction. This can be done by adopting some search strategy that guides the construction of $\text{Prod}(M, N)$ using knowledge of the input string w as well as knowledge about the source model M.

As an example, we can apply step (i) only on demand, that is, we process a transition $\mu'_2(\sigma)_{q_0,q_1q_2}$ in $\text{Prod}(M, N)$ only if we have already computed non-zero transitions of the form $\mu'_{k_1}(\sigma_1)_{q_1,w_1}$ and $\mu'_{k_2}(\sigma_2)_{q_2,w_2}$, for some $\sigma_1 \in \Sigma_{k_1}$, $w_1 \in Q^{k_1}$ and $\sigma_2 \in \Sigma_{k_2}$, $w_2 \in Q^{k_2}$ where Q is the state set of $\text{Prod}(M, N)$. The above amounts to a bottom-up strategy that is also used in the Cocke-Kasami-Younger recognition algorithm for context-free grammars (Younger, 1967).

More sophisticated strategies are also possible. For instance, one could adopt the Earley strategy developed for context-free grammar parsing (Earley, 1970). In this case, parsing is carried out in a top-down left-to-right fashion, and the binarization construction of Section 3 is carried out on the flight. This has the additional advantage that it would be possible to use WTA models that are not restricted to the special normal form of Section 3, still maintaining the cubic time complexity in the length of the input string. We do not pursue this idea any further in this paper, since our main goal here is to outline an abstract framework for parsing based on WTA models.

5.2 Probabilistic tree automata

Let us now look into specific semirings that are relevant for statistical natural language processing. The semiring of non-negative real numbers is $\mathbb{R}_{\geq 0} = (\mathbb{R}_{\geq 0}, +, \cdot, 0, 1)$. For the remainder of the section, let $M = (Q, \Sigma, \mathbb{R}_{\geq 0}, \mu, F)$ be a WTA over $\mathbb{R}_{\geq 0}$. M is **convergent** if

$$\sum_{t \in T_\Sigma} M(t) \quad < \quad \infty.$$

We say that M is a **probabilistic** tree automaton (Ellis, 1971; Magidor and Moran, 1970), or PTA for short, if $\mu_k(\sigma)_{q,q_1\cdots q_k} \in [0, 1]$ and $F(q) \in [0, 1]$, for every $\sigma \in \Sigma_k$ and $q, q_1, \ldots, q_k \in Q$. In other words, in a PTA all weights are in the range $[0, 1]$ and can be interpreted as probabilities. For a PTA M we therefore write $p_M(r) = \text{wt}(r)$ and $p_M(t) = M(t)$, for each $t \in T_\Sigma$ and $r \in \text{Run}_M(t)$.

A PTA is **proper** if $\sum_{q \in Q} F(q) = 1$ and

$$\sum_{\sigma \in \Sigma_k, k \geq 0, w \in Q^k} \mu_k(\sigma)_{q,w} = 1$$

for every $q \in Q$. Since the set of symbols is finite, we could have only required that the sum over all weights as shown with $w \in Q^k$ equals 1 for every $q \in Q$ and $\sigma \in \Sigma_k$. A simple rescaling would then be sufficient to arrive at our notion. Furthermore, a PTA is **consistent** if $\sum_{t \in T_\Sigma} p_M(t) = 1$. If a PTA is consistent, then p_M is a probability distribution over the set T_Σ.

The WTA M is **unambiguous** if for every input tree $t \in T_\Sigma$, there exists at most one $r \in \mathrm{Run}_M(t)$ such that $r(\varepsilon) \in F$ and $\mathrm{wt}_M(r) \neq 0$. In other words, in an unambiguous WTA, there exists at most one successful run for each input tree. Finally, M is in **final-state normal form** if there exists a state $q_S \in Q$ such that

- $F(q_S) = 1$,
- $F(q) = 0$ for every $q \in Q \setminus \{q_S\}$, and
- $\mu_k(\sigma)_{q,w} = 0$ if $w(i) = q_S$ for some $1 \leq i \leq k$.

We commonly denote the unique final state by q_S. For the following result we refer the reader to (Droste et al., 2005, Lemma 4.8) and (Bozapalidis, 1999, Lemma 22). The additional properties mentioned in the items of it are easily seen.

Theorem 3 *For every* WTA M *there exists an equivalent* WTA M' *in final-state normal form.*

- *If* M *is convergent (respectively, proper, consistent), then* M' *is such, too.*
- *If* M *is unambiguous, then* M' *is also unambiguous and for every* $t \in T_\Sigma$ *and* $r \in \mathrm{Run}_M(t)$ *we have* $\mathrm{wt}_{M'}(r') = \mathrm{wt}_M(r) \cdot F(r(\varepsilon))$ *where* $r'(\varepsilon) = q_S$ *and* $r'(w) = r(w)$ *for every* $w \in \mathrm{Pos}(t) \setminus \{\varepsilon\}$. □

It is not difficult to see that a proper PTA in final-state normal form is always convergent.

In statistical parsing applications we use grammar models that induce a probability distribution on the set of parse trees. In these applications, there is often the need to visit a parse tree with highest probability, among those in the parse forest obtained from the input sentence. This implements a form of disambiguation, where the most likely tree under the given model is selected, pretending that it provides the most likely syntactic analysis of the input string. In our setting, the above approach reduces to the problem of 'unfolding' a tree from a PTA $\mathrm{Prod}(M, N)$, that is assigned the highest probability.

In order to find efficient solutions for the above problem, we make the following two assumptions.

- M is in final-state normal form. By Theorem 3 this can be achieved without loss of generality.
- M is unambiguous. This restrictive assumption avoids the so-called 'spurious' ambiguity, that would result in several computations in the model for an individual parse tree.

It is not difficult to see that PTA satisfying these two properties are still more powerful than the probabilistic context-free grammar models that are commonly used in statistical natural language processing.

1: **Function** BESTPARSE(M)
2: $\mathcal{E} \leftarrow \emptyset$
3: **repeat**
4: $\quad \mathcal{A} \leftarrow \{q \mid \mu_k(\sigma)_{q,q_1\cdots q_k} > 0,\ q \notin \mathcal{E},\ q_1, \ldots, q_k \in \mathcal{E}\}$
5: $\quad$ **for all** $q \in \mathcal{A}$ **do**
6: $\quad\quad \delta(q) \leftarrow \max\limits_{\substack{\sigma \in \Sigma_k, k \geq 0 \\ q_1,\ldots,q_k \in \mathcal{E}}} \mu_k(\sigma)_{q,q_1\cdots q_k} \cdot \prod_{i=1}^{k} \delta(q_i)$
7: $\quad \mathcal{E} \leftarrow \mathcal{E} \cup \{\mathrm{argmax}_{q \in \mathcal{A}}\ \delta(q)\}$
8: **until** $q_S \in \mathcal{E}$
9: **return** $\delta(q_S)$

Figure 3: Search algorithm for the most probable parse in an unambiguous PTA M in final-state normal form.

Once more, we borrow from the literature on parsing for context-free grammars, and adapt a search algorithm developed by Knuth (1977); see also (Nederhof, 2003). The basic idea here is to generalize Dijkstra's algorithm to compute the shortest path in a weighted graph. The search algorithm is presented in Figure 3.

The algorithm takes as input a trim PTA M that recognizes at least one parse tree. We do not impose any bound on the rank of the alphabet symbols for M. Furthermore, M needs not be a proper PTA. In order to simplify the presentation, we provide the algorithm in a form that returns the largest probability assigned to some tree by M.

The algorithm records into the $\delta(q)$ variables the largest probability found so far for a run that brings M into state q, and stores these states into an agenda $\mathcal{A}$. States for which $\delta(q)$ becomes optimal are popped from $\mathcal{A}$ and stored into a set $\mathcal{E}$. Choices are made on a greedy base. Note that when a run has been found leading to an optimal probability $\delta(q)$, from our assumption we know that the associated tree has only one run that ends up in state q.

Since $\mathcal{E}$ is initially empty (line 2), only weights satisfying $\mu_0(\sigma)_{q,\varepsilon} > 0$ are considered when line 4 is executed for the first time. Later on (line 7) the largest probability is selected among all those that can be computed at this time, and the set $\mathcal{E}$ is populated. As a consequence, more states become available in the agenda in the next iteration, and new transitions can now be considered. The algorithm ends when the largest probability has been calculated for the unique final state q_S.

We now analyze the computational complexity of the algorithm in Figure 3. The 'repeat-until' loop runs at most $|Q|$ times. Entirely reprocessing set $\mathcal{A}$ at each iteration would be too expensive. We instead implement $\mathcal{A}$ as a priority heap and maintain a clock for each weight $\mu_k(\sigma)_{q,q_1\cdots q_k}$, initially set to k. Whenever a new optimal probability $\delta(q)$ becomes available through $\mathcal{E}$, we decrement the clock associated with each $\mu_k(\sigma)_{q,q_1\cdots q_k}$ by d, in case $d > 0$ occurrences of q are found in the string $q_1 \cdots q_k$. In this way, at each iteration of the 'repeat-until' loop, we can consider only those weights $\mu_k(\sigma)_{q,q_1\cdots q_k}$ with associated clock of zero, compute new values $\delta(q)$, and update the heap. For each $\mu_k(\sigma)_{q,q_1\cdots q_k} > 0$, all clock updates and the computation of quantity $\mu_k(\sigma)_{q,q_1\cdots q_k} \cdot \prod_{i=1}^{k} \delta(q_i)$ (when the associated clock becomes zero) both take an amount of time proportional to the length of the transition itself. The overall time to execute these operations is therefore linear in $|M|$. Accounting for the heap, the algorithm has overall running time in $\mathcal{O}(|M| + |Q| \log|Q|)$.

The algorithm can be easily adapted to return a tree having probability $\delta(q_S)$, if we keep a record of all transitions selected in the computation along with links from a selected transition and all of the previously selected transitions that have caused its selection. If we drop the unambiguity assumption for the PTA, then the problem of computing the best parse tree becomes NP-hard, through a reduction from similar problems for finite automata (Casacuberta and de la Higuera, 2000). In contrast, the problem of computing the probability of all parse trees of a string, also called the inside probability, can be solved in polynomial time in most practical cases and will be addressed in Subsection 5.4.

5.3 Normalization

Consider the WTA $\text{Prod}(M, N)$ obtained as in Definition 2. If N is a WSA encoding an input string w as in Subsection 5.1 and if M is a proper and consistent PTA, then $\text{Prod}(M, N)$ is a PTA as well. However, in general $\text{Prod}(M, N)$ will not be proper, nor consistent. Properness and consistency of $\text{Prod}(M, N)$ are convenient in all those applications where a statistical parsing module needs to be coupled with other statistical modules, in such a way that the composition of the probability spaces still induces a probability distribution. In this subsection we deal with the more general problem of how to transform a WTA that is convergent into a PTA that is proper and consistent. This process is called **normalization**. The normalization technique we propose here has been previously explored, in the context of probabilistic context-free grammars, in (Abney et al., 1999; Chi, 1999; Nederhof and Satta, 2003).

We start by introducing some new notions. Let us assume that M is a convergent WTA. For every $q \in Q$, we define

$$\text{wt}_M(q) = \sum_{\substack{t \in T_\Sigma, r \in \text{Run}_M(t) \\ r(\varepsilon) = q}} \text{wt}_M(r) \ .$$

Note that quantity $\text{wt}_M(q)$ equals the sum of the weights of all trees in T_Σ that would be recognized by M if we set $F(q) = 1$ and $F(p) = 0$ for each $p \in Q \setminus \{q\}$, that is, if q is the unique final state of M. It is not difficult to show that, since M is convergent, the sum in the definition of $\text{wt}_M(q)$ converges for each $q \in Q$. We will show in Subsection 5.4 that the quantities $\text{wt}_M(q)$ can be approximated to any desired precision.

To simplify the presentation, and without any loss of generality, throughout this subsection we assume that our WTA are in final-state normal form. We can now introduce the normalization technique.

Definition 3 Let $M = (Q, \Sigma, \mathbb{R}_{\geq 0}, \mu, F)$ be a convergent WTA in final-state normal form. We construct the WTA

$$\text{Norm}(M) = (Q, \Sigma, \mathbb{R}_{\geq 0}, \mu', F) \ ,$$

where for every $\sigma \in \Sigma_k$, $k \geq 0$, and $q, q_1, \ldots, q_k \in Q$

$$\mu'_k(\sigma)_{q,q_1\cdots q_k} = \mu_k(\sigma)_{q,q_1\cdots q_k} \cdot \frac{\text{wt}_M(q_1) \cdot \ldots \cdot \text{wt}_M(q_k)}{\text{wt}_M(q)} \ . \ \square$$

We now show the claimed property for our transformation.

Theorem 4 *Let M be as in Definition 3, and let $M' = \text{Norm}(M)$. Then M' is a proper and consistent* PTA, *and for every $t \in T_\Sigma$ we have $M'(t) = \frac{M(t)}{\text{wt}_M(q_S)}$.* $\square$

PROOF Clearly, M' is again in final-state normal form. An easy derivation shows that

$$\mathrm{wt}_M(q) = \sum_{\substack{\sigma\in\Sigma_k \\ q_1,\dots,q_k\in Q}} \mu_k(\sigma)_{q,q_1\cdots q_k} \cdot \prod_{i=1}^{k} \mathrm{wt}_M(q_i)$$

for every $q \in Q$. Using the previous remark, we obtain

$$\begin{aligned}
&\sum_{\sigma\in\Sigma_k, q_1,\dots,q_k\in Q} \mu'_k(\sigma)_{q,q_1\cdots q_k} \\
&= \sum_{\sigma\in\Sigma_k, q_1,\dots,q_k\in Q} \mu_k(\sigma)_{q,q_1\cdots q_k} \cdot \\
&\quad \cdot \frac{\mathrm{wt}_M(q_1)\cdot\ldots\cdot \mathrm{wt}_M(q_{k'})}{\mathrm{wt}_M(q)} \\
&= \frac{\sum_{\substack{\sigma\in\Sigma_k, \\ q_1,\dots,q_k\in Q}} \mu_k(\sigma)_{q,q_1\cdots q_k} \cdot \prod_{i=1}^{k} \mathrm{wt}_M(q_i)}{\sum_{\substack{\sigma\in\Sigma_k, \\ p_1,\dots,p_k\in Q}} \mu_k(\sigma)_{q,p_1\cdots p_k} \cdot \prod_{i=1}^{k} \mathrm{wt}_M(p_i)} \\
&= 1 \ ,
\end{aligned}$$

which proves that M' is a proper PTA.

Next, we prove an auxiliary statement. Let $t = \sigma(t_1,\dots,t_k)$ for some $\sigma \in \Sigma_k$, $k \geq 0$, and $t_1,\dots,t_k \in T_\Sigma$. We claim that

$$\mathrm{wt}_{M'}(r) = \frac{\mathrm{wt}_M(r)}{\mathrm{wt}_M(r(\varepsilon))}$$

for every $r \in \mathrm{Run}_M(t) = \mathrm{Run}_{M'}(t)$. For every $1 \leq i \leq k$, let $r_i \in \mathrm{Run}_M(t_i)$ be such that $r_i(w) = r(iw)$ for every $w \in \mathrm{Pos}(t_i)$. Then

$$\begin{aligned}
\mathrm{wt}_{M'}(r) &= \prod_{\substack{w\in\mathrm{Pos}(t) \\ \mathrm{rk}_t(w)=n}} \mu'_n(t(w))_{r(w),r(w1)\cdots r(wn)} \\
&= \mu'_k(\sigma)_{r(\varepsilon),r(1)\cdots r(k)} \cdot \prod_{i=1}^{k} \mathrm{wt}_{M'}(r_i) \\
&= \mu'_k(\sigma)_{r(\varepsilon),r_1(\varepsilon)\cdots r_k(\varepsilon)} \cdot \prod_{i=1}^{k} \frac{\mathrm{wt}_M(r_i)}{\mathrm{wt}_M(r_i(\varepsilon))} \\
&= \mu_k(\sigma)_{r(\varepsilon),r(1)\cdots r(k)} \cdot \frac{\mathrm{wt}_M(r_1)\cdot\ldots\cdot \mathrm{wt}_M(r_k)}{\mathrm{wt}_M(r(\varepsilon))} \\
&= \frac{\mathrm{wt}_M(r)}{\mathrm{wt}_M(r(\varepsilon))} \ .
\end{aligned}$$

Consequently,

$$\begin{aligned}
M'(t) &= \sum_{\substack{r\in\mathrm{Run}_{M'}(t) \\ r(\varepsilon)=q_S}} \mathrm{wt}_{M'}(r) \\
&= \sum_{\substack{r\in\mathrm{Run}_M(t) \\ r(\varepsilon)=q_S}} \frac{\mathrm{wt}_M(r)}{\mathrm{wt}_M(q_S)} = \frac{M(t)}{\mathrm{wt}_M(q_S)}
\end{aligned}$$

and

$$\begin{aligned}
\sum_{t\in T_\Sigma} M'(t) &= \sum_{\substack{t\in T_\Sigma, r\in\mathrm{Run}_{M'}(t) \\ r(\varepsilon)=q_S}} \mathrm{wt}_{M'}(r) \\
&= \sum_{\substack{t\in T_\Sigma, r\in\mathrm{Run}_M(t) \\ r(\varepsilon)=q_S}} \frac{\mathrm{wt}_M(r)}{\mathrm{wt}_M(q_S)} \\
&= \frac{\mathrm{wt}_M(q_S)}{\mathrm{wt}_M(q_S)} = 1 \ ,
\end{aligned}$$

which prove the main statement and the consistency of M', respectively. ∎

5.4 Probability mass of a state

Assume M is a convergent WTA. We have defined quantities $\mathrm{wt}_M(q)$ for each $q \in Q$. Note that when M is a proper PTA in final-state normal form, then $\mathrm{wt}_M(q)$ can be seen as the probability mass that 'rests' on state q. When dealing with such PTA, we use the notation $Z_M(q)$ in place of $\mathrm{wt}_M(q)$, and call Z_M the **partition function** of M. This terminology is borrowed from the literature on exponential or Gibbs probabilistic models.

In the context of probabilistic context-free grammars, the computation of the partition function has several applications, including the elimination of epsilon rules (Abney et al., 1999) and the computation of probabilistic distances between probability distributions realized by these formalisms (Nederhof and Satta, 2008). Besides what we have seen in Subsection 5.3, we will provide one more application of partition functions for the computations of so-called prefix probabilities in Subsection 5.5 We also add that, when computed on the Bar-Hillel automata of Section 4, the partition function provides the so-called inside probabilities of (Graehl et al., 2008) for the given states and substrings.

Let $|Q| = n$ and let us assume an arbitrary ordering $q_1,\dots,q_n$ for the states in Q. We can then rewrite the definition of $\mathrm{wt}_M(q)$ as

$$\mathrm{wt}_M(q) = \sum_{\substack{\sigma\in\Sigma_k, k\geq 0 \\ q_{i_1},\dots,q_{i_k}\in Q}} \mu_k(\sigma)_{q,q_{i_1}\cdots q_{i_k}} \cdot \prod_{j=1}^{k} \mathrm{wt}_M(q_{i_j})$$

(see proof of Theorem 4). We rename $\mathrm{wt}_M(q_i)$ with the unknown X_{q_i}, $1 \leq i \leq n$, and derive a system of n nonlinear polynomial equations of the form

$$X_{q_i} = \sum_{\substack{\sigma \in \Sigma_k, k \geq 0 \\ q_{i_1}, \ldots, q_{i_k} \in Q}} \mu_k(\sigma)_{q, q_{i_1} \cdots q_{i_k}} \cdot X_{q_{i_1}} \cdot \ldots \cdot X_{q_{i_k}} = f_{q_i}(X_{q_1}, \ldots, X_{q_n}) \ , \tag{1}$$

for each i with $1 \leq i \leq n$.

Throughout this subsection, we will consider solutions of the above system in the extended non-negative real number semiring

$$\mathbb{R}^{\infty}_{\geq 0} = (\mathbb{R}_{\geq 0} \cup \{\infty\}, +, \cdot, 0, 1)$$

with the usual operations extended to ∞. We can write the system in (1) in the compact form $\boldsymbol{X} = F(\boldsymbol{X})$, where we represent the unknowns as a vector $\boldsymbol{X} = (X_{q_1}, \ldots, X_{q_n})$ and F is a mapping of type $(\mathbb{R}^{\infty}_{\geq 0})^n \to (\mathbb{R}^{\infty}_{\geq 0})^n$ consisting of the polynomials $f_{q_i}(\boldsymbol{X})$.

We denote the vector $(0, \ldots, 0) \in (\mathbb{R}^{\infty}_{\geq 0})^n$ as $\boldsymbol{X}^0$. Let $\boldsymbol{X}, \boldsymbol{X}' \in (\mathbb{R}^{\infty}_{\geq 0})^n$. We write $\boldsymbol{X} \leq \boldsymbol{X}'$ if $X_{q_i} \leq X'_{q_i}$ for every $1 \leq i \leq n$. Since each polynomial $f_{q_i}(\boldsymbol{X})$ has coefficients represented by positive real numbers, it is not difficult to see that, for each $\boldsymbol{X}, \boldsymbol{X}' \in (\mathbb{R}^{\infty}_{\geq 0})^n$, we have $F(\boldsymbol{X}) \leq F(\boldsymbol{X}')$ whenever $\boldsymbol{X}^0 \leq \boldsymbol{X} \leq \boldsymbol{X}'$. This means that F is an order preserving, or **monotone**, mapping.

We observe that $((\mathbb{R}^{\infty}_{\geq 0})^n, \leq)$ is a complete lattice with least element $\boldsymbol{X}^0$ and greatest element $(\infty, \ldots, \infty)$. Since F is monotone on a complete lattice, by the Knaster-Tarski theorem (Knaster, 1928; Tarski, 1955) there exists a least and a greatest fixed-point of F that are solutions of $\boldsymbol{X} = F(\boldsymbol{X})$.

The Kleene theorem states that the least fixed-point solution of $\boldsymbol{X} = F(\boldsymbol{X})$ can be obtained by iterating F starting with the least element $\boldsymbol{X}^0$. In other words, the sequence $\boldsymbol{X}^k = F(\boldsymbol{X}^{k-1})$, $k = 1, 2, \ldots$ converges to the least fixed-point solution. Notice that each $\boldsymbol{X}^k$ provides an approximation for the partition function of M where only trees of depth not larger than k are considered. This means that $\lim_{k \to \infty} \boldsymbol{X}^k$ converges to the partition function of M, and the least fixed-point solution is also the sought solution. Thus, we can approximate $\mathrm{wt}_M(q)$ with $q \in Q$ to any degree by iterating F a sufficiently large number of times.

The fixed-point iteration method discussed above is also well-known in the numerical calculus literature, and is frequently applied to systems of nonlinear equations in general, because it can be easily implemented. When a number of standard conditions are met, each iteration of the algorithm (corresponding to the value of k above) adds a fixed number of bits to the precision of the approximated solution; see (Kelley, 1995) for further discussion.

Systems of the form $\boldsymbol{X} = F(\boldsymbol{X})$ where all $f_{q_i}(\boldsymbol{X})$ are polynomials with nonnegative real coefficients are called **monotone system of polynomials**. Monotone systems of polynomials associated with proper PTA have been specifically investigated in (Etessami and Yannakakis, 2005) and (Kiefer et al., 2007), where worst case results on exponential rate of convergence are reported for the fixed-point method.

5.5 Prefix probability

In this subsection we deal with one more application of the Bar-Hillel technique presented in Section 4. We show how to compute the so-called prefix probabilities, that is, the probability that a tree recognized by a PTA generates a string starting with a given prefix. Such probabilities have several applications in language modeling. As an example, prefix probabilities can be used to compute the probability distribution on the terminal symbol that follows a given prefix (under the given model).

For probabilistic context-free grammars, the problem of the computation of prefix probabilities has been solved in (Jelinek et al., 1992); see also (Persoon and Fu, 1975). The approach we propose here, originally formulated for probabilistic context-free grammars in (Nederhof and Satta, 2003; Nederhof and Satta, 2009), is more abstract than the previous ones, since it entirely rests on properties of the Bar-Hillel construction that we have already proved in Section 4.

Let $M = (Q, \Sigma, \mathbb{R}_{\geq 0}, \mu, F)$ be a proper and consistent PTA in final-state normal form, $\Delta = \Sigma_0 \setminus \{e\}$, and let $u \in \Delta^+$ be some string. We assume here that M is in the binary form discussed in Section 3. In addition, we assume that M has been preprocessed in order to remove from its recognized trees all of the unary branches as well as those branches that generate the null string ε. Although we do not discuss this construction at length in this paper, the result follows from a transformation casting weighted context-free grammars into Chomsky Normal Form (Fu and Huang, 1972; Abney et al., 1999).

We define

$$\text{Pref}(M,u) = \{t \mid t \in T_\Sigma,\ M(t) > 0,\ \text{yd}(t) = uv,\ v \in \Delta^*\} \ .$$

The **prefix probability** of u under M is defined as

$$\sum_{t \in \text{Pref}(M,u)} p_M(t) \ .$$

Let $|u| = n$. We define a WSA N_u with state set $P = \{p_0, \ldots, p_n\}$ and transition weights $\nu(p_{i-1}, u(i), p_i) = 1$ for each i with $1 \le i \le n$, and $\nu(p_n, \sigma, p_n) = 1$ for each $\sigma \in \Delta$. We also set $I(p_0) = 1$ and $F(p_n) = 1$. It is easy to see that N_u recognizes the language $\{uv \mid v \in \Delta^*\}$. Furthermore, the PTA $M_p = \text{Prod}(M, N_u)$ specified as in Definition 2 recognizes the desired tree set $\text{Pref}(M,u)$, and it preserves the weights of those trees with respect to M. We therefore conclude that $Z_{M_p}(q_S)$ is the prefix probability of u under M. Prefix probabilities can then be approximated using the fixed-point iteration method of Subsection 5.4. Rather than using an approximation method, we discuss in what follows how the prefix probabilities can be exactly computed.

Let us consider more closely the product automaton M_p, assuming that it is trim. Each state of M_p has the form $\pi = (p_i, q, p_j)$, $p_i, p_j \in P$ and $q \in Q$, with $i \le j$. We distinguish three, mutually exclusive cases.

(i) $j < n$: From our assumption that M (and thus M_p) does not have unary or ε branches, it is not difficult to see that all $Z_{M_p}(\pi)$ can be exactly computed in time $\mathcal{O}((j-i)^3)$.

(ii) $i = j = n$: We have $\pi = (p_n, q, p_n)$. Then the equations for $Z_{M_p}(\pi)$ exactly mirror the equations for $Z_M(q)$, and $Z_{M_p}(\pi) = Z_{M_p}(q)$. Because M is proper and consistent, this means that $Z_{M_p}(\pi) = 1$.

(iii) $i < j = n$: A close inspection of Definition 2 reveals that in this case the equations (1) are all linear, assuming that we have already replaced the solutions from (i) and (ii) above into the system. This is because any weight $\mu_2(\sigma)_{\pi_0, \pi_1 \pi} > 0$ in M_p with $\pi = (p_i, q, p_n)$ and $i < n$ must have $(\pi_1)_3 < n$. Quantities $Z_{M_p}(\pi)$ can then be exactly computed as the solution of a linear system of equations in time $\mathcal{O}(n^3)$.

Putting together all of the observations above, we obtain that for a proper and consistent PTA that has been preprocessed, the prefix probability of u can be computed in cubic time in the length of the prefix itself.

6 Concluding remarks

In this paper we have extended the Bar-Hillel construction to WTA, closely following the methodology proposed in (Nederhof and Satta, 2003) for weighted context-free grammars. Based on the obtained framework, we have derived several parsing algorithms for WTA, under the assumption that the input is a string rather than a tree.

As already remarked in the introduction, WTA are richer models than weighted context-free grammar, since the formers use hidden states in the recognition of trees. This feature makes it possible to define a product automaton in Definition 2 that generates exactly those trees of interest for the input string. In contrast, in the context-free grammar case the Bar-Hillel technique provides trees that must be mapped to the tree of interest using some homomorphism. For the same reason, one cannot directly convert WTA into weighted context-free grammars and then apply existing parsing algorithms for the latter formalism, unless the alphabet of nonterminal symbols is changed. Finally, our main motivation in developing a framework specifically based on WTA is that this can be extended to classes of weighted tree transducers, in order to deal with computational problems that arise in machine translation applications. We leave this for future work.

Acknowledgments

The first author has been supported by the Ministerio de Educación y Ciencia (MEC) under grant JDCI-2007-760. The second author has been partially supported by MIUR under project PRIN No. 2007TJNZRE_002.

References

S. Abney, D. McAllester, and F. Pereira. 1999. Relating probabilistic grammars and automata. In *37th Annual Meeting of the Association for Computational Linguistics, Proceedings of the Conference*, pages 542–549, Maryland, USA, June.

Y. Bar-Hillel, M. Perles, and E. Shamir. 1964. On formal properties of simple phrase structure grammars. In Y. Bar-Hillel, editor, *Language and Information: Selected Essays on their Theory and Application*, chapter 9, pages 116–150. Addison-Wesley, Reading, Massachusetts.

J. Berstel and C. Reutenauer. 1982. Recognizable formal power series on trees. *Theoret. Comput. Sci.*, 18(2):115–148.

B. Borchardt. 2005. *The Theory of Recognizable Tree Series*. Ph.D. thesis, Technische Universität Dresden.

S. Bozapalidis. 1999. Equational elements in additive algebras. *Theory Comput. Systems*, 32(1):1–33.

J. Carme, J. Niehren, and M. Tommasi. 2004. Querying unranked trees with stepwise tree automata. In *Proc. RTA*, volume 3091 of LNCS, pages 105–118. Springer.

F. Casacuberta and C. de la Higuera. 2000. Computational complexity of problems on probabilistic grammars and transducers. In L. Oliveira, editor, *Grammatical Inference: Algorithms and Applications; 5th International Colloquium, ICGI 2000*, pages 15–24. Springer.

Z. Chi. 1999. Statistical properties of probabilistic context-free grammars. *Computational Linguistics*, 25(1):131–160.

M. Droste, C. Pech, and H. Vogler. 2005. A Kleene theorem for weighted tree automata. *Theory Comput. Systems*, 38(1):1–38.

J. Earley. 1970. An efficient context-free parsing algorithm. *Communications of the ACM*, 13(2):94–102, February.

S. Eilenberg. 1974. *Automata, Languages, and Machines*, volume 59 of *Pure and Applied Math.* Academic Press.

C. A. Ellis. 1971. Probabilistic tree automata. *Information and Control*, 19(5):401–416.

Z. Ésik and W. Kuich. 2003. Formal tree series. *J. Autom. Lang. Combin.*, 8(2):219–285.

K. Etessami and M. Yannakakis. 2005. Recursive Markov chains, stochastic grammars, and monotone systems of nonlinear equations. In *22nd International Symposium on Theoretical Aspects of Computer Science*, volume 3404 of *Lecture Notes in Computer Science*, pages 340–352, Stuttgart, Germany. Springer-Verlag.

K.S. Fu and T. Huang. 1972. Stochastic grammars and languages. *International Journal of Computer and Information Sciences*, 1(2):135–170.

F. Gécseg and M. Steinby. 1984. *Tree Automata*. Akadémiai Kiadó, Budapest.

J. Graehl, K. Knight, and J. May. 2008. Training tree transducers. *Comput. Linguist.*, 34(3):391–427.

J. Högberg, A. Maletti, and H. Vogler. 2009. Bisimulation minimisation of weighted automata on unranked trees. *Fundam. Inform.* to appear.

F. Jelinek, J.D. Lafferty, and R.L. Mercer. 1992. Basic methods of probabilistic context free grammars. In P. Laface and R. De Mori, editors, *Speech Recognition and Understanding — Recent Advances, Trends and Applications*, pages 345–360. Springer-Verlag.

M. Johnson. 1998. PCFG models of linguistic tree representations. *Computational Linguistics*, 24(4):613–632.

C. T. Kelley. 1995. *Iterative Methods for Linear and Nonlinear Equations*. Society for Industrial and Applied Mathematics, Philadelphia, PA.

S. Kiefer, M. Luttenberger, and J. Esparza. 2007. On the convergence of Newton's method for monotone systems of polynomial equations. In *Proceedings of the 39th ACM Symposium on Theory of Computing*, pages 217–266.

B. Knaster. 1928. Un théorème sur les fonctions d'ensembles. *Ann. Soc. Polon. Math.*, 6:133–134.

D. E. Knuth. 1977. A generalization of Dijkstra's algorithm. *Information Processing Letters*, 6(1):1–5, February.

D. E. Knuth. 1997. *Fundamental Algorithms*. The Art of Computer Programming. Addison Wesley, 3rd edition.

M. Magidor and G. Moran. 1970. Probabilistic tree automata and context free languages. *Israel Journal of Mathematics*, 8(4):340–348.

M.-J. Nederhof and G. Satta. 2003. Probabilistic parsing as intersection. In *8th International Workshop on Parsing Technologies*, pages 137–148, LORIA, Nancy, France, April.

M.-J. Nederhof and G. Satta. 2008. Computation of distances for regular and context-free probabilistic languages. *Theoretical Computer Science*, 395(2-3):235–254.

M.-J. Nederhof and G. Satta. 2009. Computing partition functions of PCFGs. *Research on Language & Computation*, 6(2):139–162.

M.-J. Nederhof. 2003. Weighted deductive parsing and Knuth's algorithm. *Computational Linguistics*, 29(1):135–143.

E. Persoon and K.S. Fu. 1975. Sequential classification of strings generated by SCFG's. *International Journal of Computer and Information Sciences*, 4(3):205–217.

M. P. Schützenberger. 1961. On the definition of a family of automata. *Information and Control*, 4(2–3):245–270.

A. Tarski. 1955. A lattice-theoretical fixpoint theorem and its applications. *Pacific J. Math.*, 5(2):285–309.

D. H. Younger. 1967. Recognition and parsing of context-free languages in time n^3. *Information and Control*, 10:189–208.

Weighted parsing of trees

Mark-Jan Nederhof
School of Computer Science, University of St Andrews
North Haugh, St Andrews, KY16 9SX, Scotland

Abstract

We show how parsing of trees can be formalized in terms of the intersection of two tree languages. The focus is on weighted regular tree grammars and weighted tree adjoining grammars. Potential applications are discussed, such as parameter estimation across formalisms.

1 Introduction

In parsing theory, strings and trees traditionally have had a very different status. Whereas strings in general receive the central focus, the trees involved in derivations of strings are often seen as auxiliary concepts at best. Theorems tend to be about the power of grammatical formalisms to produce strings (weak generative power) rather than trees (strong generative power).

This can be explained by looking at typical applications of parsing. In compiler construction for example, one distinguishes between parse trees and (abstract) syntax trees, the former being shaped according to a grammar that is massaged to make it satisfy relatively artificial constraints, e.g. that of LALR(1), which is required by many compiler generators (Aho et al., 2007). The form of syntax trees is often chosen to simplify phases of semantic processing that follow parsing. As the machinery used in such processing is generally powerful, this offers much flexibility in the choice of the exact shape and labelling of syntax trees, as intermediate form between parsing and semantic analysis.

In the study of natural languages, parse trees have played a more important role. Whereas linguistic utterances are directly observable and trees deriving them are not, there are nevertheless traditions within linguistics that would see one structural analysis of a sentence as strongly preferred over another. Furthermore, within computational linguistics there are empirical arguments to claim certain parses are correct and others are incorrect. For example, a question answering systems may verifiably give the wrong answer if the question is parsed incorrectly. See (Jurafsky and Martin, 2000) for general discussion on the role of parsing in NLP.

Despite the relative importance of strong generative power in computational linguistics, there is still much freedom in how exactly parse trees are shaped and how vertices are labelled, due to the power of semantic analysis that typically follows parsing. This has affected much of the theoretical investigations into the power of linguistic formalisms, and where strong equivalence is considered at all, it is often "modulo relabelling" or allowing minor structural changes.

With the advent of syntax-based machine translation, trees have however gained much importance, and are even considered as the main objects of study. This is because many MT modules have trees both as input and output, which means the computational strength of such modules can be measured only in terms of the tree languages they accept and the transductions between tree languages that they implement. See for example (Knight, 2007).

In contrast, trees have always been the central issue in an important and well-established subfield of formal language theory that studies tree languages, tree automata and tree transducers (Gcseg and Steinby, 1997). The string languages generated by the relevant formalisms in this context are mostly taken to be of secondary importance, if they are considered at all.

This paper focuses on tree languages, but involves a technique that was devised for string languages, and shows how the technique carries over to tree languages. The original technique can be seen as the most fundamental idea in the field of context-free parsing, as it captures the essence of

Proceedings of the 11th International Conference on Parsing Technologies (IWPT), pages 13–24,
Paris, October 2009.

finding hierarchical structure in a linear sequence. The generalization also finds structure in a linear sequence, but now the sequence corresponds to paths in trees each leading down from a vertex to a leaf. This means that the proposed type of parsing is orthogonal to the conventional parsing of strings.

The insights this offers have the potential to create new avenues of research into the relation between formalisms that were until now considered only in isolation. We seek credence to this claim by investigating how probability distributions can be carried over from tree adjoining grammars to regular tree grammars, and vice versa.

The implication that the class of tree languages of tree adjoining grammars (TAGs) is closed under intersection with regular tree languages is not surprising, as the linear context-free tree languages (LCFTLs) are closed under intersection with regular tree languages (Kepser and Mönnich, 2006). The tree languages of TAGs form a subclass of the LCFTLs, and the main construction in the proof of the closure result for the latter can be suitably restricted to the former.

The structure of this paper is as follows. The main grammatical formalisms considered in this paper are summarized in Section 2 and Section 3 discusses a number of analyses of these formalisms that will be used in later sections. Section 4 starts by explaining how parsing of a string can be seen as the construction of a grammar that generates the intersection of two languages, and then moves on to a type of parsing involving intersection of tree languages in place of string languages.

In order to illustrate the implications of the theory, we consider how it can be used to solve a practical problem, in Section 5. A number of possible extensions are outlined in Section 6.

2 Formalisms

In this section, we recall the formalisms of weighted regular tree grammars and weighted tree adjoining grammars. We use similar notation and terminology for both, in order to prepare for Section 4, where we investigate the combination of these formalisms through intersection. As a consequence of the required unified notation, we deviate to some degree from standard definitions, without affecting generative power however.

For common definitions of weighted regular tree grammars, the reader is referred to (Graehl and Knight, 2004). Weighted tree adjoining grammars are a straightforward generalization of probabilistic (or stochastic) tree adjoining grammars, as introduced by (Resnik, 1992) and (Schabes, 1992).

For both regular tree grammars (RTGs) and tree adjoining grammars (TAGs), we will write a labeled and ordered tree as $A(\alpha)$. where A is the label of the root node, and α is a sequence of expressions of the same form that each represent an immediate subtree. In our presentation, labels do not have explicit ranks, that is, the number of children of a node is not determined by its label. This allows an interesting generalization, to be discussed in Section 6.2.

Where we are interested in the string language generated by a tree-generating grammar, we may distinguish between two kinds of labels, the *terminal labels*, which may occur only at leaves, and the *nonterminal labels*, which may occur at any node. It is customary to write terminal leaves as a instead of $a()$. The *yield* of a tree is the string of occurrences of terminal labels in it, from left to right. Note that also nonterminal labels may occur at the leaves, but they will not be included in the yield; cf. epsilon rules in context-free grammars.

2.1 Weighted regular tree grammars

A *weighted regular tree grammar* (WRTG) is a 4-tuple $G = (S, L, R, s^{\vdash})$, where S and L are two finite sets of *states* and *labels*, respectively, $s^{\vdash} \in S$ is the *initial state*, and R is a finite set of *rules*. Each rule has the form:

$$s_0 \rightarrow A(s_1 \cdots s_m) \langle w \rangle,$$

where $s_0, s_1, \ldots, s_m$ are states $(0 \leq m)$, A is a label and w is a weight.

Rewriting starts with a string containing only the initial state $s^{\vdash}$. This string is repeatedly rewritten by replacing the left-hand side state of a rule by the right-hand side of the same rule, until no state remains. It may be convenient to assume a canonical order of rewriting, for example in terms of left-most derivations (Hopcroft and Ullman, 1979).

Although alternative semirings can be considered, here we always assume that the weights of rules are non-negative real numbers, and the weight of a derivation of a tree is the product of the weights of the rule occurrences. If several (left-most) derivations result in the same tree, then the weight of that tree is given by the sum of the weights of those derivations. Where we are interested in the string language, the weights of trees with the same yield are added to obtain the weight of that yield.

A (weighted) context-free grammar can be seen as a special case of a (weighted) regular tree grammar, where the set of states equals the set of labels, and rules have the form:

$$A \to A(B_1 \cdots B_m).$$

Also the class of (weighted) tree substitution grammars (Sima'an, 1997) can be seen as a special case of (weighted) regular tree grammars, by letting the set of labels overlap with the set of states, and imposing two constraints on the allowable rules. The first constraint is that for each label that is also a state, all defining rules are of the form:

$$A \to A(s_1 \cdots s_m).$$

The second constraint is that for each state that is not a label, there is exactly one rule with that state in the left-hand side. This means that exactly one subtree (or *elementary tree*) can be built top-down out of such states, down to a level where we again encounter states that are also labels. If desired, we can exclude infinite elementary trees by imposing an additional constraint on allowed sets of rules (no cycles composed of states that are not labels); alternatively, we can demand that the grammar does not contain any useless rules, which automatically excludes such infinite elementary trees.

2.2 Weighted linear indexed grammars

Although we are mainly interested in the tree languages of tree adjoining grammars, we will use an equivalent representation in terms of linear indexed grammars, in order to obtain a uniform notation with regard to regular tree grammars.

Thus, a *weighted linear indexed grammar* (WLIG) is a 5-tuple $G = (S, I, L, R, s^{\vdash})$, where S, I and L are three finite sets of *states*, *indices* and *labels*, respectively, $s^{\vdash} \in S$ is the *initial state*, and R is a finite set of *rules*. Each rule has one of the following four forms:

1. $s_0[\circ\circ] \to A(\ s_1[\,] \cdots s_{j-1}[\,]\ s_j[\circ\circ]\ s_{j+1}[\,] \cdots s_m[\,]\ )\ \langle w \rangle$, where $s_0, s_1, \ldots, s_m$ are states ($1 \le j \le m$), A is a label and w is a weight;
2. $s[\,] \to A()\ \langle w \rangle$;
3. $s[\circ\circ] \to s'[\iota\circ\circ]\ \langle w \rangle$, where ι is an index;
4. $s[\iota\circ\circ] \to s'[\circ\circ]\ \langle w \rangle$.

The expression $\circ\circ$ may be thought of as a variable denoting a string of indices on a stack, and this variable is to be consistently substituted in the left-hand and the right-hand sides of rules upon application during rewriting. In other words, stacks are copied from the left-hand side of a rule to at most one member in the right-hand side, which we will call the *head* of that rule. The expression $[\,]$ stands for the empty stack and $[\iota\circ\circ]$ denotes a stack with top element ι. Thereby, rules of the third type implement a stack push and rules of the fourth type implement a pop. Rewriting starts from $s^{\vdash}[\,]$. The four subsets of R containing rules of the respective four forms above will be referred to as R_1, R_2, R_3 and R_4.

In terms of tree adjoining grammars, which assume a finite number of elementary trees, the intuition behind the four types of rules is as follows. Rules of the first type correspond to continued construction of the same elementary tree. Rules of the third type correspond to the initiation of a newly adjoined auxiliary tree and rules of the fourth type correspond to its completion at a foot node, returning to an embedding elementary tree that is encoded in the index that is popped. Rules of the second type correspond to construction of leaves, as in the case of regular tree grammars. See further (Vijay-Shanker and Weir, 1994) for the equivalence of linear indexed grammars and tree adjoining grammars.

Note that regular tree grammars can be seen as special cases of linear indexed grammars, by excluding rules of the third and fourth types, which means that stacks of indices always remain empty (Joshi and Schabes, 1997).

2.3 Probabilistic grammars

A weighted regular tree grammar, or weighted linear indexed grammar, respectively, is called *probabilistic* if the weights are probabilities, that is, values between 0 and 1. A probabilistic regular tree grammar (PRTG) is *proper* if for each state s, the probabilities of all rules that have left-hand side s sum to one.

Properness for a probabilistic linear indexed grammar (PLIG) is more difficult to define, due to the possible overlap of applicability between the four types of rules, listed in the section above. However, if we encode a given TAG as a LIG in a reasonable way, then a state s may occur both in left-hand sides of rules from R_1 and in left-hand sides of rules from R_3, but all other such overlap between the four types is precluded.

Intuitively, a state may represent an internal node of an elementary tree, in which case rules from both R_1 and R_3 may apply, or it may represent a non-foot leaf node, in which case a rule from R_2 may apply, or it may be a foot node, in which case a rule from R_4 may apply.

With this assumption that the only overlap in applicability is between R_1 and R_3, properness can be defined as follows.

- For each state s, either there are no rules in R_1 or R_3 with s in the left-hand side, or the sum of probabilities of all such rules equals one.

- For each state s, either there are no rules in R_2 with s in the left-hand side, or the sum of probabilities of all such rules equals one.

- For each state s and index ι, either there are no rules in R_4 with left-hand side $s[\iota\circ\circ]$, or the sum of probabilities of all such rules equals one.

We say a weighted regular tree grammar, or weighted linear indexed grammar, respectively, is *consistent* if the sum of weights of all (left-most) derivations is one. This is equivalent to saying that the sum of weights of all trees is one, and to saying that the sum of weights of all strings is one.

For each consistent WRTG (WLIG, respectively), there is an equivalent proper and consistent PRTG (PLIG, respectively). The proof lies in normalization. For WRTGs this is a trivial extension of normalization of weighted context-free grammars, as described for example by (Nederhof and Satta, 2003). For WLIGs (and weighted TAGs), the problem of normalization also becomes very similar once we consider that the set of *derivation trees* of tree adjoining grammars can be described with context-free grammars, and that this carries over to weighted derivation trees. See also (Sarkar, 1998).

WLIGs seemingly incur an extra complication, if a state may occur in combination with an index on top of the associated stack such that no rules are applicable. However, for LIGs that encode TAGs, the problem does not arise as, informally, one may always resume construction of the embedding elementary tree below the foot node of an adjoined auxiliary tree.

We say a LIG is in *TAG-normal form* if (a) at least one rule is applicable for each combination of state s and index ι such that $s[\iota\circ\circ]$ is derivable from $s^{\vdash}[\,]$, and (b) the only overlap in applicability of the four types of rules is between R_1 and R_3. Statements in what follows involving WLIGs (or PLIGs) in TAG-normal form also hold for weighted (or probabilistic) TAGs.

3 Analysis of grammars

We call a grammar rule *useless* if it cannot be part of any derivation of a tree (or of a string, in the case of grammars with an emphasis on string languages). We say a grammar is *reduced* if it does not contain useless rules.

Whereas most grammars written by hand or induced by a corpus or treebank are reduced, there are practical operations that turn reduced grammars into grammars with useless rules; we will see an example in the next section, where grammars are constructed that generate the intersection of two given languages. In order to determine whether the intersection is non-empty, it suffices to identify useless rules in the intersection grammar. If and only if *all* rules are useless, the generated language is empty.

In the case of context-free grammars (see for example (Sippu and Soisalon-Soininen, 1988)), the analysis to identify useless rules can be split into two phases:

1. a bottom-up phase to identify the grammar symbols that generate substrings, which may include the start symbol if the generated language is non-empty; and

2. a top-down phase to identify the grammar symbols that are reachable from the start symbol.

The intersection of the generating symbols and the reachable symbols gives the set of useful symbols. One can then identify useless rules as those that contain one or more symbols that are not useful.

The procedure for linear indexed grammars is similarly split into two phases, of which the first is given in Figure 1 in the form of a deduction system. The inference rules simultaneously derive

$$\frac{}{(s, s)} \left\{ s \in S \right. \qquad \text{(a)}$$

$$\frac{}{s} \left\{ s[\,] \rightarrow A() \right. \qquad \text{(b)}$$

$$\frac{s_1 \;\cdots\; s_{j-1} \; (s_j, s) \; s_{j+1} \;\cdots\; s_m}{(s_0, s)} \left\{ s_0[\circ\circ] \rightarrow A(s_1[\,] \;\cdots\; s_j[\circ\circ] \;\cdots\; s_m[\,]) \right. \qquad \text{(c)}$$

$$\frac{s_1 \;\cdots\; s_m}{s_0} \left\{ s_0[\circ\circ] \rightarrow A(s_1[\,] \;\cdots\; s_j[\circ\circ] \;\cdots\; s_m[\,]) \right. \qquad \text{(d)}$$

$$\frac{\begin{array}{c}(s_1, s_2)\\ (s_3, s_4)\end{array}}{(s_0, s_4)} \left\{ \begin{array}{l} s_0[\circ\circ] \rightarrow s_1[\iota\circ\circ] \\ s_2[\iota\circ\circ] \rightarrow s_3[\circ\circ] \end{array} \right. \qquad \text{(e)}$$

$$\frac{\begin{array}{c}(s_1, s_2)\\ s_3\end{array}}{s_0} \left\{ \begin{array}{l} s_0[\circ\circ] \rightarrow s_1[\iota\circ\circ] \\ s_2[\iota\circ\circ] \rightarrow s_3[\circ\circ] \end{array} \right. \qquad \text{(f)}$$

Figure 1: Simultaneous analysis of two kinds of subderivations in a LIG. Items (s, s') represent existence of one or more subderivations $s[\,] \rightarrow^* \alpha(s'[\,])$, where α is a tree with a gap in the form of an unresolved state s' associated with an empty stack. Furthermore, s and s' are connected through propagation of a stack of indices, or in other words, the occurrence of s' is the head of a rule, of which the left-hand side state is the head of another rule, etc., up to s. In the inference rules, items s represent existence of one or more subderivations $s[\,] \rightarrow^* \alpha$, where α is a complete tree (without any unresolved states).

two types of item. The generated language is non-empty if the item $s^{\vdash}$ can be derived.

We will explain inference rule (f), which is the most involved of the six rules. The two items in the antecedent indicate the existence of derivations $s_1[\,] \rightarrow^* \alpha(s_2[\,])$ and $s_3[\,] \rightarrow^* \beta$. Note that $s_1[\,] \rightarrow^* \alpha(s_2[\,])$ implies $s_1[\iota] \rightarrow^* \alpha(s_2[\iota])$, because an additional element in the bottom of a stack would not block an existing derivation. Hence $s_0[\,] \rightarrow s_1[\iota] \rightarrow^* \alpha(s_2[\iota]) \rightarrow \alpha(s_3[\,]) \rightarrow^* \alpha(\beta)$, which justifies the item s_0 in the consequent of the rule.

After determining which items can be derived through the deduction system, it is straightforward to identify those rules that are useful, by applying the inference rules in reverse, from consequent to antecedents, starting with $s^{\vdash}$.

The running time of the analysis is determined by how often each of the inference rules can be applied, which is bounded by the number of ways each can be instantiated with states and rules from the grammar. The six inference rules together give us $\mathcal{O}(|S| + |R_2| + |R_1| \cdot |S| + |R_1| + |R_3| \cdot |R_4| \cdot |S| + |R_3| \cdot |R_4|) = \mathcal{O}(|S| + |R_1| \cdot |S| + |R_2| + |R_3| \cdot |R_4| \cdot |S|) = |\mathcal{G}|^3$, where we assume a reasonable measure for the size $|\mathcal{G}|$ of a LIG $\mathcal{G}$, for example, the total number of occurrences of states, labels and indices in the rules.

It is not difficult to see that there is exactly one deduction of $s^{\vdash}$ in the deduction system for each complete derivation in the grammar. We leave the full proof to the interested reader, but provide the hint that items (s, s') can only play a role in a complete deduction provided s' is rewritten by a rule that pops an index from the stack. Because of this, derivations in the grammar of the form $s[\,] \rightarrow^* \alpha(s'[\,])$ or of the form $s[\,] \rightarrow^* \alpha$ can be divided in a unique way into subderivations representable by our items.

The above deduction system is conceptually very close to a system of equations that expresses the sum of weights of all derivations in the grammar, or $in(s^{\vdash})$, in terms of similar values of the form $in(s)$, which is the sum of weights of all subderivations $s[\,] \rightarrow^* \alpha$, and $in(s, s')$, which is the sum of weights of all subderivations $s[\,] \rightarrow^* \alpha(s'[\,])$. The equations are given in Figure 2.

Although the expressions look unwieldy, they

$$
\begin{aligned}
in(s_0) &= \sum_{s_0[\,] \to A()\ \langle w\rangle} w \ + \\
&\quad \sum_{s_0[\circ\circ] \to A(s_1[\,]\ \cdots\ s_j[\circ\circ]\ \cdots\ s_m[\,])\ \langle w\rangle} w \cdot in(s_1) \cdot \ldots \cdot in(s_m) \ + \\
&\quad \sum_{\substack{s_0[\circ\circ] \to s_1[\iota\circ\circ]\ \langle w\rangle \\ s_2[\iota\circ\circ] \to s_3[\circ\circ]\ \langle v\rangle}} w \cdot v \cdot in(s_1, s_2) \cdot in(s_3) \\
in(s_0, s) &= \delta(s_0 = s) \ + \\
&\quad \sum_{s_0[\circ\circ] \to A(s_1[\,]\ \cdots\ s_j[\circ\circ]\ \cdots\ s_m[\,])\ \langle w\rangle} w \cdot in(s_1) \cdot \ldots \cdot in(s_j, s) \cdot \ldots \cdot in(s_m) \ + \\
&\quad \sum_{\substack{s_0[\circ\circ] \to s_1[\iota\circ\circ]\ \langle w\rangle \\ s_2[\iota\circ\circ] \to s_3[\circ\circ]\ \langle v\rangle}} w \cdot v \cdot in(s_1, s_2) \cdot in(s_3, s)
\end{aligned}
$$

Figure 2: The sum of weights of all derivations in a WLIG, or $in(s^{\vdash})$, is defined by the smallest non-negative solution to a system of equations. The function δ with a boolean argument evaluates to 1 if the condition is true and to 0 otherwise.

express exactly the 'inside' value of the weighted context-free grammar that we can extract out of the deduction system from Figure 1, by instantiating the inference rules in all possible ways, and then taking the consequent as the left-hand side of a rule, and the antecedent as the right-hand side. The weight is the product of weights of rules that appear in the side conditions. It is possible to effectively solve the system of equations, as shown by (Wojtczak and Etessami, 2007).

In the same vein we can compute 'outside' values for weighted linear indexed grammars, as straightforward analogues of the outside values of weighted and probabilistic context-free grammars. The outside value is the sum of weights of partial derivations that may lie 'outside' a subderivation $s[\,] \to^* \alpha$ in the case of $out(s)$, or a subderivation $s[\,] \to^* \alpha(s'[\,])$ in the case of $out(s, s')$. The equations in Figure 3 again follow trivially from the view of Figure 1 as weighted context-free grammar and the usual definition of outside values.

The functions in and out are particularly useful for PLIGs in TAG-normal form, as they allow the expected number of occurrences of state s to be expressed as:

$$E(s) \;=\; in(s) \cdot out(s)$$

Similarly, the expected number of subderivations of the form $s[\,] \to^* \alpha(s'[\,])$ is:

$$E(s, s') \;=\; in(s, s') \cdot out(s, s')$$

We will return to this issue in Section 5.

4 Weighted intersection

Before we discuss intersection on the level of trees, we first show how a well-established type of intersection on the level of strings, with weighted context-free grammars and weighted finite automata (WFAs), can be trivially extended to replace CFGs with RTGs or LIGs. The intersection paradigm is originally due to (Bar-Hillel et al., 1964). Extension to tree adjoining grammars and linear indexed grammars was proposed before by (Lang, 1994) and (Vijay-Shanker and Weir, 1993b).

4.1 Intersection of string languages

Let us assume a WLIG $\mathcal{G}$ with terminal and nonterminal labels. Furthermore, we assume a weighted finite automaton $\mathcal{A}$, with an input alphabet equal to the set of terminal labels of $\mathcal{G}$. The transitions of $\mathcal{A}$ are of the form:

$$q \overset{a}{\mapsto} q'\ \langle w\rangle,$$

where q and q' are states, a is a terminal symbol, and w is a weight. To simplify the presentation,

$$
\begin{aligned}
out(s') \;=\;& \delta(s' = s^{\vdash}) \;+ \\
& \sum_{\substack{s_0[\circ\circ] \to A(s_1[] \cdots s_j[\circ\circ] \cdots s_m[])\,\langle w\rangle \\ k \in \{1,\ldots,s_{j-1},s_{j+1},\ldots,s_m\} \text{ s.t. } s' = s_k}} w \cdot out(s_0, s) \cdot in(s_j, s) \cdot \prod_{p \notin \{j,k\}} in(s_p) \;+ \\
& \sum_{\substack{s_0[\circ\circ] \to A(s_1[] \cdots s_j[\circ\circ] \cdots s_m[])\,\langle w\rangle \\ k \in \{1,\ldots,s_m\} \text{ s.t. } s' = s_k}} w \cdot out(s_0) \cdot \prod_{p \neq k} in(s_p) \;+ \\
& \sum_{\substack{s_0[\circ\circ] \to s_1[\iota\circ\circ]\,\langle w\rangle \\ s_2[\iota\circ\circ] \to s'[\circ\circ]\,\langle v\rangle}} w \cdot v \cdot out(s_0) \cdot in(s_1, s_2) \\
out(s', s) \;=\;& \sum_{\substack{s_0[\circ\circ] \to A(s_1[] \cdots s_j[\circ\circ] \cdots s_m[])\,\langle w\rangle \\ s' = s_j}} w \cdot out(s_0, s) \cdot \prod_{p \neq j} in(s_p) \;+ \\
& \sum_{\substack{s_0[\circ\circ] \to s'[\iota\circ\circ]\,\langle w\rangle \\ s[\iota\circ\circ] \to s_3[\circ\circ]\,\langle v\rangle}} w \cdot v \cdot out(s_0, s_4) \cdot in(s_3, s_4) \;+ \\
& \sum_{\substack{s_0[\circ\circ] \to s_1[\iota\circ\circ]\,\langle w\rangle \\ s_2[\iota\circ\circ] \to s'[\circ\circ]\,\langle v\rangle}} w \cdot v \cdot out(s_0, s) \cdot in(s_1, s_2) \;+ \\
& \sum_{\substack{s_0[\circ\circ] \to s'[\iota\circ\circ]\,\langle w\rangle \\ s[\iota\circ\circ] \to s_3[\circ\circ]\,\langle v\rangle}} w \cdot v \cdot out(s_0) \cdot in(s_3)
\end{aligned}
$$

Figure 3: The outside values in a WLIG.

we ignore epsilon transitions, and assume there is a unique initial state $q^{\vdash}$ and a unique final state $q^{\dashv}$.

We can construct a new WLIG $\mathcal{G}'$ whose generated language is the intersection of the language generated by $\mathcal{G}$ and the language accepted by $\mathcal{A}$. The rules of $\mathcal{G}'$ are:

1. $(q_0, s_0, q_m)[\circ\circ] \to$
   $A(\ (q_0, s_1, q_1)[] \cdots$
   $(q_{j-2}, s_{j-1}, q_{j-1})[]$
   $(q_{j-1}, s_j, q_j)[\circ\circ]$
   $(q_j, s_{j+1}, q_{j+1})[] \cdots$
   $(q_{m-1}, s_m, q_m)[]\ )\ \langle w\rangle$,
   for each rule $s_0[\circ\circ] \to A(s_1[] \cdots s_{j-1}[]\ s_j[\circ\circ]\ s_{j+1}[] \cdots s_m[])\ \langle w\rangle$ from $\mathcal{G}$ and sequence $q_0, \ldots, q_m$ of states from $\mathcal{A}$;

2. $(q, s, q)[] \to A()\ \langle w\rangle$, for each rule $s[] \to A()\ \langle w\rangle$ from $\mathcal{G}$ and state q from $\mathcal{A}$;

3. $(q, s, q')[] \to a\ \langle w \cdot v\rangle$, for each rule $s[] \to a\ \langle w\rangle$ from $\mathcal{G}$ and transition $q \overset{a}{\mapsto} q'\ \langle v\rangle$ from $\mathcal{A}$;

4. $(q, s, q')[\circ\circ] \to (q, s', q')[\iota\circ\circ]\ \langle w\rangle$, for each rule $s[\circ\circ] \to s'[\iota\circ\circ]\ \langle w\rangle$ from $\mathcal{G}$ and states q, q' from $\mathcal{A}$;

5. $(q, s, q')[\iota\circ\circ] \to (q, s', q')[\circ\circ]\ \langle w\rangle$, for each rule $s[\iota\circ\circ] \to s'[\circ\circ]\ \langle w\rangle$ from $\mathcal{G}$ and states q, q' from $\mathcal{A}$.

The new states (q, s, q') give (left-most) derivations in $\mathcal{G}'$ that each simultaneously represent one (left-most) derivation in $\mathcal{G}$ of a certain substring, starting from state s, and one sequence of transitions taking the automaton $\mathcal{A}$ from state q to state q' while scanning the same substring. The initial state of $\mathcal{G}'$ is naturally $(q^{\vdash}, s^{\vdash}, q^{\dashv})$, which derives strings in the intersection of the original two languages.

Further note that each derivation in $\mathcal{G}'$ has a weight that is the product of the weight of the corresponding derivation in $\mathcal{G}$ and the weight of the corresponding sequence of transitions in $\mathcal{A}$. This allows a range of useful applications. For example, if $\mathcal{A}$ is deterministic (the minimum requirement is in fact absence of ambiguity) and if it assigns the weight one to all transitions, then $\mathcal{G}'$ generates a set of trees that is exactly the subset of trees generated by $\mathcal{G}$ whose yields are accepted by $\mathcal{A}$. Furthermore, the weights of those derivations are preserved. If $\mathcal{G}$ is a consistent PLIG in TAG-normal form, and if $\mathcal{A}$ accepts the language of all strings containing a fixed substring x, then the sum of probabilities of all derivations in $\mathcal{G}'$ gives the substring probability of x. The effective computation of this probability was addressed in Section 3.

An even more restricted, but perhaps more familiar case is if $\mathcal{A}$ is a linear structure that accepts a single input string y of length n. Then $\mathcal{G}'$ generates exactly the set of trees generated by $\mathcal{G}$ that have y as yield. In other words, the string y is thereby parsed.

If $\mathcal{G}$ is *binary*, i.e. all rules have at most two states in the right-hand side, then $\mathcal{G}'$ has a size that is cubic in n. This may seem surprising, in the light of the awareness that practical parsing algorithms for tree adjoining grammars have a time complexity of no less than $\mathcal{O}(n^6)$. However, in order to solve the recognition problem, an analysis is needed to determine whether $\mathcal{G}'$ allows at least one derivation.

The analysis from Figure 1 requires $\mathcal{O}(|S'| + |R'_1| \cdot |S'| + |R'_2| + |R'_3| \cdot |R'_4| \cdot |S'|)$ steps, where $|S'| = \mathcal{O}(n^2)$ is the number of states of $\mathcal{G}'$, and $|R'_1| = \mathcal{O}(n^3)$, $|R'_2| = |R'_3| = |R'_4| = \mathcal{O}(n^2)$ are the numbers of rules of $\mathcal{G}'$, divided into the four main types. This leads to an overall time complexity of $\mathcal{O}(n^6)$, as expected.

The observation that recognition can be harder than parsing was made before by (Lang, 1994). The central new insight this provided was that the notion of 'parsing' is ill-defined in the literature. One may choose a form in which to capture all parses of an input allowed by a grammar, but different such forms may incur different costs of extracting individual parse trees.

In Section 6.2 we will consider the complexity of parsing and recognition if $\mathcal{G}$ is not binary.

4.2 Intersection of tree languages

We now shift our attention from strings to trees, and consider the intersection of the tree language generated by a weighted linear indexed grammar $\mathcal{G}_1$ and the tree language generated by a weighted regular tree grammar $\mathcal{G}_2$. This intersection is generated by another weighted linear indexed grammar $\mathcal{G}$, which has the following rules:

1. $(s_0, q_0)[\circ\circ] \rightarrow A(\ (s_1, q_1)[\,] \cdots (s_{j-1}, q_{j-1})[\,]\ (s_j, q_j)[\circ\circ]\ (s_{j+1}, q_{j+1})[\,] \cdots (s_m, q_m)[\,]\ )\ \langle w \cdot v \rangle$, for each rule $s_0[\circ\circ] \rightarrow A(s_1[\,] \cdots s_{j-1}[\,]\ s_j[\circ\circ]\ s_{j+1}[\,] \cdots s_m[\,])\ \langle w \rangle$ from $\mathcal{G}_1$ and each rule $q_0 \rightarrow A(q_1 \cdots q_m)\ \langle v \rangle$ from $\mathcal{G}_2$;

2. $(s, q)[\,] \rightarrow A()\ \langle w \cdot v \rangle$, for each rule $s[\,] \rightarrow A()\ \langle w \rangle$ from $\mathcal{G}_1$ and each rule $q \rightarrow A()\ \langle v \rangle$ from $\mathcal{G}_2$;

3. $(s, q)[\circ\circ] \rightarrow (s', q)[\iota\circ\circ]\ \langle w \rangle$, for each rule $s[\circ\circ] \rightarrow s'[\iota\circ\circ]\ \langle w \rangle$ from $\mathcal{G}_1$ and state q from $\mathcal{G}_2$;

4. $(s, q)[\iota\circ\circ] \rightarrow (s', q)[\circ\circ]\ \langle w \rangle$, for each rule $s[\iota\circ\circ] \rightarrow s'[\circ\circ]\ \langle w \rangle$ from $\mathcal{G}_1$ and state q from $\mathcal{G}_2$.

Much as in the previous section, each (leftmost) derivation in $\mathcal{G}$ corresponds to one (leftmost) derivation in $\mathcal{G}_1$ and one in $\mathcal{G}_2$. Furthermore, these three derivations derive the same labelled tree, and a derivation in $\mathcal{G}$ has a weight that is the product of the weights of the corresponding derivations in $\mathcal{G}_1$ and $\mathcal{G}_2$.

It can be instructive to look at special cases. Suppose that $\mathcal{G}_2$ is an unambiguous regular tree grammar of size $\mathcal{O}(n)$ generating a single tree t with n vertices, assigning weight one to all its rules. Then the above construction can be seen as *parsing* of that tree t. The sum of weights of derivations in $\mathcal{G}$ then gives the weight of the tree in $\mathcal{G}_1$. See Section 3 once more for a general way to compute this weight, as the inside value of the initial state of $\mathcal{G}$, which is naturally $(s^{\vdash}, q^{\vdash})$.

In order to do recognition of t, or in other words, to determine whether $\mathcal{G}$ allows at least one derivation, the analysis from Figure 1 can be used, which has time complexity $\mathcal{O}(|S| + |R_1| \cdot |S| + |R_2| + |R_3| \cdot |R_4| \cdot |S|)$, where $|S| = \mathcal{O}(n)$ is the number of states of $\mathcal{G}$, and the numbers of rules are $|R_1| = \mathcal{O}(n)$, $|R_2| = |R_3| = |R_4| = \mathcal{O}(n)$. Note that $|R_1| = \mathcal{O}(n)$ because we have assumed that $\mathcal{G}_2$ allows only one derivation of one tree t, hence q_0 uniquely determines $q_1, \ldots, q_m$. Overall, we obtain $\mathcal{O}(n^3)$ steps, which concurs with a known result about the complexity of TAG parsing of trees, as opposed to strings (Poller and Becker, 1998).

Another special case is if WLIG $\mathcal{G}_1$ simplifies to a WRTG (i.e. the stacks of indices remain always empty), which means we compute the intersection of two weighted regular tree grammars $\mathcal{G}_1$ and $\mathcal{G}_2$. For recognition, or in other words to decide non-emptiness of the intersection, we can still use Figure 1, although now only inference rules (b) and (d) are applicable (with a small refinement to the algorithm we can block spurious application of (a) where no rules exist that pop indices.) The complexity is determined by (d), which requires $\mathcal{O}(|\mathcal{G}_1| \cdot |\mathcal{G}_2|)$ steps.

5 Parameter estimation

PLIGs allow finer description of probability distributions than PRTG, both over string languages and over tree languages. However, the (string) parsing complexity of regular tree grammars is $\mathcal{O}(n^3)$ and that of LIGs is $\mathcal{O}(n^6)$. It may therefore be preferable for reasons of performance to do parsing with a PRTG even when a PTAGs or PLIG is available with accurately trained probabilities. Alternatively, one may do both, with a PRTG used in a first phase to heuristically reduce the search space.

This section outlines how a suitable PRTG $\mathcal{G}_2$ can be extracted out of a PLIG $\mathcal{G}_1$, assuming the underlying RTG $\mathcal{G}'_2$ without weights is already given. The tree language generated by $\mathcal{G}'_2$ may be an approximation of that generated by $\mathcal{G}_1$. The objective is to make $\mathcal{G}_2$ as close as possible to $\mathcal{G}_1$ in terms of probability distributions over trees. We assume that $\mathcal{G}'_2$ is unambiguous, that is, for each tree it generates, there is at most one derivation.

The procedure is a variant of the one described by (Nederhof, 2005). The idea is that derivations in $\mathcal{G}_1$ are mapped to those in $\mathcal{G}'_2$, via the trees in the intersection of the two tree languages. The probability distribution of states and rules in $\mathcal{G}_2$ is estimated based on the expected frequencies of states and rules from $\mathcal{G}'_2$ in the intersection.

Concretely, we turn the RTG $\mathcal{G}'_2$ into a PRTG $\mathcal{G}''_2$ that is obtained simply be assigning weight one to all rules. We then compute the intersection grammar $\mathcal{G}$ as in Section 4.2. Subsequently, the inside and outside values are computed for $\mathcal{G}$, as explained in Section 3. The expected number of occurrences of a rule in $\mathcal{G}$ of the form:

$$\begin{aligned}(s_0, q_0)[\circ\circ] \to A(\ & (s_1, q_1)[\,] \cdots \\ & (s_{j-1}, q_{j-1})[\,] \\ & (s_j, q_j)[\circ\circ] \\ & (s_{j+1}, q_{j+1})[\,] \cdots \\ & (s_m, q_m)[\,]\ )\ \langle w \cdot v \rangle,\end{aligned}$$

is given by multiplying the outside and inside probabilities and the rule probability, as usual. We get two terms however that we need to sum. The intuition is that we must count both rule occurrences used for building initial TAG trees and those used for building auxiliary TAG trees. This gives:

$$\begin{aligned}& w \cdot v \cdot out((s_0, q_0)) \cdot \prod_k in((s_k, q_k)) \ + \\ & w \cdot v \cdot \sum_{s,q} out((s_0, q_0), (s, q)) \cdot \\ & \qquad in((s_j, q_j), (s, q)) \cdot \prod_{k \neq j} in((s_k, q_k))\end{aligned}$$

By summing these expected numbers for different rules $s_0[\circ\circ] \to A(s_1[\,] \cdots s_{j-1}[\,]\ s_j[\circ\circ]\ s_{j+1}[\,] \cdots s_m[\,])$, we obtain the expected number of occurrences of $q_0 \to A(q_1 \cdots q_m)$, Let us denote this sum by $E(q_0 \to A(q_1 \cdots q_m))$. By summing these for fixed q_0, we obtain the expected number of occurrences of q_0, which we denote by $E(q_0)$. The probability of $q_0 \to A(q_1 \cdots q_m)$ in $\mathcal{G}_2$ is then set to be the ratio of $E(q_0 \to A(q_1 \cdots q_m))$ and $E(q_0)$.

By this procedure, the Kullback-Leibler distance between $\mathcal{G}_1$ and $\mathcal{G}_2$ is minimized. Although the present paper deals with very different formalisms, the proof of correctness is identical to that in (Nederhof, 2005). The reason is that in both cases the mathematical analysis must focus on the objects in the intersection (strings or trees) which may correspond to multiple derivations in the original model (here $\mathcal{G}_1$) but to a single derivation in the unambiguous model to be trained (here $\mathcal{G}_2$), and each derivation is composed of rules, whose probabilities are to be multiplied.

6 Extensions

6.1 Transduction

For various formalisms describing (string or tree) languages, there are straightforward generalizations that describe a relation between two or more languages, which is known as a transduction. The idea is that the underlying control mechanism, such as the states in regular tree grammars or linear indexed grammars, is now coupled to two or more surface forms that are synchronously produced. For example, a rule in a weighted *synchronous* regular tree grammar (WSRTG) has the form:

$$s_0 \rightarrow A(s_1 \cdots s_m), B(s_{\pi(1)} \cdots s_{\pi(m)}) \langle w \rangle,$$

where π is a permutation of $1, \ldots, m$. We can generalize this to having a third label C and a second permutation π', in order to describe simultaneous relations between three tree languages, etc. In this section we will restrict ourselves to binary relations however, and call the first surface form the input and the second surface form the output. For synchronous tree adjoining grammars, see for example (Shieber, 1994).

If we apply intersection on the input or on the output of a synchronous grammar formalism, then this is best seen as composition. This is well-known in the case of finite-state transducers and some forms of context-free transduction (Berstel, 1979), and application to a wider range of formalisms is gaining interest in the area of machine translation (Knight, 2007).

With the intersection from Section 4.2 trivially extended to composition, we can now implement composition of the form:

$$\tau_1 \circ \ldots \circ \tau_k,$$

where the different τ_j are transducers, of which $k - 1$ are (W)SRTGs and at most one is a (weighted) synchronous LIG ((W)SLIG). The result of the composition is another (W)SLIG. It should be noted that a (W)RTS (or (W)LIG) can be seen as a (W)SRTG (or (W)SLIG, respectively) that represents the identity relation on its tree language.

6.2 Binarization

In the discussion of complexity in Section 4.1, we assumed that rules are binary, that is, that they have at most two states in each right-hand side. However, whereas any context-free grammar can be transformed into a binary form (e.g. Chomsky normal form), the grammars as we have defined them cannot be. We will show that this is to a large extent a consequence of our definitions, which were motivated by presentational ease, rather than by generality.

The main problem is formed by rules of the form $s_0 \rightarrow A(s_1 \cdots s_m)$, where $m > 2$. Such long rules cannot be broken up into shorter rules of the same form, as this would require an additional labelled vertex, changing the tree language. An apparent solution lies in allowing branching rules without any label, for example $s_1 \rightarrow s_2\, s_3$. Regrettably this could create substantial computational problems for intersection of the described tree languages. As labels provide the mechanism through which to intersect tree languages, rules of the above form are somewhat similar to unit rules or epsilon rules in context-free grammars, in that they are not bound to observable elements. Branching rules furthermore have the potential to generate context-free languages, and therefore they are more pernicious to intersection, considering that emptiness of intersection of context-free languages is undecidable.

It therefore seems better to restrict branching rules $s_1 \rightarrow s_2\, s_3$ to finite-state power, for example by making these rules exclusively left-linear or right-linear. A more elegant but equivalent way of looking at this may be to have rules of the form:

$$s_0 \rightarrow A(\mathcal{R}),$$

where $\mathcal{R}$ is a regular language over states. In the case of linear indexed grammars, we would have rules of the form:

$$s[\circ\circ] \rightarrow A(\mathcal{L}\; s'[\circ\circ]\; \mathcal{R})$$

where $\mathcal{L}$ and $\mathcal{R}$ are regular languages over expressions of the form $s[\,]$. Appropriate weighted finite automata can be used to assign weights to sequences of such expressions in $\mathcal{L}$ and $\mathcal{R}$. With these extended types of rules, our construction from Section 4.2 still works. The key observation here is that regular languages are closed under intersection.

One of the implications of the above extended definitions is that labels appear not only without fixed ranks, as we have assumed from the start in Section 2, but even without a bound on the rank. Concretely, a vertex may appear with any number of children in a tree. Whereas this may be unconventional in certain areas of formal language theory, it is a well-accepted practice in the parsing of natural language to make the number of constituents of syntactic categories flexible and conceptually unbounded; see for example

(Collins, 1997). Also the literature on unranked tree automata is very relevant; see for example (Schwentick, 2007). Binarization for LIGs was considered before by (Vijay-Shanker and Weir, 1993a).

6.3 Beyond TAGs

In the light of results by (Kepser and Mönnich, 2006) it is relatively straightforward to consider larger classes of linear context-free tree grammars in place of tree-adjoining grammars, in order to generalize the construction in Section 4.2.

The generalization described in what follows seems less straightforward. Context-free languages can be characterized in terms of parse trees in which path sets (sets of strings of labels on paths from the root to a leaf) are regular. In the case of tree adjoining languages, the path sets are context-free. There is a hierarchy of classes of languages in which the third step is to consider path sets that are tree adjoining languages (Weir, 1992). In this paper, we have considered the parsing-as-intersection paradigm for the first two members of the hierarchy. It may be possible that the paradigm is also applicable to the third and following members. This avenue is yet to be pursued.

7 Conclusions

This paper has extended the parsing-as-intersection paradigm from string languages to tree languages. Probabilities, or weights in general, were incorporated in this framework in a natural way. We have discussed one particular application involving a special case of the extended paradigm.

Acknowledgements

Helpful comments by anonymous reviewers are gratefully acknowledged. The basic result from Section 4.1 as it pertains to RTGs as subclass of LIGs was discussed with Heiko Vogler, who proposed two alternative proofs. Sylvain Schmitz pointed out to me the relevance of literature on linear context-free tree languages.

References

A.V. Aho, M.S. Lam, R. Sethi, and J.D. Ullman. 2007. *Compilers: Principles, Techniques, & Tools*. Addison-Wesley.

Y. Bar-Hillel, M. Perles, and E. Shamir. 1964. On formal properties of simple phrase structure grammars. In Y. Bar-Hillel, editor, *Language and Information: Selected Essays on their Theory and Application*, chapter 9, pages 116–150. Addison-Wesley, Reading, Massachusetts.

J. Berstel. 1979. *Transductions and Context-Free Languages*. B.G. Teubner, Stuttgart.

M. Collins. 1997. Three generative, lexicalised models for statistical parsing. In *35th Annual Meeting of the Association for Computational Linguistics, Proceedings of the Conference*, pages 16–23, Madrid, Spain, July.

J. Graehl and K. Knight. 2004. Training tree transducers. In *HLT-NAACL 2004, Proceedings of the Main Conference*, Boston, Massachusetts, USA, May.

F. Gcseg and M. Steinby. 1997. Tree languages. In G. Rozenberg and A. Salomaa, editors, *Handbook of Formal Languages, Vol. 3*, chapter 1, pages 1–68. Springer, Berlin.

J.E. Hopcroft and J.D. Ullman. 1979. *Introduction to Automata Theory, Languages, and Computation*. Addison-Wesley.

A.K. Joshi and Y. Schabes. 1997. Tree-adjoining grammars. In G. Rozenberg and A. Salomaa, editors, *Handbook of Formal Languages. Vol 3: Beyond Words*, chapter 2, pages 69–123. Springer-Verlag, Berlin/Heidelberg/New York.

D. Jurafsky and J.H. Martin. 2000. *Speech and Language Processing*. Prentice-Hall.

S. Kepser and U. Mönnich. 2006. Closure properties of linear context-free tree languages with an application to optimality theory. *Theoretical Computer Science*, 354:82–97.

K. Knight. 2007. Capturing practical natural language transformations. *Machine Translation*, 21:121–133.

B. Lang. 1994. Recognition can be harder than parsing. *Computational Intelligence*, 10(4):486–494.

M.-J. Nederhof and G. Satta. 2003. Probabilistic parsing as intersection. In *8th International Workshop on Parsing Technologies*, pages 137–148, LORIA, Nancy, France, April.

M.-J. Nederhof. 2005. A general technique to train language models on language models. *Computational Linguistics*, 31(2):173–185.

P. Poller and T. Becker. 1998. Two-step TAG parsing revisited. In *Fourth International Workshop on Tree Adjoining Grammars and Related Frameworks*, pages 143–146. Institute for Research in Cognitive Science, University of Pennsylvania, August.

P. Resnik. 1992. Probabilistic tree-adjoining grammar as a framework for statistical natural language processing. In *Proc. of the fifteenth International Conference on Computational Linguistics*, pages 418–424. Nantes, August.

A. Sarkar. 1998. Conditions on consistency of probabilistic tree adjoining grammars. In *36th Annual Meeting of the Association for Computational Linguistics and 17th International Conference on Computational Linguistics*, volume 2, pages 1164–1170, Montreal, Quebec, Canada, August.

Y. Schabes. 1992. Stochastic lexicalized tree-adjoining grammars. In *Proc. of the fifteenth International Conference on Computational Linguistics*, pages 426–432. Nantes, August.

Thomas Schwentick. 2007. Automata for XML–a survey. *Journal of Computer and System Sciences*, 73:289–315.

S.M. Shieber. 1994. Restricting the weak-generative capacity of synchronous tree-adjoining grammars. *Computational Intelligence*, 10(4):371–385.

K. Sima'an. 1997. Efficient disambiguation by means of stochastic tree substitution grammars. In D. Jones and H. Somers, editors, *New Methods in Language Processing*. UCL Press, UK.

S. Sippu and E. Soisalon-Soininen. 1988. *Parsing Theory, Vol. I: Languages and Parsing*, volume 15 of *EATCS Monographs on Theoretical Computer Science*. Springer-Verlag.

K. Vijay-Shanker and D.J. Weir. 1993a. Parsing some constrained grammar formalisms. *Computational Linguistics*, 19(4):591–636.

K. Vijay-Shanker and D.J. Weir. 1993b. The use of shared forests in tree adjoining grammar parsing. In *Sixth Conference of the European Chapter of the Association for Computational Linguistics, Proceedings of the Conference*, pages 384–393, Utrecht, The Netherlands, April.

K. Vijay-Shanker and D.J. Weir. 1994. The equivalence of four extensions of context-free grammars. *Mathematical Systems Theory*, 27:511–546.

D.J. Weir. 1992. A geometric hierarchy beyond context-free languages. *Theoretical Computer Science*, 104:235–261.

D. Wojtczak and K. Etessami. 2007. PReMo: an analyzer for Probabilistic Recursive Models. In *Tools and Algorithms for the Construction and Analysis of Systems, 13th International Conference*, volume 4424 of *Lecture Notes in Computer Science*, pages 66–71, Braga, Portugal. Springer-Verlag.

Automatic Adaptation of Annotation Standards for Dependency Parsing — Using Projected Treebank as Source Corpus

Wenbin Jiang and Qun Liu

Key Lab. of Intelligent Information Processing
Institute of Computing Technology
Chinese Academy of Sciences
P.O. Box 2704, Beijing 100190, China
{jiangwenbin, liuqun}@ict.ac.cn

Abstract

We describe for dependency parsing an annotation adaptation strategy, which can automatically transfer the knowledge from a *source corpus* with a different annotation standard to the desired *target parser*, with the supervision by a *target corpus* annotated in the desired standard. Furthermore, instead of a hand-annotated one, a projected treebank derived from a bilingual corpus is used as the source corpus. This benefits the resource-scarce languages which haven't different hand-annotated treebanks. Experiments show that the target parser gains significant improvement over the baseline parser trained on the target corpus only, when the target corpus is smaller.

1 Introduction

Automatic annotation adaptation for sequence labeling (Jiang et al., 2009) aims to enhance a tagger with one annotation standard by transferring knowledge from a source corpus annotated in another standard. It would be valuable to adapt this strategy to parsing, since for some languages there are also several treebanks with different annotation standards, such as Chomskian-style Penn Treebank (Marcus et al., 1993) and HPSG LinGo Redwoods Treebank (Oepen et al., 2002) for English. However, we are not content with conducting annotation adaptation between existing different treebanks, because it would be more valuable to boost the parsers also for the resource-scarce languages, rather than only for the resource-rich ones that already have several treebanks.

Although hand-annotated treebanks are costly and scarce, it is not difficult for many languages to collect large numbers of bilingual sentence-pairs aligned to English. According to the word alignment, the English parses can be projected across to their translations, and the projected trees can be leveraged to boost parsing. Many efforts are devoted to the research on projected treebanks, such as (Lü et al., 2002), (Hwa et al., 2005) and (Ganchev et al., 2009), etc. Considering the fact that a projected treebank partially inherits the English annotation standard, some hand-written rules are designed to deal with the divergence between languages such as in (Hwa et al., 2002). However, it will be more valuable and interesting to adapt this divergence automatically and boost the existing parsers with this projected treebank.

In this paper, we investigate the automatic annotation adaptation strategy for Chinese dependency parsing, where the source corpus for adaptation is a projected treebank derived from a bilingual corpus aligned to English with word alignment and English trees. We also propose a novel, error-tolerant tree-projecting algorithm, which dynamically searches the project Chinese tree that has the largest consistency with the corresponding English tree, according to an alignment matrix rather than a single alignment. Experiments show that when the target corpus is smaller, the projected Chinese treebank, although with inevitable noise caused by non-literal translation and word alignment error, can be successfully utilized and result in significant improvement over the baseline model trained on the target corpus only.

In the rest of the paper, we first present the tree-projecting algorithm (section 2), and then the annotation adaptation strategy (section 3). After discussing the related work (section 4) we show the experiments (section 5).

2 Error-Tolerant Tree-Projecting Algorithm

Previous works making use of projected corpus usually adopt the direct-mapping method for structure projection (Yarowsky and Ngai, 2001; Hwa et al., 2005; Ganchev et al., 2009), where

Proceedings of the 11th International Conference on Parsing Technologies (IWPT), pages 25–28,
Paris, October 2009.

some filtering is needed to eliminate the inaccurate or conflicting labels or dependency edges. Here we propose a more robust algorithm for dependency tree projection. According to the alignment matrix, this algorithm dynamically searches the projected Chinese dependency tree which has the largest consistency with the corresponding English tree.

We briefly introduce the alignment matrix before describing our projecting algorithm. Given a Chinese sentence $C_{1:M}$ and its English translation $E_{1:N}$, the alignment matrix A is an $M \times N$ matrix with each element $A_{i,j}$ denoting the probability of Chinese word C_i aligned to English word E_j. Such structure potentially encodes many more possible alignments.

Using $\mathcal{C}(T_C|T_E, A)$ to denote the degree of Chinese tree T_C being consistent with English tree T_E according to alignment matrix A, the projecting algorithm aims to find

$$\hat{T_C} = \underset{T_C}{\text{argmax}}\, \mathcal{C}(T_C|T_E, A) \quad (1)$$

$\mathcal{C}(T_C|T_E, A)$ can be factorized into each dependency edge $x \rightarrow y$ in T_C, that is to say

$$\mathcal{C}(T_C|T_E, A) = \prod_{x \rightarrow y \in T_C} \mathcal{C}_e(x \rightarrow y|T_E, A) \quad (2)$$

We can obtain $\mathcal{C}_e$ by simple accumulation across all possible alignments

$$\begin{aligned} &\mathcal{C}_e(x \rightarrow y|T_E, A) \\ &= \sum_{1 \le x', y' \le |E|} A_{x,x'} \times A_{y,y'} \times \delta(x', y'|T_E) \end{aligned} \quad (3)$$

where $\delta(x', y'|T_E)$ is a 0-1 function that equals 1 only if $x' \rightarrow y'$ exists in T_E.

The searching procedure, argmax operation in equation 1, can be effectively solved by a simple, bottom-up dynamic algorithm with cube-pruning speed-up (Huang and Chiang, 2005). We omit the detailed algorithm here due to space restrictions.

3 Annotation Adaptation for Dependency Parsing

The automatic annotation adaptation strategy for sequence labeling (Jiang et al., 2009) aims to strengthen a tagger trained on a corpus annotated in one annotation standard with a larger assistant corpus annotated in another standard. We can define the purpose of the automatic annotation adaptation for dependency parsing in the same way.

Similar to that in sequence labeling, the training corpus with the desired annotation standard is called the *target corpus* while the assistant corpus annotated in a different standard is called the *source corpus*. For training, an intermediate parser, called the *source parser*, is trained directly on the source corpus and then used to parse the target corpus. After that a second parser, called the *target parser*, is trained on the target corpus with guide features extracted from the source parser's parsing results. For testing, a token sequence is first parsed by the source parser to obtain an intermediate parsing result with the source annotation standard, and then parsed by the target parser with the guide features extracted from the intermediate parsing result to obtain the final result.

The design of the guide features is the most important, and is specific to the parsing algorithm of the target parser. In this work we adopt the maximum spanning tree (MST) algorithm (McDonald et al., 2005; McDonald and Pereira, 2006) for both the source and the target parser, so the guide features should be defined on dependency edges in accordance with the edge-factored property of MST models. In the decoding procedure of the target parser, the degree of a dependency edge being supported can be adjusted by the relationship between this edge's head and modifier in the intermediate parsing result of the source parser. The most intuitionistic relationship is whether the dependency between head and modifier exists in this intermediate result. Such a bi-valued relationship is similar to that in the stacking method for combining dependency parsers (Martins et al., 2008; Nivre and McDonald, 2008). The guide features are then defined as this relationship itself as well as its combinations with the lexical features of MST models.

Furthermore, in order to explore more detailed knowledge from the source parser, we redefine the relationship as a four-valued variable which covers the following situations: *parent-child*, *child-parent*, *siblings* and *else*. With the guide features, the parameter tuning procedure of the target parser will automatically learn the regularity of using the source parser's intermediate result to guide its decision making.

4 Related Works

Many works have been devoted to obtain parsing knowledge from word aligned bilingual corpora. (Lü et al., 2002) learns Chinese bracketing knowledge via ITG alignment; (Hwa et al., 2005) and (Ganchev et al., 2009) induces dependency grammar via projection from aligned English, where some filtering is used to reduce the noise and some hand-designed rules to handle language heterogeneity.

Just recently, Smith and Eisner (2009) gave an idea similar to ours. They perform dependency projection and annotation adaptation with Quasi-Synchronous Grammar (QG) Features. Although both related to projection and annotation, there are still important differences between these two works. First, we design an error-tolerant alignment-matrix-based tree-projecting algorithm to perform whole-tree projection, while they resort to QG features to score local configurations of aligned source and target trees. Second, their adaptation emphasizes to transform a tree from one annotation standard to another, while our adaptation emphasizes to strengthen the parser using a treebank annotated in a different standard.

5 Experiments

The source corpus for annotation adaptation, that is, the projected Chinese treebank, is derived from 5.6 millions LDC Chinese-English sentence pairs. The Chinese side of the bilingual corpus is word-segmented and POS-tagged by an implementation of (Jiang et al., 2008), and the English sentences are parsed by an implementation of (McDonald and Pereira, 2006) which is instead trained on WSJ section of Penn English Treebank (Marcus et al., 1993). The alignment matrixes for sentence pairs are obtained according to (Liu et al., 2009). The English trees are then projected across to Chinese using the algorithm in section 2. Out of these projected trees, we only select 500 thousands with word count l s.t. $6 \leq l \leq 100$ and with projecting confidence $c = \mathcal{C}(T_C|T_E, A)^{1/l}$ s.t. $c \geq 0.35$. While for the target corpus, we take Penn Chinese Treebank (CTB) 1.0 and CTB 5.0 (Xue et al., 2005) respectively, and follow the traditional corpus splitting: chapters 271-300 for testing, chapters 301-325 for development, and else for training.

We adopt the 2nd-order MST model (McDonald et al., 2005) as the target parser for better performance, and the 1st-order MST model as the source parser for fast training. Both the two parsers are trained with averaged perceptron algorithm (Collins, 2002). The development set of CTB is also used to determine the best model for the source parser, conditioned on the hypothesis of larger isomorphisme between Chinese and English.

Model	P% on CTB 1	P% on CTB 5
source parser	53.28	53.28
target parser	**83.56**	**87.34**
baseline parser	82.23	87.15

Table 1: Performances of annotation adaptation with CTB 1.0 and CTB 5.0 as the target corpus respectively, as well as of the baseline parsers (2nd-order MST parsers trained on the target corpora).

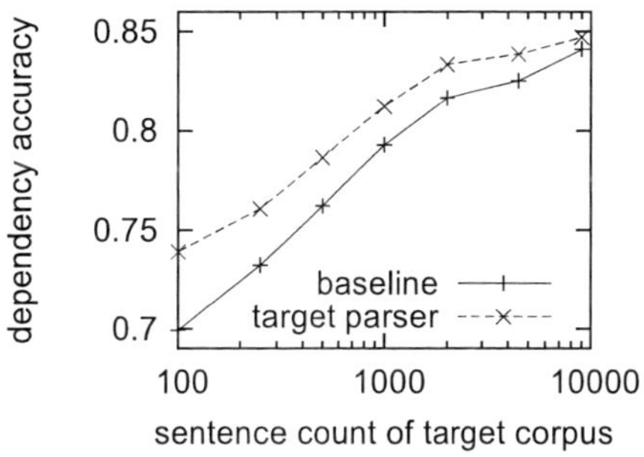

Figure 1: Performance of the target parsers with target corpora of different scales.

Table 1 shows that the experimental results of annotation adaptation, with CTB 1.0 and CTB 5.0 as the target corpus respectively. We can see that the source parsers, directly trained on the source corpora of projected trees, performs poorly on both CTB test sets (which are in fact the same). This is partly due to the noise in the projected treebank, and partly due to the heterogeneous between the CTB trees and the projected trees. On the contrary, automatic annotation adaptation effectively transfers the knowledge to the target parsers, achieving improvement on both target corpora. Especially on CTB 1.0, an accuracy increment of 1.3 points is obtained over the baseline parser.

We observe that for the much larger CTB 5.0, the performance of annotation adaptation is much lower. To further investigate the adaptation performances with target corpora of different scales, we conduct annotation adaptation on a series of target corpora which consist of different amount of dependency trees from CTB 5.0. Curves in Figure 1 shows the experimental results. We see that the smaller the training corpus is, the more significant improvement can be obtained. For example, with a target corpus composed of 2K trees, nearly 2 points of accuracy increment is achieved. This is a good news to the resource-scarce languages.

6 Conclusion and Future Works

This paper describes for dependency parsing an automatic annotation adaptation strategy. What is more important, we use a projected treebank, rather than a hand-annotated one, as the source corpus for adaptation. This is quite different from previous works on projected trees (Hwa et al., 2005; Ganchev et al., 2009), and is also more valuable than previous works of annotation adaptation (Jiang et al., 2009). Experiments show that this strategy gains improvement over baseline parsers with target corpora of different scales, especially the smaller ones. This provides a new strategy for resource-scarce languages to train high-precision dependency parsers. In the future, we will adapt this strategy to constituent parsing, which is more challenging and interesting due to the complexity of projection between constituent trees, and due to the obscurity of annotation adaptation for constituent parsing.

Acknowledgement

This project was supported by National Natural Science Foundation of China, Contracts 60603095 and 60736014, and 863 State Key Project No. 2006AA010108. We are grateful to the anonymous reviewers for their valuable suggestions. We also thank Yang Liu for sharing his codes of alignment matrix generation, and Liang Huang and Haitao Mi for helpful discussions.

References

Michael Collins. 2002. Discriminative training methods for hidden markov models: Theory and experiments with perceptron algorithms. In *Proceedings of the EMNLP*, pages 1–8, Philadelphia, USA.

Kuzman Ganchev, Jennifer Gillenwater, and Ben Taskar. 2009. Dependency grammar induction via bitext projection constraints. In *Proceedings of the 47th ACL*.

Liang Huang and David Chiang. 2005. Better k-best parsing. In *Proceedings of the IWPT*, pages 53–64.

Rebecca Hwa, Philip Resnik, Amy Weinberg, and Okan Kolak. 2002. Evaluating translational correspondence using annotation projection. In *Proceedings of the ACL*.

Rebecca Hwa, Philip Resnik, Amy Weinberg, Clara Cabezas, and Okan Kolak. 2005. Bootstrapping parsers via syntactic projection across parallel texts. In *Natural Language Engineering*, volume 11, pages 311–325.

Wenbin Jiang, Liang Huang, Yajuan Lü, and Qun Liu. 2008. A cascaded linear model for joint chinese word segmentation and part-of-speech tagging. In *Proceedings of the ACL*.

Wenbin Jiang, Liang Huang, and Qun Liu. 2009. Automatic adaptation of annotation standards: Chinese word segmentation and pos tagging–a case study. In *Proceedings of the 47th ACL*.

Yang Liu, Tian Xia, Xinyan Xiao, and Qun Liu. 2009. Weighted alignment matrices for statistical machine translation. In *Proceedings of the EMNLP*.

Yajuan Lü, Sheng Li, Tiejun Zhao, and Muyun Yang. 2002. Learning chinese bracketing knowledge based on a bilingual language model. In *Proceedings of the COLING*.

Mitchell P. Marcus, Beatrice Santorini, and Mary Ann Marcinkiewicz. 1993. Building a large annotated corpus of english: The penn treebank. In *Computational Linguistics*.

André F. T. Martins, Dipanjan Das, Noah A. Smith, and Eric P. Xing. 2008. Stacking dependency parsers. In *Proceedings of EMNLP*.

Ryan McDonald and Fernando Pereira. 2006. Online learning of approximate dependency parsing algorithms. In *Proceedings of EACL*, pages 81–88.

Ryan McDonald, Koby Crammer, and Fernando Pereira. 2005. Online large-margin training of dependency parsers. In *Proceedings of ACL*, pages 91–98.

Joakim Nivre and Ryan McDonald. 2008. Integrating graph-based and transition-based dependency parsers. In *Proceedings of ACL*.

Stephan Oepen, Kristina Toutanova, Stuart Shieber, Christopher Manning Dan Flickinger, and Thorsten Brants. 2002. The lingo redwoods treebank: Motivation and preliminary applications. In *In Proceedings of COLING*.

David Smith and Jason Eisner. 2009. Parser adaptation and projection with quasi-synchronous grammar features. In *Proceedings of EMNLP*.

Nianwen Xue, Fei Xia, Fu-Dong Chiou, and Martha Palmer. 2005. The penn chinese treebank: Phrase structure annotation of a large corpus. In *Natural Language Engineering*.

David Yarowsky and Grace Ngai. 2001. Inducing multilingual pos taggers and np bracketers via robust projection across aligned corpora. In *Proceedings of the NAACL*.

Learning Stochastic Bracketing Inversion Transduction Grammars with a Cubic Time Biparsing Algorithm

Markus Saers Joakim Nivre

Dept. of Linguistics and Philology
Uppsala University
Sweden
first.last@lingfil.uu.se

Dekai Wu

Human Language Technology Center
Dept. of Computer Science and Engineering
HKUST
Hong Kong
dekai@cs.ust.hk

Abstract

We present a biparsing algorithm for Stochastic Bracketing Inversion Transduction Grammars that runs in $O(bn^3)$ time instead of $O(n^6)$. Transduction grammars learned via an EM estimation procedure based on this biparsing algorithm are evaluated directly on the translation task, by building a phrase-based statistical MT system on top of the alignments dictated by Viterbi parses under the induced bigrammars. Translation quality at different levels of pruning are compared, showing improvements over a conventional word aligner even at heavy pruning levels.

1 Introduction

As demonstrated by Saers & Wu (2009) there is something to be gained by applying structural models such as Inversion Transduction Grammars (ITG) to the problem of word alignment. One issue is that naïve methods for inducing ITGs from parallel data can be very time consuming. We introduce a parsing algorithm for inducing Stochastic Bracketing ITGs from parallel data in $O(bn^3)$ time instead of $O(n^6)$, where b is a pruning parameter (lower = tighter pruning). We try out different values for b, and evaluate the results on a translation tasks.

In section 2 we summarize the ITG framework; in section 3 we present our algorithm, whose time complexity is analyzed in section 4. In section 5 we describe how the algorithm is evaluated, and in section 6, the empirical results are given.

2 Inversion Transduction Grammars

Inversion transductions are a theoretically interesting and empirically useful equivalence class of transductions, with expressiveness and computational complexity characteristics lying intermediate between finite-state transductions and syntax-directed transductions. An Inversion Transduction Grammar (ITG) can be used to synchronously generate sentence pairs, synchronously parse sentence pairs, or transduce from a sentence in one language to a sentence in another.[1]

The equivalence class of inversion transductions can be described by restricting Syntax-Directed Transduction Grammars (SDTG)[2] in various equivalent ways to the special cases of (a) binary SDTGs, (b) ternary SDTGs, or (c) SDTGs whose transduction rules are restricted to straight and inverted permutations only.

Thus on one hand, any binary or ternary SDTG is an ITG. Conversely, any ITG can be stated in binary two-normal form (Wu, 1997). Only three kinds of rules are present in the normal form:

$$A \rightarrow [BC]$$
$$A \rightarrow \langle BC \rangle$$
$$A \rightarrow e/f$$

On the other hand, under characterization (c), what distinguishes ITGs is that the permutation of constituents is restricted in such a way that all children of a node must be read either left-to-right, or right-to-left. The movement only applies to one of the languages, the other is fixed. Formally, an ITG is a tuple $\langle N, V, \Delta, S \rangle$, where N is a set of nonterminal symbols, Δ is a set of rewrite rules, $S \in N$ is the start symbol and $V \subseteq V_E \times V_F$ is a set of biterminal symbols, where V_E is the vocabulary of E and V_F is the vocabulary of F. We will write a biterminal as e/f, where $e \in V_E$ and $f \in V_F$. A sentence pair will be written as $\mathbf{e}/\mathbf{f}$, and a bispan as $e_{s..t}/f_{u..v}$.

Each rule $\delta \in \Delta$ is a tuple $\langle X, \gamma, \theta \rangle$ where $X \in N$ is the right hand side of the rule, $\gamma \in$

[1] All transduction grammars (a.k.a. synchronous grammars, or simply bigrammars) can be interpreted as models for generation, recognition, or transduction.

[2] SDTGs (Lewis & Stearns (1968); Aho & Ullman (1969), (1972)) are also recently called synchronous CFGs.

Proceedings of the 11th International Conference on Parsing Technologies (IWPT), pages 29–32,
Paris, October 2009.

$\{N \cup V\}^*$ is a series of nonterminal and biterminal symbols representing the production of the rule and $\theta \in \{\emptyset, [], \langle\rangle\}$ denotes the orientation (axiomatic, straight or inverted) of the rule. Straight rules are read left-to-right in both languages, while inverted rules are read left-to-right in E and right-to-left in F. The direction of the axiomatic rules is undefined, as they must be completely made up of terminals. For notational convenience, the orientation of the rule is written as surrounding the production, like so: $X \rightarrow \gamma$, $X \rightarrow [\gamma]$ and $X \rightarrow \langle\gamma\rangle$. The vocabularies of the languages may both include the empty token ϵ, allowing for deletions and insertions. The empty biterminal, ϵ/ϵ is not allowed.

2.1 Stochastic ITGs

In a Stochastic ITG (SITG), each rule is also associated with a probability, such that

$$\sum_{\gamma} Pr(X \rightarrow \gamma) = 1$$

for all $X \in N$. The probability of a derivation $S \overset{*}{\Rightarrow} \mathbf{e}/\mathbf{f}$ is defined as the production of the probabilities of all rules used. As shown by Wu (1995), it is possible to fit the parameters of a SITG to a parallel corpus via EM (expectation-maximization) estimation.

2.2 Bracketing ITGs

An ITG where there is only one nonterminal (other than the start symbol) is called a bracketing ITG (BITG). Since the one nonterminal is devoid of information, it can only be used to group its children together, imposing a bracketing on the sentence pairs.

3 Parsing SBITGs

In this section we present a biparsing algorithm for Stochastic Bracketing Inversion Transduction Grammars (SBITGs) in normal form which incorporates a pruning parameter b. The algorithm is basically an agenda-based bottom-up chart parser, where the pruning parameter controls the number of active items of a given length.

To parse a sentence pair $\mathbf{e}/\mathbf{f}$, the parser needs a chart $\mathcal{C}$ and a series of $T + V$ agendas $A_1, A_2, \ldots, A_{T+V}$, where $T = |\mathbf{e}|$ and $V = |\mathbf{f}|$. An item is defined as a nonterminal symbol (we use X to denote the anonymous nonterminal symbol of the bracketing ITG) and one span in each language, written as X_{stuv} where $0 \leq s \leq t \leq T$ corresponds to the span $e_{s..t}$ and $0 \leq u \leq v \leq V$ corresponds to the span $f_{u..v}$. The length of an item is defined as $|X_{stuv}| = (t-s)+(v-u)$. Since items are grouped by their length, highly skewed links (eg. 6:1) will be competing with very even links (eg. 4:3). Skewed links are generally bad (and should be pruned), or have a high probability (which means they are likely to survive pruning). An item may be active or passive, the active items are present in the agendas and the chart, whereas the passive items are only present in the chart.

The parser starts by asserting items from all lexical rules ($X \rightarrow e/f$), and placing them on their respective agendas. After the initial seeding, the agendas are processed in order. When an agenda is processed, it is first pruned, so that only the b best items are kept active. After pruning, the remaining active items are allowed to be extended. When extended, the item combines with an adjacent item in the chart to form a larger item. The newly created item is considered active, and added to both the chart and the appropriate agenda. Once an item has been processed it goes from being active to being passive. The process is halted when the goal item S_{0T0V} is reached, or when no active items remain. To build the forest corresponding to the parse process, back-pointers are used.

3.1 Initialization

In the initial step, the set of lexical items L is built. All lexical items $i \in L$ are then activated by placing them on their corresponding agenda $A_{|i|}$.

$$L = \left\{ X_{stuv} \;\middle|\; \begin{array}{l} 0 \leq s \leq t \leq T, \\ 0 \leq u \leq v \leq V, \\ X \rightarrow e_{s..t}/f_{u..v} \in \Delta \end{array} \right\}$$

By limiting the length of phrasal terminals to some threshold μ, the variables t and v can be limited to $s+\mu$ and $u+\mu$ respectively, limiting the complexity of the initialization step from $O(n^4)$ to $O(n^2)$.

3.2 Recursion

In the recursive step we build a set of extensions $E(i)$ for all active items i. All items in $E(i)$ are then activated by placing them on their corresponding agenda ($i \in A_{|i|}$).

$$\begin{array}{l} E(X_{stuv}) = \\ \{X_{StUv} | 0 \leq S \leq s, 0 \leq U \leq u, X_{SsUu} \in \mathcal{C}\} \quad \cup \\ \{X_{sSuU} | t \leq S \leq T, v \leq U \leq V, X_{tSvU} \in \mathcal{C}\} \quad \cup \\ \{X_{sSUv} | t \leq S \leq T, 0 \leq U \leq u, X_{tSUu} \in \mathcal{C}\} \quad \cup \\ \{X_{StuU} | 0 \leq S \leq s, v \leq U \leq V, X_{SsvU} \in \mathcal{C}\} \end{array}$$

Since we are processing the agendas in order, any item in the chart will be as long as or shorter than the item being extended. This fact can be exploited to limit the number of possible siblings explored, but has no impact on time complexity.

3.3 Viterbi parsing

When doing Viterbi parsing, all derivations but the most probable are discarded. This gives an unambiguous parse, which dictates exactly one alignment between $\mathbf{e}$ and $\mathbf{f}$. The alignment of the Viterbi parse can be used to substitute that of other word aligners (Saers and Wu, 2009) such as GIZA++ (Och and Ney, 2003).

4 Analysis

Looking at the algorithm, it is clear that there will be a total of $T + V = O(n)$ agendas, each containing items of a certain length. The items in an agenda can start anywhere in the alignment space: $O(n^2)$ possible starting points, but once the end point in one language is set, the end point in the other follows from that, adding a factor $O(n)$. This means that each agenda contains $O(n^3)$ active items. Each active item has to go through all possible siblings in the recursive step. Since the start point of the sibling is determined by the item itself (it has to be adjacent), only the $O(n^2)$ possible end points have to be explored. This means that each active item takes $O(n^2)$ time to process.

The total time is thus $O(n^6)$: $O(n)$ agendas, containing $O(n^3)$ active items, requiring $O(n^2)$ time to process. This is also the time complexity reported for ITGs in previous work (Wu, 1995; Wu, 1997).

The pruning works by limiting the number of active items in an agenda to a constant b, meaning that there are $O(n)$ agendas, containing $O(b)$ active items, requiring $O(n^2)$ time to process. This gives a total time complexity of $O(bn^3)$.

5 Evaluation

We evaluate the parser on a translation task (WMT'08 shared task[3]). In order to evaluate on a translation task, a translation system has to be built. We use the alignments from the Viterbi parses of the training corpus to substitute the alignments of GIZA++. This is the same approach as taken in Saers & Wu (2009). We will evaluate the resulting translations with two automatic metrics: BLEU (Papineni et al., 2002) and NIST (Doddington, 2002).

[3] `http://www.statmt.org/wmt08/`

6 Empirical results

In this section we describe the experimental setup as well as the outcomes.

6.1 Setup

We use the Moses Toolkit (Koehn et al., 2007) to train our phrase-based SMT models. The toolkit also includes scripts for applying GIZA++ (Och and Ney, 2003) as a word aligner. We have trained several systems, one using GIZA++ (our baseline system), one with no pruning at all, and 6 different values of b (1, 10, 25, 50, 75 and 100). We used the `grow-diag-final-and` method to extract phrases from the word alignment, and MERT (Och, 2003) to optimize the resulting model. We trained a 5-gram SRI language model (Stolcke, 2002) using the corpus supplied for this purpose by the shared task organizers. All of the above is consistent with the guidelines for building a baseline system for the WMT'08 shared task.

The translation tasks we applied the above procedure to are all taken from the Europarl corpus (Koehn, 2005). We selected the tasks German-English, French-English and Spanish-English. Furthermore, we restricted the training sentence pairs so that none of the sentences exceeded length 10. This was necessary to be able to carry out exhaustive search. The total amount of training data was roughly 100,000 sentence pairs in each language pair, which is a relatively small corpus, but by no means a toy example.

6.2 Grammar induction

It is possible to set the parameters of a SBITG by applying EM to an initial guess (Wu, 1995). As our initial guess, we used word co-occurrence counts, assuming that there was one empty token in each sentence. This gave an estimate of the lexical rules. The probability mass was divided so that the lexical rules could share half of it, while the other half was shared equally by the two structural rules ($X \rightarrow [XX]$ and $X \rightarrow \langle XX \rangle$).

Several training runs were made with different pruning parameters. The EM process was halted when a relative improvement in log-likelihood of 10^{-3} was no longer achieved over the previous iteration.

Metric	Baseline (GIZA++)	Different values of b for SBITGs: ∞	100	75	50	25	10	1
Spanish-English								
BLEU	0.2597	0.2663	**0.2671**	0.2661	0.2653	0.2655	0.2608	0.1234
NIST	6.6352	6.7407	**6.7445**	6.7329	6.7101	6.7312	6.6439	3.9705
time		03:20:00	02:40:00	02:00:00	01:20:00	00:38:00	00:17:00	00:03:10
German-English								
BLEU	0.2059	**0.2113**	0.2094	0.2091	0.2090	0.2091	0.2050	0.0926
NIST	5.8668	**5.9380**	5.9086	5.8955	5.8947	5.9292	5.8743	3.4297
time		03:40:00	02:45:00	02:10:00	01:25:00	00:41:00	00:17:00	00:03:20
French-English								
BLEU	0.2603	0.2663	0.2655	0.2668	**0.2669**	0.2654	0.2632	0.1268
NIST	6.6907	**6.8151**	6.8068	6.8068	6.8065	6.7013	6.7136	4.0849
time		03:10:00	02:45:00	02:10:00	01:25:00	00:42:00	00:17:00	00:03:25

Table 1: Results. Time measures are approximate time per iteration.

Once the EM process terminated, Viterbi parses were calculated for the training corpus, and the alignments from them outputted in the same format produced by GIZA++.

6.3 Results

The results are presented in Table 1. GIZA++ generally terminates within minutes (6–7) on the training corpora used, making it faster than any of the SBITGs (they generally required 4–6 iterations to terminate, making even the fastest ones slower than GIZA++). To put the times in perspective, about 6 iterations were needed to get the ITGs to converge, making the longest training time about 16–17 hours. The time it takes to extract the phrases and tune the model using MERT is about 14 hours for these data sets.

Looking at translation quality, we see a sharp initial rise as b grows to 10. At this point the SBITG system is on par with GIZA++. It continues to rise up to $b = 25$, but after that is more or less levels out. From this we conclude that the positive results reported in Saers & Wu (2009) hold under harsh pruning.

7 Conclusions

We have presented a SBITG biparsing algorithm that uses a novel form of pruning to cut the complexity of EM-estimation from $O(n^6)$ to $O(bn^3)$. Translation quality using the resulting learned SBITG models is improved over using conventional word alignments, even under harsh levels of pruning.

Acknowledgments

The authors are grateful for the comments made by the two anonymous reviewers. This work was funded by the Swedish National Graduate School of Language Technology, the Defense Advanced Research Projects Agency (DARPA) under GALE Contract No. HR0011-06-C-0023, and the Hong Kong Research Grants Council (RGC) under research grants GRF621008, DAG03/04.EG09, RGC6256/00E, and RGC6083/99E. Any opinions, findings and conclusions or recommendations expressed in this material are those of the authors and do not necessarily reflect the views of the Defense Advanced Research Projects Agency.

References

Alfred V. Aho and Jeffrey D. Ullman. 1969. Syntax-directed translations and the pushdown assembler. *Journal of Computer and System Sciences*, 3(1):37–56.

Alfred V. Aho and Jeffrey D. Ullman. 1972. *The Theory of Parsing, Translation, and Compiling (Volumes 1 and 2)*. Prentice-Halll, Englewood Cliffs, NJ.

George Doddington. 2002. Automatic evaluation of machine translation quality using n-gram co-occurrence statistics. In *Human Language Technology conference (HLT-2002)*, San Diego, CA.

Philipp Koehn, Hieu Hoang, Alexandra Birch, Chris Callison-Burch, Marcello Federico, Nicola Bertoldi, Brooke Cowan, Wade Shen, Christine Moran, Richard Zens, Chris Dyer, Ondrej Bojar, Alexandra Constantin, and Evan Herbst. 2007. Moses: Open source toolkit for statistical machine translation. In *ACL-2007 Demo and Poster Sessions*, pages 177–180, Prague, Jun.

Philipp Koehn. 2005. Europarl: A parallel corpus for statistical machine translation. In *Machine Translation Summit X*, Phuket, Thailand, September.

Philip M. Lewis and Richard E. Stearns. 1968. Syntax-directed transduction. *Journal of the Association for Computing Machinery*, 15(3):465–488.

Franz Josef Och and Hermann Ney. 2003. A systematic comparison of various statistical alignment models. *Computational Linguistics*, 29(1):19–52.

Franz Josef Och. 2003. Minimum error rate training in statistical machine translation. In *41st Annual Meeting of the Association for Computational Linguistics*, pages 160–167, Sapporo, Japan, Jul.

Kishore Papineni, Salim Roukos, Todd Ward, and Wei-Jing Zhu. 2002. BLEU: A method for automatic evaluation of machine translations. In *40th Annual Meeting of the Association for Computational Linguistics (ACL-2002)*, pages 311–318, Philadelphia, Jul.

Markus Saers and Dekai Wu. 2009. Improving phrase-based translation via word alignments from Stochastic Inversion Transduction Grammars. In *Proceedings of SSST-3, Third Workshop on Syntax and Structure in Statistical Translation (at NAACL HLT 2009)*, pages 28–36, Boulder, CO, Jun.

Andreas Stolcke. 2002. SRILM – an extensible language modeling toolkit. In *International Conference on Spoken Language Processing*, Denver, CO, Sep.

Dekai Wu. 1995. Trainable coarse bilingual grammars for parallel text bracketing. In *Third Annual Workshop on Very Large Corpora (WVLC-3)*, pages 69–81, Cambridge, MA, Jun.

Dekai Wu. 1997. Stochastic Inversion Transduction Grammars and bilingual parsing of parallel corpora. *Computational Linguistics*, 23(3):377–404, Sep.

Empirical lower bounds on translation unit error rate for the full class of inversion transduction grammars

Anders Søgaard
Center for Language Technology
University of Copenhagen
soegaard@hum.ku.dk

Dekai Wu
Human Language Technology Center
Hong Kong Univ. of Science and Technology
dekai@cs.ust.hk

Abstract

Empirical lower bounds studies in which the frequency of alignment configurations that cannot be induced by a particular formalism is estimated, have been important for the development of syntax-based machine translation formalisms. The formalism that has received most attention has been inversion transduction grammars (ITGs) (Wu, 1997). All previous work on the coverage of ITGs, however, concerns parse failure rates (PFRs) or sentence level coverage, which is not directly related to any of the evaluation measures used in machine translation. Søgaard and Kuhn (2009) induce lower bounds on translation unit error rates (TUERs) for a number of formalisms, incl. normal form ITGs, but not for the full class of ITGs. Many of the alignment configurations that cannot be induced by normal form ITGs can be induced by unrestricted ITGs, however. This paper estimates the difference and shows that the average reduction in lower bounds on TUER is 2.48 in absolute difference (16.01 in average parse failure rate).

1 Introduction

The first stage in training a machine translation system is typically that of aligning bilingual text. The quality of alignments is in that case of vital importance to the quality of the induced translation rules used by the system in subsequent stages. In string-based statistical machine translation, the alignment space is typically restricted by the n-grams considered in the underlying language model, but in syntax-based machine translation the alignment space is restricted by very different and less transparent structural contraints. While it is easy to estimate the consequences of restrictions to n-grams of limited size, it is less trivial to estimate the consequences of the structural constraints imposed by syntax-based machine translation formalisms. Consequently, much work has been devoted to this task (Wu, 1997; Zens and Ney, 2003; Wellington et al., 2006; Macken, 2007; Søgaard and Kuhn, 2009).

The task of estimating the consequences of the structural constraints imposed by a particular syntax-based formalism consists in finding what is often called "empirical lower bounds" on the coverage of the formalism (Wellington et al., 2006; Søgaard and Kuhn, 2009). Gold standard alignments are constructed and queried in some way as to identify complex alignment configurations, or they are parsed by an all-accepting grammar such that a parse failure indicates that no alignment could be induced by the formalism.

The assumption in this and related work that enables us to introduce a meaningful notion of alignment capacity is that simultaneously recognized words are aligned (Wu, 1997; Zhang and Gildea, 2004; Wellington et al., 2006; Søgaard and Kuhn, 2009). As noted by Søgaard (2009), this definition of alignment has the advantageous consequence that candidate alignments can be singled out by mere inspection of the grammar rules. It also has the consequence that alignments are transitive (Goutte et al., 2004), since simultaneity is transitive.

While previous work (Søgaard and Kuhn, 2009) has estimated empirical lower bounds for normal form ITGs at the level of translation units (TUER), or cepts (Goutte et al., 2004), defined as maximally connected subgraphs in alignments, nobody has done this for the full class of ITGs. What is important to understand is that while normal form ITGs can induce the same class of translations as the full class of ITGs, they do *not* induce the same class of alignments. They do not, for ex-

Proceedings of the 11th International Conference on Parsing Technologies (IWPT), pages 33–36,
Paris, October 2009. ©2009 Association for Computational Linguistics

ample, induce discontinuous translation units (see Sect. 3). Sect. 2 briefly presents some related results in the literature. Some knowledge about formalisms used in machine translation is assumed.

2 Related work

Aho and Ullman (1972) showed that 4-ary synchronous context-free grammars (SCFGs) could not be binarized, and Satta and Peserico (2005) showed that the hiearchy of SCFGs beyond ternary ones does not collapse; they also showed that the complexity of the universal recognition problem for SCFGs is NP-complete. ITGs on the other hand has a $\mathcal{O}(|G|n^6)$ solvable universal recognition problem, which coincides with the unrestricted alignment problem (Søgaard, 2009). The result extends to decoding in conjunction with a bigram language model (Huang et al., 2005).

Wu (1997) introduced ITGs and normal form ITGs. ITGs are a notational variant of the subclass of SCFGs such that all indexed nonterminals in the source side of the RHS occur in the same order or exactly in the inverse order in the target side of the RHS. It turns out that this subclass of SCFGs defines the same set of translations that can be defined by binary SCFGs. The different forms of production rules are listed below with the more restricted normal form production rules in the right column, with $\phi \in (N \cup \{e/f \mid e \in T^*, f \in T^*\})^*$ (N nonterminals and T terminals, as usual). The RHS operator $[\,]$ preserves source language constituent order in the target language, while $\langle\,\rangle$ reverses it.[1]

$$\begin{array}{lll|lll} A & \rightarrow & [\phi] & A & \rightarrow & [BC] \\ A & \rightarrow & \langle\phi\rangle & A & \rightarrow & \langle BC\rangle \\ & & & A & \rightarrow & e/f \end{array}$$

Several studies have adressed the alignment capacity of ITGs and normal form ITGs. Zens and Ney (2003) induce lower bounds on PRFs for normal form ITGs. Wellington et al. (2006) induce lower bounds on PRFs for ITGs. Søgaard and Kuhn (2009) induce lower bounds on TUER for normal form ITGs and more expressive formalisms for syntax-based machine translation. No one has, however, to the best our knowledge induced lower bounds on TUER for ITGs.

[1]One reviewer argues that our definition of full ITGs is *not* equivalent to the definition in Wu (1997), which, in the reviewer's words, allows "at most one lexical item from each language". Sect. 6 of Wu (1997), however, explicitly encourages lexical elements in rules to have more than one lexical item in many cases.

3 Experiments

As already mentioned empirical lower bounds studies differ in four important respects, namely wrt.: (i) whether they use hand-aligned or automatically aligned gold standards, (ii) the level at which they count failures, e.g. sentence, alignment or translation unit level, (iii) whether they interpret translation units disjunctively or conjunctively, and (iv) whether they induce the lower bounds (a) by running an all-accepting grammar on the gold standard data, (b) by logical characterization of the structures that can be induced by a formalism, or (c) by counting the frequency of complex alignment configurations. The advantage of (a) and (b) is that they are guaranteed to find the highest possible lower bound on the gold standard data, whereas (c) is more modular (formalism-independent) and actually tells us what configurations cause trouble.

(i) In this study we use hand-aligned gold standard data. It should be obvious why this is preferable to automatically aligned data. The only reason that some previous studies used automatically aligned data is that hand-aligned data are hard to come by. This study uses the data also used by Søgaard and Kuhn (2009), which to the best of our knowledge uses the largest collection of hand-aligned parallel corpora used in any of these studies. (ii) Failures are counted at the level of translation units as argued for in the above, but supplemented by parse failure rates for completeness. (iii) Since we count failures at the level of translation units, it is natural to interpret them conjunctively. Otherwise we would in reality count failures at the level of alignments. (iv) We use (c).

The conjunctive interpretation of translation units was also adopted by Fox (2002) and is motivated by the importance of translation units and discontinuous ones in particular to machine translation in general (Simard and colleagues, 2005; Ayan and Dorr, 2006; Macken, 2007; Shieber, 2007). In brief,

$$\text{TUER} = 1 - \frac{2|S_U \cap G_U|}{|S_U| + |G_U|}$$

where G_U are the translation units in the gold standard, and S_U the translation units produced by the system. This evaluation measure is related to consistent phrase error rate (CPER) introduced in Ayan and Dorr (2006), except that it does not only consider contiguous phrases.

3.1 Data

The characteristics of the hand-aligned gold standard parallel corpora used are presented in Figure 1. The Danish-Spanish text is part of the Copenhagen Dependency Treebank (Parole), English-German is from Pado and Lapata (2006) (Europarl), and the six combinations of English, French, Portuguese and Spanish are documented in Graca et al. (2008) (Europarl).

3.2 Alignment configurations

The full class of ITGs induces many alignment configurations that normal form ITGs do not induce, incl. discontinuous translation units (DTUs), i.e. translation units with at least one gap, double-sided DTUs, i.e. DTUs with both a gap in the source side and a gap in the target side, and multigap DTUs with arbitrarily many gaps (as long as the contents in the gap are either respect the linear order of the source side or the inverted order).

ITGs do *not* induce (i) inside-out alignments, (ii) cross-serial DTUs, (iii) what is called the "bonbon" configuration below, and (iv) multigap DTUs with mixed order in the target side. The reader is referred to Wu (1997) for discussion of inside-out alignments. (ii) and (iii) are explained below.

3.2.1 Induced configurations

DTUs are easily induced by unrestricted ITG productions, while they cannot be induced by productions in normal form. The combination of the production rules $A \rightarrow [\epsilon/ne\ B\ nothing/pas]$ and $B \rightarrow [change/modifie]$, for example, induces a DTU with a gap in the French side for the pair of substrings $\langle$*change nothing, ne modifie pas*$\rangle$.

Multigap DTUs with up to three gaps are frequent (Søgaard and Kuhn, 2009) and have shown to be important for translation quality (Simard and colleagues, 2005). While normal form ITGs do not induce multigap DTUs, ITGs induce a particular subclass of multigap DTUs, namely those that are constructed by linear or inverse interpolation.

3.2.2 Non-induced configurations

Inside-out alignments were first described by Wu (1997), and their frequency has been a matter of some debate (Lepage and Denoual, 2005; Wellington et al., 2006; Søgaard and Kuhn, 2009).

Cross-serial DTUs are made of two DTUs noncontiguous to the same side such that both have material in the gap of each other. **Bonbons** are similar, except the DTUs are non-contiguous to different sides, i.e. D has a gap in the source side that contains at least one token in E, and E has a gap in the target side that contains at least one token in D. Here's an example of a bonbon configuration from Simard et al. (2005):

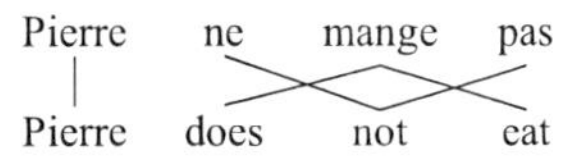

Multigap DTUs with mixed transfer are, as already mentioned multigap DTUs with crossing alignments from material in two distinct gaps.

3.3 Results

The lower bounds on TUER for the full class of ITGs are obtained by summing the ratios of inside-out alignments, cross-serial DTUs, bonbons and mixed order multigap DTUs, subtracting any overlap between these classes of configurations. The lower bounds on TUER for normal form ITGs sum ratios of inside-out aligments and DTUs subtracting any overlap. Figure 1 presents the ratio ($\times 100$), and Figure 2 presents the induced lower bounds on the full class of ITGs and normal form ITGs. Any two configurations differ *on all translation units* in order to count as two distinct configurations in these statistics. Otherwise a single translation unit could be removed to simplify two or more configurations.

4 Discussion

The usefulness of alignment error rate (AER) (Och and Ney, 2000) has been questioned lately (Fraser and Marcu, 2007); most importantly, AER does not always seem to correlate with translation quality. TUER is likely to correlate better with translation quality, since it by definition correlates with CPER (Ayan and Dorr, 2006). No large-scale experiment has been done yet to estimate the strength of this correlation.

Our study also relies on the assumption that simulatenously recognized words are aligned in bilingual parsing. The relationship between parsing and alignment can of course be complicated in ways that will alter the alignment capacity of ITG and its normal form; on some definitions the two formalisms may even become equally expressive.

5 Conclusion

It was shown that the absolute reduction in average lower bound on TUER is 2.48 for the full class of ITGs over its canonical normal form. For PRF, it is 16.01.

	Snts	TUs	IOAs	DTUs	CDTUs	Bonbons	MIX-DTUs
Da-Sp	926	6441	0.56	9.16	0.81	0.16	0.23
En-Fr	100	869	0.23	2.99	0.12	0.23	0.23
En-Ge	987	17354	1.75	5.55	0.45	0.05	0.79
En-Po	100	783	0.26	2.17	0.00	0.00	0.38
En-Sp	100	831	0.48	1.32	0.00	0.00	0.36
Po-Fr	100	862	0.23	3.13	0.58	0.00	0.46
Po-Sp	100	882	0.11	0.90	0.00	0.00	0.00
Sp-Fr	100	914	0.11	2.95	0.55	0.00	0.22

Figure 1: Characteristics of the parallel corpora and frequency of configurations ($\frac{n}{\text{TUs}} \times 100$).

	ITGs				**NF-ITGs**			
	LB-TUER	LB-PFR	Ovlp(TUs)	Ovlp(Snts)	LB-TUER	PFR	Ovlp(TUs)	Ovlp(Snts)
Da-Sp	1.58	10.37	11	10	8.54	40.50	76	32
En-Fr	0.69	6.00	1	1	2.88	22.00	3	2
En-Ge	2.75	47.32	49	42	5.24	69.30	357	236
En-Po	0.64	5.00	0	0	2.43	19.00	0	0
En-Sp	0.84	7.00	0	0	1.80	15.00	0	0
Po-Fr	1.04	9.00	2	2	3.36	24.00	0	0
Po-Sp	0.11	1.00	1	1	0.90	8.00	1	1
Sp-Fr	0.77	7.00	1	1	3.06	23.00	0	0
AV	1.05	11.59			3.53	27.60		

Figure 2: Induced lower bounds for ITGs and normal form ITGs (NF-ITGs). LB-TUER lists the lower bounds on TUER. LB-PFR lists the lower bounds on parse failure rates. Finally, the third and fourth columns list configuration overlaps at the level of translation units, resp. sentences.

References

Alfred Aho and Jeffrey Ullman. 1972. *The theory of parsing, translation and compiling*. Prentice-Hall.

Necip Ayan and Bonnie Dorr. 2006. Going beyond AER. In *COLING-ACL'06*, Sydney, Australia.

Heidi Fox. 2002. Phrasal cohesion and statistical machine translation. In *EMNLP'02*, Philadelphia, PA.

Alexander Fraser and Daniel Marcu. 2007. Measuring word alignment quality for statistical machine translation. *Computational Linguistics*, 33(3):293–303.

Cyril Goutte, Kenji Yamada, and Eric Gaussier. 2004. Aligning words using matrix factorisation. In *ACL'04*, Barcelona, Spain.

Joao Graca, Joana Pardal, Luísa Coheur, and Diamantino Caseiro. 2008. Building a golden collection of parallel multi-language word alignments. In *LREC'08*, Marrakech, Morocco.

Liang Huang, Hao Zhang, and Daniel Gildea. 2005. Machine translation as lexicalized parsing with hooks. In *IWPT'05*, pages 65–73, Vancouver, BC.

Yves Lepage and Etienne Denoual. 2005. Purest ever example-based machine translation. *Machine Translation*, 19(3–4):251–282.

Lieve Macken. 2007. Analysis of translational correspondence in view of sub-sentential alignment. In *METIS-II*, pages 9–18, Leuven, Belgium.

Franz Och and Hermann Ney. 2000. A comparison of alignment models for statistical machine translation. In *COLING'00*, Saarbrücken, Germany.

Sebastian Padó and Mirella Lapata. 2006. Optimal constituent alignment with edge covers for semantic projection. In *ACL-COLING'06*, Sydney, Australia.

Giorgio Satta and Enoch Peserico. 2005. Some computational complexity results for synchronous context-free grammars. In *HLT-EMNLP'05*, Vancouver, BC.

Stuart Shieber. 2007. Probabilistic synchronous tree-adjoining grammars for machine translation. In *SSST'07*, pages 88–95, Rochester, NY.

Michel Simard and colleagues. 2005. Translating with non-contiguous phrases. In *HLT-EMNLP'05*, Vancouver, BC.

Anders Søgaard and Jonas Kuhn. 2009. Empirical lower bounds on alignment error rates in syntax-based machine translation. In *NAACL-HLT'09, SSST-3*, Boulder, CO.

Anders Søgaard. 2009. On the complexity of alignment problems in two synchronous grammar formalisms. In *NAACL-HLT'09, SSST-3*, Boulder, CO.

Benjamin Wellington, Sonjia Waxmonsky, and Dan Melamed. 2006. Empirical lower bounds on the complexity of translational equivalence. In *ACL'06*, pages 977–984, Sydney, Australia.

Dekai Wu. 1997. Stochastic inversion transduction grammars and bilingual parsing of parallel corpora. *Computational Linguistics*, 23(3):377–403.

Richard Zens and Hermann Ney. 2003. A comparative study on reordering constraints in statistical machine translation. In *ACL'03*, Sapporo, Japan.

Hao Zhang and Daniel Gildea. 2004. Syntax-based alignment: supervised or unsupervised? In *COLING'04*, pages 418–424, Geneva, Switzerland.

Predictive Text Entry using Syntax and Semantics

Sebastian Ganslandt **Jakob Jörwall** **Pierre Nugues**
Department of Computer Science
Lund University
S-221 00 Lund, Sweden
sebastian@ganslandt.nu pierre.nugues@cs.lth.se
d02jjr@student.lth.se

Abstract

Most cellular telephones use numeric keypads, where texting is supported by dictionaries and frequency models. Given a key sequence, the entry system recognizes the matching words and proposes a rank-ordered list of candidates. The ranking quality is instrumental to an effective entry.

This paper describes a new method to enhance entry that combines syntax and language models. We first investigate components to improve the ranking step: language models and semantic relatedness. We then introduce a novel syntactic model to capture the word context, optimize ranking, and then reduce the number of keystrokes per character (KSPC) needed to write a text. We finally combine this model with the other components and we discuss the results.

We show that our syntax-based model reaches an error reduction in KSPC of 12.4% on a Swedish corpus over a baseline using word frequencies. We also show that bigrams are superior to all the other models. However, bigrams have a memory footprint that is unfit for most devices. Nonetheless, bigrams can be further improved by the addition of syntactic models with an error reduction that reaches 29.4%.

1 Introduction

The 12-key input is the most common keypad layout on cellular telephones. It divides the alphabet into eight lists of characters and each list is mapped onto one key as shown in Figure 1. Since three or four characters are assigned to a key, a single key press is ambiguous.

Figure 1: Standard 12-button keypad layout (ISO 9995-8).

1.1 Multi-tap

Multi-tap is an elementary method to disambiguate input for a 12-button keypad. Each character on a key is assigned an index that corresponds to its visual position, e.g. 'A', 1, 'B', 2, and 'C', 3 and each consecutive stroke – tap – on the same key increments the index. When the user wants to type a letter, s/he presses the corresponding key until the desired index is reached. The user then presses another key or waits a predefined time to verify that the correct letter is selected. The key sequence 8-4-4-3-3, for example, leads to the word *the*.

Multi-tap is easy to implement and no dictionary is needed. At the same time, it is slow and tedious for the user, notably when two consecutive characters are placed on the same key.

1.2 Single Tap with Predictive Text

Single tap with predictive text requires only one key press to enter a character. Given a keystroke sequence, the system proposes words using a dictionary or language modeling techniques.

Dictionary-based techniques search the words matching the key sequence in a list that is stored by the system (Haestrup, 2001). While some

Proceedings of the 11th International Conference on Parsing Technologies (IWPT), pages 37–48,
Paris, October 2009.

keystroke sequences produce a unique word, others are ambiguous and the system returns a list with all the candidates. The key sequence 8-4-3, for example, corresponds to at least three possible words: *the*, *tie*, and *vie*. The list of candidates is then sorted according to certain criteria, such as the word or character frequencies. If the word does not exist in the dictionary, the user has to fall back to multi-tap to enter it. The T9[1] commercial product is an example of a dictionary-based system (Grover et al., 1998).

LetterWise (MacKenzie et al., 2001) is a technique that uses letter trigrams and their frequencies to predict the next character. For example, pressing the key 3 after the letter bigram 'th' will select 'e', because the trigram 'the' is far more frequent than 'thd' or 'thf' in English. When the system proposes a wrong letter, the user can access the next most likely one by pressing a *next-key*. LetterWise does not need a dictionary and has a $KSPC$ of 1.1500 (MacKenzie, 2002).

1.3 Modeling the Context

Language modeling can extend the context from letter sequences to word n-grams. In this case, the system is not restricted to the disambiguation or the prediction of the typed characters. It can complete words and even predict phrases. HMS (Hasselgren et al., 2003) is an example of this that uses word bigrams in Swedish. It reports a $KSPC$ ranging from 0.8807 to 1.0108, depending on the type of text. eZiText[2] is a commercial example of a word and phrase completion system. However, having a large lexicon of bigrams still exceeds the memory capacity of many mobile devices.

Some systems use a combination of syntactic and semantic information to model the context. Gong et al. (2008) is a recent example that uses word frequencies, a part-of-speech language model, and a semantic relatedness metric. The part-of-speech language model acts as a lexical n-gram language model, but occupies much less memory since the vocabulary is restricted to the part-of-speech tagset. The semantic relatedness, modified from Li and Hirst (2005), is defined as the conditional probability of two stems appearing in the same context (the same sentence):

$$SemR(w_1|w_2) = \frac{C(stem(w_1), stem(w_2))}{C(w_2)}.$$

The three components are combined linearly and their coefficients are adjusted using a development set. Setting 1 as the limit of the $KSPC$ figure, Gong et al. (2008) reported an error reduction over the word frequency baseline of 4.6% for the semantic model, 12.6% for the part-of-speech language model, and 15.8% for the combination of both.

1.4 Syntax in Predictive Text

Beyond part-of-speech language modeling, there are few examples of systems using syntax in predictive text entry. Matiasek et al. (2002) describes a predictive text environment aimed at disabled persons, which originally relied on language models. Gustavii and Pettersson (2003) added a syntactic component to it based on grammar rules. The rules corresponded to common grammatical errors and were used to rerank the list of candidate words. The evaluation results were disappointing and the syntactic component was not added because of the large overhead it introduced (Matiasek, 2006).

In the same vein, Sundarkantham and Shalinie (2007) used grammar rules to discard infeasible grammatical constructions. The authors evaluated their system by giving it an incomplete sentence and seeing how often the system correctly guessed the next word (Shannon, 1951). They achieved better results than previously reported, although their system has not been used in the context of predictive text entry for mobile devices.

2 Predictive Text Entry Using Syntax

We propose a new technique that makes use of a syntactic component to model the word context and improve the $KSPC$ figure. It builds on Gong et al. (2008)'s system and combines a dependency grammar model with word frequencies, a part-of-speech language model, and the semantic relatedness defined in Sect. 1.3. As far as we are aware, no predictive text entry system has yet used a data-driven syntactic model of the context.

We used Swedish as our target language all over our experiments, but the results we obtained should be replicable in any other language.

[1] www.t9.com

[2] www.zicorp.com/ezitext.htm

2.1 Reranking Candidate Words

The system consists of two components. The first one disambiguates the typed characters using a dictionary and produces a list of candidate words. The second component reranks the candidate list. Although the techniques we describe could be applied to word completion, we set aside this aspect in this paper.

More formally, we frame text input as a sequence of keystrokes, $\mathbf{ks}^i = ks_1^i \ldots ks_n^i$, to enter a desired word, w_i. The words matching the key sequence in the system dictionary form an ordered set of alternatives, $match(\mathbf{ks}^i) = \{cw_0, \ldots, cw_m\}$, where it takes k extra keystrokes to reach candidate cw_k. Using our example in Sect. 1.2, a lexical ordering would yield $match(8-4-3) = \{the, tie, vie\}$, where two extra keystrokes are needed to reach *vie*.

We assign each candidate word w member of $match(\mathbf{ks}^i)$ a score

$$Score(w|Context) = \sum_{s \in S} \lambda_s \cdot s(w|Context),$$

to rerank (sort) the prediction list, where s is a scoring function from a set S, λ_s, the weight of s, and $Score(w|Context)$, the total score of w in the current context.

In this framework, optimizing predictive text entry is the task of finding the scoring functions, s, and the weights, λ_s, so that they minimize k on average.

As scoring functions, we considered lexical language models in the form of unigrams and bigrams, s_{LM1} and s_{LM2}, a part-of-speech model using sequences of part-of-speech tags of a length of up to five tags, s_{POS}, and a semantic affinity, s_{SemA}, derived from the semantic relatedness. In addition, we introduce a syntactic component in the form of a data-driven dependency syntax, s_{DepSyn} so that the complete scoring set consists of

$$S = \{s_{LM1}, s_{LM2}, s_{SemA}, s_{POS}, s_{DepSyn}\}.$$

2.2 Language and Part-of-Speech Models

The language model score is the probability of a candidate word w, knowing the sequence entered so far, $w_1, \ldots, w_i$:

$$P(w|w_1, w_2, \ldots, w_i).$$

We approximate it using unigrams, $s_{LM1}(w) = P(w)$, or bigrams, $s_{LM2}(w) = P(w|w_i)$ that we derive from a corpus using the maximum likelihood estimate. To cope with sparse data, we used a deleted interpolation so that $s_{LM2}(w) = \beta_1 P(w|w_i) + \beta_2 P(w)$, where we adjusted the values of β_1 and β_2 on a development corpus.

In practice, it is impossible to maintain a large list of bigrams on cellular telephones as it would exceed the available memory of most devices. In our experiments, the s_{LM2} score serves as an indicator of an upper-limit performance, while s_{LM1} serves as a baseline, as it is used in commercial dictionary-based products.

Part-of-speech models offer an interesting alternative to lexical models as the number of parts of speech does not exceed 100 tags in most languages. The possible number of bigrams is then at most 10,000 and much less in practice. We defined the part-of-speech model score, s_{POS} as

$$P(t|t_1, t_2, \ldots, t_i),$$

where t_i is the part of speech of w_i and t, the part of speech of the candidate word w. We used a 5-gram approximation of this probability with a simple back-off model:

$$s_{POS} = \begin{cases} P(t|t_{i-3}, \ldots, t_i) & \text{if } C(t_{i-3}, ..., t_i) \neq 0 \\ P(t|t_{i-2}, \ldots, t_i) & \text{if } C(t_{i-2}, ..., t_i) \neq 0 \\ \vdots & \\ P(t), & \text{otherwise} \end{cases}$$

We used the Granska tagger (Carlberger and Kann, 1999) to carry out the part-of-speech annotation of the word sequence.

3 Semantic Affinity

Because of their arbitrary length, language models miss possible relations between words that are semantically connected in a sentence but within a distance greater than one, two, or three words apart, the practical length of most n-grams models. Li and Hirst (2005) introduced the semantic relatedness between two words to measure such relations within a sentence. They defined it as

$$SemR(w_i, w_j) = \frac{C(w_i, w_j)}{C(w_i)C(w_j)},$$

where $C(w_i, w_j)$ is the number of times the words w_i and w_j co-occur in a sentence in the corpus, and $C(w_i)$ is the count of word w_i in the corpus. The relation is symmetrical, i.e.

$$C(w_i, w_j) = C(w_j, w_i).$$

The estimated semantic affinity of a word w is defined as:

$$SemA(w|H) = \sum_{w_j \in H} SemR(w, w_j),$$

where H is the context of the word w. In our case, H consists of words to the left of the current word.

Gong et al. (2008) used a similar model in a predictive text application with a slight modification to the $SemR$ function:

$$SemR(w_i, w_j) = \frac{C(stem(w_i), stem(w_j))}{C(stem(w_j))},$$

where the $stem(w)$ function removes suffixes from words. We refined this model further and we replaced the stemming function with a real lemmatization.

4 Dependency Parsing

Dependency syntax (Tesnière, 1966) has attracted a considerable interest in the recent years, spurred by the availability of data-driven parsers as well as annotated data in multiple languages including Arabic, Chinese, Czech, English, German, Japanese, Portuguese, or Spanish (Buchholz and Marsi, 2006; Nivre et al., 2007). We used this syntactic formalism because of its availability in many languages.

4.1 Parser Implementation

There are two main classes of data-driven dependency parsers: graph-based (McDonald and Pereira, 2006) and transition-based (Nivre, 2003). We selected Nivre's parser because of its implementation simplicity, small memory footprint, and linear time complexity. Parsing is always achieved in at most $2n - 1$ actions, where n is the length of the sentence. Both types of parser can be combined, see Zhang and Clark (2008) for a discussion.

Nivre's parser is an extension to the shift–reduce algorithm that creates a projective and acyclic graph. It uses a stack, a list of input words, and builds a set of arcs representing the graph of dependencies. The parser uses two operations in addition to shift and reduce, left-arc and right-arc:

- $Shift$ pushes the next input word onto the stack.
- *Reduce* pops the top of the stack with the condition that the corresponding word has a head.
- $LeftArc$ adds an arc from the next input word to the top of the stack and pops it.
- *RightArc* adds an arc from the top of the stack to the next input word and pushes the input word on the stack.

Table 1 shows the start and final parser states as well as the four transitions and their conditions and Algorithm 1 describes the parsing algorithm.

4.2 Features

At each step of the parsing procedure, the parser turns to a guide to decide on which transition to apply among the set {$LeftArc$, *RightArc*, $Shift$, *Reduce*}. We implemented this guide as a four-class classifier that uses features it extracts from the parser state. The features consist of words and their parts of speech in the stack, in the queue, and in the partial graph resulting from what has been parsed so far. The classifier is based on a linear logistic regression function that evaluates the transition probabilities from the features and predicts the next one.

In the learning phase, we extracted a data set of feature vectors using the gold-standard parsing procedure (Algorithm 2) that we applied to Talbanken corpus of Swedish text (Einarsson, 1976; Nilsson et al., 2005). Each vector being labeled with one of the four possible transitions. We trained the classifiers using the LIBLINEAR implementation (Fan et al., 2008) of logistic regression.

However, classes are not always separable using linear classifiers. We combined single features as pairs or triples. This emulates to some extent quadratic kernels used in support vector machines, while preserving the speed of the linear models. Table 2 shows the complete feature set to predict the transitions. A feature is defined by

- A source: S for stack and Q for the queue;
- An offset: 0 for the top of the stack and first in the queue; 1 and 2 for levels down in the stack or to the right in the queue;

Name	Action	Condition
Initialization	$\langle nil, W, \emptyset \rangle$	
Termination	$\langle S, nil, A \rangle$	
$LeftArc$	$\langle n\|S, n'\|Q, A\rangle \rightarrow \langle S, n'\|Q, A \cup \{\langle n', n\rangle\}\rangle$	$\neg\exists n'', \langle n, n''\rangle \in A$
$RightArc$	$\langle n\|S, n'\|Q, A\rangle \rightarrow \langle n'\|n\|S, Q, A \cup \langle n, n'\rangle\rangle$	$\neg\exists n'', \langle n', n''\rangle \in A$
$Reduce$	$\langle n\|S, Q, A\rangle \rightarrow \langle S, Q, A\rangle$	$\exists n', \langle n, n'\rangle \in A$
$Shift$	$\langle S, n\|Q, A\rangle \rightarrow \langle n\|S, Q, A\rangle$	

Table 1: Parser transitions. W is the original input sentence, A is the dependency graph, S is the stack, and Q is the queue. The triplet $\langle S, Q, A\rangle$ represents the parser state. n, n', and n'' are lexical tokens. The pair $\langle n', n\rangle$ represents an arc from the head n' to the dependent n.

- Possible applications of the function head, H, leftmost child, LC, or righmost child, RC;
- The value: word, w, or POS tag, t, at the specified position.

Queue	Q0w
	Q1w
	Q0t
	Q1t
	Q0tQ0w
	Q0tQ1t
	Q1wQ1t
	Q0tQ1tQ2t
	Q0wQ1tQ2t
Stack	S0t
	S0w
	S0tS0w
	S0tS1t
Stack/Queue	S0wQ0w
	Q0tS0t
	Q1tS0t
	Q0tS1t
	Q1tS1t
	S0tQ0tQ1t
	S0tQ0wQ0t
Partial Graph	S0HtS0tQ0t
	Q0LCtS0tQ0t
	Q0LCtS0tQ0w
	S0RCtS0tQ0t
	S0RCtS0tQ0w

Table 2: Feature model for predicting parser actions with combined features.

4.3 Calculating Graph Probabilities

Nivre (2006) showed that every terminating transition sequence $A_1^m = (a_1, ..., a_m)$ applied to a sentence $W_1^n = (w_1, ..., w_n)$ defines exactly one parse tree G. We approximated the probability $P(G|W_1^n)$ of a dependency graph G as $P(A_1^m|W_1^n)$ and we estimated the probability of G as the product of the transition probabilities, so that

$$\begin{aligned} P_{Parse}(G|W_1^n) &= P(A_1^m|W_1^n) \\ &= \prod_{k=1}^{m} P(a_k|A_1^{k-1}, W_1^{\phi(k-1)}), \end{aligned}$$

where a_k is member of the set $\{LeftArc$, $RightArc$, $Shift$, $Reduce\}$ and $\phi(k)$ corresponds to the index of the current word at transition k.

We finally approximated the term $A_1^{k-1}, W_1^{\phi(k-1)}$ to the feature set and computed probability estimates using the logistic regression output.

4.4 Beam Search

We extended Nivre's parser with a beam search to mitigate error propagation that occurs with a deterministic parser (Johansson and Nugues, 2006). We maintained N parser states in parallel and we applied all the possible transitions to each state. We scored each transition action and we ranked the states with the product of the action's probabilities leading to this state. Algorithm 3 outlines beam search with a diameter of N.

An alternative to training parser transitions using local features is to use an online learning algorithm (Johansson and Nugues, 2007; Zhang and Clark, 2008). The classifiers are then computed over the graph that has already been built instead of considering the probability of a single transition.

4.5 Evaluation

We evaluated our dependency parser separately from the rest of the application and Table 3 shows the results. We optimized our parameter selection for the unlabeled attachment score (UAS). This explains the relatively high difference with the labeled attachment score (LAS): about –8.6.

Table 3 also shows the highest scores obtained on the same Talbanken corpus of Swedish text (Einarsson, 1976; Nilsson et al., 2005) in the CoNLL-X evaluation (Buchholz and Marsi, 2006): 89.58 for unlabeled attachments (Corston-Oliver and Aue, 2006) and 84.58 for labeled attachments (Nivre et al., 2006). CoNLL-X systems were optimized for the LAS category.

The figures we reached were about 1.10% below those reported in CONLL-X for the UAS category. However our results are not directly comparable as the parsers or the classifiers in CONLL-X have either a higher complexity or are more time-consuming. We chose linear classifiers over kernel machines as it was essential to our application to run on mobile devices with limited resources in both CPU power and memory size.

This paper			CONLL-X	
Beam width	LAS	UAS	LAS	UAS
1	79.45	88.05	84.58	89.54
2	79.76	88.41		
4	79.75	88.40		
8	79.77	88.41		
16	79.78	88.42		
32	79.77	88.41		
64	79.79	88.44		

Table 3: Parse results on the Swedish Talbanken corpus obtained for this paper as well as the best reported results in CONLL-X on the same corpus (Buchholz and Marsi, 2006).

5 Dependencies to Predict the Next Word

We built a syntactic score to measure the grammatical relevance of a candidate word w in the current context, that is the word sequence so far $w_1, ..., w_i$. We defined it as the weighted sum of three terms: the score of the partial graph resulting from the analysis of the words to the left of the candidate word and the scores of the link from w to its head, $h(w)$, using their lexical forms and their parts of speech:

$$s_{DepSyn}(w) = \lambda_1 P_{Parse}(G(w)|w_1, ..., w_i, w) + \lambda_2 P_{Link}(w, h(w)) + \lambda_3 P_{Link}(POS(w), POS(h(w))),$$

where $G(w)$ is the partial graph representing the word sequence $w_1, ..., w_i, w$. The P_{Link} terms are intended to give an extra-weight to the probability of an association between the predicted word and a possible head to the left of it. They hint at the strength of the ties between w and the words before it.

We used the transition probabilities described in Sect. 4.3 to compute the score of the partial graph, yielding

$$P_{Parse}(G(w)|w_1, ..., w_i, w) = \prod_{k=1}^{j} P(a_k),$$

where $a_1, ..., a_j$ is the sequence of transition actions producing $G(w)$ and $P(a_k)$, the probability output of transition k given by the logistic regression engine.

The last two terms $P_{Link}(w, h(w))$ and $P_{Link}(POS(w), POS(h(w)))$ are computed from counts in the training corpus using maximum likelihood estimates:

$$P_{Link}(w, h(w)) = \frac{C(Link(w, h(w)) + 1}{\sum_{w_l \in PW} C(Link(w_l, h(w_l)))} + |PW|$$

and

$$P_{Link}(POS(w), POS(h(w))) = \frac{C(Link(POS(w), POS(h(w)))) + 1}{\sum_{w_l \in PW} C(Link(POS(w_l), h(POS(w_l))))} + |PW|,$$

where $PW = match(\mathbf{ks}^i)$, is the set of predicted words for the current key sequence.

If the current word w has not been assigned a head yet, we default $h(w)$ to the root of the graph and $POS(h(w))$ to the $ROOT$ value.

6 Experiments and Results

6.1 Experimental Setup

Figure 2 shows an overview of the three stages to produce and evaluate our models: training, tuning, and testing. Ideally, we would have trained the classifiers on a corpus matching a text entry application. However, as there is no large available SMS corpus in Swedish, we used the Stockholm-Umeå corpus (SUC) (Ejerhed and Källgren, 1997). SUC is balanced and the largest available POS-tagged corpus in Swedish with more than 1 million words.

We parsed the corpus and we divided it randomly into a training set (80%), a development set (10%), and a test set (10%). The training set was used to gather statistics on word n-grams, POS n-grams, collocations, lemma frequencies, dependent/head relations. We discarded hapaxes: relations and sequences occurring only once. We used lemmas instead of stems in the semantic relatedness score, $SemR$, because stemming is less appropriate in Swedish than in English.

We used the development set to find optimal weights for the scoring functions, resulting in the lowest KSPC. We ran an exhaustive search using all possible linear combinations with increments of 0.1, except for two functions, where this was too coarse. We used 0.01 then.

We applied the resulting linear combinations of scoring functions to the test set. We first compared the frequency-based disambiguation acting as a baseline to linear combinations involving or not involving syntax, but always excluding bigrams. Table 4 shows the most significant combinations. We then compared a set of other combinations with the bigram model. They are shown in Table 6.

6.2 Metrics

We redefined the KSPC metric of MacKenzie (2002), since the number of characters needed to input a word is now dependent on the word's left context in the sentence. Let $S = (w_1, \ldots, w_n) \in L$ be a sentence in the test corpus. The KSPC for the test corpus then becomes

$$KSPC = \frac{\sum_{S \in L} \sum_{w \in S} KS(w|LContext(w, S))}{\sum_{S \in L} \sum_{w \in S} Chars(w)}$$

where $KS(w|LContext)$ is the number of key strokes needed to enter a word in a given context, $LContext(w, S)$ is the left context of w in S, and $Chars(w)$ is the number of characters in w.

Another performance measure is the disambiguation accuracy (DA), which is the percentage of words that are correctly disambiguated after all the keys have been pressed

$$DA = \frac{\sum_{S \in L} \sum_{w \in S} PredHit(w|LContext(w, S))}{\#w},$$

where $PredHit(w|Context) = 1$ if w is the top prediction and 0 otherwise, and $\#w$, the total number of words in L. A good DA means that the user can more often simply accept the default proposed word instead of navigating the prediction list for the desired word.

As scoring tokens, we chose to keep the ones that actually have the ability to differentiate the models, i.e. we did not count the KSPC and DA for words that were not in the dictionary. Neither did we count white spaces, nor the punctuation marks.

All our measures are without word or phrase completion. This means that the lower-limit figure for $KSPC$ is 1.

6.3 Results

As all the KSPC figures are close to 1, we computed the error reduction rate (ERR), i.e. the reduction in the number of extra keystrokes needed beyond one. We carried out all the optimizations considering KSPC, but we can observe that KSPC ERR and DA ERR strongly correlate.

Table 5 shows the results with scoring functions using the word frequencies. The columns include KSPC and DA together with KSPC ERR and DA ERR compared with the baseline. Table 7 shows the respective results when using a bigram-based disambiguation instead of just frequency. The ERR is still compared to the word frequency baseline but attention should also be drawn on the relative increases: how much the new models can improve bigram-based disambiguation.

7 Discussion

We can observe from the results that a model based on dependency grammars improves the prediction considerably. The $DepSyn$ model is actually the most effective one when applied together with the frequency counts. Furthermore, the improvements from the POS, $SemA$, and $DepSyn$ model are almost disjunct, as the combined model improvement matches the sum of their respective individual contributions.

The 4.2% ERR observed when adding the $SemA$ model is consistent with the result from

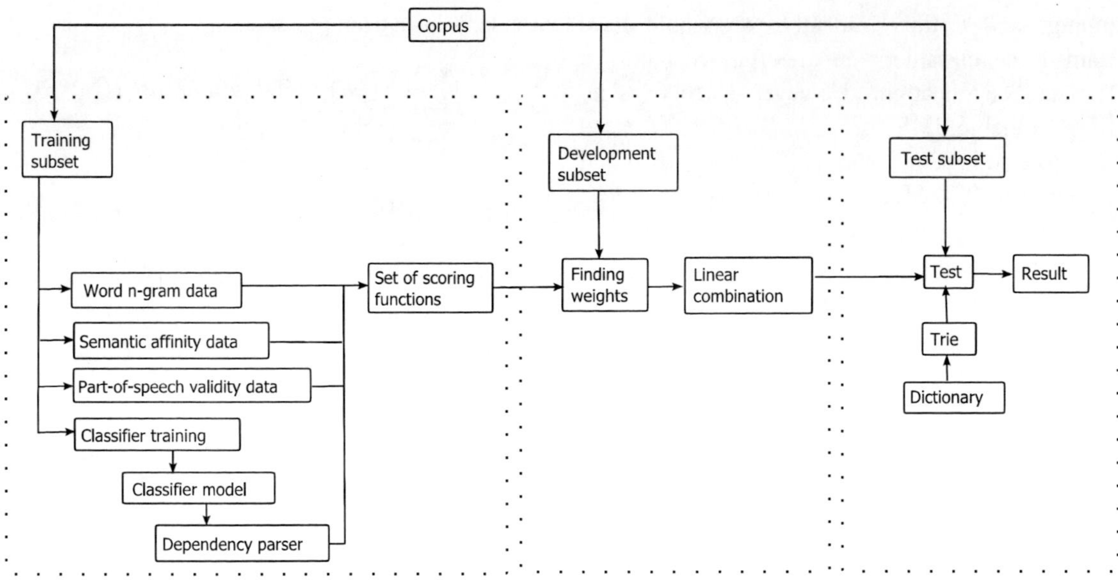

Figure 2: System architecture, where the set of scoring functions is $S = \{s_{LM}, s_{SemA}, s_{POS}, s_{DepSyn}\}$ and the linear combination is $= \sum_{s \in S} \lambda_s \cdot s(w)$.

Gong et al. (2008), where a 4.6% ERR was found. On the other hand, the POS model only contributed 4.7% ERR in our case, whereas Gong et al. (2008) observed 12.6%. One possible explanation for this is that they clustered related POS tags into 19 groups reducing the sparseness problem. By performing this grouping, we can effectively ignore morphological and lexical features that have no relevance, when deciding which word should come next. Other possible explanations include that our backoff model is not well suited for this problem or that the POS sequences are not an applicable model for Swedish.

The bigram language model has the largest impact on the performance. The ERR for bigrams alone is higher than all the other models combined. Still, the other models have the ability to contribute on top of the bigram model. For example, the POS model increases the ERR by about 5% both when using bigram- and frequency-based disambiguation, suggesting that this information is not captured by the bigrams. On the other hand, $DepSyn$ increases the ERR by a more modest 3% when using bigrams instead of 7% with word frequencies. This is likely due to the fact that about half of the dependency links only stretch to the next preceding or succeeding word in the corpus.

The most effective combination of models are the bigrams together with the POS sequence and the dependency structure, both embedding syntactic information. With this combination, we were able to reduce the number of erroneous disambiguations as well as extra keystrokes by almost one third.

8 Further Work

SMS texting, which is the target of our system, is more verbal than the genres gathered in the Stockholm-Umeå corpus. The language models of a final application would then change considerably from the ones we extracted from the SUC. A further work would be to collect a SMS corpus and replicate the experiments: retrain the models and obtain the corresponding performance figures.

Moreover, we carried out our implementation and simulations on desktop computers. The POS model has an estimated size of 700KB (Gong et al., 2008). The P_{Parse} term of the $DepSyn$ model can be made as small as the feature model. We expect the optimized size of this model to be under 100KB in an embedded environment. The size of the lexical variant of P_{Link} is comparable to the bigram model. This could however be remedied by using the probability of the action that constructed this last link. The computational power required by LIBLINEAR is certainly within the reach of modern hand-held devices. However, a prototype simulation with real hardware conditions would be needed to prove an implementability on mobile devices.

Finally, a user might perceive subtle differences in the presentation of the words compared with that of popular commercial products. Gutowitz (2003) noted the reluctance to single-tap input methods because of their "unpredictable" behavior. Introducing syntax-based disambiguation could increase this perception. A next step would be to carry out usability studies and assess this element.

References

Sabine Buchholz and Erwin Marsi. 2006. CoNLL-X shared task on multilingual dependency parsing. In *Proceedings of the Tenth Conference on Computational Natural Language Learning (CoNLL-X)*, pages 149–164, New York City.

Johan Carlberger and Viggo Kann. 1999. Implementing an efficient part-of-speech tagger. *Software – Practice and Experience*, 29(2):815–832.

Simon Corston-Oliver and Anthony Aue. 2006. Dependency parsing with reference to slovene, spanish and swedish. In *Proceedings of the Tenth Conference on Computational Natural Language Learning (CoNLL-X)*, pages 196–200, New York City, June.

Jan Einarsson. 1976. Talbankens skriftspråkskonkordans. Technical report, Lund University, Institutionen för nordiska språk, Lund.

Eva Ejerhed and Gunnel Källgren. 1997. Stockholm Umeå Corpus version 1.0, SUC 1.0.

Rong-En Fan, Kai-Wei Chang, Cho-Jui Hsieh, Xiang-Rui Wang, and Chih-Jen Lin. 2008. LIBLINEAR: A library for large linear classification. *Journal of Machine Learning Research*, 9:1871–1874.

Jun Gong, Peter Tarasewich, and I. Scott MacKenzie. 2008. Improved word list ordering for text entry on ambiguous keypads. In *NordiCHI '08: Proceedings of the 5th Nordic conference on Human-computer interaction*, pages 152–161, Lund, Sweden.

Dale L. Grover, Martin T. King, and Clifford A. Kushler. 1998. Reduced keyboard disambiguating computer. U.S. Patent no. 5,818,437.

Ebba Gustavii and Eva Pettersson. 2003. A Swedish grammar for word prediction. Technical report, Department of Linguistics, Uppsala University.

Howard Gutowitz. 2003. Barriers to adoption of dictionary-based text-entry methods; a field study. In *Proceedings of the Workshop on Language Modeling for Text Entry Systems (EACL 2003)*, pages 33–41, Budapest.

Jan Haestrup. 2001. Communication terminal having a predictive editor application. U.S. Patent no. 6,223,059.

Jon Hasselgren, Erik Montnemery, Pierre Nugues, and Markus Svensson. 2003. HMS: A predictive text entry method using bigrams. In *Proceedings of the Workshop on Language Modeling for Text Entry Methods (EACL 2003)*, pages 43–49, Budapest.

Richard Johansson and Pierre Nugues. 2006. Investigating multilingual dependency parsing. In *Proceedings of the Tenth Conference on Computational Natural Language Learning (CONLL-X)*, pages 206–210, New York.

Richard Johansson and Pierre Nugues. 2007. Incremental dependency parsing using online learning. In *Proceedings of the CoNLL Shared Task Session of EMNLP-CoNLL*, pages 1134–1138, Prague, June 28-30.

Jianhua Li and Graeme Hirst. 2005. Semantic knowledge in word completion. In *Assets '05: Proceedings of the 7th international ACM SIGACCESS conference on Computers and accessibility*, pages 121–128, Baltimore.

I. Scott MacKenzie, Hedy Kober, Derek Smith, Terry Jones, and Eugene Skepner. 2001. LetterWise: Prefix-based disambiguation for mobile text input. In *14th Annual ACM Symposium on User Interface Software and Technology*, Orlando, Florida.

I. Scott MacKenzie. 2002. KSPC (keystrokes per character) as a characteristic of text entry techniques. In *Proceedings of the Fourth International Symposium on Human Computer Interaction with Mobile Devices*, pages 195–210, Heidelberg, Germany.

Johannes Matiasek, Marco Baroni, and Harald Trost. 2002. FASTY – A multi-lingual approach to text prediction. In *ICCHP '02: Proceedings of the 8th International Conference on Computers Helping People with Special Needs*, pages 243–250, London.

Johannes Matiasek. 2006. The language component of the FASTY predictive typing system. In Karin Harbusch, Kari-Jouko Raiha, and Kumiko Tanaka-Ishii, editors, *Efficient Text Entry*, number 05382 in Dagstuhl Seminar Proceedings, Dagstuhl, Germany.

Ryan McDonald and Fernando Pereira. 2006. Online learning of approximate dependency parsing algorithms. In *Proceedings of the 11th Conference of the European Chapter of the Association for Computational Linguistics (EACL)*, pages 81–88, Trento.

Jens Nilsson, Johan Hall, and Joakim Nivre. 2005. MAMBA meets TIGER: Reconstructing a Swedish treebank from antiquity. In *Proceedings of the NODALIDA Special Session on Treebanks*, Joensuu, Finland.

Joakim Nivre, Johan Hall, Jens Nilsson, Gülsen Eryigit, and Svetoslav Marinov. 2006. Labeled pseudo-projective dependency parsing with support vector machines. In *Proceedings of the Tenth Conference on Computational Natural Language Learning (CoNLL-X)*, pages 221–225, June.

Joakim Nivre, Johan Hall, Sandra Kübler, Ryan McDonald, Jens Nilsson, Sebastian Riedel, and Deniz Yuret. 2007. The CoNLL 2007 shared task on dependency parsing. In *Proceedings of the CoNLL Shared Task Session of EMNLP-CoNLL 2007*, pages 915–932, Prague.

Joakim Nivre. 2003. An efficient algorithm for projective dependency parsing. In *Proceedings of the 8th International Workshop on Parsing Technologies (IWPT)*, pages 149–160, Nancy.

Joakim Nivre. 2006. *Inductive Dependency Parsing*. Springer, Dordrecht, The Netherlands.

Claude Elwood Shannon. 1951. Prediction and entropy of printed English. *The Bell System Technical Journal*, pages 50–64, January.

K. Sundarkantham and S. Mercy Shalinie. 2007. Word predictor using natural language grammar induction technique. *Journal of Theoretical and Applied Information Technology*, 3:1–8.

Lucien Tesnière. 1966. *Éléments de syntaxe structurale*. Klincksieck, Paris, 2e edition.

Yue Zhang and Stephen Clark. 2008. A tale of two parsers: Investigating and combining graph-based and transition-based dependency parsing using beam-search. In *Proceedings of the 2008 Conference on Empirical Methods in Natural Language Processing*, pages 562–571, Hawaii, October 25–27.

Algorithm 1 Nivre's algorithm.

```
Queue ⇐ W
Stack ⇐ nil
while ¬Queue.isEmpty() do
   features ⇐ ExtractFeatures()
   action ⇐ guide.Predict(features)
   if action = RightArc ∧ canRightArc() then
      RightArc()
   else if action = LeftArc ∧ canLeftArc() then
      LeftArc
   else if action = Reduce ∧ canReduce() then
      Reduce()
   else
      Shift()
   end if
end while
return(A)
```

Algorithm 2 Reference parsing.

```
Queue ⇐ W
Stack ⇐ nil
while ¬Queue.isEmpty() do
   x ⇐ ExtractFeatures()
   if ⟨Stack.peek(), Queue.get(0)⟩ ∈ A ∧ canRightArc() then
      t ⇐ RightArc
   else if ⟨Queue.get(0), Stack.peek()⟩ ∈ A ∧ canLeftArc() then
      t ⇐ LeftArc
   else if ∃w ∈ Stack : ⟨w, Queue.get(0)⟩ ∈ A∨ ⟨Queue.get(0), w⟩ ∈ A) ∧ canReduce() then
      t ⇐ Reduce
   else
      t ⇐ Shift
   end if
   store training example ⟨x, t⟩
end while
```

Algorithm 3 Beam parse.

```
Agenda.add(InititalParserState)
while ¬done do
   for parserState ∈ Agenda do
      Output.add(parserState.doLeftArc())
      Output.add(parserState.doRightArc())
      Output.add(parserState.doReduce())
      Output.add(parserState.doShift())
   end for
   Sort(Output)
   Clear(Agenda)
   Take N best parse trees from Output and put in Agenda.
end while
Return best item in Agenda.
```

Configuration	Scoring model	*DepSyn* weights
F1 baseline	$1 \times LM1$ (Word frequencies)	–
F2	$0.9 \times LM1 + 0.1 \times POS$	–
F3	$0.7 \times LM1 + 0.3 \times SemA$	–
F4	$0.6 \times LM1 + 0.4 \times DepSyn$	(0.3, 0.7, 0.0)
F5	$0.6 \times LM1 + 0.1 \times POS + 0.3 \times DepSyn$	(0.0 1.0 0.0)
F6	$0.5 \times LM1 + 0.2 \times SemA + 0.3 \times DepSyn$	(0.2 0.7 0.1)
F7	$0.4 \times LM1 + 0.1 \times POS + 0.3 \times DepSyn + 0.2 \times SemA$	(0.2, 0.8, 0.0)

Table 4: The different combinations of scoring models using frequency-based disambiguation as a baseline. The *DepSyn* weight triples corresponds to $(\lambda_1, \lambda_2, \lambda_3)$ in Sect. 5.

Configuration	KSPC	DA	KSPC ERR	DA ERR
F1	1.015559	94.15%	0.00%	0.00%
F2	1.014829	94.31%	4.69%	2.72%
F3	1.014902	94.36%	4.22%	3.62%
F4	1.014462	94.56%	7.05%	7.04%
F5	1.013625	94.75%	12.43%	10.28%
F6	1.014159	94.62%	9.00%	8.10%
F7	1.013438	94.86%	13.63%	12.16%

Table 5: Results for the disambiguation based on word frequencies together with the semantic and syntactic models.

Configuration	Scoring model	Bigram weights	*DepSyn* weights
B1	$1 \times LM2$ (Bigram frequencies)	(0.9, 0.1)	–
B2	$0.9 \times LM2 + 0.1 \times POS$	(0.8, 0.2)	–
B3	$0.95 \times LM2 + 0.05 \times SemA$	(0.8, 0.2)	–
B4	$0.9 \times LM2 + 0.1 \times DepSyn$	(0.8, 0.2)	(0.2, 0.8, 0.0)
B5	$0.8 \times LM2 + 0.1 \times POS + 0.1 \times SemA$	(0.8, 0.2)	–
B6	$0.81 \times LM2 + 0.08 \times POS + 0.11 \times DepSyn$	(0.8, 0.2)	(0.2, 0.8, 0.0)

Table 6: The different combinations of scoring models using bigram-based disambiguation as baseline. In addition to the *DepSyn* weights, this table also shows the language model interpolation weights, β_1 and β_2 described in Sect. 2.2.

Label	KSPC	DA	KSPC ERR	DA ERR
B1	1.012159254	95.48%	21.85%	22.81%
B2	1.011434213	95.75%	26.51%	27.41%
B3	1.011860573	95.50%	23.77%	23.20%
B4	1.011698693	95.62%	24.81%	25.19%
B5	1.011146932	95.80%	28.36%	28.23%
B6	1.010980592	95.91%	29.43%	30.09%

Table 7: Results for the disambiguation based on bigrams plus the semantic and syntactical models. The error reduction rate is relative to the word frequency baseline.

Parsing Formal Languages using Natural Language Parsing Techniques

Jens Nilsson* **Welf Löwe*** **Johan Hall†*** **Joakim Nivre†***
*Växjö University, School of Mathematics and Systems Engineering, Sweden
†Uppsala University, Department of Linguistics and Philology, Sweden
{jens.nilsson|welf.lowe|johan.hall|joakim.nivre}@vxu.se

Abstract

Program analysis tools used in software maintenance must be robust and ought to be accurate. Many data-driven parsing approaches developed for natural languages are robust and have quite high accuracy when applied to parsing of software. We show this for the programming languages Java, C/C++, and Python. Further studies indicate that post-processing can almost completely remove the remaining errors. Finally, the training data for instantiating the generic data-driven parser can be generated automatically for formal languages, as opposed to the manually development of treebanks for natural languages. Hence, our approach could improve the robustness of software maintenance tools, probably without showing a significant negative effect on their accuracy.

1 Introduction

Software engineering, especially software maintenance, is supported by numerous program analysis tools. Maintenance tasks include program comprehension (understanding unknown code for fixing bugs or further development), quality assessment (judging code, e.g., in code reviews), and reverse-engineering (reifying the design documents for given source code). To extract information from the programs, the tools first parse the program code and produce an abstract syntax tree (AST) for further analysis and abstraction (Strein et al., 2007). As long as the program conforms to the syntax of a programming language, classical parsing techniques known from the field of compiler construction may be applied. This, however, cannot be assumed in general, as the programs to analyze can be incomplete, erroneous, or conform to a (yet unknown) dialect or version of the language. Despite error stabilization, classical parsers then lose a lot of information or simply break down. This is unsatisfactory for tools supporting maintenance. Therefore, quite some effort has gone into the development of robust parsers of programs for these tools (cf. our related work section 5). This effort, however, has to be repeated for every programming language.

The development of *robust* parsers is of special interest for languages like C/C++ due to their numerous dialects in use (Anderson, 2008). Also, tools for languages frequently coming in new versions, like Java, benefit from robust parsing. Finally, there are languages like HTML where existing browsers are forgiving if documents do not adhere to the formal standard with the consequence that there exist many formally erroneous documents. In such cases, robust parsing is even a prerequisite for tool-supported maintenance.

The *accuracy* of parsing is a secondary goal in the context of software maintenance. Tasks like program comprehension, quality assessment, and reverse-engineering are fuzzy by their nature. There is no well-defined notion of correctness—rather an empirical answer to the question: Did it help the software engineers in fulfilling their tasks? Moreover, the information provided to the engineers abstracts anyway from the concrete program syntax and semantics, i.e., inaccuracies in the input may disappear in the output. Finally, program analyses are often heuristics themselves, approximating computationally hard problems like pattern matching and optimal clustering.

The natural language processing (NLP) community has for many years developed parsing technology that is both completely robust and highly accurate. The present approach applies this technology to programming languages. It is robust in the sense that, for each program, the parser always gives a meaningful model even for slightly incorrect and incomplete programs. The approach is,

Proceedings of the 11th International Conference on Parsing Technologies (IWPT), pages 49–60,
Paris, October 2009. ©2009 Association for Computational Linguistics

however, not accurate to 100%, i.e., even correct programs may lead to slightly incorrect models. As we will show, it is quite accurate when applied to programming languages.

The data-driven dependency parsing approach applied here only needs correct examples of the source and the expected analysis model. Then it automatically trains and adapts a generic parser. As we will show, training data for adapting to a new programming language can even be generated automatically. Hence, the effort for creating a parser for a new programming language is quite small.

The basic idea – applying natural language parsing to programming languages – has been presented to the program maintenance community before (Nilsson et al., 2009). This paper contributes with experimental results on

1. data-driven dependency parsing of the programming languages C/C++, Java, and Python,

2. transformations between dependency structure and phrase structure adapted to programming languages,

3. generic parser model selection and its effect on parsing accuracy.

Section 2 gives an introduction to the parsing technology applied here. In section 3, the preparation of the training examples necessary is described, while section 4 presents the experimental results. Section 5 discusses related work in information extraction for software maintenance. We end with conclusions and future work in section 6.

2 NLP Background

Dependency structure is one way of representing the syntax of natural languages. Dependency trees form labeled, directed and rooted trees, as shown in figure 1. One essential difference compared to context-free grammar is the absence of nonterminals. Another difference is that the syntactic structure is composed of lexical tokens (also called terminals or words) linked by binary and directed relations called *dependencies*. Each token in the figure is labeled with a part-of-speech, shown at the bottom of the figure. Each dependency relation is also labeled.

The parsing algorithm used in the experiments of section 4, known as the Nivre's arc-eager al-

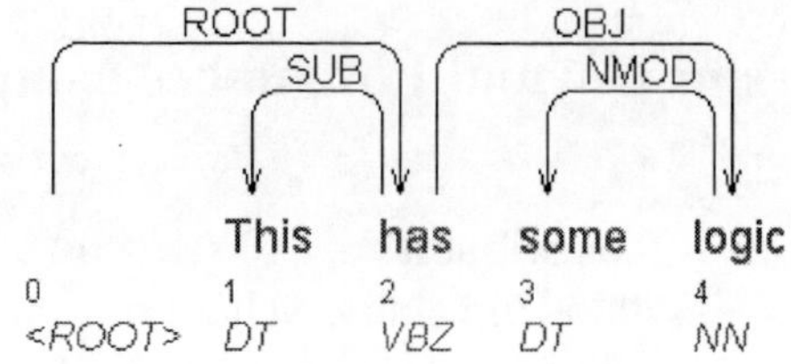

Figure 1: Sentence with a dependency tree.

gorithm (Nivre, 2003), can produce such dependency trees. It bears a resemblance to the shift-reduce parser for context-free grammars, with the most apparent difference being that terminals (not nonterminals) are pushed onto the stack. Parser configurations are represented by a stack, a list of (remaining) input tokens, and the (current) set of arcs for the dependency tree. Similar to the shift-reduce parser, the construction of syntactic structure is created by a sequence of transitions. The parser starts with an empty stack and terminates when the input queue is empty, parsing input from left to right. It has four transitions (**Left-Arc**, **Right-Arc**, **Reduce** and **Shift**), manipulating these data structures. The algorithm has a linear time complexity as it is guaranteed to terminate after at most $2n$ transitions, given that the length of the input sentence is n.

In contrast to a parser guided by a grammar (e.g., ordinary shift-reduce parsing for context-free grammars), this parser is guided by a classifier induced from empirical data using machine learning (Nivre et al., 2004). Hence, the parser requires training data containing dependency trees. In other words, the parser has a training phase where the training data is used by the training module in order to learn the correct sequence of transitions. The training data can contain dependency trees for sentences of any language irrespectively of whether the language is a natural or formal one.

The training module produces the correct transition sequences using the dependency trees of the training data. These correct parser configurations and transition sequences are then provided as training data to a classifier, which predicts the correct transitions (including a dependency label for **Left-Arc**, **Right-Arc**) given parser configurations. A parser configuration contains a vast amount of information located in the data-structures. It is therefore necessary to abstract it into a set of features. Possible features are word forms and parts-of-speech of tokens on the stack and in the list of input tokens, and dependency labels of dependency arcs created so far.

The parser produces exactly one syntactic analysis for every input, even if the input does not conform to a grammar. The price we have to pay for this robustness is that any classifier is bound to commit errors even if the input is acceptable according to a grammar.

3 General Approach

In section 2, we presented a parsing algorithm for producing dependency trees for natural languages. Here we will show how it can be used to produce syntactic structures for programming languages. Since the framework requires training data forming correct dependency trees, we need an approach for converting source code to dependency trees.

The general approach can be divided into two phases, training and production. In order to be able to perform both these phases in this study, we need to adapt natural language parsing to the needs of information extraction from programming language code, i.e., we need to automatically produce training data. Therefore, we apply:

(a) **Source Code ⇒ Syntax Tree**: the classical approach for generating syntax trees for correct and complete source code of a programming language.

(b) **Syntax Tree ⇒ Dependency Tree**: an approach for encoding the syntax trees as dependency trees adapted to programming languages.

(c) **Dependency Tree ⇒ Syntax Tree**: an approach to convert the dependency trees back to syntax trees.

These approaches have been accomplished as presented below. In the training phase, we need to train and adapt the generic parsing approach to a specific programming language. Therefore:

(1) **Generate training data** automatically by producing syntax trees and then dependency trees for correct programs using approaches (a) and (b).

(2) **Train** the generic parser with the training data.

This automated training phase needs to be done for every new programming language we adapt to.

Finally, in the production phase, we extract the information from (not necessarily correct and complete) programs:

(3) **Parse** the new source code into dependency trees.

(4) **Convert** the dependency trees into syntax trees using approach (c).

This automated production phase needs to be executed for every project we analyze.

Steps (2) and (3) have already been discussed in section 2 for parsing natural languages. They can be generalized to parsing programming languages as described in section 3.1. Both the training phase and the production phase are complete, once the steps (a)–(c) have been accomplished. We present them in sections 3.2, 3.3, and 3.4, respectively.

3.1 Adapting the Input

As mentioned, the parsing algorithm described in section 2 has been developed for natural languages, which makes it necessary to resolve a number of issues that arise when the parser is adapted for source code as input. First, the parsing algorithm takes a sequence of words as input, and for simplicity, we map the tokens in a programming language to words.

One slightly more problematic issue is how to define a "sentence" in source code. A natural language text syntactically decomposes into a sequence of sentences in a relatively natural way. But is there also a natural way of splitting source code into sentences? The most apparent approach may be to define a sentence as a compilation unit, that is, a file of source code. This can however result in practical problems since a sentence in a natural language text is usually on average between 15–25 words long, partially depending on the author and the type of text. The sequence of tokens in a source file may on the other hand be much longer. Time complexity is usually in practice of less importance when the average sentence length is as low as in natural languages, but that is hardly the case when there can be several thousands tokens in a sentence to parse.

Other approaches could for instance be to let one method be a sentence. However, then we need to deal with other types of source code constructions explicitly. We have in this study for simplicity let one compilation unit be one sentence. This is possible in practice due to the linear time complexity of the parsing algorithm of section 2, a quite unusual property compared to other NLP parsers guided by machine learning with state-of-the-art accuracy.

3.2 Source Code ⇒ Syntax Tree

In order to produce training data for the parser for a programming language, an analyzer that constructs syntax trees for correct and complete source code of the programming language is needed. We are in this study focusing on Java, Python and C/C++, and consequently need one such analyzer for each language. For example, figure 2 shows the concrete syntax tree of the following fragments of Java:

Example (1):

```
public String getName() {
   return name;
}
```

Example (2):

```
while (count > 0) {
   stack[--count]=null;
}
```

We also map the output of the lexical analyzer to the parts-of-speech for the words (e.g., `Identifier` for `String` and `getName`). All source code comments and indentation information (except for Python where the indentation conveys hierarchical information) have been excluded from the syntax trees. All string and character literals have also been mapped to "string" and "char", respectively. This does not entail that the approach is lossy, since all this information can be retained in a post-processing step, if necessary. As pointed out by, for instance, Collard et al. (2003), comments and indentation may among other things be of interest when trying to understand source code.

3.3 Syntax Tree ⇒ Dependency Tree

Here we will discuss the conversion of syntax trees into dependency trees. We use a method that has been successfully applied for natural languages for converting syntax trees into a *convertible* dependency tree that makes it possible to perform the inverse conversion, meaning that information about the syntax tree is saved in complex arc labels (Hall and Nivre, 2008). We also present results in section 4 using the dependency trees that cannot be used for the inverse conversion, which we call *non-convertible* dependency trees.

The conversion is performed in a two-step approach. First, the algorithm traverses the syntax tree from the root and identifies the head-child and the terminal head for all nonterminals in a recursive depth-first search. To identify the head-child for each nonterminal, the algorithm uses heuristics called *head-finding rules*, inspired by, for instance, Magerman (1995). Three head-finding strategies have been investigated. For each nonterminal:

1. FREQ: Let the element with the most frequently occurring name be the head, but exclude the token ';' as a potential head. If two tokens have the same frequency, let the leftmost occurring element be the head.

2. LEFT: let the leftmost terminal in the entire subtree of the nonterminal be the head of all other elements.

3. RIGHT: let the rightmost terminal in the entire subtree of the nonterminal be the head of all other elements.

The dependency trees in figures 3 and 4 use LEFT and FREQ. LEFT and RIGHT induce that all arcs are pointing to the right and left, respectively. The head-finding rules for FREQ are automatically created by counting the children's names for each distinct non-terminal name in the syntax trees of the training data. The priority list is then compiled by ordering the elements by descending frequency for each distinct non-terminal name. For instance, given that the syntax trees are grammatically correct, every non-terminal `While` will contain the tokens `(`, `)` and `while`. These tokens have thus the highest priority, and `while` therefore becomes the head in the lower dependency tree of figure 4. This is the same as choosing the left-most mandatory element for each left-hand side in the grammar. An interesting observation is that binary operators and the copy assignment operator become the heads of their operands for FREQ, which is the case for < and = in figure 4. Note also that the element names of terminals act as part-of-speech tags, e.g., the part-of-speech for `String` is `Identifier`.

In the second step, a dependency tree is created according to the identified terminal heads. The arcs in the convertible dependency tree are labeled with complex arc labels, where each complex arc label consists of two sublabels:

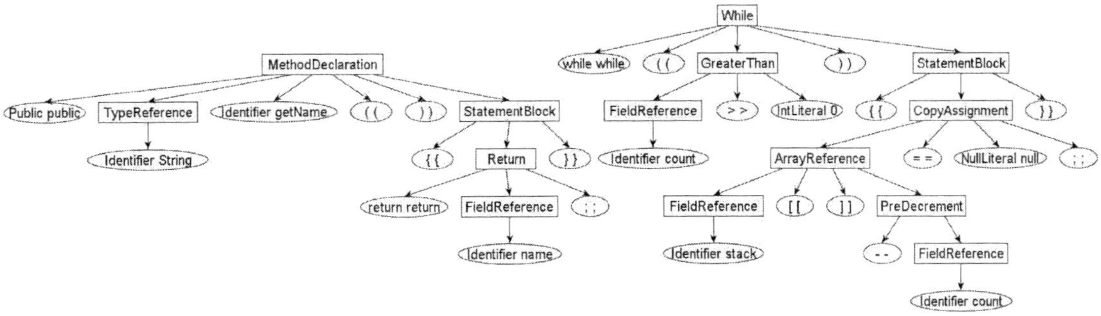

Figure 2: Syntax trees for examples (1) and (2).

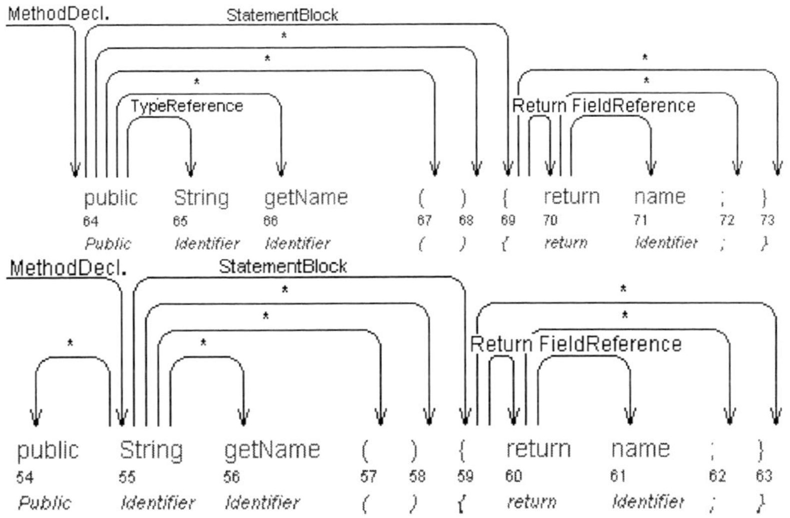

Figure 3: Non-convertible dependency trees for example (1) using LEFT (upper) and FREQ (lower).

1. Encode the dependent spine, i.e., the sequence of nonterminal labels from the dependent terminal to the highest nonterminal where the dependent terminal is the terminal head; "|" separates the nonterminal labels,

2. Encode the attachment point in the head spine, a non-negative integer value a, which means that the dependent spine is attached a steps up in the head spine.

By encoding the arc labels with these two sublabels, it is possible to perform the inverse conversion, (see subsection 3.4).

The non-convertible dependency labels allow us to reduce the complexity of the arc labels, making the learning problem simpler due to fewer distinct arc labels. This may result in a higher accuracy during parsing and can be used as input for further processing directly without taking the detour back to syntax trees. This can be motivated by the fact that all information in the syntax trees is usually not needed anyway in many reverse engineering tasks, but labels indicating method calls and declarations – the most important information for most program comprehension tasks – are preserved. This is exemplified by the fact that both dependency structures in figure 3 contain the label `MethodsDecl.`. We thus believe that all the necessary information is also captured in this less informative dependency tree. Each dependency label is the highest nonterminal name of the spine, that is, the single nonterminal name that is closest to its head. The non-convertible dependency label also excludes the attachment point value, making the learning problem even simpler. Figures 3 and 4 show the non-convertible dependency labels of the syntax trees (or phrase structure trees) in the same figures, where each label contains just a single nonterminal name of the original syntax trees.

3.4 Dependency Tree ⇒ Syntax Tree

The inverse conversion is a bottom-up and top-down process on the convertible dependency tree

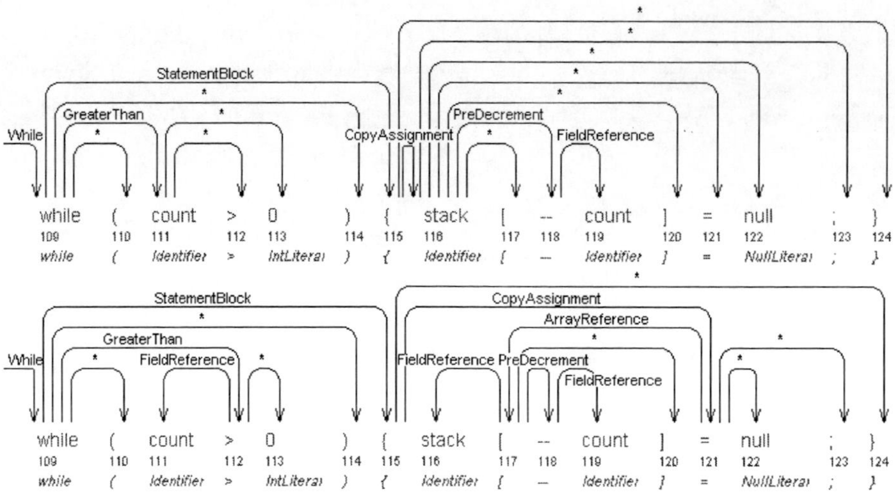

Figure 4: Non-convertible dependency trees for example (2) using LEFT (upper) and FREQ (lower).

(must contain complex arc labels). First, the algorithm visits every terminal in the convertible dependency tree and restores the spines of nonterminals with labels for each terminal using the information in the first sublabel of the incoming arc. Thus, the bottom-up process results in a spine of zero or more arcs from each terminal to the highest nonterminal of which the terminal is the terminal head. Secondly, the spines are weaved together according to the arcs of the dependency tree. This is achieved by traversing the dependency tree recursively from the root using a pre-order depth-first search, where the dependent spine is attached to its head spine or to the root of the syntax tree. The attachment point a, given by the second sublabel, specifies the number of nonterminals between the terminal head and the attachment nonterminal.

4 Experiments

We will in this section present parsing experiments and evaluate the accuracy of the syntax trees produced by the parser. As mentioned in section 2, the parsing algorithm is robust in the sense that it always produces a syntactic analysis no matter the input, but it can commit errors even for correct input. This section investigates the accuracy for correct input, when varying feature set, head-finding rules and language. We begin with the experimental setup.

4.1 Experimental Setup

The open-source software MaltParser (maltparser.org) (Nivre et al., 2006) is used in the experiments. It contains an implementation of the parsing algorithm, as well as an implementation of the conversion strategy from syntax trees to dependency trees and back, presented in subsections 3.3 and 3.4. It comes with the machine learner LIBSVM (Chang and Lin, 2001), producing the most accurate results for parsing natural languages compared to other evaluated machine learners (Hall et al., 2006). LIBSVM requires training data. The source files of the following projects have been converted into dependency trees:

- For Java: Recoder 0.83 (Gutzmann et al., 2007), using all source files in the directory "src" (having 400 source files with 92k LOC and 335k tokens).
- For C/C++: Elsa 2005.08.22b (McPeak, 2005), where 1389 source files were used, including the 978 C/C++ benchmark files in the distribution (thus comprising 1389 source files with 265k LOC and 691k tokens).
- For Python: Natural Language Toolkit 0.9.5 (Bird et al., 2008), where all source files in the directory "nltk" were used (having 160 source files with 65k LOC and 280k tokens).

To construct the syntax tree for the source code file of Recoder, we have used Recoder. It creates an abstract syntax tree for a source file, but we are currently interested in the concrete syntax tree with all the original tokens. In this first conversion step, the tokens of the syntax trees are thus retained. For example, the syntax trees in figure 2 are generated by Recoder.

The same strategy was adopted for Elsa with the difference that CDT 4.0.3, a plug-in to the Eclipse IDE to produce syntax trees for source code of C/C++, was used for producing the abstract syntax trees.[1] It produces abstract syntax trees just like Recoder, so the concrete syntax trees have also been created by retaining the tokens.

The Python 2.5 interpreter is actually shipped with an analyzer that produces concrete syntax trees (using the Python imports `from _ast import PyCF_ONLY_AST` and `import parser`), which we have utilized for the Python project above. Hence, no additional processing is needed in order prepare the concrete syntax trees as training data.

For the experiments, the source files have been divided into a training set T and a development test set D, where the former comprises 80% of the dependency trees and the latter 10%. The remaining 10% (E) has been left untouched for later use. The source files have been ordered alphabetically by the file names including the path. The dependency trees have then been distributed into the data sets in a pseudo-randomized way. Every tenth dependency tree starting at index 9 (i.e. dependency trees 9, 19, 29, ...) will belong to D, and every tenth dependency trees starting at index 0 to E. The remaining trees constitute the training set T.

4.2 Metrics

The standard evaluation metric for parse trees for natural languages based on context-free grammar is F-score, the harmonic mean of precision and recall. F-score compares constituents – defined by triples $\langle i, j, XP\rangle$ spanning between terminals i and j – derived from the test data with those derived from the parser. A constituent in the parser output matches a constituent in the test data when they span over the same terminals in the input string. Recall is the ratio of matched constituents over all constituents in the test data. Precision is the ratio of matched constituents over all constituents found by the parser. F-score comes in two versions, one unlabeled (F_U) and one labeled (F_L), where each correct constituent in the latter also must have the correct nonterminal name (i.e., XP). The metric is implemented in Evalb (Collins and Sekine, 2008).

[1] It is worth noting that CDT failed to produce syntax trees for 2.2% of these source files, which were consequently excluded from the experiments. This again indicates the difficult of parsing C/C++ due to its different dialects.

	F_L			F_U		
	FR	LE	RI	FR	LE	RI
UL	82.1	93.5	74.6	92.3	97.9	90.6
L	89.7	97.7	80.8	95.8	99.3	92.1

Table 1: F-score for various parser models and head-finding rules for Java, where FR = FREQ, LE = LEFT and RI = RIGHT.

The standard evaluation metric measuring accuracy for dependency parsing for natural language is, on the other hand, labeled (AS_L) and unlabeled (AS_U) attachment score. AS_U is the ratio of tokens attached to its correct head. AS_L is the same as AS_U with the additional requirement that the dependency label should be correct as well.

4.3 Results

This section presents the parsing results. The first experiment was conducted for Java, using the inverse transformation back to syntax trees. Two feature models are evaluated, one unlexicalized feature sets (**UL**) containing 13 parts-of-speech and 4 dependency label features, and one lexicalized feature sets (**L**) containing all these 17 features and 13 additional word form features, developed by manual feature optimization. Table 1 compares these two feature sets, as well as the different head-finding rules discussed previously.

The figures give a clear answer to the question whether lexical information is beneficial or not. Every figure in the row **L** is higher than its corresponding figure in the row **UL**. This means that names of variables, methods, classes, etc., actually contain valuable information for the classifier. This is in contrast to ordinary syntactic parsing using a grammar of programming languages where all names are mapped to the same value (e.g. Identifier), and, e.g., integer constants to IntLiteral, before the parse. One potential contributing factor of the difference is the naming conventions that programmers normally follow. For example, naming classes, class attributes and local variables, etc. using typical methods names, such as `equals` in Java, is usually avoided by programmers.

It is just as clear that the choice of head-finding strategy is very important. For both F_L and F_U, the best choice is with a wide margin LEFT, followed by FREQ. RIGHT is consequently the least accurate one. A higher amount of arcs pointing to the right seems to be beneficial for the strategy of

	AS_L			AS_U		
	FR	LE	RI	FR	LE	RI
CO	87.6	96.6	86.6	90.9	98.2	90.7
NC	91.0	99.1	89.5	92.1	99.7	90.7

Table 2: Attachment score for Java and the lexical feature set, where *CO* = convertible and *NC* = non-convertible dependency trees.

	Python		C/C++	
	F_L	F_U	F_L	F_U
UL	91.5	92.1	95.6	96.4
L	99.1	99.2	96.5	96.9

Table 3: F-score for various parser models and head-finding rules LEFT for Python and C/C++.

parsing from left to right.

Table 1 can be compared to the accuracy on the parser output before conversion from dependency trees to syntax trees. This is shown in the first row (*CO*) of table 2, where all information in the complex dependency label is concatenated and placed in the dependency label. The relationships between the head-finding strategies remain the same, but it is worth noting that the accuracies for FREQ and RIGHT are closer to each other, entailing a more difficult conversion to syntax trees for the latter. The first row can also be compared to the second row (*NC*) in the same table, showing the accuracies when training and parsing with non-convertible dependency trees. One observation is that each figure in *NC* is higher than its corresponding figure in *CO* (even AS_U for RIGHT with more decimals), probably attributed to the lower burden on the parser. Both AS_U and AS_L are above 99% for the non-convertible dependency trees using LEFT.

We can see that choosing an appropriate representation of syntactic structure to be used during parsing is just as important for programming languages as for natural languages, when using data-driven natural language parsers (Bikel, 2004).

The parser output in table 1 can more easily be used as input to existing program comprehension tools, normally requiring abstract syntax trees. However, the highly accurate output for LEFT using non-convertible dependency trees could be worth using instead, but it requires some additional processing.

In order to investigate the language independence of our approach, table 3 contains the corresponding figures as in table 1 for Python and C/C++, restricted to LEFT, which is the best head-finding strategy for these languages as well. Again, each lexicalized feature set (**L**) outperforms its corresponding unlexicalized feature set (**UL**). Python has higher F_L and virtually the same F_U as Java, whereas C/C++ has the lowest accuracies for **L**. However, the **UL** figures are not far behind the **L** figures for C/C++, and C/C++ has in fact higher F_L for **UL** compared to Java and Python. These results can maybe be explained by the fact that C/C++ has less verbose syntax than both Java and Python, making the lexical features less informative.

The F_L figures for Java, Python and C/C++ using LEFT can also be compared to the corresponding figures in Nilsson et al. (2009). They use the same data sets but a slightly different head-finding strategy. Instead of selecting the leftmost element (terminal or non-terminal) as in LEFT, they always select the leftmost terminal, resulting in F_L=99.5 for Java, F_L=98.3 for Python and F_L=96.5 for C/C++. That is, our results are slightly lower for Java, higher for Python, and slightly higher for C/C++. The same holds for F_U as well. That is, having only arcs pointing to the right results in high accuracy for all languages (which is the case for `Left` described in section 3), but small deviations from this head-finding strategy can in fact be beneficial for some languages.

We are not aware of any similar studies for programming languages[2] so we compare the results to natural language parsing. First, the figures in table 2 for dependency structure are better than figures reported for natural languages. Some natural languages are easier to parse than others, and the parsing results of the CoNLL shared task 2007 (Nivre et al., 2007) for dependency structure indicate that English and Catalan are relatively easy, with AS_L around 88-89% and AS_U around 90-94% for the best dependency parsers.

Secondly, compared to parsing German with phrase structure with the same approach as here, with F_U = 81.4 and F_L = 78.7%, and Swedish, with F_U = 76.8 and F_L = 74.0 (Hall and Nivre,

[2] A comparative experiment using another data-driven NLP parser for context-free grammar could be of theoretical interest. However, fast parsing time is important in program comprehension tasks, and data-driven NLP parsers for context-free grammar have worse than a linear time complexity. As, e.g., the Java project has 838 tokens per source file, linear time complexity is a prerequisite in practice.

	Correct Label	Parsing Label
66	FieldReference	VariableReference
25	VariableReference	FieldReference
12	MethodDeclaration	LocalVariableDeclaration
9	Conditional	FieldReference
5	NotEquals	MethodReference
4	Plus	MethodReference
4	Positive	*
4	LessThan	FieldReference
4	GreaterOrEquals	FieldReference
4	Divide	FieldReference
4	Modulo	FieldReference
4	LessOrEquals	FieldReference
3	Equals	NotEquals
3	LessOrEquals	Equals
3	NotEquals	Equals

Table 4: Confusion matrix for Java using non-convertible dependency trees with LEFT, ordered by descending frequency.

2008), the figures reported in tables 1 and 3 are also much better. It is however worth noting that natural languages are more complex and less regular compared to programming languages. Although it remains to be shown, we conjecture that these figures are sufficiently high for a large number of program comprehension tasks.

4.4 Error Analysis

This subsection will study the result for Java with non-convertible dependency trees (*NC*) and LEFT, in order to get a deeper insight into the types of errors that the parser commits. Specifically, the labeling mistakes caused by the parser are investigated here. This is done by producing a confusion matrix based on the dependency labels. That is, how often does a parser confuse label X with label Y. This is shown in table 4 for the 15 most common errors.

The two most frequent errors show that the parser confuses *FieldReference* and *VariableReference*. A *FieldReference* refers to a class attribute whereas a *VariableReference* could refer to either an attribute or a local variable. The parser mixes a reference to a class attribute with a reference that could also be a local variable or vice versa. The error is understandable, since the parser obviously has no knowledge about where the variables are declared. This is an error that type and name analysis can easily resolve. On the use-occurrence of a name (reference), analysis looks up for both possible define-occurrences of the name (declaration), first a *LocalVariableDeclaration* and then a *FieldDeclaration*. It uses the one that is found first.

Another type of confusion involves declarations, where a *MethodDeclaration* is misinterpreted as a *LocalVariableDeclaration*. This type of error can be resolved by a simple post-processing step: a *LocalVariableDeclaration* followed by opening parenthesis (always recognized correctly) is a *MethodDeclaration*.

Errors that involve binary operators, e.g., *Conditional*, *NotEqual*, *Plus*, are at rank 4 and below in the list of the most frequent errors. They are most likely a result of the incremental left-to-right parsing strategy. The whole expression should be labeled in accordance with its binary operator (see `count > 0` in figure 4 for LEFT), but is incorrectly labeled as either *MethodReference*, *FieldReference* or some other operator instead. The references actually occur in the left-hand side subexpression of the binary operators. This means that subexpressions and bracketing were recognized correctly, but the type of the top expression node was mixed up. Extending the lookahead in the list of remaining input tokens, making it possible for the classifier in the parser to look at even more yet unparsed tokens, might be one possible solution. However, these errors are by and large relatively harmless anyway. Hence, no correction is in practice needed.

Figure 5 displays some typical mistakes for the example program fragment

```
return (fw.unitIndex == unitIndex &&
        fw.unitIndex.equals(unitList));
```

The parser mixes up a *ParenthesizedExpression* with a *Conditional*, a boolean *ParenthesizedExpression* only occurring in conditional statements and expressions. Then it incorrectly assigns the label *Equals* to the arc between the first left parenthesis and the first `fw` instead of the correct label *LogicalAnd*. It mixes up the type of the whole expression, an *Equals*- (i.e., `==`) is taken for an *LogicalAnd*-expression (i.e., `&&`). Finally, the two *FieldReferences* are taken as more general *VariableReferences*, which is corrigible as discussed.

In addition to a possible error correction in a post-processing step, the parsing errors could disappear due to the abstraction of subsequent analyses as commonly used in software maintenance tools. For instance, without any error correction, the type reference graphs of our test program, the correct one and the one constructed using the not quite correct parsing results, are identical.

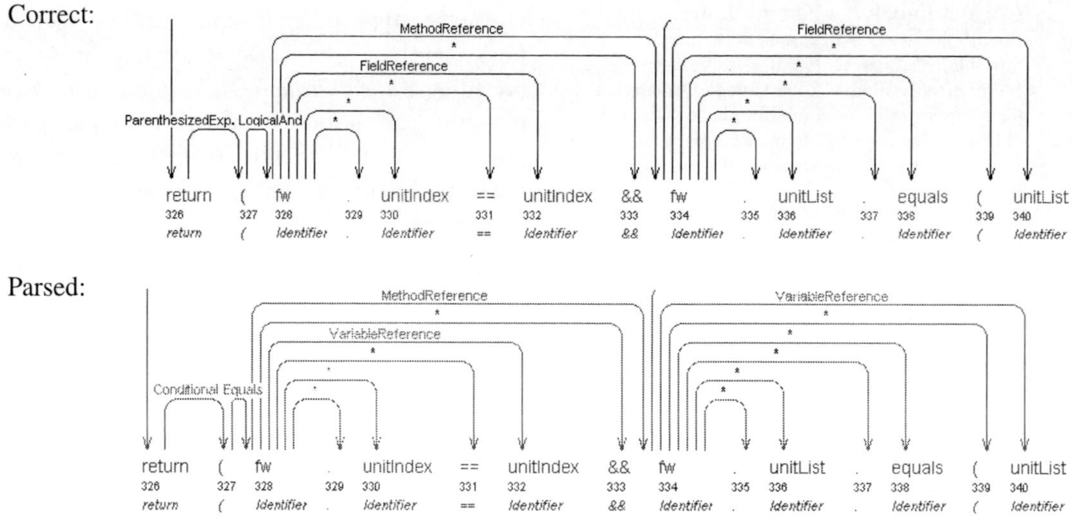

Figure 5: Typical errors for LEFT using by non-convertible dependency trees.

5 Related Work

Classical parsers for formal languages have been known for many years. They (conventionally) accept a context-free language defined by a context-free grammar. For each program, the parsers produce a phrase structure referred to as an abstract syntax tree (AST) which is also defined by a context-free language. Parsers including error stabilization and AST-constructors can be generated from context-free grammars for parsers (Kastens et al., 2007). A parser for a new language still requires the development of a complex specification. Moreover, error stabilization often throws away large parts of the source – it is robust but does not care about maximizing accuracy.

Breadth-First Parsing (Ophel, 1997) was designed to provide better error stabilization than traditional parsers and parser generators. It uses a two phase approach: the first phase identifies high-level entities – the second phase parses the structure with these entities as root nonterminals (axioms).

Fuzzy Parsing (Koppler, 1997) was designed to efficiently develop parsers by performing the analysis on selected parts of the source instead of the whole input. It is specified by a set of (sub)grammars each with their own axioms. The actual approach is then similar to Breadth-First Parsing: it scans for instances of the axioms and then parses according to the grammar. It makes parsing more robust in the sense that it ignores source fragments – including missing parts, errors and deviations therein – that subsequent analyses abstract from anyway. A prominent tool using the fuzzy parsing approach for information extraction in reverse-engineering tools is Sniff (Bischofberger, 1992) for analyzing C++ code.

Island grammars (Moonen, 2001) generalize on Fuzzy Parsing. Parsing is controlled by two grammar levels (island and sea) where the sea-level is used when no island-level production applies. The island-level corresponds to the sub-grammars of fuzzy parsing. Island grammars have been applied in reverse-engineering, specifically, to bank software (Moonen, 2002).

Syntactic approximation based on lexical analysis was developed with the same motivation as our work: when maintenance tools need syntactic information but the documents could not be parsed for some reason, hierarchies of regular expression analyses could be used to approximate the information with high accuracy (Murphy and Notkin, 1995; Cox and Clarke, 2003). Their information extraction approach is characterized as "lightweight" in the sense that it requires little specification effort.

A similar robust and light-weight approach for information extraction constructs XML formats (JavaML and srcML) from C/C++/Java programs first, before further processing with XML tools like Xpath (Badros, 2000; Collard et al., 2003). It combines lexical and context free analyses. Lexical pattern matching is also used in combination with context free parsing in order to extract facts from semi-structured specific comments and configuration specifications in frameworks (Knodel and Pinzger, 2003).

TXL is a rule-based language defining information extraction and transformation rules for formal languages (Cordy et al., 1991). It makes it possible to incrementally extend the rule base and to adapt to language dialects and extensions. As the rules are context-sensitive, TXL goes beyond the lexical and context-free approaches discussed before.

The fundamental difference of our approach compared to lexical, context-free, and context-sensitive approaches (and combinations thereof) is that we use *automated* machine learning instead of *manual* specification for defining and adapting the information extraction.

General NLP techniques have been applied for extracting facts from general source code comments to support software maintenance (Etzkorn et al., 1999). Comments are extracted from source code using classical lexical analysis; additional information is extracted (and then added) with classical compiler front-end technology.

NLP has also been applied to other information extraction tasks in software maintenance to analyze unstructured or very large information sources, e.g., for analyzing requirement specifications (Sawyer et al., 2002), in clone detection (Marcus and Maletic, 2001; Grant and Cordy, 2009), and to connect program documentation to source code (Marcus and Maletic, 2003).

6 Conclusions and Future Work

In this paper, we applied natural language parsing techniques to programming languages. One advantage is that it offers *robustness*, since it always produces some output even if the input is incorrect or incomplete. Completely correct analysis can, however, not be guaranteed even for correct input. However, the experiments showed that accuracy is in fact close to 100%.

In contrast to robust information extractors used so far for formal languages, the approach presented here is rapidly adaptable to new languages. We *automatically generate* the language specific information extractor using machine learning and training of a generic parsing, instead of *explicitly specifying* the information extractor using grammar and transformation rules. Also the training data can be generated automatically. This could increase the development efficiency of parsers, since no language specification has to be provided, only examples.

Regarding accuracy, the experiments showed that selecting the syntactic base representation used by the parser internally has a major impact. Incorporating, for instance, class, method and variable names in the set of features of the parser improves the accuracy more than expected. The detailed error analysis showed that many errors committed by the parser are forgivable, as they are anyway abstracted in later processing phases. Other errors are easily corrigible. We can also see that the best results presented here are much higher than the best parsing results for natural languages.

Besides efficient information extractor development, efficient parsing itself is important. Applied to programs which can easily contain several million lines of code, a parser with more than linear time complexity is not acceptable. The data-driven parser utilized here has linear parsing time.

These results are only the first (promising) step towards natural language parsing leveraging information extraction for software maintenance. However, the only way to really evaluate the usefulness of the approach is to use its output as input to client analyses, e.g., software measurement and architecture recovery, which we plan to do in the future. Another direction for future work is to apply the approach to more dialects of C/C++, such as analyzing correct, incomplete, and erroneous programs for both standard C and its dialects.

References

Paul Anderson. 2008. 90 % Perspiration: Engineering Static Analysis Techniques for Industrial Applications. In *Proceedings of the 8th IEEE International Working Conference on Source Code Analysis and Manipulation*, pages 3–12.

Greg J. Badros. 2000. JavaML: a Markup Language for Java Source Code. In *Proceedings of the 9th International World Wide Web conference on Computer networks : the international journal of computer and telecommunications networking*, pages 159–177.

Daniel M. Bikel. 2004. Intricacies of Collins' Parsing Model. *Computational Linguistics*, 30(4):479–511.

Steven Bird, Edward Loper, and Ewan Klein. 2008. Natural Language Toolkit (NLTK) 0.9.5. http://nltk.org/.

Walter R. Bischofberger. 1992. Sniff: A Pragmatic Approach to a C++ Programming Environment. In *USENIX C++ Conference*, pages 67–82.

Chih-Chung Chang and Chih-Jen Lin. 2001. LIBSVM: A Library for Support Vector Machines.

Michael L. Collard, Huzefa H. Kagdi, and Jonathan I. Maletic. 2003. An XML-Based Lightweight C++ Fact Extractor. In *11th IEEE International Workshop on Program Comprehension*, pages 134–143.

Michael Collins and Satoshi Sekine. 2008. Evalb. http://nlp.cs.nyu.edu/evalb/.

James R. Cordy, Charles D. Halpern-Hamu, and Eric Promislow. 1991. TXL: a Rapid Prototyping System for Programming Language Dialects. *Computer Languages*, 16(1):97–107.

Anthony Cox and Charles L. A. Clarke. 2003. Syntactic Approximation Using Iterative Lexical Analysis. In *Proceedings of the 11th IEEE International Workshop on Program Comprehension*, pages 154–163.

Letha H. Etzkorn, Lisa L. Bowen, and Carl G. Davis. 1999. An Approach to Program Understanding by Natural Language Understanding. *Natural Language Engineering*, 5(3):219–236.

Scott Grant and James R. Cordy. 2009. Vector Space Analysis of Software Clones. In *Proceedings of the IEEE 17th International Conference on Program Comprehension*, pages 233–237.

Tobias Gutzmann, Dirk Heuzeroth, and Mircea Trifu. 2007. Recoder 0.83. http://recoder.sourceforge.net/.

Johan Hall and Joakim Nivre. 2008. Parsing Discontinuous Phrase Structure with Grammatical Functions. In *Proceedings of GoTAL*, pages 169–180.

Johan Hall, Joakim Nivre, and Jens Nilsson. 2006. Discriminative Classifiers for Deterministic Dependency Parsing. In *Proceedings of COLING-ACL*, pages 316–323.

Uwe Kastens, Anthony M. Sloane, and William M. Waite. 2007. *Generating Software from Specifications*. Jones and Bartlett Publishers.

Jens Knodel and Martin Pinzger. 2003. Improving Fact Extraction of Framework-Based Software Systems. In *Proceedings of 10th Working Conference on Reverse Engineering*, pages 186–195.

Rainer Koppler. 1997. A Systematic Approach to Fuzzy Parsing. *Software - Practice and Experience*, 27(6):637–649.

David M. Magerman. 1995. Statistical Decision-tree Models for Parsing. In *Proceedings of ACL*, pages 276–283.

Andrian Marcus and Jonathan I. Maletic. 2001. Identification of High-Level Concept Clones in Source Code. In *Proceedings of the 16th IEEE international conference on Automated software engineering*, page 107.

Andrian Marcus and Jonathan I. Maletic. 2003. Recovering Documentation-to-Source-Code Traceability Links using Latent Semantic Indexing. In *Proceedings of the 25th International Conference on Software Engineering*, pages 125–135.

Scott McPeak. 2005. Elsa: The Elkhound-based C/C++ Parser. http://www.cs.berkeley.edu/~smcpeak.

Leon Moonen. 2001. Generating Robust Parsers using Island Grammars. In *Proceedings of the 8th Working Conference on Reverse Engineering*, pages 13–22.

Leon Moonen. 2002. Lightweight Impact Analysis using Island Grammars. In *Proceedings of the 10th International Workshop on Program Comprehension*, pages 219–228.

Gail C. Murphy and David Notkin. 1995. Lightweight Source Model Extraction. *SIGSOFT Software Engineering Notes*, 20(4):116–127.

Jens Nilsson, Welf Löwe, Johan Hall, and Joakim Nivre. 2009. Natural Language Parsing for Fact Extraction from Source Code. In *Proceedings of 17th IEEE International Conference on Program Comprehension*, pages 223–227.

Joakim Nivre, Johan Hall, and Jens Nilsson. 2004. Memory-based Dependency Parsing. In *Proceedings of CoNLL*, pages 49–56.

Joakim Nivre, Johan Hall, and Jens Nilsson. 2006. MaltParser: A Data-Driven Parser-Generator for Dependency Parsing. In *Proceedings of LREC*, pages 2216–2219.

Joakim Nivre, Johan Hall, Sanda Kübler, Ryan McDonald, Jens Nilsson, Sebastian Riedel, and Deniz Yuret. 2007. The CoNLL 2007 Shared Task on Dependency Parsing. In *Proceedings of CoNLL/ACL*, pages 915–932.

Joakim Nivre. 2003. An Efficient Algorithm for Projective Dependency Parsing. In *Proceedings of IWPT*, pages 149–160.

John Ophel. 1997. Breadth-First Parsing. citeseerx.ist.psu.edu/viewdoc/summary?doi=10.1.1.50.3035.

Pete Sawyer, Paul Rayson, and Roger Garside. 2002. REVERE: Support for Requirements Synthesis from Documents. *Information Systems Frontiers*, 4(11):343–353.

Dennis Strein, Rüdiger Lincke, Jonas Lundberg, and Welf Löwe. 2007. An Extensible Meta-Model for Program Analysis. *IEEE Transactions on Software Engineering*, 33(9):592–607.

An Incremental Earley Parser for Simple Range Concatenation Grammar

Laura Kallmeyer and **Wolfgang Maier**
Collaborative Research Center 833
University of Tübingen
Tübingen, Germany
{lk,wmaier}@sfs.uni-tuebingen.de

Abstract

We present an Earley-style parser for simple range concatenation grammar, a formalism strongly equivalent to linear context-free rewriting systems. Furthermore, we present different filters which reduce the number of items in the parsing chart. An implementation shows that parses can be obtained in a reasonable time.

1 Introduction

Linear context-free rewriting systems (LCFRS) (Vijay-Shanker et al., 1987), the equivalent multiple context-free grammars (MCFG) (Seki et al., 1991) and simple range concatenation grammars (sRCG) (Boullier, 1998) have recently attracted an increasing interest in the context of natural language processing. For example, Maier and Søgaard (2008) propose to extract simple RCGs from constituency treebanks with crossing branches while Kuhlmann and Satta (2009) propose to extract LCFRS from non-projective dependency treebanks. Another application area of this class of formalisms is biological computing (Kato et al., 2006).

This paper addresses the symbolic parsing of sRCG/LCFRS. Starting from the parsing algorithms presented in Burden and Ljunglöf (2005) and Villemonte de la Clergerie (2002), we propose an incremental Earley algorithm for simple RCG. The strategy is roughly like the one pursued in Villemonte de la Clergerie (2002). However, instead of the automaton-based formalization in Villemonte de la Clergerie's work, we give a general formulation of an incremental Earley algorithm, using the framework of parsing as deduction. In order to reduce the search space, we introduce different types of filters on our items. We have implemented this algorithm and tested it on simple RCGs extracted from the German treebanks Negra and Tiger.

In the following section, we introduce simple RCG and in section 3, we present an algorithm for symbolic parsing of simple RCG. Section 4 then presents different filtering techniques to reduce the number of items. We close discussing future work.

2 Grammar Formalism

A **range concatenation grammar (RCG)** is a 5-tuple $G = (N, T, V, P, S)$. N is a finite set of non-terminals (predicate names) with an arity function dim: $N \rightarrow \mathbb{N}^+$, T and V are disjoint finite sets of terminals and variables. P is a finite set of clauses of the form $\psi_0 \rightarrow \psi_1 \ldots \psi_m$, where $m \geq 0$ and each of the $\psi_i, 0 \leq i \leq m$, is a predicate of the form $A_i(\alpha_1^i, \ldots, \alpha_{dim(A)}^i)$. Each $\alpha_j^i \in (T \cup V)^*$, $1 \leq j \leq dim(A)$ and $0 \leq i \leq k$, is an argument. As a shorthand notation for $A_i(\alpha_1, \ldots, \alpha_{dim(A)})$, we use $A_i(\vec{\alpha})$. $S \in N$ is the start predicate name with $dim(S) = 1$.

Note that the order of right-hand side (RHS) predicates in a clause is of no importance. Subclasses of RCGs are introduced for further reference: An RCG $G = (N, T, V, P, S)$ is **simple** if for all $c \in P$, it holds that every variable X occurring in c occurs exactly once in the left-hand side (LHS) and exactly once in the RHS, and each argument in the RHS of c contains exactly one variable. A simple RCG is **ordered** if for all $\psi_0 \rightarrow \psi_1 \cdots \psi_m \in P$, it holds that if a variable X_1 precedes a variable X_2 in a ψ_i, $1 \leq i \leq m$, then X_1 also precedes X_2 in ψ_0. The ordering requirement does not change the expressive power, i.e., ordered simple RCG is equivalent to simple RCG (Villemonte de la Clergerie, 2002). An RCG is **ε-free** if it either contains no ε-rules or there is exactly one rule $S(\varepsilon) \rightarrow \varepsilon$ and S does not appear in any of the righthand sides of the rules in the grammar. A rule is an ε-rule if one of the arguments

Proceedings of the 11th International Conference on Parsing Technologies (IWPT), pages 61–64,
Paris, October 2009.

of the lefthand side is the empty string ε. (Boullier, 1998) shows that for every simple RCG, one can construct an equivalent ε-free simple RCG. An RCG $G = (N, T, V, P, S)$ is a k-**RCG** if for all $A \in N$, $dim(A) \leq k$.

The language of RCGs is based on the notion of **range**. For a string $w_1 \cdots w_n$ a range is a pair of indices $\langle i, j \rangle$ with $0 \leq i \leq j \leq n$, i.e., a string span, which denotes a substring $w_{i+1} \cdots w_j$ in the source string or a substring $v_{i+1} \cdots v_j$ in the target string. Only consecutive ranges can be concatenated into new ranges. Terminals, variables and arguments in a clause are bound to ranges by a substitution mechanism. An **instantiated** clause is a clause in which variables and arguments are consistently replaced by ranges; its components are **instantiated predicates**. For example $A(\langle g \cdots h \rangle) \rightarrow B(\langle g+1 \cdots h \rangle)$ is an instantiation of the clause $A(aX_1) \rightarrow B(X_1)$ if the target string is such that $w_{g+1} = a$. A **derive** relation $\Rightarrow$ is defined on strings of instantiated predicates. If an instantiated predicate is the LHS of some instantiated clause, it can be replaced by the RHS of that instantiated clause. The language of an RCG $G = (N, T, V, P, S)$ is the set $L(G) = \{w_1 \cdots w_n \mid S(\langle 0, n \rangle) \stackrel{*}{\Rightarrow} \varepsilon\}$, i.e., an input string $w_1 \cdots w_n$ is recognized if and only if the empty string can be derived from $S(\langle 0, n \rangle)$. In this paper, we are dealing only with ordered simple RCGs. The ordering requirement does not change the expressive power (Villemonte de la Clergerie, 2002). Furthermore, without loss of generality, we assume that for every clause, there is a $k \geq 0$ such that the variables occurring in the clause are exactly $X_1, \ldots, X_k$.

We define derivation trees for simple RCGs as unordered trees whose internal nodes are labelled with predicate names and whose leaves are labelled with ranges such that all internal nodes are licensed by RCG clause instantiations: given a simple RCG G and a string w, a tree $D = \langle V, E, r \rangle$ is a **derivation tree** of $w = a_1 \ldots a_n$ iff 1. there are exactly n leaves in D labelled $\langle 0, 1 \rangle, \ldots, \langle n-1, n \rangle$ and 2. for all $v_0 \in V$ with $v_1, \ldots, v_n \in V$, $n \geq 1$ being all vertices with $\langle v_0, v_i \rangle \in E$ ($1 \leq i \leq n$) such that the leftmost range dominated by v_i precedes the leftmost range dominated by v_{i+1} ($1 \leq i < n$): there is a clause instantiation $A_0(\vec{\rho_0}) \rightarrow A_1(\vec{\rho_1}) \ldots A_n(\vec{\rho_n})$ such that a) $l(v_i) = A_i$ for $0 \leq i \leq n$ and b) the yield of the leaves dominates by v_i is $\vec{\rho_i}$.

3 Parsing

Our parsing algorithm is a modification of the "incremental algorithm" of Burden and Ljunglöf (2005) with a strategy very similar to the strategy adopted by *Thread Automata* (Villemonte de la Clergerie, 2002). It assumes the grammar to be ordered and ε-free. We refrain from supporting non-ε-free grammars since the treebank grammars used with our implementation are all ε-free. However, note that only minor modifications would be necessary in order to support non-ε-free grammars (see below).

We process the arguments of LHS of clauses incrementally, starting from an S-clause. Whenever we reach a variable, we move into the clause of the corresponding RHS predicate (**predict** or **resume**). Whenever we reach the end of an argument, we **suspend** this clause and move into the parent clause that has called the current one. In addition, we treat the case where we reach the end of the last argument and move into the parent as a special case. Here, we first **convert** the item into a passive one and then **complete** the parent item with this passive item. This allows for some additional factorization.

The item form for passive items is $[A, \vec{\rho}]$ where A a predicate of some arity k, $\vec{\rho}$ is a range vector of arity k. The item form for active items: $[A(\vec{\phi}) \rightarrow A_1(\vec{\phi_1}) \ldots A_m(\vec{\phi_m}), pos, \langle i, j \rangle, \vec{\rho}]$ where $A(\vec{\phi}) \rightarrow A_1(\vec{\phi_1}) \ldots A_m(\vec{\phi_m}) \in P$; $pos \in \{0, \ldots, n\}$ is the position up to which we have processed the input; $\langle i, j \rangle \in \mathbb{N}^2$ marks the position of our dot in the arguments of the predicate A: $\langle i, j \rangle$ indicates that we have processed the arguments up to the jth element of the ith argument; $\vec{\rho}$ is an range vector containing the bindings of the variables and terminals occurring in the lefthand side of the clause ($\vec{\rho}(i)$ is the range the ith element is bound to). When first predicting a clause, it is initialized with a vector containing only symbols "?" for "unknown". We call such a vector (of appropriate arity) $\vec{\rho}_{init}$. We introduce an additional piece of notation. We write $\vec{\rho}(X)$ for the range bound to the variable X in $\vec{\rho}$. Furthermore, we write $\vec{\rho}(\langle i, j \rangle)$ for the range bound to the jth element in the ith argument of the clause lefthand side.

Applying a range vector $\vec{\rho}$ containing variable bindings for a given clause c to the argument vector of the lefthand side of c means mapping the ith element in the arguments to $\vec{\rho}(i)$ and concatenating adjacent ranges. The result is defined iff every argument is thereby mapped to a range.

We start by **predicting** the S-predicate:

$$\frac{}{[S(\vec{\phi}) \rightarrow \bullet\vec{\Phi}, 0, \langle 1, 0\rangle, \vec{\rho}_{init}]} \; S(\vec{\phi}) \rightarrow \vec{\Phi} \in P$$

Scan: Whenever the next symbol after the dot is the next terminal in the input, we can scan it:

$$\frac{[A(\vec{\phi}) \rightarrow \vec{\Phi}, pos, \langle i, j\rangle, \vec{\rho}]}{[A(\vec{\phi}) \rightarrow \vec{\Phi}, pos+1, \langle i, j+1\rangle, \vec{\rho}']} \; \vec{\phi}(i, j{+}1) = w_{pos+1}$$

where $\vec{\rho}'$ is $\vec{\rho}$ updated with $\vec{\rho}(i, j+1) = \langle pos, pos+1\rangle$.

In order to support ε-free grammars, one would need to store the pair of indices a ε is mapped to in the range vector, along with the mappings of terminals and variables. The indices could be obtained through a **Scan-**ε operation, parallel to the **Scan** operation.

Predict: Whenever our dot is left of a variable that is the first argument of some RHS predicate B, we predict new B-clauses:

$$\frac{[A(\vec{\phi}) \rightarrow \ldots B(X, \ldots) \ldots, pos, \langle i, j\rangle, \vec{\rho}_A]}{[B(\vec{\psi}) \rightarrow \vec{\Psi}, pos, \langle 1, 0\rangle, \vec{\rho}_{init}]}$$

with the side condition $\vec{\phi}(i, j+1) = X, B(\vec{\psi}) \rightarrow \vec{\Psi} \in P$.

Suspend: Whenever we arrive at the end of an argument that is not the last argument, we suspend the processing of this clause and we go back to the item that was used to predict it.

$$\frac{[B(\vec{\psi}) \rightarrow \vec{\Psi}, pos', \langle i, j\rangle, \vec{\rho}_B], \quad [A(\vec{\phi}) \rightarrow \ldots B(\vec{\xi}) \ldots, pos, \langle k, l\rangle, \vec{\rho}_A]}{[A(\vec{\phi}) \rightarrow \ldots B(\vec{\xi}) \ldots, pos', \langle k, l+1\rangle, \vec{\rho}]}$$

where the dot in the antecedent A-item precedes the variable $\vec{\xi}(i)$, $|\vec{\psi}(i)| = j$ (the ith argument has length j and has therefore been completely processed), $|\vec{\psi}| < i$ (the ith argument is not the last argument of B), $\vec{\rho}_B(\vec{\psi}(i)) = \langle pos, pos'\rangle$ and for all $1 \leq m < i$: $\vec{\rho}_B(\vec{\psi}(m)) = \vec{\rho}_A(\vec{\xi}(m))$. $\vec{\rho}$ is $\vec{\rho}_A$ updated with $\vec{\rho}_A(\vec{\xi}(i)) = \langle pos, pos'\rangle$.

Convert: Whenever we arrive at the end of the last argument, we convert the item into a passive one:

$$\frac{[B(\vec{\psi}) \rightarrow \vec{\Psi}, pos, \langle i, j\rangle, \vec{\rho}_B]}{[B, \rho]} \; \begin{array}{l} |\vec{\psi}(i)| = j, |\vec{\psi}| = i, \\ \vec{\rho}_B(\vec{\psi}) = \rho \end{array}$$

Complete: Whenever we have a passive B item we can use it to move the dot over the variable of the last argument of B in a parent A-clause that was used to predict it.

$$\frac{[B, \vec{\rho}_B], [A(\vec{\phi}) \rightarrow \ldots B(\vec{\xi}) \ldots, pos, \langle k, l\rangle, \vec{\rho}_A]}{[A(\vec{\phi}) \rightarrow \ldots B(\vec{\xi}) \ldots, pos', \langle k, l+1\rangle, \vec{\rho}]}$$

where the dot in the antecedent A-item precedes the variable $\vec{\xi}(|\vec{\rho}_B|)$, the last range in $\vec{\rho}_B$ is $\langle pos, pos'\rangle$, and for all $1 \leq m < |\vec{\rho}_B|$: $\vec{\rho}_B(m) = \vec{\rho}_A(\vec{\xi}(m))$. $\vec{\rho}$ is $\vec{\rho}_A$ updated with $\vec{\rho}_A(\vec{\xi}(|\vec{\rho}_B|)) = \langle pos, pos'\rangle$.

Resume: Whenever we are left of a variable that is not the first argument of one of the RHS predicates, we resume the clause of the RHS predicate.

$$\frac{[A(\vec{\phi}) \rightarrow \ldots B(\vec{\xi}) \ldots, pos, \langle i, j\rangle, \vec{\rho}_A], \quad [B(\vec{\psi}) \rightarrow \vec{\Psi}, pos', \langle k-1, l\rangle, \vec{\rho}_B]}{[B(\vec{\psi}) \rightarrow \vec{\Psi}, pos, \langle k, 0\rangle, \vec{\rho}_B]}$$

where $\vec{\phi}(i)(j+1) = \vec{\xi}(k), k > 1$ (the next element is a variable that is the kth element in $\vec{\xi}$, i.e., the kth argument of B), $|\vec{\psi}(k-1)| = l$, and $\vec{\rho}_A(\vec{\xi}(m)) = \vec{\rho}_B(\vec{\psi})(m)$ for all $1 \leq m \leq k-1$.

The **goal item** has the form $[S, \langle 0, n\rangle]$.

Note that, in contrast to a purely bottom-up CYK algorithm, the Earley algorithm presented here is prefix valid, provided that the grammar does not contain useless symbols.

4 Filters

During parsing, various optimizations known from (P)CFG parsing can be applied. More concretely, because of the particular form of our simple RCGs, we can use several filters to reject items very early that cannot lead to a valid parse tree for a given input $w = w_1 \ldots w_n$.

Since our grammars are ε-free, we know that each variable or occurrence of a terminal in the clause must cover at least one terminal in the input. Furthermore, since separations between arguments are generated only in cases where between two terminals belonging to the yield of a non-terminal, there is at least one other terminals that is not part of the yield, we know that between different arguments of a predicate, there must be at least one terminal in the input. Consequently, we obtain as a filtering condition on the validity of an active item that the length of the remaining input must be greater or equal to the number of variables and terminal occurrences plus the number of argument separations to the right of the dot in the left-hand side of the clause. More formally, an active item $[A(\vec{\phi}) \rightarrow A_1(\vec{\phi_1}) \ldots A_m(\vec{\phi_m}), pos, \langle i, j\rangle, \vec{\rho}]$ satisfies the **length filter** iff

$$\begin{array}{l} (n - pos) \\ \geq (|\vec{\phi}(i)| - j) + \Sigma_{k=i+1}^{dim(A)} |\vec{\phi}(k)| + (dim(A) - i) \end{array}$$

The length filter is applied to results of **predict**, **resume**, **suspend** and **complete**.

A second filter, first proposed in Klein and Manning (2003), checks for the presence of required preterminals. In our case, we assume the preterminals to be treated as terminals, so this filter amounts to checking for the presence of all terminals in the predicted part of a clause (the part to the right of the dot) in the remaining input. Furthermore, we check that the terminals appear in the predicted order and that the distance between two of them is at least the number of variables/terminals and argument separations in between. In other words, an active item $[A(\vec{\phi}) \to A_1(\vec{\phi_1}) \dots A_m(\vec{\phi_m}), pos, \langle i, j \rangle, \vec{\rho}]$ satisfies the **terminal filter** iff we can find an injective mapping $f_T : Term = \{\langle k, l \rangle \mid \vec{\phi}(k)(l) \in T$ and either $k > i$ or $(k = i$ and $l > j)\} \to \{pos + 1, \dots, n\}$ such that

1. $w_{f_T(\langle k,l \rangle)} = \vec{\phi}(k)(l)$ for all $\langle k, l \rangle \in Term$;
2. for all $\langle k_1, l_1 \rangle, \langle k_2, l_2 \rangle \in Term$ with $k_1 = k_2$ and $l_1 < l_2$: $f_T(\langle k_2, l_2 \rangle) \geq f_T(\langle k_1, l_1 \rangle) + (l_2 - l_1)$;
3. for all $\langle k_1, l_1 \rangle, \langle k_2, l_2 \rangle \in Term$ with $k_1 < k_2$: $f_T(\langle k_2, l_2 \rangle) \geq f_T(\langle k_1, l_1 \rangle) + (|\vec{\phi}(k_1)| - l_1) + \Sigma_{k=k_1+1}^{k_2-1} |\vec{\phi}(k)| + l_2 + (k_2 - k_1)$.

Checking this filter amounts to a linear traversal of the part of the lefthand side of the clause that is to the right of the dot. We start with index $i = pos + 1$, for every variable or gap we increment i by 1. For every terminal a, we search the next a in the input, starting at position i. If it occurs at position j, then we set $i = j$ and continue our traversal of the remaining parts of the lefthand side of the clause.

The preterminal filter is applied to results of the **predict** and **resume** operations.

We have implemented the incremental Earley parser with the filtering conditions on items. In order to test it, we have extracted simple RCGs from the first 1000 sentences of Negra and Tiger (with removed punctuation) using the algorithm described in Maier and Søgaard (2008) and parsed the sentences 1001-1100 with it. The grammars contained 2474 clauses (Negra) and 2554 clauses (Tiger). The following table contains the total number of sentences for different length and resp. the number of sentences for which a parse was found, along with the average parsing times of those that had a parse:

	Negra		Tiger	
	parse/tot	av. t.	parse/tot	av. t.
$\lvert w \rvert \leq 20$	73/84	0.40 sec.	50/79	0.32
$20 \leq \lvert w \rvert \leq 35$	14/16	2.14 sec.	10/19	2.16

5 Conclusion and Future Work

We have presented an Earley-style algorithm for simple range concatenation grammar, formulated as deduction system. Furthermore, we have presented a set of filters on the chart reducing the number of items. An implementation and a test with grammars extracted from treebanks showed that reasonable parsing times can be achieved.

We are currently working on a probabilistic k-best extension of our parser which resumes comparable work for PCFG (Huang and Chiang, 2005). Unfortunately, experiments with the Earley algorithm have shown that with grammars of a reasonable size for data-driven parsing ($> 15,000$ clauses), an exhaustive parsing is no longer efficient, due to the highly ambiguous grammars. Algorithms using only passive items seem more promising in this context since they facilitate the application of A* parsing techniques.

References

Pierre Boullier. 1998. Proposal for a natural language processing syntactic backbone. Rapport de Recherche RR-3342, INRIA.

Håkan Burden and Peter Ljunglöf. 2005. Parsing linear context-free rewriting systems. In *Proceedings of IWPT 2005*.

Liang Huang and David Chiang. 2005. Better k-best parsing. In *Proceedings of IWPT 2005*.

Yuki Kato, Hiroyuki Seki, and Tadao Kasami. 2006. Stochastic multiple context-free grammar for RNA pseudoknot modeling. In *Proceedings of TAG+8*.

Dan Klein and Christopher D. Manning. 2003. A* Parsing: Fast Exact Viterbi Parse Selection. In *Proceedings of HLT-NAACL*.

Marco Kuhlmann and Giorgio Satta. 2009. Treebank grammar techniques for non-projective dependency parsing. In *Proceedings of EACL*.

Wolfgang Maier and Anders Søgaard. 2008. Treebanks and mild context-sensitivity. In *Proceedings of Formal Grammar 2008*.

Hiroyuki Seki, Takahashi Matsumura, Mamoru Fujii, and Tadao Kasami. 1991. On multiple context-free grammars. *Theoretical Computer Science*.

K. Vijay-Shanker, David Weir, and Aravind Joshi. 1987. Characterising structural descriptions used by various formalisms. In *Proceedings of ACL*.

Eric Villemonte de la Clergerie. 2002. Parsing mildly context-sensitive languages with thread automata. In *Proceedings of COLING*.

Deductive Parsing with Interaction Grammars

Joseph Le Roux
NCLT, School of Computing,
Dublin City University
jleroux@computing.dcu.ie

Abstract

We present a parsing algorithm for Interaction Grammars using the deductive parsing framework. This approach brings new perspectives to this problem, departing from previous methods which rely on constraint-solving techniques.

1 Introduction

An Interaction Grammar (IG) (Guillaume and Perrier, 2008) is a lexicalized grammatical formalism that primarily focuses on valency, explicitly expressed using polarities decorating syntagms. These polarities and the use of underspecified structures naturally lead parsing to be viewed as a constraint-solving problem – for example (Bonfante et al.) reduce the parsing problem to a graph-rewriting problem in (2003) .

However, in this article we depart from this approach and present an algorithm close to (Earley, 1970) for context-free grammars. We introduce this algorithm using the standard framework of deductive parsing (Shieber et al., 1995).

This article is organised as follows: we first present IGs (section 2), then we describe the algorithm (section 3). Finally we discuss some technical points and conclude (sections 4 and 5).

2 Interaction Grammars

We briefly introduce IGs as in (Guillaume and Perrier, 2008)[1]. However, we omit polarized feature structures, for the sake of exposition.

2.1 Polarized Tree Descriptions

The structures associated with words by the lexicon are Polarized Tree Descriptions (PTDs). They represent fragments of parse trees. The nodes of these structures are labelled with a category and a polarity. IGs use 4 polarities, $\mathbb{P} = \{\rightarrow, \leftarrow, =, \sim\}$, namely positive, negative, neutral and virtual.

A multiset of polarities is *superposable*[2] if it contains at most one $\rightarrow$ and at most one $\leftarrow$.

A multiset of polarities is *saturated* if it contains either (1) one $\rightarrow$, one $\leftarrow$ and any number of $\sim$ and $=$, or (2) zero $\rightarrow$, zero $\leftarrow$, any number of $\sim$ and at least one $=$.

The two previous definitions can be extended to nodes: a multiset of nodes is saturated (resp. superposable) if all the elements have the same category and if the induced multiset of polarities is saturated (resp. superposable).

A PTD is a DAG with four binary relations: the immediate dominance $>$, the general dominance $>^*$, the immediate precedence $\prec$ and the general precedence $\prec^+$. A valid PTD is a PTD where (1) $>$ and $>^*$ define a tree structure[3] , (2) $\prec$ and $\prec^+$ are restricted to couples of nodes having the same ancestor by $>$, and (3) one leaf is the anchor. In the rest of this paper, all PTDs will be valid.

We now introduce some notations : if $n >^* m$, we say that m is constrained by n and for a set of nodes $\mathcal{N}$, we define $\mathcal{N}^{\maltese} = \{N | \exists M \in \mathcal{N}, M \maltese N\}$ where $\maltese$ is a binary relation.

2.2 Grammars

An IG is a tuple $\mathcal{G} = \{\Sigma, \mathbb{C}, S, \mathcal{P}, phon\}$, where Σ is the terminal alphabet, $\mathbb{C}$ the non-terminal alphabet, $S \in \mathbb{C}$ the initial symbol, $\mathcal{P}$ is a set of PTDs with node labels in $\mathbb{C} \times \mathbb{P}$, and $phon$ is a function from anchors in $\mathcal{P}$ to Σ.

The structure obtained from parsing is a *syntactic tree*, a totally ordered tree in which all nodes are labelled with a non-terminal. We call $lab(A)$ the label of node A. If a leaf L is labelled with a terminal, this terminal is denoted $word(L)$.

[1] This paper also discusses the linguistic motivations behind IGs.

[2] This name comes from the *superposition* introduced in previous presentations of IGs.

[3] For readers familiar with D-Tree Grammars (Rambow et al., 1995), $>$ adds an i-edge while $>^*$ adds a d-edge.

Proceedings of the 11th International Conference on Parsing Technologies (IWPT), pages 65–68,
Paris, October 2009.

We will write $M \gg N$ if the node M is the mother of N and $N \gg [N_1, \ldots, N_k]$ if the N is the mother of the ordered list of nodes $[N_1, \ldots, N_k]$. The order between siblings can also be expressed using the relation $\prec\!\prec$: $M \prec\!\prec N$ means that N is the immediate successor of M. $\prec\!\prec^+$ is the transitive closure of $\prec\!\prec$ and $\gg^*$ the reflexive transitive closure of $\gg$.

We define the phonological projection PP of a node as : $PP(M) = [t]$ if $M \gg []$ and $word(M) = t$, or $PP(M) = [PP(N_1) \ldots PP(N_k)]$ if $M \gg [N_1, \ldots, N_k]$

A syntactic tree T is a *model* for a multiset $\mathcal{D}$ of PTDs if there exists a total function I from nodes in $\mathcal{D}$ ($\mathcal{ND}$) to nodes in T ($\mathcal{NT}$). I must respect the following conditions, where variables M, N range over $\mathcal{ND}$ and A, B over $\mathcal{NT}$:

1. $I^{-1}(A)$ is saturated and non-empty.
2. if $M > N$ then $I(M) \gg I(N)$
3. if $M >^* N$ then $I(M) \gg^* I(N)$
4. if $M \prec N$ then $I(M) \prec\!\prec I(N)$
5. if $M \prec^+ N$ then $I(M) \prec\!\prec^+ I(N)$
6. if $A \gg B$ then there exists $M \in I^{-1}(A)$ and $N \in I^{-1}(B)$ such that $M > N$
7. $lab(A) = lab(M)$ for all $M \in I^{-1}(A)$
8. if $phon(M) = w$ then $PP(I(M)) = [w]$

Given an IG $\mathcal{G} = \{\Sigma, \mathbb{C}, S, \mathcal{P}, phon\}$ and a sentence $s = w_1, \ldots, w_n$ in Σ^*, a syntactic tree T is a parse tree for s if there exists a multiset of PTDs $\mathcal{D}$ from $\mathcal{P}$ such that the root node R of T is labelled with S and $PP(R) = [w_1, \ldots, w_n]$. The language generated by $\mathcal{G}$ is the set of strings in Σ^* for which there is a parse tree.

3 Parsing Algorithm

We use the deductive parsing framework (Shieber et al., 1995). A state of the parser is encoded as an item, created by applying deductive rules. Our algorithm resembles the Earley algorithm for CFGs and uses the same rules : prediction, scanning and completion.

3.1 Items

Items $[A(H, N, F) \to \alpha \bullet \beta, i, j, (O, U, D)]$ consist of a dotted rule, 2 position indexes and a 3-tuple of sets of constrained nodes.

The dotted rule $A(H, N, F) \to \alpha \bullet \beta$ means that there exists a node A in the parse tree with antecedents $H \cup N \cup F$. Elements of the sequence α are also nodes of the parse tree. For the sequence β, the elements have the form $B_k(H_k)$ where B_k is a node of the parse tree and H_k is a subset of its antecedents, the predicted antecedents.

This item asserts that a syntactic tree can be partially built from the input grammar and sentence, that contains $A \gg [A_1 \ldots A_k B_1 \ldots B_l]$ and that $PP(A_1) \circ \cdots \circ PP(A_k) = [m_{i+1} \ldots m_j]$.

The proper use of constrained nodes is managed by O, U and D:

- Nodes in D are available in prediction to find antecedents for new parse tree nodes.
- Nodes in O must be used in a sub-parse. To use an item as a completer, O must be empty.
- U contains constrained nodes that have been used in a prediction, and for which the constraining nodes have not been completed yet.

Moreover, we will use 3 additional symbols: $\top$ as the left-hand side of the axiom item which can be seen as a dummy root, and ■ or ♦ that mark items for which prediction is not terminated.

We will need sequences of antecedents that respect the order relations of an IG. Given a set of nodes $\mathcal{N}$, we define the set of all these orderings:

$$
\begin{aligned}
&ord(\mathcal{N}) = \{[\mathcal{N}_1 \ldots \mathcal{N}_k] | \\
&(\mathcal{N}_i)_{1 \le i \le k} \text{ is a partition of } \mathcal{N} \wedge \\
&1 \le i \le k, \mathcal{N}_i \text{ is superposable} \wedge \\
&\text{if } n_1, n_2 \in \mathcal{N} \text{ and } n_1 \prec n_2 \text{ then} \\
&\quad \exists 1 \le j < k \text{ s.t. } n_1 \in \mathcal{N}_j \text{ and } n_2 \in \mathcal{N}_{j+1} \wedge \\
&\text{if } n_1, n_2 \in \mathcal{N} \text{ and } n_1 \prec^+ n_2 \text{ then} \\
&\quad \exists 1 \le i < j \le k \text{ s.t. } n_1 \in \mathcal{N}_i \text{ and } n_2 \in \mathcal{N}_j\}
\end{aligned}
$$

3.2 Deductive Rules

In this section, we assume an input sentence $s = w_1, \ldots, w_n$ and a IG $\mathcal{G} = \{\Sigma, \mathbb{C}, S, \mathcal{P}, phon\}$.

Axiom This rule creates the first item. It prepares the prediction of a node of category S starting at position 0 without constrained nodes.

$$\frac{}{[\top \to \bullet S(\emptyset), 0, 0, (\emptyset, \emptyset, \emptyset)]} ax$$

Prediction This rule initializes a sub-parse. We divide it in three in order to introduce the different constraints one at a time.

$$\frac{[A(H,N,F) \rightarrow \alpha \bullet C(H_C)\beta, i, j, (O,U,D)]}{[C(H_C,\emptyset,\emptyset) \rightarrow \blacksquare, j, j, (\emptyset, U, D \cup O)]} p_1$$

In this first step, we initialize a new sub-parse at the current position j where C will be the predicted node that we want to find antecedents for. If some antecedents H_C have already been predicted we use them. The nodes in O, that must be used in one of the sub-parse of A, become available as possible antecedents for C.

$$\frac{[C(H_C,\emptyset,\emptyset) \rightarrow \blacksquare, j, j, (\emptyset, U_1, D_1)]}{[C(H_C,N_C,\emptyset) \rightarrow \blacklozenge, j, j, (\emptyset, U_2, D_2)]} p_2$$

$$\begin{cases} H_C \cup N_C \neq \emptyset \\ H_C \cup N_C \text{ is superposable} \\ N_C \subset D_1 \cup \text{roots}(\mathcal{P}) \\ D_2 = D_1 - N_C \\ U_2 = U_1 \cup (D_1 \cap N_C) \end{cases}$$

In this second step, new antecedents for C are added from the set N_C, chosen among available nodes in D_1 and root nodes from the PTDs of the grammar. The 3 node sets are then updated. Constrained nodes that have been chosen as antecedents for C are not available anymore and are added to the set of used constrained nodes.

$$\frac{[C(H_C,N_C,\emptyset) \rightarrow \blacklozenge, j, j, (\emptyset, U, D)]}{[C(H_C,N_C,F_C) \rightarrow \bullet\gamma, j, j, (O, U, D)]} p_3$$

$$\begin{cases} H_C \cup N_C \cup F_C \text{ is saturated} \\ \gamma \in ord((H_C \cup N_C \cup F_C)^{>}) \\ F_C = \bigcup_i Q_i, Q_0 \subseteq (H_C \cup N_C)^{>^*}, Q_{i+1} \subseteq Q_i^{>^*} \\ O = (H_C \cup N_C \cup F_C)^{>^*} - F_C \\ \text{no anchor node in } H_C \cup N_C \cup F_C \end{cases}$$

In this last step of prediction, we can choose new antecedents for C among nodes constrained by antecedents already chosen in the previous steps in order to saturate them. This choice is recursive : each added antecedent triggers the possibility of choosing the nodes it constrains. The second part of this step consists of predicting the shape of the tree. We need to order and superpose the daughter nodes of the antecedents in such a way that ordering relations in PTDs are respected: an element of $ord((H_C \cup N_C \cup F_C)^{>})$ is chosen.

Finally, the nodes that must be used in a sub-parse are the ones that are constrained by antecedents of C and not antecedents themselves.

Scan This is the rule that checks predictions against the input string. It is similar to the previous rule, but one (and only one) of the antecedents must be an anchor.

$$\frac{[C(H_C,N_C,\emptyset) \rightarrow \blacklozenge, j, j, (\emptyset, U, D)]}{[C(H_C,N_C,F_C) \rightarrow \bullet, j, j+1, (\emptyset, U, D)]} s$$

$$\begin{cases} H_C \cup N_C \cup F_C \text{ is saturated} \\ (H_C \cup N_C \cup F_C)^{>} = \emptyset \\ F_C = \bigcup_i Q_i, Q_0 \subseteq (H_C \cup N_C)^{>^*}, Q_{i+1} \subseteq Q_i^{>^*} \\ (H_C \cup N_C \cup F_C)^{>^*} - F_C = \emptyset \\ \text{one anchor } a \text{ in } H_C \cup N_C \cup F_C \\ phon(a) = w_{j+1} \end{cases}$$

If the expected terminal is read on the input string, parsing can proceed. Note that antecedents for C should not constrain nodes that are not antecedents of C themselves.

Completion This rule extends a parse by combining it with a complete sub-parse.

$$\frac{\begin{array}{l}[A(H,N,F) \rightarrow \alpha \bullet C(H_c)\beta, i, j, (O_1,U_1,D_1)] \\ [C(H_C,N_C,F_C) \rightarrow \gamma\bullet, j, k, (\emptyset, U_2, D_2)]\end{array}}{[A(H,N,F) \rightarrow \alpha C \bullet \beta, i, k, (O_3,U_3,D_3)]} c$$

$$\begin{cases} N_C \subseteq D_1 \cup O_1 \cup \mathcal{P} \\ D_2 \subseteq (D_1 \cup O_1) - N_C \\ U_1 \subseteq U_2 \\ O_3 = O_1 - U_2 \\ D_3 = D_1 - U_2 \\ U_3 = U_2 - O_1 \end{cases}$$

We have to make sure that the second hypothesis is a sub-parse for the first : (1) the set of available nodes in the sub-parse must be a subset of the available nodes for current parse, (2) the set of used nodes in the main parse must be a subset of the used nodes in the sub-parse and (3) used nodes constrained by the first hypothesis disappear.

Goal Parsing is successful if the following item is created : $[\top \rightarrow S\bullet, 0, n, (\emptyset,\emptyset,\emptyset)]$.

4 Discussion

4.1 Consistency and completeness

An item $[A(H,N,F) \rightarrow \alpha \bullet \beta, i, j, (O,U,D)]$ asserts the following invariants :

- A and the elements α_l of α are models for saturated sets of nodes. Conditions 1, 7 and 3 (reflexive case) of a model are respected.

- Elements β_k of β are superposable. Then we have $\beta_k \subseteq (A^{-1})^{>}$ (conditions 2 and 6).

- the sequence $\alpha\beta$ is compatible with the order relations from the PTDs (conditions 4 and 5).

- $PP(\alpha_1) \circ \ldots \circ PP(\alpha_l) = [w_{i+1} \cdots w_j]$

- a node N in U is a constrained node in relation $>^*$ with a node such that condition 3 holds.

These invariants can be checked by induction on rules. Hence, such an item asserts there exists a function J from the nodes of a subset of the PTDs of an IG to a syntactic tree with its root labelled by S and phonological projection $w_1 \ldots w_j$. This function has the same properties as the function I for models but conditions 2 to 5 only apply if both nodes are in the domain of J. The parsing process extends the domain until (1) all the nodes of each PTD selected are used and (2) the input string has been read completely. Then J defines a syntactic tree which is a parse tree.

4.2 Sources of non-determinism

The parsing problem in IGs is a NP-hard problem (Bonfante et al., 2003). Our presentation lets us see several sources of non-determinism.

In p_2, new antecedents are chosen among available nodes and root nodes of PTDs from the input grammar. There is an exponential number of such choices. However, IGs are lexicalized : only PTDs associated with a word in the sentence will be used and efficient lexical filters have been developed for IGs (Bonfante et al., 2006) that drastically decrease the number of PTDs to consider.

In p_3 and s, constrained nodes can be chosen as antecedents (nodes in F_C). There is again an exponential number of such choices. But in existing IGs, nodes have at most one successor by $>^*$ and there is no chain of nodes in relation by $>^*$. Consequently, $|F_C|$ can be bounded by $|H_C \cup N_C|$.

In p_3, daughters must be partitioned. Instead of building all these partitions in p_3 and generating many useless items, one can think of a lazy approach like the one proposed by (Nederhof et al., 2003) for pomset-CFGS.

It can be noticed that the completion rule, while having the most positional indexes, is not a particular source of non-determinism.

5 Conclusion

We presented a parsing algorithm for IGs. Although we used a simplified version without polarized feature structures, adding a unification mechanism shouldn't be an issue. The novelty of this presentation is the use of deductive parsing for a formalism developed in the model-theoretic framework (Pullum and Scholz, 2001).

This change of perspective provides new insights on the causes of non-determinism. It is a first step to a precise complexity study of the problem. In the future, it will be interesting to search for algorithmical approximations to improve efficiency. Another way to overcome NP-hardness is to restrict superpositions, as in (k-)TT-MCTAGs (Kallmeyer and Parmentier, 2008).

References

G. Bonfante, B. Guillaume, and G. Perrier. 2003. Analyse syntaxique électrostatique. *Traitement Automatique des Langues*, 44(3).

G. Bonfante, J. Le Roux, and G. Perrier. 2006. Lexical disambiguation with polarities and automata. In *Proceedings of CIAA*.

J. Earley. 1970. An efficient context-free parsing algorithm. *Communications of the ACM*, 13(2):94–102.

B. Guillaume and G. Perrier. 2008. Interaction Grammars. Research Report RR-6621, INRIA.

L. Kallmeyer and Y. Parmentier. 2008. On the relation between TT-MCTAG and RCG. In *Proceedings of LATA*.

M.J. Nederhof, G. Satta, and S. Shieber. 2003. Partially ordered multiset context-free grammars and ID/LP parsing. In *Proceedings of IWPT*.

G. Pullum and B. Scholz. 2001. On the distinction between model-theoretic and generative-enumerative syntactic frameworks. In *Proccedings of LACL*.

O. Rambow, K. Vijay-Shanker, and D. Weir. 1995. D-tree grammars. In *Proceedings of ACL*.

S. Shieber, Y. Schabes, and F. Pereira. 1995. Principles and implementation of deductive parsing. *Journal of Logic Programming*, 24(1–2):3–36.

Synchronous Rewriting in Treebanks

Laura Kallmeyer
University of Tübingen
Tübingen, Germany
lk@sfs.uni-tuebingen.de

Wolfgang Maier
University of Tübingen
Tübingen, Germany
wo.maier@uni-tuebingen.de

Giorgio Satta
University of Padua
Padova, Italy
satta@dei.unipd.it

Abstract

Several formalisms have been proposed for modeling trees with discontinuous phrases. Some of these formalisms allow for synchronous rewriting. However, it is unclear whether synchronous rewriting is a necessary feature. This is an important question, since synchronous rewriting greatly increases parsing complexity. We present a characterization of recursive synchronous rewriting in constituent treebanks with discontinuous annotation. An empirical investigation reveals that synchronous rewriting is actually a necessary feature. Furthermore, we transfer this property to grammars extracted from treebanks.

1 Introduction

Discontinuous phrases are frequent in natural language, particularly in languages with a relatively free word order. Several formalisms have been proposed in the literature for modeling trees containing such phrases. These include non-projective dependency grammar (Nivre, 2006), discontinuous phrase structure grammar (DPSG) (Bunt et al., 1987), as well as linear context-free rewriting systems (LCFRS) (Vijay-Shanker et al., 1987) and the equivalent formalism of simple range concatenation grammar (sRCG) (Boullier, 2000). Kuhlmann (2007) uses LCFRS for non-projective dependency trees. DPSG have been used in Plaehn (2004) for data-driven parsing of treebanks with discontinuous constituent annotation. Maier and Søgaard (2008) extract sRCGs from treebanks with discontinuous constituent structures.

Both LCFRS and sRCG can model discontinuities and allow for synchronous rewriting as well. We speak of synchronous rewriting when two or more context-free derivation processes are instantiated in a synchronous way. DPSG, which has also been proposed for modeling discontinuities, does not allow for synchronous rewriting because the different discontinuous parts of the yield of a non-terminal are treated locally, i.e., their derivations are independent from each other. So far, synchronous rewriting has not been empirically motivated by linguistic data from treebanks. In this paper, we fill this gap by investigating the existence of structures indicating synchronous rewriting in treebanks with discontinuous annotations. The question of whether we can find evidence for synchronous rewriting has consequences for the complexity of parsing. In fact, parsing with synchronous formalisms can be carried out in time polynomial in the length of the input string, with a polynomial degree depending on the maximum number of synchronous branches one can find in derivations (Seki et al., 1991).

In this paper, we characterize synchronous rewriting as a property of trees with crossing branches and in an empirical evaluation, we confirm that treebanks do contain recursive synchronous rewriting which can be linguistically motivated. Furthermore, we show how this characterization transfers to the simple RCGs describing these trees.

2 Synchronous Rewriting Trees in German treebanks

By **synchronous rewriting** we indicate the synchronous instantiation of two or more context-free derivation processes. As an example, consider the language $L = \{a^n b^n c^n d^n \mid n \geq 1\}$. Each of the two halves of some $w \in L$ can be obtained through a stand-alone context-free derivation, but for w to be in L the two derivations must be synchronized somehow. For certain tasks, synchronous rewriting is a desired property for a formalism. In machine translation, e.g., synchronous

Proceedings of the 11th International Conference on Parsing Technologies (IWPT), pages 69–72,
Paris, October 2009.

rewriting is extensively used to model the synchronous dependence between the source and target languages (Chiang, 2007). The question we are concerned with in this paper is whether we can find instances of recursive synchronous rewriting in treebanks that show discontinuous phrases.

We make the assumption that, if the annotation of a treebank allows to express synchronous rewriting, then all cases of synchronous rewriting are present in the annotation. This means that, on the one hand, there are no cases of synchronous rewriting that the annotator "forgot" to encode. Therefore unrelated cases of parallel iterations in different parts of a tree are taken to be truly unrelated. On the other hand, if synchronous rewriting is annotated explicitely, then we take it to be a case of true synchronous rewriting, even if, based on the string, it would be possible to find an analysis that does not require synchronous rewriting. This assumption allows us to concentrate only on explicit cases of synchronous rewriting .

We concentrate on German treebanks annotated with trees with crossing branches. In such trees, synchronous rewriting amounts to cases where different components of a non-terminal category develop in parallel. In particular, we search for cases where the parallelism can be iterated. An example is the relative clause in (1), found in TIGER. Fig. 1 gives the annotation. As can be seen in the annotation, we have two VP nodes, each of which has a discontinuous span consisting of two parts. The two parts are separated by lexical material not belonging to the VPs. The two components of the second VP (*Pop-Idol* and *werden*) are included in the two components of the first, higher, VP (*genausogut auch Pop-Idol* and *werden können*). In other words, the two VP components are rewritten in parallel containing again two smaller VP components.

(1) ...der genausogut auch Pop-Idol hätte werden können
...who as well also pop-star AUX become could
"who could as well also become a pop-star"

Let us assume the following definitions: We map the elements of a string to their positions. We then say that the yield Υ of a node n in a tree is the set of all indices i such that n dominates the leaf labeled with the ith terminal. A yield Υ has a gap if there are $i_1 < i_2 < i_3$ such that $i_1, i_3 \in \Upsilon$ and $i_2 \notin \Upsilon$. For all $i, j \in \Upsilon$ with $i < j$, the set $\Upsilon_{\langle i,j \rangle} = \{k \mid i \leq k \leq j\}$ is a component of Υ if $\Upsilon_{\langle i,j \rangle} \subseteq \Upsilon$ and $i-1 \notin \Upsilon$ and $j+1 \notin \Upsilon$. We order the components of Υ such that $\Upsilon_{\langle i_1,j_1 \rangle} < \Upsilon_{\langle i_2,j_2 \rangle}$ if $i_1 < i_2$.

Trees showing **recursive synchronous rewriting** can be characterized as follows: We have a non-terminal node n_1 with label A whose yield has a gap. n_1 dominates another node n_2 with label A such that for some $i \neq j$, the ith component of the yield of n_2 is contained in the ith component of the yield of n_1 and similar for the jth component. We call the path from n_1 to n_2 a **recursive synchronous rewriting segment (RSRS)**.

Table 1 shows the results obtained from searching for recursive synchronous rewriting in the German TIGER and NeGra treebanks. In a preprocessing step, punctuation has been removed, since it is directly attached to the root node and therefore not included in the annotation.

	TIGER	NeGra
number of trees	40,013	20,597
total num. of RSRS in all trees	1476	600
av. RSRS length in all trees	2.13	2.12
max. RSRS length in all trees	5	4

Table 1: Synchronous rewriting in treebanks

Example (1) shows that we find instances of recursive synchronous rewriting where each of the rewriting steps adds something to both of the parallel components. (1) was not an isolated case.

The annotation of (1) in Fig. 1 could be turned into a context-free structure if the lowest node dominating the material in the gap while not dominating the synchronous rewriting nodes (here VAFIN) is attached lower, namely below the lower VP node. (Note however that there is good linguistic motivation for attaching it high.) Besides such cases, we even encountered cases where the discontinuity cannot be removed this way. An example is (2) (resp. Fig. 2) where we have a gap containing an NP such that the lowest node dominating this NP while not dominating the synchronous rewriting nodes has a daughter to the right of the yields of the synchronous rewriting nodes, namely the extraposed relative clause. This structure is of the type $a^n c b^n d$, where a and b depend on each other in a left-to-right order and can be nested, and c and d also depend on each other and must be generated together. This is a structure that requires synchronous rewriting, even on the basis of the string language. Note that the nesting of VPs can be iterated, as can be seen in (3).

(2) ...ob auf deren Gelände der Typ von
...whether on their premises the type of

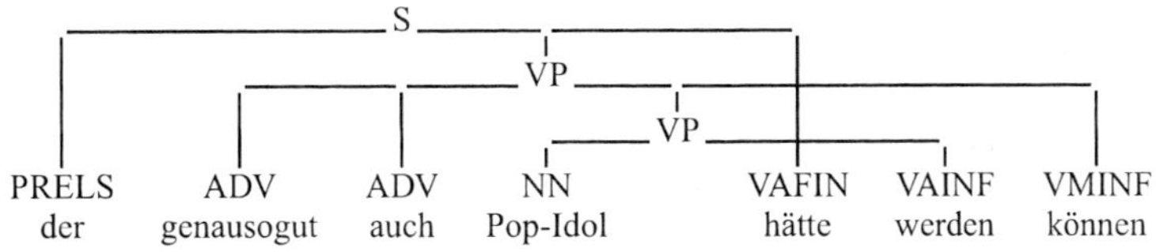

Figure 1: Example for recursive synchronous rewriting

Abstellanlage gebaut werden könne, der ...
parking facility built be could, which ...
"whether on their premises precisely the type of parking facility could be built, which ..."

(3) ...ob auf deren Gelände der Typ von
...whether on their premises the type of
Abstellanlage eigentlich hätte schon gebaut werden
parking facility actually had already built be
sollen, der ...
should, which ...
"whether on their premises precisely the type of parking facility should actually already have been built, which ..."

As a conclusion from these empirical results, we state that to account for the data we can find in treebanks with discontinuities, i.e., with crossing branches, we need a formalism that can express synchronous rewriting.

3 Synchronous Rewriting in Grammars Extracted from Treebanks

In the following, we will use simple RCG (which are equivalent to LCFRS) to model our treebank annotations. We extract simple RCG rewriting rules from NeGra and TIGER and check them for the possibility to generate recursive synchronous rewriting.

A **simple RCG** (Boullier, 2000) is a tuple $G = (N, T, V, P, S)$ where a) N is a finite set of predicate names with an arity function dim: $N \to \mathbb{N}$, b) T and V are disjoint finite sets of terminals and variables, c) P is a finite set of clauses of the form

$$A(\alpha_1, \dots, \alpha_{dim(A)}) \to A_1(X_1^{(1)}, \dots, X_{dim(A_1)}^{(1)}) \cdots A_m(X_1^{(m)}, \dots, X_{dim(A_m)}^{(m)})$$

for $m \geq 0$ where $A, A_1, \dots, A_m \in N$, $X_j^{(i)} \in V$ for $1 \leq i \leq m, 1 \leq j \leq dim(A_i)$ and $\alpha_i \in (T \cup V)^*$ for $1 \leq i \leq dim(A)$, and e) $S \in N$ is the start predicate name with $dim(S) = 1$. For all $c \in P$, it holds that every variable X occurring in c occurs exactly once in the left-hand side (LHS) and exactly once in the RHS. A simple RCG $G = (N, T, V, P, S)$ is a simple k-**RCG** if for all $A \in N$, $dim(A) \leq k$.

For the definition of the language of a simple RCG, we borrow the LCFRS definitions here: Let $G = \langle N, T, V, P, S \rangle$ be a simple RCG. For every $A \in N$, we define the yield of A, $yield(A)$ as follows:

a) For every $A(\vec{\alpha}) \to \varepsilon$, $\vec{\alpha} \in yield(A)$;

b) For every clause

$$A(\alpha_1, \dots, \alpha_{dim(A)}) \to A_1(X_1^{(1)}, \dots, X_{dim(A_1)}^{(1)}) \cdots A_m(X_1^{(m)}, \dots, X_{dim(A_m)}^{(m)})$$

and all $\vec{\tau_i} \in yield(A_i)$ for $1 \leq i \leq m$, $\langle f(\alpha_1), \dots, f(\alpha_{dim(A)}) \rangle \in yield(A)$ where f is defined as follows:

(i) $f(t) = t$ for all $t \in T$,

(ii) $f(X_j^{(i)}) = \vec{\tau_i}(j)$ for all $1 \leq i \leq m, 1 \leq j \leq dim(A_i)$ and

(iii) $f(xy) = f(x)f(y)$ for all $x, y \in (T \cup V)^+$.

c) Nothing else is in $yield(A)$.

The language is then $\{w \mid \langle w \rangle \in yield(S)\}$.

We are using the algorithm from Maier and Søgaard (2008) to extract simple RCGs from NeGra and TIGER. For the tree in Fig. 1, the algorithm produces for instance the following clauses:

PRELS(der) $\to \varepsilon$
ADV(genausogut) $\to \varepsilon$
...
S($X_1X_2X_3X_4$) $\to$ PRELS(X_1)VP$_2$(X_1,X_4) VAFIN(X_3)
VP$_2$($X_1X_2X_3$,X_4X_5) $\to$ ADV(X_1) ADV(X_2) VP$_2$(X_3,X_4) VMINF(X_5)
VP$_2$(X_1,X_2) $\to$ NN(X_1) VAINF(X_2)

We distinguish different usages of the same category depending on their numbers of yield components. E.g., we distinguish non-terminals VP$_1$, VP$_2$, ... depending on the arity of the VP. We define $cat(A)$ for $A \in N$ as the category of A, independent from the arity, e.g., cat(VP$_2$) =VP.

In terms of simple RCG, synchronous rewriting means that in a single clause distinct variables occurring in two different arguments of the LHS predicate are passed to two different arguments of the same RHS predicate. We call this **recursive**

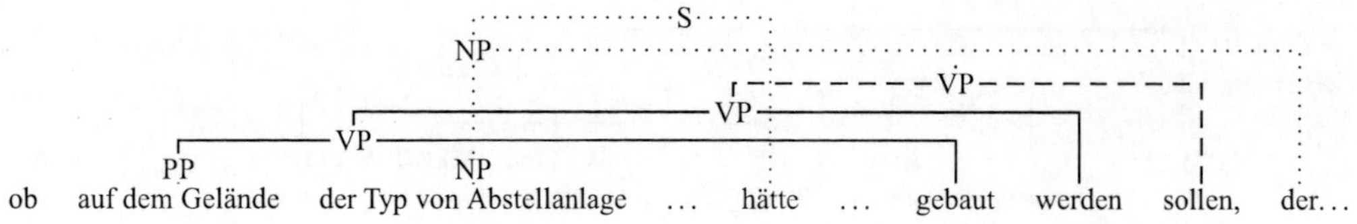

Figure 2: Iterable treebank example for synchronous rewriting

if, by a sequence of synchronous rewriting steps, we can reach the same two arguments of the same predicate again. Derivations using such cycles of synchronous rewriting lead exactly to the recursive synchronous rewriting trees characterized in section 2. In the following, we check to which extent the extracted simple RCG allows for such cycles.

In order to detect synchronous rewriting in a simple k-RCG G, we build a labeled directed graph $\mathcal{G} = (V_\mathcal{G}, E_\mathcal{G}, l)$ from the grammar with $V_\mathcal{G}$ a set of nodes, $E_\mathcal{G}$ a set of arcs and $l : V_\mathcal{G} \rightarrow N' \times \{0, \ldots, k\} \times \{0, \ldots, k\}$ where $N' = \{cat(A) \mid A \in N\}$ a labeling function. $\mathcal{G}$ is constructed as follows. For each clause $A_0(\vec{\alpha}) \rightarrow A_1(\vec{\alpha_1}) \ldots A_m(\vec{\alpha_m}) \in P$ we consider all pairs of variables X_s, X_t for which the following conditions hold: (i) X_s and X_t occur in different arguments i and j of A_0, $1 \leq i < j \leq dim(A_0)$; *and* (ii) X_s and X_t occur in different arguments q and r of the same occurrence of predicate A_p in the RHS, $1 \leq q < r \leq dim(A_p)$ and $1 \leq p \leq m$. For each of these pairs, two nodes with labels $[cat(A_0), i, j]$ and $[cat(A_p), q, r]$, respectively, are added to $V_\mathcal{G}$ (if they do not yet exist, otherwise we take the already existing nodes) and a directed arc from the first node to the second node is added to $E_\mathcal{G}$. The intuition is that an arc in $\mathcal{G}$ represents one or more clauses from the grammar in which a gap between two variables in the LHS predicate is transferred to the same RHS predicate. To detect recursive synchronous rewriting, we then need to discover all elementary cycles in $\mathcal{G}$, i.e., all cycles in which no vertex appears twice. In order to accomplish this task efficiently, we exploit the algorithm presented in Johnson (1975). On a grammar extracted from NeGra (19,100 clauses), the algorithm yields a graph with 28 nodes containing 206,403 cycles of an average length of 12.86 and a maximal length of 28.

4 Conclusion

The starting point of this paper was the question whether synchronous rewriting is a necessary feature of grammer formalisms for modelling natural languages. In order to answer this question, we have characterized synchronous rewriting in terms of properties of treebank trees with crossing branches. Experiments have shown that recursive cases of synchronous rewriting occur in treebanks for German which leads to the conclusion that, in order to model these data, we need formalisms that allow for synchronous rewriting. In a second part, we have extracted a simple RCG from these treebanks and we have characterized the grammar properties that are necessary to obtain recursive synchronous rewriting. We then have investigated the extent to which a grammar extracted from NeGra allows for recursive synchronous rewriting.

References

Pierre Boullier. 2000. Range concatenation grammars. In *Proceedings of IWPT*.

Harry Bunt, Jan Thesingh, and Ko van der Sloot. 1987. Discontinuous constituents in trees, rules and parsing. In *Proceedings of EACL*.

David Chiang. 2007. Hierarchical phrase-based translation. *Computational Linguistics*.

Donald B. Johnson. 1975. Finding all the elementary circuits of a directed graph. *SIAM Journal on Computing*.

Marco Kuhlmann. 2007. *Dependency Structures and Lexicalized Grammars*. Dissertation, Saarland University.

Wolfgang Maier and Anders Søgaard. 2008. Treebanks and mild context-sensitivity. In *Proceedings of Formal Grammar*.

Joakim Nivre. 2006. *Inductive Dependency Parsing*. Springer.

Oliver Plaehn. 2004. Computing the most probable parse for a discontinuous phrase-structure grammar. In *New developments in parsing technology*. Kluwer.

H. Seki, T. Matsumura, M. Fujii, and T. Kasami. 1991. On multiple context-free grammars. *Theoretical Computer Science*.

K. Vijay-Shanker, David Weir, and Aravind Joshi. 1987. Characterising structural descriptions used by various formalisms. In *Proceedings of ACL*.

An Improved Oracle for Dependency Parsing with Online Reordering

Joakim Nivre[⋆†] **Marco Kuhlmann**[⋆] **Johan Hall**[⋆]
[⋆]Uppsala University, Department of Linguistics and Philology, SE-75126 Uppsala
[†]Växjö University, School of Mathematics and Systems Engineering, SE-35195 Växjö
E-mail: FIRSTNAME.LASTNAME@lingfil.uu.se

Abstract

We present an improved training strategy for dependency parsers that use online reordering to handle non-projective trees. The new strategy improves both efficiency and accuracy by reducing the number of swap operations performed on non-projective trees by up to 80%. We present state-of-the-art results for five languages with the best ever reported results for Czech.

1 Introduction

Recent work on dependency parsing has resulted in considerable progress with respect to both accuracy and efficiency, not least in the treatment of discontinuous syntactic constructions, usually modeled by *non-projective* dependency trees. While non-projective dependency relations tend to be rare in most languages (Kuhlmann and Nivre, 2006), it is not uncommon that up to 25% of the sentences have a structure that involves at least one non-projective relation, a relation that may be crucial for an adequate analysis of predicate-argument structure. This makes the treatment of non-projectivity central for accurate dependency parsing.

Unfortunately, parsing with unrestricted non-projective structures is a hard problem, for which exact inference is not possible in polynomial time except under drastic independence assumptions (McDonald and Satta, 2007), and most data-driven parsers therefore use approximate methods (Nivre et al., 2006; McDonald et al., 2006). One recently explored approach is to perform online reordering by swapping adjacent words of the input sentence while building the dependency structure. Using this technique, the system of Nivre (2009) processes unrestricted non-projective structures with state-of-the-art accuracy in observed linear time.

The normal procedure for training a transition-based parser is to use an oracle that predicts an optimal transition sequence for every dependency tree in the training set, and then approximate this oracle by a classifier. In this paper, we show that the oracle used for training by Nivre (2009) is suboptimal because it eagerly swaps words as early as possible and therefore makes a large number of unnecessary transitions, which potentially affects both efficiency and accuracy. We propose an alternative oracle that reduces the number of transitions by building larger structures before swapping, but still handles arbitrary non-projective structures.

2 Background

The fundamental reason why sentences with non-projective dependency trees are hard to parse is that they contain dependencies between non-adjacent substructures. The basic idea in online reordering is to allow the parser to swap input words so that all dependency arcs can be constructed between adjacent subtrees. This idea is implemented in the transition system proposed by Nivre (2009). The first three transitions of this system (LEFT-ARC, RIGHT-ARC, and SHIFT) are familiar from many systems for transition-based dependency parsing (Nivre, 2008). The only novelty is the SWAP transition, which permutes two nodes by moving the second-topmost node from the stack back to the input buffer while leaving the top node on the stack.

To understand how we can parse sentences with non-projective dependency trees, in spite of the fact that dependencies can only be added between nodes that are adjacent on the stack, note that, for any sentence x with dependency tree G, there is always some permutation x' of x such that G is projective with respect to x'. There may be more than one such permutation, but Nivre (2009) defines the canonical *projective* order $<_G$ for x given G as the order given by an inorder traversal of G that respects the order $<$ between a node and its direct dependents. This is illustrated in Figure 1, where the words of a sentence with a non-projective tree

Proceedings of the 11th International Conference on Parsing Technologies (IWPT), pages 73–76,
Paris, October 2009.

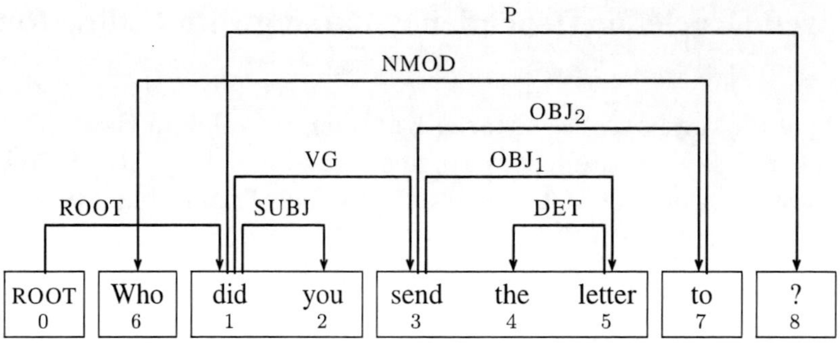

Figure 1: Dependency tree for an English sentence with projective order annotation.

have been annotated with their positions in the projective order; reading the words in this order gives the permuted string *Did you send the letter who to?*

3 Training Oracles

In order to train classifiers for transition-based parsing, we need a *training oracle*, that is, a function that maps every dependency tree T in the training set to a transition sequence that derives T. While every complete transition sequence determines a unique dependency tree, the inverse does not necessarily hold. This also means that it may be possible to construct different training oracles. For simple systems that are restricted to projective dependency trees, such differences are usually trivial, but for a system that allows online reordering there may be genuine differences that can affect both the efficiency and accuracy of the resulting parsers.

3.1 The Old Oracle

Figure 2 defines the original training oracle τ_1 proposed by Nivre (2009). This oracle follows an *eager* reordering strategy; it predicts SWAP in every configuration where this is possible. The basic insight in this paper is that, by postponing swaps and building as much of the tree structure as possible before swapping, we can significantly decrease the length of the transition sequence for a given sentence and tree. This may benefit the *efficiency* of the parser trained using the oracle, as each transition takes a certain time to predict and to execute. Longer transition sequences may also be harder to learn than shorter ones, which potentially affects the *accuracy* of the parser.

3.2 A New Oracle

While it is desirable to delay a SWAP transition for as long as possible, it is not trivial to find the right time point to actually do the swap. To see this, consider the dependency tree in Figure 1. In a parse of this tree, the first configuration in which swapping is possible is when who_6 and did_1 are the two top nodes on the stack. In this configuration we can delay the swap until *did* has combined with its subject *you* by means of a RIGHT-ARC transition, but if we do not swap in the second configuration where this is possible, we eventually end up with the stack $[\text{ROOT}_0, who_6, did_1, send_3, to_7]$. Here we cannot attach *who* to *to* by means of a LEFT-ARC transition and get stuck.

In order to define the new oracle, we introduce an auxiliary concept. Consider a modification of the oracle τ_1 from Figure 2 that cannot predict SWAP transitions. This oracle will be able to produce valid transition sequences only for *projective* target trees; for non-projective trees, it will fail to reconstruct all dependency arcs. More specifically, a parse with this oracle will end up in a configuration in which the set of constructed dependency arcs forms a *set* of projective dependency trees, not necessarily a single such tree. We call the elements of this set the *maximal projective components* of the target tree. To illustrate the notion, we have drawn boxes around nodes in the same component in Figures 1.

Based on the concept of maximal projective components, we define a new training oracle τ_2, which delays swapping as long as the next node in the input is in the same maximal projective component as the top node on the stack. The definition of the new oracle τ_2 is identical to that of τ_1 except that the third line is replaced by "SWAP if $c = ([\sigma|i, j], [k|\beta], A_c)$, $j <_G i$, and $\text{MPC}(j) \neq \text{MPC}(k)$", where $\text{MPC}(i)$ is the maximal projective component of node i. As a special case, τ_2 predicts SWAP if $j <_G i$ and the buffer B is empty.

$$\tau_1(c) = \begin{cases} \text{LEFT-ARC}_l & \text{if } c = ([\sigma|i,j], B, A_c), (j,l,i) \in A \text{ and } A^i \subseteq A_c \\ \text{RIGHT-ARC}_l & \text{if } c = ([\sigma|i,j], B, A_c), (i,l,j) \in A \text{ and } A^j \subseteq A_c \\ \text{SWAP} & \text{if } c = ([\sigma|i,j], B, A_c) \text{ and } j <_G i \\ \text{SHIFT} & \text{otherwise} \end{cases}$$

Figure 2: Training oracle τ_1 for an arbitrary target tree $G = (V_x, A)$, following the notation of Nivre (2009), where $c = (\Sigma, B, A_c)$ denotes a configuration c with stack Σ, input buffer B and arc set A_c. We write A^i to denote the subset of A that only contains the outgoing arcs of the node i. (Note that A_c is the arc set in configuration c, while A is the arc set in the target tree G.)

For example, in extracting the transition sequence for the target tree in Figure 1, the new oracle will postpone swapping of *did* when *you* is the next node in the input, but not postpone when the next node is *send*. We can show that a parser informed by the new training oracle can always proceed to a terminal configuration, and still derive all (even non-projective) dependency trees.

4 Experiments

We now test the hypothesis that the new training oracle can improve both the accuracy and the efficiency of a transition-based dependency parser. Our experiments are based on the same five data sets as Nivre (2009). The training sets vary in size from 28,750 tokens (1,534 sentences) for Slovene to 1,249,408 tokens (72,703 sentences) for Czech, while the test sets all consist of about 5,000 tokens.

4.1 Number of Transitions

For each language, we first parsed the training set with both the old and the new training oracle. This allowed us to compare the number of SWAP transitions needed to parse all sentences with the two oracles, shown in Table 1. We see that the reduction is very substantial, ranging from 55% (for Czech) to almost 84% (for Arabic). While this difference does not affect the asymptotic complexity of parsing, it may reduce the number of calls to the classifier, which is where transition-based parsers spend most of their time.

4.2 Parsing Accuracy

In order to assess whether the reduced number of SWAP transitions also has a positive effect on parsing accuracy, we trained two parsers for each of the five languages, one for each oracle. All systems use SVM classifiers with a polynomial kernel with features and parameters optimized separately for each language and training oracle. The training data for these classifiers consist only of the sequences derived by the oracles, which means that the parser has no explicit notion of projective order or maximal projective components at parsing time.

Table 2 shows the labeled parsing accuracy of the parsers measured by the overall attachment score (AS), as well as labeled precision, recall and (balanced) F-score for non-projective dependencies.[1] For comparison, we also give results for the two best performing systems in the original CoNLL-X shared task, Malt (Nivre et al., 2006) and MST (McDonald et al., 2006), as well as the combo system MST_{Malt}, (Nivre and McDonald, 2008).

Looking first at the overall labeled attachment score, we see that the new training oracle consistently gives higher accuracy than the old one, with differences of up to 0.5 percentage points (for Arabic and Slovene), which is substantial given that the frequency of non-projective dependencies is only 0.4–1.9%. Because the test sets are so small, none of the differences is statistically significant (McNemar's test, $\alpha = .05$), but the consistent improvement over all languages nevertheless strongly suggests that this is a genuine difference.

In relation to the state of the art, we note that the parsers with online reordering significantly outperform Malt and MST on Czech and Slovene, and MST on Turkish, and have significantly lower scores than the combo system MST_{Malt} only for Arabic and Danish. For Czech, the parser with the new oracle actually has the highest attachment score ever reported, although the difference with respect to MST_{Malt} is not statistically significant.

Turning to the scores for non-projective dependencies, we again see that the new oracle consistently gives higher scores than the old oracle, with

[1] These metrics are not meaningful for Arabic as the test set only contains 11 non-projective dependencies.

	Arabic	Czech	Danish	Slovene	Turkish
Old (τ_1)	1416	57011	8296	2191	2828
New (τ_2)	229	26208	1497	690	1253
Reduction (%)	83.8	55.0	82.0	68.5	55.7

Table 1: Number of SWAP transitions for the old (τ_1) and new (τ_2) training oracle.

	Arabic	Czech				Danish				Slovene				Turkish			
System	**AS**	**AS**	**P**	**R**	**F**	**AS**	**P**	**R**	**F**	**AS**	**P**	**R**	**F**	**AS**	**P**	**R**	**F**
Old (τ_1)	67.2	82.5	74.7	**72.9**	73.8	84.2	30.0	30.0	30.0	75.2	33.3	26.4	29.5	64.7	12.5	11.4	11.9
New (τ_2)	67.5	**82.7**	**79.3**	71.0	**79.3**	84.3	38.2	32.5	35.1	75.7	**60.6**	**27.6**	**37.9**	65.0	14.3	**13.2**	**13.7**
Malt	66.7	78.4	76.3	57.9	65.8	84.8	45.8	27.5	34.4	70.3	45.9	20.7	25.1	65.7	**16.7**	9.2	11.9
MST	66.9	80.2	60.5	61.7	61.1	84.8	54.0	**62.5**	57.9	73.4	33.7	26.4	29.6	63.2	–	11.8	–
MST_{Malt}	**68.6**	82.3	63.9	69.2	66.1	**86.7**	**63.0**	60.0	**61.5**	**75.9**	31.6	**27.6**	29.5	**66.3**	11.1	9.2	10.1

Table 2: Labeled attachment score (AS) overall; precision (P), recall (R) and balanced F-score (F) for non-projective dependencies. Old = τ_1; New = τ_2; Malt = Nivre et al. (2006), MST = McDonald et al. (2006), MST_{Malt} = Nivre and McDonald (2008).

the single exception that the old one has marginally higher recall for Czech. Moreover, the reordering parser with the new oracle has higher F-score than any other system for all languages except Danish. Especially the result for Czech, with 79.3% precision and 71.0% recall, is remarkably good, making the parser almost as accurate for non-projective dependencies as it is for projective dependencies. It seems likely that the good results for Czech are due to the fact that Czech has the highest percentage of non-projective structures in combination with the (by far) largest training set.

5 Conclusion

We have presented a new training oracle for the transition system originally presented in Nivre (2009). This oracle postpones swapping as long as possible but still fulfills the correctness criterion. Our experimental results show that the new training oracle can reduce the necessary number of swaps by more than 80%, and that parsers trained in this way achieve higher precision and recall on non-projective dependency arcs as well as higher attachment score overall. The results are particularly good for languages with a high percentage of non-projective dependencies, with an all-time best over all metrics for Czech.

An interesting theoretical question is whether the new oracle defined in this paper is optimal with respect to minimizing the number of swaps. The answer turns out to be negative, and it is possible to reduce the number of swaps even further by generalizing the notion of maximal projective components to maximal components that may be non-projective. However, the characterization of these generalized maximal components is non-trivial, and is therefore an important problem for future research.

References

Marco Kuhlmann and Joakim Nivre. 2006. Mildly non-projective dependency structures. In *Proceedings of the COLING/ACL 2006 Main Conference Poster Sessions*, pages 507–514.

Ryan McDonald and Giorgio Satta. 2007. On the complexity of non-projective data-driven dependency parsing. In *Proceedings of IWPT*, pages 122–131.

Ryan McDonald, Kevin Lerman, and Fernando Pereira. 2006. Multilingual dependency analysis with a two-stage discriminative parser. In *Proceedings of CoNLL*, pages 216–220.

Joakim Nivre and Ryan McDonald. 2008. Integrating graph-based and transition-based dependency parsers. In *Proceedings of ACL*, pages 950–958.

Joakim Nivre, Johan Hall, Jens Nilsson, Gülsen Eryiğit, and Svetoslav Marinov. 2006. Labeled pseudo-projective dependency parsing with support vector machines. In *Proceedings of CoNLL*, pages 221–225.

Joakim Nivre. 2008. Algorithms for deterministic incremental dependency parsing. *Computational Linguistics*, 34:513–553.

Joakim Nivre. 2009. Non-projective dependency parsing in expected linear time. In *Proceedings of ACL-IJCNLP*.

Two stage constraint based hybrid approach to free word order language dependency parsing

Akshar Bharati, Samar Husain, Dipti Misra and Rajeev Sangal
Language Technologies Research Centre, IIIT-Hyderabad, India
{samar, dipti, sangal}@mail.iiit.ac.in

Abstract

The paper describes the overall design of a new two stage constraint based hybrid approach to dependency parsing. We define the two stages and show how different grammatical construct are parsed at appropriate stages. This division leads to selective identification and resolution of specific dependency relations at the two stages. Furthermore, we show how the use of hard constraints and soft constraints helps us build an efficient and robust hybrid parser. Finally, we evaluate the implemented parser on Hindi and compare the results with that of two data driven dependency parsers.

1 Introduction

Due to the availability of annotated corpora for various languages since the past decade, data driven parsing has proved to be immensely successful. Unlike English, however, most of the parsers for morphologically rich free word order (MoR-FWO) languages (such as Czech, Turkish, Hindi, etc.) have adopted the dependency grammatical framework. It is well known that for MoR-FWO languages, dependency framework provides ease of linguistic analysis and is much better suited to account for their various structures (Shieber, 1975; Mel'Cuk, 1988; Bharati et al., 1995). The state of the art parsing accuracy for many MoR-FWO languages is still low compared to that of English. Parsing experiments (Nivre et al., 2007; Hall et al., 2007) for these languages have pointed towards various reasons for this low performance. For Hindi[1], (a) *difficulty in extracting relevant linguistic cues*, (b) *non-projectivity*, (c) *lack of explicit cues*, (d) *long distance dependencies*, (e) *complex linguistic phenomena*, and (f) *less corpus size*, have been suggested (Bharati et al., 2008) for low performance. The approach proposed in this paper shows how one can minimize these adverse effects and argues that a hybrid approach can prove to be a better option to parsing such languages. There have been, in the past, many attempts to parsing using constraint based approaches. Some recent works include (Debusmann et al., 2004; Schröder, 2002; Bharati et al., 1993).

The paper describes the overall design of a new two stage constraint based hybrid approach to dependency parsing. We define the two stages and show how different grammatical construct are parsed at appropriate stages. This division leads to selective identification and resolution of specific dependency relations at two different stages. Furthermore, we show how the use of hard constraints (H-constraints) and soft constraints (S-constraints) helps us build an efficient and robust hybrid parser. Specifically, H-constraints incorporate the knowledge base of the language and S-constraints are weights corresponding to various constraints. These weights are automatically learnt from an annotated treebank. Finally, we evaluate the implemented parser on Hindi and compare the results with that of two data driven dependency parsers.

2 Two Stage Parsing

The parser tries to analyze the given input sentence, which has already been POS tagged and chunked[2], in 2 stages; it first tries to extract intra-clausal[3] dependency relations. These relations generally correspond to the argument structure of the verb, noun-noun genitive relation, infinitive-verb relation, infinitive-noun relation, adjective-noun, adverb-verb relations, etc. In the 2nd stage it then tries to handle more complex relations such as conjuncts, relative clause, etc. What this

[1] Hindi is a verb final language with free word order and a rich case marking system. It is one of the official languages of India, and is spoken by ~800 million people.

[2] A chunk is a set of adjacent words which are in dependency relation with each other, and are connected to the rest of the words by a single incoming arc. The parser marks relations between the head of the chunks (inter-chunk relations); this is done to avoid local details and can be thought as a device for modularity.

[3] A clause is a group of word such that the group contains a single finite verb chunk.

Proceedings of the 11th International Conference on Parsing Technologies (IWPT), pages 77–80,
Paris, October 2009. ©2009 Association for Computational Linguistics

essentially means is a 2-stage resolution of dependencies, where the parser selectively resolves the dependencies of various lexical heads at their appropriate stage, for example verbs in the 1st stage and conjuncts and inter-verb relations in the 2nd stage. The key ideas of the proposed layered architecture are: (1) There are two layers stages, (2) the 1st stage handles intra-clausal relations, and the 2nd stage handles inter-clausal relations, (3) the output of each layer is a linguistically valid partial parse that becomes, if necessary, the input to the next layer, and (4) the output of the final layer is the desired full parse.

By following the above approach we are able to get 4-fold advantage, (1) Each layer in effect does linguistically valid partial parsing, (2) by dividing the labels into different functional sets (intra-clausal and inter-clausal) we localize the dependencies that need to be identified, hence the problem of long distance dependencies is minimizes, (3) by attacking the problem in a modular way, i.e. handling only individual clauses at 1st stage, we reduce non-projective structures significantly, and (4) the two stage constraint based approach can easily capture complex linguistic cues that are difficult to learn via the data-driven parsers. We'll revisit these points in Section 5. The 1st stage output for example 1 is shown in figure 1 (a).

Eg. 1: *mai ghar gayaa kyomki mai*
'I' 'home' 'went' 'because' 'I'
bimaar thaa
'sick' 'was'
'I went home because I was sick'

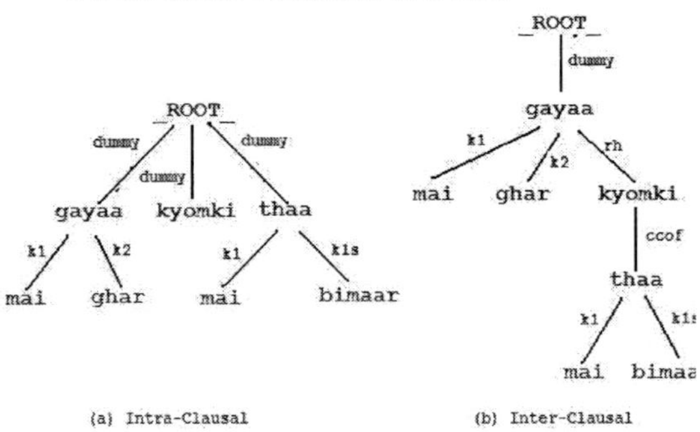

Figure 1. Eg 1 (a): 1st stage output, (b): 2nd stage final parse

In figure 1a, the parsed matrix clause subtree '*mai ghar gayaa*' and the subordinate clause are attached to _ROOT_. The subordinating conjunct '*kyomki*' is also seen attached to the _ROOT_. _ROOT_ ensures that the parse we get after each stage is connected and takes all the analyzed 1st stage sub-trees along with unprocessed nodes as its children. The dependency tree thus obtained in the 1st stage is partial, but linguistically sound. Later in the 2nd stage the relationship between various clauses are identified. The 2nd stage parse for the above sentences is also shown in figure 1b. Note that under normal conditions the 2nd stage does not modify the parse sub-trees obtained from the 1st stage, it only establishes the relations between the clauses.

3 Hard and Soft Constraints

Both 1st and 2nd stage described in the previous section use linguistically motivated constraints. These *hard* constraints (H-constraints) reflect that aspect of the grammar that in general cannot be broken. H-constraints comprise of lexical and structural knowledge of the language. The H-constraints are converted into integer programming problem and solved (Bharati et al., 1995). The solution(s) is/are valid parse(s). The *soft* constraints (S-constraints) on the other hand are learnt as weights from an annotated treebank. They reflect various preferences that a language has towards various linguistic phenomena. They are used to prioritize the parses and select the best parse. Both H & S constraints reflect the linguistic realities of the language and together can be thought as the grammar of a language. Figure 2 shows the overall design of the proposed parser schematically.

3.1 Hard Constraints

The core language knowledge being currently considered that cannot be broken without the sentence being called ungrammatical is named H-constraints. There can be multiple parses which can satisfy these H-constraints. This indicates the ambiguity in the sentence if only the limited knowledge base is considered. Stated another way, H-constraints are insufficient to restrict multiple analysis of a given sentence and that more knowledge (semantics, other preferences, etc.) is required to curtain the ambiguities. Moreover, we know that many sentences are syntactically ambiguous unless one uses some pragmatic knowledge, etc. For all such constructions there are multiple parses. As described earlier, H-constraints are used during intra-clausal (1st stage) and inter-clausal (2nd stage) analysis (cf. Figure 2). They are used to form a constraint graph which is converted into integer programming equalities (or inequalities). These are then solved to get the final solution graph(s). Some of the H-constraints are: (1) *Structural constraints* (ensuring the solution graph to be a tree,

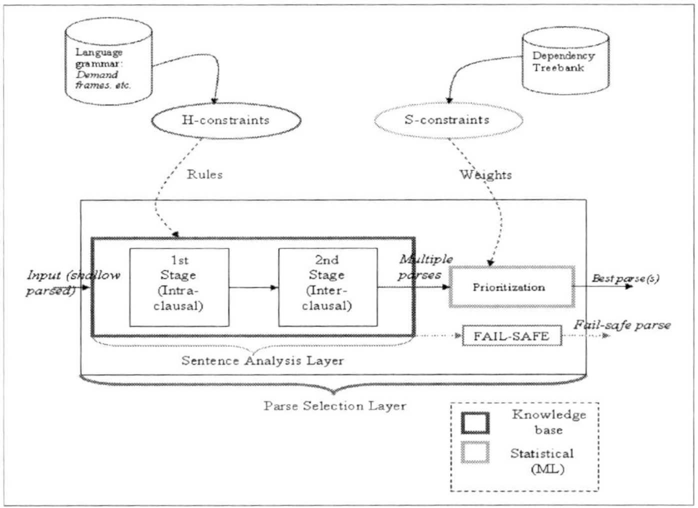

Figure 2. Overall parser design

removing implausible language specific ungrammatical structures, etc.), (2) *Lexicon* (linguistic demands of various heads), and (3) *Other lexical constraints* (some language specific characteristics), etc.

3.2 Soft Constraints

The S-constraints on the other hand are the constraints which can be broken, and are used in the language as preferences. These are used during the prioritization stage. Unlike the H-constraints that are derived from a knowledge base and are used to form a constraint graph, S-constraints have weights assigned to them. These weights are automatically learnt using a manually annotated dependency treebank. The tree with the maximum overall score is the best parse. Some such S-constraints are, (1) *Order of the arguments*, (2) *Relative position of arguments w.r.t. the verb*, (3) *Agreement principle*, (4) *Alignment of prominence scale*, and (5) *Structural preferences/General graph properties* (mild non-projectivity, valency, dominance, etc.), etc.

4 Evaluation

Malt Parser (version 0.4) (Nivre et al., 2007), and MST Parser (version 0.4b) (McDonald et al., 2005) have been tuned for Hindi by Bharati et al. (2008). Parsers were trained on a subset of a Hindi Treebank (Begum et al., 2008a). We use the same experimental setup (parameters, features, etc.) used by them and compare the results of the two data driven parsers with that of the proposed constraint based hybrid parser (CBP) on the same dataset[4] in terms of unlabeled attachments (UA), label (L) and labeled attachment (LA) accuracy. In Table 1, CBP' shows the performance of the system when a basic prioritizer is used, while CBP'' shows it for the best parse that is available in the first 25 parses. CBP gives the accuracy when the 1st parse is selected. We show CBP'' to show that a good parse is available in as few as the first 25 parses and that once the prioritizer is further improved the overall performance will easily cross CBP''.

	UA	LA	L
CBP	86.1	63	65
CBP'	87.69	69.67	72.39
CBP''	**90.1**	***75***	***76.9***
MST	*87.8*	70.4	72.3
Malt	86.6	68.0	70.6

Table 1. Parser Evaluation

5 Observations

The initial results show that the proposed parser performs better than the state-of-the-art data driven Hindi parsers. There are various reasons why we think that the proposed approach is better suited to parsing MoR-FWO. (1) Complex linguistic cues can easily be encoded as part of various constraints. For example, it has been shown by Bharati et al. (2008) that, for Hindi, complex agreement patterns, though present in the data, are not being learnt by data driven parsers. Such patterns along with other idiosyncratic language properties can be easily incorporated as constraints, (2) Making clauses as basic parsing unit drastically reduces non-projective

[4] For details on the corpus type, annotation scheme, tagset, etc. see Begum et al. (2008a).

sentences. Experiments in parsing MoR-FOW have shown that such non-projective sentences impede parser performances (Bharati et al., 2008; Hall et al., 2007). Note that there will still remain some intra-clausal non-projective structures in the 1st stage, but they will be short distance dependencies, (3) Use of H-constraints and S-constraints together reflect the grammar of a language. The rules in the form of H-constraints are complemented by the weights of S-constraints learnt from the annotated corpus, (4) 2 stage parsing lends itself seamlessly to parsing complex sentences by modularizing the task of overall parsing, (5) the problem of label bias (Bharati et al., 2008) faced by the data driven Hindi parsers for some cases does not arise here as contextually similar entities are disambiguated by tapping in hard to learn features, (6) Use of clauses as basic parsing units reduces the search space at both the stages, (7) Parsing closely related languages will become easy.

The performance of our parser is affected due to the following reasons, (a) *Small lexicon (linguistic demands of various heads)*: The total number of such demand frames which the parser currently uses is very low. There are a total of around 300 frames, which have been divided into 20 verb classes (Begum et al., 2008b). As the coverage of this lexicon increases, the efficiency will automatically increase. (b) *Unhandled constructions*: The parser still doesn't handle some constructions, such as the case when a conjunct takes another conjunct as its dependent, and (c) *Prioritization mistakes*: As stated earlier the prioritizer being used is basic and is still being improved. The overall performance will increase with the improvement of the prioritizer.

6 Conclusion

In this paper we proposed a new two stage constraint based hybrid approach to dependency parsing. We showed how by modularizing the task of overall parsing into 2 stages we can overcome many problems faced by data driven parsing. We showed how in the 1st stage only intra-clausal dependencies are handled and later in the 2nd stage the inter-clausal dependencies are identified. We also briefly described the use of H-constraints and S-constraints. We argued that such constraints complement each other in getting the best parse and that together they represent the grammar of the language. We evaluated our system for Hindi with two data driven parsers. Initial results show that the proposed parser performs better than those parsers. Finally, we argued why the proposed hybrid approach is better suited to handle the challenges posed by MoR-FWO and gave few pointers as how we can further improve our performance.

The proposed parser is still being improved at various fronts. To begin with a prioritization mechanism has to be improved. We need to enrich the verb frame lexicon along with handling some unhandled constructions. This will be taken up as immediate future work.

References

R. Begum, S. Husain, A. Dhwaj, D. Sharma, L. Bai, and R. Sangal. 2008a. Dependency annotation scheme for Indian languages. *Proc. of IJCNLP08.*

R. Begum, S. Husain, D. Sharma and L. Bai. 2008b. Developing Verb Frames in Hindi. *Proc. of LREC08.*

A. Bharati, S. Husain, B. Ambati, S. Jain, D. Sharma and R. Sangal. 2008. Two Semantic features make all the difference in Parsing accuracy. *Proc. of ICON-08.*

A. Bharati and R. Sangal. 1993. Parsing Free Word Order Languages in the Paninian Framework. *Proc. of ACL: 93.*

A. Bharati, V. Chaitanya and R. Sangal. 1995. *Natural* Language *Processing: A Paninian Perspective,* Prentice-Hall of India, New Delhi.

R. Debusmann, D. Duchier and G. Kruijff. 2004. Extensible dependency grammar: A new methodology. *Proceedings of the Workshop on Recent Advances in Dependency Grammar*, pp. 78–85.

J. Hall, J. Nilsson, J. Nivre, G. Eryigit, B. Megyesi, M. Nilsson and M. Saers. 2007. Single Malt or Blended? A Study in Multilingual Parser Optimization. *Proc. of EMNLP-CoNLL shared task 2007.*

R. McDonald, F. Pereira, K. Ribarov, and J. Hajic. 2005. Non-projective dependency parsing using spanning tree algorithms. *Proc. of HLT/EMNLP.*

I. A. Mel'Cuk. 1988. Dependency *Syntax: Theory and Practice,* State University Press of New York.

J. Nivre, J. Hall, J. Nilsson, A. Chanev, G. Eryigit, S. Kübler, S. Marinov and E Marsi. 2007. MaltParser: A language-independent system for data-driven dependency parsing. *NLE.*

S. M. Shieber. 1985. Evidence against the context-freeness of natural language. In *Linguistics and Philosophy*, p. 8, 334–343.

I. Schröder. 2002. *Natural Language Parsing with Graded Constraints.* PhD thesis, Hamburg Univ.

Analysis of Discourse Structure with Syntactic Dependencies and Data-Driven Shift-Reduce Parsing

Kenji Sagae
USC Institute for Creative Technologies
Marina del Rey, CA 90292 USA
sagae@ict.usc.edu

Abstract

We present an efficient approach for discourse parsing within and across sentences, where the unit of processing is an entire document, and not a single sentence. We apply shift-reduce algorithms for dependency and constituent parsing to determine syntactic dependencies for the sentences in a document, and subsequently a Rhetorical Structure Theory (RST) tree for the entire document. Our results show that our linear-time shift-reduce framework achieves high accuracy and a large improvement in efficiency compared to a state-of-the-art approach based on chart parsing with dynamic programming.

1 Introduction

Transition-based dependency parsing using shift-reduce algorithms is now in wide use for dependency parsing, where the goal is to determine the syntactic structure of sentences. State-of-the-art results have been achieved for syntactic analysis in a variety of languages (Bucholz and Marsi, 2006). In contrast to graph-based approaches, which use edge-factoring to allow for global optimization of parameters over entire tree structures using dynamic programming or maximum spanning tree algorithms (McDonald et al., 2005) transition-based models are usually optimized at the level of individual shift-reduce actions, and can be used to drive parsers that produce competitive accuracy using greedy search strategies in linear time.

Recent research in data-driven shift-reduce parsing has shown that the basic algorithms used for determining dependency trees (Nivre, 2004) can be extended to produce constituent structures (Sagae and Lavie, 2005), and more general dependency graphs, where words can be linked to more than one head (Henderson et al., 2008; Sagae and Tsujii, 2008). A remarkably similar parsing approach, which predates the current wave of interest in data-driven shift-reduce parsing sparked by Yamada and Matsumoto (2003) and Nivre and Scholz (2004), was proposed by Marcu (1999) for data-driven *discourse parsing*, where the goal is to determine the rhetorical structure of a document, including relationships that span multiple sentences. The linear-time shift-reduce framework is particularly well suited for discourse parsing, since the length of the input string depends on document length, not sentence length, making cubic run-time chart parsing algorithms often impractical.

Soricut and Marcu (2003) presented an approach to discourse parsing that relied on syntactic information produced by the Charniak (2000) parser, and used a standard bottom-up chart parsing algorithm with dynamic programming to determine discourse structure. Their approach greatly improved on the accuracy of Marcu's shift-reduce approach, showing the value of using syntactic information in discourse analysis, but recovered only discourse relations within sentences.

We present an efficient approach to discourse parsing using syntactic information, inspired by Marcu's application of a shift-reduce algorithm for discourse analysis with Rhetorical Structure Theory (RST), and Soricut and Marcu's use of syntactic structure to help determine discourse structure. Our transition-based discourse parsing framework combines elements from Nivre (2004)'s approach to dependency parsing, and Sagae and Lavie (2005)'s approach to constituent parsing. Our results improve on accuracy over existing approaches for data-driven RST parsing, while also improving on speed over Soricut and Marcu's chart parsing approach, which produces state-of-the-art results for RST discourse relations within sentences.

Proceedings of the 11th International Conference on Parsing Technologies (IWPT), pages 81–84,
Paris, October 2009.

2 Discourse analysis with the RST Discourse Treebank

The discourse parsing approach presented here is based on the formalization of Rhetorical Structure Theory (RST) (Mann and Thompson, 1988) used in the RST Discourse Treebank (Carlson et al., 2003). In this scheme, the discourse structure of a document is represented as a tree, where the leaves are contiguous spans of text, called *elementary discourse units*, or EDUs. Each node in the tree corresponds to a contiguous span of text formed by concatenation of the spans corresponding to the node's children, and represents a rhetorical relation (*attribution*, *enablement*, *elaboration*, *consequence*, etc.) between these text segments. In addition, each node is marked as a *nucleus* or as a *satellite*, depending on whether its text span represents an essential unit of information, or a supporting or background unit of information, respectively. While the notions of *nucleus* and *satellite* are in some ways analogous to *head* and *dependent* in syntactic dependencies, RST allows for multi-nuclear relations, where two nodes marked as *nucleus* can be linked into one node.

Our parsing framework includes three components: (1) syntactic dependency parsing, where standard techniques for sentence-level parsing are applied; (2) discourse segmentation, which uses syntactic and lexical information to segment text into EDUs; and (3) discourse parsing, which produces a discourse structure tree from a string of EDUs, also benefiting from syntactic information. In contrast to the approach of Soricut and Marcu (2003), which also includes syntactic parsing, discourse segmentation and discourse parsing, our approach assumes that the unit of processing for discourse parsing is an entire document, and that discourse relations may exist within sentences as well as across sentences, while Soricut and Marcu's processes one sentence at a time, independently, finding only discourse relations within individual sentences. Parsing entire documents at a time is made possible in our approach through the use of linear-time transition-based parsing. An additional minor difference is that in our approach syntactic information is represented using dependencies, while Soricut and Marcu used constituent trees.

2.1 Syntactic parsing and discourse segmentation

Assuming the document has been segmented into sentences, a task for which there are approaches with very high accuracy (Gillick, 2009), we start by finding the dependency structure for each sentence. This includes part-of-speech (POS) tagging using a CRF tagger trained on the Wall Street Journal portion of the Penn Treebank, and transition-based dependency parsing using the shift-reduce arc-standard algorithm (Nivre, 2004) trained with the averaged perceptron (Collins, 2002). The dependency parser is also trained with the WSJ Penn Treebank, converted to dependencies using the head percolation rules of Yamada and Matsumoto (2003).

Discourse segmentation is performed as a binary classification task on each word, where the decision is whether or not to insert an EDU boundary between the word and the next word. In a sentence of length n, containing the words $w_1, w_2 \dots w_n$, we perform one classification per word, in order. For word w_i, the binary choice is whether to insert an EDU boundary between w_i and w_{i+1}. The EDUs are then the words between EDU boundaries (assuming boundaries exist in the beginning and end of each sentence).

The features used for classification are: the current word, its POS tag, its dependency label, and the direction to its head (whether the head appears before or after the word); the previous two words, their POS tags and dependency labels; the next two words, their POS tags and dependency labels; the direction from the previous word to its head; the leftmost dependent to the right of the current word, and its POS tag; the rightmost dependent to the left of the current word, and its POS tag; whether the head of the current word is between the previous EDU boundary and the current word; whether the head of the next word is between the previous EDU boundary and the current word. In addition, we used templates that combine these features (in pairs or triples). Classification was done with the averaged perceptron.

2.2 Transition-based discourse parsing

RST trees can be represented in a similar way as constituent trees in the Penn Treebank, with a few differences: the trees represent entire documents, instead of single sentences; the leaves of the trees are EDUs consisting of one or more contiguous words; and the node labels contain nucleus/satellite status, and possibly the name of a discourse relation. Once the document has been segmented into a sequence of EDUs, we use a transition-based constituent parsing approach (Sagae and Lavie, 2005) to build an RST tree for the document.

Sagae and Lavie's constituent parsing algorithm uses a stack that holds subtrees, and consumes the input string (in our case, a sequence of EDUs) from left to right, using four types of actions: (1) *shift*, which removes the next token from the input string, and pushes a subtree containing exactly that token onto the stack; (2) *reduce-unary-LABEL*, which pops the stack, and push onto it a new subtree where a node with label *LABEL* dominates the subtree that was popped (3) *reduce-left-LABEL*, and (4) *reduce-right-LABEL*, which each pops two items from the stack, and pushes onto it a new subtree with root *LABEL*, which has as right child the subtree previously on top of the stack, and as left child the subtree previously immediately below the top of the stack. The difference between *reduce-left* and *reduce-right* is whether the head of the new subtree comes from the left or right child. The algorithm assumes trees are lexicalized, and in our use of the algorithm for discourse parsing, heads are entire EDUs, and not single words.

Our process for lexicalization of discourse trees, which is required for the parsing algorithm to function properly, is a simple percolation of "head EDUs," performed in the same way as lexical heads can be assigned in Penn Treebank-style trees using a head percolation table (Collins, 1999). To determine head EDUs, we use the nucleus/satellite status of nodes, as follows: for each node, the leftmost child with nucleus status is the head; if no child is a nucleus, the leftmost satellite is the head. Most nodes have exactly two children, one nucleus and one satellite. The parsing algorithm deals only with binary trees. We use the same binarization transform as Sagae and Lavie, converting the trees in the training set to binary trees prior to training the parser, and converting the binary trees produced by the parser at run-time into *n*-ary trees.

As with the dependency parser and discourse segmenter, learning is performed using the averaged perceptron. We use similar features as Sagae and Lavie, with one main difference: since there is usually no single head-word associated with each node, but a EDU that contains a sequence of words, we use the dependency structure of the EDU to determine what lexical features and POS tags should be used as features associated with each RST tree node. In place of the head-word and POS tag of the top four items on the stack, and the next four items in the input, we use subsets of the words and POS tags in the EDUs for each of those items. The subset of words (and POS tags) that represent an EDU contain the first two and last words in the EDU, and each word in the EDU whose head is outside of the EDU. In the vast majority of EDUs, this subset of words with heads outside the EDU (the *EDU head set*) contains a single word. In addition, we extract these features for the top three (not four) items on the stack, and the next three (not four) words in the input. For the top two items on the stack, in addition to subsets of words and POS tags described above, we also take the words and POS tags for the leftmost and rightmost children of each word in the EDU head set. Finally, we use feature templates that combine these and other individual features from Sagae and Lavie, who used a polynomial kernel and had no need for such templates (at the cost of increased time for both training and running).

3 Results

To test our discourse parsing approach, we used the standard training and testing sections of the RST Discourse Treebank and the compacted 18-label set described by Carlson et al. (2003). We used approximately 5% of the standard training set as a development set.

Our part-of-speech tagger and syntactic parser were *not* trained using the standard splits of the Penn Treebank for those tasks, since there are documents in the RST Discourse Treebank test section that are included in the usual training sets for POS taggers and parsers. The POS tagger and syntactic parser were then trained on sections 2 to 21 of the WSJ Penn Treebank, excluding the specific documents used in the test section of the RST Discourse Treebank.

Table 1 shows the precision, recall and f-score of our discourse segmentation approach on the test set, compared to that of Soricut and Marcu (2003) and Marcu (1999). In all cases, results were obtained with automatically produced syntactic structures. We also include the total time required for syntactic parsing (required in our

	Prec.	Recall	F-score	Time
Marcu99	83.3	77.1	80.1	-
S&M03	83.5	82.7	83.1	361s
this work	**87.4**	**86.0**	**86.7**	**40s**

Table 1: Precision, recall, f-score and time for discourse segmenters, tested on the RST Discourse Treebank. Time includes syntactic parsing, Charniak (2000) for S&M03, and our implemetation of Nivre arc-standard for our segmenter.

	F-score	Time
Marcu99	37.2	-
S&M03	49.0	481s
this work	**52.9**	**69s**
human	77.0	-

Table 2: F-score for bracketing of RST discourse trees on the test set of the RST Discourse Treebank, and total time (syntactic parsing, segmentation and discourse parsing) required to parse the test set (S&M03 and our approach were run on the same hardware).

segmentation approach and Soricut and Marcu's) and segmentation. For comparison with previous results, we include only segmentation within sentences (if all discourse boundaries are counted, including sentence boundaries, our f-score is 92.9).

Using our discourse segmentation and transition-based discourse parsing approach, we obtain 42.9 precision and 46.2 recall (44.5 f-score) for all discourse structures in the test set. Table 2 shows f-score of labeled bracketing for discourse relations *within sentences* only, for comparison with previously published results. We note that human performance on this task has f-score 77.0.

While our f-score is still far below that of human performance, we have achieved a large gain in speed of processing compared to a state-of-the-art approach.

4 Conclusion

We have presented an approach to discourse analysis based on transition-based algorithms for dependency and constituent trees. Dependency parsing is used to determine the syntactic structure of text, which is then used in discourse segmentation and parsing. A simple discriminative approach to segmentation results in an overall improvement in discourse parsing f-score, and the use of a linear-time algorithm results in an a large improvement in speed over a state-of-the-art approach.

Acknowledgments

The work described here has been sponsored by the U.S. Army Research, Development, and Engineering Command (RDECOM). Statements and opinions expressed do not necessarily reflect the position or the policy of the United States Government, and no official endorsement should be inferred.

References

Buchholz, S. and Marsi, E. 2006. CoNLL-X shared task on multilingual dependency parsing. In *Proc. of CoNLL 2006 Shared Task.*

Carlson, L., Marcu, D., and Okurowski, M. E. 2003. Building a discourse-tagged corpus in the framework of Rhetorical Structure Theory. In J. van Kuppevelt and R. W. Smith, editors, *Current and New Directions in Discourse and Dialogue.* Kluwer Academic Publishers.

Charniak, E. 2000. A maximum-entropy-inspired parser. In *Proc. of NAACL.*

Collins, M. 1999. *Head-driven statistical models for natural language processing.* PhD dissertation, University of Pennsylvania.

Collins, M. 2002. Discriminative Training Methods for Hidden Markov Models: Theory and Experiments with Perceptron Algorithms. In *Proc. of EMNLP.* Philadelphia, PA.

Gillick, D. 2009. Sentence Boundary Detection and the Problem with the U.S. In *Proc. of the NAACL HLT: Short Papers.* Boulder, Colorado.

Henderson, J., Merlo, P., Musillo, G., Titov, I. 2008. A Latent Variable Model of Synchronous Parsing for Syntactic and Semantic Dependencies. *In Proc. of CoNLL 2008 Shared Task*, Manchester, UK.

Mann, W. C. and Thompson, S. A. 1988. Rhetorical Structure Theory: toward a functional theory of text organization. *Text*, 8(3):243-281.

Marcu, D. 1999. A decision-based approach to rhetorical parsing. In *Proc. of the Annual Meeting of the Association for Computational Linguistics.*

McDonald, R., Pereira, F., Ribarov, K., and Hajic, J. 2005. Non-projective dependency parsing using spanning tree algorithms. In *Proc. of HLT/EMNLP.*

Nivre, J. 2004. Incrementality in Deterministic Dependency Parsing. In *Incremental Parsing: Bringing Engineering and Cognition Together* (workshop at ACL-2004). Barcelona, Spain.

Nivre, J. and Scholz, M. 2004. Deterministic Dependency Parsing of English Text. In *Proc. of COLING.*

Sagae, K. and Lavie, A. 2005. A classifier-based parser with linear run-time complexity. In *Proc. of IWPT.*

Sagae, K. and Tsujii, J. 2008. Shift-reduce dependency DAG parsing. In *Proc. of COLING.*

Soricut, R. and Marcu, D. 2003. Sentence level discourse parsing using syntactic and lexical information. In *Proc. of NAACL.* Edmonton, Canada.

Yamada, H. and Matsumoto, Y. 2003. Statistical dependency analysis with support vector machines. In *Proc. of IWPT.*

Evaluating Contribution of Deep Syntactic Information to Shallow Semantic Analysis

Sumire Uematsu **Jun'ichi Tsujii**
Graduate School of Information Science and Technology
The University of Tokyo
{uematsu,tsujii}@is.s.u-tokyo.ac.jp

Abstract

This paper presents shallow semantic parsing based only on HPSG parses. An HPSG-FrameNet map was constructed from a semantically annotated corpus, and semantic parsing was performed by mapping HPSG dependencies to FrameNet relations. The semantic parsing was evaluated in a Senseval-3 task; the results suggested that there is a high contribution of syntactic information to semantic analysis.

1 Introduction

This paper presents semantic parsing based only on HPSG parses, and examines the contribution of the syntactic information to semantic analysis.

In computational linguistics, many researchers have studied the relationship between syntax and semantics. Its quantitative analysis was formalized as semantic parsing, or semantic role labeling, and has attracted the attention of researchers.

Recently, an improvement in the accuracy and robustness of "deep parsers" has enabled us to directly map deep syntactic dependencies to semantic relations. Deep parsers are based on linguistically expressive grammars; e.g. HPSG, LFG, etc, and less affected by syntactic alternations such as passivization. Their results are therefore expected to closely relate to semantic annotations. For example, the sentences in figure 1 share the same set of semantic roles, and the roles have one-to-one relations to deep syntactic dependencies in the sentences. However, the results of the deep parsers are represented in complex structures, shown in figure 3, and cannot be straightforwardly compared to semantic annotations.

In order to directly map the deep dependencies to semantic relations, we adapted the corpus analysis method of (Frank and Semecký, 2004) for the semantic parsing using HPSG parses. We performed the semantic parsing by mapping paths in HPSG parses to semantic predicate-argument relations. The analysis of the HPSG paths for the predicate-argument pairs, and the preliminary result of the semantic parsing indicate the contribution of syntactic analysis to semantic parsing.

2 Related Work

Besides (Frank and Semecký, 2004)'s work, as mentioned above, there have been several studies on the relationship between deep syntax and semantic parsing. Although the studies did not focus on direct mappings between deep syntax and shallow semantics, they suggested a strong relationship between the two. (Miyao and Tsujii, 2004) evaluated the accuracy of an HPSG parser against PropBank semantic annotations, and showed that the HPSG dependants correlated with semantic arguments of the PropBank, particularly with "core" arguments. In (Gildea and Hockenmaier, 2003) and (Zhang et al., 2008), features from deep parses were used for semantic parsing, together with features from CFG or dependency parses. The deep features were reported to contribute to a performance gain.

3 Syntactic and Semantic Parsing

Some semantic relations are easily identified by using syntactic parsing while others are more difficult. This section presents easy and difficult cases in syntax-semantics map construction.

Trivial when using syntactic analysis: Syntactic parsing, including CFG analysis, detects semantic similarity of sentences sharing similar phrase structures. For the example sentences a) and b) in figure 1, the parsing provides similar phrase structures, and therefore gives the same syntactic dependency to occurrences of each role.

Trivial when using deep analysis: Deep parsing reveals the semantic similarity of sentences

Proceedings of the 11th International Conference on Parsing Technologies (IWPT), pages 85–88,
Paris, October 2009.

a) …, I$_{Communicator}$ **praise** them$_{Evaluee}$ for being 99 percent perfect$_{Reason}$.
b) …, but he$_{Communicator}$ **praised** the Irish premier$_{Evaluee}$ for making a ``sensible'' speech$_{Reason}$.
c) The child$_{Evaluee}$ is **praised** for having a dry bed$_{Reason}$ and …
d) …, She$_{Communicator}$ was supposed, therefore, to **praise** him$_{Evaluee}$ and then …

Figure 1: Sentences with a set of semantic roles for the predicate *praise*.

e) It$_{Evaluee}$ received high **praise**, …
f) Alice$_{Wearer}$'s **dress**
g) Versace's **dress**

Figure 2: Example phrases for section 3.

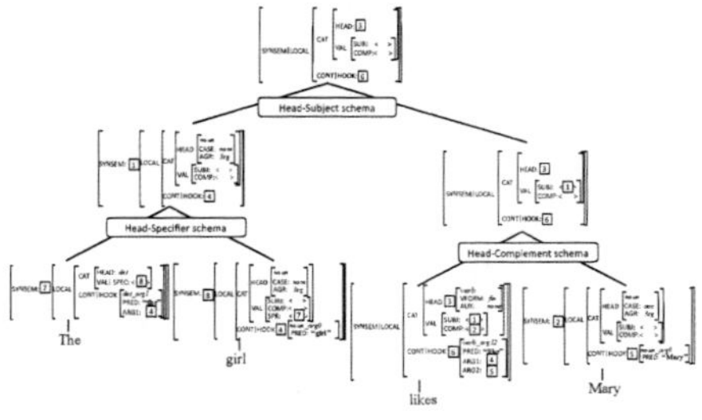

Figure 3: An HPSG parse for *The girl likes Mary.*

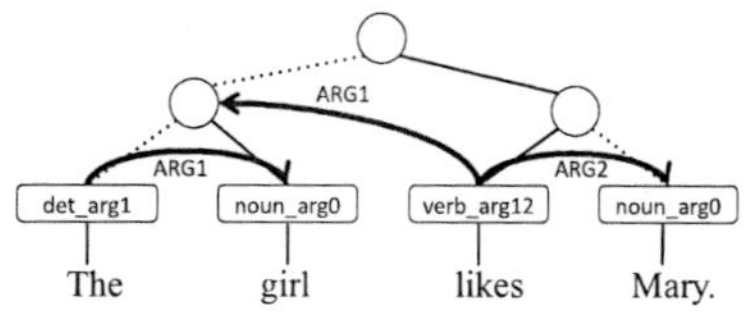

Figure 4: A simplified representation of figure 3.

containing complex syntactic phenomena, which is not easily detected by CFG analysis. The sentences c) and d) in figure 1 contain passivization and object raising, while deep parsing provides one dependency for each role in the figure.

Not trivial even when using deep analysis: Some semantic arguments are not direct syntactic dependants of their predicates - especially of noun predicates. In sentence e) in figure 2, the *Evaluee* phrase depends on the predicate *praise*, through the support verb *receive*. The deep analysis would be advantageous in capturing such dependencies, because it provides *receive* with direct links to the phrases of the role and the predicate.

Problematic when using only syntactic analysis: Sometimes, the semantic role of a phrase is strongly dependent on the type of the mentioned entity, rather than on the syntactic dependency. In phrases f) and g) in figure 2, the phrases *Alice* and *Versace*, have the same syntactic relation to the predicate *dress*. However, the *Wearer* role is given only to the former phrase.

4 A Wide-Coverage HPSG Parser

We employed a wide-coverage HPSG parser for semantic parsing, and used deep syntactic dependencies encoded in a Predicate Argument Structure (PAS) in each parse node.

In our experiments, the parser results were considered as graphs, as illustrated by figures 3 and 4, to extract HPSG dependencies conveniently. The graph is obtained by ignoring most of the linguistic information in the original parse nodes, and by adding edges directing to the PAS dependants. The PAS information is represented in the graph, by the terminal nodes' *PAS types*, e.g. *verb_arg12*, etc., and by the added edges. Note that the interpretation of the edge labels depends on the PAS type. If the PAS type is *verb_arg12*, the *ARG2* dependant is the object of the transitive verb or its equivalence (the subject of the passive, etc.). If the PAS type is *prep_arg12*, then the dependant is the NP governed by the preposition node.

5 Semantic Parsing Based on FrameNet

We employed FrameNet (FN) as a semantic corpus. Furthermore, we evaluated our semantic parsing on the SRL task data of Senseval-3 (Litkowski, 2004), which consists of FN annotations.

In FN, semantic *frames* are defined, and each frame is associated with predicates that evoke the frame. For instance, the verb and noun *praise* are predicates of the *Judgment_communication* frame, and they share the same set of semantic roles.

The Senseval-3 data is a standard for evaluation of semantic parsing. The task is defined as identifying phrases and their semantic roles for a given sentence, predicate, and frame. The data includes *null instantiations* of roles[1], which are "conceptually salient", but do not appear in the text.

6 Methods

The semantic parsing using an HPSG-FN map consisted of the processes shown in figure 5.

[1] An example of a null instantiation is the *Communicator* role in the sentence, "All in all the conference was **acclaimed** as a considerable success."

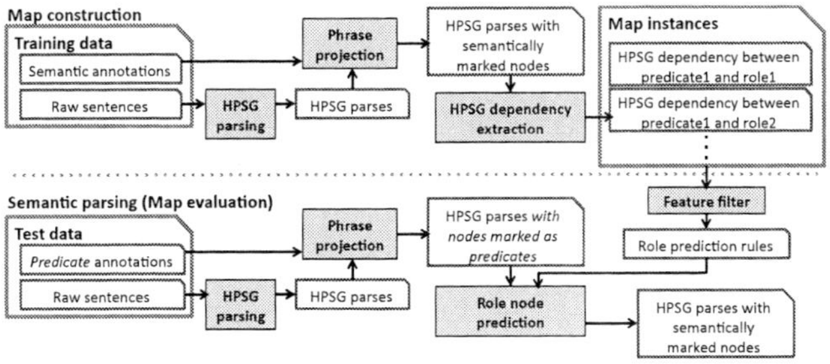

Figure 5: Processes in the map construction and evaluation.

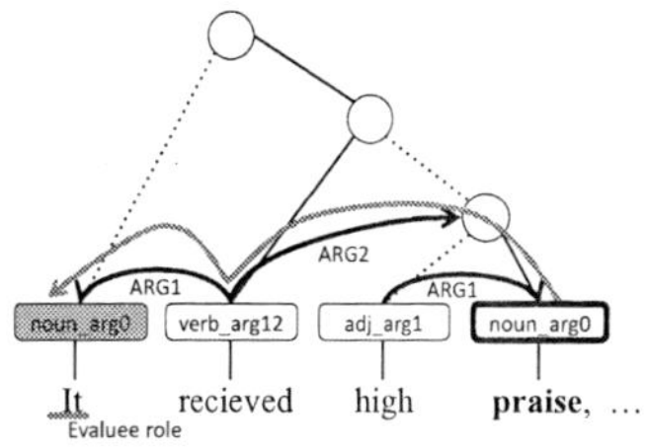

Figure 6: an HPSG path for a semantic relation.

Predicate base: The base form of the semantic predicate word. (*praise* in the case of figure 6).
Predicate type: The *PAS type* of the HPSG terminal node for the predicate - see section 4. (*noun_arg0* in figure 6).
Intermediate word base: The base form of the *intermediate word*, corresponding to a terminal passed by the path, and satisfying pre-defined conditions. The word may be a support verb. - see figure 6. (*receive* in figure 6).
Intermediate word type: The *PAS type* of the *intermediate word*. (*verb_arg12* in figure 6).
Dependency label sequence: The labels of the path's edges. We omitted labels presenting head-child relations, for identifying a phrase with another phrase sharing the same head word. (*Reverse of ARG2, ARG1* in figure 6).

Table 1: Features used to represent a HPSG path.

Filter	Pred. base	Pred. type	Inter. base	Inter. type	Dep. label
Same	√	√	√	√	√
AllInter	√	√		√	√
AllPred		√	√	√	√
AllPred-AllInter		√		√	√

Table 2: Syntactic features for role prediction.

Phrase projection: Because we used FN annotations, which are independent of any syntactic framework, role phrases needed to be projected to appropriate HPSG nodes. We projected the phrases based on *maximal projection*, which was generally employed, with heads defined in the HPSG.

HPSG dependency extraction: As an HPSG dependency for a predicate-argument pair, we used the shortest path between the predicate node and the argument node in the HPSG parse. The path was then represented by pre-defined features, listed in table 1. The search for the shortest path was done in the simplified graph of the HPSG parse (see figure 4), with the edges denoting deep dependencies, and head-child relations. An instance of the HPSG-FN map consisted of the path's features, the *FN frame*, and the *role label*.

Role node prediction: The role prediction was based on simple rules with scores. The rules were obtained by filtering features of the map instances. Table 2 shows the feature filters. The score of a rule was the number of map instances matching the rule's features. In the test, for each node of a HPSG parse, the role label with the highest score was selected as the result, where the score of a label was that of the rule providing the label.

7 Experiments

For the experiments, we employed a wide coverage HPSG parser, Enju version 2.3.1[2], and the data for the Semantic Role Labeling task of Senseval-3.

7.1 Analysis of Map Instances

We extracted 41,193 HPSG-FN map instances from the training set, the training data apart from the development set. The instances amounted to 97.7 % (41,193 / 42,163) of all the non-null instantiated roles in the set, and HPSG paths were short for many instances. Paths to syntactic arguments were almost directly mapped to semantic roles, while roles for other phrases were more ambiguous.

The length distribution of HPSG paths: 64 % (26410 / 41193) of the obtained HPSG paths were length-one, and 8 % (3390 / 41193) were length-two, due to the effect of direct links provided by HPSG parsing. The length of a path was defined

[2]http://www-tsujii.is.s.u-tokyo.ac.jp/enju/

Pred.	Freq.	Feature representation	Interpretation
Verb	3792	verb_arg12/–/–/ARG2	The object of the transitive predicate
	3191	verb_arg12/–/–/ARG1	The subject of the transitive predicate
Noun	7468	noun_arg0/–/–/–	NP headed by the predicate
	1161	noun_arg0/of/prep_arg12/Rev-ARG1	The PP headed by "of", attaching to the predicate
Adj	1595	adj_arg1/–/–/ARG1	The modifiee of the predicate
	274	verb_arg12/–/–/ARG2	The modifiee of the predicate treated as a verb

Table 3: Most frequent syntactic paths extracted for predicates of each POS.

as the number of the labels in the **Dep. label seq.** of the path. Most of the one-length paths were paths directing to syntactic arguments, and to PPs attaching to the predicates. The two-length paths included paths using support verbs (see figure 6).

Most frequent HPSG dependencies: The most frequent paths are shown in table 3; syntactic dependencies are presented and counted as taples of **Pred. type**, **Inter. base**, **Inter. type**, and **Dep. label seq.** The interpretation column describes the syntactic dependencies for the taples. Note that the column denotes normalized dependencies, in which *object* indicates objects of active voice verbs, subjects of passive-voiced verbs, etc.

7.2 Performance of Semantic Parsing

Finally, semantic parsing was evaluated on the test data. Table 4 shows the overall performance. The scores were measured by the Senseval-3 official script, in the *restrictive* setting, and can be directly compared to other systems' scores. Since our preliminary system of semantic parsing ignored null instantiations of roles, it lost around 0.10 point of the recalls. We believe that such instantiations may be separately treated. Although the system was based on only the syntactic information, and was very naïve, the system's performance was promising, and showed the high contribution of syntactic dependencies for semantic parsing.

8 Conclusion

This paper presents semantic parsing based on only HPSG parses, and investigates the contribution of syntactic information to semantic parsing.

We constructed an HPSG-FN map by finding the HPSG paths that corresponded to semantic relations, and used it as role prediction rules in semantic parsing. The semantic parsing was evaluated on the SRL task data of Senseval-3. Although the preliminary system used only the syntactic information, the performance was promising, and

Rule set	Prec.	Overlap	Recall
Same	0.799	0.783	0.518
AllInter	0.599	0.586	0.589
AllPred	0.472	0.462	0.709
AllPred-AllInter	0.344	0.335	0.712
Senseval-3 best	0.899	0.882	0.772
Senseval-3 4th best	0.802	0.784	0.654

Table 4: Semantic parsing result on the test data.

indicated that syntactic dependencies may make significant contribution to semantic analysis.

This paper also suggests a limit of the semantic analysis based purely on syntax. A next step for accurate HPSG-FN mapping could be analysis of the interaction between the HPSG-FN map and other information, such as named entity types which were shown to be effective in many studies.

Acknowledgments

This work was partially supported by Grant-in-Aid for Specially Promoted Research (MEXT, Japan) and Special Coordination Funds for Promoting Science and Technology (MEXT, Japan).

References

Anette Frank and Jiří Semecký. 2004. Corpus-based induction of an LFG syntax-semantics interface for frame semantic processing. In *Proc. of International Workshop on Linguistically Interpreted Corpora*.

Daniel Gildea and Julia Hockenmaier. 2003. Identifying semantic roles using combinatory categorial grammar. In *Proc. of EMNLP*.

Ken Litkowski. 2004. Senseval-3 task: Automatic labeling of semantic roles. In *Proc. of Senseval-3*.

Yusuke Miyao and Jun'ichi Tsujii. 2004. Deep linguistic analysis for the accurate identification of predicate-argument relations. In *Proc. of Coling*.

Yi Zhang, Rui Wang, and Hans Uszkoreit. 2008. Hybrid learning of dependency structures from heterogeneous linguistic resources. In *Proc. of CoNLL*.

Weight pushing and binarization for fixed-grammar parsing

Matt Post and **Daniel Gildea**
Department of Computer Science
University of Rochester
Rochester, NY 14627

Abstract

We apply the idea of *weight pushing* (Mohri, 1997) to CKY parsing with fixed context-free grammars. Applied after rule binarization, weight pushing takes the weight from the original grammar rule and pushes it down across its binarized pieces, allowing the parser to make better pruning decisions earlier in the parsing process. This process can be viewed as generalizing weight pushing from transducers to hypergraphs. We examine its effect on parsing efficiency with various binarization schemes applied to tree substitution grammars from previous work. We find that weight pushing produces dramatic improvements in efficiency, especially with small amounts of time and with large grammars.

1 Introduction

Fixed grammar-parsing refers to parsing that employs grammars comprising a finite set of rules that is fixed before inference time. This is in contrast to markovized grammars (Collins, 1999; Charniak, 2000), variants of tree-adjoining grammars (Chiang, 2000), or grammars with wildcard rules (Bod, 2001), all of which allow the construction and use of rules not seen in the training data. Fixed grammars must be binarized (either explicitly or implicitly) in order to maintain the $\mathcal{O}(n^3|G|)$ (n the sentence length, $|G|$ the grammar size) complexity of algorithms such as the CKY algorithm.

Recently, Song et al. (2008) explored different methods of binarization of a PCFG read directly from the Penn Treebank (the Treebank PCFG), showing that binarization has a significant effect on both the number of rules and new nonterminals introduced, and subsequently on parsing time. This variation occurs because different binarization schemes produce different amounts of shared rules, which are rules produced during the binarization process from more than one rule in the original grammar. Increasing sharing reduces the amount of state that the parser must explore. Binarization has also been investigated in the context of parsing-based approaches to machine translation, where it has been shown that paying careful attention to the binarization scheme can produce much faster decoders (Zhang et al., 2006; Huang, 2007; DeNero et al., 2009).

The choice of binarization scheme will not affect parsing results if the parser is permitted to explore the whole search space. In practice, however, this space is too large, so parsers use pruning to discard unlikely hypotheses. This presents a problem for bottom-up parsing algorithms because of the way the probability of a rule is distributed among its binarized pieces: The standard approach is to place all of that probability on the top-level binarized rule, and to set the probabilities of lower binarized pieces to 1.0. Because these rules are reconstructed from the bottom up, pruning procedures do not have a good estimate of the complete cost of a rule until the entire original rule has been reconstructed. It is preferable to have this information earlier on, especially for larger rules.

In this paper we adapt the technique of *weight pushing* for finite state transducers (Mohri, 1997) to arbitrary binarizations of context-free grammar rules. Weight pushing takes the probability (or, more generally, the weight) of a rule in the original grammar and pushes it down across the rule's binarized pieces. This helps the parser make bet-

Proceedings of the 11th International Conference on Parsing Technologies (IWPT), pages 89–98,
Paris, October 2009.

ter pruning decisions, and to make them earlier in the bottom-up parsing process. We investigate this algorithm with different binarization schemes and grammars, and find that it improves the time vs. accuracy tradeoff for parsers roughly proportionally to the size of the grammar being binarized.

This paper extends the work of Song et al. (2008) in three ways. First, weight pushing further reduces the amount of time required for parsing. Second, we apply these techniques to Tree Substitution Grammars (TSGs) learned from the Treebank, which are both larger and more accurate than the context-free grammar read directly from the Treebank.[1] Third, we examine the interaction between binarization schemes and the inexact search heuristic of beam-based and k-best pruning.

2 Weight pushing

2.1 Binarization

Not all binarization schemes are equivalent in terms of efficiency of representation. Consider the grammar in the lefthand column of Figure 1 (rules 1 and 2). If this grammar is right-binarized or left-binarized, it will produce seven rules, whereas the optimal binarization (depicted) produces only 5 rules due to the fact that two of them are shared. Since the complexity of parsing with CKY is a function of the grammar size as well as the input sentence length, and since in practice parsing requires significant pruning, having a smaller grammar with maximal shared substructure among the rules is desirable.

We investigate two kinds of binarization in this paper. The first is right binarization, in which nonterminal pairs are collapsed beginning from the two rightmost children and moving leftward. The second is a greedy binarization, similar to that of Schmid (2004), in which the most frequently occurring (grammar-wide) nonterminal pair is collapsed in turn, according to the algorithm given in Figure 2.

Binarization must ensure that the product of the probabilities of the binarized pieces is the same as that of the original rule. The easiest way to do this is to assign each newly-created binarized rule a probability of 1.0, and give the top-level rule the complete probability of the original rule. In the following subsection, we describe a better way.

[1]The mean rule rank in a Treebank PCFG is 2.14, while the mean rank in our sampled TSG is 8.51. See Table 1.

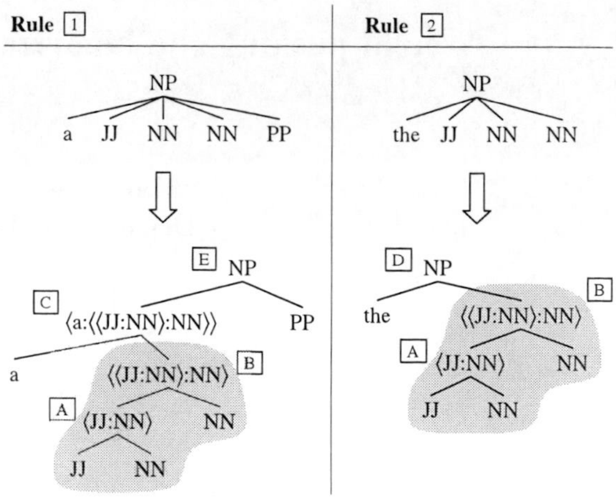

Figure 1: A two-rule grammar. The greedy binarization algorithm produces the binarization shown, with the shared structure highlighted. Binarized rules A, B, and C are initially assigned a probability of 1.0, while rules D and E are assigned the original probabilities of rules 2 and 1, respectively.

2.2 Weight pushing

Spreading the weight of an original rule across its binarized pieces is complicated by sharing, because of the constraint that the probability of shared binarized pieces must be set so that the product of their probabilities is the same as the original rule, for each rule the shared piece participates in. Mohri (1997) introduced *weight pushing* as a step in the minimization of weighted finite-state transducers (FSTs), which addressed a similar problem for tasks employing finite-state machinery. At a high level, weight pushing moves the weight of a path towards the initial state, subject to the constraint that the weight of each path in the FST is unchanged. To do weight pushing, one first computes for each state q in the transducer the shortest distance $d(q)$ to any final state. Let $\sigma(q, a)$ be the state transition function, deterministically transitioning on input a from state q to state $\sigma(q, a)$. Pushing adjusts the weight of each edge $w(e)$ according to the following formula:

$$w'(e) = d(q)^{-1} \times w(e) \times d(\sigma(q, a)) \quad (1)$$

Mohri (1997, §3.7) and Mohri and Riley (2001) discuss how these operations can be applied using various semirings; in this paper we use the $(\max, \times)$ semiring. The important observation for our purposes is that pushing can be thought of as a sequence of local operations on individual nodes

```
1: function GREEDYBINARIZE(P)
2:     while RANK(P) > 2 do
3:         κ := UPDATECOUNTS(P)
4:         for each rule X → x_1 x_2 ··· x_r do
5:             b := argmax_{i∈(2···r)} κ[x_{i−1}, x_i]
6:             l := ⟨x_{b−1} : x_b⟩
7:             add l → x_{b−1} x_b to P
8:             replace x_{b−1} x_b with l in rule
9: function UPDATECOUNTS(P)
10:     κ := {}                          ▷ a dictionary
11:     for each rule X → x_1 x_2 ··· x_r ∈ P do
12:         for i ∈ (2 ··· r) do
13:             κ[x_{i−1}, x_i]++
        return κ
```

Figure 2: A greedy binarization algorithm. The rank of a grammar is the rank of its largest rule. Our implementation updates the counts in κ more efficiently, but we present it this way for clarity.

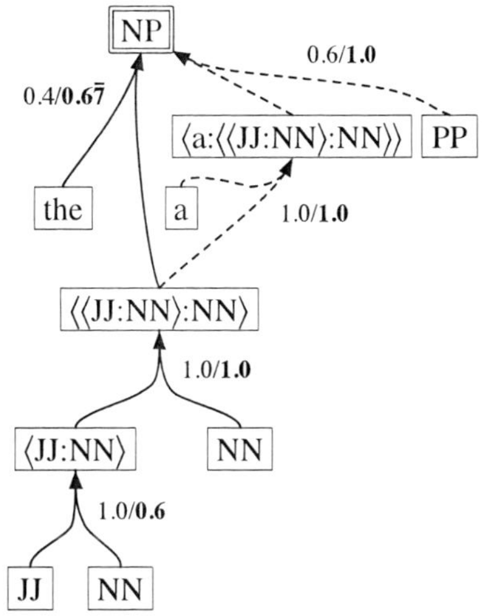

Figure 3: The binarized rules of Figure 1 arranged in a shared hypergraph forest. Each hyperedge is labeled with its weight before/**after** pushing.

q, shifting a constant amount of weight $d(q)^{-1}$ from q's outgoing edges to its incoming edges.

Klein and Manning (2003) describe an encoding of context-free grammar rule binarization that permits weight pushing to be applied. Their approach, however, works only with left or right binarizations whose rules can be encoded as an FST. We propose a form of weight pushing that works for arbitrary binarizations. Weight pushing across a grammar can be viewed as generalizing pushing from weighted transducers to a certain kind of weighted hypergraph. To begin, we use the following definition of a hypergraph:

Definition. A *hypergraph* H is a tuple $\langle V, E, F, R\rangle$, where V is a set of nodes, E is a set of hyperedges, $F \subset V$ is a set of final nodes, and R is a set of permissible weights on the hyperedges. Each hyperedge $e \in E$ is a triple $\langle T(e), h(e), w(e)\rangle$, where $h(e) \in V$ is its head node, $T(e)$ is a sequence of tail nodes, and $w(e)$ is its weight.

We can arrange the binarized rules of Figure 1 into a shared hypergraph forest (Figure 3), with nodes as nonterminals and binarized rules as hyperedges. We distinguish between final and nonfinal nodes and hyperedges. Nonfinal nodes are those in $V - F$. Nonfinal hyperdges E_{NF} are those in $\{e : h(e) \in V - F\}$, that is, all hyperedges whose head is a nonfinal node. Because all nodes introduced by our binarization procedure expand deterministically, each nonfinal node is the head of no more than one such hyperedge. Initially, all nonfinal hyperedges have a probability of 1, and final hyperedges have a probability equal to the that of the original unbinarized rule. Each path through the forest exactly identifies a binarization of a rule in the original grammar, and hyperpaths overlap where binarized rules are shared.

Weight pushing in this hypergraph is similar to weight pushing in a transducer. We consider each nonfinal node v in the graph and execute a local operation that moves weight in some way from the set of edges $\{e : v \in T(e)\}$ (v's outgoing hyperedges) to the edge e_h for which $v = h(e)$ (v's incoming hyperedge).

A critical difference from pushing in transducers is that a node in a hyperpath may be used more than once. Consider adding the rule NP→JJ NN JJ NN to the binarized two-rule grammar we have been considering. Greedy binarization could[2] binarize it in the following manner

$$\begin{aligned} \text{NP} &\rightarrow \langle\text{JJ:NN}\rangle\ \langle\text{JJ:NN}\rangle \\ \langle\text{JJ:NN}\rangle &\rightarrow \text{JJ NN} \end{aligned}$$

which would yield the hypergraph in Figure 4. In order to maintain hyperpath weights, a pushing procedure at the ⟨JJ:NN⟩ node must pay attention to the number of times it appears in the set of tail nodes of each outgoing hyperedge.

[2]Depending on the order in which the argmax variable i of Line 5 from the algorithm in Figure 2 is considered. This particular binarization would not have been produced if the values $2 \ldots r$ were tested sequentially.

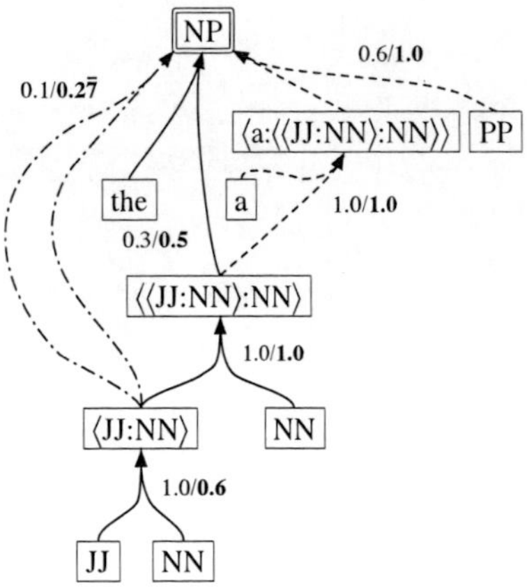

Figure 4: A hypergraph containing a hyperpath representing a rule using the same binarized piece twice. Hyperedge weights are again shown before/**after** pushing.

1: **function** DiffuseWeights(P_{BIN}, Π)
2: $\quad R :=$ bottom-up sort of P_{BIN}
3: $\quad$ **for** each rule $r \in R$ **do**
4: $\quad\quad r.\mathrm{pr} := \max\{ \sqrt[c(r,p)]{p.\mathrm{pr}} : p \in \Pi(r)\}$
5: $\quad\quad$ **for** each rule $p \in \Pi(r)$ **do**
6: $\quad\quad\quad p.\mathrm{pr} := p.\mathrm{pr}/r.\mathrm{pr}^{c(r,p)}$

Figure 6: Maximal weight pushing algorithm applied to a binarized grammar, P_{BIN}. Π is a dictionary mapping from an internal binary rule to a list of top-level binary rules that it appeared under.

With these similarities and differences in mind, we can define the local weight pushing procedure. For each nonfinal node v in the hypergraph, we define e_h as the edge for which $h(e) = v$ (as before), $P = \{e : v \in T(e)\}$ (the set of outgoing hyperedges), and $c(v, T(e))$ as the number of times v appears in the sequence of tail nodes $T(e)$. The minimum amount of probability available for pushing is then

$$\max\{ \sqrt[c(v,T(e))]{w(e)} : e \in P\} \quad (2)$$

This amount can then be multiplied into $w(e_h)$ and divided out of each edge $e \in P$. This max is a lower bound because we have to ensure that the amount of probability we divide out of the weight of each outgoing hyperedge is *at least as large as* that of the maximum weight.

While finite state transducers each have a unique equivalent transducer on which no further pushing is possible, defined by Equation 1, this is not the case when operating on hypergraphs. In this generalized setting, the choice of which tail nodes to push weight across can result in different final solutions. We must define a strategy for choosing among sequences of pushing operations, and for this we now turn to a discussion of the specifics of our algorithm.

2.3 Algorithm

We present two variants. *Maximal* pushing, analogous to weight pushing in weighted FSTs, pushes the original rule's weight down as far as possible. Analysis of interactions between pruning and maximal pushing discovered situations where maximal pushing resulted in search error (see §4.2). To address this, we also discuss *nthroot* pushing, which attempts to distribute the weight more evenly across its pieces, by taking advantage of the fact that Equation 2 is a lower bound on the amount of probability available for pushing.

The algorithm for maximal pushing is listed in Figure 6, and works in the following manner. When binarizing we maintain, for each binarized piece, a list of all the original rules that share it. We then distribute that original rule's weight by considering each of these binarized pieces in bottom-up topological order and setting the probability of the piece to the maximum (remaining) probability of these parents. This amount is then divided out of each of the parents, and the process continues. See Figure 5 for a depiction of this process. Note that, although we defined pushing as a local operation between adjacent hyperedges, it is safe to move probability mass from the top-level directly to the bottom (as we do here). Intuitively, we can imagine this as a series of local pushing operations on all intervening nodes; the end result is the same.

For nthroot pushing, we need to maintain a dictionary δ which records, for each binary piece, the rank (number of items on the rule's righthand side) of the original rule it came from. This is accomplished by replacing line 4 in Figure 6 with

$$r.\mathrm{pr} := \max\{ \sqrt[(\delta(p)-1)\cdot c(r,p)]{p.\mathrm{pr}} : p \in \Pi(r)\}$$

Applying weight pushing to a binarized PCFG results in a grammar that is not a PCFG, because rule probabilities for each lefthand side no longer sum to one. However, the tree distribution, as well as the conditional distribution P(tree|string) (which are what matter for parsing) are unchanged. To show this, we argue from the algorithm in Figure 6, demonstrating that, for

step	A	B	C	D	E
0	1.0	1.0	1.0	x	y
1	$\max(x, y)$	$\cdot$	$\cdot$	$\frac{x}{\max(x,y)}$	$\frac{y}{\max(x,y)}$
2	$\cdot$	$\max(z_{1,D}, z_{1,E})$	$\cdot$	$\frac{z_{1,D}}{\max(z_{1,D},z_{1,E})}$	$\frac{z_{1,D}}{\max(z_{1,D},z_{1,E})}$
3	$\cdot$	$\cdot$	$\max(z_{2,D}, z_{2,E})$	$\frac{z_{2,D}}{\max(z_{2,D},z_{2,E})}$	$\frac{z_{2,E}}{\max(z_{2,D},z_{2,E})}$
4	$\cdot$	$\cdot$	$\cdot$	$\cdot$	$\cdot$

Figure 5: Stepping through the maximal weight pushing algorithm for the binarized grammar in Figure 1. Rule labels A through E were chosen so that the binarized pieces are sorted in topological order. A $(\cdot)$ indicates a rule whose value has not changed from the previous step, and the value $z_{r,c}$ denotes the value in row r column c.

each rule in the original grammar, its probability is equal to the product of the probabilities of its pieces in the binarized grammar. This invariant holds at the start of the algorithm (because the probability of each original rule was placed entirely at the top-level rule, and all other pieces received a probability of 1.0) and is also true at the end of each iteration of the outer loop. Consider this loop. Each iteration considers a single binary piece (line 3), determines the amount of probability to claim from the parents that share it (line 4), and then removes this amount of weight from each of its parents (lines 5 and 6). There are two important considerations.

1. A binarized rule piece may be used more than once in the reconstruction of an original rule; this is important because we are assigning probabilities to binarized rule *types*, but rule reconstruction makes use of binarized rule *tokens*.

2. Multiplying together two probabilities results in a lower number: when we shift weight p from the parent rule to (n instances of) a binarized piece beneath it, we are creating a new set of probabilities p_c and p_p such that $p_c^n \cdot p_p = p$, where p_c is the weight placed on the binarized rule type, and p_p is the weight we leave at the parent. This means that we must choose p_c from the range $[p, 1.0]$.[3]

In light of these considerations, the weight removed from each parent rule in line 6 must be greater than or equal to each parent sharing the binarized rule piece. To ensure this, line 4 takes the maximum of the $c(r, p)$th root of each parent's probability, where $c(r, p)$ is the number of times binarized rule token r appears in the binarization of p.

Line 4 breaks the invariant, but line 6 restores it for each parent rule the current piece takes part in. From this it can be seen that weight pushing does not change the product of the probabilities of the binarized pieces for each rule in the grammar, and hence the tree distribution is also unchanged.

We note that, although Figures 3 and 4 show only one final node, any number of final nodes can appear if binarized pieces are shared across different top-level nonterminals (which our implementation permits and which does indeed occur).

3 Experimental setup

We present results from four different grammars:

1. The standard Treebank probabilistic context-free grammar (PCFG).

2. A "spinal" tree substitution grammar (TSG), produced by extracting n lexicalized subtrees from each length n sentence in the training data. Each subtree is defined as the sequence of CFG rules from leaf upward all sharing the same lexical head, according to the Magerman head-selection rules (Collins, 1999). We detach the top-level unary rule, and add in counts from the Treebank CFG rules.

3. A "minimal subset" TSG, extracted and then refined according to the process defined in Bod (2001). For each height h, $2 \leq h \leq 14$, 400,000 subtrees are randomly sampled from the trees in the training data, and the counts

[3]The upper bound of 1.0 is set to avoid assigning a negative weight to a rule.

grammar	# rules	rank		
		median	mean	max
PCFG	46K	1	2.14	51
spinal	190K	3	3.36	51
sampled	804K	8	8.51	70
minimal	2,566K	10	10.22	62

Table 1: Grammar statistics. A rule's rank is the number of symbols on its right-hand side.

grammar	unbinarized	right	greedy
PCFG	46K	56K	51K
spinal	190K	309K	235K
sampled	804K	3,296K	1,894K
minimal	2,566K	15,282K	7,981K

Table 2: Number of rules in each of the complete grammars before and after binarization.

are summed. From these counts we remove (a) all unlexicalized subtrees of height greater than six and (b) all lexicalized subtrees containing more than twelve terminals on their frontier, and we add all subtrees of height one (i.e., the Treebank PCFG).

4. A sampled TSG produced by inducing derivations on the training data using a Dirichlet Process prior (described below).

The sampled TSG was produced by inducing a TSG derivation on each of the trees in the training data, from which subtree counts were read directly. These derivations were induced using a collapsed Gibbs sampler, which sampled from the posterior of a Dirichlet process (DP) defined over the subtree rewrites of each nonterminal. The DP describes a generative process that prefers small subtrees but occasionally produces larger ones; when used for inference, it essentially discovers TSG derivations that contain larger subtrees only if they are frequent in the training data, which discourages model overfitting. See Post and Gildea (2009) for more detail. We ran the sampler for 100 iterations with a stop probability of 0.7 and the DP parameter $\alpha = 100$, accumulating subtree counts from the derivation state at the end of all the iterations, which corresponds to the $(100, 0.7, \leq 100)$ grammar from that paper.

All four grammar were learned from all sentences in sections 2 to 21 of the Wall Street Journal portion of the Penn Treebank. All trees were preprocessed to remove empty nodes and nonterminal annotations. Punctuation was retained. Statistics for these grammars can be found in Table 1. We present results on sentences with no more than forty words from section 23.

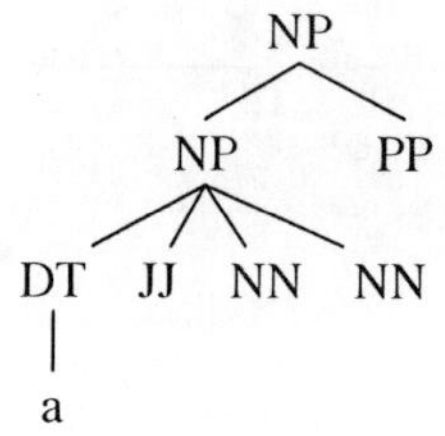

Figure 7: Rule 1 in Figure 1 was produced by flattening this rule from the sampled grammar.

Our parser is a Perl implementation of the CKY algorithm.[4] For the larger grammars, memory limitations require us to remove from consideration all grammar rules that could not possibly take part in a parse of the current sentence, which we do by matching the rule's frontier lexicalization pattern against the words in the sentence. All unlexicalized rules are kept. This preprocessing time is not included in the parsing times reported in the next section.

For pruning, we group edges into equivalence classes according to the following features:

- span (s, t) of the input
- level of binarization (0,1,2+)

The level of binarization refers to the height of a nonterminal in the subtree created by binarizing a CFG rule (with the exception that the root of this tree has a binarization level of 0). The naming scheme used to create new nonterminals in line 6 of Figure 2 means we can determine this level by counting the number of left-angle brackets in the nonterminal's name. In Figure 1, binarized rules D and E have level 0, C has level 3, B has level 2, and A has level 1.

Within each bin, only the β highest-weight items are kept, where $\beta \in (1, 5, 10, 25, 50)$ is a parameter that we vary during our experiments. Ties are broken arbitrarily. Additionally, we maintain a beam within each bin, and an edge is pruned if its score is not within a factor of 10^{-5} of the highest-scoring edge in the bin. Pruning takes place when the edge is added and then again at the end of each

[4]It is available from `http://www.cs.rochester.edu/~post/`.

span in the CKY algorithm (but before applying unary rules).

In order to binarize TSG subtrees, we follow Bod (2001) in first flattening each subtree to a depth-one PCFG rule that shares the subtree's root nonterminal and leaves, as depicted in Figure 7. Afterward, this transformation is reversed to produce the parse tree for scoring. If multiple TSG subtrees have identical mappings, we take only the most probable one. Table 2 shows how grammar size is affected by binarization scheme.

We note two differences in our work that explain the large difference between the scores reported for the "minimal subset" grammar in Bod (2001) and here. First, we did not implement the smoothed "mismatch parsing", which introduces new subtrees into the grammar at parsing time by allowing lexical leaves of subtrees to act as wildcards. This technique reportedly makes a large difference in parsing scores (Bod, 2009). Second, we approximate the most probable parse with the single most probable derivation instead of the top 1,000 derivations, which Bod also reports as having a large impact (Bod, 2003, §4.2).

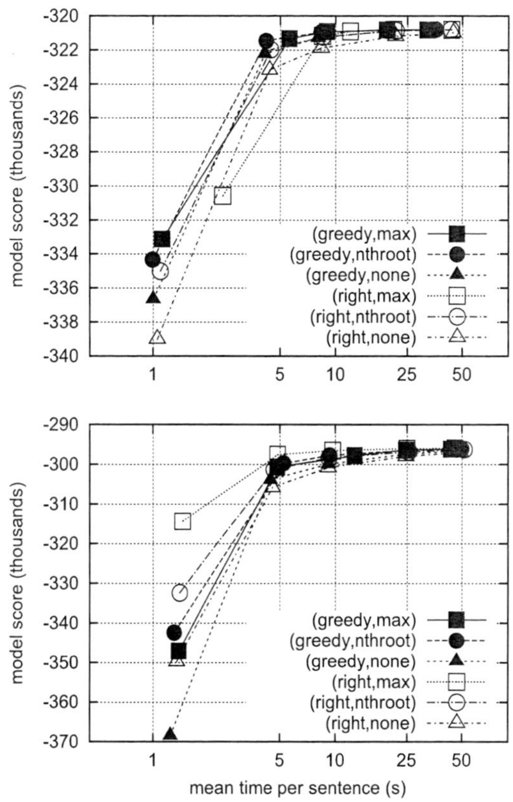

Figure 8: Time vs. model score for the PCFG (top) and the sampled grammar (bottom). Note that the y-axis range differs between plots.

4 Results

Figure 8 displays search time vs. model score for the PCFG and the sampled grammar. Weight pushing has a significant impact on search efficiency, particularly for the larger sampled grammar. The spinal and minimal graphs are similar to the PCFG and sampled graphs, respectively, which suggests that the technique is more effective for the larger grammars.

For parsing, we are ultimately interested in accuracy as measured by F_1 score.[5] Figure 9 displays graphs of time vs. accuracy for parses with each of the grammars, alongside the numerical scores used to generate them. We begin by noting that the improved search efficiency from Figure 8 carries over to the time vs. accuracy curves for the PCFG and sampled grammars, as we expect. Once again, we note that the difference is less pronounced for the two smaller grammars than for the two larger ones.

4.1 Model score vs. accuracy

The tables in Figure 9 show that parser accuracy is not always a monotonic function of time; some of the runs exhibited peak performance as early as at a bin size of $\beta = 10$, and then saw drops in scores when given more time. We examined a number of instances where the F_1 score for a sentence was lower at a higher bin setting, and found that they can be explained as modeling (as opposed to search) errors. With the PCFG, these errors were standard parser difficulties, such as PP attachment, which require more context to resolve. TSG subtrees, which have more context, are able to correct some of these issues, but introduce a different set of problems. In many situations, larger bin settings permitted erroneous analyses to remain in the chart, which later led to the parser's discovery of a large TSG fragment. Because these fragments often explain a significant portion of the sentence more cheaply than multiple smaller rules multiplied together, the parser prefers them. More often than not, they are useful, but sometimes they are overfit to the training data, and result in an incorrect analysis despite a higher model score.

Interestingly, these dips occur most frequently for the heuristically extracted TSGs (four of six

[5] $F_1 = \frac{2 \cdot P \cdot R}{P+R}$, where P is precision and R recall.

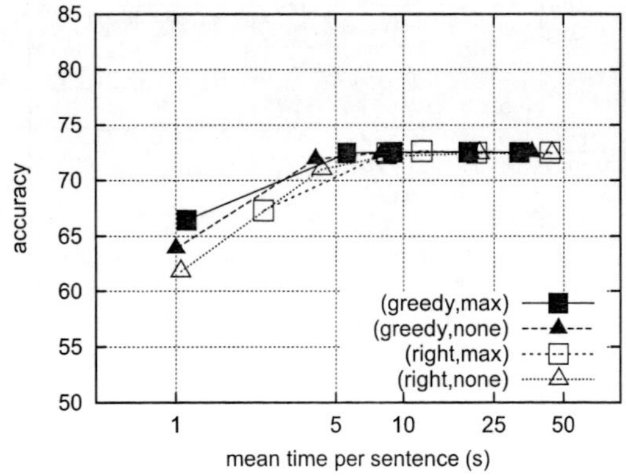

PCFG

run	1	5	10	25	50
■ (g,m)	66.44	72.45	72.54	72.54	72.51
● (g,n)	65.44	72.21	72.47	72.45	72.47
▲ (g,-)	63.91	71.91	72.48	72.51	72.51
□ (r,m)	67.30	72.45	72.61	72.47	72.49
○ (r,n)	64.09	71.78	72.33	72.45	72.47
△ (r,-)	61.82	71.00	72.18	72.42	72.41

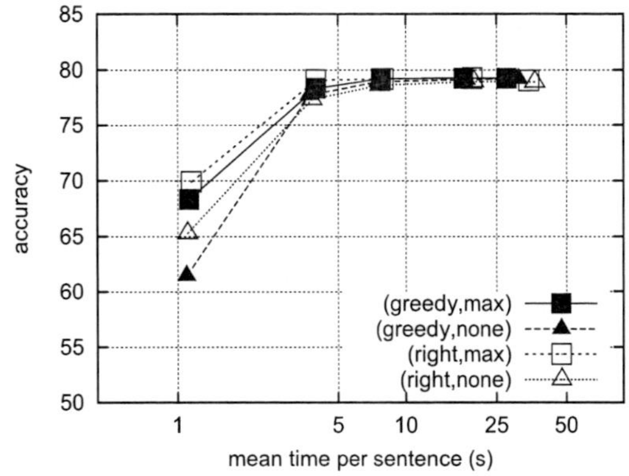

spinal

run	1	5	10	25	50
■ (g,m)	68.33	78.35	79.21	79.25	79.24
● (g,n)	64.67	78.46	79.04	79.07	79.09
▲ (g,-)	61.44	77.73	78.94	79.11	79.20
□ (r,m)	69.92	79.07	79.18	79.25	79.05
○ (r,n)	67.76	78.46	79.07	79.04	79.04
△ (r,-)	65.27	77.34	78.64	78.94	78.90

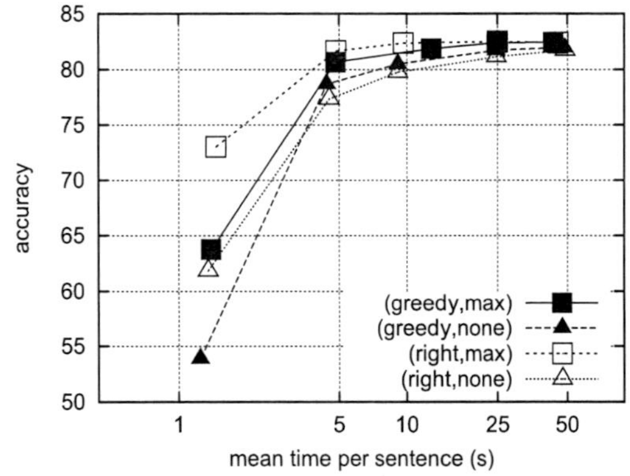

sampled

run	1	5	10	25	50
■ (g,m)	63.75	80.65	81.86	82.40	82.41
● (g,n)	61.87	79.88	81.35	82.10	82.17
▲ (g,-)	53.88	78.68	80.48	81.72	81.98
□ (r,m)	72.98	81.66	82.37	82.49	82.40
○ (r,n)	65.53	79.01	80.81	81.91	82.13
△ (r,-)	61.82	77.33	79.72	81.13	81.70

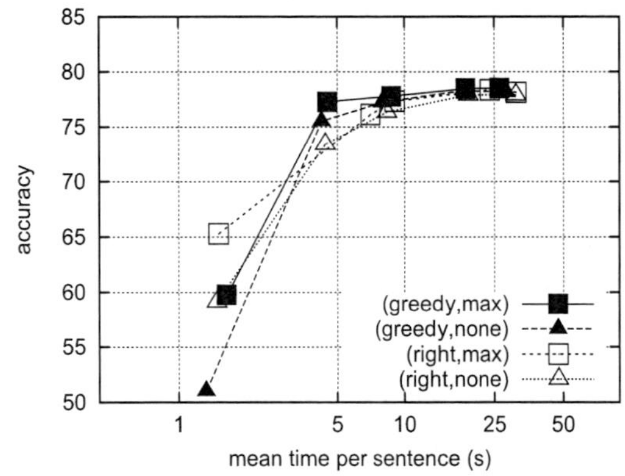

minimal

run	1	5	10	25	50
■ (g,m)	59.75	77.28	77.77	78.47	78.52
● (g,n)	57.54	77.12	77.82	78.35	78.36
▲ (g,-)	51.00	75.52	77.21	78.30	78.13
□ (r,m)	65.29	76.14	77.33	78.34	78.13
○ (r,n)	61.63	75.08	76.80	77.97	78.31
△ (r,-)	59.10	73.42	76.34	77.88	77.91

Figure 9: Plots of parsing time vs. accuracy for each of the grammars. Each plot contains four sets of five points ($\beta \in (1, 5, 10, 25, 50)$), varying the binarization strategy (right (r) or greedy (g)) and the weight pushing technique (maximal (m) or none (-)). The tables also include data from nthroot (n) pushing.

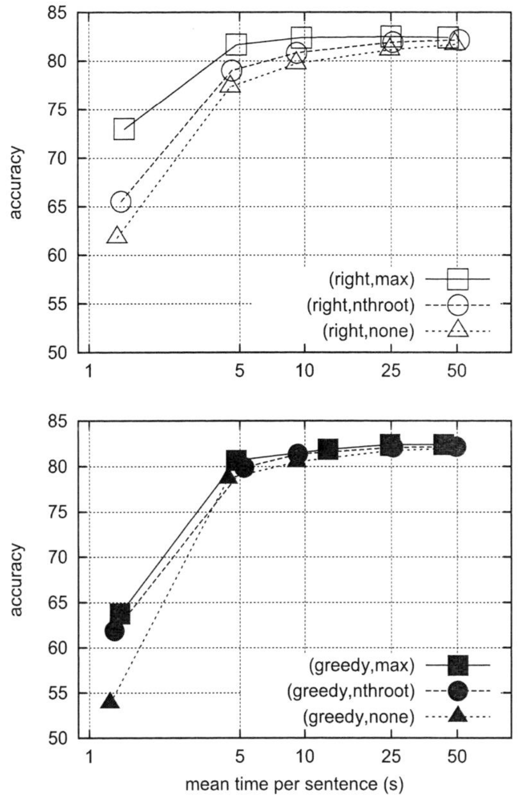

Figure 10: Time vs. accuracy (F_1) for the sampled grammar, broken down by binarization (right on top, greedy on bottom).

runs for the spinal grammar, and two for the minimal grammar) and for the PCFG (four), and least often for the model-based sampled grammar (just once). This may suggest that rules selected by our sampling procedure are less prone to overfitting on the training data.

4.2 Pushing

Figure 10 compares the nthroot and maximal pushing techniques for both binarizations of the sampled grammar. We can see from this figure that there is little difference between the two techniques for the greedy binarization and a large difference for the right binarization. Our original motivation in developing nthroot pushing came as a result of analysis of certain sentences where maximal pushing and greedy binarization resulted in the parser producing a lower model score than with right binarization with no pushing. One such example was binarized fragment [A] from Figure 1; when parsing a particular sentence in the development set, the correct analysis required the rule from Figure 7, but greedy binarization and maximal pushing resulted in this piece getting pruned early in the search procedure. This pruning happened because maximal pushing allowed too much weight to shift down for binarized pieces of competing analyses relative to the correct analysis. Using nthroot pushing solved the search problem in that instance, but in the aggregate it does not appear to be helpful in improving parser efficiency as much as maximal pushing. This demonstrates some of the subtle interactions between binarization and weight pushing when inexact pruning heuristics are applied.

4.3 Binarization

Song et al. (2008, Table 4) showed that CKY parsing efficiency is not a monotonic function of the number of constituents produced; that is, enumerating fewer edges in the dynamic programming chart does not always correspond with shorter run times. We see here that efficiency does not always perfectly correlate with grammar size, either. For all but the PCFG, right binarization improves upon greedy binarization, regardless of the pushing technique, despite the fact that the right-binarized grammars are always larger than the greedily-binarized ones.

Weight pushing and greedy binarization both increase parsing efficiency, and the graphs in Figures 8 and 9 suggest that they are somewhat complementary. We also investigated left binarization, but discontinued that exploration because the results were nearly identical to that of right binarization. Another popular binarization approach is head-outward binarization. Based on the analysis above, we suspect that its performance will fall somewhere among the binarizations presented here, and that pushing will improve it as well. We hope to investigate this in future work.

5 Summary

Weight pushing increases parser efficiency, especially for large grammars. Most notably, it improves parser efficiency for the Gibbs-sampled tree substitution grammar of Post and Gildea (2009).

We believe this approach could alo benefit syntax-based machine translation. Zhang et al. (2006) introduced a synchronous binarization technique that improved decoding efficiency and accuracy by ensuring that rule binarization avoided gaps on both the source and target sides (for rules where this was possible). Their binarization was designed to share binarized pieces among rules, but their approach to distributing weight was the default (nondiffused) case found in this paper to be least efficient: The entire weight of the original rule is placed at the top binarized rule and all internal rules are assigned a probability of 1.0.

Finally, we note that the weight pushing algorithm described in this paper began with a PCFG and ensured that the tree distribution was not changed. However, weight pushing need not be limited to a probabilistic interpretation, but could be used to spread weights for grammars with discriminatively trained features as well, with necessary adjustments to deal with positively and negatively weighted rules.

Acknowledgments We thank the anonymous reviewers for their helpful comments. This work was supported by NSF grants IIS-0546554 and ITR-0428020.

References

Rens Bod. 2001. What is the minimal set of fragments that achieves maximal parse accuracy? In *Proceedings of the 39th Annual Conference of the Association for Computational Linguistics (ACL-01)*, Toulouse, France.

Rens Bod. 2003. Do all fragments count? *Natural Language Engineering*, 9(4):307–323.

Rens Bod. 2009. Personal communication.

Eugene Charniak. 2000. A maximum-entropy-inspired parser. In *Proceedings of the 2000 Meeting of the North American chapter of the Association for Computational Linguistics (NAACL-00)*, Seattle, Washington.

David Chiang. 2000. Statistical parsing with an automatically-extracted tree adjoining grammar. In *Proceedings of the 38th Annual Conference of the Association for Computational Linguistics (ACL-00)*, Hong Kong.

Michael John Collins. 1999. *Head-driven Statistical Models for Natural Language Parsing*. Ph.D. thesis, University of Pennsylvania, Philadelphia.

John DeNero, Mohit Bansal, Adam Pauls, and Dan Klein. 2009. Efficient parsing for transducer grammars. In *Proceedings of the 2009 Meeting of the North American chapter of the Association for Computational Linguistics (NAACL-09)*, Boulder, Colorado.

Liang Huang. 2007. Binarization, synchronous binarization, and target-side binarization. In *North American chapter of the Association for Computational Linguistics Workshop on Syntax and Structure in Statistical Translation (NAACL-SSST-07)*, Rochester, NY.

Dan Klein and Christopher D. Manning. 2003. A* parsing: Fast exact Viterbi parse selection. In *Proceedings of the 2003 Meeting of the North American chapter of the Association for Computational Linguistics (NAACL-03)*, Edmonton, Alberta.

Mehryar Mohri and Michael Riley. 2001. A weight pushing algorithm for large vocabulary speech recognition. In *European Conference on Speech Communication and Technology*, pages 1603–1606.

Mehryar Mohri. 1997. Finite-state transducers in language and speech processing. *Computational Linguistics*, 23(2):269–311.

Matt Post and Daniel Gildea. 2009. Bayesian learning of a tree substitution grammar. In *Proceedings of the 47th Annual Meeting of the Association for Computational Linguistics (ACL-09)*, Suntec, Singapore.

Helmut Schmid. 2004. Efficient parsing of highly ambiguous context-free grammars with bit vectors. In *Proceedings of the 20th International Conference on Computational Linguistics (COLING-04)*, Geneva, Switzerland.

Xinying Song, Shilin Ding, and Chin-Yew Lin. 2008. Better binarization for the CKY parsing. In *2008 Conference on Empirical Methods in Natural Language Processing (EMNLP-08)*, Honolulu, Hawaii.

Hao Zhang, Liang Huang, Daniel Gildea, and Kevin Knight. 2006. Synchronous binarization for machine translation. In *Proceedings of the 2006 Meeting of the North American chapter of the Association for Computational Linguistics (NAACL-06)*, New York, NY.

Co-Parsing with Competitive Models

Lidia Khmylko
Natural Language Systems Group
University of Hamburg, Germany
khmylko@informatik.uni-hamburg.de

Kilian A. Foth
smartSpeed GmbH & Co. KG
Hamburg, Germany
kilian.foth@smartspeed.com

Wolfgang Menzel
Natural Language Systems Group
University of Hamburg, Germany
menzel@informatik.uni-hamburg.de

Abstract

We present an asymmetric approach to a run-time combination of two parsers where one component serves as a predictor to the other one. Predictions are integrated by means of weighted constraints and therefore are subject to preferential decisions. Previously, the same architecture has been successfully used with predictors providing partial or inferior information about the parsing problem. It has now been applied to a situation where the predictor produces exactly the same type of information at a fully competitive quality level. Results show that the combined system outperforms its individual components, even though their performance in isolation is already fairly high.

1 Introduction

Machine learning techniques for automatically acquiring processing models from a data collection and traditional methods of eliciting linguistic knowledge from human experts are usually considered as two alternative roadmaps towards natural language processing solutions. Since the resulting components exhibit quite different performance characteristics with respect to coverage, robustness and output quality, they might be able to provide some kind of complementary information, which could even lead to a notable degree of synergy between them when combined within a single system solution.

For the task of dependency parsing, the high potential for such a synergy has indeed been demonstrated already (e.g. Zeman and Žabokrtský (2005), Foth and Menzel (2006)).

A popular approach for combining alternative decision procedures is voting (Zeman and Žabokrtský, 2005). It makes use of a symmetric architecture, where a meta component chooses from among the available candidate hypotheses by means of a (weighted) voting scheme. Such an approach not only requires the target structures of all components to be of the same kind, but in case of complex structures like parse trees also requires sophisticated decision procedures which are able to select the optimal hypotheses with respect to additional global constraints (e.g. the tree property). Since this optimization problem has to be solved by the individual parser anyhow, an asymmetric architecture suggests itself as an alternative.

In asymmetric architectures, a master component, i.e. a full fledged parser, is solely in charge of deciding on the target structure, whilst the others (so called helper or predictor components) provide additional evidence which is integrated into the global decision by suitable means. Such a scheme has been extensively investigated for the Weighted Constraint Dependency Grammar, WCDG (Foth, 2006). External evidence from the predictor components is integrated by means of constraints, which check for compatibility between a local structure and a prediction, and penalize this hypothesis in case of a conflict. So far, however, all the additional information sources which have been considered in this research differed considerably from the master component: They either focused on particular aspects of the parsing problem (e.g. POS tagging, chunking, PP attachment), or used a simplified scheme for structural annotation (e.g. projective instead of non-projective trees).

This paper takes one step further by investigating the same architecture under the additional condition that (1) the helper component provides the

Proceedings of the 11th International Conference on Parsing Technologies (IWPT), pages 99–107,
Paris, October 2009.

very same kind of target structure as the master, and (2) the quality levels of each of the components in isolation are considered.

As a helper component MSTParser (McDonald, 2006), a state-of-the-art dependency parser for non-projective structures based on a discriminative learning paradigm, is considered. The accuracy of MSTParser differs insignificatly from that of WCDG with all the previously used helper components active.

Section two introduces WCDG with a special emphasis on the soft integration of external evidence while section three describes MSTParser which is used as a new predictor component. Since parsing results for these systems have been reported in quite different experimental settings we first evaluate them under comparable conditions and provide the results of using MSTParser as a guiding predictor for WCDG in section four and discuss whether the expected synergies have really materialized. Section five concentrates on a comparative error analysis.

2 WCDG

The formalism of a Constraint Dependency Grammar was first introduced by Maruyama (1990) and suggests modeling natural language with the help of constraints. Schröder (2002) has extended the approach to Weighted Constraint Dependency Grammar, WCDG, where weights are used to further disambiguate between competing structural alternatives. A WCDG models natural language as labeled dependency trees and is entirely declarative. It has no derivation rules — instead, constraints license well-formed tree structures. The reference implementation of WCDG for the German language used for the experiments described below contains about $1,000$ manually compiled constraints.[1]

Every constraint of the WCDG carries a *weight*, also referred to as a *penalty*, in the interval from zero to one, a lower value of the weight reflects its greater importance. Constraints having zero weights are referred to as *hard* and are used for prohibitive rules. Constraints with a weight greater than zero, also called *defeasible*, may express universal principles or vague preferences for language phenomena.

Attempts have been made to compute the weights of a WCDG automatically by observing which weight vectors perform best on a given corpus, but the computations did not bring any significant improvements to the manually assigned scored (Schröder et al., 2001). Empirically, the absolute values of defeasible constraints usually do not matter greatly as long as the relative importance of the rules remains preserved so that typical constructions are preferred, but seldom variations are also allowed. Thus, the values of weights of the WCDG constraints have to be determined by the grammar writer experimentally.

If a set of dependency edges in a parse found by the system violates any of the constraints, it is registered as a *constraint violation* between the structure and the rules of the language. The *score* of an analysis is the product of all the weights for constraint violations occurring in the structure. It becomes possible to differentiate between the quality of different parse results: the analysis with a higher score is considered preferable. Although, under these conditions, an analysis having only a few grave conflicts may be preferred by the system against another one with a great number of smaller constraint violations, but it ensures that an analysis which violates any of the hard constraints always receives the lowest possible score.

The parsing problem is being treated in the WCDG system as a Constraint Satisfaction Problem. While a complete search is intractable for such a problem, *transformation-based solution methods* provide a reliable heuristic alternative. Starting with an initial guess about the optimal tree, changes of labels, subordinations, or lexical variants are applied, with constraint violations used as a control mechanism guiding the transformation process (Foth et al., 2000).

A transformation-based search cannot guarantee to find the best solution to the constraint satisfaction problem. Compared to the resource requirements of a complete search, however, it is not only more efficient, but can also be interrupted at any time. Even if interrupted, it will always return an analysis, together with a list of constraint violations it was not able to remove. The algorithm terminates on its own if no violated constraints with a weight above a predefined threshold remain. Alternatively, a timeout condition can be imposed.

The same kind of constraints that describe grammar rules, can also be used as an interface

[1] Freely available from `http://nats-www.informatik.uni-hamburg.de/view/CDG/DownloadPage`

to external predictor components. Thus, the formalism turned out to be flexible enough to incorporate other sources of knowledge into the decision process on the optimal structural interpretation. Foth and Menzel (2006) have reported about five additional statistical components that have been successfully integrated into WCDG: POS tagger, chunker, supertagger, PP attacher and a shift-reduce oracle parser. They have also shown that the accuracy improves if multiple components interact and consistent predictions no longer can be guaranteed. Even thought previously integrated predictor components have an accuracy that is mostly — with the exception of the tagger — below that of the parser itself, WCDG not only avoids error propagation successfully, it also improves its results consistently with each component added.

3 MSTParser

MSTParser (McDonald, 2006) is a state-of-the-art language independent data-driven parser. It processes the input in two separate stages. In the first, the dependency structure is determined, labeling is applied to it successively in the second. The reasons of its efficiency lie in the successful combination of discriminative learning with graph-based solution methods for the parsing problem.

In this edge-factored graph-based model, each edge of the dependency graph is assigned a real-valued score by its linear model. The score of the graph is defined as the sum of its edge scores.

If a scoring function for edges is known, the parsing problem becomes equivalent to finding the highest scoring directed spanning tree in the complete graph over the given sentence, and the correct parse can be obtained by searching the space of valid dependency graphs for a tree with a maximum score.

This formalism allows to find efficient solutions for both projective and non-projective trees. When only features over single edges are taken into account, the complexity falls to $O(n^2)$ (McDonald et al., 2005).

Not only a single edge, but also adjacent edges may be included into the scoring function. As a result, intractability problems arise for the non-projective algorithm, but an efficient approximate algorithm based on exhaustive search is provided for this case (McDonald et al., 2006). This algorithm was also used for our experiments.[2]

The parsing model of MSTParser has the advantage that it can be trained globally and eventually be applied with an exact inference algorithm. On the other hand, the parser has only limited access to the history of parsing decisions. To avoid complexity problems, the scores (and the feature representations) are restricted to a single edge or adjacent edges. Outsourcing labeling into a separate stage comes at the price of not being able to combine knowledge about the label and the structure it is attached to. Such combined evidence, however, might be helpful for some disambiguation problems.

4 Guiding WCDG by Predictions of MSTParser

MSTParser predictions are integrated into the decision procedure of WCDG by means of two additional constraints, which monitor each dependency hypothesis for being in accord with the prediction and penalize it if a mismatch has been found. One of the constraints checks the attachment point being the same, while the other takes care of the dependency label.

To properly adjust the weights of these constraints, it has to be determined how valuable the information of the predictor is relative to the information already present in the system. This gradation is needed to establish a balance between the influence of the grammar and the predictor. According to the scoring principles of WCDG, a low weight strongly deprecates all deviations from the prediction, thus forcing the system to follow them almost without exception. Higher weights, on the other hand, enable the grammar to override a prediction. This, however, also means that predictions have less guiding effect of the transformation process. Typically for WCDG, the best suitable weights have to be tuned on development data.

To determine the best constraint weights the WCDG grammar has been extended with three additional constraints similar to those used for the shift-reduce predictor in the previous experiments (Foth, 2006). Two of them advise WCDG on the structural information available from the MSTParser result and one fetches the edge label predicted.

As a result of these experiments, the optimum

[2]MSTParser is freely available from `http://sourceforge.net/projects/mstparser`

weight for the attachment predictions has been adjusted to 0.75. Compared to a weight of 0.9 for the shift-reduce parser, this is a rather strong influence, which also reflects the differences in the reliability of these two information sources. With a weight of 0.9, the integration of the label predictions is considerably weaker, which is consistent with their lower degree of accuracy.

Evaluation

The most common general measures for the quality of dependency trees are *structural accuracy* that points out the percentage of words correctly attached to their head word, and *labeled accuracy* which is the ratio of the correctly attached words which also have the correct label. Still, it is difficult to directly compare the results reported for different parsers, as the evaluation results are influenced by the data used during the experiment, the domain of the data, and different annotation guidelines. Moreover, the particular kind of POS information might be relevant, which either can be obtained from the manual annotations or be provided by a real tagger. Even such a condition as the treatment of punctuation has not yet become a standard. Following the evaluation procedure in the CoNLL-X shared task (Buchholz and Marsi, 2006), we will not include punctuation into the performance measures, as was done in previous WCDG experiments (Foth and Menzel, 2006). The source of POS tagging information will need to be specified in each individual case.

All the evaluations were performed on a thousand sentences ($18,602$ – $19,601$) from the NEGRA treebank, the same data set that was previously used in the performance evaluations of WCDG, e.g. in (Foth, 2006). The NEGRA treebank is a collection of newspaper articles; in the original, it stores phrase structure annotations. These have been automatically translated into dependency trees and then manually corrected to bring them in accord with the annotation guidelines of WCDG. The major difference consists in a different treatment of non-projectivity, where WCDG only allows non-projectivity in the attachment of verbal arguments, relative clauses and coordinations, i.e., the cases where it helps to decrease ambiguity. Furthermore, corrections were applied when the annotations of NEGRA itself turned out to be inconsistent (usually in connection with co-ordinated or elliptical structures, adverbs and subclauses).

Unfortunately, these manually corrected data were only available for a small part ($3,000$ sentences) of the NEGRA corpus, which is not sufficient for training MSTParser on WCDG-conforming tree structures. Previous evaluations of the MSTParser have used much larger training sets. E.g., during the CoNLL-X shared task 39,216 sentences from the TIGER Treebank (Brants et al., 2002) were used.

Therefore, we used $20,000$ sentences from the online archive of `www.heise.de` as an alternative training set. They have been manually annotated according to the WCDG guidelines (and are referred to `heiseticker` in the following)[3]. The texts in this corpus are all from roughly the same domain as in NEGRA, and although very many technical terms and proper nouns are used, the sentences have only a slightly longer mean length compared to the NEGRA corpus.

Using POS tags from the gold annotations, MSTParser achieves 90.5% structural and 87.5% labeled accuracy on the aforementioned NEGRA test set (Table 1). Even a model trained on the inconsistent NEGRA data excluding the test set reaches state-of-the-art 90.5 and 87.3% for structural and labeled accuracy respectively, despite the obvious mismatch between training and test data. This performance is almost the same as the $90.4\%/87.3\%$ reported on the TIGER data during the CoNLL-X 2006 shared task.

Experiment	structural	labeled
MSTParser-h	90.5	87.5
MSTParser-N	90.5	87.3
MSTParser(CoNLL-X)	90.4	87.3
WCDG + MST	92.9	91.3
WCDG + MST + 5P	93.3	92.0

Table 1: Structural/labeled accuracy results with POS tagging from the gold standard. WCDG — no statistical enhancements used. MSTParser-h — MSTParser trained on the `heiseticker`. MSTParser-N — MSTParser trained on NEGRA. 5P — with all five statistical predictors of WCDG.

As is to be expected, if a real POS tagger is used in the experiments with MSTParser, the accuracy is reduced quite expectedly by approximately one

[3]The `heiseticker` dependency treebank is under preparation and will be available soon.

percent to 89.5%/86.0% (Table 2 (B)). All the results obtained with a real POS tagger are summarized in Table 2. For comparison, under the same evaluation conditions, the performance of WCDG with different predictors is summarized in Table 2 (A).

	Experiment	structural	labeled
(A)	**WCDG**	**88.0**	**86.0**
	CP	88.6	86.5
	PP	89.4	87.3
	ST	90.8	89.2
	SR	90.0	88.4
	PP+SR	90.2	88.6
	ST+SR	91.0	89.4
	ST+PP	90.8	89.2
	5P	**91.3**	**90.0**
(B)	**MSTParser**	**89.5**	**86.0**
(C)	**WCDG + MST**	**92.0**	**90.5**
	PP	92.0	90.6
	CP	92.1	90.6
	SR	92.2	90.6
	ST	92.4	90.9
	CP+SR	92.3	90.7
	CP+ST	92.6	91.0
	ST+SR	92.9	91.4
	PP+CP+ST	92.6	91.1
	PP+ST+SR	92.8	91.3
	CP+ST+SR	92.9	91.4
	5P	**92.9**	**91.4**

Table 2: Structural/labeled accuracy results with a real POS tagger. (A) WCDG experiments with different statistical enhancements (B) MSTParser experiment with a real POS tagger. (C) Combined experiments of WCDG and MSTParser with other statistical enhancements of WCDG. CP — chunker, ST — supertagger, PP — prepositional attacher, SR — shift-reduce oracle parser, 5P — POS + CP + PP + ST + SR.

The combined experiments in which MSTParser was used as a predictor for WCDG have achieved higher accuracy than each of the combined components in isolation: the structural accuracy rises to 92.0% while the labeled accuracy also gets over the 90%-boundary (WCDG + MST experiment in Table 2 (C)) .

Finally, the MSTParser predictor was evaluated in combination with the other predictors available for WCDG. The results of the experiments are shown in Table 2 (C). Every combination of MSTParser with other predictors (first four experiments) improves the accuracy. The increase is highest (0.4%) for the combination with the supertagger. This confirms earlier experiments with WCDG, in which the supertagger also contributed the largest gains.

The experimental results again confirm that WCDG is a reliable platform for information integration. Although the use of multiple predictors does not lead to an accumulation of the individual improvements, the performance of predictor combinations is always higher that using them separately. A maximum performance of 92.9%/91.4% is reached with all the six available predictors active. For comparison, the same experiment with POS tags from the gold standard has achieved even better results of 93.3%/92.0% (Table 1).

Unfortunately, the PP attacher brings accuracy reductions when it is working parallel to the shift-reduce predictor (experiment PP + CP + SR in Table 2 (C)). This effect has already been observed in the experiments that combined the two alone (experiment PP + SR in Table 2 (A)). When MST was combined with the PP attacher (experiment PP in Table 2 (C)), the increase of the performance was also below a tenth of a percent. The possible reasons why the use of an additional information source does not improve the performance in this case may be the disadvantages of the PP attacher compared to a full parser.

5 Error Analysis

A very useful property of WCDG is that it not only can be used as a parser, but also as a diagnostic tool for dependency structures. Applied to a given dependency tree, any constraint violation reported by the constraint solver indicates an inconsistency between the structure and the WCDG constraint grammar.

Among the most frequent hard constraint violations found in the MSTParser results are double subjects, double objects and direct objects in passive, projectivity violations, conjunctions without a clause as well as subordinate clause without conjunction.

These findings are in line with the analysis of

McDonald and Nivre (2007). For example, the errors in distinguishing noun complements of the verb may be due to the fact that MSTParser is more precise for longer dependency arcs and has no access to the parsing history.

In absolute figures, MSTParser commits 1509 attachment errors of which 902 are corrected by WCDG. On the other hand, WCDG adds another 542 errors of its own, so that the final result still contains 1149 errors.

For most labels, accuracy of the predictor combination is higher than in each of the parsers alone. A particularly large gain has been observed for coordinated elements (KON and CJ), subordinate (NEB) and relative (REL) clauses, indirect accusative objects (OBJA), genitive modifiers (GMOD) and apposition (APP). Table 3) summarizes the values of structural precision, the ratio of the number of correct attachment of a given label to the number of all the predictions for that label made by the parser, and label recall, the ratio between the number of correct labeling decisions and desired labeling.

In this respect, the increase in the structural precision of the PP attachment seems worth mentioning. MSTParser attaches 79.3% of PPs correctly on the used test set. Although MSTParser does not use any special PP-attachment resolution mechanisms, it is comparable with the result of WCDG combined with the PP attacher that achieves 78.7% structural precision for PP edges.

If MSTParser is trained on NEGRA excluding the test set — the rest of NEGRA lacking consistence mentioned above — it performs even better, attaching 80.4% of PP-s correctly. Thus, MSTParser as a statistical parser trained on a full corpus becomes a strong competitor for a PP attacher that has been trained on restricted four-tuples input.

As for the errors in the MSTParser output that are most often corrected in the hybrid experiment, this happens for both the structural precision and label recall of most verb complements, such as direct and indirect objects, or clausal objects as well as for subordinate and relative clauses for such subordinate clauses.

It even comes to one case in which the synergy took place in spite of the incorrect predictions. Although MSTParser has predicted possessive modifiers more seldom than WCDG alone (the label recall of MSTParser for possessive modification was over 5% below that of WCDG) its structural precision and label recall in the combined experiment are by around 6% greater than WCDG result.

	(1)		(2)		(3)	
Label	*p*	*r*	*p*	*r*	*p*	*r*
DET	98.4	99.3	98.7	99.5	99.3	99.5
PN	97.4	97.4	98.0	98.0	98.0	98.7
PP	67.6	98.1	78.3	97.4	80.1	98.5
ADV	76.6	94.7	79.4	95.4	82.2	97.2
SUBJ	94.0	90.9	91.3	86.4	95.8	94.0
ATTR	95.2	95.8	97.7	98.2	98.3	98.4
S	89.2	90.1	89.3	90.5	90.5	91.0
AUX	95.9	94.2	98.6	97.8	98.7	97.6
OBJA	87.9	83.9	83.8	72.5	92.5	88.7
APP	85.1	88.5	88.9	90.9	90.9	94.0
KON	78.9	88.1	78.9	88.3	86.0	89.2
CJ	85.6	86.5	90.9	91.4	93.0	93.5
GMOD	90.7	90.7	89.0	85.3	96.3	95.8
KONJ	88.6	91.9	91.9	95.7	95.1	95.7
PRED	90.3	75.0	85.4	60.4	91.7	76.4
NEB	68.9	82.8	73.0	66.4	79.5	90.2
REL	64.8	77.9	59.0	77.0	68.9	86.9

Table 3: Per label structural precision (*p*, %) and label recal (*r*, %) in comparison for the experiments with the real POS tagger (1) WCDG, (2) MSTParser, (3) WCDG combined with MSTParser

Cases in which WCDG performs worse with the predictor than its predictor alone can hardly be found. Still, one may observe many cases in which the predictor has a negative influence on the performance of WCDG, such as for different kinds of objects (indirect objects, object clauses and infinitive objects) and parenthetic matrix clauses. For all, the result of MSTParser was below that of the baseline WCDG with only the POS tagger active. Same can be said about the labeled accuracy for split verb prefixes and nominal time expressions. This worsening effect can be attributed to the lower values of the WCDG constraints for the corresponding labels and edges than for the MSTParser predictor. Thus, the search could not find a decision scoring better than that when the MSTParser prediction has been followed.

Around 15% of the sentences in the test set are

not projective. The accuracy of MSTParser on the projective sentences of the test set is higher than that on the non-projective sentences by more than 3 percent (Table 4), although these values cannot be compared directly as the mean length of non-projective sentences is longer (25.0 vs. 15.3 words).

Experiment	Non-proj.	Proj.
MSTParser (POS)	88.2	91.7
WCDG (POS)	87.2	90.2
WCDG (POS + SR)	88.7	92.2
WCDG (POS + MST)	91.3	93.6

Table 4: Structural accuracy, (%), for different parsing runs for non-projective vs. projective sentences.

MSTParser generally tends to find many more non-projective edges than the data has, while the precision remains restricted. The number of non-projective edges was determined by counting how often an edge crosses some other edge. Thus, if a non-projective edge crossed three other edges the number of non-projective edges equals three. For MSTParser experiments with a real POS tagger (MSTParser POS-experiment in Table 5), the non-projective edge recall, the ratio of the non-projective edges found in the experiment to the corresponding value in the gold standard, is at 23% and non-projective edge precision, the ratio of the correctly found non-projective edges to all non-projective edges found, is also only 36% (second column in Table 5).

	Edges		Sentences	
Experiment	*r*	*p*	*r*	*p*
MSTParser (POS)	23	36	35	44
WCDG (POS)	37	53	51	63
WCDG (POS + SR)	41	47	57	55
WCDG (POS + MST)	48	53	61	61

Table 5: Recall (*r*, %) and precision (*p*, %) of the non-projective edges and sentences for different parsing runs.

Precision and recall of non-projective sentences is a less rigid measure. If at least one edge-crossing is correctly identified in a non-projective sentence, it is added to the correctly identified non-projective sentences, even if the identified edge-crossing is not the one annotated in the gold standard and the ratios are calculated respectively (right column of Table 5). Under these relaxed conditions, MSTParser correctly identifies slightly less than a half of the non-projective sentences and over a third of non-projective edges. In fact, WCDG under the same conditions (WCDG POS-experiment in Table 5) has a non-projective sentence precision of 63% and a non-projective edge precision of 53%. Still, WCDG misses a considerable amount of non-projectivities. More importantly, as the present shift-reduce predictor has not been designed for non-projective parsing, its inclusion reduces the non-projective sentence and edge precision of WCDG — to 55% and 47% respectively — WCDG (POS+SR) in Table 5.

The expected benefits for the non-projective sentences have not yet been observed to the full extent. The precision of the combined system to find non-projective sentences and edges remained limited by the performance that WCDG was able to achieve alone (WCDG (POS+MST) in Table 5). While MSTParser in many cases predicts non-projectivity correctly WCDG is seldom capable of accepting this external evidence. On the contrary, WCDG often accepts an incorrect projective solution of the predictor instead of relying on its own cues. In its interaction with external predictors WCDG should typically decide about the alternatives.

6 Related Work

So far, approaches to hybrid parsing have been mainly based on the idea of a post-hoc selection which can be carried out for either complete parses, or individual constituents and dependency edges, respectively. The selection component itself can be based on heuristics, like a majority vote. Alternatively, a second-level classifier is trained to decide which component to trust under which conditions and therefore the approach is often referred to as classifier stacking.

In a series of experiments, Henderson and Brill (1999) combined three constituency-based parsers by a selection mechanism for either complete parsing results (parser switching) or individual constituents (parse hybridization), using both a heuristic decision rule as well as a naïve Bayesian classifier in each case. Among the heuristics considered were majority votes for constituents and a similarity-based measure for complete trees. Tests on Penn Treebank data showed a clear improvement of the combined results over the best individual parser. Constituent selection outperformed the complete parse selection scheme, and Bayesian selection was slightly superior.

Instead of coupling different data-driven parsers which all provide comparable analyses for complete sentences, Rupp et al. (2000) combined differently elaborated structural descriptions (namely chunks and phrase structure trees) obtained by data-driven components with the output of a HPSG-parser. Driven by the requirements of the particular application (speech-to-speech translation), the focus was not only on parse selection, but also on combining incomplete results. However, no quantitative evaluation of the results has been published.

Zeman and Žabokrtský (2005) applied the selection idea to dependency structures and extended it by using more context features. They combined seven different parsers for Czech, among them also a system based on a manually compiled rule set. Some of the individual parsers had a fairly poor performance, but even a simple voting scheme on single edges contributed a significant improvement while the best results have been obtained for a combination that did not include the worst components. Alternatively the authors experimented with a trained selection component which not only had access to the alternative local parsing results, but also to their structural context. Neither a memory-based approach nor a model based on decision trees did result in further gains.

In two separate experiments, Sagae and Lavie (2006) combined a number of dependency and constituent parsers, respectively. They created a new weighted search space from the results of the individual component parsers using different weighting schemes for the candidates. They then reparsed this search space and found a consistent improvement for the dependency structures, but not for the constituent-based ones.

While all these approaches attempt to integrate the available evidence at parse time, Nivre and McDonald (2008) pursued an alternative architecture, where integration is achieved already at training time. They combined the two state-of-the-art data-driven dependency parsers, MaltParser (Nivre et al., 2006) and MSTParser (McDonald et al., 2006), by integrating the features of each of the classifiers into the parsing model of the other one at training time. Since the two parsers are based on quite different model types (namely a history-based vs. a structure-based one), they exhibit a remarkable complementary behavior (McDonald and Nivre, 2007). Accordingly, significant mutual benefits have been observed. Note, however, that one of the major benefits of MaltParser, its incremental left-to-right processing, is sacrificed under such a combination scheme.

Martins et al. (2008) use stacked learning to overcome the restriction to the single-edge features in both MaltParser and MSTParser. They suggest an architecture with two layers, where the output of a standard parser in the first level provides new features for a parser in the subsequent level. During the training phase, the second parser learns to correct mistakes made by the first one. It allows to involve higher-order predicted edges to simulate non-local features in the second parser. The results are competitive with McDonald and Nivre (2007) while $O(n^2)$ runtime of the spanning tree algorithm is preserved.

7 Conclusion

Integrating MSTParser as a full predictor with WCDG is beneficial for both of them. Since these systems take their decisions based on completely different sources of knowledge, combining both helps avoid many mistakes each of them commits in isolation. Altogether, with a real POS tagger, an accuracy level of 92.9%/91.3% has been reached (the last row in Table 2 (C)), which is higher than what any of the parsers achieved alone. With POS tagging from the gold standard, the accuracy has been at 93.3%/92.0% (the last row in Table 1). To the knowledge of the authors, these accuracy values are also better than any previous parsing results on the NEGRA test set.

WCDG can profit from the combination not only with ancillary predictors for specific parsing subtasks, but also with another full parser. This result was achieved even though the second parser is very similar to WCDG with respect to both the richness and the accuracy of its target structures. The probable reason lies in the considerable difference in the error profiles of both systems as regards specific linguistic phenomena. WCDG was also used as a diagnostic tool for the errors of MSTParser.

Possibly, a higher degree of synergy could be

achieved if a stronger coupling of the components were established by also using the scores of MSTParser as additional information for WCDG, reflecting the intuitive notion of preference or plausibility of the predictions. This could be done for the optimal parse tree alone as well as for the complete hypothesis space. Alternatively, the output of MSTParser can be used as a initial state for the transformation procedure of WCDG. Vice versa, MSTParser could be enriched with additional features based on the output of WCDG, similar to the feature-based integration of data-driven parsers evaluated by Nivre and McDonald (2008).

At the moment, the integration constraints treats all attachment and label predictions as being uniformly reliable. To individualize them with respect to their type or origin could not only make the system sensitive to qualitative differences between predictions (for instance, with respect to different labels). It would also allow the parser to accommodate multiple oracle predictors and to carefully distinguish between typical configurations in which one prediction should be preferred over an alternative one. MaltParser (Nivre et al., 2006) is certainly a good candidate for carrying out such experiments.

References

Sabine Brants, Stefanie Dipper, Silvia Hansen, Wolfgang Lezius, and George Smith. 2002. The TIGER treebank. In: *Proceedings of the First Workshop on Treebanks and Linguistic Theories (TLT)*, pages 24–41.

Sabine Buchholz and Erwin Marsi. 2006. CoNLL-X shared task on multilingual dependency parsing. In *Proc. CoNLL*, pages 149 – 164.

Kilian A. Foth and Wolfgang Menzel. 2006. Hybrid parsing: using probabilistic models as predictors for a symbolic parser. In *Proc. 21st Int. Conference on Computational Linguistics and ACL-44*, pages 321–328.

Kilian A. Foth, Wolfgang Menzel, and Ingo Schröder. 2000. A Transformation-based Parsing Technique with Anytime Properties. In *4th Int. Workshop on Parsing Technologies, IWPT-2000*, pages 89 – 100.

Kilian A. Foth. 2006. *Hybrid Methods of Natural Language Analysis*. Doctoral thesis, Hamburg University.

John C. Henderson and Eric Brill. 1999. Exploiting diversity in natural language processing: Combining parsers. In *Proceedings 4th Conference on Empirical Methods in Natural Language Processing*, pages 187–194.

André F. T. Martins, Dipanjan Das, Noah A. Smith, and Eric P. Xing. 2008. Stacking Dependency Parsers. In *Proc. of the 2008 Conf. on Empirical Methods in Natural Language Processing*, pages 157 – 166.

Hiroshi Maruyama. 1990. Structural disambiguation with constraint propagation. In *Proc. 28th Annual Meeting of the ACL (ACL-90)*, pages 31–38.

Ryan McDonald and Joakim Nivre. 2007. Characterizing the errors of data-driven dependency parsing models. In *Proc. EMNLP-CoNLL*, pages 122 – 131.

Ryan McDonald, Fernando Pereira, Kiril Ribarov, and Jan Hajič. 2005. Non-projective dependency parsing using spanning tree algorithms. In *Proc. HLT/EMNLP*, pages 523 – 530.

Ryan McDonald, Kevin Lerman, and Fernando Pereira. 2006. Multilingual dependency analysis with a two-stage discriminative parser. In *Proc. CoNLL*, pages 216 – 220.

Ryan McDonald. 2006. *Discriminative Learning and Spanning Tree Algorithms for Dependency Parsing*. PhD dissertation, University of Pennsylvania.

Joakim Nivre and Ryan McDonald. 2008. Integrating graph-based and transition-based dependency parsers. In *Proc. ACL-08: HLT*, pages 950–958.

Joakim Nivre, Johan Hall, Jens Nilsson, Gülsen Eryiğit, and Svetoslav Marinov. 2006. Labelled pseudo-projective dependency parsing with support vector machines. In *Proc. CoNLL-2006*, pages 221–225.

Christopher G. Rupp, Jörg Spilker, Martin Klarner, and Karsten L. Worm. 2000. Combining analyses from various parsers. In Wolfgang Wahlster, editor, *Verbmobil: Foundations of Speech-to-Speech Translation*, pages 311–320. Springer-Verlag, Berlin etc.

Kenji Sagae and Alon Lavie. 2006. Parser combinations by reparsing. In *Proc. HLT/NAACL*, pages 129–132.

Ingo Schröder. 2002. *Natural Language Parsing with Graded Constraints*. Ph.D. thesis, Dept. of Computer Science, University of Hamburg, Germany.

Ingo Schröder, Horia F. Pop, Wolfgang Menzel, and Kilian A. Foth. 2001. *Learning grammar weights using genetic algorithms*. In *Proc. Euroconference Recent Advances in Natural Language Processing*, pages 235 – 239.

Daniel Zeman and Zdeněk Žabokrtský. 2005. Improving parsing accuracy by combining diverse dependency parsers. In *Proc. 9th International Workshop on Parsing Technologies (IWPT-2005)*, pages 171–178, Vancouver, B.C.

Capturing Consistency between Intra-clause and Inter-clause Relations in Knowledge-rich Dependency and Case Structure Analysis

Daisuke Kawahara
National Institute of Information and Communications Technology,
3-5 Hikaridai Seika-cho, Soraku-gun,
Kyoto, 619-0289, Japan
dk@nict.go.jp

Sadao Kurohashi
Graduate School of Informatics,
Kyoto University,
Yoshida-Honmachi, Sakyo-ku,
Kyoto, 606-8501, Japan
kuro@i.kyoto-u.ac.jp

Abstract

We present a method for dependency and case structure analysis that captures the consistency between intra-clause relations (i.e., case structures or predicate-argument structures) and inter-clause relations. We assess intra-clause relations on the basis of case frames and inter-clause relations on the basis of transition knowledge between case frames. Both knowledge bases are automatically acquired from a massive amount of parses of a Web corpus. The significance of this study is that the proposed method selects the best dependency and case structure that are consistent within each clause and between clauses. We confirm that this method contributes to the improvement of dependency parsing of Japanese.

1 Introduction

The approaches of dependency parsing basically assess the likelihood of a dependency relation between two words or phrases and subsequently collect all the assessments for these pairs as the dependency parse of the sentence. To improve dependency parsing, it is important to consider as broad a context as possible, rather than a word/phrase pair.

In the recent evaluation workshops (shared tasks) of multilingual dependency parsing (Buchholz and Marsi, 2006; Nivre et al., 2007), transition-based and graph-based methods achieved good performance by incorporating rich context. Transition-based dependency parsers consider the words following the word under consideration as features of machine learning (Kudo and Matsumoto, 2002; Nivre and Scholz, 2004; Sassano, 2004). Graph-based dependency parsers consider sibling and grandparent nodes, i.e., second-order and higher-order features (McDonald and Pereira, 2006; Carreras, 2007; Nakagawa, 2007).

It is desirable to consider a wider-range phrase, clause, or a whole sentence, but it is difficult to judge whether the structure of such a wide-range expression is linguistically correct. One of the reasons for this is the scarcity of the knowledge required to make such a judgment. When we use the Penn Treebank (Marcus et al., 1993), which is one of the largest corpora among the available analyzed corpora, as training data, even bi-lexical dependencies cannot be learned sufficiently (Bikel, 2004). To circumvent such scarcity, for instance, Koo et al. (2008) proposed the use of word classes induced by clustering words in a large raw corpus. They succeeded in improving the accuracy of a higher-order dependency parser.

On the other hand, some researchers have proposed other approaches where linguistic units such as predicate-argument structures (also known as case structures and logical forms) are considered instead of arbitrary nodes such as sibling nodes. To solve the problem of knowledge scarcity, they learned knowledge of such predicate-argument structures from a very large number of automatically analyzed corpora (Abekawa and Okumura, 2006; Kawahara and Kurohashi, 2006b). While Abekawa and Okumura (2006) used only co-occurrence statistics of verbal arguments, Kawahara and Kurohashi (2006b) assessed predicate-argument structures by checking case frames, which are semantic frames that are automatically compiled for each predicate sense from a large raw corpus. These methods outperformed the accuracy of supervised dependency parsers.

In such linguistically-motivated approaches, well-formedness within a clause was considered, but coherence between clauses was not considered. Even if intra-clause relations (i.e., a predicate-argument structure within a clause) are

Proceedings of the 11th International Conference on Parsing Technologies (IWPT), pages 108–116,
Paris, October 2009.

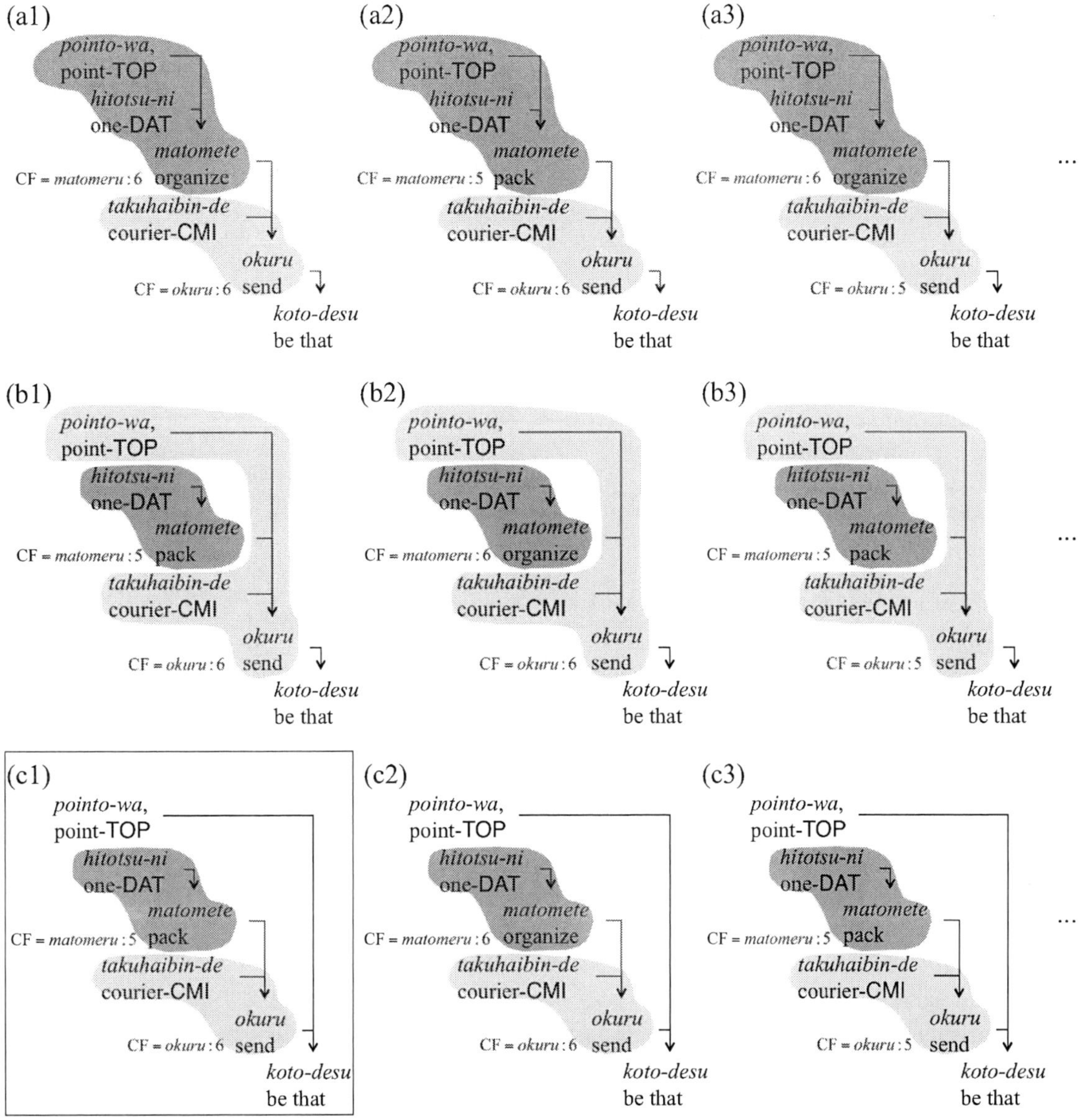

Figure 1: Possible dependency and case structures of sentence (1).

optimized, they might not be optimum when looking at clause pairs or sequences. To improve the accuracy of dependency parsing, we propose a method for dependency and case structure analysis that considers the consistency between intra-clause and inter-clause relations. This method analyzes intra-clause relations on the basis of *case frames* and inter-clause relations on the basis of *transition knowledge* between case frames. These two knowledge sources are automatically acquired from a massive amount of parses of a Web corpus.

The contributions of this paper are two-fold. First, we acquire transition knowledge not between verbs or verb phrases but between case frames, which are semantically disambiguated representations. Second, we incorporate the transition knowledge into dependency and case structure analysis to capture the consistency between intra-clause and inter-clause relations.

The remainder of this paper is organized as follows. Section 2 illustrates our idea. Section 3 describes a method for acquiring the transition knowledge. Section 4 explains the proposed method of incorporating the acquired transition knowledge into a probabilistic model of dependency and case structure analysis. Section 5 reports experimental results. Section 6 gives the conclusions.

2 Idea of Capturing Consistency between Intra-clause and Inter-clause Relations

We propose a method for generative dependency parsing that captures the consistency between intra-clause and inter-clause relations.

Figure 1 shows the ambiguities of dependency and case structure of *pointo-wa* (point-TOP) in the following sentence:

(1) *pointo-wa, hitotsu-ni matomete*
point-TOP one-DAT pack

takuhaibin-de okuru koto-desu
courier-CMI send be that

(The point is that (we) pack (one's baggage) and send (it) using courier service.)

The correct structure is (c1), which is surrounded by the dotted rectangle. Structures (c2), (c3) and so on have the same dependency structure as (c1), but have incorrect case structures, in which incorrect case frames are selected. Note that *matomeru*:5, *okuru*:6 and so on in the figure represent the IDs of the case frames.

The parser of Kawahara and Kurohashi (2006b) (and also conventional Japanese parsers) erroneously analyzes the head of *pointo-wa* (point-TOP)[1] as *matomete* (organize), whereas the correct head is *koto-desu* (be that), as shown in structure (a1) in Figure 1.

This error is caused by the incorrect selection of the case frame *matomeru*:6 (organize), which is shown in Table 1. This case frame locally matches the input predicate-argument structure "*pointo-wa hitotsu-ni matomeru*" (organize points). Therefore, this method considers only intra-clause relations, and falls into local optimum.

If we consider the wide range of two clauses, this error can be corrected. In structure (a1) in Figure 1, the generative probability of case frame transition, $P(matomeru{:}6|okuru{:}6)$, is considered. This probability value is very low, because there are few relations between the case frame *matomeru*:6 (organize) and the case frame *okuru*:6 (send baggage) in corpora.

Consequently, structure (c1) is chosen as the correct one, where both intra-clause and inter-clause relations can be interpreted by the *case frames* and the *transition knowledge* between case frames.

[1]In this paper, we use the following abbreviations: NOM (nominative), ACC (accusative), ABL (ablative), CMI (comitative) and TOP (topic marker).

Table 1: Case frame examples for *matomeru* and *okuru*. "CS" represents case slot. Argument words are written only in English. "<num>" represents the class of numerals.

case frame ID	CS	example words
⋮	⋮	⋮
matomeru:5 (pack)	*ga*	I, person, ...
	wo	baggage, luggage, variables, ...
	ni	<num>, pieces, compact, ...
matomeru:6 (organize)	*ga*	doctor, ...
	wo	point, singularity, ...
	ni	<num>, pieces, below, ...
⋮	⋮	⋮
okuru:1 (send)	*ga*	person, I, ...
	wo	mail, message, information, ...
	ni	friend, address, direction, ...
	de	mail, post, postage, ...
⋮	⋮	⋮
okuru:6 (send)	*ga*	woman, ...
	wo	baggage, supply, goods, ...
	ni	person, Japan, parental house, ...
	de	mail, post, courier, ...
⋮	⋮	⋮

3 Acquiring Transition Knowledge between Case Frames

We automatically acquire large-scale transition knowledge of inter-clause relations from a raw corpus. The following two points are different from previous studies on the acquisition of inter-clause knowledge such as entailment/synonym knowledge (Lin and Pantel, 2001; Torisawa, 2006; Pekar, 2006; Zanzotto et al., 2006), verb relation knowledge (Chklovski and Pantel, 2004), causal knowledge (Inui et al., 2005) and event relation knowledge (Abe et al., 2008):

- the unit of knowledge is disambiguated and generalized

  The unit in previous studies was a verb or a verb phrase, in which verb sense ambiguities still remain. Our unit is case frames that are semantically disambiguated.

- the variation of relations is not limited

  Although previous studies focused on limited kinds of semantic relations, we comprehensively collect generic relations between clauses.

In this section, we first describe our unit of transition knowledge, case frames, briefly. We then detail the acquisition method of the transition knowledge, and report experimental results. Finally, we refer to related work to the acquisition of such knowledge.

3.1 The Unit of Transition Knowledge: Case Frames

In this paper, we regard case frames as the unit of transition knowledge. Case frames are constructed from unambiguous structures and are semantically clustered according to their meanings and usages. Therefore, case frames can be a less ambiguous and more generalized unit than a verb and a verb phrase. Due to these characteristics, case frames are a suitable unit for acquiring transition knowledge and weaken the influence of data sparseness.

3.1.1 Automatic Construction of Case Frames

We employ the method of Kawahara and Kurohashi (2006a) to automatically construct case frames. In this section, we outline the method for constructing the case frames.

In this method, a large raw corpus is automatically parsed, and the case frames are constructed from argument-head examples in the resulting parses. The problems in automatic case frame construction are syntactic and semantic ambiguities. In other words, the parsing results inevitably contain errors, and verb senses are intrinsically ambiguous. To cope with these problems, case frames are gradually constructed from reliable argument-head examples.

First, argument-head examples that have no syntactic ambiguity are extracted, and they are disambiguated by a pair comprising a verb and its closest case component. Such pairs are explicitly expressed on the surface of the text and can be considered to play an important role in conveying the meaning of a sentence. For instance, examples are distinguished not by verbs (e.g., "*tsumu*" (load/accumulate)), but by pairs (e.g., "*nimotsu-wo tsumu*" (load baggage) and "*keiken-wo tsumu*" (accumulate experience)). argument-head examples are aggregated in this manner, and they yield basic case frames.

Thereafter, the basic case frames are clustered in order to merge similar case frames, including similar case frames that are made from scrambled sentences. For example, since "*nimotsu-wo tsumu*" (load baggage) and "*busshi-wo tsumu*" (load supply) are similar, they are clustered together. The similarity is measured by using a distributional thesaurus based on the study described in Lin (1998).

3.2 Acquisition of Transition Knowledge from Large Corpus

To acquire the transition knowledge, we collect the clause pairs in a large raw corpus that have a dependency relation and represent them as pairs of case frames. For example, from the following sentence, a case frame pair, (*matomeru*:5, *okuru*:6), is extracted.

(2) *nimotsu-wo* *matomete,* *takuhaibin-de*
baggage-ACC pack courier-CMI

okutta
sent

(packed one's baggage and sent (it) using courier service)

These case frames are determined by applying a conventional case structure analyzer (Kawahara and Kurohashi, 2006b), which selects the case frames most similar to the input expressions "*nimotu-wo matomeru*" (pack baggage) and "*takuhaibin-de okuru*" (send with courier service) from among the case frames of *matomeru* (organize/settle/pack/...) and *okuru* (send/remit/see off/...); some of the case frames of *matomeru* and *okuru* are listed in Table 1.

We adopt the following steps to acquire the transition knowledge between case frames:

1. Apply dependency and case structure analysis to assign case frame IDs to each clause in a large raw corpus.
2. Collect clause pairs that have a dependency relation, and represent them as pairs of case frame IDs.
3. Count the frequency of each pair of case frame IDs; these statistics are used in the analysis described in Section 4.

At step 2, we collect both syntactically ambiguous and unambiguous relations in order to alleviate data sparseness. The influence of a small number of dependency parsing errors would be hidden by a large number of correct (unambiguous) relations.

Table 2: Examples of automatically acquired transition knowledge between case frames.

pairs of case frame IDs	meaning	freq.
(*okuru*:1, *okuru*:6)	(send mails, send baggage)	186
(*aru*:1, *okuru*:6)	(have, send baggage)	150
(*suru*:1, *okuru*:6)	(do, send baggage)	134
(*issyoda*:10, *okuru*:6)	(get together, send baggage)	118
(*kaku*:1, *okuru*:6)	(write, send baggage)	115
⋮	⋮	⋮
(*matomeru*:5, *okuru*:6)	(pack, send baggage)	12
(*dasu*:3, *okuru*:6)	(indicate, send baggage)	12
⋮	⋮	⋮

3.3 Experiments of Acquiring Transition Knowledge between Case Frames

To obtain the case frames and the transition knowledge between case frames, we first built a Japanese Web corpus by using the method of Kawahara and Kurohashi (2006a). We first crawled 100 million Japanese Web pages, and then, we extracted and unduplicated Japanese sentences from the Web pages. Consequently, we developed a Web corpus consisting of 1.6 billion Japanese sentences.

Using the procedure of case frame construction presented in Section 3.1.1, we constructed case frames from the whole Web corpus. They consisted of 43,000 predicates, and the average number of case frames for a predicate was 22.2.

Then, we acquired the transition knowledge between case frames using 500 million sentences of the Web corpus. The resulting knowledge consisted of 108 million unique case frame pairs. Table 2 lists some examples of the acquired transition knowledge. In the acquired transition knowledge, we can find various kinds of relation such as entailment, cause-effect and temporal relations.

Let us compare this result with the results of previous studies. For example, Chklovski and Pantel (2004) obtained 29,165 verb pairs for several semantic relations in VerbOcean. The transition knowledge acquired in this study is several thousand times larger than that in VerbOcean. It is very difficult to make a meaningful comparison, but it can be seen that we have succeeded in acquiring generic transition knowledge on a large scale.

3.4 Related Work

In order to realize practical natural language processing (NLP) systems such as intelligent dialog systems, a lot of effort has been made to develop world knowledge or inference knowledge. For example, in the CYC (Lenat, 1995) and Open Mind (Stork, 1999) projects, such knowledge has been obtained manually, but it is difficult to manually develop broad-coverage knowledge that is sufficient for practical use in NLP applications.

On the other hand, the automatic acquisition of such inference knowledge from corpora has attracted much attention in recent years. First, semantic knowledge between entities has been automatically obtained (Girju and Moldovan, 2002; Ravichandran and Hovy, 2002; Pantel and Pennacchiotti, 2006). For example, Pantel and Pennacchiotti (2006) proposed the Espresso algorithm, which iteratively acquires entity pairs and extraction patterns using reciprocal relationship between entities and patterns.

As for the acquisition of the knowledge between events or clauses, which is most relevant to this study, many approaches have been adopted to acquire entailment knowledge. Lin and Pantel (2001) and Szpektor and Dagan (2008) learned entailment rules based on distributional similarity between instances that have a relation to a rule. Torisawa (2006) extracted entailment knowledge using coordinated verb pairs and noun-verb co-occurrences. Pekar (2006) also collected entailment knowledge with discourse structure constraints. Zanzotto et al. (2006) obtained entailment knowledge using nominalized verbs.

There have been some studies on relations other than entailment relations. Chklovski and Pantel (2004) obtained verb pairs that have one of five semantic relations by using a search engine. Inui et al. (2005) classified the occurrences of the Japanese connective marker *tame*. Abe et al.

(2008) learned event relation knowledge for two semantic relations. They first gave seed pairs of verbs or verb phrases and extracted the patterns that matched these seed pairs. Subsequently, by using the Espresso algorithm (Pantel and Pennacchiotti, 2006), this process was iterated to augment both instances and patterns. The acquisition unit in these studies was a verb or a verb phrase.

In contrast to these studies, we obtained generic transition knowledge between case frames without limiting target semantic relations.

4 Incorporating Transition Knowledge into Dependency and Case Structure Analysis

We employ the probabilistic generative model of dependency and case structure analysis (Kawahara and Kurohashi, 2006b) as a base model. We incorporate the obtained transition knowledge into this base parser.

Our model assigns a probability to each possible dependency structure, T, and case structure, L, of the input sentence, S, and outputs the dependency and case structure that have the highest probability. In other words, the model selects the dependency structure T_{best} and the case structure L_{best} that maximize the probability $P(T, L|S)$ or its equivalent, $P(T, L, S)$, as follows:

$$\begin{aligned}(T_{best}, L_{best}) &= \text{argmax}_{(T,L)} P(T, L|S) \\ &= \text{argmax}_{(T,L)} \frac{P(T, L, S)}{P(S)} \\ &= \text{argmax}_{(T,L)} P(T, L, S). \quad (1)\end{aligned}$$

The last equation follows from the fact that $P(S)$ is constant.

In the model, a clause (or predicate-argument structure) is considered as a generation unit and the input sentence is generated from the end of the sentence. The probability $P(T, L, S)$ is defined as the product of the probabilities of generating clauses C_i as follows:

$$P(T, L, S) = \prod\nolimits_{C_i \in S} P(C_i|C_h), \quad (2)$$

where C_h is the modifying clause of C_i. Since the Japanese language is head final, the main clause at the end of a sentence does not have a modifying head; we account for this by assuming C_h = EOS (End Of Sentence).

The probability $P(C_i|C_h)$ is defined in a manner similar to that in Kawahara and Kurohashi (2006b). However, the difference between the probability in the above-mentioned study and that in our study is the generative probability of the case frames, i.e., the probability of generating a case frame CF_i from its modifying case frame CF_h. The base model approximated this probability as the product of the probability of generating a predicate v_i from its modifying predicate v_h and the probability of generating a case frame CF_i from the predicate v_i as follows:

$$\begin{aligned}&P(CF_i|CF_h) \approx \\ &\quad P(v_i|v_h) \times P(CF_i|v_i). \quad (3)\end{aligned}$$

Our proposed model directly estimates the probability $P(CF_i|CF_h)$ and considers the transition likelihood between case frames. This probability is calculated from the transition knowledge between case frames using maximum likelihood.

In practice, to avoid the data sparseness problem, we interpolate the probability $P(CF_i|CF_h)$ with the probability of generating predicates, $P(v_i|v_h)$, as follows:

$$\begin{aligned}&P'(CF_i|CF_h) \approx \\ &\quad \lambda P(CF_i|CF_h) + (1-\lambda)P(v_i|v_h), \quad (4)\end{aligned}$$

where λ is determined using the frequencies of the case frame pairs, (CF_i, CF_h), in the same manner as in Collins (1999).

5 Experiments

We evaluated the dependency structures that were output by our new dependency parser. The case frames used in these experiments are the same as those described in Section 3.3, which were automatically constructed from 1.6 billion Japanese sentences obtained from the Web.

In this study, the parameters related to unlexical types were calculated from the Kyoto University Text Corpus, which is a small tagged corpus of newspaper articles, and lexical parameters were obtained from a large Web corpus. To evaluate the effectiveness of our model, our experiments were conducted using sentences obtained from the Web. As a test corpus, we used 759 Web sentences[2], which were manually annotated using the same criteria as those in the case of the Kyoto University Text Corpus. We also used the Kyoto University Text Corpus as a development corpus to optimize some smoothing parameters. The system

[2]The test set was not used to construct case frames and estimate probabilities.

Table 3: The dependency accuracies in our experiments.

	syn	syn+case	syn+case+cons
all	4,555/5,122 (88.9%)	4,581/5,122 (89.4%)	4,599/5,122 (89.8%)
NP→VP	2,115/2,383 (88.8%)	2,142/2,383 (89.9%)	2,151/2,383 (90.3%)
NP→NP	1,068/1,168 (91.4%)	1,068/1,168 (91.4%)	1,068/1,168 (91.4%)
VP→VP	779/928 (83.9%)	777/928 (83.7%)	783/928 (84.4%)
VP→NP	579/623 (92.9%)	579/623 (92.9%)	582/623 (93.4%)

input was automatically tagged using the JUMAN morphological analyzer [3].

We used two baseline systems for the purposes of comparison: a rule-based dependency parser (Kurohashi and Nagao, 1994) and the probabilistic generative model of dependency and case structure analysis (Kawahara and Kurohashi, 2006b)[4]. We use the above-mentioned case frames also in the latter baseline parser, which also requires automatically constructed case frames.

5.1 Evaluation of Dependency Structures

We evaluated the obtained dependency structures in terms of phrase-based dependency accuracy — the proportion of correct dependencies out of all dependencies[5].

Table 3 lists the dependency accuracies. In this table, "syn" represents the rule-based dependency parser, "syn+case" represents the probabilistic parser of syntactic and case structure (Kawahara and Kurohashi, 2006b)[6], and "syn+case+cons" represents our proposed model. In the table, the dependency accuracies are classified into four categories on the basis of the phrase classes (VP: verb phrase[7] and NP: noun phrase) of a dependent and its head. The parser "syn+case+cons" significantly outperformed the two baselines for "all" (McNemar's test; $p < 0.05$). In particular, the accuracy of the intra-clause (predicate-argument) relations ("NP→VP") was improved by 1.5% from "syn" and by 0.4% from "syn+case." These improvements are due to the incorporation of the transition knowledge into syntactic/case structure analysis.

In order to compare our results with a state-of-the-art discriminative dependency parser, we input the test corpus into an SVM-based Japanese dependency parser, CaboCha[8](Kudo and Matsumoto, 2002), which was trained using the Kyoto University Text Corpus. Its dependency accuracy was 88.6% (4,540/5,122), which is close to that of "syn." This low accuracy is attributed to the lack of knowledge of both intra-clause and inter-clause relations. Another cause of the low accuracy is the out-of-domain training corpus. In other words, the parser was trained on a newspaper corpus, while the test corpus was obtained from the Web because a tagged Web corpus that is large enough to train a supervised parser is not available.

5.2 Discussions

Figure 2 shows some improved analyses; here, the dotted lines represent the results of the analysis performed using the baseline "syn + case," and the solid lines represent the analysis performed using the proposed method, "syn+case+cons." These sentences are incorrectly analyzed by the baseline but correctly analyzed by the proposed method. For example, in sentence (a), the head of *gunegunemichi-wo* (winding road-ACC) was correctly analyzed as *yurareru* (be jolted). This is because the case frame of "*basu-ni yurareru*" (be jolted by bus) is likely to generate *tatsu* (stand) that does not take the *wo* (ACC) slot. In this manner, by considering the transition knowledge between case frames, the selection of case frames became accurate, and thus, the accuracy of the dependencies within clauses (predicate-argument structures) was improved.

In the case of the dependencies between predicates (VP→VP), however, only small improve-

[3] http://nlp.kuee.kyoto-u.ac.jp/nl-resource/juman-e.html

[4] http://nlp.kuee.kyoto-u.ac.jp/nl-resource/knp-e.html

[5] Since Japanese is head-final, the second to last phrase unambiguously depends on the last phrase. However, we include such dependencies into our evaluation as in most of previous studies.

[6] The accuracy described in Kawahara and Kurohashi (2006b) is different from that of this paper due to the different evaluation measure excluding the unambiguous dependencies of the second last phrases.

[7] VP includes not only verbs but also adjectives and nouns with copula.

[8] http://chasen.org/~taku/software/cabocha/

(a)	*gunegunemichi-wo*	*tattamama*	*basu-ni*	*yurareru*	*toko-wo*	*kakugoshimashita.*
	winding road-ACC	stand	bus-DAT	be jolted	(that)-ACC	be resolved

(be resolved to be jolted standing on the bus by the winding road.)

(b)	*nanika-wo*	*eru*	*tame-ni*	*suteta*	*mono-nimo*	*miren-wo*	*nokoshiteiru.*
	something-ACC	get	for	discarded	thing-also	lingering desire-ACC	retain

(retain a lingering desire also for the thing that was discarded to get something.)

(c)	*senbei-no*	*hako-wa,*	*kankaku-wo*	*akete*	*chinretsusareteiruno-ga*	*mata*	*yoi.*
	rice cracker-GEN	box-TOP	interval-ACC	place	be displayed-NOM	also	good

(It is also good that boxes of rice cracker are displayed placing an interval.)

Figure 2: Improved examples.

(d)	*ketsuron-kara*	*itteshimaeba,*	*kaitearukoto-wa*	*machigattenaishi,*	*juyouna*	*kotodato-wa*	*wakaru.*
	conclusion-ABL	say	content-TOP	not wrong	important	(that)-TOP	understand

(Saying from conclusions, the content is not wrong and (I) understand that (it) is important)

Figure 3: An erroneous example.

ments were achieved by using the transition knowledge between case frames. This is mainly because the heads of the predicates are intrinsically ambiguous in many cases.

For example, in sentence (d) in Figure 3, the correct head of *itteshimaeba* (say) is *wakaru* (understand) as designated by the solid line, but our model incorrectly judged the head to be *machigatteinaishi,* (not wrong) as designated by the dotted line. However, in this case, both the phrases that are being modified are semantically related to the modifier. To solve this problem, it is necessary to re-consider the evaluation metrics of dependency parsing.

6 Conclusion

In this paper, we have described a method for acquiring the transition knowledge of inter-clause relations and a method for incorporating this knowledge into dependency and case structure analysis. The significance of this study is that the proposed parsing method selects the best dependency and case structures that are consistent within each clause and between clauses. We confirmed that this method contributed to the improvement of the dependency parsing of Japanese.

The case frames that are acquired from 1.6 billion Japanese sentences have been made freely available to the public[9]. In addition, we are preparing to make the acquired transition knowledge accessible on the Web.

In future, we will investigate the iteration of knowledge acquisition and parsing based on the acquired knowledge. Since our parser is a generative model, we are expecting a performance gain by the iteration. Furthermore, we would like to explore the use of the transition knowledge between case frames to improve NLP applications such as recognizing textual entailment (RTE) and sentence generation.

References

Shuya Abe, Kentaro Inui, and Yuji Matsumoto. 2008. Acquiring event relation knowledge by learning cooccurrence patterns and fertilizing cooccurrence samples with verbal nouns. In *Proceedings of IJCNLP2008*, pages 497–504.

Takeshi Abekawa and Manabu Okumura. 2006. Japanese dependency parsing using co-occurrence information and a combination of case elements. In *Proceedings of COLING-ACL2006*, pages 833–840.

Daniel M. Bikel. 2004. Intricacies of Collins' parsing model. *Computational Linguistics*, 30(4):479–511.

[9] http://nlp.kuee.kyoto-u.ac.jp/nl-resource/caseframe-e.html

Sabine Buchholz and Erwin Marsi. 2006. CoNLL-X shared task on multilingual dependency parsing. In *Proceedings of CoNLL-X*, pages 149–164.

Xavier Carreras. 2007. Experiments with a higher-order projective dependency parser. In *Proceedings of EMNLP-CoNLL2007 Shared Task*, pages 957–961.

Timothy Chklovski and Patrick Pantel. 2004. VerbOcean: Mining the web for fine-grained semantic verb relations. In *Proceedings of EMNLP2004*, pages 33–40.

Michael Collins. 1999. *Head-Driven Statistical Models for Natural Language Parsing*. Ph.D. thesis, University of Pennsylvania.

Roxana Girju and Dan Moldovan. 2002. Mining answers for causation questions. In *Proceedings of AAAI Spring Symposium.*

Takashi Inui, Kentaro Inui, and Yuji Matsumoto. 2005. Acquiring causal knowledge from text using the connective marker tame. *ACM Transactions on Asian Language Information Processing (ACM-TALIP)*, 4(4):435–474.

Daisuke Kawahara and Sadao Kurohashi. 2006a. Case frame compilation from the web using high-performance computing. In *Proceedings of LREC2006.*

Daisuke Kawahara and Sadao Kurohashi. 2006b. A fully-lexicalized probabilistic model for Japanese syntactic and case structure analysis. In *Proceedings of HLT-NAACL2006*, pages 176–183.

Terry Koo, Xavier Carreras, and Michael Collins. 2008. Simple semi-supervised dependency parsing. In *Proceedings of ACL-08:HLT*, pages 595–603.

Taku Kudo and Yuji Matsumoto. 2002. Japanese dependency analysis using cascaded chunking. In *Proceedings of CoNLL2002*, pages 29–35.

Sadao Kurohashi and Makoto Nagao. 1994. A syntactic analysis method of long Japanese sentences based on the detection of conjunctive structures. *Computational Linguistics*, 20(4):507–534.

Douglas B. Lenat. 1995. CYC: A large-scale investment in knowledge infrastructure. *Communications of the ACM*, 38(11):32–38.

Dekang Lin and Patrick Pantel. 2001. DIRT - discovery of inference rules from text. In *Proceedings of ACM SIGKDD Conference on Knowledge Discovery and Data Mining*, pages 323–328.

Dekang Lin. 1998. Automatic retrieval and clustering of similar words. In *Proceedings of COLING-ACL98*, pages 768–774.

Mitchell Marcus, Beatrice Santorini, and Mary Marcinkiewicz. 1993. Building a large annotated corpus of English: the Penn Treebank. *Computational Linguistics*, 19(2):313–330.

Ryan McDonald and Fernando Pereira. 2006. Online learning of approximate dependency parsing algorithms. In *Proceedings of EACL2006*, pages 81–88.

Tetsuji Nakagawa. 2007. Multilingual dependency parsing using global features. In *Proceedings of EMNLP-CoNLL2007 Shared Task*, pages 952–956.

Joakim Nivre and Mario Scholz. 2004. Deterministic dependency parsing of English text. In *Proceedings of COLING2004*, pages 64–70.

Joakim Nivre, Johan Hall, Sandra Kübler, Ryan McDonald, Jens Nilsson, Sebastian Riedel, and Deniz Yuret. 2007. The CoNLL 2007 shared task on dependency parsing. In *Proceedings of EMNLP-CoNLL2007*, pages 915–932.

Patrick Pantel and Marco Pennacchiotti. 2006. Espresso: Leveraging generic patterns for automatically harvesting semantic relations. In *Proceedings of COLING-ACL2006*, pages 113–120.

Viktor Pekar. 2006. Acquisition of verb entailment from text. In *Proceedings of HLT-NAACL2006*, pages 49–56.

Deepak Ravichandran and Eduard Hovy. 2002. Learning surface text patterns for a question answering system. In *Proceedings of ACL2002*, pages 41–47.

Manabu Sassano. 2004. Linear-time dependency analysis for Japanese. In *Proceedings of COLING2004*, pages 8–14.

David G. Stork. 1999. Character and document research in the open mind initiative. In *Proceedings of International Conference on Document Analysis and Recognition*, pages 1–12.

Idan Szpektor and Ido Dagan. 2008. Learning entailment rules for unary templates. In *Proceedings of COLING2008*, pages 849–856.

Kentaro Torisawa. 2006. Acquiring inference rules with temporal constraints by using Japanese coordinated sentences and noun-verb co-occurrences. In *Proceedings of HLT-NAACL2006*, pages 57–64.

Fabio Massimo Zanzotto, Marco Pennacchiotti, and Maria Teresa Pazienza. 2006. Discovering asymmetric entailment relations between verbs using selectional preferences. In *Proceedings of COLING-ACL2006*, pages 849–856.

Constructing parse forests that include exactly the n-best PCFG trees

Pierre Boullier[1], **Alexis Nasr**[2] **and Benoît Sagot**[1]
1. Alpage, INRIA Paris-Rocquencourt & Université Paris 7
Domaine de Voluceau — Rocquencourt, BP 105 — 78153 Le Chesnay Cedex, France
{Pierre.Boullier,Benoit.Sagot}@inria.fr
2. LIF, Univ. de la Méditerrannée
163, avenue de Luminy - Case 901 — 13288 Marseille Cedex 9, France
Alexis.Nasr@lif.univ-mrs.fr

Abstract

This paper describes and compares two algorithms that take as input a shared PCFG parse forest and produce shared forests that contain exactly the n most likely trees of the initial forest. Such forests are suitable for subsequent processing, such as (some types of) reranking or LFG f-structure computation, that can be performed ontop of a shared forest, but that may have a high (e.g., exponential) complexity w.r.t. the number of trees contained in the forest. We evaluate the performances of both algorithms on real-scale NLP forests generated with a PCFG extracted from the Penn Treebank.

1 Introduction

The output of a CFG parser based on dynamic programming, such as an Earley parser (Earley, 1970), is a compact representation of all syntactic parses of the parsed sentence, called a *shared parse forest* (Lang, 1974; Lang, 1994). It can represent an exponential number of parses (with respect to the length of the sentence) in a cubic size structure. This forest can be used for further processing, as reranking (Huang, 2008) or machine translation (Mi et al., 2008).

When a CFG is associated with probabilistic information, as in a Probabilistic CFG (PCFG), it can be interesting to process only the n most likely trees of the forest. Standard state-of-the-art algorithms that extract the n best parses (Huang and Chiang, 2005) produce a collection of trees, losing the factorization that has been achieved by the parser, and reproduce some identical sub-trees in several parses.

This situation is not satisfactory since post-parsing processes, such as reranking algorithms or attribute computation, cannot take advantage of this lost factorization and may reproduce some identical work on common sub-trees, with a computational cost that can be exponentally high.

One way to solve the problem is to prune the forest by eliminating sub-forests that do not contribute to any of the n most likely trees. But this over-generates: the pruned forest contains more than the n most likely trees. This is particularly costly for post-parsing processes that may require in the worst cases an exponential execution time w.r.t. the number of trees in the forest, such as LFG f-structures construction or some advanced reranking techniques. The experiments detailed in the last part of this paper show that the over-generation factor of pruned sub-forest is more or less constant (see 6): after pruning the forest so as to keep the n best trees, the resulting forest contains approximately $10^3 n$ trees. At least for some post-parsing processes, this overhead is highly problematic. For example, although LFG parsing can be achieved by computing LFG f-structures on top of a c-structure parse forest with a reasonable efficiency (Boullier and Sagot, 2005), it is clear that a 10^3 factor drastically affects the overall speed of the LFG parser.

Therefore, simply pruning the forest is not an adequate solution. However, it will prove useful for comparison purposes.

The new direction that we explore in this paper is the production of shared forests that contain *exactly* the n most likely trees, avoiding both the explicit construction of n different trees and the over-generation of pruning techniques. This can be seen as a transduction which is applied on a forest and produces another forest. The transduction applies some local transformations on the structure of the forest, developing some parts of the forest when necessary.

The structure of this paper is the following. Section 2 defines the basic objects we will be dealing with. Section 3 describes how to prune a shared

Proceedings of the 11th International Conference on Parsing Technologies (IWPT), pages 117–128,
Paris, October 2009.

forest, and introduces two approaches for building shared forests that contain exactly the n most likely parses. Section 4 describes experiments that were carried out on the Penn Treebank and section 5 concludes the paper.

2 Preliminaries

2.1 Instantiated grammars

Let $G = \langle \mathcal{N}, \mathcal{T}, \mathcal{P}, S \rangle$ be a context-free grammar (CFG), defined in the usual way (Aho and Ullman, 1972). Throughout this paper, we suppose that we manipulate only non-cyclic CFGs,[1] but they may (and usually do) include ε-productions. Given a production $p \in \mathcal{P}$, we note $\mathrm{lhs}(p)$ its left-hand side, $\mathrm{rhs}(p)$ its right-hand side and $|p|$ the length of $\mathrm{rhs}(p)$. Moreover, we note $\mathrm{rhs}_k(p)$, with $1 \leq k \leq |p|$, the kth symbol of $\mathrm{rhs}(p)$. We call A-production any production $p \in \mathcal{P}$ of G such that $\mathrm{lhs}(p) = A$.

A complete derivation of a sentence $w = t_1 \ldots t_{|w|}$ $(\forall i \leq |w|, t_i \in \mathcal{T})$ w.r.t. G is of the form $S \overset{*}{\underset{G,w}{\Rightarrow}} \alpha A \beta \underset{G,w}{\Rightarrow} \alpha X^1 X^2 \ldots X^r \beta \overset{*}{\underset{G,w}{\Rightarrow}} w$. By definition, $A \rightarrow X^1 X^2 \ldots X^r$ is a production of G. Each of A, X^1, X^2, ..., X^r spans a unique occurrence of a substring $t_{i+1} \ldots t_j$ of w, that can be identified by the corresponding *range*, noted $i..j$. A complete derivation represents a *parse tree* whose yield is w, in which each symbol X of range $i..j$ roots a subtree whose yield is $t_{i+1} \ldots t_j$ (i.e., a derivation of the form $X \overset{*}{\underset{G,w}{\Rightarrow}} t_{i+1} \ldots t_j$).

Let us define the *w-instantiation* operation (or *instantiation*). It can be applied to symbols and productions of G, and to G itself, w.r.t. a string w. It corresponds to the well-known intersection of G with the linear automaton that corresponds to the string w. We shall go into further detail for terminology, notation and illustration purposes.

An *instantiated non terminal symbol* is a triple noted $A_{i..j}$ where $A \in \mathcal{N}$ and $0 \leq i \leq j \leq |w|$. Similarly, an *instantiated terminal symbol* is a triple noted $T_{i..j}$ where $T \in \mathcal{T}$ and $0 \leq i \leq j = i + 1 \leq |w|$. An *instantiated symbol*, terminal or non terminal, is noted $X_{i..j}$. For any instantiated symbol $X_{i..j}$, i (resp. j) is called its *lower bound* (resp. *upper bound*), and can be extracted by the operator $\mathrm{lb}()$ (resp. $\mathrm{ub}()$).

An *instantiated production* (or *instantiated rule*) is a context-free production $A_{i..j} \rightarrow X^1_{i_1..j_1} X^2_{i_2..j_2} \ldots X^r_{i_r..j_r}$ whose left-hand side is an instantiated non terminal symbol and whose right-hand side is a (possibly empty) sequence of instantiated (terminal or non terminal) symbols, provided the followings conditions hold:

1. the indexes involved are such that $i = i_1$, $j = j_r$, and $\forall l$ such that $1 \leq l < r$, $j_l = i_{l+1}$;
2. the corresponding non-instantiated production $A \rightarrow X^1 X^2 \ldots X^r$ is a production of G.

If $\mathrm{lhs}(p) = A_{i..j}$, we set $\mathrm{lb}(p) = i$ and $\mathrm{ub}(p) = j$.

In a complete derivation $S \overset{*}{\underset{G,w}{\Rightarrow}} \alpha A \beta \underset{G,w}{\Rightarrow} \alpha X^1 X^2 \ldots X^r \beta \overset{*}{\underset{G,w}{\Rightarrow}} w$, any symbol X that spans the range $i..j$ can be replaced by the instantiated symbols $X_{i..j}$. For example, the axiom S can be replaced by the instantiated axiom $S_{0..|w|}$ in the head of the derivation. If applied to the whole derivation, this operation creates an *instantiated derivation*, whose rewriting operations define a particular set of instantiated productions. Given G and w, the set of all instantiated productions involved in at least one complete derivation of w is unique, and noted $\mathcal{P}_w$. An instantiated derivation represents an *instantiated parse tree*, i.e., a parse tree whose node labels are instantiated symbols. In an instantiated parse tree, each node label is unique, and therefore we shall not distinguish between a node in an instantiated parse tree and its label (i.e., an instantiated symbol).

Then, the *w-instantiated grammar* G_w for G and w is a CFG $\langle \mathcal{N}_w, \mathcal{T}_w, \mathcal{P}_w, S_{0..|w|} \rangle$ such that:

1. $\mathcal{P}_w$ is defined as explained above;
2. $\mathcal{N}_w$ is a set of instantiated non terminal symbols;
3. $\mathcal{T}_w$ is a set of instantiated terminal symbols.

It follows from the definition of $\mathcal{P}_w$ that (instantiated) symbols of G_w have the following properties: $A_{i..j} \in \mathcal{N}_w \Leftrightarrow A \overset{*}{\underset{G,w}{\Rightarrow}} t_{i+1} \ldots t_j$, and $T_{i..j} \in \mathcal{T}_w \Leftrightarrow T = t_j$.

The w-instantiated CFG G_w represents *all* parse trees for w in a shared (factorized) way. It is the grammar representation of the parse forest of w

[1] Actually, cyclic CFG can be treated as well, but not cyclic parse forests. Therefore, if using a cyclic CFG which, on a particular sentence, builds a cyclic parse forest, cycles have to be removed before the algorithms descibed in the next sections are applied. This is the case in the SYNTAX system (see below).

w.r.t. G.[2] In fact, $\mathcal{L}(G_w) = \{w\}$ and the set of parses of w with respect to G_w is isomorphic to the set of parses of w with respect to G, the isomorphism being the w-instantiation operation. The *size* of a forest is defined as the size of the grammar that represents it, i.e., as the number of symbol occurrences in this grammar, which is defined as the number of productions plus the sum of the lengths of all right-hand sides.

Example 1: First running example.

Let us illustrate these definitions by an example. Given the sentence $w =$ the boy saw a man with a telescope *and the grammar G (that the reader has in mind), the instantiated productions of* G_w *are:*

$Det_{0..1} \to the_{0..1}$	$N_{1..2} \to boy_{1..2}$
$NP_{0..2} \to Det_{0..1}\ N_{1..2}$	$V_{2..3} \to saw_{2..3}$
$Det_{3..4} \to a_{3..4}$	$N_{4..5} \to man_{4..5}$
$NP_{3..5} \to Det_{3..4}\ N_{4..5}$	$Prep_{5..6} \to with_{5..6}$
$Det_{6..7} \to a_{6..7}$	$N_{7..8} \to telescope_{7..8}$
$NP_{6..8} \to Det_{6..7}\ N_{7..8}$	$PP_{5..8} \to Prep_{5..6}\ NP_{6..8}$
$NP_{3..8} \to NP_{3..5}\ PP_{5..8}$	$VP_{2..8} \to V_{2..3}\ NP_{3..8}$
$VP_{2..5} \to V_{2..3}\ NP_{3..5}$	$VP_{2..8} \to VP_{2..5}\ PP_{5..8}$
$S_{0..8} \to NP_{0..2}\ VP_{2..8}$	

They represent the parse forest of w according to G. This parse forest contains two trees, since there is one ambiguity: $VP_{2..8}$ *can be rewritten in two different ways.*

The instantiated grammar G_w can be represented as an hypergraph (as in (Klein and Manning, 2001) or (Huang and Chiang, 2005)) where the instantiated symbols of G_w correspond to the vertices of the hypergraph and the instantiated productions to the hyperarcs.

We define the *extension* of an instantiated symbol $X_{i..j}$, noted $\mathcal{E}(X_{i..j})$, as the set of instantiated parse trees that have $X_{i..j}$ as a root. The set of all parse trees of w w.r.t. G is therefore $\mathcal{E}(S_{0..|w|})$. In the same way, we define the extension of an instantiated production $X_{i..j} \to \alpha$ to be the subset of $\mathcal{E}(X_{i..j})$ that corresponds to derivations of the form $X_{i..j} \underset{G,w}{\Rightarrow} \alpha \underset{G,w}{\overset{*}{\Rightarrow}} t_{i+1} \ldots t_j$ (i.e., trees rooted in $X_{i..j}$ and where the daughters of the node $X_{i..j}$ are the symbols of α).

2.2 Forest traversals

Let us suppose that we deal with non-cyclic forests, i.e., we only consider forests that are represented by a non-recursive instantiated CFG. In this case, we can define two different kinds of forest traversals.

A *bottom-up traversal* of a forest is a traversal with the following constraint: an $A_{i..j}$-production is visited if and only if all its instantiated right-hand side symbols have already been visited; the instantiated symbol $A_{i..j}$ is visited once all $A_{i..j}$-productions have been visited. The bottom-up visit starts by visiting all instantiated productions with right-hand sides that are empty or contain only (instantiated) terminal symbols.

A *top-down traversal* of a forest is a traversal with the following constraint: a node $A_{i..j}$ is visited if and only if all the instantiated productions in which it occurs in right-hand side have already been visited; once an instantiated production $A_{i..j}$ has been visited, all its $A_{i..j}$-productions are visited as well. Of course the top-down visit starts by the visit of the axiom $S_{0..|w|}$.

2.3 Ranked instantiated grammar

When an instantiated grammar $G_w = \langle \mathcal{N}_w, \mathcal{T}_w, \mathcal{P}_w, S_{0..|w|} \rangle$ is built on a PCFG, every parse tree in $\mathcal{E}(S_{0..|w|})$ has a probability that is computed in the usual way (Booth, 1969). We might be interested in extracting the kth most likely tree of the forest represented by G_w,[3] without *unfolding* the forest, i.e., without enumerating trees. In order to do so, we need to add some extra structure to the instantiated grammar. The augmented instantiated grammar will be called a *ranked instantiated grammar*.

This extra structure takes the form of *n-best tables* that are associated with each instantiated non terminal symbol (Huang and Chiang, 2005), thus leading to *ranked instantiated non terminal symbols*, or simply *instantiated symbols* when the context is non ambiguous. A ranked instantiated non terminal symbol is written $\langle A_{i..j}, \mathcal{T}(A_{i..j}) \rangle$, where $\mathcal{T}(A_{i..j})$ is the n-best table associated with the instantiated symbol $A_{i..j}$.

$\mathcal{T}(A_{i..j})$ is a table of at most n entries. The k-th entry of the table, noted e, describes how to build the k-th most likely tree of $\mathcal{E}(A_{i..j})$. This tree will be called the k-th extention of $A_{i..j}$, noted $\mathcal{E}_k(A_{i..j})$. More precisely, e indicates the instantiated $A_{i..j}$-production p such that $\mathcal{E}_k(A_{i..j}) \in \mathcal{E}(p)$. It indicates furthermore which trees of the exten-

[2] In particular, if G is a binary grammar, its w-instantiation (i.e., the parse forest of w) has a size $\mathcal{O}(|w|^3)$, whereas it represents a potentially exponential number of parse trees w.r.t $|w|$ since we manipulate only non-cyclic grammars.

[3] In this paper, we shall use the kth *most likely tree* and *the tree of rank* k as synonyms.

sions of p's right-hand side symbols must be combined together in order to build $\mathcal{E}_k(A_{i..j})$.

We also define the m,n-extension of $A_{i..j}$ as follows: $\mathcal{E}_{m,n}(A_{i..j}) = \cup_{m \leq k \leq n} \mathcal{E}_k(A_{i..j})$.

Example 2: n-best tables for the first running example.

Let us illustrate this idea on our first running example. Recall that in Example 1, the symbol $VP_{2..8}$ can be rewritten using the two following productions :

$$VP_{2..8} \rightarrow V_{2..3} \quad NP_{3..8}$$
$$VP_{2..8} \rightarrow VP_{2..5} \quad PP_{5..8}$$

$\mathcal{T}(VP_{2..8})$ has the following form:

1	P_1	$VP_{2..8} \rightarrow V_{2..3}\, NP_{3..8}$	$\langle 1,1 \rangle$	1
2	P_2	$VP_{2..8} \rightarrow VP_{2..5}\, PP_{5..8}$	$\langle 1,1 \rangle$	1

This table indicates that the most likely tree associated with $VP_{2..8}$ (line one) has probability P_1 and is built using the production $VP_{2..8} \rightarrow V_{2..3}\, NP_{3..8}$ by combining the most likely tree of $\mathcal{E}(V_{2..3})$ (indicated by the first 1 in $\langle 1,1 \rangle$) with the most likely tree of $\mathcal{E}(NP_{3..8})$ (indicated by the second 1 in $\langle 1,1 \rangle$). It also indicates that the most likely tree of $\mathcal{E}(VP_{2..8})$ is the most likely tree of $\mathcal{E}(VP_{2..8} \rightarrow V_{2..3}\, NP_{3..8})$ (indicated by the presence of 1 in the last column of entry 1) and the second most likely tree of $\mathcal{E}(VP_{2..8})$ is the most likely tree of $\mathcal{E}(VP_{2..8} \rightarrow VP_{2..5}\, PP_{5..8})$. This last integer is called the local rank of the entry.

More formally, the entry $\mathcal{T}(A_{i..j})[k]$ is defined as a 4-tuple $\langle P_k, p_k, \vec{v_k}, l_k \rangle$ where k is the rank of the entry, P_k is the probability of the tree $\mathcal{E}_k(A_{i..j})$, p_k is the instantiated production such that $\mathcal{E}_k(A_{i..j}) \in \mathcal{E}(p_k)$, $\vec{v_k}$ is a tuple of $|\mathrm{rhs}(p_k)|$ integers and l_k is the local rank.

The tree $\mathcal{E}_k(A_{i..j})$ is rooted by $A_{i..j}$, and its daughters root $N = |\mathrm{rhs}(p_k)|$ subtrees that are $\mathcal{E}_{\vec{v_k}[1]}(\mathrm{rhs}_1(p_k)), \ldots, \mathcal{E}_{\vec{v_k}[N]}(\mathrm{rhs}_N(p_k))$.

Given an instantiated symbol $A_{i..j}$ and an instantitated production $p \in P(A_{i..j})$, we define the n-best table of p to be the table composed of the entries $\langle P_k, p_k, \vec{v_k}, l_k \rangle$ of $\mathcal{T}(A_{i..j})$ such that $p_k = p$.

Example 3: Second running example.

The following is a standard PCFG (probabilities are shown next to the corresponding clauses).

$S \rightarrow A\,B$	1		
$A \rightarrow A1$	0.7	$A1 \rightarrow a$	1
$A \rightarrow A2$	0.3	$A2 \rightarrow a$	1
$B \rightarrow B1$	0.6	$B1 \rightarrow b$	1
$B \rightarrow B2$	0.4	$B2 \rightarrow b$	1

The instantiation of the underlying (non-probabilistic) CFG grammar by the input text $w = a\,b$ is the following.

$$S_{1..3} \rightarrow A_{1..2}\, B_{2..3}$$

$A_{1..2} \rightarrow A1_{1..2}$	$A1_{1..2} \rightarrow a_{1..2}$
$A_{1..2} \rightarrow A2_{1..2}$	$A2_{1..2} \rightarrow a_{1..2}$
$B_{2..3} \rightarrow B1_{2..3}$	$B1_{2..3} \rightarrow b_{2..3}$
$B_{2..3} \rightarrow B2_{2..3}$	$B2_{2..3} \rightarrow b_{2..3}$

This grammar represents a parse forest that contains four different trees, since on the one hand one can reach (parse) the instantiated terminal symbol $a_{1..2}$ through A1 or A2, and on the other hand one can reach (parse) the instantiated terminal symbol $b_{1..2}$ through B1 or B2. Therefore, when discussing this example in the remainder of the paper, each of these four trees will be named accordingly: the tree obtained by reaching a through Ai and b through Bj (i and j are 1 or 2) shall be called $T_{i,j}$.

The corresponding n-best tables are trivial (only one line) for all instantiated symbols but $A_{1..2}$, $B_{2..3}$ and $S_{1..3}$. That of $A_{1..2}$ is the following 2-line table.

1	0.7	$A \rightarrow A1$	$\langle 1 \rangle$	1
2	0.3	$A \rightarrow A2$	$\langle 1 \rangle$	1

The n-best table for $B_{2..3}$ is similar. The n-best table for $S_{1..3}$ is:

1	0.42	$S_{1..3} \rightarrow A_{1..2}\, B_{2..3}$	$\langle 1,1 \rangle$	1
2	0.28	$S_{1..3} \rightarrow A_{1..2}\, B_{2..3}$	$\langle 1,2 \rangle$	2
3	0.18	$S_{1..3} \rightarrow A_{1..2}\, B_{2..3}$	$\langle 2,1 \rangle$	3
4	0.12	$S_{1..3} \rightarrow A_{1..2}\, B_{2..3}$	$\langle 2,2 \rangle$	4

Thanks to the algorithm sketched in section 2.4, these tables allow to compute the following obvious result: the best tree is $T_{1,1}$, the second-best tree is $T_{1,2}$, the third-best tree is $T_{2,1}$ and the worst tree is $T_{2,2}$.

If $n = 3$, the pruned forest over-generates: all instantiated productions take part in at least one of the three best trees, and therefore the pruned forest is the full forest itself, which contains four trees.

We shall use this example later on so as to illustrate both methods we introduce for building forests that contain exactly the n best trees, without overgenerating.

2.4 Extracting the kth-best tree

An efficient algorithm for the extraction of the n-best trees is introduced in (Huang and Chiang, 2005), namely the authors' algorithm 3, which is a re-formulation of a procedure originally proposed by (Jiménez and Marzal, 2000). Contrarily to (Huang and Chiang, 2005), we shall sketch this algorithm with the terminology introduced above (whereas the authors use the notion of hypergraph). The algorithm relies on the n-best tables described above: extracting the kth-best tree consists in extending the n-best tables as much as necessary by computing all lines in each n-best table up to those that concern the kth-best tree.[4]

The algorithm can be divided in two sub-algorithms: (1) a bottom-up traversal of the forest for extracting the best tree; (2) a top-down traversal for extracting the kth-best tree provided the $(k-1)^{\text{th}}$-best has been already extracted.

The extraction of the best tree can be seen as a bottom-up traversal that initializes the n-best tables: when visiting a node $A_{i..j}$, the best probability of each $A_{i..j}$-production is computed by using the tables associated with each of their right-hand side symbols. The best of these probabilities gives the first line of the n-best table for $A_{i..j}$ (the result for other productions are stored for possible later use). Once the traversal is completed (the instantiated axiom has been reached), the best tree can be easily output by following recursively where the first line of the axiom's n-best table leads to.

Let us now assume we have extracted all k'-best trees, $1 \leq k' < k$, for a given $k \leq n$. We want to extract the kth-best tree. We achieve this recursively by a top-down traversal of the forest. In order to start the construction of the kth-best tree, we need to know the following:

- which instantiated production p must be used for rewriting the instantiated axiom,
- for each of p's right-hand side symbols $A_{i..j}$, which subtree rooted in $A_{i..j}$ must be used; this subtree is identified by its *local rank* $k_{A_{i..j}}$, i.e., the rank of its probability among all subtrees rooted in $A_{i..j}$.

This information is given by the kth line of the n-best table associated with the instantiated axiom. If this k^{th} line has not been filled yet, it is computed recursively.[5] Once the kth line of the n-best table is known, i.e., p and all $k_{A_{i..j}}$'s are known, the rank k is added to p's so-called *rankset*, noted $\rho(p)$. Then, the top-down traversal extracts recursively for each $A_{i..j}$ the appropriate subtree as defined by $k_{A_{i..j}}$. After having extracted the n-th best tree, we know that a given production p is included in the kth-best tree, $1 \leq k \leq n$, if and only if $k \in \rho(p)$.

3 Computing sub-forests that only contain the n best trees

Given a ranked instantiated grammar G_w, we are interested in building a new instantiated grammar which contains exactly the n most likely trees of $\mathcal{E}(G_w)$. In this section, we introduce two algorithms that compute such a grammar (or forest). Both methods rely on the construction of new symbols, obtained by decorating instantiated symbols of G_w.

An empirical comparison of the two methods is described in section 4. In order to evaluate the size of the new constructed grammars (forests), we consider as a lower bound the so-called *pruned forest*, which is the smallest sub-grammar of the initial instantiated grammar that includes the n best trees. It is built simply by pruning productions with an empty rankset: no new symbols are created, original instantiated symbols are kept. Therefore, it is a lower bound in terms of size. However, the pruned forest usually overgenerates, as illustrated by Example 3.

3.1 The ranksets method

The algorithm described in this section builds an instantiated grammar G_w^n by decorating the symbols of G_w. The new (decorated) symbols have the form $A_{i..j}^{\rho}$ where ρ is a set of integers called a *rankset*. An integer r is a *rank* iff we have $1 \leq r \leq n$.

The starting point of this algorithm is set of n-best tables, built as explained in section 2.4, without explicitely unfolding the forest.

[4] In the remainder of this paper, we shall use "extracting the kth-best tree" as a shortcut for "extending the n-best tables up to what is necessary to extract the kth-best tree" (i.e., we do not necessarily really build or print the kth-best tree).

[5] Because the $k-1^{\text{th}}$-best tree has been computed, this n-best table is filled exactly up to line $k-1$. The kth line is then computed as follows: while constructing the k'^{th}-best trees for each k' between 1 and $k-1$, we have identified many possible rewritings of the instantiated axiom, i.e., many (production, right-hand side local ranks) pairs; we know the probability of all these rewritings, although only some of them consitute a line of the instantiated axiom's n-best table; we now identify new rewritings, starting from known rewritings and incrementing only one of their local ranks; we compute (recursively) the probability of these newly identified rewritings; the rewriting that has the best probability among all those that are not yet a line of the n-best table is then added: it is its kth line.

A preliminary top-down step uses these n-best tables for building a parse forest whose non-terminal symbols (apart from the axiom) have the form $A^{\rho}_{i..j}$ where ρ is a singleton $\{r\}$: the sub-forest rooted in $A^{\{r\}}_{i..j}$ contains only one tree, that of local rank r. Only the axiom is not decorated, and remains unique. Terminal symbols are not affected either.

At this point, the purpose of the algorithm is to merge productions with identical right-hand sides, whenever possible. This is achieved in a bottom-up fashion as follows. Consider two symbols $A^{\rho_1}_{i..j}$ and $A^{\rho_2}_{i..j}$, which differ only by their underlying ranksets. These symbols correspond to two different production sets, namely the set of all $A^{\rho_1}_{i..j}$-productions (resp. $A^{\rho_2}_{i..j}$-productions). Each of these production sets define a set of right-hand sides. If these two right-hand side sets are identical we say that $A^{\rho_1}_{i..j}$ and $A^{\rho_2}_{i..j}$ are *equivalent*. In that case introduce the rankset $\rho = \rho_1 \cup \rho_2$ and create a new non-terminal symbol $A^{\rho}_{i..j}$. We now simply replace all occurrences of $A^{\rho_1}_{i..j}$ and $A^{\rho_2}_{i..j}$ in left- and right-hand sides by $A^{\rho}_{i..j}$. Of course (newly) identical productions are erased. After such a transformation, the newly created symbol may appear in the right-hand side of productions that now only differ by their left-hand sides; the factorization spreads to this symbol in a bottom-up way. Therefore, we perform this transformation until no new pair of equivalent symbols is found, starting from terminal leaves and percolating bottom-up as far as possible.

Example 4: Applying the ranksets method to the second running example.

Let us come back to the grammar of Example 3, and the same input text $w = a\,b$ as before. As in Example 3, we consider the case when we are interested in the $n = 3$ best trees.

Starting from the instantiated grammar and the n-best tables given in Example 3, the preliminary top-down step builds the following forest (for clarity, ranksets have not been shown on symbols that root sub-forests containing only one tree):

$$S_{1..3} \rightarrow A^{\{1\}}_{1..2}\, B^{\{1\}}_{2..3}$$

$$S_{1..3} \rightarrow A^{\{1\}}_{1..2}\, B^{\{2\}}_{2..3}$$

$$S_{1..3} \rightarrow A^{\{2\}}_{1..2}\, B^{\{1\}}_{2..3}$$

$$A^{\{1\}}_{1..2} \rightarrow A1_{1..2} \qquad A1_{1..2} \rightarrow a_{1..2}$$

$$A^{\{2\}}_{1..2} \rightarrow A2_{1..2} \qquad A2_{1..2} \rightarrow a_{1..2}$$

$$B^{\{1\}}_{2..3} \rightarrow B1_{2..3} \qquad B1_{2..3} \rightarrow b_{2..3}$$

$$B^{\{2\}}_{2..3} \rightarrow B2_{2..3} \qquad B2_{2..3} \rightarrow b_{2..3}$$

In this example, the bottom-up step doesn't factorize out any other symbols, and this is therefore the final output of the ranksets method. It contains 2 more productions and 3 more symbols than the pruned forest (which is the same as the original forest), but it contains exactly the 3 best trees, contrarily to the pruned forest.

3.2 The rectangles method

In this section only, we assume that the grammar G is binary (and therefore the forest, i.e., the grammar G_w, is binary). Standard binarization algorithms can be found in the litterature (Aho and Ullman, 1972).

The algorithm described in this section performs, as the preceding one, a decoration of the symbols of G_w. The new (decorated) symbols have the form $A^{x,y}_{i..j}$, where x and y denote ranks such that $1 \leq x \leq y \leq n$. The semantics of the decoration is closely related to the x, y extention of $A_{i..j}$, introduced in 2.3:

$$\mathcal{E}(A^{x,y}_{i..j}) = \mathcal{E}_{x,y}(A_{i..j})$$

It corresponds to ranksets (in the sense of the previous section) that are intervals: $A^{x,y}_{i..j}$ is equivalent to the previous section's $A^{\{x,x+1,\dots,y-1,y\}}_{i..j}$. In other words, the sub-forest rooted with $A^{x,y}_{i..j}$ contains exactly the trees of the initial forest, rooted with $A_{i..j}$, which rank range from x to y.

The algorithm performs a top-down traversal of the initial instantiated grammar G_w. This traversal also takes as input two parameters x and y. It starts with the symbol $S_{0..|w|}$ and parameters 1 and n. At the end of the traversal, a new decorated forest is built which contains exactly n most likely the parses. During the traversal, every instantiated symbol $A_{i..j}$ will give birth to decorated instantiated symbols of the form $A^{x,y}_{i..j}$ where x and y are determined during the traversal. Two different actions are performed depending on whether we are visiting an instantiated symbol or an instantiated production.

3.2.1 Visiting an instantiated symbol

When visiting an instantiated symbol $A_{i..j}$ with parameters x and y, a new decorated instantiated symbol $A_{i..j}^{x,y}$ is created and the traversal continues on the instantiated productions of $P(A_{i..j})$ with parameters that have to be computed. These parameters depend on how the elements of $\mathcal{E}_{x,y}(A_{i..j})$ are "distributed" among the sets $\mathcal{E}(p)$ with $p \in P(A_{i..j})$. In other words, we need to determine x_k's and y_k's such that:

$$\mathcal{E}_{x,y}(A_{i..j}) = \bigcup_{p_k \in P(A_{i..j})} \mathcal{E}_{x_k,y_k}(p_k)$$

The idea can be easily illustrated on an example. Suppose we are visiting the instantiated symbol $A_{i..j}$ with parameters 5 and 10. Suppose also that $A_{i..j}$ can be rewritten using the two instantiated productions p_1 and p_2. Suppose finally that the 5 to 10 entries of $\mathcal{T}(A_{i..j})$ are as follows[6]:

5	p_1	4
6	p_2	2
7	p_2	3
8	p_1	5
9	p_2	4
10	p_1	6

This table says that $\mathcal{E}_5(A_{i..j}) = \mathcal{E}_4(p_1)$ i.e. the 5th most likely analysis of $\mathcal{E}(A_{i..j})$ is the 4th most likely analysis of $\mathcal{E}(p_1)$ and $\mathcal{E}_6(A_{i..j}) = \mathcal{E}_2(p_2)$ and so on. From this table we can deduce that:

$$\mathcal{E}_{5,10}(A_{i..j}) = \mathcal{E}_{4,6}(p_1) \cup \mathcal{E}_{2,4}(p_2)$$

The traversal therefore continues on p_1 and p_2 with parameters $4, 6$ and $2, 4$.

3.2.2 Visiting an instantiated production

When visiting an instantiated production p of the form $A_{i..j} \rightarrow B_{i..l}\ C_{l..j}$ with parameters x and y, a collection of q instantiated productions p_r of the form $A_{i..j}^{x,y} \rightarrow B_{i..l}^{x_r^1,x_r^2}\ C_{l..j}^{y_r^1,y_r^2}$, with $1 \leq r \leq q$, are built, where the parameters $x_r^1, x_r^2, y_r^1, y_r^2$ and q have to be computed.

Once the parameters q and $x_r^1, x_r^2, y_r^1, y_r^2$ with $1 \leq r \leq q$, have been computed, the traversal continues independently on $B_{i..l}$ with parameters x_r^1 and x_r^2 and on $C_{l..j}$ with parameters y_r^1 and y_r^2.

[6]Only the relevant part of the table have been kept in the figure.

The computation of the parameters x_r^1, x_r^2, y_r^1 and y_r^2 for $1 \leq r \leq q$, is the most complex part of the algorithm, it relies on the three notions of *rectangles*, *q-partitions* and *n-best matrices*, which are defined below.

Given a 4-tuple of parameters $x_r^1, x_r^2, y_r^1, y_r^2$, a rectangle is simply a pairing of the form $\langle\langle x_r^1, x_r^2\rangle, \langle y_r^1, y_r^2\rangle\rangle$. A rectangle can be interpreted as a couple of rank ranges : $\langle x_r^1, y_r^1\rangle$ and $\langle x_r^2, y_r^2\rangle$. It denotes the cartesian product $[x_r^1, x_r^2] \times [y_r^1, y_r^2]$.

Let $\langle\langle x_1^1, x_1^2\rangle, \langle y_1^1, y_1^2\rangle\rangle, \ldots, \langle\langle x_q^1, x_q^2\rangle, \langle y_q^1, y_q^2\rangle\rangle$ be a collection of q rectangles. It will be called a *q-partition* of the instantiated production p iff the following is true:

$$\mathcal{E}_{x,y}(p) = \bigcup_{1 \leq r \leq q} \mathcal{E}(A_{i..j}^{x,y} \rightarrow B_{i..l}^{x_r^1,x_r^2}\ C_{l..j}^{y_r^1,y_r^2})$$

To put it differently, this definition means that $\langle\langle x_1^1, x_1^2\rangle, \langle y_1^1, y_1^2\rangle\rangle, \ldots, \langle\langle x_q^1, x_q^2\rangle, \langle y_q^1, y_q^2\rangle\rangle$ is a q partition of p if any tree of $\mathcal{E}(B_{i..l}^{x_r^1,x_r^2})$ combined with any tree of $\mathcal{E}(C_{l..j}^{y_r^1,y_r^2})$ is a tree of $\mathcal{E}_{x,y}(p)$ and, conversely, any tree of $\mathcal{E}_{x,y}(p)$ is the combination of a tree of $\mathcal{E}(B_{i..l}^{x_r^1,x_r^2})$ and a tree of $\mathcal{E}(C_{l..j}^{y_r^1,y_r^2})$.

The *n-best matrix* associated with an instantiated production p, introduced in (Huang and Chiang, 2005), is merely a two dimensional representation of the n-best table of p. Such a matrix, represents how the n most likely trees of $\mathcal{E}(p)$ are built. An example of an n-best matrix is represented in figure 1. This matrix says that the first most likely tree of p is built by combining the tree $\mathcal{E}_1(B_{i..l})$ with the tree $\mathcal{E}_1(C_{l..j})$ (there is a 1 in the cell of coordinate $\langle 1, 1\rangle$). The second most likely tree is built by combining the tree $\mathcal{E}_1(B_{i..l})$ and $\mathcal{E}_2(C_{l..j})$ (there is a 2 in the cell of coordinate $\langle 1, 2\rangle$) and so on.

$C_{l..j}$

$B_{i..l}$	1	2	3	4	5	6
1	1	2	6	8	14	15
2	3	5	11	13	18	29
3	4	9	12	17	24	30
4	7	10	20	21	26	33
5	16	19	22	25	27	35
6	23	28	31	32	34	36

Figure 1: n-best matrix

An n-best matrix M has, by construction, the remarkable following properties:

$$M(i,y) < M(x,y)\ \forall i\ 1 \leq i < x$$
$$M(x,j) < M(x,y)\ \forall j\ 1 \leq j < y$$

Given an n-best matrix M of dimensions $d = X \cdot Y$ and two integers x and y such that $1 \leq x < y \leq d$, M can be decomposed into three regions:

- the *lower region*, composed of the cells which contain ranks i with $1 \leq i < x$
- the *intermediate region*, composed of the cells which contain ranks i with $x \leq i \leq y$
- the *upper region*, composed of the cells which contain ranks i such that $y < i \leq d$.

The three regions of the matrix of figure 1, for $x = 4$ and $y = 27$ have been delimited with bold lines in figure 2.

$C_{l..j}$

$B_{i..l}$	1	2	3	4	5	6
1	1	2	6	8	14	15
2	3	5	11	13	18	29
3	4	9	12	17	24	30
4	7	10	20	21	26	33
5	16	19	22	25	27	35
6	23	28	31	32	34	36

Figure 2: Decomposition of an n-best matrix into a lower, an intermediate and an upper region with parameters 4 and 27.

It can be seen that a rectangle, as introduced earlier, defines a *sub-matrix* of the n-best matrix. For example the rectangle $\langle\langle 2,5\rangle,\langle 2,5\rangle\rangle$ defines the sub-matrix which north west corner is $M(2,2)$ and south east corner is $M(5,5)$, as represented in figure 3.

When visiting an instantiated production p, having M as an n-best matrix, with the two parameters x and y, the intermediate region of M, with respect to x and y, contains, by definition, all the ranks that we are interested in (the ranks ranging from x to y). This region can be partitioned into a collection of disjoint rectangular regions. Each such partition therefore defines a collection of rectangles or a q-partition.

The computation of the parameters x_r^1, y_r^1, x_r^2 and y_r^2 for an instantiated production p therefore boils down to the computation of a partition of the intermediate region of the n-best matrix of p.

$C_{l..j}$

$B_{i..l}$	2			5
2	5	11	13	18
	9	12	17	24
	10	20	21	26
5	19	22	25	27

Figure 3: The sub-matrix corresponding to the rectangle $\langle\langle 2,5\rangle,\langle 2,5\rangle\rangle$

We have represented schematically, in figure 4, two 4-partitions and a 3-partition of the intermediate region of the matrix of figure 2. The leftmost (resp. rightmost) partition will be called the vertical (resp. horizontal) partition. The middle partition will be called an optimal partition, it decomposes the intermediate region into a minimal number of sub-matrices.

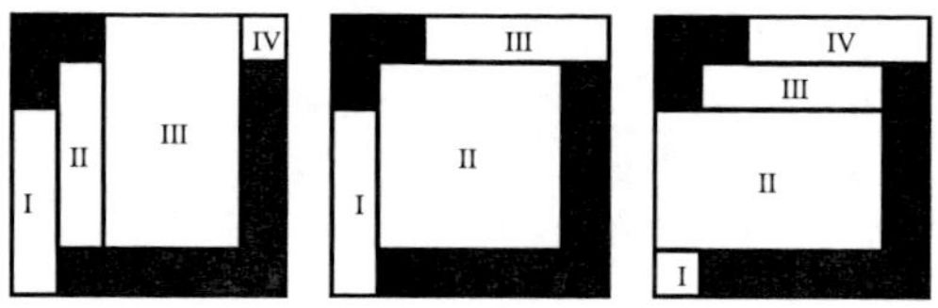

Figure 4: Three partitions of an n-best matrix

The three partitions of figure 4 will give birth to the following instantiated productions:

- Vertical partition
  $A_{i..j}^{4,27} \rightarrow B_{i..l}^{3,6}\, C_{l..j}^{1,1}$ $\quad A_{i..j}^{4,27} \rightarrow B_{i..l}^{2,5}\, C_{l..j}^{2,2}$
  $A_{i..j}^{4,27} \rightarrow B_{i..l}^{1,5}\, C_{l..j}^{3,5}$ $\quad A_{i..j}^{4,27} \rightarrow B_{i..l}^{1,1}\, C_{l..j}^{6,6}$
- Optimal partition
  $A_{i..j}^{4,27} \rightarrow B_{i..l}^{1,1}\, C_{l..j}^{3,6}$ $\quad A_{i..j}^{4,27} \rightarrow B_{i..l}^{2,5}\, C_{l..j}^{2,5}$
  $A_{i..j}^{4,27} \rightarrow B_{i..l}^{3,6}\, C_{l..j}^{1,1}$
- Horizontal partition
  $A_{i..j}^{4,27} \rightarrow B_{i..l}^{1,1}\, C_{l..j}^{3,6}$ $\quad A_{i..j}^{4,27} \rightarrow B_{i..l}^{2,2}\, C_{l..j}^{2,5}$
  $A_{i..j}^{4,27} \rightarrow B_{i..l}^{3,5}\, C_{l..j}^{1,5}$ $\quad A_{i..j}^{4,27} \rightarrow B_{i..l}^{6,6}\, C_{l..j}^{1,1}$

Vertical and horizontal partition of the intermediate region of a n-best matrix can easily be computed. We are not aware of an efficient method that computes an optimal partition. In the implementation used for experiments described in section 4, a simple heuristic has been used which computes horizontal and vertical partitions and keeps the partition with the lower number of parts.

The size of the new forest is clearly linked to the partitions that are computed: a partition with a lower number of parts will give birth to a lower number of decorated instantiated productions and therefore a smaller forest. But this optimization is local, it does not take into account the fact that an instantiated symbol may be shared in the initial forest. During the computation of the new forest, an instantiated production p can therefore be visited several times, with different parameters. Several partitions of p will therefore be computed. If a rectangle is shared by several partitions, this will tend to decrease the size of the new forest. The global optimal must therefore take into account all the partitions of an instantiated production that are computed during the construction of the new forest.

Example 5: Applying the rectangles method to the second running example.

We now illustrate more concretely the rectangles method on our second running example introduced in Example 3. Let us recall that we are interested in the $n = 3$ *best trees, the original forest containing 4 trees.*

As said above, this method starts on the instantiated axiom $S_{1..3}$*. Since it is the left-hand side of only one production, this production is visited with parameters* $1, 3$*. Moreover, its* n*-best table is the same as that of* $S_{1..3}$*, given in Example 3. We show here the corresponding* n*-best matrix, with the empty lower region, the intermediate region (cells corresponding to ranks 1 to 3) and the upper region:*

		$B_{2..3}$	
		1	2
$A_{1..2}$	1	1	2
	2	3	4

As can be seen on that matrix, there are two optimal 2-partitions, namely the horizontal and the vertical partitions, illustrated as follows:

Let us arbitrarily chose the vertical partition. It gives birth to two $S_{1..3}$*-productions, namely:*

$$S^{1,3}_{1..3} \rightarrow A^{1,2}_{1..2}\, B^{1,1}_{2..3}$$
$$S^{1,3}_{1..3} \rightarrow A^{1,1}_{1..2}\, B^{2,2}_{2..3}$$

Since this is the only non-trivial step while applying the rectangles algorithm to this example, we can now give its final result, in which the axiom's (unnecessary) decorations have been removed:

$$S_{1..3} \rightarrow A^{1,2}_{1..2}\, B^{\{1,1\}}_{2..3}$$
$$S_{1..3} \rightarrow A^{1,1}_{1..2}\, B^{\{2,2\}}_{2..3}$$

$$A^{1,2}_{1..2} \rightarrow A1_{1..2} \qquad A1_{1..2} \rightarrow a_{1..2}$$
$$A^{1,2}_{1..2} \rightarrow A2_{1..2} \qquad A2_{1..2} \rightarrow a_{1..2}$$
$$B^{1,2}_{2..3} \rightarrow B1_{2..3} \qquad B1_{2..3} \rightarrow b_{2..3}$$
$$B^{2,2}_{2..3} \rightarrow B2_{2..3} \qquad B2_{2..3} \rightarrow b_{2..3}$$

Compared to the forest built by the ranksets algorithm, this forest has one less production and one less non-terminal symbol. It has only one more production than the over-generating pruned forest.

4 Experiments on the Penn Treebank

The methods described in section 3 have been tested on a PCFG G extracted from the Penn Treebank (Marcus et al., 1993). G has been extracted naively: the trees have been decomposed into binary context free rules, and the probability of every rule has been estimated by its relative frequency (number of occurrences of the rule divided by the number of occurrences of its left hand side). Rules occurring less than 3 times and rules with probabilities lower than 3×10^{-4} have been eliminated. The grammar produced contains 932 non terminals and $3,439$ rules.[7]

The parsing has been realized using the SYNTAX system which implements, and optimizes, the Earley algorithm (Boullier, 2003).

The evaluation has been conducted on the $1,845$ sentences of section 1, which constitute our test set. For every sentence and for increasing values of n, an n-best sub-forest has been built using the rankset and the rectangles method.

The performances of the algorithms have been measured by the average *compression rate* they

[7]We used this test set only to generate practical NLP forests, with a real NLP grammar, and evaluate the performances of our algorithms for constucting sub-forests that contain only the n-best trees, both in terms of compression rate and execution time. Therefore, the evaluation carried out here has nothing to do with the usual evaluation of the precision and recall of parsers based on the Penn Treebank. In particular, we are not interested here in the accuracy of such a grammar, its only purpose is to generate parse forests from which n-best sub-forests will be built.

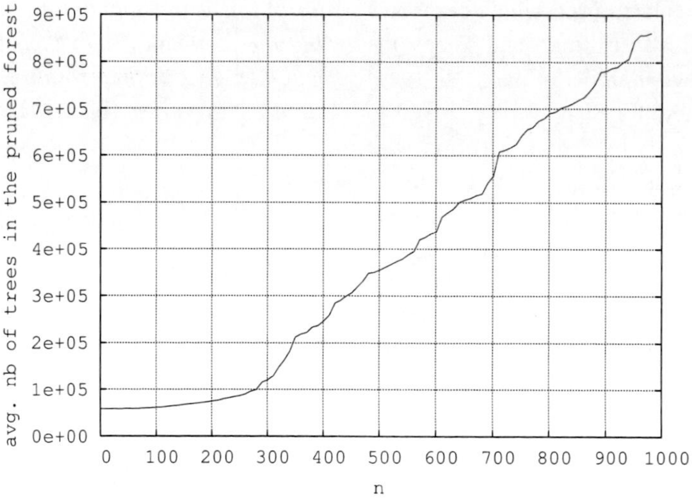

Figure 5: Overgeneration of the pruned n-best forest

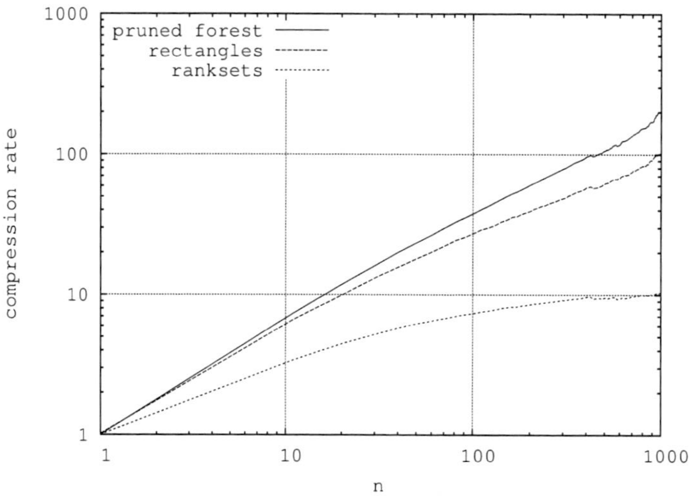

Figure 6: Average compression rates

achieve for different values of n. The compression rate is obtained by dividing the size of the n-best sub-forest of a sentence, as defined in section 2, by the size of the (unfolded) n-best forest. The latter is the sum of the sizes of all trees in the forest, where every tree is seen as an instantiated grammar, its size is therefore the size of the corresponding instantiated grammar.

The size of the n-best forest constitutes a natural upper bound for the representation of the n-best trees. Unfortunately, we have no natural lower bound for the size of such an object. Nevertheless, we have computed the compression rates of the pruned n-best forest and used it as an imperfect lower bound. As already mentioned, its imperfection comes from the fact that a pruned n-best forest contains more trees than the n best ones. This overgeneration appears clearly in Figure 5 which shows, for increasing values of n, the average number of trees in the n-best pruned forest for all sentences in our test set.

Figure 6 shows the average compression rates achieved by the three methods (forest pruning, rectangles and ranksets) on the test set for increasing values of n. As predicted, the performances lie between 1 (no compression) and the compression of the n-best pruned forest. The rectangle method outperforms the ranksets algorithm for every value of n.

The time needed to build an 100-best forest with the rectangle and the ranksets algorithms is shown in Figure 7. This figure shows the average parsing

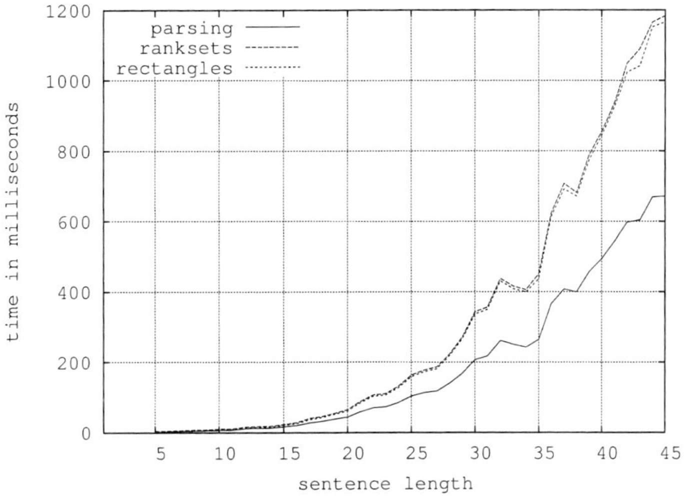

Figure 7: Processing time

time for sentences of a given length, as well as the average time necessary for building the 100-best forest using the two aforementioned algorithms. This time includes the parsing time i.e. it is the time necessary for parsing a sentence and building the 100-best forest. As shown by the figure, the time complexities of the two methods are very close.

5 Conclusion and perspectives

This work presented two methods to build n-best sub-forests. The so called rectangle methods showed to be the most promising, for it allows to build efficient sub-forests with little time overhead. Future work will focus on computing optimized partitions of the n-best matrices, a crucial part of the rectangle method, and adapting the method to arbitrary (non binary) CFG. Another line of research will concentrate on performing re-ranking of the n-best trees directly on the sub-forest.

Acknowledgments

This research is supported by the French National Research Agency (ANR) in the context of the SEQUOIA project (ANR-08-EMER-013).

References

Alfred V. Aho and Jeffrey D. Ullman. 1972. *The Theory of Parsing, Translation, and Compiling*, volume 1. Prentice-Hall, Englewood Cliffs, NJ.

Taylor L. Booth. 1969. Probabilistic representation of formal languages. In *Tenth Annual Symposium on Switching and Automata Theory*, pages 74–81.

Pierre Boullier and Philippe Deschamp. 1988. Le système SYNTAX™ - manuel d'utilisation. http://syntax.gforge.inria.fr/syntax3.8-manual.pdf.

Pierre Boullier and Benot Sagot. 2005. Efficient and robust LFG parsing: SXLFG. In *Proceedings of IWPT'05*, Vancouver, Canada.

Pierre Boullier. 2003. Guided Earley parsing. In *Proceedings of IWPT'03*, pages 43–54.

Jay Earley. 1970. An efficient context-free parsing algorithm. *Communication of the ACM*, 13(2):94–102.

Liang Huang and David Chiang. 2005. Better k-best parsing. In *Proceedings of IWPT'05*, pages 53–64.

Liang Huang. 2008. Forest reranking: Discriminative parsing with non-local features. In *Proceedings of ACL'08*, pages 586–594.

Víctor M. Jiménez and Andrés Marzal. 2000. Computation of the n best parse trees for weighted and stochastic context-free grammars. In *Proceedings of the Joint IAPR International Workshops on Advances in Pattern Recognition*, pages 183–192, London, United Kingdom. Springer-Verlag.

Dan Klein and Christopher D. Manning. 2001. Parsing and hypergraphs. In *Proceedings of IWPT'01*.

Bernard Lang. 1974. Deterministic techniques for efficient non-deterministic parsers. In J. Loeckx, editor, *Proceedings of the Second Colloquium on Automata, Languages and Programming*, volume 14 of *Lecture Notes in Computer Science*, pages 255–269. Springer-Verlag.

Bernard Lang. 1994. Recognition can be harder then parsing. *Computational Intelligence*, 10:486–494.

Mitchell P. Marcus, Beatrice Santorini, and Mary Ann Marcinkiewicz. 1993. Building a large annotated corpus of English: The Penn treebank. *Computational Linguistics*, 19(2):313–330, June.

Haitao Mi, Liang Huang, and Qun Liu. 2008. Forest-based translation. In *Proceedings of ACL-08: HLT*, pages 192–199.

Hebrew Dependency Parsing: Initial Results

Yoav Goldberg and **Michael Elhadad**
Ben Gurion University of the Negev
Department of Computer Science
POB 653 Be'er Sheva, 84105, Israel
{yoavg,elhadad}@cs.bgu.ac.il

Abstract

We describe a newly available Hebrew Dependency Treebank, which is extracted from the Hebrew (constituency) Treebank. We establish some baseline unlabeled dependency parsing performance on Hebrew, based on two state-of-the-art parsers, MST-parser and MaltParser. The evaluation is performed both in an artificial setting, in which the data is assumed to be properly morphologically segmented and POS-tagged, and in a real-world setting, in which the parsing is performed on automatically segmented and POS-tagged text. We present an evaluation measure that takes into account the possibility of incompatible token segmentation between the gold standard and the parsed data. Results indicate that (a) MST-parser performs better on Hebrew data than MaltParser, and (b) both parsers do not make good use of morphological information when parsing Hebrew.

1 Introduction

Hebrew is a Semitic language with rich morphological structure and free constituent order.

Previous computational work addressed unsupervised Hebrew POS tagging and unknown word resolution (Adler, 2007), Hebrew NP-chunking (Goldberg et al., 2006), and Hebrew constituency parsing (Tsarfaty, 2006; Golderg et al., 2009). Here, we focus on Hebrew dependency parsing.

Dependency-parsing got a lot of research attention lately, in part due to two CoNLL shared tasks focusing on multilingual dependency parsing (Buchholz and Erwin, 2006; Nivre et al., 2007). These tasks include relatively many parsing results for Arabic, a Semitic language similar to Hebrew. However, parsing accuracies for Arabic usually lag behind non-semitic languages. Moreover, while there are many published results, we could not find any error analysis or even discussion of the results of Arabic dependency parsing models, or the specific properties of Arabic making it easy or hard to parse in comparison to other languages.

Our aim is to evaluate current state-of-the-art dependency parsers and approaches on Hebrew dependency parsing, to understand some of the difficulties in parsing a Semitic language, and to establish a strong baseline for future work.

We present the first published results on Dependency Parsing of Hebrew.

Some aspects that make Hebrew challenging from a parsing perspective are:

Affixation Common prepositions, conjunctions and articles are prefixed to the following word, and pronominal elements often appear as suffixes. The segmentation of prefixes and suffixes is often ambiguous and must be determined in a specific context only. In term of dependency parsing, this means that the dependency relations occur not between space-delimited tokens, but instead between sub-token elements which we'll refer to as segments. Furthermore, any mistakes in the underlying token segmentations are sure to be reflected in the parsing accuracy.

Relatively free constituent order The ordering of constituents inside a phrase is relatively free. This is most notably apparent in the verbal phrases and sentential levels. In particular, while most sentences follow an SVO order, OVS and VSO configurations are also possible. Verbal arguments can appear before or after the verb, and in many ordering. For example, the message "went from Israel to Thailand" can be expressed as "went to Thailand from Israel", "to Thailand went from Israel", "from Israel went to Thailand", "from Israel to Thailand went" and "to Thailand from Israel went". This results in long and flat VP and S structures and a fair amount of sparsity, which suggests

Proceedings of the 11th International Conference on Parsing Technologies (IWPT), pages 129–133,
Paris, October 2009.

that a dependency representations might be more suitable to Hebrew than a constituency one.

Rich templatic morphology Hebrew has a very productive morphological structure, which is based on a root+template system. The productive morphology results in many distinct word forms and a high out-of-vocabulary rate, which makes it hard to reliably estimate lexical parameters from annotated corpora. The root+template system (combined with the unvocalized writing system) makes it hard to guess the morphological analyses of an unknown word based on its prefix and suffix, as usually done in other languages.

Unvocalized writing system Most vowels are not marked in everyday Hebrew text, which results in a very high level of lexical and morphological ambiguity. Some tokens can admit as many as 15 distinct readings, and the average number of possible morphological analyses per token in Hebrew text is 2.7, compared to 1.4 in English (Adler, 2007). This means that on average, every token is ambiguous with respect to its POS and morphological features.

Agreement Hebrew grammar forces morphological agreement between Adjectives and Nouns (which should agree in Gender and Number and definiteness), and between Subjects and Verbs (which should agree in Gender and Number).

2 Hebrew Dependency Treebank

Our experiments are based on the Hebrew Dependency Treebank (henceforth DepTB), which we derived from Version 2 of the Hebrew Constituency Treebank (Guthmann et al., 2009) (henceforth TBv2). We briefly discuss the conversion process and the resulting Treebank:

Parent-child dependencies TBv2 marks several kinds of dependencies, indicating the mother-daughter percolation of features such as number, gender, definiteness and accusativity. See (Guthmann et al., 2009) for the details. We follow TBv2's HEAD, MAJOR and MULTIPLE dependency marking in our-head finding rules. When these markings are not available we use head finding rules in the spirit of Collins. The head-finding rules were developed by Reut Tsarfaty and used in (Tsarfaty and Sima'an, 2008). We slightly extended them to handle previously unhandled cases. Some conventions in TBv2 annotations resulted in bad dependency structures. We identified these constructions and transformed the tree structure,

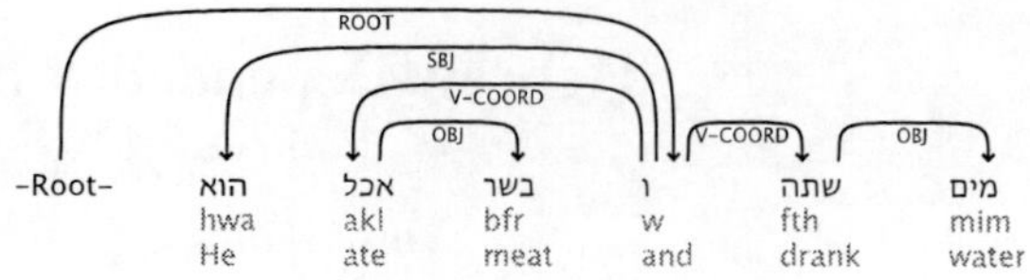

Figure 1: Coordinated Verbs

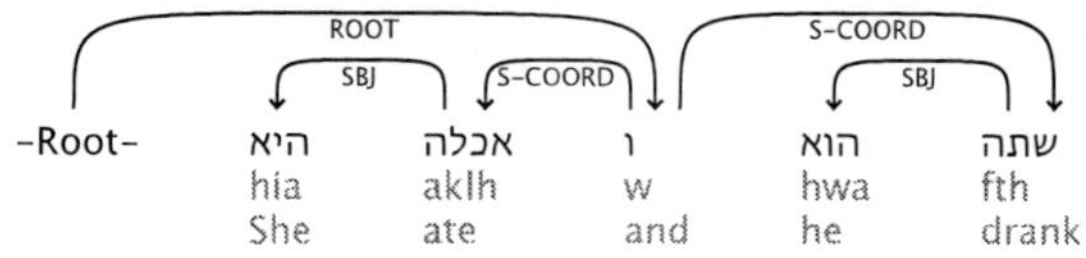

Figure 2: Coordinated Sentence

either manually or automatically, prior to the dependency extraction process.

The conversion process revealed some errors and inconsistencies in TBv2, which we fixed.

We take relativizers as the head S and SBAR, and prepositions as the heads of PPs. In the case the parent of a word X is an empty element, we take the parent of the empty element as the parent of X instead. While this may result in non-projective structures, in practice all but 34 of the resulting trees are projective.

We take conjunctions to be the head of a coordinated structure, resulting in dependency structures such as the one in Figures 1 and 2. Notice how in Figure 1 the parent of the subject "הוא/He" is the coordinator "ו/and", and not one of the verbs. While this makes things harder for the parser, we find this representation to be much cleaner and more expressive than the usual approach in which the first coordinated element is taken as the head of the coordinated structure.[1]

Dependency labels TBv2 marks 3 kinds of functional relations: Subject, Object and Complementizer. We use these in our conversion process, and label dependencies as being SBJ, OBJ or CMP, as indicated in TBv2. We also trivially mark the ROOT dependency, and introduce the relations INF_PREP, AT_INF POS_INF RB_INF between a base word and its suffix for the cases of suffix-inflected prepositions, accusative suffixes, possessive suffixes and inflected-adverbs, respectively. Still, most dependency relations remain unlabeled. We are currently seeking a method of reliably labeling the remaining edges with a rich set

[1] A possible alternative would be to allow multiple parents, as done in (de Marneffe et al., 2006), but current parsing algorithms require the output to be tree structured.

of relations. However, in the current work we focus on the unlabeled dependency structure.

POS tags The Hebrew Treebank follows a syntactic tagging scheme, while other Hebrew resources prefer a more morphological/dictionary-based scheme. For a discussion of these two tagging schemes in the context of parsing, see (Goldberg et al., 2009). In DepTB, we kept the two tagsets, and each token has two POS tags associated with it. However, as current dependency parsers rely on an external POS tagger, we performed all of our experiments only with the morphological tagset, which is what our tagger produces.

3 The Parsing Models

To establish some baseline results for Hebrew dependency parsing, we experiment with two parsing models, the graph-based MST-parser (McDonald, 2006) and the transition-based MaltParser (Nivre et al., 2006). These two parsers represent the current mainstream approaches for dependency parsing, and each was shown to provide state-of-the-art results on many languages (CoNLL Shared Task 2006, 2007).

Briefly, a graph-based parsing model works by assigning a score to every possible attachment between a pair (or a triple, for a second-order model) of words, and then inferring a global tree structure that maximizes the sum of these local scores. Transition-based models work by building the dependency graph in a sequence of steps, where each step is dependent on the next input word(s), the previous decisions, and the current state of the parser. For more details about these parsing models as well as a discussion on the relative benefits of each model, see (McDonald and Nivre, 2007).

Contrary to constituency-based parsers, dependency parsing models expect a morphologically segmented and POS tagged text as input.

4 Experiments

Data We follow the train-test-dev split established in (Tsarfaty and Sima'an, 2008). Specifically, we use Sections 2-12 (sentences 484-5724) of the Hebrew Dependency Treebank as our training set, and report results on parsing the development set, Section 1 (sentences 0-483). We do not evaluate on the test set in this work.

The data in the Treebank is segmented and POS-tagged. All of the models were trained on the gold-standard segmented and tagged data. When evaluating the parsing models, we perform two sets of evaluations. The first one is an oracle experiment, assuming gold segmentation and tagging is available. The second one is a real-world experiment, in which we segment and POS-tag the test-set sentences using the morphological disambiguator described in (Adler, 2007; Goldberg et al., 2008) prior to parsing.

Parsers and parsing models We use the freely available implementation of MaltParser[2] and MSTParser[3], with default settings for each of the parsers.

For MaltParser, we experiment both with the default feature representation (MALT) and the feature representation used for parsing Arabic in CoNLL 2006 and 2007 multilingual dependency parsing shared tasks (MALT-ARA).

For MST parser, we experimented with first-order (MST1) and second-order (MST2) models.

We varied the amount of lexical information available to the parser. Each of the parsers was trained on 3 datasets: LEXFULL, in which all the lexical items are available, LEX20, in which lexical items appearing less than 20 times in the training data were replaced by an OOV token, and LEX100 in which we kept only lexical items appearing more than 100 times in training.

We also wanted to control the effect of the rich morphological information available in Hebrew (gender and number marking, person, and so on). To this end, we trained and tested each model either with all the available morphological information (+MORPH) or without any morphological information (-MORPH).

Evaluation Measure We evaluate the resulting parses in terms of unlabeled accuracy – the percent of correctly identified (child,parent) pairs[4]. To be precise, we calculate:

$$\frac{number\_of\_correctly\_identified\_pairs}{number\_of\_pairs\_in\_gold\_parse}$$

For the oracle case in which the gold-standard token segmentation is available for the parser, this is the same as the traditional unlabeled-accuracy evaluation metric. However, in the real-word setting in which the token segmentation is done automatically, the yields of the gold-standard and the

[2] http://w3.msi.vxu.se/~jha/maltparser/

[3] http://sourceforge.net/projects/mstparser/

[4] All the results are macro averaged. The micro-averaged numbers are about 2 percents higher for all cases.

	Features	MST1	MST2	MALT	MALT-ARA
-MORPH	Full Lex	83.60	84.31	80.77	80.32
	Lex 20	82.99	84.52	79.69	79.40
	Lex 100	82.56	83.12	78.66	78.56
+MORPH	Full Lex	83.60	84.39	80.77	80.73
	Lex 20	83.60	84.77	79.69	79.84
	Lex 100	83.23	83.80	78.66	78.56

Table 1: Unlabeled dependency accuracy with **oracle** token segmentation and POS-tagging.

	Features	MST1	MST2	MALT	MALT-ARA
-MORPH	Full Lex	75.64	76.38	73.03	72.94
	Lex 20	75.48	76.41	72.04	71.88
	Lex 100	74.97	75.49	70.93	70.73
+MORPH	Full Lex	73.90	74.62	73.03	73.43
	Lex 20	73.56	74.41	72.04	72.30
	Lex 100	72.90	73.78	70.93	70.97

Table 2: Unlabeled dependency accuracy with **automatic** token segmentation and POS-tagging.

automatic parse may differ, and one needs to decide how to handle the cases in which one or more elements in the identified (child,parent) pair are not present in the gold-standard parse. Our evaluation metric penalizes these cases by regarding any such case as a mistake.

5 Results and Analysis

Results are presented in Tables 1 and 2.

It seems that the graph-based parsers perform better than the transitions-based ones. We attribute this to 2 factors: first, our representation of coordinated structure is hard to capture with a greedy local search as performed by a transition-based parser, because we need to defer many attachment decisions until the final coordinator is revealed. The global inference of the graph-based parser is much more robust to these kinds of structure. Indeed, when evaluating the gold-morphology, fully-lexicalized models on a subset of the test-set (314 sentences) which does not have coordinated structures, the accuracy of MALT improves in 3.98% absolute (from 80.77 to 84.75), while MST improves only in 2.66% absolute (from 83.60 to 86.26). Coordination is hard for both parsing models, but more so to the transition based MALT.

Second, it might be hard for a transition-based parser to handle the free constituent order of Hebrew, as it has no means of generalizing from the training set to various possible constituent ordering. The graph-based parser's features and inference method do not take constituent order into account, making it more suitable for free constituent order language.

As expected, the Second-order graph based models perform better than the first-order ones. Surprisingly, the Arabic-optimized feature-set do not perform better than the English one for the transition-based parsers. Overall, morphological information seems to contribute very little (if at all) to any of the parsers in the gold-morphology (oracle) setting. MALTARA gets some benefit from the morphological information in the fully-lexicalized case, while the MST variants benefit from morphology in the lexically-pruned models.

Overall, full lexicalization is not needed. Indeed, less lexicalized LEX20 2nd-order graph-based models perform better than the fully lexicalized ones. This strengthens our intuition that robust lexical statistics are hard to acquire from small annotated corpora, even more so for a language with productive morphology such as Hebrew.

Moving from the oracle morphological disambiguation to an automatic one greatly hurts the performance of all the models. This is in line with results for Hebrew constituency parsing, where going from gold segmentation to a parser derived one caused a similar drop in accuracy (Golderg et al., 2009). This suggests that we should either strive to improve the tagging accuracy, or perform joint inference for parsing and morphological disambiguation. We believe the later would be a better way to go, but it is currently unsupported in state-of-the-art dependency parsing algorithms.

Interestingly, in the automatic morphological disambiguation setting MALTARA benefits a little from the addition of morpological features, while the MST models perform better *without* these features.

6 Conclusions

We presented the first results for unlabeled dependency parsing of Hebrew, with two state-of-the-art dependency parsing models of different families. We experimented both with gold morphological information, and with an automatically derived one. It seems that graph-based models have a slight edge in parsing Hebrew over current transition-based ones. Both model families are not currently making good use of morphological information.

References

Meni Adler. 2007. *Hebrew Morphological Disambiguation: An Unsupervised Stochastic Word-based Approach*. Ph.D. thesis, Ben-Gurion University of the Negev, Beer-Sheva, Israel.

Sabine Buchholz and Marsi Erwin. 2006. CoNLL-X shared task on multilingual dependency parsing. In *Proc. of CoNLL*.

Marie-Catherine de Marneffe, Bill MacCartney, and Christopher D. Manning. 2006. Generating typed dependency parses from phrase structure parses. In *Proc. of LREC*.

Yoav Goldberg, Meni Adler, and Michael Elhadad. 2006. Noun phrase chunking in hebrew: Influence of lexical and morphological features. In *Proc. of COLING/ACL*.

Yoav Goldberg, Meni Adler, and Michael Elhadad. 2008. EM can find pretty good HMM POS-Taggers (when given a good start). In *Proc. of ACL*.

Yoav Golderg, Reut Tsarfaty, Meni Adler, and Michael Elhadad. 2009. Enhancing unlexicalized parsing performance using a wide coverage lexicon, fuzzy tag-set mapping, and EM-HMM-based lexical probabilities. In *Proc of EACL*.

Noemie Guthmann, Yuval Krymolowski, Adi Milea, and Yoad Winter. 2009. Automatic annotation of morpho-syntactic dependencies in a modern hebrew treebank. In *Proc of TLT*.

Ryan McDonald and Joakim Nivre. 2007. Characterizing the errors of data-driven dependency parsing models. In *Proc. of EMNLP*.

Ryan McDonald. 2006. *Discriminative Training and Spanning Tree Algorithms for Dependency Parsing*. Ph.D. thesis, University of Pennsylvania.

Joakim Nivre, Johan Hall, and Jens Nillson. 2006. MaltParser: A data-driven parser-generator for dependency parsing. In *Proc. of LREC*.

Joakim Nivre, Johan Hall, Sandra Kubler, Ryan McDonald, Jens Nilsson, Sebastian Riedel, and Deniz Yuret. 2007. The CoNLL 2007 shared task on dependency parsing. In *Proc. of the EMNLP-CoNLL*.

Reut Tsarfaty and Khalil Sima'an. 2008. Relational-realizational parsing. In *Proc. of CoLING*, August.

Reut Tsarfaty. 2006. Integrated morphological and syntactic disambiguation for modern hebrew. In *Proceedings of ACL-SRW*.

Scalable Discriminative Parsing for German

Yannick Versley
SFB 833
Universität Tübingen
versley@sfs.uni-tuebingen.de

Ines Rehbein
Dep. of Computational Linguistics
Universität des Saarlandes
rehbein@coli.uni-sb.de

Abstract

Generative lexicalized parsing models, which are the mainstay for probabilistic parsing of English, do not perform as well when applied to languages with different language-specific properties such as free(r) word order or rich morphology. For German and other non-English languages, linguistically motivated complex treebank transformations have been shown to improve performance within the framework of PCFG parsing, while generative lexicalized models do not seem to be as easily adaptable to these languages.

In this paper, we show a practical way to use grammatical functions as first-class citizens in a discriminative model that allows to extend annotated treebank grammars with rich feature sets without having to suffer from sparse data problems. We demonstrate the flexibility of the approach by integrating unsupervised PP attachment and POS-based word clusters into the parser.

1 Introduction

To capture the semantic relations inherent in a text, parsing has to recover both structural information and grammatical functions, which commonly coincide in English, but not in freer word order languages such as German. Instead one has to make use of morphological features in addition to exploiting ordering preferences such as the (violatable) default ordering of (*subject*<)*dative*<*accusative*.

Because of this fact, many successful approaches for German PCFG parsing (Schiehlen, 2004; Dubey, 2005; Versley, 2005) use *annotated treebank grammars* where the constituent trees from the treebank are enriched with further linguistic information that allows an adequate reconstruction of syntactic relationships, suggesting that probabilistic context-free grammars are an adequate tool for parsing these languages.

In the ACL 2008 workshop on Parsing German (Kübler, 2008), Rafferty and Manning (2008) used a lexicalized PCFG parser using markovization and parent annotation, but no linguistically inspired transformations; Rafferty and Manning did quite well on constituents, but were not successful in reconstructing grammatical functions, with results considerably worse than for other submissions in the shared task.

The framework we present in this paper – annotated treebank grammars with a discriminative model that allows lexicalization based on grammatical function assignment, as well as the addition of features based on unsupervised learning, including PP attachment and word clusters – shows that it is possible to achieve good improvements over generative lexicalized models by using the additional flexibility gained over standard lexicalized PCFG models. Our approach offers more flexibility than generative PCFG models, while computational costs for development and practical use are still acceptable. While we only present results for German, we are confident that the results carry over to other languages where annotated treebank grammars have been used successfully.

2 Parsing German with Morphology and Valence Information

As a base parser, we use BitPar (Schmid, 2004), a fast unlexicalized PCFG parser based on a first pass where non-probabilistic bottom-up parsing and top-down filtering is carried out efficiently by storing the chart in bit vectors, and construct the probabilistic chart only after top-down filtering. We use an annotated treebank PCFG that is de-

Proceedings of the 11th International Conference on Parsing Technologies (IWPT), pages 134–137,
Paris, October 2009.

rived from the Tiger treebank and largely inspired by earlier work on annotated treebank grammars for German (Schiehlen, 2004; Dubey, 2005; Versley, 2005).

Subcategorization With respect to the treebank grammar, we refine the node labels with linguistically important information that is only implicit in the treebank but would be tedious (and pointless) to annotate by hand:

Firstly, we annotate NPs by case; clause nodes (S and VP) are subcategorized by the clause type (*fin,inf,izu,rel*), and NPs and PPs with a relative pronoun are marked. Comparative phrases (e.g., *bigger [than a house]*, marked as NP in Tiger and TüBa-D/Z) are marked by adding a "CC" ending to the node label. Finally, auxiliaries are split according to their verb lemma into sein (*be*), haben (*have*), werden (*become*).

To aid the identification of noun phrase case, we add information related to case/number/gender syncretism to the preterminal labels of determiners, nouns, and adjectives (for details, see Versley, 2005) that allows to accurately determine the set of possible cases while keeping the size of the tagset relatively small .

Verb Valence We use information from the lexicon of the WCDG parser for German (Foth and Menzel, 2006) to mark verbs according to the arguments that they can take. While the WCDG lexicon contains more information, we only encode the possibility of accusative and dative complements, ignoring entries for genitive or clausal complements.

Markovization with Argument Marking It has been noted consistently (Klein and Manning, 2003; Schiehlen, 2004) that using markovization - replacing the original treebank rules by an approximation that only considers a limited context window of one or two siblings - improves results at least for a constituency-based evaluation. However, in some cases this simple markovization scheme leads to undesirable results including sentences with multiple subjects, as predicative arguments also have nominative case. To avoid this, we additionally mark which arguments have already been seen, yielding node labels such as `S_fin<VVFIN_a<RNP_a<sa` in the case of a partial constituent for a finite sentence (`S_fin`) expanding to the right (`<R`) where both subject (`s`) and accusative object (`a`) have already been seen.

Unknown Words For the base PCFG parse, we use a decision tree with 43 regular expressions as features, five of which are tailored towards recognizing the past and *zu*-infinitive form of separable prefix verbs (*ab*arbeiten ⇒ *ab*<u>ge</u>arbeitet, *ab*<u>zu</u>arbeiten), which cannot be recognized by considering suffixes only. The extended part of speech tags for verbs (which contain valency information) are interpolated between the distribution at the concrete leaf of the decision tree and the global valency distribution for the (coarse) part-of-speech tag.

Additionally, we use SMOR (Schmid et al., 2004) in conjunction with the verb lexicon and a gazetteer list containing person and location names to determine possible fine-grained part-of-speech tags for unknown words.

Restoring Grammatical Functions Adding edge labels to the nodes in PCFG parsing easily creates sparse data problems, as reported by Rafferty and Manning (2008), who witness a drop in constituent F-measure (excluding grammatical function labels) when they include function labels in the symbols of their PCFG. On the other hand, the informativity of grammatical function labels for the contents of the node does not always justify their cost in terms of data sparseness. Thus, we chose an approach where we include linguistically relevant information in the node labels (see above), and use the finer categorization to restore the grammatical function labels automatically: Using the most frequent function label sequence associated with a rule yields good results even in the presence of markovization, where some of the surrounding context is lost. Furthermore, this approach allows us to use the grammatical function label assignments in the subsequent discriminative model, thus yielding typed dependencies rather than the unlabeled dependencies that are used in the lexicalization model of the Stanford parser.

3 Discriminative Parsing

Generative parsing models are based on few distributions that use different feature combinations based on smoothing; incorporating additional features into these is very difficult at best.

As a result, the use of external preferences in such parsers is usually limited to approaches that reattach dependents in the output of the parser rather than integrating them in the parsing process.

Settings	no GFs	with GFs
Rafferty and Manning (2008)	77.40	NA
—, training with GFs	72.09	60.48
markov[unlex]	74.66	62.47
markov+parent[unlex]	73.94	61.63
markovGF[unlex]	75.00	63.58
markov[lex]	77.68	66.05
markovGF[lex]	77.55	66.69
markovGF[+pp]	**78.43**	**67.90**

Table 1: Evaluation results: PARSEVAL F_1 on PaGe development set

fW-w-*pos*, CW-w-*pos*	word form, cluster
f-s_p, fS-s_p-*size*	node label, node size$^{(1)}$
f-s_p-*RHS*	rule expansion
LD*dir*-s_p-s_d-hs_d	daughter attachment
LH-s_p-s_d-hs_d-hl_d	head projection
Ld*dir*-hs_p-hs_d	dependency (pos-pos)
Ld*dir*-hs_p-hs_d-*dist*	attachment length$^{(1)}$
Le*dir*-hs_p-hs_d-hl_d	dependency (pos-lemma)
Lf*dir*-hs_p-hl_p-hs_d	dependency (pos-lemma)
Lf*dir*-hs_p-hl_p-hs_d-*GF*	typed dep. (lemma-pos)
Lh*GF*-hc_p-hl_p-hc_d-hl_d	typed dep. (lemma-lemma)
MIpp-*prep*, MIpp0-*prep*	PP attach (noun)
MIppV-*prep*, MIppV0-*prep*	PP attach (verb)

^{1}) node sizes and attachment distances are discretized.
dir: one of H(head), L/R(head dep), B/I/E(nonheaded dep)
$s_{p/d}$ constituent symbol (parent/dep), $hs_{p/d}$ head cat, hc head cat (coarse), hl head lemma

Table 2: List of Features

Discriminative parsing for unification-based grammar commonly uses the conditional random field formulation introduced by Miyao and Tsujii (2002) and Geman and Johnson (2002), which uses local features to select a parse from a packed forest. The much larger cost in terms of memory and time compared to generative models has until recently made this approach largely unattractive (but see Finkel et al., 2008, who distributes the learning process over several powerful machines).

An alternative use of discriminative models has been to incorporate global features, either by reranking (e.g. Charniak and Johnson, 2005, or Kübler et al., 2009 for German) or by beam search over a pruned parse forest (Huang, 2008). However, Huang shows that a discriminative model using only local features reaps most of the benefits of the global model and performs at a similar level than earlier reranking-based approaches, pointing to the fact that local ambiguities often result in the n-best list not containing the correct parse.

The model we propose here extracts a pruned parse forest from a simple unlexicalized parser and then uses a factored discriminative model to apply a rich set of features using the lexicalized parse tree and its typed dependencies.

CRF parsing on pruned forests We extract a pruned forest that contains exactly those nodes and edges that can occur in trees that have a probability $\geq p_{best} \cdot t$, where in practice a threshold of $t = 10^{-3}$ ensures that no good parse is pruned away while at the same time, the resulting forest has only few nodes and edges.

For training, we extract an *oracle* tree, which is selected according to a combination of correct (annotated grammar) constituents, the absence of incorrect constituents, and the likelihood of the tree, to account for the fact that the forest does not always contain the exact gold tree. We then use the AMIS maximum entropy learner of Miyao and Tsujii (2002) to learn the discriminative model by creating a forest from a grammar learned on the remaining 4/5 of the training data.

Efficiency Parsing using the discriminative model is quite efficient, with a memory consumption for the whole system at about 270MB, including the data used to determine the corpus derived features (word clusters, mutual information statistics, semantic role clusters). Parsing speed is at 1.65sec./sentence on a 1.5GHz Pentium M, against 1.84sec./sent for BitPar alone when not using the tag filter for unknown words.

The time needed for learning can be reduced by keeping the pruned parse charts and only rerunning the part of lexicalization and discriminative feature extraction; when reusing the old parameters as a starting point for AMIS' model estimation, the turn-around time including feature extraction is below two hours.

3.1 Clustering for unknown words

To improve the behaviour on unknown words where morphological analyzer and regular expressions do not yield informative preferences, we exploit a large, part-of-speech-tagged corpus to induce clusters which provide robust information that is useful even in our case where preterminals in the PCFG are finer than standard POS tags.

The following features were gathered and used by weighting by the pointwise mutual information between the word and feature occurrences:

The **context** feature retrieves windows of high-frequent words surrounding the word in question (e.g. *der_mit* for 'der *Mann* mit den Blumen').

The **context2** feature retrieves windows of one high-frequent word and one part-of-speech tag surrounding the word in question (e.g. *der_NN* for 'der *schöne* Mann').

The **postag** feature simply retrieves the part-of-speech tag that is assigned to the word.

The result of using the repeated bisecting k-means implementation of CLUTO (Steinbach et al., 2000) on the resulting features yields syntactically sensible clusters containing years, money sums, last names, or place names.

3.2 Unsupervised PP Attachment and Subject-Object preferences

We used simple part-of-speech tag patterns to gather statistics on the association between nouns and immediately following prepositions, as well as between prepositions and closely following verbs on the DE-WaC corpus (Baroni and Kilgariff, 2006), an 1.7G words sample of the German-language WWW. The mutual information values for PP attachment are made available to the parser as features that are weighted by the mutual information value.

4 Evaluation and Discussion

To evaluate our approach, we use the dataset used for the ACL-2008 Parsing German Workshop (Kübler, 2008) that contains 26,116 sentences of the TIGER treebank (Brants et al., 2002), in a 8:1:1 split of training, testing, and evaluation data, and validate our approach on the development data, where the results published by Rafferty and Manning (2008) provide a useful comparison. All our experiments are done using tags automatically assigned by the parser, which reaches a tagging accuracy of about 97.5% according to the EVALB output.

We find that our final model, combining augmenting the treebank labels with lingustic information in addition to lexicalization and unsupervised PP attachment works better than the best-performing models of Rafferty and Manning, with a very large improvement in grammatical functions that is only surpassed by the Berkeley Parser (Petrov and Klein, 2008), showing that our combination of annotated treebank grammars with a factored discriminative model not only allows great control and flexibility for experimenting with the inclusion of novel features, but also yields very good results compared with the state of the art for German (see table 1 for results on the Tiger treebank). Preliminary results on TüBa-D/Z with a subset of the transformations of Versley (2005) show the same tendency as the results for Tiger, with 91.3% for constituents only, and 80.1% including function labels (compared to 88.9% and 77.2% for the Stanford parser).

Future work will investigate the impact of including additional features into the discriminative parsing model.

References

Baroni, M. and Kilgariff, A. (2006). Large linguistically-processed web corpora for multiple languages. In *EACL 2006*.

Brants, S., Dipper, S., Hansen, S., Lezius, W., and Smith, G. (2002). The TIGER treebank. In *Proc. TLT 2002*.

Charniak, E. and Johnson, M. (2005). Coarse-to-fine n-best parsing and maxent discriminative reranking. In *Proc. ACL 2005*.

Dubey, A. (2005). What to do when lexicalization fails: parsing German with suffix analysis and smoothing. In *ACL-2005*.

Finkel, J. R., Kleeman, A., and Manning, C. D. (2008). Efficient, feature-based, conditional random field parsing. In *ACL/HLT-2008*.

Foth, K. and Menzel, W. (2006). Hybrid parsing: Using probabilistic models as predictors for a symbolic parser. In *ACL 2006*.

Geman, S. and Johnson, M. (2002). Dynamic programming for parsing and estimation of stochastic unification-based grammars. In *ACL 2002*.

Huang, L. (2008). Forest reranking: Discriminative parsing with non-local features. In *HLT/ACL 2008*.

Klein, D. and Manning, C. D. (2003). Accurate unlexicalized parsing. In *ACL 2003*.

Kübler, S. (2008). The PaGe 2008 shared task on parsing German. In *Proceedings of the ACL-2008 Workshop on Parsing German*.

Kübler, S., Hinrichs, E., Maier, W., and Klett, E. (2009). Parsing coordinations. In *EACL 2009*.

Miyao, Y. and Tsujii, J. (2002). Maximum entropy estimation for feature forests. In *HLT 2002*.

Petrov, S. and Klein, D. (2008). Parsing German with latent variable grammars. In *Parsing German Workshop at ACL-HLT 2008*.

Rafferty, A. and Manning, C. D. (2008). Parsing three German treebanks: Lexicalized and unlexicalized baselines. In *ACL'08 workshop on Parsing German*.

Schiehlen, M. (2004). Annotation strategies for probabilistic parsing in German. In *Proc. Coling 2004*.

Schmid, H. (2004). Efficient parsing of highly ambiguous context-free grammars with bit vectors. In *Proc. Coling 2004*.

Schmid, H., Fitschen, A., and Heid, U. (2004). SMOR: A German computational morphology covering derivation, composition and inflection. In *Proceedings of LREC 2004*.

Steinbach, M., Karypis, G., and Kumar, V. (2000). A comparison of document clustering techniques. In *KDD Workshop on Text Mining*.

Versley, Y. (2005). Parser evaluation across text types. In *Proceedings of the Fourth Workshop on Treebanks and Linguistic Theories (TLT 2005)*.

Improving generative statistical parsing with semi-supervised word clustering

Marie Candito and Benoît Crabbé
Université Paris 7/INRIA (Alpage), 30 rue du Château des Rentiers, 75013 Paris

Abstract

We present a semi-supervised method to improve statistical parsing performance. We focus on the well-known problem of lexical data sparseness and present experiments of word clustering prior to parsing. We use a combination of lexicon-aided morphological clustering that preserves tagging ambiguity, and unsupervised word clustering, trained on a large unannotated corpus. We apply these clusterings to the French Treebank, and we train a parser with the PCFG-LA unlexicalized algorithm of (Petrov et al., 2006). We find a gain in French parsing performance: from a baseline of F_1=86.76% to F_1=87.37% using morphological clustering, and up to F_1=88.29% using further unsupervised clustering. This is the best known score for French probabilistic parsing. These preliminary results are encouraging for statistically parsing morphologically rich languages, and languages with small amount of annotated data.

1 Introduction

Lexical information is known crucial in natural language parsing. For probabilistic parsing, one main drawback of the plain PCFG approach is to lack sensitivity to the lexicon. The symbols accessible to context-free rules are part-of-speech tags, which encode generalizations that are too coarse for many parsing decisions (for instance subcategorization information is generally absent from tagsets). The lexicalized models first proposed by Collins reintroduced words at every depth of a parse tree, insuring that attachments receive probabilities that take lexical information into account. On the other hand, (Matsuzaki et al., 2005) have proposed probabilistic CFG learning with latent annotation (hereafter PCFG-LA), as a way to automate symbol splitting in unlexicalized probabilistic parsing (cf. adding latent annotations to a symbol is comparable to splitting this symbol). (Petrov et al., 2006) rendered the method usable in practice, with a tractable technique to retain only the beneficial splits.

We know that both lexicalized parsing algorithm and PCFG-LA algorithm suffer from lexical data sparseness. For lexicalized parsers, (Gildea, 2001) shows that bilexical dependencies parameters are almost useless in the probabilistic scoring of parser because they are too scarce.
For PCFG-LA, we have previously studied the lexicon impact on this so-called "unlexicalized" algorithm, for French parsing (Crabbé and Candito, 2008), (Candito et al., 2009). We have tested a totally unlexicalized parser, trained on a treebank where words are replaced by their POS tags. It obtains a parseval F_1=86.28 (note that it induces perfect tagging). We compared it to a parser trained with word+tag as terminal symbols (to simulate a perfect tagging), achieving F_1=87.79. This proves that lexical information is indeed used by the "unlexicalized" PCFG-LA algorithm: some lexical information percolates through parse trees via the latent annotations.

We have also reported a slight improvement (F_1=88.18) when word forms are clustered on a morphological basis, into lemma+tag clusters. So PCFG-LA uses lexical information, but it is too sparse, hence it benefits from word clustering. Yet the use of lemma+tag terminals supposes tagging prior to parsing. We propose here to apply rather a deterministic supervised morphological clustering that preserves tagging ambiguities, leaving it to the parser to disambiguate POS tags.

We also investigate the use of unsupervised word clustering, obtained from unannotated text. It has been proved useful for parsing by (Koo et al., 2008) and their work directly inspired ours. They have shown that parsing improves when cluster information is used as features in a discriminative training method that learns dependency parsers. We investigate in this paper the use of such clusters in a generative approach to probabilistic phrase-structure parsing, simply by replacing each token by its cluster.

Proceedings of the 11th International Conference on Parsing Technologies (IWPT), pages 138–141,
Paris, October 2009.

We present in section 2 the treebank instantiation we use for our experiments, the morphological clustering in section 3, and the Brown algorithm for unsupervised clustering in section 4. Section 5 presents our experiments, results and discussion. Section 6 discusses related work. Section 7 concludes with some ideas for future work.

2 French Treebank

For our experiments, we use the French Treebank (hereafter FTB) (Abeillé et al., 2003), containing 12531 sentences of the newspaper *Le Monde*. We started with the treebank instantiation defined in (Crabbé and Candito, 2008), where the rich original annotation containing morphological and functional information is mapped to a plain phrase-structure treebank with a tagset of 28 POS tags.

In the original treebank, 17% of the tokens belong to a compound, and compounds range from very frozen multi word expressions like *y compris* (literally *there included*, meaning *including*) to syntactically regular entities like *loi agraire* (*land law*). In most of the experiments with the FTB, each compound is merged into a single token: `(P (CL y) (A compris))` is merged as `(P y_compris)`. But because our experiments aim at reducing lexical sparseness but also at augmenting lexical coverage using an unannotated corpus, we found it necessary to make the unannotated corpus tokenisation and the FTB tokenisation consistent. To set up a robust parser, we chose to avoid recognizing compounds that exhibit syntactically regular patterns. We create a new instance of the treebank (hereafter FTB-UC), where syntactically regular patterns are "undone" (Figure 1). This reduces the number of distinct compounds in the whole treebank from 6125 to 3053.

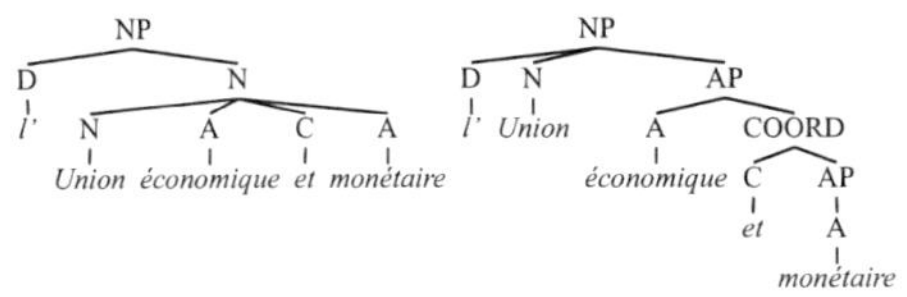

Figure 1: A NP with a compound (left) changed into a regular structure with simple words (right)

3 Morphological clustering

The aim of this step is to reduce lexical sparseness caused by inflection, without hurting parsability, and without committing ourselves as far as ambiguity is concerned. Hence, a morphological clustering using lemmas is not possible, since lemma assignment supposes POS disambiguation. Further, information such as mood on verbs is necessary to capture for instance that infinitive verbs have no overt subject, that participial clauses are sentence modifiers, etc... This is encoded in the FTB with different projections for finite verbs (projecting sentences) versus non finite verbs (projecting VPpart or VPinf).

We had the intuition that the other inflection marks in French (gender and number for determiners, adjectives, pronouns and nouns, tense and person for verbs) are not crucial to infer the correct phrase-structure projected by a given word[1].

So to achieve morphological clustering, we designed a process of *desinflection*, namely of removing some inflection marks. It makes use of the Lefff, a freely available rich morphological and syntactic French lexicon (Sagot et al., 2006), containing around 116000 lemmas (simple and compounds) and 535000 inflected forms. The desinflection is as follows: for a token t to *desinflect*, if it is known in the lexicon, for all the inflected lexical entries le of t, try to get corresponding singular entries. If for all the le, corresponding singular entries exist and all have the same form, then replace t by the corresponding singular. For instance for wt=*entrées* (ambiguous between *entrances* and *entered*, fem, plural), the two lexical entries are *[entrées/N/fem/plu]* and *[entrées/V/fem/plu/part/past]*[2], each have a corresponding singular lexical entry, with form *entrée*.

Then the same process applies to map feminine forms to corresponding masculine forms. This allows to change *mangée* (*eaten*, fem, sing) into *mangé* (*eaten*, masc, sing). But for the form *entrée*, ambiguous between N and Vpastpart entries, only the participle has a corresponding masculine entry (with form *entré*). In that case, in order to preserve the original ambiguity, *entrée* is not replaced by *entré*. Finite verb forms, when unambiguous with other POS, are mapped to second person plural present indicative corresponding forms. This choice was made in order to avoid creating ambiguity: the second person plural forms end with a very typical *-ez* suffix, and the resulting form is very unlikely ambiguous. For the first

[1]For instance, French oral comprehension does not seem to need plural marks very much, since a majority of French singular forms have their corresponding plural form pronounced in the same way.

[2]This is just an example and not the real Lefff format.

token of a sentence, if unknown in the lexicon, the algorithm tries to desinflect the low case corresponding form.

This desinflection reduces the number of distinct tokens in the FTB-UC from 27143 to 20268.

4 Unsupervised word clustering

We chose to use the (Brown et al., 1992) hard clustering algorithm, which has proven useful for various NLP tasks, such as dependency parsing (Koo et al., 2008) or named entity recognition (Liang, 2005). The algorithm to obtain C clusters is as follows: each of the C most frequent tokens of the corpus is assigned its own distinct cluster. For the (C+1)th most frequent token, create a (C+1)th cluster. Then for each pair among the C+1 resulting clusters, merge the pair that minimizes the loss in the likelihood of the corpus, according to a bigram language model defined on the clusters. Repeat this operation for the (C+2)th most frequent token, etc... This results in a hard clustering into C clusters. The process can be continued to further merge pairs of clusters among the C clusters, ending with a unique cluster for the whole vocabulary. This can be traced to obtain a binary tree representing the merges of the C clusters. A cluster can be identified by its path within this binary tree. Hence, clusters can be used at various levels of granularity.

5 Experiments and discussion

For the Brown clustering algorithm, we used Percy Liang's code[3], run on the *L'Est Républicain* corpus, a 125 million word journalistic corpus, freely available at CNRTL[4]. The corpus was tokenised[5], segmented into sentences and desinflected using the process described in section 3. We ran the clustering into 1000 clusters for the desinflected forms appearing at least 20 times.

We tested the use of word clusters for parsing with the Berkeley algorithm (Petrov et al., 2006). Clustering words in this case has a double advantage. First, it augments the known vocabulary, which is made of all the forms of all the clusters appearing in the treebank. Second, it reduces sparseness for the latent annotations learning on the lexical rules of the PCFG-LA grammar.

We used Petrov's code, adapted to French by (Crabbé and Candito, 2008), for the suffixes used to classify unknown words, and we used the same training(80%)/dev(10%)/test(10%) partition. We used the FTB-UC treebank to train a baseline parser, and three other parsers by changing the terminal symbols used in training data:

desinflected forms: as described in section 3

clusters + cap: each desinflected form is replaced by its cluster bit string. If the desinflected form has no corresponding cluster (it did not appear 20 times in the unannotated corpus), a special cluster UNKC is used. Further, a _C suffix is added if the form starts with a capital.

clusters + cap + suffixes: same as before, except that 9 additional features are used as suffixes to the cluster: if form is all digits, ends with *ant*, or *r*, or *ez* (cf. this is how end desinflected forms of unambiguous finite verbs), ...

We give in table 1 parsing performance in terms of labeled precision/recall/Fscore, and also the more neutral unlabeled attachment score (UAS)[6].

The desinflection process does help: benefits from reducing data sparseness exceed the loss of agreement markers. Yet tagging decreases a little, and this directly impacts the dependency score, because the dependency extraction uses head propagation rules that are sensitive to tagging. In the same way, the use of bare clusters increases labeled recall/precision, but the tagging accuracy decreases, and thus the UAS. This can be due to the coarseness of the clustering method, which sometimes groups words that have different POS (for instance among a cluster of infinite verbs, one may find a present participle). The quality of the clusters is more crucial in our case than when clusters are features, whose informativity is discriminatively learnt. This observation led us to append a restricted set of suffixes to the clusters, which gives us the best results for now.

6 Related work

We already mentioned that we were inspired by the success of (Koo et al., 2008) in using word clusters as features for the discriminative learning of dependency parsers. Another approach to augment the known vocabulary for a generative prob-

[3] *http://www.eecs.berkeley.edu/ pliang/software*

[4] *http://www.cnrtl.fr/corpus/estrepublicain*

[5] The 200 most frequent compounds of the FTB-UC were systematically recognized as one token.

[6] In all metrics punctuation tokens are ignored and all results are for sentences of less than 40 words. Note that we used the FTB-UC treebank. There are mors tokens in sentences than in the FTB with all compounds merged, and baseline F_1 scores are a little higher (86.79 versus 86.41).

terminal symbols	LP	LR	F_1	UAS	Vocab. size	Tagging Acc.
inflected forms (baseline)	86.94	86.65	86.79	91.00	27143	96.90
desinflected forms	87.42	87.32	87.37	91.14	20268	96.81
clusters + cap	88.08	87.50	87.79	91.12	1201	96.37
clusters + cap + suffixes	88.43	88.14	**88.29**	**91.68**	1987	**97.04**

Table 1: Parsing performance when training and parsing use clustered terminal symbols

abilistic parser is the one pursued in (Goldberg et al., 2009). Within a plain PCFG, the lexical probabilities for words that are rare or absent in the treebank are taken from an external lexical probability distribution, estimated using a lexicon and the Baulm-Welch training of an HMM tagger. This is proved useful to better parse Hebrew.

7 Conclusion and future work

We have tested the very simple method of replacing inflected forms by clusters of forms in a generative probabilistic parser. This crude technique has surprisingly good results and offers a very cheap and simple way to augment the vocabulary seen at training time. It seems interesting to try the technique on other generative approaches such as lexicalized probabilistic parsing.

We plan to optimize the exact shape of terminal symbols to use. Bare unsupervised clusters are unsatisfactory, and we have seen that adding simple suffixes to the clusters improved performance. Learning such suffixes is a path to explore. Also, the hierarchical organization of the clusters could be used, in the generative approach adopted here, by modulating the granularity of the clusters depending on their frequency in the treebank.

We also need to check to what extent the desinflection step helps for taking advantage of the very local information captured by the Brown clustering.Finally, we could try using other kinds of clustering, such as the approach of (Lin, 1998), which captures similarity between syntactic dependencies beared by nouns and verbs.

8 Acknowledgements

The authors truly thank Percy Liang and Slav Petrov for providing their code for respectively Brown clustering and PCFG-LA. This work was supported by the French National Research Agency (SEQUOIA project ANR-08-EMER-013).

References

Anne Abeillé, Lionel Clément, and François Toussenel, 2003. *Building a Treebank for French*. Kluwer, Dordrecht.

Peter F. Brown, Vincent J. Della, Peter V. Desouza, Jennifer C. Lai, and Robert L. Mercer. 1992. Class-based n-gram models of natural language. *Computational linguistics*, 18(4):467–479.

Marie Candito, Benoit Crabbé, and Djamé Seddah. 2009. On statistical parsing of french with supervised and semi-supervised strategies. In *EACL 2009 Workshop Grammatical inference for Computational Linguistics*, Athens, Greece.

Benoit Crabbé and Marie Candito. 2008. Expériences d'analyse syntaxique statistique du français. In *Actes de la 15ème Conférence sur le Traitement Automatique des Langues Naturelles (TALN'08)*, pages 45–54, Avignon, France.

Daniel Gildea. 2001. Corpus variation and parser performance. In *Proc. of EMNLP'01*, pages 167–202, Pittsburgh, USA.

Yoav Goldberg, Reut Tsarfaty, Meni Adler, and Michael Elhadad. 2009. Enhancing unlexicalized parsing performance using a wide coverage lexicon, fuzzy tag-set mapping, and EM-HMM-based lexical probabilities. In *Proc. of EACL-09*, pages 327–335, Athens, Greece.

Terry Koo, Xavier Carreras, and Michael Collins. 2008. Simple semi-supervised dependency parsing. In *Proc. of ACL-08*, Columbus, USA.

Percy Liang. 2005. Semi-supervised learning for natural language. In *MIT Master's thesis*, Cambridge, USA.

Dekang Lin. 1998. Automatic retrieval and clustering of similar words. In *Proc. of ACL-98*, pages 768–774, Montreal, Canada.

Takuya Matsuzaki, Yusuke Miyao, and Jun'ichi Tsujii. 2005. Probabilistic cfg with latent annotations. In *Proc. of ACL-05*, pages 75–82, Ann Arbor, USA.

Slav Petrov, Leon Barrett, Romain Thibaux, and Dan Klein. 2006. Learning accurate, compact, and interpretable tree annotation. In *Proc. of ACL-06*, Sydney, Australia.

Benoît Sagot, Lionel Clément, Éric Villemonte de La Clergerie, and Pierre Boullier. 2006. The Lefff 2 syntactic lexicon for french: architecture, acquisition, use. In *Proc. of LREC'06*, Genova, Italy.

Application of feature propagation to dependency parsing

Kepa Bengoetxea Koldo Gojenola
IXA NLP Group, Technical School of Engineering, Bilbao
University of the Basque Country, Plaza La Casilla 3, 48012, Bilbao
kepa.bengoetxea@ehu.es, koldo.gojenola@ehu.es

Abstract

This paper presents a set of experiments performed on parsing the Basque Dependency Treebank. We have applied feature propagation to dependency parsing, experimenting the propagation of several morphosyntactic feature values. In the experiments we have used the output of a parser to enrich the input of a second parser. Both parsers have been generated by Maltparser, a freely data-driven dependency parser generator. The transformations, combined with the pseudoprojective graph transformation, obtain a LAS of 77.12% improving the best reported results for Basque.

1 Introduction

This work presents several experiments performed on dependency parsing of the Basque Dependency Treebank (BDT, Aduriz et al. 2003). We have experimented the idea of feature propagation through dependency arcs, in order to help the parser. Feature propagation has been used in classical unification-based grammars as a means of propagating linguistic information through syntax trees. We apply this idea in the context of inductive dependency parsing, combining a reduced set of linguistic principles that express feature propagation among linguistic elements with Maltparser (Nivre et al. 2007a), an automatic dependency parser generator.

We have concentrated on propagating several morphosyntactic feature values from: a) auxiliary verbs to the main verb, b) the last constituent to the head noun, in noun phrases c) the last conjunct to the conjunction, in coordination.

This work was developed in the context of dependency parsing exemplified by the CoNLL shared task on dependency parsing in years 2006 and 2007 (Nivre et al. 2007b), where several systems had to compete analyzing data from a typologically varied range of 11 languages. The treebanks for all languages were standardized using a previously agreed CoNLL-X format (see Figure 1). BDT was one of the evaluated treebanks, which will allow a direct comparison of results.

Many works on treebank parsing have dedicated an effort to the task of pre-processing training trees (Nilsson et al. 2007). When these approaches have been applied to dependency parsing several works (Nilsson et al. 2007; Bengoetxea and Gojenola 2009) have concentrated on modifying the structure of the dependency tree, changing the shape of the graph. In contrast, rather than modifying the tree structure, we will experiment changing the information contained in the nodes of the tree. This approach requires having an initial dependency tree in order to apply the feature propagation process, which will be obtained by means of a standard trained model. This way, the features will be propagated through some incorrect dependency arcs, and the process will be dependent on the reliability of the initial arcs. After enriching the tree, a second parsing model will try to use this new information to improve the standard model. This process can also be seen as an example of stacked learning (Martins et al. 2008, Nivre and McDonald 2008) where a second parser is used to improve the performance of a first one.

The rest of the paper is organized as follows. Section 2 presents the main resources used in this work. Section 3 presents three different proposals for the propagation of the most important morphological features. Next, section 4 will evaluate the results of each transformation, and the last section outlines the main conclusions.

2 Resources

This section will describe the main elements that have been used in the experiments. First, subsection 2.1 will present the Basque Dependency Treebank data, while subsection 2.2 will describe the main characteristics of Maltparser, a state of the art and data-driven dependency parser.

2.1 The Basque Dependency Treebank

The BDT can be considered a pure dependency treebank, as its initial design considered that all the dependency arcs would connect sentence tokens. Although this decision had consequences on the annotation process, its simplicity is also an advantage when applying several of the most

Proceedings of the 11th International Conference on Parsing Technologies (IWPT), pages 142–145,
Paris, October 2009.

Index	Word	Lemma	Category	Subcategory	Features	Head	Dependency
1	etorri	etorri	V	V	_	3	lot
2	dela	izan	AUXV	AUXV	SC:CMP|SUBJ:3S	1	auxmod
3	eta	eta	CONJ	CONJ	_	6	ccomp_obj
4	joan	joan	V	V	_	3	lot
5	dela	izan	AUXV	AUXV	SC:CMP|SUBJ:3S	4	auxmod
6	esan	esan	V	V	_	0	ROOT
7	zien	*edun	AUXV	AUXV	SUBJ:3S|OBJ:3P	6	auxmod
8	mutil	mutil	NOUN	NOUN	_	6	ncsubj
9	txikiak	txiki	ADJ	ADJ	CASE:ERG|NUM:S	8	ncmod
10	.	.	PUNT	PUNT_PUNT	_	9	PUNC

Figure 1: Example of a BDT sentence in the CONLL-X format

(V = main verb, AUXV = auxiliary verb, SC = subordinated clause, CMP = completive, ccomp_obj = clausal complement object, SUBJ:3S: subject in 3rd person sing., OBJ:3P: object in 3rd person pl.).

efficient parsing algorithms. The treebank consists of 55,469 tokens forming 3,700 sentences, 334 of which were used as test data.

```
(1) Etorri (come) dela (that-has) eta
  (and) joan  (go) dela (that-has) esan
  (tell) zien (did) mutil (boy)
  txikiak(the-little)
He told the little boy that he has come
and he has gone
```

Figure 1 contains an example of a sentence (1), annotated in the CoNLL-X format. The text is organized in eight tab-separated columns: word-number, form, lemma, category , subcategory, morphological features, and the dependency relation (headword + dependency). Basque is an agglutinative language and it presents a high power to generate inflected word-forms. The information in Figure 1 has been simplified due to space reasons, as typically the Features column will contain many morphological features, which are relevant for parsing.

2.2 Maltparser

Maltparser (Nivre et al. 2007a) is a state of the art dependency parser that has been successfully applied to typologically different languages and treebanks. While several variants of the base parser have been implemented, we will use one of its standard versions (Maltparser version 0.4). The parser obtains deterministically a dependency tree in linear-time in a single pass over the input. To determine which is the best action at each parsing step, the parser uses history-based feature models and discriminative machine learning. In all the following experiments, we made use of a SVM classifier. The specification of the features used for learning can in principle be any kind of data in Figure 1 (such as word-form, lemma, category or morphological features).

3 Experiments

We applied the following steps:

a) Application of feature propagation to the training data, using the gold standard arcs, obtaining a "enriched training data".

b) Training Maltparser on the "enriched training data" to generate a "enriched parser".

c) Training Maltparser with the training data, without any transformation, to generate a "standard parser".

d) Parse the test data with the "standard parser", obtaining the "standard output".

e) Apply feature propagation to the "standard output", using the dependency arcs given by the parser (with some incorrect arcs), obtaining the "standard parser's enriched output".

f) Finally, parsing the "standard parser's enriched output" with the "enriched parser",

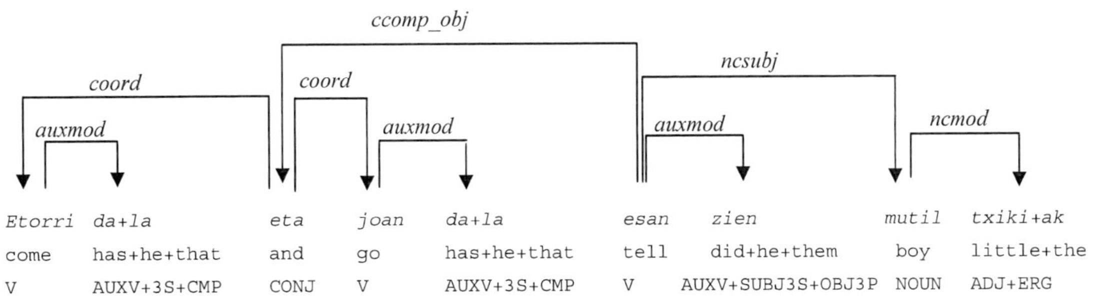

Figure 2: Dependency tree for the sentence in Figure 1.

(V = main verb; AUXV: auxiliary verb; CMP: completive subordinated mark; CONJ: conjunction; ERG: ergative case).

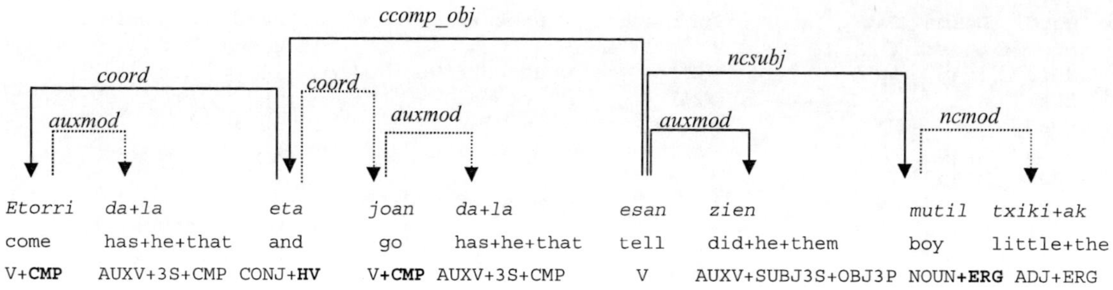

Figure 3: Dependency tree after propagating the morphological features.

evaluating the output with the gold test data.

We have applied three types of feature propagation of the most important morphological feature values: a) from auxiliary verbs to the main verb (verb phrases) b) from post-modifiers to the head noun (noun phrases) c) from the last conjunct to the conjunction (coordination). This was done because Basque is a head final language, where many relevant features are located at the end of constituents. Figure 3 shows (dotted lines) the arcs that will propagate features from child to parent. The three transformations will be described in the following subsections.

3.1 Verb compounds

In BDT the verbal elements are organized around the main verb, but much syntactically relevant verbal information, like subordination type, aspect, tense and agreement usually appear attached to the auxiliary verb, which is the dependent. Its main consequence for parsing is that the elements bearing the relevant information for parsing are situated far in the tree with respect to their head. In Figure 2, we can see that the morpheme *–la*, indicating a subordinated completive sentence, appears down in the tree, and this could affect the correct attachment of the two coordinated verbs to the conjunction (*eta*), as conjunctions should link elements showing similar grammatical features (*-la* in this example). Similarly, it could affect the decision about the dependency type of *eta* (and) with respect to the main verb *esan* (to say), as the dependency relation ccomp_obj is defined by means of the *–la* (completive) morpheme, far down in the tree.

Figure 3 shows the effect of propagating the completive feature value (CMP) from the auxiliary verb to the main verb through the auxmod (auxiliary modifier) relation.

3.2 Noun Phrases

In noun phrases and postpositional phrases, the most important morphological feature values (case and number) are situated in the last post-modifier after the noun. Figure 3 shows the effect of propagating the ergative (ERG) case feature value from the adjective (the last constituent of the noun phrase) to the noun through the relation ncmod (non-clausal modifier).

3.3 Coordination

Coordination in BDT was annotated in the so called Prague Style, where the conjunction is taken as the head, and the conjuncts depend on it. Basque is head final, so usually the last conjunct contains syntactically relevant features. We experimented the promotion of the category, case and subordination information from the last conjunct to the conjunction. In the example in Figure 3, the conjunction (*eta*) receives a new feature (HV for Head:Verb) from its dependent. This can be seen as an alternative to (Nilsson et al. 2007) who transform dependency arcs.

4 Evaluation

Evaluation was performed dividing the treebank in three sets: training set (45,000 tokens), development and test sets (5,000 tokens each). Training and testing of the system have been performed on the same datasets presented at the CoNLL 2007 shared task, which will allow for a direct comparison. Table 1 presents the Labeled Attachment Score (LAS) of the different tests on development and test data. The first row presents the best system score (76.94% LAS) in CoNLL 2007. This system combined six variants of a base parser (Maltparser). The second row shows the single Maltparser approach which obtained the fifth position. Row 3 presents Bengoetxea and Gojenola's results (76.80% LAS) when applying graph transformations (pseudo-projective, coordination and verb groups) to Basque, in the spirit of Nilsson et al. (2007). Row 4 shows our results after applying several feature optimizations, which we will use as our baseline.

		LAS			
	System	Development		Test	
1	Nivre et al. 2007b (CoNLL 2007)	-		76.94%	
2	Hall et al. 2007 (CoNLL 2007)			74.99%	
3	Bengoetxea and Gojenola 2009			76.80%	
4	Feature optimization (baseline)	77.46%		75.07%	
5	Proj	78.16%	(+0.70)	*75.99%	(+0.92)
6	P_{VG}	78.14%	(+0.68)	75.54%	(+0.47)
7	P_{COOR}	77.36%	(-0.10)	75.22%	(+0.15)
8	P_{CAS}	77.32%	(-0.14)	74.86%	(-0.21)
9	$P_{VG} + P_{CAS}$	78.53%	(+1.09)	75.42%	(+0.35)
10	$P_{COOR} + P_{VG} + P_{CAS}$	78.31%	(+0.85)	*75.93%	(+0.86)
11	$P_{COOR} + P_{VG}$	78.25%	(+0.79)	*75.93%	(+0.86)
12	Proj + P_{VG}	78.91%	(+1.45)	*76.12%	(+1.05)
13	Proj + P_{VG} + P_{COOR} + P_{CAS}	78.31%	(+0.85)	***77.12%**	(+2.05)

Table 1. Evaluation results

(Proj: Pseudo-projective, P_{VG}, P_{CAS}, P_{COOR}: Propagation on verb compounds, case (NPs) and coordination; *: statistically significant in McNemar's test with respect to labeled attachment score with $p < 0.01$)

Feature propagation in verb groups (P_{VG}) improves LAS in almost 0.5% (row 6 in Table 1). While coordination and case propagation do not improve significantly the accuracy by themselves (rows 7 and 8), their combination with P_{VG} (verb groups) significantly increases LAS (+0.86%, see row 10). Looking at the accuracy of the dependency arcs used for feature propagation, auxiliary verbs are the most reliable elements, as their arcs (linking it to its head, the main verb) have 97% precision and 98% recall. This is in accord with P_{VG} giving the biggest increase, while arcs related to coordination (63% precision and 65% recall) give a more modest contribution.

BDT contains 2.9% of nonprojective arcs, so we experimented the effect of combining the pseudoprojective transformation (Nilsson et al. 2007) with feature propagation, obtaining a LAS of 77.12%, the best reported results for the BDT.

5 Conclusions

We have performed a set of experiments using the output of a parser to enrich the input of a second parser, propagating the relevant morphological feature values through dependency arcs. The best system, after applying three types of feature propagation, obtains a 77.12% LAS (2.05% improvement over the baseline) on the test set, which is the best reported result for Basque dependency parsing, improving the better published result for a combined parser (76.94%).

Acknowledgements

This research was supported by the Basque Government (EPEC-RS, S-PE08UN48) and the University of the Basque Country (EHU-EJIE, EJIE07/05).

References

I. Aduriz, M. J. Aranzabe, J. M. Arriola, A. Atutxa, A. Diaz de Ilarraza, A. Garmendia and M. Oronoz. 2003. *Construction of a Basque dependency treebank*. Treebanks and Linguistic Theories.

Kepa Bengoetxea and Koldo Gojenola. 2009. *Exploring Treebank Transformations in Dependency Parsing*. Proceedings of RANLP'2009.

Johan Hall, Jens Nilsson, Joakim Nivre J., Eryigit G., Megyesi B., Nilsson M. and Saers M. 2007. *Single Malt or Blended? A Study in Multilingual Parser Optimization*. Proceedings of the CoNLL Shared Task EMNLP-CoNLL.

André F. T. Martins, Dipanjan Das, Noah A. Smith, Eric P. Xing. 2008. *Stacking Dependency Parsing*. EMNLP-2008.

Jens Nilsson, Joakim Nivre and Johan Hall. 2007. *Tree Transformations for Inductive Dependency Parsing*. Proceedings of the 45th ACL.

Joakim Nivre, Johan Hall, Jens Nilsson, Chanev A., Gülsen Eryiğit, Sandra Kübler, Marinov S., and Edwin Marsi. 2007a. *MaltParser: A language-independent system for data-driven dependency* parsing. Natural Language Engineering.

Joakim Nivre, Johan Hall, Sandra Kübler, Ryan McDonald, Jens Nilsson, Sebastian Riedel and Deniz Yuret. 2007b. *The CoNLL 2007 Shared Task on Dependency Parsing*. EMNLP-CoNLL.

Joakim Nivre and Ryan McDonald. 2008. *Integrating graphbased and transition-based dependency parsers*. ACL-2008.

Guessing the Grammatical Function of a Non-Root F-Structure in LFG

Anton Bryl
CNGL,
Dublin City University,
Dublin 9, Ireland

Josef van Genabith
CNGL,
Dublin City University,
Dublin 9, Ireland

Yvette Graham
NCLT,
Dublin City University,
Dublin 9, Ireland

{abryl,josef,ygraham}@computing.dcu.ie

Abstract

Lexical-Functional Grammar (Kaplan and Bresnan, 1982) f-structures are bilexical labelled dependency representations. We show that the Naive Bayes classifier is able to guess missing grammatical function labels (i.e. bilexical dependency labels) with reasonably high accuracy (82–91%). In the experiments we use f-structure parser output for English and German Europarl data, automatically "broken" by replacing grammatical function labels with a generic UNKNOWN label and asking the classifier to restore the label.

1 Introduction

The task of labeling unlabelled dependencies, a sub-task of dependency parsing task, can occur in transfer-based machine translation (when only an inexact match can be found in the training data for the given SL fragment) or in parsing where the system produces fragmented output. In such cases it is often reasonably straightforward to guess which fragments are dependent on which other fragments (e.g. in transfer-based MT). What is harder to guess are the labels of the dependencies connecting the fragments.

In this paper we systematically investigate the labelling task by automatically deleting function labels from Lexical-Functional Grammar-based parser output for German and English Europarl data, and then restoring them using a Naive Bayes classifier trained on attribute names and attribute values of the f-structure fragments. We achieve 82% (German) to 91% (English) accuracy for both single and multiple missing function labels.

The paper is organized as follows: in Section 2 we define the problem and the proposed solution more formally. Section 3 details the experimental evaluations, and in Section 4 we present our conclusions.

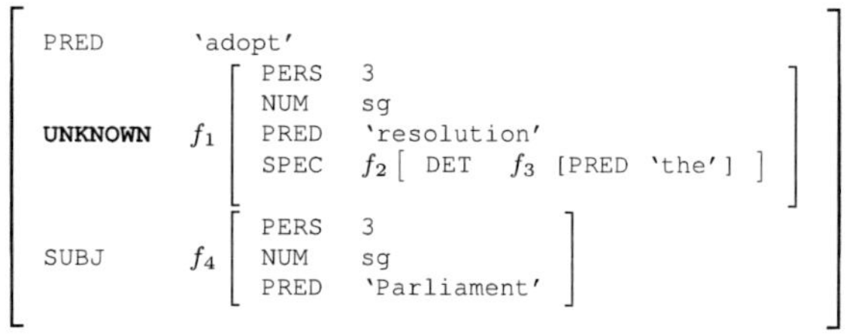

Figure 1: Example of a "broken" f-structure (simplified). The sentence is *'Parliament adopted the resolution.'* The missing function of f_1 is OBJ.

2 Guessing Unknown Grammatical Functions

Let us introduce some useful definitions. By dependent f-structure of the parent f-structure f_P we mean an f-structure f_d which bears a grammatical function within f_P, or belongs to a set which bears a grammatical function within f_P. E.g., in Figure 1 f_2 is a dependent f-structure of f_1. In this paper we will not distinguish between these two situations, but simply refer to multiple f-structures bearing the same function within the same parent for set-valued grammatical functions. $C(\phi, f_P)$ denotes the number of dependent f-structures of f_P which bear the grammatical function ϕ in f_P (either directly or as members of a set).

Let us formalize the simple case when the grammatical function of only one dependent f-structure is missing. Let F_P be the set of f-structures which have a dependent f-structure with an UNKNOWN label instead of the grammatical function. Let Φ be the set of all grammatical functions of the given grammar. We need a guessing function $G : F_P \to \Phi$, such that $G(f_P)$ is a meaningful replacement for the UNKNOWN label in f_P. As the set Φ is finite, the problem is evidently a classification task.

F-structures are characterized by attributes some of which potentially carry information about the f-structure's grammatical function, even if

Proceedings of the 11th International Conference on Parsing Technologies (IWPT), pages 146–149,
Paris, October 2009.

Language	N-GF	N-DEP	AVG-DEP	MIN-DEP	MAX-DEP
English	24	9724	1.57	1	5
German	39	10910	1.55	1	5

Table 1: Data used in the evaluation. **N-GF** is the number of different grammatical functions occurring in the dataset. **N-DEP** is the number of dependent f-structures in the test set. **AVG-DEP**, **MIN-DEP**, **MAX-DEP** is the average, min. and max. number of dependant structures per parent in the test set.

we observe these attributes completely separately from each other. For example, it seems likely that an f-structure with an `ATYPE` attribute is an `ADJUNCT`, while an f-structure which has `CASE` is probably a `SUBJ` or an `OBJ`. Given this, Naive Bayes appears to be a promising solution here. Below we describe a way to adapt this classifier to the problem of grammatical function guessing.

Let $\Phi_P \subseteq \Phi$ be the set of grammatical functions which are already present in f_P. Let $\Xi = \{\xi_1..\xi_n\}$ be the set of features, and let $X = \{x_1..x_n\}$ be the values of these features for the f-structure f_d for which the function should be guessed. Then the answer ϕ_d is chosen as follows:

$$\phi_d = \arg\max_{\phi \in \Phi} \left(p(\phi) M_P(\phi) \prod_{i=1}^{n} p(\xi_i = x_i | \phi) \right) \quad (1)$$

$$M_P(\phi) = \begin{cases} p(C(\phi, f_P) > 1), \textit{ if } \phi \in \Phi_P \\ 1, \textit{otherwise} \end{cases} \quad (2)$$

where the probabilities are estimated from the training data. Equation (2) states that if ϕ is already present in the parent f-structure, the probability of ϕ being set-valued is considered.

We propose two ways of building the feature set Ξ. First, it is possible to consider the presence/absence of each particular attribute in f_d as a binary feature. Second, it is possible to consider atomic attribute values as features as well. To give a motivating example, in many languages the value of `CASE` is extremely informative when distinguishing objects from subjects. We use only those atomic attribute values which do not represent words. E.g., `NUM`, `PRED` or `NUM=sg` are features, while `PRED='resolution'` is not a feature. This distinction prevents the feature set from growing too large and thus the probability estimates from being too inaccurate.

If grammatical functions are missing for several dependent f-structures, it is possible to use the same approach, guessing the missing functions one by one. In general, however, these decisions will not be independent. To illustrate this, let us consider a situation when the functions are to be guessed for two dependent f-structures of the same parent f-structure, `OBJ` being the correct answer for the first and `SUBJ` for the second. If the guesser returns `SUBJ` for the first of the two, this answer will not only be incorrect, but also decrease the probability of the correct answer for the second by decreasing M_P(`SUBJ`) in Equation (1). This suggests that in such cases maximization of the joint probability of the values of all the missing functions may be a better choice.

3 Experimental Evaluation

We present two experiments which assess the accuracy of the proposed approach and compare different variants of it in order to select the best, and an additional one which assesses the usefulness of the approach for practical machine translation.

3.1 Data Used in the Evaluation

For our experiments we used sentences from the German-English part of the Europarl corpus (Koehn, 2005) parsed into f-structures with the XLE parser (Kaplan et al., 2002) using English (Riezler et al., 2002) and German (Butt et al., 2002) LFGs. We parsed only sentences of length 5–15 words. For the first two experiments, we picked 2000 sentences for training and 1000 for testing for both languages. We ignored robustness features (`FIRST`, `REST`), functions related to c-structure constraints (`MOTHER`, `LEFT_SISTER`, etc.), and `TOPIC`. Of the remaining functions, we considered only those occurring in the PREDs-only part of f-structure. If a dependent f-structure has multiple functions within the same parent f-structure, only the first function occurring in the description is considered. This does not unduely influence the results, as the grammatical function of an f-structure, after exclusion of `TOPIC`, carries multiple labels in only about 2% of the cases in the English data and about 1% in the German data. In Table 1 we provide some useful statistics to help the reader interpret the results of the experiments.

Language	MF	NB-CASE	NB-N	NB-N&V
English	36.3%	56.7%	85.6%	91.6%
German	23.4%	51.0%	74.8%	82.5%

Table 2: Experiment 1: Guessing a Single Missing Grammatical Function. **MF** is the pick-most-frequent classifier. **NB-CASE** is Naive Bayes (NB) with only CASE values used as features. **NB-N** is NB with only attribute names used as features. **NB-N&V** is NB with both attribute names and atomic attribute values used as features.

3.2 Experiment 1: Guessing a Single Missing Grammatical Function

The goal of this experiment is to evaluate the accuracy of the Bayesian guesser in the case when the grammatical function is unknown only for one dependent f-structure, and to assess whether the inclusion of attribute values into the feature set improves the results, and whether attributes other than CASE are useful.

Procedure. As a baseline, we used a pick-most-frequent algorithm **MF** which considers only the function's prior probability and the presence of this function in the parent (returning to Equations (1) and (2), **MF** is in fact Naive Bayes with an empty feature set Ξ). The guesser was evaluated in three variants: **NB-CASE** with the feature set formed only from the values of CASE attributes (if the f-structure has no CASE feature, the classifier degenerates to **MF**), **NB-N** with the feature set formed only from attribute names, and **NB-N&V** with the feature set formed from both attribute names and values. All grammatical functions in the test set were used as test cases. At each step in the evaluation, one function was removed and then guessed by each algorithm. For both languages the test set was split into 10 non-intersecting subsets with approximately equal numbers of grammatical functions in each, and the values obtained for the 10 subsets were further used to assess the statistical significance of the differences in the results with the paired Student's t-test.

Results. Table 2 presents the results. For both English and German all the three versions of the classifier clearly outperform the baseline, and even the advantage of **NB-CASE** over the baseline is statistically significant at the 0.5% level for both languages. However, **NB-CASE** performs much worse than **NB-N** and **NB-N&V** (their advantage over **NB-CASE** is statistically significant at the 0.5% level for both languages), confirming that CASE is not the only feature which is useful in our task. The increase in accuracy brought about by including the atomic attribute values into the feature space is visible and significant at the same level. The increase is somewhat more pronounced for German than for English. For English the inclusion of attribute values into the feature space affects primarily the accuracy of SUBJ vs. OBJ decisions. For German, the accuracy notably increases for telling SUBJ, OBJ and ADJ-GEN from one another.

Language	MF	NB-S	NB-J
English	22.0%	90.4%	91.2%
German	17.1%	81.4%	82.1%

Table 3: Experiment 2: Guessing Multiple Missing Functions. **MF** is the pick-most-frequent classifier. **NB-S** and **NB-J** are one-by-one and join-probability-based Naive Bayesian guessers.

3.3 Experiment 2: Guessing Multiple Missing Grammatical Functions

The goal of this experiment is to assess the accuracy of the Bayesian guesser for multiple missing grammatical functions within one parent f-structure, and to compare the accuracy of one-by-one vs. joint-probability-based guessing. Our evaluation procedure models the extreme case when the functions are unknown for *all* the dependent f-structures of a particular parent.

Procedure. As a baseline, we use the same algorithm **MF** as in Experiment 1, applied to the missing grammatical functions one by one. Two Bayesian guessers are evaluated, **NB-S** guessing the missing grammatical functions one by one, and **NB-J** guessing them all at once by maximizing the joint probability of the values. Both Bayesian guessers use attribute names and values as features. All grammatical functions in the test set were used as test cases. At each step of the experiment, the grammatical functions of all the dependent f-structures of a particular parent were removed simultaneously, and then guessed with each of the algorithms considered in this experiment. Statistical significance was assessed in the same way as in Experiment 1.

Results. Table 3 presents the accuracy scores. The one-by-one guesser and the joint-probability-based guesser perform nearly equally well, resulting in accuracy levels very close to those obtained in Experiment 1 for f-structures with a single missing function. Joint-probability-based guessing achieves an advantage which is statistically significant at the 0.5% level for both languages but is not exceeding 1% absolute improvement. For both languages errors typically occur in distinguishing `OBJ` vs. `SUBJ` and `ADJUNCT` vs. `MOD`, and additionally in `XCOMP` vs. `OBJ` for English.

3.3.1 Experiment 3: Postprocessing the Output of an MT Decoder

The goal of this experiment is to see how the method influences the results of an SMT system.

Procedure. For this experiment we use the Sulis SMT system (Graham et al., 2009), and a decoder, which selects the transfer rules by maximizing the source-to-target probability of the complete translation. Such a decoder, though simple, allows us to create a realistic environment for evaluation. From the f-structures produced by the decoder, candidate sentences are generated with XLE, and then the one best translation is selected for each sentence using a language model. The function guesser is used to postprocess the output of the decoder before sentence generation. In the experiment, the function guesser uses both attribute names and values to make a guess. Guessing of multiple missing functions is performed one-by-one, as joint guessing complicates the algorithm and leads to a very small improvement in accuracy. The function guesser is trained on 3000 sentences, which are a subset of the set used for inducing the transfer rules. The overall MT system is evaluated both with and without function guessing on 500 held-out sentences, and the quality of the translation is measured using the BLEU metric (Papineni et al., 2002). We also calculate the number of sentences for which the generator output is unempty.

Results. The system without function guesser produced results for 364 sentences out of 500, with BLEU score equal to 5.69%; with function guesser the number of successfully generated sentences increases to 433, with BLEU improving to 6.95%. Thus, the absolute increase of BLEU score brought about by the guesser is 1.24%. This suggests that the algorithm succeeds on real data and is useful in grammar-based machine translation.

4 Conclusion

In this paper we addressed the problem of restoring unknown grammatical functions in automatically generated f-structures. We proposed to view this problem as a classification task and to solve it with the Naive Bayes classifier, using the names and the values of the attributes of the dependent f-structure to construct the feature set.

The approach was evaluated on English and German data, and showed reasonable accuracy, restoring the missing functions correctly in about 91% of the cases for English and about 82% for German. It is tempting to interpret the differences in accuracy for English and German as reflecting the complexity of grammatical function assignment for the two languages. It is not clear, however, whether the differences are due to differences in the grammars or in the underlying data.

The experiments reported here use LFG-type representations. However, nothing much in the method is specific to LFG, and therefore we are confident that our method also applies to other dependency-based representations.

Acknowledgments

The research presented here was supported by Science Foundation Ireland grant 07/CE2/I1142 under the CNGL CSET programme.

References

M. Butt, H. Dyvik, T. H. King, H. Masuichi, and C. Rohrer. 2002. The parallel grammar project. In *COLING'02, Workshop on Grammar Engineering and Evaluation*.

Y. Graham, A. Bryl, and J. van Genabith. 2009. F-structure transfer-based statistical machine translation. In *LFG'09 (To Appear)*.

R. Kaplan and J. Bresnan. 1982. Lexical functional grammar, a formal system for grammatical represenation. *The Mental Representation of Grammatical Relations*, pages 173–281.

R. M. Kaplan, T. H. King, and J. T. Maxwell III. 2002. Adapting existing grammars: the XLE experience. In *COLING'02, Workshop on Grammar Engineering and Evaluation*.

P. Koehn. 2005. Europarl: A parallel corpus for statistical machine translation. In *MT Summit X*, pages 79–86.

K. Papineni, S. Roukos, T. Ward, and W. Zhu. 2002. BLEU: a method for automatic evaluation of machine translation. In *ACL'02*, pages 311–318.

S. Riezler, T. H. King, R. M. Kaplan, R. Crouch, J. T. Maxwell III, and M. Johnson. 2002. Parsing the wall street journal using a lexical-functional grammar and discriminative estimation techniques. In *ACL'02*, pages 271–278.

Cross Parser Evaluation and Tagset Variation : a French Treebank Study

Djamé Seddah[†], Marie Candito[‡] and Benoît Crabbé[‡]

[†] Université Paris-Sorbonne
LALIC & INRIA (ALPAGE)
28 rue Serpente
F-75006 Paris — France

[‡] Université Paris 7
INRIA (ALPAGE)
30 rue du Château des Rentiers
F-75013 Paris — France

Abstract

This paper presents preliminary investigations on the statistical parsing of French by bringing a complete evaluation on French data of the main probabilistic lexicalized and unlexicalized parsers first designed on the Penn Treebank. We adapted the parsers on the two existing treebanks of French (Abeillé et al., 2003; Schluter and van Genabith, 2007). To our knowledge, mostly all of the results reported here are state-of-the-art for the constituent parsing of French on every available treebank. Regarding the algorithms, the comparisons show that lexicalized parsing models are outperformed by the unlexicalized Berkeley parser. Regarding the treebanks, we observe that, depending on the parsing model, a tag set with specific features has direct influence over evaluation results. We show that the adapted lexicalized parsers do not share the same sensitivity towards the amount of lexical material used for training, thus questioning the relevance of using only one lexicalized model to study the usefulness of lexicalization for the parsing of French.

1 Introduction

The development of large scale symbolic grammars has long been a lively topic in the French NLP community. Surprisingly, the acquisition of probabilistic grammars aiming at stochastic parsing, using either supervised or unsupervised methods, has not attracted much attention despite the availability of large manually syntactic annotated data for French. Nevertheless, the availability of the Paris 7 French Treebank (Abeillé et al., 2003), allowed (Dybro-Johansen, 2004) to carry out the extraction of a Tree Adjoining Grammar (Joshi, 1987) and led (Arun and Keller, 2005) to induce the first effective lexicalized parser for French. Yet, as noted by (Schluter and van Genabith, 2007), the use of the treebank was "challenging". Indeed, before carrying out successfully any experiment, the authors had to perform a deep restructuring of the data to remove errors and inconsistencies. For the purpose of building a statistical LFG parser, (Schluter and van Genabith, 2007; Schluter and van Genabith, 2008) have re-annotated a significant subset of the treebank with two underlying goals: (1) designing an annotation scheme that matches as closely as possible the LFG theory (Kaplan and Bresnan, 1982) and (2) ensuring a more consistent annotation. On the other hand, (Crabbé and Candito, 2008) showed that with a new released and corrected version of the treebank[1] it was possible to train statistical parsers from the original set of trees. This path has the advantage of an easier reproducibility and eases verification of reported results.

With the problem of the usability of the data source being solved, the question of finding one or many accurate language models for parsing French raises. Thus, to answer this question, this paper reports a set of experiments where five algorithms, first designed for the purpose of parsing English, have been adapted to French: a PCFG parser with latent annotation (Petrov et al., 2006), a Stochastic Tree Adjoining Grammar parser (Chiang, 2003), the Charniak's lexicalized parser (Charniak, 2000) and the Bikel's implementation of Collins' Model 1 and 2 (Collins, 1999) described in (Bikel, 2002). To ease further comparisons, we report results on two versions of the treebank: (1) the last version made available in December 2007, hereafter FTB , and described in (Abeillé and Barrier, 2004) and the (2) LFG inspired version of (Schluter and van Genabith, 2007).

The paper is structured as follows : After a brief presentation of the treebanks, we discuss the use-

[1] This has been made available in December 2007.

Proceedings of the 11th International Conference on Parsing Technologies (IWPT), pages 150–161,
Paris, October 2009. ©2009 Association for Computational Linguistics

fulness of testing different parsing frameworks over two parsing paradigms before introducing our experimental protocol and presenting our results. Finally, we discuss and compare with related works on cross-language parser adaptation, then we conclude.

2 Treebanks for French

This section provides a brief overview to the corpora on which we report results: the French Treebank (FTB) and the Modified French Treebank (MFT).

2.1 The French Treebank

THE FRENCH TREEBANK is the first treebank annotated and manually corrected for French. It is the result of a supervised annotation project of newspaper articles from *Le Monde* (Abeillé and Barrier, 2004). The corpus is annotated with labelled constituent trees augmented with morphological annotations and functional annotations of verbal dependents as shown below :

```
<SENT>
  <NP fct="SUJ">
    <w cat="D" lemma="le" mph="ms" subcat="def">le</w>
    <w cat="N" lemma="bilan" mph="ms" subcat="C">bilan</w>
  </NP>
  <VN>
    <w cat="ADV" lemma="ne" subcat="neg">n'</w>
    <w cat="V" lemma="être" mph="P3s" subcat="">est</w>
  </VN>
  <AdP fct="MOD">
    <w compound="yes" cat="ADV" lemma="peut-être">
      <w catint="V">peut</w>
      <w catint="PONCT">-</w>
      <w catint="V">être</w>
    </w>
    <w cat="ADV" lemma="pas" subcat="neg">pas</w>
  </AdP>
  <AP fct="ATS">
    <w cat="ADV" lemma="aussi">aussi</w>
    <w cat="A" lemma="sombre" mph="ms" subcat="qual">sombre</w>
  </AP>
  <w cat="PONCT" lemma="." subcat="S">.</w>
</SENT>
```

Figure 1: Simplified example of the FTB: "Le bilan n'est peut-être pas aussi sombre." *(i.e. The result is perhaps not as bleak)*

Though the original release (*in 2000*) consists of 20,648 sentences, the subset of 12351 functionally annotated sentences is known to be more consistently annotated and therefore is the one used in this work. Its key properties, compared with the Penn Treebank (hereafter PTB, (Marcus et al., 1994)), are the following :

Size: The FTB consists of 385,458 tokens and 12,351 sentences, that is the third of the PTB. It also entails that the average length of a sentence is 27.48 tokens. By contrast the average sentence length in the PTB is 24 tokens.

Inflection: French morphology is richer than English and leads to increased data sparseness issues for the purpose of statistical parsing. There are 24,098 types in the FTB, entailing an average of 16 tokens occurring for each type.

A Flat Annotation Scheme: Both the FTB and the PTB are annotated with constituent trees. However, the annotation scheme is flatter in the FTB. For instance, there are no VPs for finite verbs and only one sentential level for clauses or sentences whether or not introduced by a complementizer. Only *verbal nucleus* (VN) is annotated and comprises the verb, its clitics, auxiliaries, adverbs and surrounding negation.

While X-bar inspired constituents are supposed to contain all the syntactic information, in the FTB the shape of the constituents does not necessarily express unambiguously the *type* of dependency existing between a head and a dependent appearing in the same constituent. Yet, this is crucial to extract the underlying predicate-argument structures. This has led to a "flat" annotation scheme, completed with functional annotations that inform on the type of dependency existing between a verb and its dependents. This was chosen for French to reflect, for instance, the possibility to mix post-verbal modifiers and complements (Figure 2), or to mix post-verbal subject and post-verbal indirect complements : a post verbal NP in the FTB can correspond to a temporal modifier, (most often) a direct object, or an inverted subject, and all cases, other subcategorized complements may appear.

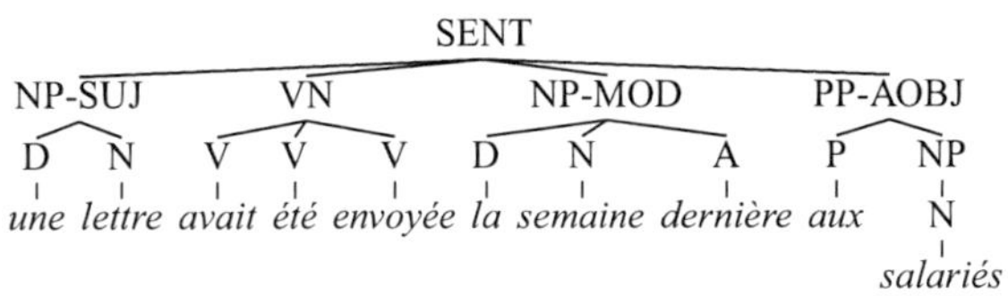

(a) A letter had been sent last week to the employees

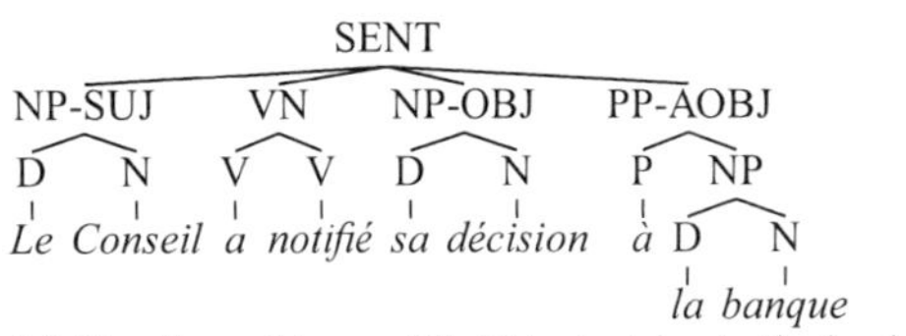

(b) The Council has notified his decision to the bank

Figure 2: Two examples of post-verbal NPs : a temporal modifier (a) and a direct object (b)

Compounds: Compounds are explicitly annotated and very frequent in the treebank: 14.52% of tokens are part of a compound (see the compound *peut-être 'perhaps'* in Figure 1). They include digit numbers (written with spaces in French) (e.g. *10 000*), frozen compounds (eg. *pomme de terre 'potato'*) but also named entities or sequences whose meaning is compositional but where insertion is rare or difficult (e.g. *garde d'enfant 'child care'*). As noted by (Arun and Keller, 2005), compounds in French may exhibit ungrammatical sequences of tags as in *à la va vite* 'in a hurry' : Prep+ Det+ finite verb + adverb or can include "words" which do not exist outside a compound (e.g *hui* in *aujourd'hui* 'today'). Therefore, compounds receive a two-level annotation : constituent parts are described in a subordinate level using the same POS tagset as the genuine compound POS. This makes it more difficult to extract a proper grammar from the FTB without merged compounds[2]. This is why, following (Arun and Keller, 2005) and (Schluter and van Genabith, 2007), all the treebanks used in this work contain compounds.

2.2 The Modified French Treebank

THE MODIFIED FRENCH TREEBANK (MFT) has been derived from the FTB by (Schluter and van Genabith, 2008) as a basis for a PCFG-based Lexical Functional Grammar induction process (Cahill et al., 2004) for French. The corpus is a subset of 4739 sentences extracted from the original FTB. The MFT further introduces formal differences of two kinds with respect to the original FTB: structural and labeling modifications.
Regarding structural changes, the main transformations include increased rule stratification (Fig. 3), coordination raising (Fig. 5).

Moreover, the MFT's authors introduced new treatments of linguistic phenomena that were not covered by their initial source treebank. Those include, for example, analysis for 'It'-cleft constructions.[3] Since the MFT was designed for the purpose of improving the task of grammar induction, the MFT's authors also refined its tag set by propagating information (such as mood features added to VN node labels), and added functional paths[4] to the original function labels. The modifications introduced in the MFT meet better the formal requirements of the LFG architecture set up

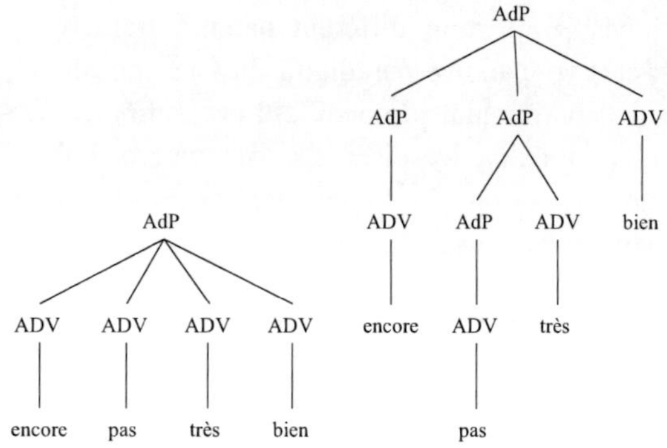

Figure 3: Increased stratification in the MFT : *"encore pas très bien"* ('still not very well')

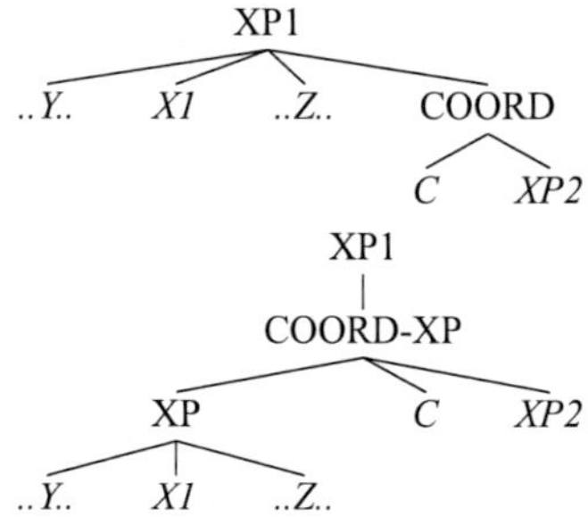

Figure 5: Coordinated structures in the general case, for FTB (up) and MFT (down)

by (Cahill et al., 2004) and reduce the size of the grammars extracted from the treebank. MFT has also undergone a phase of error mining and an extensive manual correction.

2.3 Coordination in French Treebanks

One of the key differences between the two French treebanks is the way they treat coordinate structures. Whereas the FTB represents them with an adjunction of a COORD phrase as a sister or a daughter of the coordinated element, the MFT introduces a treatment closer to the one used in the PTB to describe such structures. As opposed to (Arun and Keller, 2005) who decided to transform the FTB's coordinations to match the PTB's analysis, the COORD label is not removed but extended to include the coordinated label (Fig. 5).

In Figure 5, we show the general coordination structure in the FTB, and the corresponding modified structure in the MFT. A more complicated modification concerns the case of *VP coordinations*. (Abeillé et al., 2003) argue for a flat representation with no VP-node for French, and this is

[2]Consider the case of the compound *peut-être 'perhaps'* whose POS is ADV, its internal structure (Fig. 1) would lead to a CFG rule of the form ADV ⟶ V V.

[3]See pages 2-3 of (Schluter and van Genabith, 2007) for details.

[4]Inspired by the LFG framework (Dalrymple, 2001).

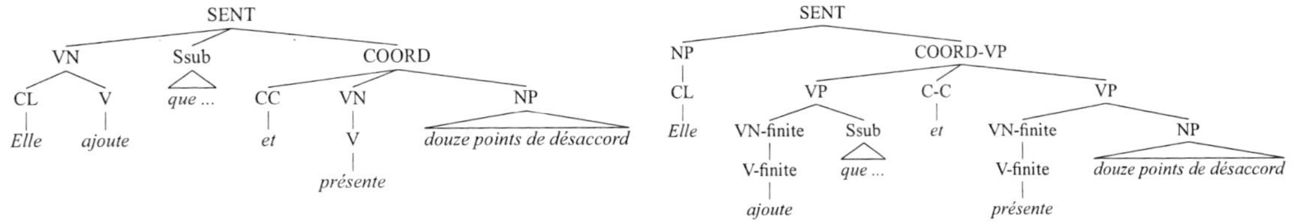

Figure 4: Two representations of "VP coordinations" for the sentence *She adds that ... and presents twelve sticking points*: in the FTB (left) and in the MFT (right)

particularly justified in some cases of subject-verb inversion. Nevertheless, VP phrases are used in the FTB for non-finite VPs only (nodes VPinf and VPpart). In the MFT, finite VPs were introduced to handle *VP coordinations*. In those cases, the FTB annotation scheme keeps a flat structure (Figure 4, left), where the COORD phrase has to be interpreted as a coordinate of the VN node; whereas finite VP nodes are inserted in the MFT (Figure 4, right).

2.4 Summary

In Table 2, we describe the annotation schemes of the treebanks and we provide in Table 1 a numeric summary of some relevant different features between these two treebanks. The reported numbers take into account the base syntactic category labels without functions, part-of-speech tags without any morpho-syntactic information (ie. no 'gender' or number').

properties	FTB	MFT
# of sentences	12351	4739
Average sent. length	27.48	28.38
Average node branching	2.60	2.11
PCFG size (without term. prod.)	14874	6944
# of NT symbols	13	39
# of POS tags	15	27

Table 1: Treebanks Properties

3 Parsing Algorithms

Although Probabilistic Context Free Grammars (PCFG) are a baseline formalism for probabilistic parsing, it is well known that they suffer from two problems: (a) The independence assumptions made by the model are too strong, and (b) For Natural Language Parsing, they do not take into account lexical probabilities. To date, most of the results on statistical parsing have been reported for English. Here we propose to investigate how to apply these techniques to another language – French – by testing two distinct enhancements

	FTB	MFT
POS tags	A ADV C CL D ET I N P P+D P+PRO PONCT PREF PRO V	A A_card ADV ADV_int ADVne A_int CC CL C_S D D_card ET I N N_card P P+D PONCT P+PRO_rel PREF PRO PRO_card PRO_int PRO_rel V_finite V_inf V_part
NT labels	AP AdP COORD NP PP SENT Sint Srel Ssub VN VPinf VPpart	AdP AdP_int AP AP_int COORD_XP COORD_UC COORD_unary NC NP NP_int NP_rel PP PP_int PP_rel SENT Sint Srel Ssub VN_finite VN_inf VN_part VP VPinf VPpart VPpart_rel

Table 2: FTB's and MFT's annotation schemes

over the bare PCFG model carried out by two class of parser models: an unlexicalized model attempting to overcome problem (a) and 3 different lexicalized models attempting to overcome PCFG's problems (a) and (b)[5].

3.1 Lexicalized algorithms

The first class of algorithms used are lexicalized parsers of (Collins, 1999; Charniak, 2000; Chiang, 2003). The insight underlying the lexicalized algorithms is to model lexical dependencies between a governor and its dependants in order to improve attachment choices.

Even though it has been proven numerous times that lexicalization was useful for parsing the *Wall Street Journal* corpus (Collins, 1999; Charniak, 2000), the question of its relevance for other languages has been raised for German (Dubey and Keller, 2003; Kübler et al., 2006) and for French

[5]Except (Chiang, 2003) which is indeed a TREE INSERTION GRAMMAR (Schabes and Waters, 1995) parser but which must extract a lexicalized grammar from the set of context free rules underlying a treebank.

(Arun and Keller, 2005) where the authors argue that French parsing benefits from lexicalization but the treebank flatness reduces its impact whereas (Schluter and van Genabith, 2007) argue that an improved annotation scheme and an improved treebank consistency should help to reach a reasonable state of the art. As only Collins' models 1 & 2 have been used for French as instances of lexicalised parsers, we also report results from the history-based generative parser of (Charniak, 2000) and the Stochastic Tree Insertion Grammar parser of (Chiang, 2003) as well as (Bikel, 2002)'s implementation of the Collins' models 1 & 2 (Collins, 1999). Most of the lexicalized parsers we use in this work are well known and since their releases, almost ten years ago, their core parsing models still provide state-of-the-art performance on the standard test set for English.[6] We insist on the fact that one of the goals of this work was to evaluate raw performance of well known parsing models on French annotated data. Thus, we have not considered using more complex parsing architectures that makes use of reranking (Charniak and Johnson, 2005) or self-training (McClosky et al., 2006) in order to improve the performance of a raw parsing model. Furthermore, studying and designing a set of features for a reranking parser was beyond the scope of this work. However, we did use some of these models in a non classical way, leading us to explore a Collins' model 2 variation, named model X, and a Stochastic Tree Adjoining Grammar (Schabes, 1992; Resnik, 1992) variant[7], named Spinal Stochastic Tree Insertion Grammars (hereafter SPINAL STIG), which was first used to validate the heuristics used by our adaptation of the Bikel's parser to French. The next two subsections introduce these variations.

Collins' Model 2 variation During the exploratory phase of this work, we found out that a specific instance of the Collins' model 2 leads to significantly better performance than the canonical model when applied to any of the French Treebanks. The difference between those two models relies on the way probabilities associated to so-called "modifier non terminals" nodes are handled by the generative model.

To explain the difference, let us recall that a lexicalized PCFG can roughly be described as a set of stochastic rules of the form: $\boxed{P \rightarrow L_n\ L_{n-1}\ ..L_1\ H\ R_1\ ..\ R_{m-1}\ R_m}$ where L_i, H, R_i and P are all lexicalized non terminals; P inherits its head from H (Bikel, 2004). The Collins' model 2 deterministically labels some nodes of a rule to be arguments of a given Head and the remaining nodes are considered to be modifier non terminals (hereafter MNT).

In this model, given a left-hand side symbol, the head and its arguments are first generated and then the MNT are generated from the head outward. In Bikel's implementation of Collins's model 2 (Bikel, 2004), the MNT parameter class is the following (for clarity, we omit the *verb intervening*, *subcat* and *side* features which are the same in both classes) :

- model 2 (canonical) :
  $\boxed{p(M(t)_i|P, H, w_h, t_h, map(M_{i-1}))}$
  Where $M(t)_i$ is the POS tag of the ith MNT, P the parent node label, H the head node label, w_h the head word and t_h its POS tag. $map(M_{i-1})$ is a mapped version of the previously-generated modifier added to the conditioning context (see below for its definition).

$$map(M_i) = \begin{cases} +START+ & \text{if } i = 0 \\ CC & \text{if } M_i = CC \\ +PUNC+ & \text{if } M_i =, \\ & \text{or } M_i =: \\ +OTHER+ & \text{otherwise} \end{cases}$$

Whereas in the model we call X [8], the mapping version of the previously generated non terminal is replaced by a complete list of all previously generated non terminals.

- Model X :
  $\boxed{p(M(t)_i|P, H, w_h, t_h, (M_{i-1}, ..., M_{i-k}))}$

The FTB being flatter than the PTB, one can conjecture that giving more context to generate MNT will improve parsing accuracy, whereas clustering MNT in a X-bar scheme must help to reduce data sparseness. Note that the Model X, to the best of our knowledge, is not documented but included in Bikel's parser.

[6] Section 23 of the Wall Street Journal section of the PTB.

[7] The formalism actually used in this parser is a context free variant of Tree Adjoining Grammar, Tree Insertion Grammars (TIG), first introduced in (Schabes and Waters, 1995).

[8] See file NonTerminalModelStructure1.java in Bikel's parser source code at http://www.cis.upenn.edu/~dbikel/download/dbparser/1.2/install.sh.

The spinal STIG model In the case of the STIG parser implementation, having no access to an argument adjunct table leads it to extract a grammar where almost all elementary trees consist of a suite of unary productions from a lexical anchor to its maximal projection (i.e. spine[9]). Therefore extracted trees have no substitution node.
Moreover, the probability model, being split between lexical anchors and tree templates, allows a very coarse grammar that contains, for example, only 83 tree templates for one treebank instantiation, namely the FTB-CC (cf. section 5). This behavior, although not documented[10], is close to Collins' model 1, which does not use any argument adjunct distinction information, and led to results interesting enough to be integrated as the "Chiang Spinal" model in our parser set. It should be noted that, recently, the use of similar models has been independently proposed in (Carreras et al., 2008) with the purpose of getting a richer parsing model that can use non local features and in (Sangati and Zuidema, 2009) as a mean of extracting a Lexicalized Tree Substitution Grammar. In their process, the first extracted grammar is actually a spinal STIG.

3.2 Unlexicalized Parser

As an instance of an unlexicalized parser, the last algorithm we use is the Berkeley unlexicalized parser (BKY) of (Petrov et al., 2006). This algorithm is an evolution of treebank transformation principles aimed at reducing PCFG independence assumptions (Johnson, 1998; Klein and Manning, 2003).

Treebank transformations may be of two kinds (1) structure transformation and (2) labelling transformations. The Berkeley parser concentrates on (2) by recasting the problem of acquiring an optimal set of non terminal symbols as an semi-supervised learning problem by learning a PCFG with Latent annotations (PCFG-LA): given an observed PCFG induced from the treebank, the latent grammar is generated by combining every non terminal of the observed grammar to a predefined set H of latent symbols. The parameters of the latent grammar are estimated from the actual treebank trees (or *observed trees*) using a specific instanciation of EM.

4 Experimental protocol

In this section, we specify the settings of the parsers for French, the evaluation protocol and the different instantiations of the treebanks we used for conducting the experiments.

4.1 Parsers settings

Head Propagation table All lexicalized parsers reported in this paper use head propagation tables. Adapting them to the French language requires to design French specific head propagation rules. To this end, we used those described by (Dybro-Johansen, 2004) for training a Stochastic Tree Adjoining Grammar parser on French. From this set, we built a set of meta-rules that were automatically derived to match each treebank annotation scheme.
As the Collins Model 2 and the STIG model need to distinguish between argument and adjunct nodes to acquire subcategorization frames probabilities, we implemented an argument-adjunct distinction table that takes advantage of the function labels annotated in the treebank. This is one of the main differences with the experiments described in (Arun and Keller, 2005) and (Dybro-Johansen, 2004) where the authors had to rely only on the very flat treebank structure without function labels, to annotate the arguments of a head.

Morphology and typography adaptation Following (Arun and Keller, 2005), we adapted the morphological treatment of unknown words proposed for French when needed (BKY's and BIKEL's parser). This process clusters unknown words using typographical and morphological information. Since all lexicalized parsers contain specific treatments for the PTB typographical convention, we automatically converted the original punctuation parts of speech to the PTB's punctuation tag set.

4.2 Experimental details

For the BKY parser, we use the Berkeley implementation, with an initial horizontal markovization h=0, and 5 split/merge cycles. For the COLLINS' MODEL, we use the standard parameters set for the model 2, without any argu-

[9] Not to be confused with the "spine" in the Tree Adjunct Grammar (Joshi, 1987) framework which is the path from a foot node to the root node.

[10] We mistakenly "discovered" this obvious property during the preliminary porting phase.

ment adjunct distinction table, as a rough emulation of the COLLINS MODEL 1. The same set of parameters used for COLLINS' MODEL 2 is used for the MODEL X except for the parameters "Mod{Nonterminal,Word}ModelStructureNumber" set to 1 instead of 2.

4.3 Protocol

For all parsers, we report parsing results with the following experimental protocol: a treebank is divided in 3 sections : test (first 10%), development (second 10%) and training (remaining 80%). The MFT partition set is the canonical one (3800 sentences for training, 509 for the dev set and the last 430 for the test set). We systematically report the results with compounds merged. Namely, we preprocess the treebank in order to turn each compound into a single token both for training and test.

4.4 Evaluation metrics

Constituency Evaluation: we use the standard labeled bracketed PARSEVAL metric for evaluation (Black et al., 1991), along with unlabeled dependency evaluation, which is described as a more annotation-neutral metric in (Rehbein and van Genabith, 2007). In the remainder of this paper, we use PARSEVAL as a shortcut for Labeled Brackets results on sentence of length 40 or less.
Dependency Evaluation: unlabeled dependencies are computed using the (Lin, 1995) algorithm, and the Dybro Johansens's head propagation rules cited above[11]. The unlabeled dependency accuracy gives the percentage of input words (excluding punctuation) that receive the correct head. All reported evaluations in this paper are calculated on sentences of length less than 40 words.

4.5 Baseline : Comparison using minimal tagsets

We compared all parsers on three different instances, but still comparable versions, of both the FTB and the MFT. In order to establish a baseline, the treebanks are converted to a minimal tag set (only the major syntactic categories.) without any other information (no mode propagation as in the MFT) except for the BIKEL's parser in Collins' model 2 (resp. model X) and the STIG parser (i.e. STIG-pure) whose models needs function labels to perform.
Note that by stripping all information from the node labels in the treebanks, we do not mean to compare the shape of the treebanks or their *parsability* but rather to present an overview of parser performance on each treebank regardless of tagset optimizations. However, in each experiment we observe that the BKY parser significantly outperforms the other parsers in all metrics.
As the STIG parser presents non statistically significant PARSEVAL results differences between its two modes (PURE & SPINAL) with a f-score p-value of 0.32, for the remaining of the paper we will only present results for the STIG's parser in "spinal" mode.

		FTB-min	MFT-min
COLLINS MX	PARSEVAL	81.65	79.19
	UNLAB. DEP	88.48	84.96
COLLINS M2	PARSEVAL	80.1	78.38
	UNLAB. DEP	87.45	84.57
COLLINS M1	PARSEVAL	77.98	76.09
	UNLAB. DEP	85.67	82.83
CHARNIAK	PARSEVAL	82,44	81.34
	UNLAB. DEP	88.42	84.90
CHIANG-SPINAL	PARSEVAL	80.66	80.74
	UNLAB. DEP	87.92	85,14
BKY	PARSEVAL	84,93	83.16
	UNLAB. DEP	90.06	87.29
CHIANG-PURE	PARSEVAL	80.52	79.56
	UNLAB. DEP	87,95	85.02

Table 3: Labeled F_1 scores for unlexicalised and lexicalised parsers on treebanks with minimal tagsets

5 Cross parser evaluation of tagset variation

In (Crabbé and Candito, 2008), the authors showed that it was possible to accurately train the Petrov's parser (Petrov et al., 2006) on the FTB using a more fine grained tag set. This tagset, named CC[12] annotates the basic non-terminal labels with verbal mood information, and wh-features. Results were shown to be state of the art with a F_1 parseval score of 86.42% on less than 40 words sentences.
To summarize, the authors tested the impact of tagset variations over the FTB using constituency measures as performance indicators.
Knowing that the MFT has been built with PCFG-based LFG parsing performance in mind (Schluter

[11] For this evaluation, the gold constituent trees are converted into pseudo-gold dependency trees (that may contain errors). Then parsed constituent trees are converted into parsed dependency trees, that are matched against the pseudo-gold trees.

[12] TREEBANKS+ in (Crabbé and Candito, 2008).

and van Genabith, 2008) but suffers from a small training size and yet allows surprisingly high parsing results (PARSEVAL F-score (<=40) of 79.95 % on the MFT gold standard), one would have wished to verify its

performance with more annotated data.

However, some semi-automatic modifications brought to the global structure of this treebank cannot be applied, in an automatic and reversible way, to the FTB. Anyway, even if we cannot evaluate the influence of a treebank structure to another, we can evaluate the influence of one tagset to another treebank using handwritten conversion tools. In order to evaluate the relations between tagsets and parsing accuracy on a given treebank, we extract the optimal tagsets[13] from the FTB, the CC tagset and we convert the MFT POS tags to this tagset. We then do the same for the FTB on which we apply the MFT's optimal tagset (ie. SCHLU). Before introducing the results of our experiments, we briefly describe these tagsets.

1. **min** : Preterminals are simply the main categories, and non terminals are the plain labels
2. **cc** : (Crabbé and Candito, 2008) best tagset. Preterminals are the main categories, concatenated with a wh- boolean for A, ADV, PRO, and with the mood for verbs (there are 6 moods). No information is propagated to non terminal symbols. This tagset is shown in Table 4, and described in (Crabbé and Candito, 2008).

ADJ ADJWH ADV ADVWH CC CLO CLR CLS CS DET DETWH ET I NC NPP P P+D P+PRO PONCT PREF PRO PROREL PROWH V VIMP VINF VPP VPR VS

Table 4: CC tagset

3. **schlu** : N. Schluter's tagset (Table 2. Preterminals are the main categories, plus an inf/finite/part verbal distinction, and int/card/rel distinction on N, PRO, ADV, A. These distinctions propagate to non terminal nodes projected by the lexical head. Non terminals for coordinating structures are split according to the type of the coordinated phrases.

Results of these experiments, presented in Table 5, show that BKY displays higher performances in every aspects (constituency and dependency, except for the MFT-SCHLU). Regardless of the parser type, we note that unlabeled dependency scores are higher with the SCHLU tagset than with the CC tagset. That can be explained by the finest granularity of the SCHLU based rule set compared to the other tagset's rules. As these rules have all been generated from meta description (a general COORD label rewrites into COORD_vfinite, COORD_Sint, etc..) their coverage and global accuracy is higher. For example the FTB-CC contains 18 head rules whereas the FTB-SCHLU contains 43 rules.

Interestingly, the ranking of lexicalized parsers w.r.t PARSEVAL metrics shows that CHARNIAK has the highest performance over both treebank tagsets variation even though the MFT's table (table 5) exhibits a non statistically significant variation between CHARNIAK and STIG-spinal on PARSEVAL evaluation of the MFT-CC.[14]

One the other hand, unlabeled dependency evaluations over lexicalized parsers are different among treebanks. In the case of the FTB, CHARNIAK exhibits the highest F-score (FTB-CC: 89.7, FTB-SCHLU: 89.67) whereas SPINAL STIG performs slightly better on the MFT-SCHLU (MFT-CC: 86,7, MFT-SCHLU: 87.16). Note that both tested variations of the Collins' model 2 display very high unlabeled dependency scores with the SCHLU tagset.

6 Related Works

As we said in the introduction, the initial work on the FTB has been carried by (Dybro-Johansen, 2004) in order to extract Tree Adjunct Grammars from the treebank. Although parsing results were not reported, she experienced the same argument adjunct distinction problem than (Arun and Keller, 2005) due to the treebank flatness and the lack of functional labels in this version. This led Arun to modify some node annotations (VNG to distinguish nodes dominating subcategorized subject clitics and so on) and to add bigrams probabilities to the language model in order to enhance the overall COLLINS' MODEL' performance. Although our treebanks cannot be compared (20.000 sentences for Arun's one vs 12351 for the FTB), we report his best PARSEVAL results (<=40): 80.65 LP, 80.25 LR, 80.45 F1.

However, our results are directly comparable with

[13] W.r.t constituent parsing accuracy

[14] Precision P-value = 0.1272 and Recall = 0.06.

Parser	Parseval		Dependency		Parseval		Dependency	
	MFTCC	MFTSCH.	MFTCC	MFTSCH.	FTBCC	FTBSCH.	FTBCC	FTBSCH.
Collins (MX)	80.2	80.96	85.97	**87.98**	82.52	82.65	88.96	89.12
Collins (M2)	78.56	79.91	84.84	87.43	80.8	79.56	87.94	87.87
Collins (M1)	74	78.49	81.31	85.94	79.16	78.51	86.66	86.93
Charniak	82.5	82.66	86.45	86.94	84.27	83.27	89.7	89.67
Chiang (Sp)	82.6	81.97	86.7	87.16	81.73	81.54	88.85	89.02
Bky	**83.96**	**82.86**	**87.41**	86.87	**86.02**	**84.95**	**90.48**	**90.73**

Table 5: Evaluation Results: MFT-CC vs MFT-SCHLU and FTB-CC vs FTB-SCHLU

(Schluter and van Genabith, 2007) whose best PARSEVAL F-score on raw text is 79.95 and our best 82.86 on the MFT-SCHLU.

PARSER	FTBARUN	MFTSCHLU
Arun (acl05)	**80.45**	-
Arun (this paper)	**81.08**	-
Schluter (pacling07)	-	**79.95**
Collins (Mx)	81.5	80,96
Collins (M2)	79.36	79,91
Collins (M1)	77.82	-
Charniak	82.35	82,66
Chiang (Sp)	80.94	81,86
Bky	84.03	82.86

Table 6: Labeled bracket scores on Arun's FTB version and on the MFT

In order to favour a "fair" comparison between our work and (Arun and Keller, 2005), we also ran their best adaptation of the COLLINS MODEL 2 on their treebank version using our own head rules set[15] and obtained 81.08% of F_1 score (Table 6). This shows the important influence of a fine grained head rules set and argues in favor of data driven induction of this kind of heuristics. Even though it was established, in (Chiang and Bikel, 2002), that unsupervised induction of head rules did not lead to improvement over an extremely hand crafted head rules set, we believe that for resource poor languages, such methods could lead toward significant improvements over parsing accuracy. Thus, the new unsupervised head rules induction method presented in (Sangati and Zuidema, 2009) seems very promising for this topic.
However, it would be of interest to see how the Arun's model would perform using the MODEL X parameter variations.

7 Discussion

Regarding the apparent lack of success of a genuine COLLINS' MODEL 2 (in most cases, its performance is worse than the other parsers w.r.t to constituent parsing accuracy) when trained on a treebank with annotated function labels, we suspect that this is caused by the increased data sparseness added by these annotations. The same can be said about the pure STIG model, whose results are only presented on the FTB-MIN because the differences between the spinal model and itself were too small and most of the time not statistically significant. In our opinion, there might be simply not enough data to accurately train a pure COLLINS' MODEL 2 on the FTB with function labels used for clues to discriminate between argument and adjuncts. Nevertheless, we do not share the commonly accepted opinion about the potential lack of success of lexicalized parsers.
To the best of our knowledge, most adaptations of a lexicalized model to a western language have been made with Dan Bikel's implementation of COLLINS' MODELS.[16]
In fact, the adaptations of the CHARNIAK and BKY's models exhibit similar magnitudes of performances for French as for English. Evidence of lexicalization usefulness is shown through a learning curve (Figure 6) obtained by running some of our parsers in perfect tagging mode. This experiment was done in the early stages of this work, the goal was to see how well the parsers would behave with the same head rules and the same set of parameters. We only compared the parsers that could be used without argument adjunct distinction table (ie. COLLIN'S MODEL 1, SPINAL STIG, CHARNIAK and BKY).

For this earlier experiment, our implementation of the COLLINS MODEL 1 actually corresponds to the MODEL X without an argument adjunct distinction table. More precisely, the absence of argument nodes, used for the acquisition of subcategorization frames features, makes the MODEL X parsing model consider all the nodes of a rule, ex-

[15]Due to the lack of function annotation labels in this treebank, (Arun and Keller, 2005)'s argument distinction table was used for this experiment.

[16]Note that the CHARNIAK's parser has been adapted for Danish (Zeman and Resnik, 2008) ; the authors report a 80.20 F_1 score for a specific instance of the Danish Treebank.

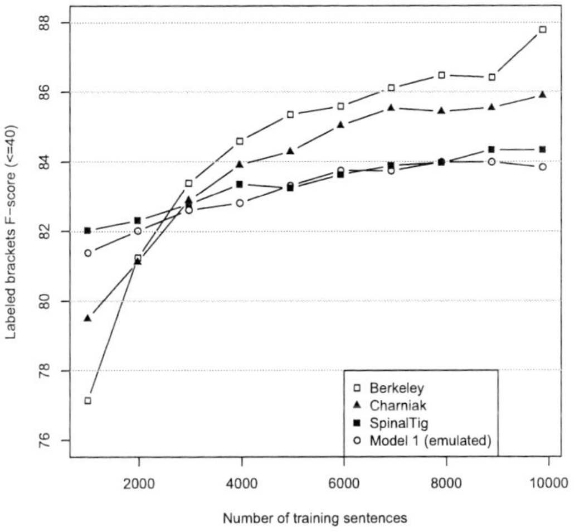

Figure 6: Learning Curve experiment results for parsers in perfect tagging mode

cept the head, as Modifier Non Terminal nodes (MNTs). Hence, because of the impossibility to extract subcategorization frames, the generation of a MNT depends mainly on the parent head word and on the whole list of previously generated MNTs. One can suppose that training on small treebanks would lead this distribution to be sparse, therefore most of the discriminant information would come from less specific distributions. Namely the ones conditioned on the head pos tag and on the last previously generated MNT as shown in this model back-off structure (Table 7).

Back-off level	$p(M(t)_i \mid \cdots)$
0	$P, H, w_h, t_h, \langle M_{i-1}, ..., M_{i-k} \rangle$
1	P, H, t_h, M_{i-1}
2	P, H, f

Table 7: MODEL X simplified parameter class for MNTs

$M(t)_i$ is the POS tag of the ith MNT, P the parent node label, H the head node label, w_h the head word, t_h its POS tag, $\langle M_{i-1}, ..., M_{i-k} \rangle$ the list of previously generated MNTs and f a flag stating if the current node is the first MNT to be generated.

Interestingly, in the SPINAL STIG model, almost all the extracted trees are spinal and consequently are handled by an operation called *Sister Adjunction* whose probability model for a given root node of an elementary tree, also conditions its generation upon the label of the previously generated tree (Chiang, 2003). Furthermore, the second component of the *Sister Adjunction*'s back-off structure (Table 8) is made coarser by the removing of the lexical anchor of the tree where a sister-adjunction is to occur.

Studying in depth the respective impact of these features on the performance of both models is outside the scope of this paper, nevertheless we note that their back-off structures are based on similar principles: a deletion of the main lexical information and a context limited to the root label of the previously generated tree (resp. MNT node label for the MODEL X). This can explain why these formally different parsers display almost the same learning curves (Fig. 6) and more over why they surprisingly exhibit few sensitivity to the amount of lexical material used for training.

Back-off level	$P_{sa}(\gamma \mid \cdots)$
0	$\tau_\eta, \omega_\eta, \eta_\eta, i, X$
1	$\tau_\eta, \eta_\eta, i, X$
2	$\overline{\tau}_\eta, \eta_\eta, i$

Table 8: SPINAL STIG parameter class for Sister-adjoining tree templates (Chiang, 2003)

γ is the tree to be generated on the sister adjunction site (η_η, i) of the tree template τ_η, ω_η is the lexical anchor of τ_η, $\overline{\tau}_\eta$ is τ_η stripped from its anchor POS tag and X is the root label of the previous tree to sister-adjoin at the site (η_η, i).

However, the learning curve also shows that the CHARNIAK's[17] and BKY's parsers have almost parallel curves whereas this specific COLLIN'S MODEL 1 parser and the SPINAL STIG model have very similar shape and seem to reach an upper limit very quickly.[18] The last two parsers having also very similar back-off models (Chiang, 2003), we wonder (1) if we are not actually comparing them because of data sparseness issues and (2) if the small size of commonly used treebanks does not lead the community to consider lexicalized models, via the lone COLLINS' MODELS, as inappropriate to parse other languages than *Wall Street Journal* English.

[17] As opposed to the other parsers, the Charniak's parser tagging accuracy did not reach the 100% limit, 98.32% for the last split. So the comparison is not really fair but we believe that the visible tendency still stands.

[18] We are of course aware that the curve's values are also function of the amount of new productions brought by the increased treebank size. That should be of course taken into account.

Regarding the remarkable performance of the BKY algorithm, it remains unclear why exactly it systematically outperforms the other lexicalized algorithms. We can only make a few remarks about that. First, the algorithm is totally disjoint from the linguistic knowledge, that is entirely taken from the treebank, except for the suffixes used for handling unknown words. This is not true of the Collins' or Charniak's models, that were set up with the PTB annotation scheme in mind. Another point concerns the amount of data necessary for an accurate learning. We had the intuition that lexicalized algorithms would have benefited more than BKY from the training data size increase. Yet the BKY's learning curve displays a somewhat faster progression than lexicalized algorithms such as the SPINAL STIG and our specific instance of the COLLINS' MODEL 1.
In our future work, we plan to conduct self-training experiments using discriminative rerankers on very large French corpora to study the exact impact of the lexicon on this unlexicalized algorithm.

8 Conclusion

By adapting those parsers to French and carrying out extensive evaluation over the main characteristics of the treebank at our disposal, we prove indeed that probabilistic parsing was efficient enough to provide accurate parsing results for French. We showed that the BKY model establishes a high performance level on parsing results. Maybe more importantly we emphasized the importance of tag set model to get distinct state of the art evaluation metrics for FTB parsing, namely the SCHLU tagset to get more accurate unlabeled dependencies and the CC tagset to get better constituency parses. Finally, we showed that the lexicalization debate could benefit from the inclusion of more lexicalized parsing models.

9 Acknowledgments

This work was supported by the ANR Sequoia (ANR-08-EMER-013). We heartily thank A. Arun, J. van Genabith an N. Schluter for kindly letting us use our parsers on their treebanks. Thanks to the anonymous reviewers for their comments. All remaining errors are ours. We thank J. Wagner for his help and we would like to acknowledge the Centre for Next Generation Localization (www.cngl.ie) for providing access to one of its high-memory nodes.

References

Anne Abeillé and Nicolas Barrier. 2004. Enriching a french treebank. In *Proceedings of Language Ressources and Evaluation Conference (*LREC*)*, Lisbon.

Anne Abeillé, Lionel Clément, and François Toussenel, 2003. *Building a Treebank for French*. Kluwer, Dordrecht.

Abhishek Arun and Frank Keller. 2005. Lexicalization in crosslinguistic probabilistic parsing: The case of french. In *Proceedings of the 43rd Annual Meeting of the Association for Computational Linguistics*, pages 306–313, Ann Arbor, MI.

Daniel M. Bikel. 2002. Design of a multi-lingual, parallel-processing statistical parsing engine. In *Proceedings of the second international conference on Human Language Technology Research*, pages 178–182. Morgan Kaufmann Publishers Inc. San Francisco, CA, USA.

Daniel M. Bikel. 2004. Intricacies of Collins' Parsing Model. *Computational Linguistics*, 30(4):479–511.

E. Black, S. Abney, D. Flickinger, C. Gdaniec, R. Grishman, P. Harrison, D. Hindle, R. Ingria, F. Jelinek, J. Klavans, M. Liberman, M. Marcus, S. Roukos, B. Santorini, and T. Strzalkowski. 1991. A procedure for quantitatively comparing the syntactic coverage of english grammars. In *Proceedings of the DARPA Speech and Natural Language Workshop*, pages 306–311, San Mateo (CA). Morgan Kaufman.

Aoife Cahill, Michael Burke, Ruth O'Donovan, Josef van Genabith, and Andy Way. 2004. Long-Distance Dependency Resolution in Automatically Acquired Wide-Coverage PCFG-Based LFG Approximations. In *Proceedings of the 42nd Annual Meeting of the Association for Computational Linguistics*, pages 320–327, Barcelona, Spain.

Xavier Carreras, Mickael Collins, and Terry Koo. 2008. TAG, dynamic programming, and the perceptron for efficient, feature-rich parsing. In *Proceedings of the Twelfth Conference on Computational Natural Language Learning (CoNLL)*, pages 9–16.

Eugene Charniak and Mark Johnson. 2005. Coarse-to-fine n-best parsing and maxent discriminative reranking. In *Proceedings of the 43rd Annual Meeting of the Association for Computational Linguistics (ACL 2005)*, Ann Arbor (MI).

Eugene Charniak. 2000. A maximum-entropy-inspired parser. In *Proceedings of the 1st Annual Meeting of the North American Chapter of the ACL (NAACL)*, Seattle.

David Chiang and Daniel M. Bikel. 2002. Recovering latent information in treebanks. In *Proceedings of COLING'02, 19th International Conference on Computational Linguistics*, Taipei, Taiwan, August.

David Chiang, 2003. *Statistical Parsing with an Automatically Extracted Tree Adjoining Grammar*, chapter 16, pages 299–316. CSLI Publications.

Michael Collins. 1999. *Head Driven Statistical Models for Natural Language Parsing*. Ph.D. thesis, University of Pennsylvania, Philadelphia.

Benoit Crabbé and Marie Candito. 2008. Expériences d'analyse syntaxique statistique du français. In *Actes de la 15ème Conférence sur le Traitement Automatique des Langues Naturelles (TALN'08)*, pages 45–54, Avignon, France.

Mary Dalrymple. 2001. *Lexical-Functional Grammar*, volume 34 of *Syntax and Semantics*. San Diego, CA; London. Academic Press.

Amit Dubey and Frank Keller. 2003. Probabilistic parsing for german using sister-head dependencies. In *In Proceedings of the 41st Annual Meeting of the Association for Computational Linguistics*, pages 96–103.

Ane Dybro-Johansen. 2004. Extraction automatique de grammaires à partir d'un corpus français. Master's thesis, Université Paris 7.

Mark Johnson. 1998. PCFG models of linguistic tree representations. *Computational Linguistics*, 24(4):613–632.

Aravind K. Joshi. 1987. Introduction to tree adjoining grammar. In A. Manaster-Ramer, editor, *The Mathematics of Language*. J. Benjamins.

R. Kaplan and J. Bresnan. 1982. Lexical-functional grammar: A formal system for grammarical representation. In J. Bresnan, editor, *The Mental Representation of Grammatical Relations*, pages 173–281. Mass.: MIT Press.

Dan Klein and Christopher D. Manning. 2003. Accurate unlexicalized parsing. In *Proceedings of the 41st Annual Meeting on Association for Computational Linguistics-Volume 1*, pages 423–430. Association for Computational Linguistics Morristown, NJ, USA.

Sandra Kübler, Erhard W. Hinrichs, and Wolfgang Maier. 2006. Is it really that difficult to parse german? In *Proceedings of the 2006 Conference on Empirical Methods in Natural Language Processing*, pages 111–119, Sydney, Australia, July. Association for Computational Linguistics.

Dekang Lin. 1995. A dependency-based method for evaluating broad-coverage parsers. In *International Joint Conference on Artificial Intelligence*, pages 1420–1425, Montreal.

Mitchell P. Marcus, Beatrice Santorini, and Mary Ann Marcinkiewicz. 1994. Building a large annotated corpus of english: The penn treebank. *Computational Linguistics*, 19(2):313–330.

David McClosky, Eugene Charniak, and Mark Johnson. 2006. Effective self-training for parsing. In *Proceedings of the Human Language Technology Conference of the NAACL, Main Conference*, pages 152–159, New York City, USA, June. Association for Computational Linguistics.

Slav Petrov, Leon Barrett, Romain Thibaux, and Dan Klein. 2006. Learning accurate, compact, and interpretable tree annotation. In *Proceedings of the 21st International Conference on Computational Linguistics and 44th Annual Meeting of the Association for Computational Linguistics*, Sydney, Australia, July. Association for Computational Linguistics.

Ines Rehbein and Josef van Genabith. 2007. Treebank annotation schemes and parser evaluation for german. In *Proceedings of the 2007 Joint Conference on Empirical Methods in Natural Language Processing and Computational Natural Language Learning (EMNLP-CoNLL)*, Prague.

Philip Resnik. 1992. Probabilistic tree-adjoining grammars as a framework for statistic natural language processing. *COLING'92, Nantes, France.*

F. Sangati and W. Zuidema. 2009. Unsupervised methods for head assignments. In *Proceedings of the 12th Conference of the European Chapter of the ACL (EACL 2009)*, pages 701–709, Athens, Greece. Association for Computational Linguistics.

Y. Schabes and R.C. Waters. 1995. Tree Insertion Grammar: Cubic-Time, Parsable Formalism that Lexicalizes Context-Free Grammar without Changing the Trees Produced. *Computational Linguistics*, 21(4):479–513.

Yves Schabes. 1992. Stochastic Lexicalized Tree Adjoining Grammars. In *Proceedings of the 14th conference on Computational linguistics*, pages 425–432, Nantes, France. Association for Computational Linguistics.

Natalie Schluter and Josef van Genabith. 2007. Preparing, restructuring, and augmenting a french treebank: Lexicalised parsers or coherent treebanks? In *Proceedings of PACLING 07*.

Natalie Schluter and Josef van Genabith. 2008. Treebank-based acquisition of lfg parsing resources for french. In European Language Resources Association (ELRA), editor, *Proceedings of the Sixth International Language Resources and Evaluation (LREC'08)*, Marrakech, Morocco, may.

Daniel Zeman and Philip Resnik. 2008. Cross-language parser adaptation between related languages. In *Proceedings of IJCNLP 2008 Workshop on NLP for Less Privileged Languages*, Hajdarábádu, India.

Transition-Based Parsing of the Chinese Treebank using a Global Discriminative Model

Yue Zhang
Oxford University
Computing Laboratory
yue.zhang@comlab.ox.ac.uk

Stephen Clark
Cambridge University
Computer Laboratory
stephen.clark@cl.cam.ac.uk

Abstract

Transition-based approaches have shown competitive performance on constituent and dependency parsing of Chinese. State-of-the-art accuracies have been achieved by a deterministic shift-reduce parsing model on parsing the Chinese Treebank 2 data (Wang et al., 2006). In this paper, we propose a global discriminative model based on the shift-reduce parsing process, combined with a beam-search decoder, obtaining competitive accuracies on CTB2. We also report the performance of the parser on CTB5 data, obtaining the highest scores in the literature for a dependency-based evaluation.

1 Introduction

Transition-based statistical parsing associates scores with each decision in the parsing process, selecting the parse which is built by the highest scoring sequence of decisions (Briscoe and Carroll, 1993; Nivre et al., 2006). The parsing algorithm is typically some form of bottom-up shift-reduce algorithm, so that scores are associated with actions such as *shift* and *reduce*. One advantage of this approach is that the parsing can be highly efficient, for example by pursuing a greedy strategy in which a single action is chosen at each decision point.

The alternative approach, exemplified by Collins (1997) and Charniak (2000), is to use a chart-based algorithm to build the space of possible parses, together with pruning of low-probability constituents and the Viterbi algorithm to find the highest scoring parse. For English dependency parsing, the two approaches give similar results (McDonald et al., 2005; Nivre et al., 2006). For English constituent-based parsing using the Penn Treebank, the best performing transition-based parser lags behind the current state-of-the-art (Sagae and Lavie, 2005). In contrast, for Chinese, the best dependency parsers are currently transition-based (Duan et al., 2007; Zhang and Clark, 2008). For constituent-based parsing using the Chinese Treebank (CTB), Wang et al. (2006) have shown that a shift-reduce parser can give competitive accuracy scores together with high speeds, by using an SVM to make a single decision at each point in the parsing process.

In this paper we describe a global discriminative model for Chinese shift-reduce parsing, and compare it with Wang et al.'s approach. We apply the same shift-reduce procedure as Wang et al. (2006), but instead of using a local classifier for each transition-based action, we train a generalized perceptron model over complete sequences of actions, so that the parameters are learned in the context of complete parses. We apply beam search to decoding instead of greedy search. The parser still operates in linear time, but the use of beam-search allows the correction of local decision errors by global comparison. Using CTB2, our model achieved Parseval F-scores comparable to Wang et al.'s approach. We also present accuracy scores for the much larger CTB5, using both a constituent-based and dependency-based evaluation. The scores for the dependency-based evaluation were higher than the state-of-the-art dependency parsers for the CTB5 data.

2 The Shift-Reduce Parsing Process

The shift-reduce process used by our beam-search decoder is based on the greedy shift-reduce parsers of Sagae and Lavie (2005) and Wang et al. (2006).

Proceedings of the 11th International Conference on Parsing Technologies (IWPT), pages 162–171,
Paris, October 2009.

The process assumes binary-branching trees; section 2.1 explains how these are obtained from the arbitrary-branching trees in the Chinese Treebank.

The input is assumed to be segmented and POS tagged, and the word-POS pairs waiting to be processed are stored in a queue. A stack holds the partial parse trees that are built during the parsing process. A parse *state* is defined as a $\langle$stack,queue$\rangle$ pair. Parser actions, including SHIFT and various kinds of REDUCE, define functions from states to states by shifting word-POS pairs onto the stack and building partial parse trees.

The actions used by the parser are:

- SHIFT, which pushes the next word-POS pair in the queue onto the stack;
- REDUCE–unary–X, which makes a new unary-branching node with label X; the stack is popped and the popped node becomes the child of the new node; the new node is pushed onto the stack;
- REDUCE–binary–{L/R}–X, which makes a new binary-branching node with label X; the stack is popped twice, with the first popped node becoming the right child of the new node and the second popped node becoming the left child; the new node is pushed onto the stack;
- TERMINATE, which pops the root node off the stack and ends parsing. This action is novel in our parser. Sagae and Lavie (2005) and Wang et al. (2006) only used the first three transition actions, setting the final state as all incoming words having been processed, and the stack containing only one node. However, there are a small number of sentences (14 out of 3475 from the training data) that have unary-branching roots. For these sentences, Wang's parser will be unable to produce the unary-branching roots because the parsing process terminates as soon as the root is found. We define a separate action to terminate parsing, allowing unary reduces to be applied to the root item before parsing finishes.

The trees built by the parser are lexicalized, using the head-finding rules from Zhang and Clark (2008). The left (L) and right (R) versions of the REDUCE-binary rules indicate whether the head of the new node is to be taken from the left or right child. Note also that, since the parser is building binary trees, the X label in the REDUCE rules can be one of the temporary constituent labels, such as NP*, which are needed for the binarization process described in Section 2.1. Hence the number of left and right binary reduce rules is the number of constituent labels in the binarized grammar.

Wang et al. (2006) give a detailed example showing how a segmented and POS-tagged sentence can be incrementally processed using the shift-reduce actions to produce a binary tree. We show this example in Figure 1.

```
for node Y = X_1..X_m ∈ T :
  if m > 2 :
    find the head node X_k(1 ≤ k ≤ m) of Y
    m' = m
    while m' > k and m' > 2 :
      new node Y* = X_1..X_{m'-1}
      Y ← Y* X_{m'}
      m' = m' - 1
    n' = 1
    while n' < k and k - n' > 1 :
      new node Y* = X_{n'}..X_k
      Y ← X_{n'} Y*
      n' = n' + 1
```

Figure 2: the binarization algorithm with input T

2.1 The binarization process

The algorithm in Figure 2 is used to map CTB trees into binarized trees, which are required by the shift-reduce parsing process. For any tree node with more than two child nodes, the algorithm works by first finding the head node, and then processing its right-hand-side and left-hand-side, respectively. The head-finding rules are taken from Zhang and Clark (2008). $Y = X_1..X_m$ represents a tree node Y with child nodes $X_1...X_m (m \geq 1)$.

The label of the newly generated node Y^* is based on the constituent label of the original node Y, but marked with an asterix. Hence binarization enlarges the set of constituent labels. We call the constituents marked with * *temporary* constituents. The binarization process is reversible, in that output from the shift-reduce parser can be unbinarized into CTB format, which is required for evaluation.

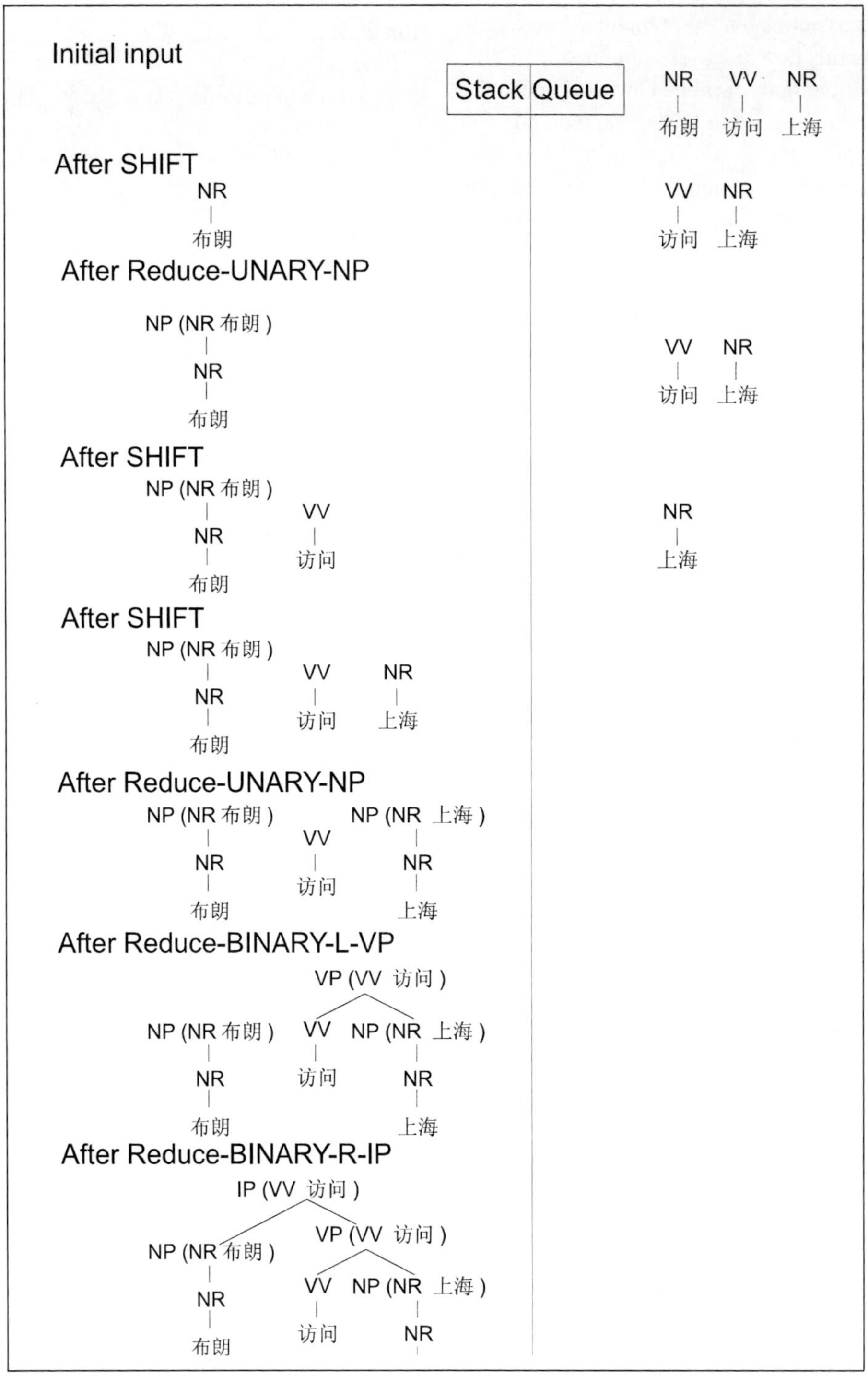

Figure 1: An example shift-reduce parsing process, adopted from Wang et al. (2006)

2.2 Restrictions on the sequence of actions

Not all sequences of actions produce valid binarized trees. In the deterministic parser of Wang et al. (2006), the highest scoring action predicted by the classifier may prevent a valid binary tree from being built. In this case, Wang et al. simply return a partial parse consisting of all the subtrees on the stack.

In our parser a set of restrictions is applied which guarantees a valid parse tree. For example, two simple restrictions are that a SHIFT action can only be applied if the queue of incoming words

Variables: state item $item = (S, Q)$, where
S is stack and Q is incoming queue;
the agenda $agenda$;
list of state items $next$;
Algorithm:
  for $item \in agenda$:
    if $item$.score = $agenda$.bestScore and
    $item$.isFinished:
      $rval = item$
      break
    next = []
    for $move \in item$.legalMoves:
      next.push(item.TakeAction(move))
    agenda = next.getBBest()
Outputs: $rval$

Figure 3: the beam-search decoding algorithm

is non-empty, and the binary reduce actions can only be performed if the stack contains at least two nodes. Some of the restrictions are more complex than this; the full set is listed in the Appendix.

3 Decoding with Beam Search

Our decoder is based on the incremental shift-reduce parsing process described in Section 2. We apply beam-search, keeping the B highest scoring state items in an agenda during the parsing process. The agenda is initialized with a state item containing the starting state, i.e. an empty stack and a queue consisting of all word-POS pairs from the sentence.

At each stage in the decoding process, existing items from the agenda are progressed by applying legal parsing actions. From all newly generated state items, the B highest scoring are put back on the agenda. The decoding process is terminated when the highest scored state item in the agenda reaches the final state. If multiple state items have the same highest score, parsing terminates if any of them are finished. The algorithm is shown in Figure 3.

4 Model and Learning Algorithm

We use a linear model to score state items. Recall that a parser state is a $\langle$stack,queue$\rangle$ pair, with the stack holding subtrees and the queue holding incoming words waiting to be processed. The score for state item Y is defined by:

$$Score(Y) = \vec{w} \cdot \Phi(Y) = \sum_i \lambda_i f_i(Y)$$

where $\Phi(Y)$ is the global feature vector from Y, and $\vec{w}$ is the weight vector defined by the model. Each element from $\Phi(Y)$ represents the global count of a particular feature from Y. The feature set consists of a large number of features which pick out various configurations from the stack and queue, based on the words and subtrees in the state item. The features are described in Section 4.1. The weight values are set using the generalized perceptron algorithm (Collins, 2002).

Inputs: training examples (x_i, y_i)
Initialization: set $\vec{w} = 0$
Algorithm:
  for $t = 1..T$, $i = 1..N$:
    $z_i = parse(x_i, \vec{w})$
    if $z_i \neq y_i$:
      $\vec{w} = \vec{w} + \Phi(y_i) - \Phi(z_i)$
Outputs: $\vec{w}$

Figure 4: the perceptron learning algorithm

The perceptron algorithm is shown in Figure 4. It initializes weight values as all zeros, and uses the current model to decode training examples (the *parse* function in the pseudo-code). If the output is correct, it passes on to the next example. If the output is incorrect, it adjusts the weight values by adding the feature vector from the gold-standard output and subtracting the feature vector from the parser output. Weight values are updated for each example (making the process *online*) and the training data is iterated over T times. In order to avoid overfitting we used the now-standard averaged version of this algorithm (Collins, 2002).

We also apply the *early update* modification from Collins and Roark (2004). If the agenda, at any point during the decoding process, does not contain the correct partial parse, it is not possible for the decoder to produce the correct output. In this case, decoding is stopped early and the weight values are updated using the highest scoring partial parse on the agenda.

4.1 Feature set

Table 1 shows the set of feature templates for the model. Individual features are generated from

Description	Feature templates
Unigrams	S_0tc, S_0wc, S_1tc, S_1wc,
	S_2tc, S_2wc, S_3tc, S_3wc,
	N_0wt, N_1wt, N_2wt, N_3wt,
	S_0lwc, S_0rwc, S_0uwc,
	S_1lwc, S_1rwc, S_1uwc,
Bigrams	S_0wS_1w, S_0wS_1c, S_0cS_1w, S_0cS_1c,
	S_0wN_0w, S_0wN_0t, S_0cN_0w, S_0cN_0t,
	N_0wN_1w, N_0wN_1t, N_0tN_1w, N_0tN_1t
	S_1wN_0w, S_1wN_0t, S_1cN_0w, S_1cN_0t,
Trigrams	$S_0cS_1cS_2c$, $S_0wS_1cS_2c$,
	$S_0cS_1wS_2c$, $S_0cS_1cS_2w$,
	$S_0cS_1cN_0t$, $S_0wS_1cN_0t$,
	$S_0cS_1wN_0t$, $S_0cS_1cN_0w$
Bracket	S_0wb, S_0cb
	S_0wS_1cb, S_0cS_1wb, S_0cS_1cb
	S_0wN_0tb, S_0cN_0wb, S_0cN_0tb
Separator	S_0wp, S_0wcp, S_0wq, S_0wcq,
	S_1wp, S_1wcp, S_1wq, S_1wcq
	S_0cS_1cp, S_0cS_1cq

Table 1: Feature templates

these templates by first instantiating a template with particular labels, words and tags, and then pairing the instantiated template with a particular action. In the table, the symbols S_0, S_1, S_2, and S_3 represent the top four nodes on the stack, and the symbols N_0, N_1, N_2 and N_3 represent the first four words in the incoming queue. S_0L, S_0R and S_0U represent the left and right child for binary branching S_0, and the single child for unary branching S_0, respectively; w represents the lexical head token for a node; c represents the label for a node. When the corresponding node is a terminal, c represents its POS-tag, whereas when the corresponding node is non-terminal, c represents its constituent label; t represents the POS-tag for a word.

The context S_0, S_1, S_2, S_3 and N_0, N_1, N_2, N_3 for the feature templates is taken from Wang et al. (2006). However, Wang et al. (2006) used a polynomial kernel function with an SVM and did not manually create feature combinations. Since we used the linear perceptron algorithm we manually combined Unigram features into Bigram and Trigram features.

The "Bracket" row shows bracket-related features, which were inspired by Wang et al. (2006). Here brackets refer to left brackets including “（”, ““” and “《” and right brackets including “）”, “”” and “》”. In the table, b represents the matching status of the last left bracket (if any) on the stack. It takes three different values: 1 (no matching right bracket has been pushed onto stack), 2 (a matching right bracket has been pushed onto stack) and 3 (a matching right bracket has been pushed onto stack, but then popped off).

The "Separator" row shows features that include one of the separator punctuations (i.e. “，”, “。”, “、” and “；”) between the head words of S_0 and S_1. These templates apply only when the stack contains at least two nodes; p represents a separator punctuation symbol. Each unique separator punctuation between S_0 and S_1 is only counted once when generating the global feature vector. q represents the count of any separator punctuation between S_0 and S_1.

Whenever an action is being considered at each point in the beam-search process, templates from Table 1 are matched with the context defined by the parser state and combined with the action to generate features. Negative features, which are the features from incorrect parser outputs but not from any training example, are included in the model. There are around a million features in our experiments with the CTB2 dataset.

Wang et al. (2006) used a range of other features, including rhythmic features of S_0 and S_1 (Sun and Jurafsky, 2003), features from the most recently found node that is to the left or right of S_0 and S_1, the number of words and the number of punctuations in S_0 and S_1, the distance between S_0 and S_1 and so on. We did not include these features in our parser, because they did not lead to improved performance during development experiments.

5 Experiments

The experiments were performed using the Chinese Treebank 2 and Chinese Treebank 5 data. Standard data preparation was performed before the experiments: empty terminal nodes were removed; any non-terminal nodes with no children were removed; any unary $X \rightarrow X$ nodes resulting from the previous steps were collapsed into one X node.

For all experiments, we used the EVALB tool[1] for evaluation, and used labeled recall (LR), labeled precision (LP) and $F1$ score (which is the

[1] http://nlp.cs.nyu.edu/evalb/

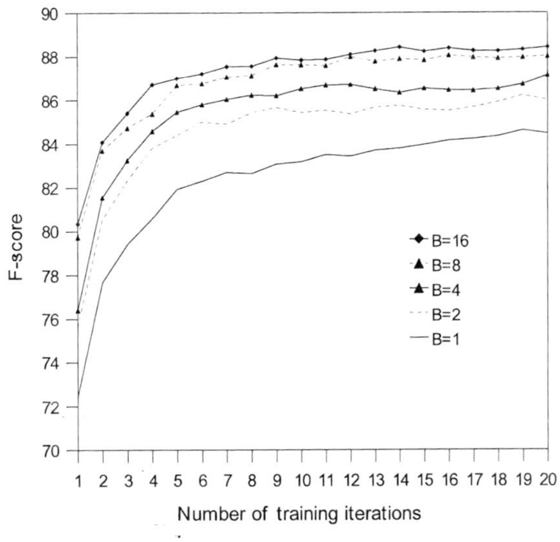

Figure 5: The influence of beam-size

	Sections	Sentences	Words
Training	001–270	3475	85,058
Development	301–325	355	6,821
Test	271–300	348	8,008

Table 2: The standard split of CTB2 data

harmonic mean of LR and LP) to measure parsing accuracy.

5.1 The influence of beam-size

Figure 5 shows the accuracy curves using different beam-sizes for the decoder. The number of training iterations is on the x-axis with F-score on the y-axis. The tests were performed using the development test data and gold-standard POS-tags. The figure shows the benefit of using a beam size greater than 1, with comparatively little accuracy gain being obtained beyond a beam size of 8. Hence we set the beam size to 16 for the rest of the experiments.

5.2 Test results on CTB2

The experiments in this section were performed using CTB2 to allow comparison with previous work, with the CTB2 data extracted from Chinese Treebank 5 (CTB5). The data was split into training, development test and test sets, as shown in Table 2, which is consistent with Wang et al. (2006) and earlier work. The tests were performed using both gold-standard POS-tags and POS-tags automatically assigned by a POS-tagger. We used our

Model	LR	LP	$F1$
Bikel Thesis	80.9%	84.5%	82.7%
Wang 2006 SVM	87.2%	88.3%	87.8%
Wang 2006 Stacked	88.3%	88.1%	88.2%
Our parser	89.4%	90.1%	89.8%

Table 3: Accuracies on CTB2 with gold-standard POS-tags

own implementation of the perceptron-based tagger from Collins (2002).

The results of various models measured using sentences with less than 40 words and using gold-standard POS-tags are shown in Table 3. The rows represent the model from Bikel and Chiang (2000), Bikel (2004), the SVM and ensemble models from Wang et al. (2006), and our parser, respectively. The accuracy of our parser is competitive using this test set.

The results of various models using automatically assigned POS-tags are shown in Table 4. The rows in the table represent the models from Bikel and Chiang (2000), Levy and Manning (2003), Xiong et al. (2005), Bikel (2004), Chiang and Bikel (2002), the SVM model from Wang et al. (2006) and the ensemble system from Wang et al. (2006), and the parser of this paper, respectively. Our parser gave comparable accuracies to the SVM and ensemble models from Wang et al. (2006). However, comparison with Table 3 shows that our parser is more sensitive to POS-tagging errors than some of the other models. One possible reason is that some of the other parsers, e.g. Bikel (2004), use the parser model itself to resolve tagging ambiguities, whereas we rely on a POS tagger to accurately assign a single tag to each word. In fact, for the Chinese data, POS tagging accuracy is not very high, with the perceptron-based tagger achieving an accuracy of only 93%. The beam-search decoding framework we use could accommodate joint parsing and tagging, although the use of features based on the tags of incoming words complicates matters somewhat, since these features rely on tags having been assigned to all words in a pre-processing step. We leave this problem for future work.

In a recent paper, Petrov and Klein (2007) reported LR and LP of 85.7% and 86.9% for sentences with less than 40 words and 81.9% and 84.8% for all sentences on the CTB2 test set, re-

	≤ 40 words				≤ 100 words				Unlimited			
	LR	LP	$F1$	POS	LR	LP	$F1$	POS	LR	LP	$F1$	POS
Bikel 2000	76.8%	77.8%	77.3%	-	73.3%	74.6%	74.0%	-	-	-	-	-
Levy 2003	79.2%	78.4%	78.8%	-	-	-	-	-	-	-	-	-
Xiong 2005	78.7%	80.1%	79.4%	-	-	-	-	-	-	-	-	-
Bikel Thesis	78.0%	81.2%	79.6%	-	74.4%	78.5%	76.4%	-	-	-	-	-
Chiang 2002	78.8%	81.1%	79.9%	-	75.2%	78.0%	76.6%	-	-	-	-	-
Wang 2006 SVM	78.1%	81.1%	79.6%	92.5%	75.5%	78.5%	77.0%	92.2%	75.0%	78.0%	76.5%	92.1%
Wang 2006 Stacked	79.2%	81.1%	80.1%	92.5%	76.7%	78.4%	77.5%	92.2%	76.2%	78.0%	77.1%	92.1%
Our parser	80.2%	80.5%	80.4%	93.5%	76.5%	77.7%	77.1%	93.1%	76.1%	77.4%	76.7%	93.0%

Table 4: Accuracies on CTB2 with automatically assigned tags

≤ 40 words				Unlimited			
LR	LP	$F1$	POS	LR	LP	$F1$	POS
87.9%	87.5%	87.7%	100%	86.9%	86.7%	86.8%	100%
80.2%	79.1%	79.6%	94.1%	78.6%	78.0%	78.3%	93.9%

Table 5: Accuracies on CTB5 using gold-standard and automatically assigned POS-tags

	Sections	Sentences	Words
Set A	001–270	3,484	84,873
Set B	Set A; 400–699	6,567	161,893
Set C	Set B; 700–931	9,707	236,051

Table 6: Training sets with different sizes

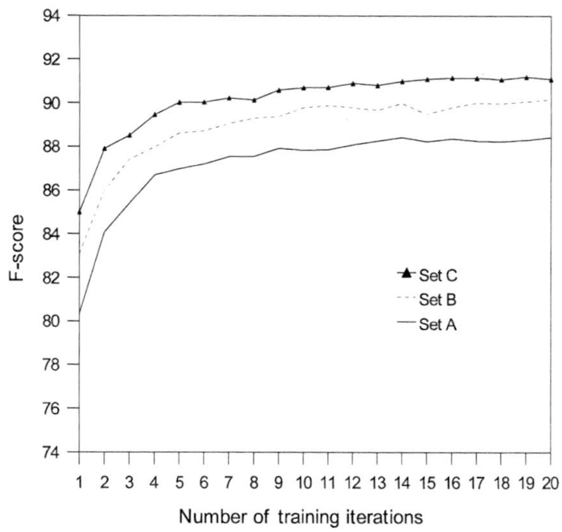

Figure 6: The influence of the size of training data

spectively. These results are significantly better than any model from Table 4. However, we did not include their scores in the table because they used a different training set from CTB5, which is much larger than the CTB2 training set used by all parsers in the table. In order to make a comparison, we split the data in the same way as Petrov and Klein (2007) and tested our parser using automatically assigned POS-tags. It gave LR and LP of 82.0% and 80.9% for sentences with less than 40 words and 77.8% and 77.4% for all sentences, significantly lower than Petrov and Klein (2007), which we partly attribute to the sensitivity of our parser to pos tag errors (see Table 5).

5.3 The effect of training data size

CTB2 is a relatively small corpus, and so we investigated the effect of adding more training data from CTB5. Intuitively, more training data leads to higher parsing accuracy. By using increased amount of training sentences (Table 6) from CTB5 with the same development test data (Table 2), we draw the accuracy curves with different number of training iterations (Figure 6). This experiment confirmed that the accuracy increases with the amount of training data.

Another motivation for us to use more training data is to reduce overfitting. We invested considerable effort into feature engineering using CTB2, and found that a small variation of feature templates (e.g. changing the feature template S_0cS_1c from Table 1 to S_0tcS_1tc) can lead to a comparatively large change (up to 1%) in the accuracy. One possible reason for this variation is the small size of the CTB2 training data. When performing experiments using the larger set B from Table 6, we observed improved stability relative to small feature changes.

	Sections	Sentences	Words
Training	001–815; 1001–1136	16,118	437,859
Dev	886–931; 1148–1151	804	20,453
Test	816–885; 1137–1147	1,915	50,319

Table 7: Standard split of CTB5 data

	Non-root	Root	Complete
Zhang 2008	86.21%	76.26%	34.41%
Our parser	86.95%	79.19%	36.08%

Table 8: Comparison with state-of-the-art dependency parsing using CTB5 data

5.4 Test accuracy using CTB5

Table 5 presents the performance of the parser on CTB5. We adopt the data split from Zhang and Clark (2008), as shown in Table 7. We used the same parser configurations as Section 5.2.

As an additional evaluation we also produced dependency output from the phrase-structure trees, using the head-finding rules, so that we can also compare with dependency parsers, for which the highest scores in the literature are currently from our previous work in Zhang and Clark (2008). We compare the dependencies read off our constituent parser using CTB5 data with the dependency parser from Zhang and Clark (2008). The same measures are taken and the accuracies with gold-standard POS-tags are shown in Table 8. Our constituent parser gave higher accuracy than the dependency parser. It is interesting that, though the constituent parser uses many fewer feature templates than the dependency parser, the features do include constituent information, which is unavailable to dependency parsers.

6 Related work

Our parser is based on the shift-reduce parsing process from Sagae and Lavie (2005) and Wang et al. (2006), and therefore it can be classified as a transition-based parser (Nivre et al., 2006). An important difference between our parser and the Wang et al. (2006) parser is that our parser is based on a discriminative learning model with global features, whilst the parser from Wang et al. (2006) is based on a local classifier that optimizes each individual choice. Instead of greedy local decoding, we used beam search in the decoder.

An early work that applies beam search to constituent parsing is Ratnaparkhi (1999). The main difference between our parser and Ratnaparkhi's is that we use a global discriminative model, whereas Ratnaparkhi's parser has separate probabilities of actions chained together in a conditional model.

Both our parser and the parser from Collins and Roark (2004) use a global discriminative model and an incremental parsing process. The major difference is the use of different incremental parsing processes. To achieve better performance for Chinese parsing, our parser is based on the shift-reduce parsing process. In addition, we did not include a generative baseline model in the discriminative model, as did Collins and Roark (2004).

Our parser in this paper shares similarity with our transition-based dependency parser from Zhang and Clark (2008) in the use of a discriminative model and beam search. The main difference is that our parser in this paper is for constituent parsing. In fact, our parser is one of only a few constituent parsers which have successfully applied global discriminative models, certainly without a generative baseline as a feature, whereas global models for dependency parsing have been comparatively easier to develop.

7 Conclusion

The contributions of this paper can be summarized as follows. First, we defined a global discriminative model for Chinese constituent-based parsing, continuing recent work in this area which has focused on English (Clark and Curran, 2007; Carreras et al., 2008; Finkel et al., 2008). Second, we showed how such a model can be applied to shift-reduce parsing and combined with beam search, resulting in an accurate linear-time parser. In standard tests using CTB2 data, our parser achieved comparable Parseval F-score to the state-of-the-art systems. Moreover, we observed that more training data lead to improvements on both accuracy and stability against feature variations, and reported performance of the parser using CTB5 data. By converting constituent-based output to dependency relations using standard head-finding rules, our parser also obtained the highest scores for a CTB5 dependency evaluation in the literature.

Due to the comparatively low accuracy for Chinese POS-tagging, the parsing accuracy dropped significantly when using automatically assigned POS-tags rather than gold-standard POS-tags. In our further work, we plan to investigate possible methods of joint POS-tagging and parsing under the discriminative model and beam-search framework.

A discriminative model allows consistent training of a wide range of different features. We showed in Zhang and Clark (2008) that it was possible to combine graph and transition-based dependency parser into the same global discriminative model. Our parser framework in this paper allows the same integration of graph-based features. However, preliminary experiments with features based on graph information did not show accuracy improvements for our parser. One possible reason is that the transition actions for the parser in this paper already include graph information, such as the label of the newly generated constituent, while for the dependency parser in Zhang and Clark (2008), transition actions do not contain graph information, and therefore the use of transition-based features helped to make larger improvements in accuracy. The integration of graph-based features for our shift-reduce constituent parser is worth further study.

The source code of our parser is publicly available at http://www.sourceforge.net/projects/zpar.[2]

Appendix

The set of restrictions which ensures a valid binary tree is shown below. The restriction on the number of consecutive unary rule applications is taken from Sagae and Lavie (2005); it prevents infinite running of the parser by repetitive use of unary reduce actions, and ensures linear time complexity in the length of the sentence.

- the shift action can only be performed when the queue of incoming words is not empty;
- when the node on top of the stack is temporary and its head word is from the right child, no shift action can be performed;
- the unary reduce actions can be performed only when the stack is not empty;
- a unary reduce with the same constituent label ($Y \rightarrow Y$) is not allowed;
- no more than three unary reduce actions can be performed consecutively;
- the binary reduce actions can only be performed when the stack contains at least two nodes, with at least one of the two nodes on top of stack (with R being the topmost and L being the second) being non-temporary;
- if L is temporary with label X^*, the resulting node must be labeled X or X^* and left-headed (i.e. to take the head word from L); similar restrictions apply when R is temporary;
- when the incoming queue is empty and the stack contains only two nodes, binary reduce can be applied only if the resulting node is non-temporary;
- when the stack contains only two nodes, temporary resulting nodes from binary reduce must be left-headed;
- when the queue is empty and the stack contains more than two nodes, with the third node from the top being temporary, binary reduce can be applied only if the resulting node is non-temporary;
- when the stack contains more than two nodes, with the third node from the top being temporary, temporary resulting nodes from binary reduce must be left-headed;
- the terminate action can be performed when the queue is empty, and the stack size is one.

[2]The make target for the parser in this paper is chinese.conparser.

References

Daniel M. Bikel and David Chiang. 2000. Two statistical parsing models applied to the Chinese Treebank. In *Proceedings of SIGHAN Workshop*, pages 1–6, Morristown, NJ, USA.

Daniel M. Bikel. 2004. *On the Parameter Space of Generative Lexicalized Statistical Parsing Models.* Ph.D. thesis, University of Pennsylvania.

Ted Briscoe and John Carroll. 1993. Generalized probabilistic LR parsing of natural language (corpora) with unification-based grammars. *Computational Linguistics*, 19(1):25–59.

Xavier Carreras, Michael Collins, and Terry Koo. 2008. Tag, dynamic programming, and the perceptron for efficient, feature-rich parsing. In *Proceedings of CoNLL*, pages 9–16, Manchester, England, August.

Eugene Charniak. 2000. A maximum-entropy-inspired parser. In *Proceedings of NAACL*, pages 132–139, Seattle, WA.

David Chiang and Daniel M. Bikel. 2002. Recovering latent information in treebanks. In *Proceedings of COLING.*

Stephen Clark and James R. Curran. 2007. Wide-coverage efficient statistical parsing with CCG and log-linear models. *Computational Linguistics*, 33(4):493–552.

Michael Collins and Brian Roark. 2004. Incremental parsing with the perceptron algorithm. In *Proceedings of ACL*, pages 111–118, Barcelona, Spain, July.

Michael Collins. 1997. Three generative, lexicalised models for statistical parsing. In *Proceedings of the 35th Meeting of the ACL*, pages 16–23, Madrid, Spain.

Michael Collins. 2002. Discriminative training methods for hidden markov models: Theory and experiments with perceptron algorithms. In *Proceedings of EMNLP*, pages 1–8, Philadelphia, USA, July.

Xiangyu Duan, Jun Zhao, and Bo Xu. 2007. Probabilistic models for action-based Chinese dependency parsing. In *Proceedings of ECML/ECPPKDD*, Warsaw, Poland, September.

Jenny Rose Finkel, Alex Kleeman, and Christopher D. Manning. 2008. Efficient, feature-based, conditional random field parsing. In *Proceedings of ACL/HLT*, pages 959–967, Columbus, Ohio, June. Association for Computational Linguistics.

Roger Levy and Christopher D. Manning. 2003. Is it harder to parse Chinese, or the Chinese Treebank? In *Proceedings of ACL*, pages 439–446, Sapporo, Japan, July.

Ryan McDonald, Koby Crammer, and Fernando Pereira. 2005. Online large-margin training of dependency parsers. In *Proceedings of ACL*, pages 91–98, Ann Arbor, Michigan, June.

Joakim Nivre, Johan Hall, Jens Nilsson, Gülşen Eryiğit, and Svetoslav Marinov. 2006. Labeled pseudo-projective dependency parsing with support vector machines. In *Proceedings of CoNLL*, pages 221–225, New York City, June.

Slav Petrov and Dan Klein. 2007. Improved inference for unlexicalized parsing. In *Proceedings of HLT/NAACL*, pages 404–411, Rochester, New York, April. Association for Computational Linguistics.

Adwait Ratnaparkhi. 1999. Learning to parse natural language with maximum entropy models. *Machine Learning*, 34(1-3):151–175.

Kenji Sagae and Alon Lavie. 2005. A classifier-based parser with linear run-time complexity. In *Proceedings of IWPT*, pages 125–132, Vancouver, British Columbia, October.

Honglin Sun and Daniel Jurafsky. 2003. The effect of rhythm on structural disambiguation in Chinese. In *Proceedings of SIGHAN Workshop.*

Mengqiu Wang, Kenji Sagae, and Teruko Mitamura. 2006. A fast, accurate deterministic parser for Chinese. In *Proceedings of COLING/ACL*, pages 425–432, Sydney, Australia.

Deyi Xiong, Shuanglong Li, Qun Liu, Shouxun Lin, and Yueliang Qian. 2005. Parsing the Penn Chinese Treebank with semantic knowledge. In *Proceedings of IJCNLP.*

Yue Zhang and Stephen Clark. 2008. A tale of two parsers: investigating and combining graph-based and transition-based dependency parsing using beam-search. In *Proceedings of EMNLP*, pages 562–571, Hawaii, USA, October.

Grammar Error Detection with Best Approximated Parse

Jean-Philippe Prost
LIFO, Université d'Orléans
INRIA Lille - Nord Europe
Jean-Philippe.Prost@univ-orleans.fr

Abstract

In this paper, we propose that grammar error detection be disambiguated in generating the connected parse(s) of optimal merit for the full input utterance, in overcoming the cheapest error. The detected error(s) are described as violated grammatical constraints in a framework for Model-Theoretic Syntax (MTS). We present a parsing algorithm for MTS, which only relies on a grammar of well-formedness, in that the process does not require any extra-grammatical resources, additional rules for constraint relaxation or error handling, or any recovery process.

1 Introduction

Grammar error detection is a crucial part of NLP applications such as Grammar Checking or Computer-Assisted Language Learning (CALL). The problem is made highly ambiguous depending on which context is used for interpreting, and thus pinpointing, the error. For example, a phrase may look perfectly fine when isolated (*e.g. brief interview*), but is erroneous in a specific context (*e.g.* in **The judge grants brief interview to this plaintiff*, or in **The judges brief interview this plaintiff*). Robust partial parsing is often not enough to precisely desambiguate those cases. The solution we prescribe is to point out the error(s) as a set of violated (atomic) constraints of minimal cost, along with the structural context used for measuring that cost. Given an ungrammatical input string, the aim is then to provide an approximated rooted parse tree for it, along with a description of all the grammatical constraints it violates. For example, Figure 1 illustrates an approximated parse for an ill-formed sentence in French, and the error being detected in that context. Property Grammar (Blache, 2001) provides an elegant framework for that purpose.

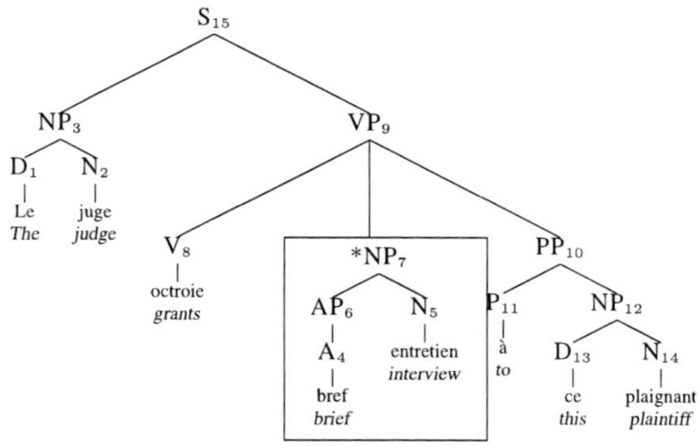

Figure 1: Approximated parse for an erroneous French sentence (the Noun '*entretien*' requires a Determiner).

Most of the relevant approaches to robust knowledge-based parsing addresses the problem as a recovery process. More specifically, we observe three families of approaches in that respect: those relying on grammar *mal-rules* in order to specify how to correctly parse what ought to be ungrammatical (Bender et al., 2004; Foster, 2007); those relying on constraint relaxation according to specified relaxation rules (Douglas and Dale, 1992); and those relying on constraint relaxation with no relaxation rules, along with a recovery process based on weighted parsing (Fouvry, 2003; Foth et al., 2005). The first two are actually quite similar, in that, through their use of extra-grammatical rules, they both extend the grammar's coverage with a set of ought-to-be-ungrammatical utterances. The main drawback of those approaches is that when faced with unexpected input at best their outcome remains unknown, at worst the parsing process fails. With robust weighted parsing, on the other hand, that problem does not occur. The recovery process consists of filtering out structures with respect to their weights or the weights of the constraints being relaxed. However, these strategies usually can not discriminate between grammatical and ungrammatical sentences. The reason for that comes

Proceedings of the 11th International Conference on Parsing Technologies (IWPT), pages 172–175,
Paris, October 2009.

from the fact that grammaticality is disconnected from grammar consistency: since the grammar contains contradicting (universal) constraints, no conclusion can be drawn with regard to the grammaticality of a syntactic structure, which violates part of the constraint system. The same problem occurs with Optimality Theory. In a different fashion, Fouvry weighs unification constraints according to "how much information it contains". However, relaxation only seems possible for those unification constraints: error patterns such as word order, co-occurrence, uniqueness, mutual exclusion, ... can not be tackled. The same restriction is observed in VanRullen (2005), though to a much smaller extent in terms of unrelaxable constraints.

What we would like is (i) to detect *any* type of errors, and present them as conditions of well-formedness being violated in solely relying on the knowledge of a grammar of well-formedness—as opposed to an *error grammar* or *mal-rules*, and (ii) to present, along-side the violated constraints, an approximated parse for the full sentence, which may explain which errors have been found and overcome. We propose here a parsing algorithm which meets these requirements.

NP (*Noun Phrase*)	
Features	Property Type : Properties
[AVM]	*obligation* : NP: $\triangle$(N $\vee$ PRO)
	uniqueness : NP: D!
	: NP: N!
	: NP: PP!
	: NP: PRO!
	linearity : NP: D $\prec$ N
	: NP: D $\prec$ PRO
	: NP: D $\prec$ AP
	: NP: N $\prec$ PP
	requirement : NP: N $\Rightarrow$ D
	: NP: AP $\Rightarrow$ N
	exclusion : NP: N $\not\Leftrightarrow$ PRO
	dependency : NP: N$\begin{bmatrix}\text{GEND } \boxed{1} \\ \text{NUM } \boxed{2}\end{bmatrix} \rightsquigarrow$ D$\begin{bmatrix}\text{GEND } \boxed{1} \\ \text{NUM } \boxed{2}\end{bmatrix}$

Table 1: NP specification in Property Grammar

2 Property Grammar

The framework we are using for knowledge representation is Property Grammar (Blache, 2001) (PG), whose model-theoretical semantics was formalised by Duchier et al. (2009). Intuitively, a PG grammar decomposes what would be rewriting rules of a generative grammar into atomic syntactic properties — a *property* being represented as a boolean constraint. Take, for instance, the rewriting rule NP $\rightarrow$ D N. That rule implicitely informs on different properties (for French): (1) NP has a D child; (2) the D child is unique; (3) NP has an N child; (4) the N child is unique; (5) the D child precedes the N child; (6) the N child requires the D child. PG defines a set of axioms, each axiom corresponding to a constraint type. The properties above are then specified in the grammar as the following constraints: (1) NP : $\triangle$ D; (2) NP : D!; (3) NP : $\triangle$ N; (4) NP : N!; (5) NP : D $\prec$ N; (6) NP : N $\Rightarrow$ D. These constraints can be independently violated. A PG grammar is traditionally presented as a collection of Categories (or Constructions), each of them being specified by a set of constraints. Table 1 shows an example of a category. The class of models we are working with is made up of trees labelled with categories, whose surface realisations are the sentences σ of language. A syntax tree of the realisation of the well-formed sentence σ is a *strong* model of the PG grammar $\mathcal{G}$ iff it satisfies every constraint in $\mathcal{G}$. The loose semantics also allows for constraints to be relaxed. Informally, a syntax tree of the realisation of the ill-formed sentence σ is a *loose* model of $\mathcal{G}$ iff it maximises the proportion of satisfied constraints in $\mathcal{G}$ with respect to the total number of evaluated ones for a given category. The set of violated constraints provides a description of the detected error(s).

3 Parsing Algorithm

The class of models is further restricted to constituent tree structures with no pairwise intersecting constituents, satisfying at least one constraint. Since the solution parse must have a single root, should a category not be found for a node a wildcard (called *Star*) is used instead. The Star category is not specified by any constraint in the grammar.

We introduce an algorithm for Loose Satisfaction Chart Parsing (LSCP), presented as Algorithm 1. We have named our implementation of it *Numbat*. LSCP is based on the probabilistic CKY, augmented with a process of *loose constraint satisfaction*. However, LSCP differs from CKY in various respects. While CKY requires a grammar in Chomsky Normal Form (CNF), LSCP takes an ordinary PG grammar, since no equivalent of the CNF exists for PG. Consequently, LSCP generates n-ary structures. LSCP also uses scores of *merit* instead of probabilities for the constituents. That score can be optimised, since it only factors through the influence of the constituent's immediate descendants.

Steps 1 and 2 enumerate all the possible and

Algorithm 1 Loose Satisfaction Chart Parsing

/* Initialisation */
Create and clear the chart π: every score in π is set to 0

/* Base case: populate π with POS-tags for each word */
for $i \leftarrow 1$ **to** *num_words*
  for (each POS-category T of w_i)
    if $\texttt{merit}(T) \geq \pi[i, 1, T]$ **then**
      Create constituent w_i^T, whose category is T
      $\pi[i, 1, T] \leftarrow \{w_i^T, \texttt{merit}(w_i^T)\}$

/* Recursive case */
/* Step 1: SELECTION of the current reference span */
for *span* $\leftarrow 1$ **to** *num_words*
  for *offset* $\leftarrow 1$ **to** *num_words* $-$ *span* $+ 1$
    end $\leftarrow$ *offset* $+$ *span* $- 1$
    $K \leftarrow \emptyset$
/* Step 2: ENUMERATION of all the configurations */
    for (every set partition $\mathcal{P}$ in [*offset*, ..., *end*])
      $K_{\mathcal{P}} \leftarrow \texttt{buildConfigurations}(\mathcal{P})$
      $K \leftarrow K \cup K_{\mathcal{P}}$
/* Step 3: CHARACTERISATION of the constraint system from the grammar */
      for (every configuration $\mathcal{A} \in K_{\mathcal{P}}$)
        $\chi_{\mathcal{A}} \leftarrow \texttt{characterisation}(\mathcal{A})$
/* Step 4: PROJECTION into categories */
        /* $\mathcal{C}_{\mathcal{A}}$ is a set of candidate constituents */
        $\mathcal{C}_{\mathcal{A}} \leftarrow \texttt{projection}(\chi_{\mathcal{A}})$
        $\texttt{checkpoint}(\mathcal{C}_{\mathcal{A}})$
/* Step 5: MEMOISATION of the optimal candidate constituent */
        for (every candidate constituent $x \in \mathcal{C}_{\mathcal{A}}$, of construction C)
          if $\texttt{merit}(x) \geq \pi[\textit{offset}, \textit{span}, C]$ **then**
            $\pi[\textit{offset}, \textit{span}, C] \leftarrow \{x, \texttt{merit}(x)\}$
    if $\pi[\textit{offset}, \textit{span}] = \emptyset$ **then**
      $\pi[\textit{offset}, \textit{span}] \leftarrow$ preferred forest in K

legal configurations of optimal sub-structures already stored in the chart for a given span and offset. At this stage, a configuration is a tree with an unlabelled root. Note that Step 2 actually does not calculate all the set partitions, but only the legal ones, *i.e.* those which are made up of subsets of contiguous elements. Step 3 evaluates the constraint system, using a configuration as an assignment. The characterisation process is implemented with Algorithm 2. Step 4 consists of making a category judgement for a configuration, on the basis of which constraints are satisfied and violated, in order to label its root. The process is a simple table lookup, the grammar being indexed by properties. Step 5 then memoises the optimal sub-structures for every possible category. Note that the uniqueness of the solution is not guaranteed, and there may well be many different parses with exact same merit for a given input utterance.

Algorithm 2 Characterisation Function

function $\texttt{characterisation}(\mathcal{A} = \langle c_1, \ldots, c_n \rangle$: assignment, $\mathcal{G}$: grammar)
  returns the set of evaluated properties relevant to $\mathcal{A}$,
  and the set of projected categories for $\mathcal{A}$.

/* For storing the result characterisation: */
create and clear $\chi_{\mathcal{A}}$[*property*]: table of *boolean*, indexed by *property*
/* For storing the result projected categories: */
create and clear $\mathcal{C}_{\mathcal{A}}$: set of *category*
/* For temporarily storing the properties to be evaluated: */
create and clear S: set of *property*

for (*mask* $\in [1 \ldots 2^n - 1]$)
  key $\leftarrow \texttt{applyBinaryMask}(\mathcal{A}, \textit{mask})$
  if (*key* is in the set of indexes for $\mathcal{G}$) **then**
    /* Properties are retrieved from the grammar, then evaluated */
    $S \leftarrow \mathcal{G}[\textit{key}].\texttt{getProperties()}$
    $\chi_{\mathcal{A}} \leftarrow \texttt{evaluate}(S)$
    /* Projection Step: fetch the categories to be projected */
    $\mathcal{C}_{\mathcal{A}} \leftarrow \mathcal{G}[\textit{key}].\texttt{getDominantCategories()}$
return $\chi_{\mathcal{A}}, \mathcal{C}_{\mathcal{A}}$

The *key* is a hash-code of a combination of constructions, used for fetching the constraints this combination is concerned with.

Should the current cell in the chart not being populated with any constituents, a preferred forest of partial parses (= Star category) is used instead. The preferred forest is constructed on the fly (as part of `buildConfigurations`); a pointer is maintained to the preferred configuration during enumeration. The preference goes to: (i) the constituents with the widest span; (ii) the least overall number of constituents. This translates heuristically into a *preference score* p_F computed as follows (where F is the forest, and C_i its constituents): $p_F = \textit{span} \cdot (\texttt{merit}(C_i) + \textit{span})$. In that way, LSCP always delivers a parse for any input. The technique is somehow similar to the one of Riezler et al. (2002), where *fragment parses* are allowed for achieving increased robustness, although their solution requires the standard grammar to be augmented with a *fragment grammar.*

4 Evaluation

In order to measure *Numbat*'s ability to (i) detect errors in an ungrammatical sentence, and (ii) build the best approximated parse for it, *Numbat* should, ideally, be evaluated on a corpus of both well-formed and ill-formed utterances annotated with spannnig phrase structures. Unfortunately, such a Gold Standard is not available to us. The development of adequate resources is central to future works. In order to (partially) overcome that problem we have carried out two distinct evaluations: one aims to measure *Numbat*'s performance on grammatical sentences, and the other one on ungrammatical sentences. Evaluation 1, whose results are reported in Table 2, follows the protocol devised for the EASY evaluation campaign of parsers of French (Paroubek et al., 2003), with a subset of the campaign's corpus. For comparison, Table 3 reports the performance measured under the same circumstances for two other parsers: a shallow one (VanRullen, 2005) also based on PG, and a stochastic one (VanRullen et al., 2006). The grammar used for that evaluation was developed by VanRullen (2005). Evaluation 2 was run on

	Precision	Recall	F
Total	**0.7835**	**0.7057**	**0.7416**
general_lemonde	0.8187	0.7515	0.7837
general_mlcc	0.7175	0.6366	0.6746
general_senat	0.8647	0.7069	0.7779
litteraire	0.8124	0.7651	0.788
mail	0.7193	0.6951	0.707
medical	0.8573	0.678	0.757
oral_delic	0.6817	0.621	0.649
questions_amaryllis	0.8081	0.7432	0.7743
questions_trec	0.8208	0.7069	0.7596

Table 2: EASY scores of *Numbat* (Eval. 1)

	Precision	Recall	F
shallow parser	0.7846	0.8376	0.8102
stochastic parser	0.9013	0.8978	0.8995

Table 3: Comparative EASY scores

a corpus of unannotated ungrammatical sentences (Blache et al., 2006), where each of the ungrammatical sentences (amounting to 94% of the corpus) matches a controlled error pattern. Five expert annotators were asked whether the solution trees were possible and acceptable syntactic parses for their corresponding sentence. Specific instructions were given to make sure that the judgement does not hold on the grammatical acceptability of the surface sentence as such, but actually on the parse associated with it. For that evaluation VanRullen's grammar was completed with nested categories (since the EASY annotation scheme only has chunks). Given the nature of the material to be assessed here, the Precision and Recall measurements had to be modified. The total number of input sentences is interpreted as the number of *predictions*; the number of COMPLETE structures is interpreted as the number of *observations*; and the number of structures evaluated as CORRECT by human judges is interpreted as the number of correct solutions. Hence the following formulations and scores: Precision=CORRECT/COMPLETE=0.74; Recall=CORRECT/Total=0.68; F=0.71. 92% of the corpus is analysed with a complete structure; 74% of these complete parses were judged as syntactically correct. The Recall score indicates that the correct parses represent 68% of the corpus. In spite of a lack of a real baseline, these scores compare with those of grammatical parsers.

5 Conclusion

In this paper, we have proposed to address the problem of grammar error detection in providing a set of violated syntactic properties for an ill-formed sentence, along with the best structural context in the form of a connected syntax tree. We have introduced an algorithm for Loose Satisfaction Chart Parsing (LSCP) which meets those requirements, and presented performance measures for it. Future work includes optimisation of LSCP and validation on more appropriate corpora.

Acknowledgement

Partly funded by ANR-07-MDCO-03 (CRoTAL).

References

E. M. Bender, D. Flickinger, S. Oepen, A. Walsh, and T. Baldwin. 2004. Arboretum: Using a precision grammar for grammar checking in CALL. In *Proc. of InSTIL/ICALL2004*, volume 17, page 19.

P. Blache, B. Hemforth, and S. Rauzy. 2006. Acceptability Prediction by Means of Grammaticality Quantification. In *Proc. of CoLing/ACL*, pages 57–64. ACL.

P. Blache. 2001. *Les Grammaires de Propriétés : des contraintes pour le traitement automatique des langues naturelles*. Hermès Sciences.

S. Douglas and R. Dale. 1992. Towards Robust PATR. In *Proc. of CoLing*, volume 2, pages 468–474. ACL.

D. Duchier, J-P. Prost, and T-B-H. Dao. 2009. A Model-Theoretic Framework for Grammaticality Judgements. In *To appear in Proc. of FG'09*, volume 5591 of *LNCS*. FOLLI, Springer.

J. Foster. 2007. Real bad grammar: Realistic grammatical description with grammaticality. *Corpus Linguistics and Lingustic Theory*, 3(1):73–86.

K. Foth, W. Menzel, and I. Schröder. 2005. Robust Parsing with Weighted Constraints. *Natural Language Engineering*, 11(1):1–25.

F. Fouvry. 2003. Constraint relaxation with weighted feature structures. pages 103–114.

P. Paroubek, I. Robba, and A. Vilnat. 2003. EASY: An Evaluation Protocol for Syntactic Parsers. www.limsi.fr/RS2005/chm/lir/lir11/ (08/2008).

S. Riezler, T. H. King, R. M. Kaplan, R. Crouch, J. T. III Maxwell, and M. Johnson. 2002. Parsing the Wall Street Journal using a Lexical-Functional Grammar and Discriminative Estimation Techniques. In *Proc. of ACL*, pages 271–278. ACL.

T. VanRullen, P. Blache, and J-M. Balfourier. 2006. Constraint-Based Parsing as an Efficient Solution: Results from the Parsing Evaluation Campaign EASy. In *Proc. of LREC*, pages 165–170.

T. VanRullen. 2005. *Vers une analyse syntaxique à granularité variable*. Thèse de doctorat.

The effect of correcting grammatical errors on parse probabilities

Joachim Wagner
CNGL
School of Computing
Dublin City University, Ireland
jwagner@computing.dcu.ie

Jennifer Foster
NCLT
School of Computing
Dublin City University, Ireland.
jfoster@computing.dcu.ie

Abstract

We parse the sentences in three parallel error corpora using a generative, probabilistic parser and compare the parse probabilities of the most likely analyses for each grammatical sentence and its closely related ungrammatical counterpart.

1 Introduction

The syntactic analysis of a sentence provided by a parser is used to guide the interpretation process required, to varying extents, by applications such as question-answering, sentiment analysis and machine translation. In theory, however, parsing also provides a grammaticality judgement as shown in Figure 1. Whether or not a sentence is grammatical is determined by its parsability with a grammar of the language in question.

The use of parsing to determine whether a sentence is grammatical has faded into the background as hand-written grammars aiming to describe only the grammatical sequences in a language have been largely supplanted by treebank-derived grammars. Grammars read from treebanks tend to overgenerate. This overgeneration is unproblematic if a probabilistic model is used to rank analyses and if the parser is not being used to provide a grammaticality judgement. The combination of grammar size, probabilistic parse selection and smoothing techniques results in high robustness to errors and broad language coverage, desirable properties in applications requiring a syntactic analysis of any input, regardless of noise. However, for applications which rely on a parser's ability to distinguish grammatical sequences from ungrammatical ones, e.g. grammar checkers, overgenerating grammars are perhaps less useful as they fail to reject ungrammatical strings.

A naive solution might be to assume that the probability assigned to a parse tree by its probabilistic model could be leveraged in some way to determine the sentence's grammaticality. In this paper, we explore one aspect of this question by using three parallel error corpora to determine the effect of common English grammatical errors on the parse probability of the most likely parse tree returned by a generative probabilistic parser.

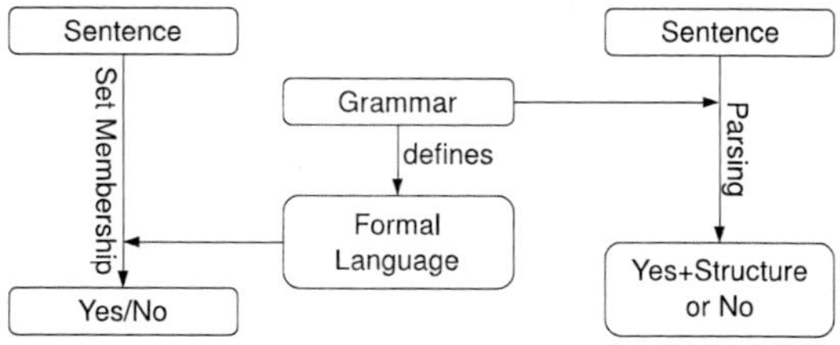

Figure 1: Grammaticality and formal languages

2 Related Work

The probability of a parse tree has been used before in error detection systems. Sun *et al.* (2007) report only a very modest improvement when they include a parse probability feature in their system whose features mostly consist of linear sequential patterns. Lee and Seneff (2006) detect ungrammatical sentences by comparing the parse probability of a possibly ill-formed input sentence to the parse probabilities of candidate corrections which are generated by arbitrarily deleting, inserting and substituting articles, prepositions and auxiliaries and changing the inflection of verbs and nouns. Foster *et al.* (2008) compare the parse probability returned by a parser trained on a regular treebank to the probability returned by the same parser trained on a "noisy" treebank and use the difference to decide whether the sentence is ill-formed.

Research in the field of psycholinguistics has explored the link between frequency and grammaticality, often focusing on borderline acceptable sentences (see Crocker and Keller (2006) for a discussion of the literature). Koonst-Garboden and Jaeger (2003) find a weak correlation between the

Proceedings of the 11th International Conference on Parsing Technologies (IWPT), pages 176–179,
Paris, October 2009.

frequency ratios of competing surface realisations and human acceptability judgements. Hale (2003) calculates the information-theoretic load of words in sentences assuming that they were generated according to a probabilistic grammar and finds that these values are good predictors for observed reading time and other measures of cognitive load.

3 Experimental Setup

The aim of this experiment is to find out to what extent ungrammatical sentences behave differently from correct sentences as regards their parse probabilities. There are two types of corpora we study: two parallel error corpora that consist of authentic ungrammatical sentences and manual corrections, and a parallel error corpus that consists of authentic grammatical sentences and automatically induced errors. Using parallel corpora allows us to compare pairs of sentences that have the same or very similar lexical content and differ only with respect to their grammaticality. A corpus with automatically induced errors is included because such a corpus is much larger and controlled error insertion allows us to examine directly the effect of a particular error type.

The first parallel error corpus contains 1,132 sentence pairs each comprising an ungrammatical sentence and a correction (Foster, 2005). The sentences are taken from written texts and contain either one or two grammatical errors. The errors include those made by native English speakers. We call this the Foster corpus. The second corpus is a learner corpus. It contains transcribed spoken utterances produced by learners of English of varying L1s and levels of experience in a classroom setting. Wagner et al. (2009) manually corrected 500 sentences of the transcribed utterances, producing a parallel error corpus which we call Gonzaga 500. The third parallel corpus contains 199,600 sentences taken from the British National Corpus and ungrammatical sentences produced by introducing errors of the following five types into the original BNC sentences: errors involving an extra word, errors involving a missing word, real-word spelling errors, agreement errors and errors involving an incorrect verbal inflection.

All sentence pairs in the three parallel corpora are parsed using the June 2006 version of the first-stage parser of Charniak and Johnson (2005), a lexicalised, generative, probabilistic parser achieving competitive performance on Wall Street Journal text. We compare the probability of the highest ranked tree for the grammatical sentence in the pair to the probability of the highest ranked tree for the ungrammatical sentence.

4 Results

Figure 2 shows the results for the Foster corpus. For ranges of 4 points on the logarithmic scale, the bars depict how many sentence pairs have a probability ratio within the respective range. For example, there are 48 pairs (5th bar from left) for which the correction has a parse probability which is between 8 and 12 points lower than the parse probability of its erroneous original, or, in other words, for which the probability ratio is between e^{-12} and e^{-8}. 853 pairs show a higher probability for the correction vs. 279 pairs which do not. Since the probability of a tree is the product of its rule probabilities, sentence length is a factor. If we focus on corrections that do not change the sentence length, the ratio sharpens to 414 vs. 90 pairs. Ungrammatical sentences do often receive lower parse probabilities than their corrections.

Figure 3 shows the results for the Gonzaga 500. Here we see a picture similar to the Foster corpus although the peak for the range from $e^0 = 1$ to $e^4 \approx 54.6$ is more pronounced. This time there are more cases where the parse probability drops despite a sentence being shortened and vice versa. Overall, 348 sentence pairs show an increased parse probability, 152 do not. For sentences that stay the same length the ratio is 154 to 34, or 4.53:1, for this corpus which is almost identical to the Foster corpus (4.60:1).

How do these observations translate to the artificial parallel error corpus created from BNC data? Figure 4 shows the results for the BNC data. In order to keep the orientation of the graph as before, we change the sign by looking at decrements instead of increments. Also, we swap the keys for shortened and lengthened sentences. Clearly, the distribution is wider and moved to the right. The peak is at the bar labelled 10. Accordingly, the ratio of the number of sentence pairs above and below the zero line is much higher than before (overall 32,111 to $167,489 = 5.22$, for same length only 8,537 to $111,171 = 13.02$), suggesting that our artificial errors might have a stronger effect on parse probability than authentic errors. Another possible explanation is that the BNC data only contains five error types, whereas the range of

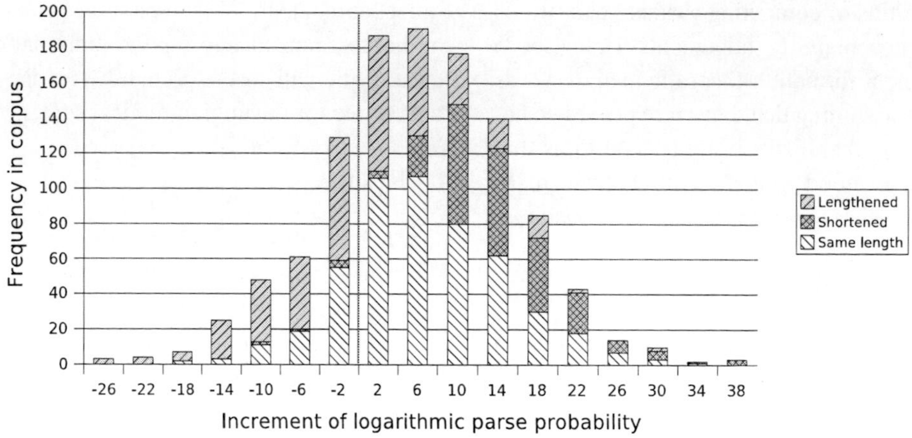

Figure 2: Effect of correcting erroneous sentences (Foster corpus) on the probability of the best parse. Each bar is broken down by whether and how the correction changed the sentence length in tokens. A bar labelled x covers ratios from e^{x-2} to e^{x+2} (exclusive).

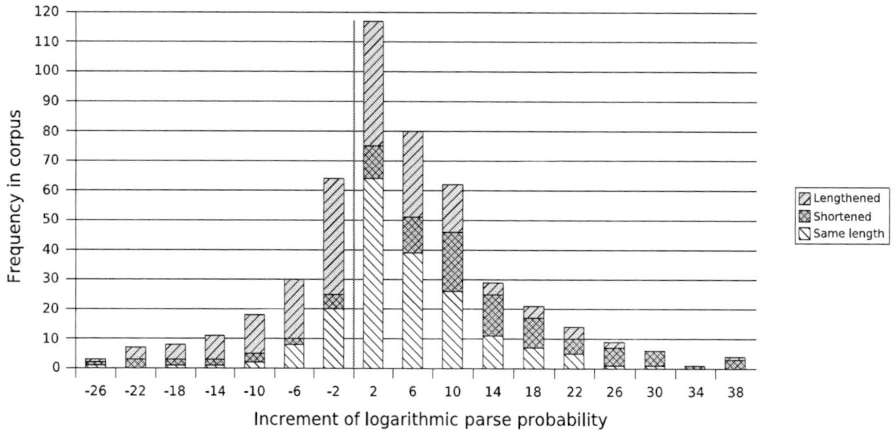

Figure 3: Effect of correcting erroneous sentences (Gonzaga 500 corpus) on the probability of the best parse.

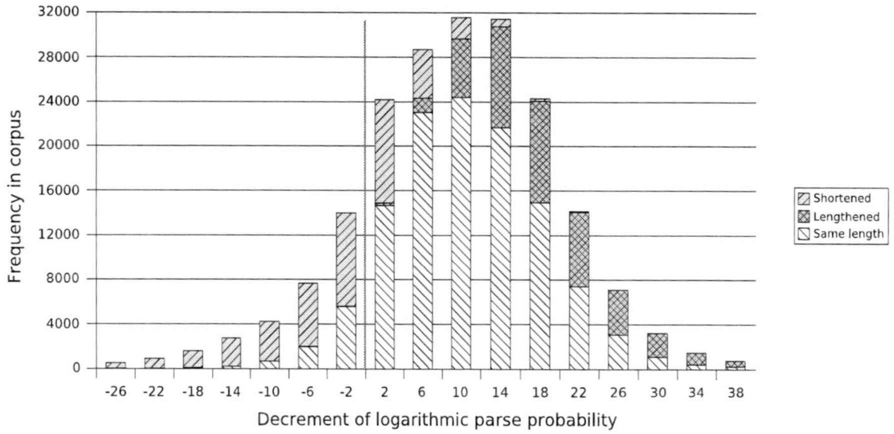

Figure 4: Effect of inserting errors into BNC sentences on the probability of the best parse.

errors in the Foster and Gonzaga corpus is wider.

Analysing the BNC data by error type and looking firstly at those error types that do not involve a change in sentence length, we see that:

- 96% of real-word spelling errors cause a reduction in parse probability.
- 91% of agreement errors cause a reduction in parse probability. Agreement errors involving articles most reliably decrease the probability.
- 92% of verb form errors cause a reduction. Changing the form from present participle to past participle[1] is least likely to cause a reduction, whereas changing it from past participle to third singular is most likely.

The effect of error types which change sentence length is more difficult to interpret. Almost all of the extra word errors cause a reduction in parse probability and it is difficult to know whether this is happening because the sentence length has increased or because an error has been introduced. The errors involving missing words do not systematically result in an increase in parse probability – 41% of them cause a reduction in parse probability, and this is much more likely to occur if the missing word is a function word (article, auxiliary, preposition).

Since the Foster corpus is also error-annotated, we can also examine its results by error type. This analysis broadly agrees with that of the BNC data, although the percentage of ill-formed sentences for which there is a reduction in parse probability is generally lower (see Fig. 2 vs. Fig. 4).

5 Conclusion

We have parsed the sentences in three parallel error corpora using a generative, probabilistic parser and examined the parse probability of the most likely analysis of each sentence. We find that grammatical errors have some negative effect on the probability assigned to the best parse, a finding which corroborates previous evidence linking sentence grammaticality to frequency. In our experiment, we approximate sentence probability by looking only at the most likely analysis – it might be useful to see if the same effect holds if we sum over parse trees. To fully exploit parse or sentence probability in an error detection system, it is necessary to fully account for the effect on probability of 1) non-structural factors such as sentence length and 2) *particular* error types. This study represents a contribution towards the latter.

[1] This raises the issue of covert errors, resulting in grammatical sentence structures. Lee and Seneff (2008) give the example *I am **prepared** for the exam* which was produced by a learner of English instead of *I am **preparing** for the exam*. These occur in authentic error corpora and cannot be completely avoided when automatically introducing errors.

Acknowledgements

We are grateful to James Hunter from Gonzaga University for providing us with a learner corpus. We thank Josef van Genabith and the reviewers for their comments and acknowledge the Irish Centre for High-End Computing for the provision of computational facilities. The BNC is distributed by Oxford University Computing Services.

References

Eugene Charniak and Mark Johnson. 2005. Course-to-fine n-best-parsing and maxent discriminative reranking. In *Proceedings of ACL*.

Matthew W. Crocker and Frank Keller. 2006. Probabilistic grammars as models of gradience in language processing. In Gisbert Fanselow, C. Féry, R. Vogel, and M. Schlesewsky, editors, *Gradience in Grammar: Generative Perspectives*, pages 227–245. Oxford University Press.

Jennifer Foster, Joachim Wagner, and Josef van Genabith. 2008. Adapting a WSJ-trained parser to grammatically noisy text. In *Proceedings of ACL*.

Jennifer Foster. 2005. *Good Reasons for Noting Bad Grammar: Empirical Investigations into the Parsing of Ungrammatical Written English*. Ph.D. thesis, University of Dublin, Trinity College.

John Hale. 2003. The information conveyed by words in sentences. *Journal of Psycholinguistic Research*, 32(2):101–123.

Andrew Koontz-Garboden and T. Florian Jaeger. 2003. An empirical investigation of the frequency-grammaticality correlation hypothesis. Student essay received or downloaded on 2006-03-13.

John Lee and Stephanie Seneff. 2006. Automatic grammar correction for second-language learners. In *Interspeech 2006 - 9th ICSLP*, pages 1978–1981.

John Lee and Stephanie Seneff. 2008. Correcting misuse of verb forms. In *Proceedings of ACL*.

Guihua Sun, Xiaohua Liu, Gao Cong, Ming Zhou, Zhongyang Xiong, John Lee, and Chin-Yew Lin. 2007. Detecting erroneous sentences using automatically mined sequential patterns. In *Proc. of ACL*.

Joachim Wagner, Jennifer Foster, and Josef van Genabith. 2009. Judging grammaticality: Experiments in sentence classification. *CALICO Journal*, 26(3).

Effective Analysis of Causes and Inter-dependencies of Parsing Errors

Tadayoshi Hara[1] **Yusuke Miyao**[1] **Jun'ichi Tsujii**[1,2,3]
[1]Department of Computer Science, University of Tokyo
Hongo 7-3-1, Bunkyo-ku, Tokyo, 113-0033, JAPAN
[2]School of Computer Science, University of Manchester
[3]NaCTeM (National Center for Text Mining)
{harasan,yusuke,tsujii}@is.s.u-tokyo.ac.jp

Abstract

In this paper, we propose two methods for analyzing errors in parsing. One is to classify errors into categories which grammar developers can easily associate with defects in grammar or a parsing model and thus its improvement. The other is to discover inter-dependencies among errors, and thus grammar developers can focus on errors which are crucial for improving the performance of a parsing model.

The first method uses patterns of errors to associate them with categories of causes for those errors, such as errors in scope determination of coordination, PP-attachment, identification of antecedent of relative clauses, etc. On the other hand, the second method, which is based on re-parsing with one of observed errors corrected, assesses inter-dependencies among errors by examining which other errors were to be corrected as a result if a specific error was corrected.

Experiments show that these two methods are complementary and by being combined, they can provide useful clues as to how to improve a given grammar.

1 Introduction

In any kind of complex systems, analyzing causes of errors is a crucial step for improving its performance. In recent sophisticated parsing technologies, the step of error analysis has been becoming more and more convoluted and time-consuming, if not impossible. While common performance evaluation measures such as F-values are useful to compare the performance of systems or evaluate improvement of a system, they hardly give useful clues as to how to improve a system. Evaluation measures usually assume uniform units such as the number of correctly or incorrectly recognized constituent boundaries and their labels, or in a similar vein, dependency links among words and their labels, and then compute single values such as the F-value. These values do not give any insights as to where the weaknesses exist in a parsing model. As a result, the improvement process takes the form of time consuming trial-error cycles.

Once grammar developers know the actual distribution of errors across different categories such as PP-attachment, complement/adjunct distinction, gerund/participle distinction, etc., they can think of focused and systematic improvement of a parsing model.

Another problem of the F-value in terms of uniform units is that it does not take inter-dependencies among errors into consideration. In particular, for parsers based on grammar formalisms such as LFG (Kaplan and Bresnan, 1995), HPSG (Pollard and Sag, 1994), or CCG (Steedman, 2000), units (eg. single predicate-argument links) are inter-related through hierarchical structures and structure sharing assumed by these formalisms. Single errors are inherently propagated to other sets of errors. This is also the case, though to a lesser extent, for parsing models in which shallow parsing is followed by another component for semantic label assignment.

In order to address these two issues, we propose two methods in this paper. One is to recognize cause categories of errors and the other is to capture inter-dependencies among errors. The former method defines various patterns of errors to identify categories of error causes. The latter method re-parses a sentence with a single target error corrected, and regards the errors which are corrected in re-parse as errors dependent on the target.

Although these two methods are implemented for a specific parser using HPSG (Miyao and Tsujii, 2005; Ninomiya et al., 2006), the same ideas can be applied to any type of parsing models.

Proceedings of the 11th International Conference on Parsing Technologies (IWPT), pages 180–191,
Paris, October 2009.

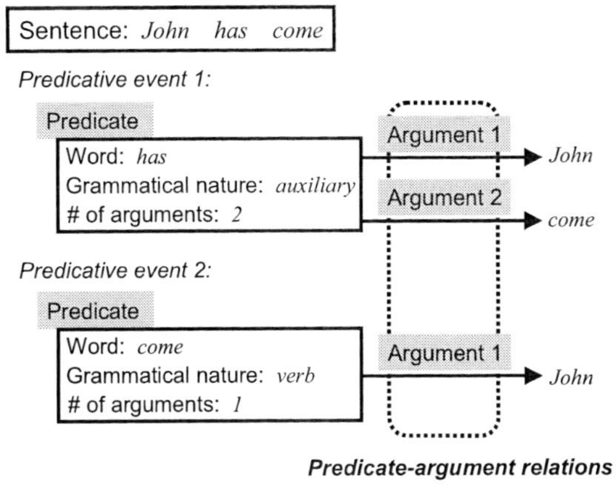

Figure 1: Predicate-argument relations

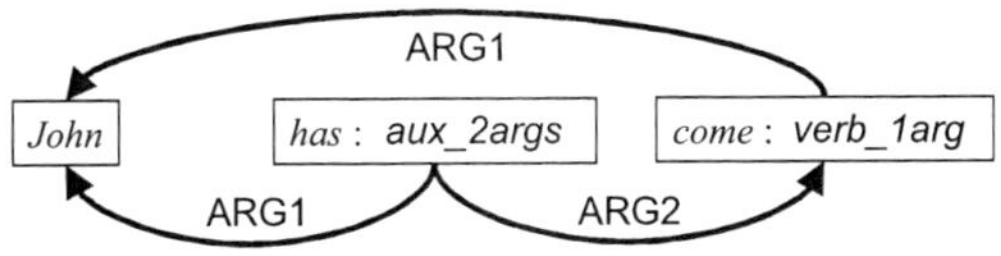

Figure 2: Representation of predicate-argument relations

In the following, Section 2 introduces a parser and its evaluation metrics, Section 3 illustrates difficulties in analyzing parsing errors based on common evaluation measures, and Section 4 proposes the two methods for effective error analysis. Section 5 presents experimental results which show how our methods work for analyzing actual parsing errors. Section 6 and Section 7 illustrate further application of these methods to related topics. Section 8 summarizes this research and indicates some of future directions.

2 A parser and its evaluation

A parser is a system which interprets given sentences in terms of structures derived from syntactic or in some cases semantic viewpoints, and structures constructed as a result are used as essential information for various tasks of natural language processing such as information extraction, machine translation, and so on.

In this paper, we address issues involved in improving the performance of a parser which produces structural representations deeper than surface constituent structures. Such a parser is called a "deep parser." In many deep parsers, the output structure is defined by a linguistics-based grammar framework such as CFG, CCG (Steedman, 2000), LFG (Kaplan and Bresnan, 1995) or HPSG

Abbr.	Full	Abbr.	Full
aux	auxiliary	*conj*	conjunction
prep	prepositional	*lgs*	logical subject
verb	verb	*app*	apposition
coord	coordination	*relative*	relative
det	determiner	*_Narg(s)*	takes N arguments
adj	adjunction	*_mod*	modifies a word

Table 1: Descriptions for predicate types

(Pollard and Sag, 1994). Alternatively, some deep parsing models assume staged processing in which a stage of shallow parsing is followed by a stage of semantic role labeling, which assigns labels indicating semantic relationships between predicates and their arguments. In either case, we assume a parser to produce a single "deep" structural representation for a given sentence, which is chosen from a set of possible interpretations as the most probable one by a disambiguation model.

For evaluation of the performance of a parser, various metrics have been introduced according to the structure captured by a given grammar formalism or a system of semantic labels. In most cases, instead of examining correctness for a whole structure, a parser is evaluated in terms of the F-value which shows how correctly it recognizes relationships among words and assigns "labels" to the relationships in the structure. In this paper, we assume a certain type of "predicate-argument relation."

In this measurement, a structure given for a sentence is decomposed into a set of predicative words and their arguments. A predicate takes other words as its arguments. In our representation, the arguments are labeled by semantically neutral labels such as ARGn(n = 1...5) and MOD. In this representation, a basic unit is a triplet, such as

<Predicate:PredicateType,
ArgumentLabel,
Argument>,

where "Predicate" and "Argument" are surface words. As shown in the examples in Section 4, "PredicateType" bears extra information concerning the syntactic construction in which the triplet is embedded. ARG1-ARG5 express relations between a Head and its complement, while MOD expresses a relation between an Adjunct and its modifiee. Since all dependency relations are expressed by triplets, triplets contain not only semantic de-

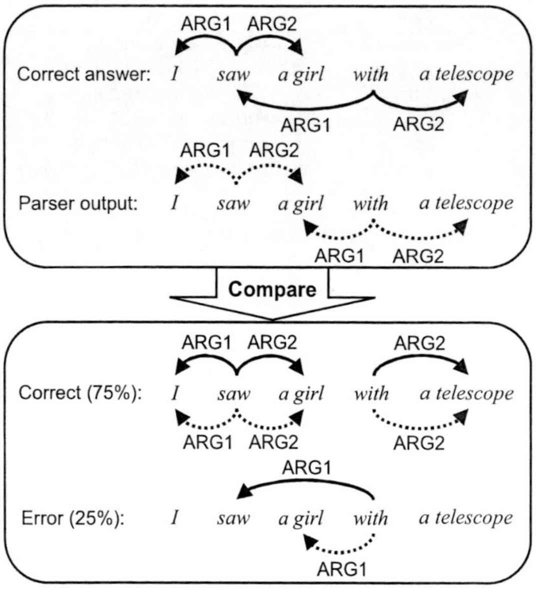

Figure 3: An example of parsing performance evaluations

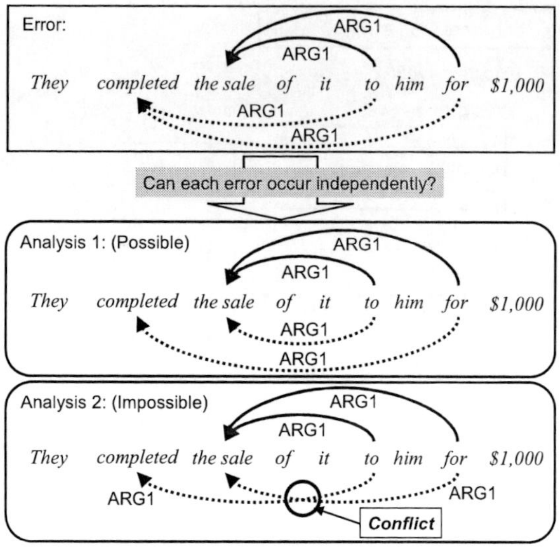

Figure 4: Sketch of error propagation

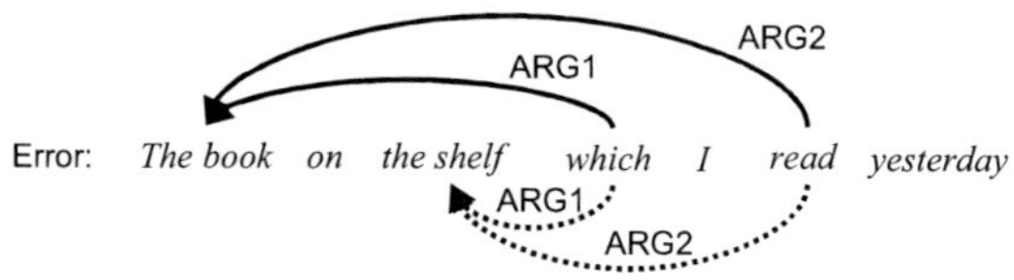

Figure 5: Parsing errors around one relative clause attachment

pendencies but also many dependencies which are essentially syntactic in nature. Figure 1 shows an example used in Miyao and Tsujii (2005) and Ninomiya et al. (2006).

This example shows predicate-argument relations for "*John has come.*" There are two predicates in this sentence, "*has*" and "*come*". The word "*has*", which is used as an auxiliary verb, takes two words, "*John*" and "*come*", as its arguments, and therefore two triplets of predicate-argument relation, <*has* ARG1 *John*> and <*has* ARG2 *come*>. As for the predicative word "*come*", we have one triplet <*come* ARG1 *John*>. Note that, in this HPSG analysis, the auxiliary verb "*has*" is analyzed in such a way that it takes one NP as subject and one VP as complement, and that the subject of the auxiliary verb is shared by the verb ("*come*") in VP as its subject (Figure 2). The fact that "*has*" in this sentence is an auxiliary verb is indicated by the "PredicateType", *aux_2args*. A "PredicateType" consists of a type and the number of arguments it takes (Table 1).

3 Difficulties in analyzing parsing errors

Figure 3 shows an example of the evaluation of the parser based on these predicate-argument relations. Note that the predicate types are abbreviated in this figure. In the sentence "*I saw a girl with a telescope*", there should be four triplets for the two predicates, "*saw*" and "*with*," each of which takes two arguments. Although the parser output does indeed contain four triplets, the first argument of "*with*" is not the correct one. Thus, this output is erroneous, with the F-value of 75%.

While the F-value thus computed is fine for capturing the performance of a parser, it does not offer any help for improving its performance.

First, because it does not give any indication on what portion of erroneous triplets are in PP-attachment, complement/adjunct distinction, gerund/participle distinction, etc., one cannot determine which part of a parsing model should be improved. In order to identify error categories, we have to manually compare a parsing output with a correct parse and classify them. Consider again the example in Figure 3. We can easily observe that "ARG1" of predicate "*with*" was mistaken. In this case, the word linked via "ARG1" represents a modifiee of the prepositional phrase, and thereby we conclude that the error is in PP-attachment. While the process looks straightforward for this simple sentence and error, to perform such a manual inspection for all sentences and more complex types of errors is costly, and becomes inhibitive when the size of a test set of sentences is realistically large.

Another problem with the F-value is that it ignores inter-dependencies among errors. Since the F-value does not consider inter-dependencies, one cannot determine which errors are more crucial than others in terms of the performance of the system as a whole.

A simple example of inter-dependency is shown in Figure 4. "ARG1" of "*for*" and "*to*" were mistaken by a parser, both of which can be classified as PP-attachments as in Figure 3. However, the two errors are not independent. The former error can occur by itself (Analysis 1) while the latter cannot because of the structural conflict with the former (Analysis 2). The occurrence of the latter error thus forces the former.

Moreover, inter-dependency in a deep parser based on linguistics-based formalisms can be complicated. Error propagation is ingrained in grammar itself. Consider Figure 5. In this example, a wrong decision on the antecedent of a relative clause results in a wrong triplet of the predicate in the embedded clause with the antecedent. That is, the two erroneous triplets, one of the "ARG1" of "*which*" and the other of the "ARG2" of "*read*," were caused by a single wrong decision of the antecedent of a relative clause. Such a propagation of errors can be even more complicated, for example, when the predicate in the relative clause is a control verb.

In the following section we propose two methods for analyzing errors. Although both methods are implemented for the specific parser *Enju* (Miyao and Tsujii, 2005; Ninomiya et al., 2006), the same ideas can be implemented for any parsing model.

4 Methods for effective error analysis

4.1 Recognizing categories of error causes

While the Enju parser produces rich feature structures as output, the performance is evaluated by the F-value in terms of basic units of predicate-argment structure. As we illustrated in Section 2, the basic unit is a triplet in the following form.

<Predicate:PredicateType,
ArgumentLabel,
Argument>

We illustrated in Section 2 how we can identify errors in PP-attachment simply by examining a

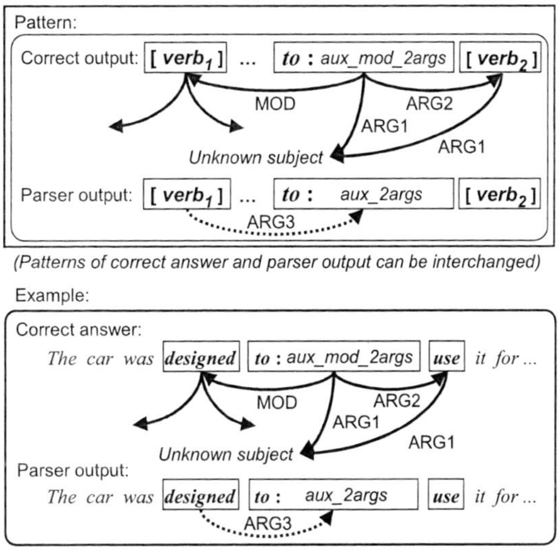

Figure 6: Pattern for "To-infinitive for modifier/argument of verb"

triplet produced by the parser with the corresponding triplet in the gold standard parse.

However, in more complex cases, we have to consider a set of mismatched triplets collectively in order to map errors to meaningful error causes. The following are typical examples of error causes and pattern rules which identify them.

(1) Interpretation of Infinitival Clauses as Adjunct or Complement

Two different types of interpretations of the infinitival clauses are explicitly indicated by "PredicateType." Consider the following two sentences.

(a) [Infinitival clause as an adjunct of the main clause]

The car was designed (by John) to use it for business trips.

(b) [Infinitival clause as an argument of catenative verb]

The car is designed to run fast.

In both sentences, "*to*" is treated as a predicate to represent the infinitival clauses in triplets. However, Enju marks the "PredicateType" of (a) as "*aux-mod-2args*," while it marks the predicate simply as "*aux-2args*" in (b). Furthermore, the linkage between the main clause and the infinitival clause is treated differently. In (a), the infinitival clause takes the main clause with relation MOD, while in (b) the main clause takes the infinitival

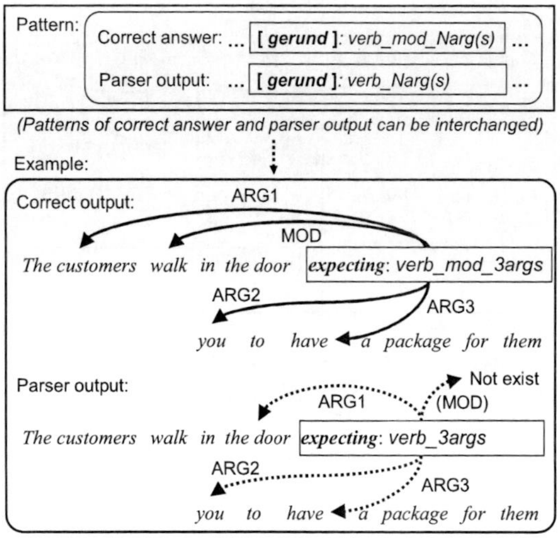

Figure 7: Pattern for "Gerund acts as modifier or not"

clause as ARG3. Furthermore, in the catenative verb interpretation of "*designed*", the deep object (the surface subject in this example) fills ARG1 of the verb in the infinitival clause (complement), while in the adjunct interpretation, the deep subject which is missing in this sentence occupies the same role. Consequently, a single erroneous choice between these two interpretations results in a set of mismatched triplets.

We recognize such a set of mismatched triplets by a pattern rule (Figure 6) and map them to this type of error cause.

(2) Interpretation of Gerund-Participle interpretations

A treatment similar to (1) is taken for different interpretations of Gerund. Interpretation as Adjunct of a main clause is signaled by the "PredicateType" *verb-mod-**, while an interpretation as a modifier of a noun is represented by the "PredicateType" *verb* (Figure 7).

(3) Interpretation of "*by*"

A prepositional phrase with "*by*" in a passive clause can be interpreted as a deep subject, while the same phrase can be interpreted as an ordinary PP phrase that is used as an adjunct. The first interpretation is marked by the "PredicateType" *lgs* (logical subject) which takes only one argument. The relationship between the passivized verb and the deep subject is captured by ARG1 which goes

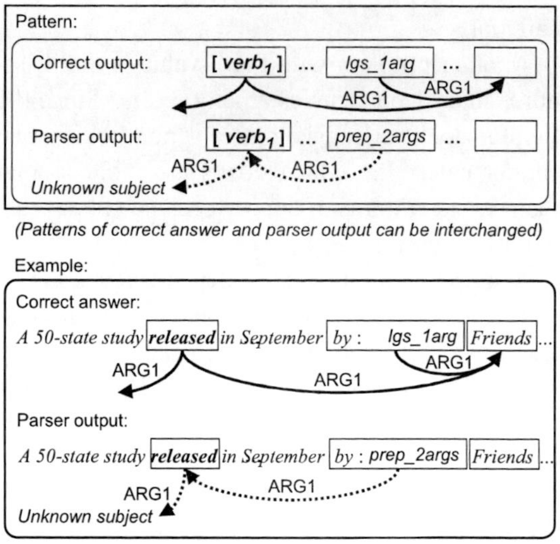

Figure 8: Pattern for "Subject for passive sentence or not"

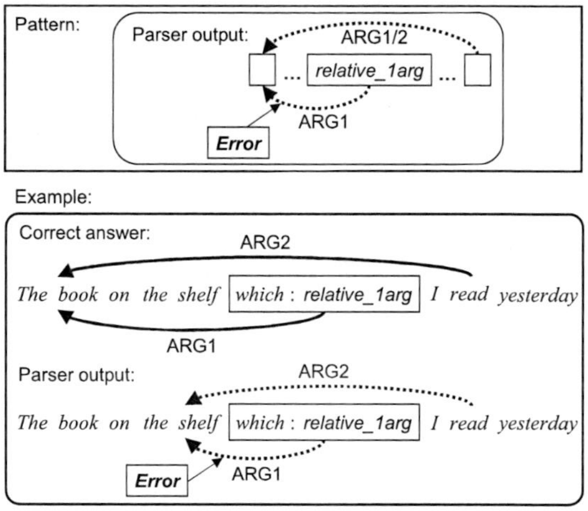

Figure 9: Pattern for "Relative clause attachment"

from the verb to the noun phrase. On the other hand, in the interpretation as an ordinary PP, the preposition as predicate links the main verb and NP via ARG1 and ARG2, respectively (Figure 8).

Again, a set of mismatched triplets should be mapped to a single cause of errors via a pattern rule.

(4) Antecedent of a Relative Clause

This type of error is manifested by two mismatched triplets with different predicates. This is because a wrong choice of antecedent for a relative clause results in a wrong link for the trace of the relative clause.

Since a relative clause pronoun is treated as a

Cause categories	Patterns
[Argument selection]	
Prepositional attachment	ARG1 of *prep_**
Adjunction attachment	ARG1 of *adj_**
Conjunction attachment	ARG1 of *conj_**
Head selection for noun phrase	ARG1 of *det_**
Coordination	ARG1/2 of *coord_**
[Predicate type selection]	
Preposition/Adjunction	*prep_** ↔ *adj_**
Gerund acts as modifier/not	*verb_mod_Narg(s)* ↔ *verb_Narg(s)*
Coordination/conjunction	*coord_** ↔ *conj_**
# of arguments for preposition	*prep_Marg(s)* ↔ *prep_Narg(s)*
Adjunction/adjunctive noun	*adj_** ↔ *noun_**
[More structural errors]	
To-infinitive for modifier/argument of verb	see Figure 6
Subject for passive sentence/not	see Figure 8
[Others]	
Comma	any error around ","
Relative clause attachment	see Figure 9

Table 2: Defined patterns for cause categories

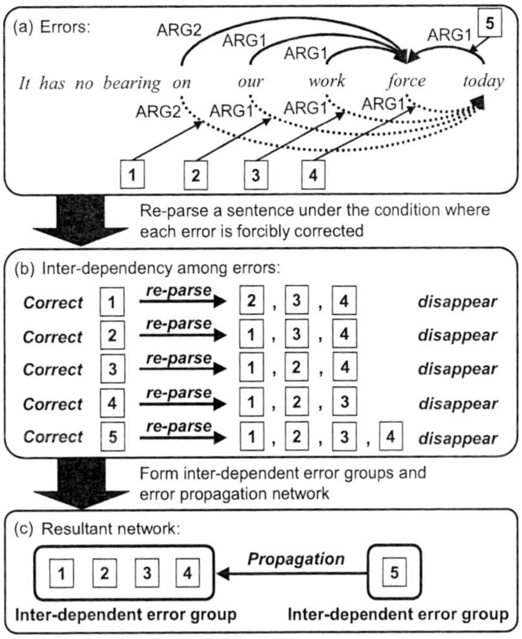

Figure 10: Schema of capturing inter-dependencies

predicate which takes the antecedent as its single argument, identification of error type can be done simply by looking at ARG1. However, since the errors usually propagate to the triplets that contain their traces, we have to map them together to the single error (Figure 9).

Table 2 shows the errors across different types which our current version of pattern rules can identify.

4.2 Capturing inter-dependencies among errors

Some inter-dependencies among erroneous triplets are ingrained in grammar, such as the case of antecedent of a relative clause in (4) in Section 4.1. Some are caused by general constraints such as the projection principle in dependency structure (Figure 4 in Section 2).

Regardless of causes of dependencies, to recognize inter-dependencies among errors is a crucial step of effective error analysis.

Our method consists of the following four steps:

[Step 1] Re-parsing a target sentence: A given sentence is re-parsed under the condition where an error is forcibly corrected.

[Step 2] Forming a network of inter-dependencies of errors: By comparing the new parse result (a set of triplets) with the initial parse result, this step creates a directed graph of errors in the initial parse. A directed link shows that correction of the error in the starting node produces a new parse result in which the error in the receiving node of the link disappears.

[Step 3] Forming groups of inter-dependent errors: This step recognizes a group of inter-dependent errors which forms a directed circle in the network created by [Step 2].

[Step 4] Forming a network of error propagation: This step creates a new network by reducing each of inter-dependent error groups of [Step 3] to a single node.

Figure 10 illustrates how these steps work. In this example, while "*today*" should modify the noun phrase "*our work force*", the initial parse wrongly takes "*today*" as the head noun of the whole noun phrase. As a result, there are five errors; three wrong outputs, "ARG2" of "*on*" (Error 1), "ARG1" of "*our*" (Error 2) and "ARG1" of "*work*" (Error 3). There is an extra triplet for "ARG1" of "*force*" (Error 4), and a triplet for "ARG1" of "today" (Error 5) is missing (Figure 10 (a)).

Figure 10 (b) shows inter-dependencies among the errors recognized by [Step 2], and Figure 10

Cause categories of errors	# of	
	Errors	**Locations**
Classified	**2,078**	**1,671**
[Argument selection]		
Prepositional attachment	579	579
Adjunction attachment	261	261
Conjunction attachment	43	40
Head selection for noun phrase	30	30
Coordination	202	184
[Predicate type selection]		
Preposition/Adjunction	108	54
Gerund acts as modifier/not	84	31
Coordination/conjunction	54	27
# of arguments for preposition	51	17
Adjunction/adjunctive noun	13	13
[More structural errors]		
To-infinitive for modifier/argument of verb	120	22
Subject for passive sentence/not	8	3
[Others]		
Comma	444	372
Relative clause attachment	102	38
Unclassified	**2,631**	–
Total	**4,709**	–

Table 3: Errors classified into cause categories

(c) shows what the resultant network looks like. An inter-dependent error group of 1, 2, 3 and 4 is recognized by [Step 3] and represented as a single node. Error 5 is propagated to this node in the final network.

5 Experiments

We applied our methods to the analyses of actual errors produced by Enju. This version of Enju was trained on the Penn Treebank (Marcus et al., 1994) Section 2-21.

5.1 Observation of identified cause categories

We first parsed sentences in PTB Section 22, and based on the observation of errors, we defined the patterns in Section 4. We then parsed sentences in Section 0. The errors in Section 0 were mapped to error cause categories by the pattern rules created for Section 22.

Table 3 summarizes the distribution across the causes of errors. The left and right numbers in the table show the number of erroneous triplets classified into the categories and the frequency of the patterns matched, respectively. The table shows that, with the 14 pattern rules, we successfully observed 1,671 hits and 2,078 erroneous triplets are dealt with by these hits. This amounts to more than 40% erroneous triplets (2,078/4,709). Since this was the first attempt, we expect the coverage can be easily improved by adding new patterns.

Evaluated sentences (erroneous)	1,811 (1,009)
Errors (Correctable)	4,709 (3,085)
Inter-dependent error groups	1,978
Correction propagations	501
F-score (LP/LR)	90.69 (90.78/90.59)

Table 4: Summary of inter-dependencies

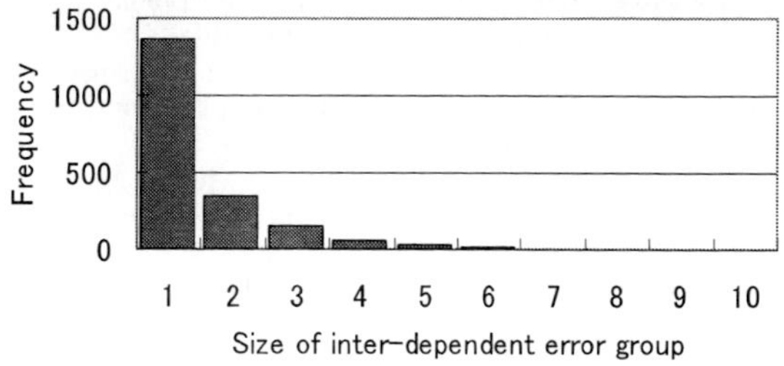

Figure 11: Frequency of each size of inter-dependent error group

From the table, we can observe that a significant portion of errors is covered by simple types of error causes such as PP-attachment and Adjunct attachment. They are simple in the sense that the number of erroneous triplets treated and the frequency of the pattern application coincide. However, their conceived significance may be overrated. These simple types may constitute parts of more complex error causes. Furthermore, since pattern rules for these simple causes are easy to prepare and have already been covered by the current version, most of the remaining 60% of the erroneous triplets are likely to require patterns for more complex causes.

On the other hand, patterns for complex causes collect more erroneous triplets once they are fired. This tendency is more noticeable in structural patterns of errors. For example, in "To-infinitive for modifier/argument of verb," there were only 22 hits for the pattern, while the number of erroneous triplets is 120. This implies five triplets per hit. This is because, in a deep parser, a wrong choice between adjunct or complement interpretations of a to-infinitival clause affects the interpretation of implicit arguments in the clause through control. Though expected, such detailed observations show how differences between shallow and deep parsers may affect evaluation methods and the methods of analyzing errors.

5.2 Observation of inter-dependencies

In the inter-dependency experiments we performed, some errors could not be forcibly corrected by our method. This was because the parser

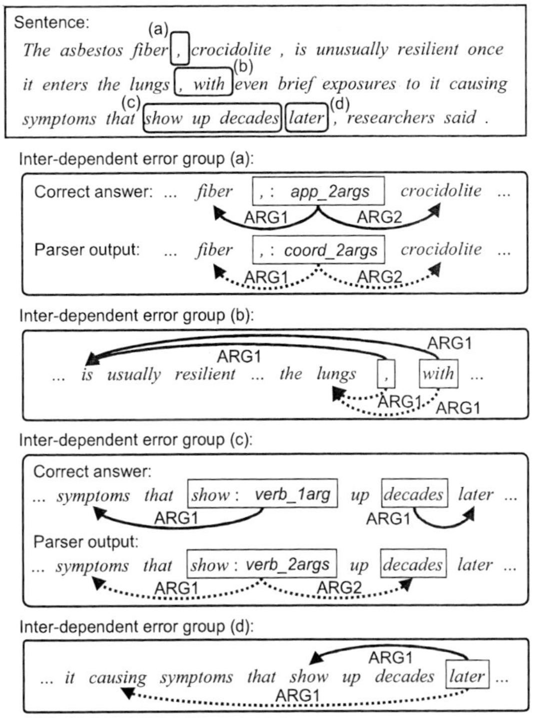

Figure 12: Obtained inter-dependent error groups

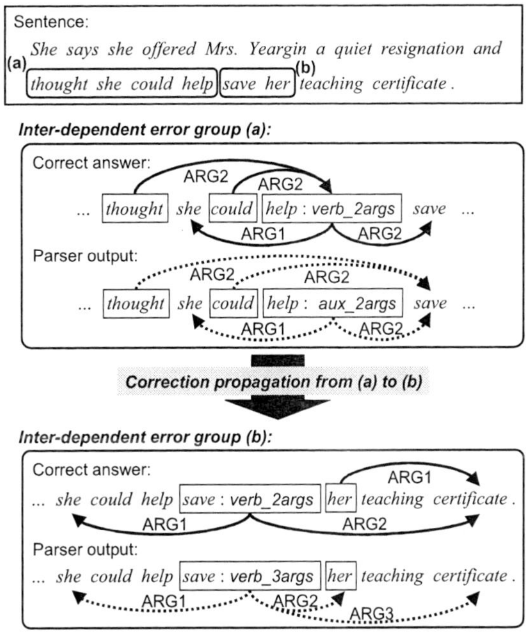

Figure 13: Correction propagation between obtained inter-dependent error groups

we use prunes less probable parse substructures during parsing. In some cases, even if we gave a large positive value to a triplet which should be included in the final parse, parsing paths which can contain the triplet were pruned before. In this research, we ignored such errors as "*uncorrectable*" ones, and focused on the remaining "*correctable*" errors.

Table 4 shows a summary of the analysis. As the previous experiment, Enju produced 4,709 errors for Section 0, of which 3,085 were correctable. By applying the method illustrated in Section 4.2, we obtained 1,978 inter-dependent error groups and 501 correction propagation relationships among the groups.

Figure 11 shows the frequency of the size of inter-dependent error groups. About half of the groups contain only single errors which could have only one-way correction propagations with other errors or were completely independent of other errors.

Figure 12 shows an example of the extracted inter-dependent error groups. For the sentence shown at the top, Enju gave seven errors. By applying the method in Section 4.2, these errors were grouped into four inter-dependent error groups (a) to (d), and no correction propagations were detected among them. Group (a) contains two errors on the comma's local behavior as apposition or coordination. Group (b) contains the errors on the words which give almost the same attachment behaviors. Group (c) contains the errors on whether the verb "*show*" took "*decades*" as its object or not. Group (d) contains an error on the attachment of the adverb "*later*". Regardless of the overlap of the regions in the sentence for (c) and (d), our approach successfully grouped the errors into two independent groups. The method shows that the errors in each group are inter-dependent, but errors in one group are independent of those in another. This enables us to concentrate on each of the co-occurring error groups separately, without minding the errors in other groups.

Figure 13 shows another example. In this example, eight errors for a sentence were classified into two inter-dependent error groups (a) and (b). Moreover, it shows that the correction of group (a) results in correction of group (b).

The errors in group (a) were related to the choice as to whether "*help*" had an auxiliary or a pure verbal role. The errors in group (b) were related with the choice as to whether "*save*" took only one object ("*her teaching certificate*") or two objects ("*her*" and "*teaching certificate*"). Between group (a) and (b), no "structural" con-

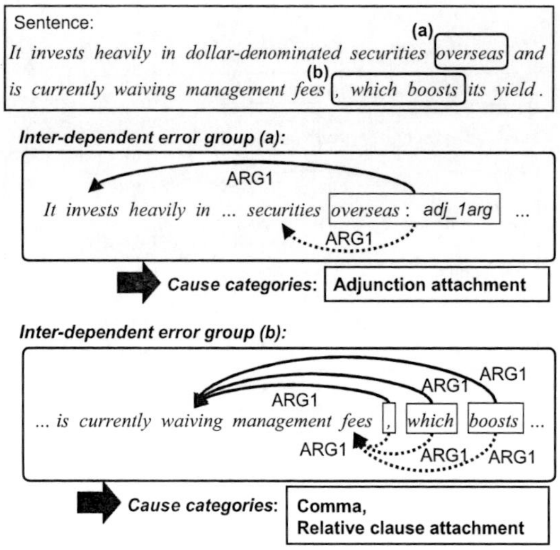

Figure 14: Combining our two methods (1)

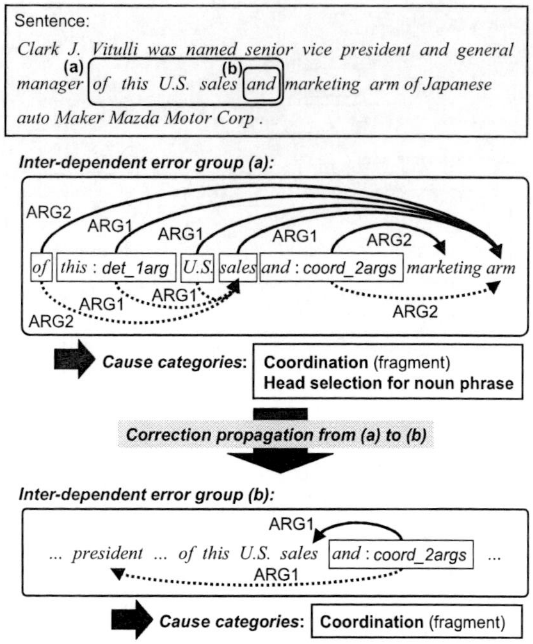

Figure 15: Combining our two methods (2)

flict could arise when correcting only each of the groups. We could then hypothesize that the correction propagation between the two groups were caused by the disambiguation model.

By dividing the errors into minimal units and clarifying the effects of correcting a target error, we can conclude that the inter-dependent group (a) should be handled first for effective improvement of the parser. In such a way, obtained inter-dependencies among errors can suggest an effective strategy for parser improvement.

5.3 Combination of the two methods

By combining the two methods described in Section 4.1 and 4.2, we can see how each error cause affects the performance of a parser. The results are summarized in Table 5. The leftmost column in the table shows the numbers of errors in terms of triplets, which are the same as the leftmost column in Table 3.

The "*independence rate*" shows the ratio of erroneous triplets in the category which are not affected by correction of other erroneous triplets. On the other hand, the "*correction effect*" shows how many erroneous triplets would be corrected if one of the erroneous triplets in the category was corrected. These two columns are computed by using the error propagation network constructed in Section 4.2. That is, by using the network we obtain the number of erroneous triplets to be corrected if a given erroneous triplet in the category was corrected, sum up these numbers and then calculate the average number of expected side-effect correction per erroneous triplet in the category.

Figure 14 shows an example of *independent* errors. For the sentence at the top, the parser produced four errors. The method in Section 4.2 successfully discovered two inter-dependent error groups (a) and (b). There was no error propagation relation between the two groups. On the other hand, the method in Section 4.1 associated all of these four errors with the categories of "Adjunction attachment," "Comma" and "Relative clause attachment," and the error for the "Adjunction attachment" corresponds to the inter-dependent error group (a). Because this group is not a receiving node of any propagation in the network, the error is regarded as an "*independent*" one.

Independent errors mean that, if a new parsing model could correct them, the correction would not be destroyed by other errors which remain in the new parsing model.

The *correction effect* shows the opposite and desirable effect of the nature of the dependency among errors which the propagation network represents. This means that, if one of erroneous triplets in the category was corrected, the correction would be amplified through propagation, and as a result other errors would also be corrected.

We show an example of the correction effect in Figure 15. In the figure, the parser had six errors; three false outputs for ARG1 of "*and*," "*this*" and

Cause categories of errors	# of errors	Independence rate (%)	Correction effect (%)	Expected range of error correction
[Argument selection]				
Prepositional attachment	579	74.8	144.3	625.0 - 835.5
Adjunction attachment	261	56.6	179.6	265.3 - 468.8
Conjunction attachment	43	36.4	239.4	37.5 - 102.9
Head selection for noun phrase	30	0.0	381.8	0.0 - 114.5
Coordination	202	42.5	221.2	189.9 - 446.8
[Predicate type selection]				
Preposition/Adjunction	108	41.7	158.3	71.3 - 171.0
Gerund acts as modifier/not	84	46.2	159.0	61.7 - 133.0
Coordination/conjunction	54	44.4	169.4	40.6 - 91.5
# of arguments for preposition	51	95.8	108.3	52.9 - 55.2
Adjunction/adjunctive noun	13	75.0	125.0	12.2 - 16.3
[More structural errors]				
To-infinitive for modifier/argument of verb	120	36.0	116.0	50.1 - 139.2
Subject for passive sentence/not	8	37.5	112.5	3.4 - 9.0
[Others]				
Comma	444	39.5	194.4	341.0 - 863.1
Relative clause attachment	102	32.1	141.7	46.4 - 144.5

Table 5: Correction propagations between errors for each cause category and the other errors

"*U.S.*," two false outputs for ARG2 of "*of*" and "*and*," and a missing output for ARG1 of "*sales*." Our method for inter-dependencies classified these errors into two inter-dependent error groups (a) and (b), and extracted an correction propagation from (a) to (b). Our method for cause categories, on the other hand, associated two errors of "*and*" with the category "Coordination" and one error of "*this*" with the category "Head selection for noun phrase." When we correct an error in the interdependent error group (a), the correction leads to not only correction of the other errors in (a) but also correction of the error in (b) via correction propagation from (a) to (b). Therefore, a correction effect of an error in group (a) results in 6.0.

On the basis of the above considerations, we estimated the range of the effect which an error correction in each category has. The minimum of expected correction range in Table 5 is given by the product of the number of erroneous triplets in the category, the independence rate and the correction effect. On the other hand, the maximum is given by the product of the number of erroneous triplets in the category and the correction effect. This assumes that all corrections made in the category are not cancelled by other errors, while the figure in the minimum are based on the assumption that all corrections made in the category, except for the independent ones, are cancelled by other errors.

Table 5 would thus suggest which categories should be resolved with high priority, from three points of view: the number of errors in the category, the number of independent errors, and the correction effect.

6 Further applications of our methods

In this section, as an example of the further application of our methods, we attempt to analyze parsing behaviors in domain adaptation from the viewpoints of error cause categories.

In Hara et al. (2007), we proposed a method for adapting Enju to a target domain, and then succeeded in improving the parser performance for the GENIA corpus (Kim et al., 2003), a biomedical domain. Table 6 summarizes the parsing results for three types of settings respectively: parsing PTB with Enju ("Enju for PTB"), parsing GENIA with Enju ("Enju for GENIA"), and parsing GENIA with the adapted model ("Adapted for GENIA"). We then analyzed the performance transition among these settings from the viewpoint of the cause categories given in Section 4.1 (Table 7). In order to compare the error frequencies among different settings, we took the percentage of target errors in all of the evaluated triplets. The signed values between the two settings show how much the errors increased when moving from the left settings to the right ones.

When we focus on the transition from "Enju for PTB" to "Enju for GENIA," we can observe that the change in the domain resulted in a different distribution of error causes. The errors for most categories increased, and in particular, the errors for "Prepositional attachment" and "Coordi-

	Enju for PTB	Enju for GENIA	Adapted for GENIA
Evaluated sentences	1,811	842	842
Evaluated triplets	44,934	22,230	22,230
Errors	4,709	3,120	2,229
F-score (LP/LR)	90.69 (90.78/90.59)	87.41 (87.60/87.22)	90.93 (91.10/90.76)

Table 6: Summary of parsing performances for domain and model variations

Cause categories of errors	Rate of errors against total examined relations in test set (%)				
	Enju for PTB	⟶	**Enju for GENIA**	⟶	**Adapted for GENIA**
Classified	**4.62**	+2.60↗	**7.22**	−1.80↘	**5.42**
[Argument selection]					
Prepositional attachment	1.29	**+0.93**↗	2.22	**−0.64**↘	1.58
Adjunction attachment	0.58	**+0.38**↗	0.96	**−0.20**↘	0.76
Conjunction attachment	0.10	**−0.04**↘	0.06	**−0.04**↘	0.02
Head selection for noun phrase	0.07	**+0.17**↗	0.24	**−0.06**↘	0.18
Coordination	0.45	**+0.59**↗	1.04	**−0.25**↘	0.79
[Predicate type selection]					
Preposition/Adjunction	0.24	**+0.08**↗	0.32	**−0.06**↘	0.26
Gerund acts as modifier/not	0.19	**−0.07**↘	0.12	**+0.01**↗	0.13
Coordination/conjunction	0.12	**±0.00**→	0.12	**−0.07**↘	0.05
# of arguments for preposition	0.11	**−0.02**↘	0.09	**±0.00**↘	0.09
Adjunction/adjunctive noun	0.03	**+0.19**↗	0.22	**−0.08**↘	0.14
[More structural errors]					
To-infinitive for modifier/argument of verb	0.27	**+0.02**↗	0.29	**−0.09**↘	0.20
Subject for passive sentence/not	0.02	**+0.34**↗	0.36	**+0.01**↗	0.37
[Others]					
Comma	0.99	**−0.03**↘	0.96	**−0.31**↘	0.65
Relative clause attachment	0.23	**+0.05**↗	0.28	**−0.03**↘	0.25
Unclassified	**5.86**	+0.96↗	**6.82**	−2.22↘	**4.60**
Total (Classified + Unclassified)	**10.48**	+3.56↗	**14.04**	−4.01↘	**10.03**

Table 7: Error distributions for domain and model variations

nation" increased remarkably. On the other hand, the transition from "Enju for GENIA" to "Adapted for GENIA" shows that their adaptation method succeeded in reducing the errors for most categories to some extent. However, for "Prepositional attachment," "Coordination," and "Subject for passive sentence or not," there were still noticeable gaps in error distribution between "Enju for PTB" and "Adapted for GENIA." This would mean that the adapted model requires further performance improvement if we expect the same level of performances for those categories as the parser originally obtained in PTB.

We could thus capture some biases of cause categories which occur in domain transition or in domain adaptation, which would not be clarified by F-score evaluation methods. With inter-dependencies given by the method described in Section 4.2, the above analysis would be useful for effectively exploring further adaptation.

7 Related works

Although there have been many researchers who analyzed errors in their own systems in the experiments, there has been little research which focused on error analysis itself.

In the field of parsing, McDonald and Nivre (2007) compared parsing errors between graph-based and transition-based parsers. They considered accuracy transitions from various points of view, and the obtained statistical data suggested that error propagation seemed to occur in the graph structures of parsing outputs. Our research proceeded one step further and attempted to reveal the nature of the propagations. In examining the combination of the two types of parsing, they utilized approaches similar to our method for capturing inter-dependencies of errors. They allowed a parser to give only structures produced by the parsers and utilized the ideas for evaluating the parser's potentials, whereas we utilized it for observing error propagations.

Dredze et al. (2007) showed that many of the parsing errors in domain adaptation tasks may come from inconsistencies between the annotations of training resources. This would suggest that just error comparisons without considering the inconsistencies could lead to a misunderstanding of what happens in domain transitions. The summarized error cause categories and inter-dependencies given by our methods would be useful clues for extracting such domain-dependent error phenomena.

When we look into other research areas in natural language processing, Giménez and Màrquez (2008) proposed an automatic error analysis approach in machine translation (MT) technologies. They developed a metric set which could capture features in MT outputs at different linguistic levels with different levels of granularity. Like we considered parsing systems, they explored ways to resolve costly and rewardless error analysis in the MT field. One of their objectives was to enable researchers to easily obtain detailed linguistic reports on the behavior of their systems, and to concentrate on analyses for the system improvements.

8 Conclusion

We proposed two methods for analyzing parsing errors. One is to assign errors to cause categories, and the other is to capture inter-dependencies among errors. The first method defines error patterns to identify cause categories and then associates errors involved in the patterns with the corresponding categories. The second method re-parses a sentence with a target error corrected, and regards errors corrected together as dependent on the target.

In our experiments with an HPSG parser, we successfully associated more than 40% of the errors with 14 cause categories, and captured 1,978 inter-dependent error groups. Moreover, the combination of our methods gave a more detailed error analysis for effective improvement of the parser.

In our future work, we would give more pattern rules for classifying a large percentage of errors into cause categories, and incorporate *uncorrectable* errors into inter-dependency analysis. After improving the analytical facilities of our individual methods, we would explore the possibility of combining the methods for obtaining more powerful and detailed clues on how to improve parsing performance.

Acknowledgments

This work was partially supported by Grant-in-Aid for Specially Promoted Research (MEXT, Japan).

References

Mark Dredze, John Blitzer, Partha Pratim Talukdar, Kuzman Ganchev, João V. Graça, and Fernando Pereira. 2007. Frustratingly hard domain adaptation for dependency parsing. In *Proceedings of the CoNLL Shared Task Session of the 2007 Joint Conference on Empirical Methods in Natural Language Processing and Computational Natural Language Learning (EMNLP-CoNLL)*, pages 1051–1055.

Jesús Giménez and Lluís Màrquez. 2008. Towards heterogeneous automatic mt error analysis. In *Proceedings of the Sixth International Language Resources and Evaluation (LREC'08)*, pages 1894–1901.

Tadayoshi Hara, Yusuke Miyao, and Jun'ichi Tsujii. 2007. Evaluating impact of re-training a lexical disambiguation model on domain adaptation of an hpsg parser. In *Proceedings of 10th International Conference on Parsing Technologies (IWPT 2007)*, pages 11–22.

Ronald M. Kaplan and Joan Bresnan. 1995. Lexical-functional grammar: A formal system for grammatical representation. *Formal Issues in Lexical-Functional Grammar*, pages 29–130.

Jin-Dong Kim, Tomoko Ohta, Yuka Teteisi, and Jun'ichi Tsujii. 2003. GENIA corpus - a semantically annotated corpus for bio-textmining. *Bioinformatics*, 19(suppl. 1):i180–i182.

Mitchell Marcus, Grace Kim, Mary Ann Marcinkiewicz, Robert Macintyre, Ann Bies, Mark Ferguson, Karen Katz, and Britta Schasberger. 1994. The Penn Treebank: Annotating predicate argument structure. In *Proceedings of ARPA Human Language Technology Workshop*.

Ryan McDonald and Joakim Nivre. 2007. Characterizing the errors of data-driven dependency parsing models. In *Proceedings of the 2007 Joint Conference on Empirical Methods in Natural Language Processing and Computational Natural Language Learning (EMNLP-CoNLL)*, pages 122–131.

Yusuke Miyao and Jun'ichi Tsujii. 2005. Probabilistic disambiguation models for wide-coverage HPSG parsing. In *Proceedings of the 43rd Annual Meeting on Association for Computational Linguistics (ACL)*, pages 83–90.

Takashi Ninomiya, Takuya Matsuzaki, Yoshimasa Tsuruoka, Yusuke Miyao, and Jun'ichi Tsujii. 2006. Extremely lexicalized models for accurate and fast HPSG parsing. In *Proceedings of the 2006 Conference on Empirical Methods in Natural Language Processing (EMNLP)*, pages 155–163.

Carl J. Pollard and Ivan A. Sag. 1994. *Head-Driven Phrase Structure Grammar*. University of Chicago Press.

Mark Steedman. 2000. *The Syntactic Process*. THE MIT Press.

Clustering Words by Syntactic Similarity Improves Dependency Parsing of Predicate-Argument Structures

Kenji Sagae and **Andrew S. Gordon**
Institute for Creative Technologies
University of Southern California
13274 Fiji Way
Marina del Rey, CA 90292
{sagae,gordon}@ict.usc.edu

Abstract

We present an approach for deriving syntactic word clusters from parsed text, grouping words according to their unlexicalized syntactic contexts. We then explore the use of these syntactic clusters in leveraging a large corpus of trees generated by a high-accuracy parser to improve the accuracy of another parser based on a different formalism for representing a different level of sentence structure. In our experiments, we use phrase-structure trees to produce syntactic word clusters that are used by a predicate-argument dependency parser, significantly improving its accuracy.

1 Introduction

Syntactic parsing of natural language has advanced greatly in recent years, in large part due to data-driven techniques (Collins, 1999; Charniak, 2000; Miyao and Tsujii, 2005; McDonald et al., 2005; Nivre et al., 2007) coupled with the availability of large treebanks. Several recent efforts have started to look for ways to go beyond what individual annotated data sets and individual parser models can offer, looking to combine diverse parsing models, develop cross-framework interoperability and evaluation, and leverage the availability of large amounts of text available. Two research directions that have produced promising improvements on the accuracy of data-driven parsing are: (1) combining different parsers using ensemble techniques, such as voting (Henderson and Brill, 1999; Sagae and Lavie, 2006; Hall et al., 2007) and stacking (Nivre and McDonald, 2008; Martins et al., 2008), and (2) semi-supervised learning, where unlabeled data (plain text) is used in addition to a treebank (McClosky et al., 2006; Koo et al., 2008).

In this paper we explore a new way to obtain improved parsing accuracy by using a large amount of unlabeled text and two parsers that use different ways of representing syntactic structure. In contrast to previous work where automatically generated constituent trees were used directly to train a constituent parsing model (McClosky et al., 2006), or where word clusters were derived from a large corpus of plain text to improve a dependency parser (Koo et al., 2008), we use a large corpus of constituent trees (previously generated by an accurate constituent parser), which we use to produce *syntactically derived clusters* that are then used to improve a transition-based parser that outputs dependency graphs that reflect predicate-argument structure where words may be dependents of more than one parent. This type of representation is more general than dependency trees (Sagae and Tsujii, 2008; Henderson et al., 2008), and is suitable for representing both surface relations and long-distance dependencies (such as control, it-cleft and tough movement).

The first contribution of this work is a novel approach for deriving syntactic word clusters from parsed text, grouping words by the general syntactic contexts where they appear, and not by n-gram word context (Brown et al., 1992) or by immediate dependency context (Lin, 1998). Unlike in clustering approaches that rely on *lexical context* (either linear or grammatical) to group words, resulting in a notion of word similarity that blurs syntactic and semantic characteristics of lexical items, we use *unlexicalized syntactic context*, so that words are clustered based only on their syntactic behavior. This way, we attempt to generate clusters that are more conceptually similar to part-of-speech tags or supertags

Proceedings of the 11th International Conference on Parsing Technologies (IWPT), pages 192–201,
Paris, October 2009.

(Bangalore and Joshi, 1999), but organized hierarchically to provide tagsets with varying levels of granularity.

Our second contribution is a methodology for leveraging a high-accuracy parser to improve the accuracy of a parser that uses a different formalism (that represents different structural information), without the need to process the input with both parsers at run-time. In our experiments, we show that we can improve the accuracy of a fast dependency parser for predicate-argument structures by using a corpus which was previously automatically annotated using a highly accurate but considerably slower phrase-structure tree parser. This is accomplished by using the slower parser only to parse the data used to create the syntactic word clusters. During run-time, the dependency parser uses these clusters, which encapsulate syntactic knowledge from the phrase-structure parser. Although our experiments focus on the use of phrase-structure and dependency parsers, the same framework can be easily applied to data-driven parsing using other syntactic formalisms, such as CCG or HPSG.

2 Clustering by Syntactic Similarity

We developed a new approach to clustering words according to their syntactic similarity. Our method involves the use of hierarchical agglomerate clustering techniques using the calculated *syntactic* distance between words. Syntactic distance between words is computed as the cosine distance between vector representations of the frequency of unique parse tree paths emanating from the word in a corpus of parse trees. In this research, we employ a novel encoding of syntactic parse tree paths that includes direction information and non-terminal node labels, but does not include lexical information or part-of-speech tags. Consequently, the resulting hierarchy groups words that appear in similar places in similar parse trees, regardless of its assigned part-of-speech tag. In this section we describe our approach in detail.

2.1 Parse tree path representation

Gordon and Swanson (2007) first described a corpus-based method for calculating a measure of syntactic similarity between words, and demonstrated its utility in improving the performance of a syntax-based Semantic Role Labeling system. The central idea behind their approach was that *parse tree paths* could be used as features for describing a word's grammatical behavior.

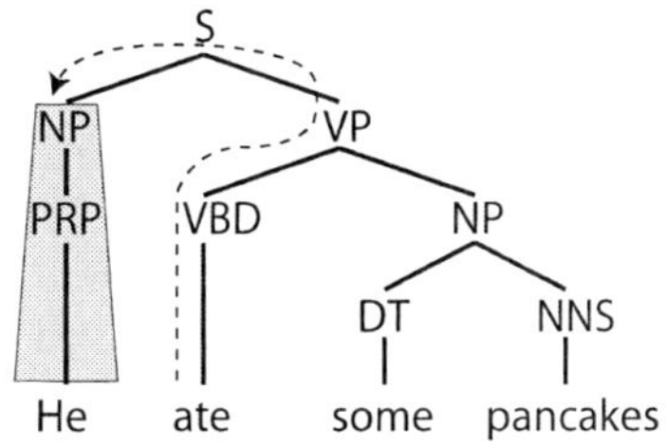

Figure 1: An example parse tree path from the verb *ate* to the argument NP *He*, represented as $\uparrow$VBD$\uparrow$VP$\uparrow$S$\downarrow$NP.

Parse tree paths are descriptions of tree transitions from a terminal (e.g. a verb) to a different node in a constituent parse tree of a sentence. Parse tree paths gained popularity in early Semantic Role Labeling research (Gildea and Jurafsky, 2002), where they were used as features describing the relationship between a verb and a particular semantic role label. For example, Figure 1 illustrates a parse tree path between a verb and a semantically related noun phrase.

Gordon and Swanson viewed parse tree paths as features that could be used to describe the syntactic contexts of words in a corpus. In their approach, all of the possible parse tree paths that begin at a given word were identified in a large set of automatically generated constituent parse trees. The normalized frequency counts of unique parse tree paths were combined into a feature vector that describes the location that the given word appears in the set of parse trees. This syntactic profile was then compared with other profiles using a cosine distance function, producing a quantitative value of word similarity. In this manner, the syntactic similarity between the verb "pluck" and the verb "whisk" was calculated as 0.849.

One drawback of the approach of Gordon and Swanson was the inclusion of part-of-speech tags in the encoding of the parse tree paths. As a consequence, the cosine distance between words of different classes was always zero, regardless of their similarities in the remainder of the paths. To correct this problem in our current research, we removed part-of-speech tags from the encoding of parse tree paths, deleting the tag that begins each path and replacing tags when they appear at the end of a path with a generic terminal label.

A second drawback of the approach of Gordon and Swanson is that the path directionality is underspecified. Consider the parse tree paths that emanate from each of the words "some" and "pancakes" in Figure 1. In the original encoding, the paths for each of these words would be identical (if the part of speech tags were removed), despite their unique locations in this parse tree. To correct this problem in our current research, we elaborated the original set of two path identifiers (↑ and ↓) to a set of six tags that included information about the direction of the transition. Up-Right (↗) and Down-Left (↙) transition are used to and from nodes that are the first constituent of a non-terminal. Up-Left (↖) and Down-Right (↘) transitions are used to and from nodes that are the last constituent of a non-terminal. Transitions to and from all other constituent nodes are labeled Up-Middle (↑) or Down-Middle (↓), accordingly. For example, we represent the parse tree path depicted in Figure 1 as: ↗VP↖S↙NP.

2.2 Profiles for BLLIP WSJ Corpus words

As in the previous work of Gordon and Swanson (2007), we characterize the syntactic properties of words as the normalized frequency of unique parse tree paths emanating from the word in a large corpus of syntactic parse trees.

In our research, we used the Brown Laboratory for Linguistic Information Processing (BLLIP) 1987-89 WSJ Corpus Release 1 (Charniak et al., 2000), which contains approximately 30 million words of Wall Street Journal news articles, parsed with Charniak (2000) parser. Although the trees in the BLLIP corpus are enriched with function tags and empty nodes, we remove this information, leaving only the trees produced by the Charniak parser. We identified the top five thousand most frequent words (or, more generally, *types*, since these also include other sequences of characters, such as numbers and punctuation) in this corpus, treating words that differed in capitalization or in assigned part-of-speech tag as separate types. These five thousand types correspond to approximately 85% of the tokens in the BLLIP corpus. For each token instance of each of these five thousand types, we identified every occurring parse tree path emanating from the token in each of the sentences in which it appeared. The most frequent type was the comma, which appeared 2.2 million times and produced 118 million parse tree paths. The least frequent token in this set was the singular noun "pollution," with 731 instances producing 35,185 parse tree paths.

To generate syntactic profiles for a given type, the frequency of unique parse tree paths was tabulated, and then normalized by dividing this frequency by the number of tokens of that type in the corpus. To reduce the dimensionality of these normalized frequency vectors, parse tree paths that appeared in less than 0.2% of the instances were ignored. This threshold value produced vectors with dimensionality that was comparable across all five thousand types, and small enough to process given our available computational resources. The mean vector size was 2,228 dimensions, with a standard deviation of 734.

2.3 Distance calculation and clustering

Pairwise distances between each of the five thousand types were computed as the cosine distance between their profile vectors. We then grouped similar types using hierarchical agglomerate clustering techniques, where distance between clusters is calculated as mean distance between elements of each cluster (average link clustering).

The three most similar types (the first 2 clustering steps) consisted of the capitalized subordinating conjunctions "Although," "While," and "Though." The two most dissimilar types (the last to be included in any existing cluster) were the symbol "@" and the question mark.

2.4 Cluster label selection

Hierarchical agglomerate clustering produces a binary-branching tree structure, where each branch point is ordered according to a similarity value between 0 and 1. In our clustering of the top five thousand most frequent types in the BLLIP corpus, there are five thousand leaf nodes representing individual tokens, and 4999 branch points that cluster these types into a single tree. We label each of these 4999 branch points, and treat these cluster labels as features of the types that they dominate. For example, the singular noun "house" participates in 114 clusters of increasing size. The syntactic features of this type can therefore be characterized by 114 cluster labels, which overlap with varying degrees with other tokens in the set.

We view these cluster labels as conceptually similar to traditional part-of-speech tags in that they are indicative of the syntactic contexts in which words are likely to appear. Because words are clustered based on their unlexicalized syntactic contexts, the resulting clusters are more likely to reflect purely syntactic information than are clusters derived from lexical context, such as adjacent words (Brown et al., 1992) or immediate head-word (Lin, 1998). However, the extent to which these syntactic contexts are specified can vary from a more general to a more fine-grained level than that of parts-of-speech. As clusters become more fine-grained, they become more similar to supertags (Bangalore and Joshi, 1999). Clusters that represent more specific syntactic contexts can encode information about, for example, subcategorization. As these labels are derived empirically from a large corpus of syntactic parse trees, they accurately represent syntactic distinctions in real discourse at different granularities, in contrast to the single arbitrary granularity of theoretically derived part-of-speech tags used in existing treebanks (Marcus et al., 1993).

While it is sometimes useful to view types as having multiple part-of-speech tags at different levels of granularity (e.g. the 114 tags for the token "house"), it is often useful to select a single level of granularity to use across all tokens. For example, it is useful to know which one of the 114 cluster labels for "house" to use if exactly 100 part-of-speech distinctions are to be made among tokens in the set. These cluster labels can be identified by slicing the tree at the level for which there are exactly 100 branches, then using the label of the first branch point in each branch as the label for all of its leaf-node types, or the leaf-node itself in the case where no further branching exists. Given our hierarchical clustering, there are five thousand different ways to slice the tree in this manner, yielding sets of cluster labels (and un-clustered types) that vary in size from 1 to 5000. We identified these sets for use in the experiments described in the next sections.

Figure 2 shows a dendrogram representation of the cluster tree when it is sliced to produce exactly 60 clusters, 19 of which are individual types. For the other 41 clusters, we show only the most frequent word in the cluster and the number of additional words in the cluster. The scale line in the lower left of Figure 2 indicates the horizontal length of a calculated similarity between clusters of 0.1.

3 Transition-based dependency parsing with word clusters

The clusters obtained with the approach described in section 2 provide sets of syntactic tags with varying levels of granularity. Previous work by Koo et al. (2008) and Miller et al. (2004) suggests that different levels of cluster granularity may be useful in natural language

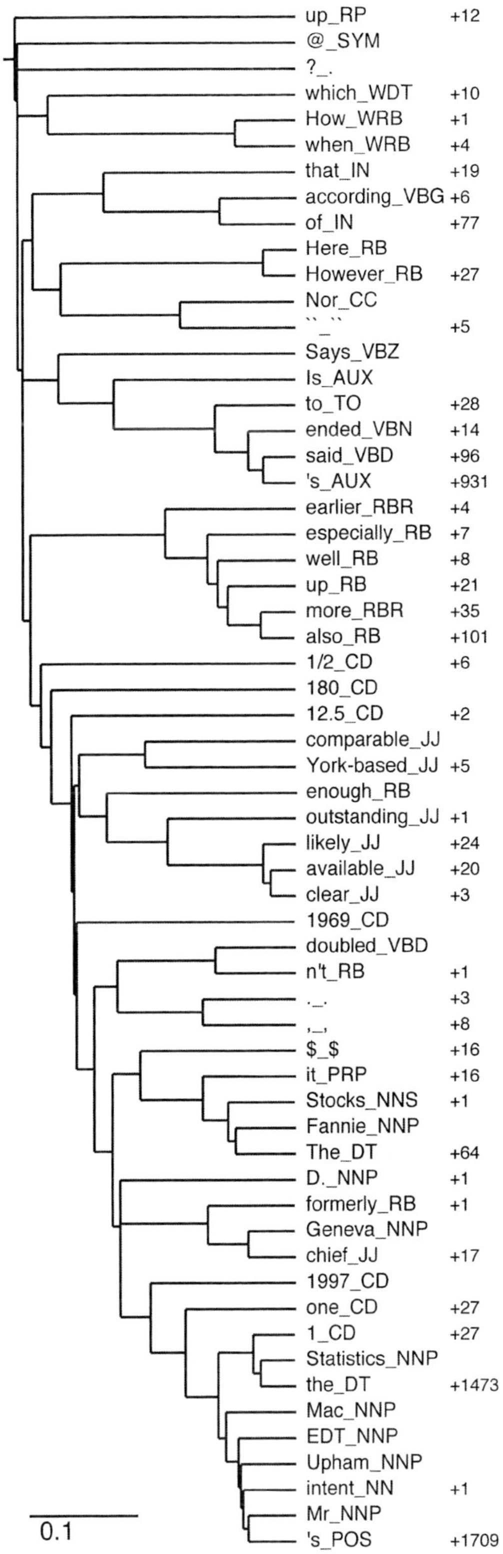

Figure 2: A hierarchical clustering of the top five thousand tokens in the BLLIP corpus, cut at 60 clusters.

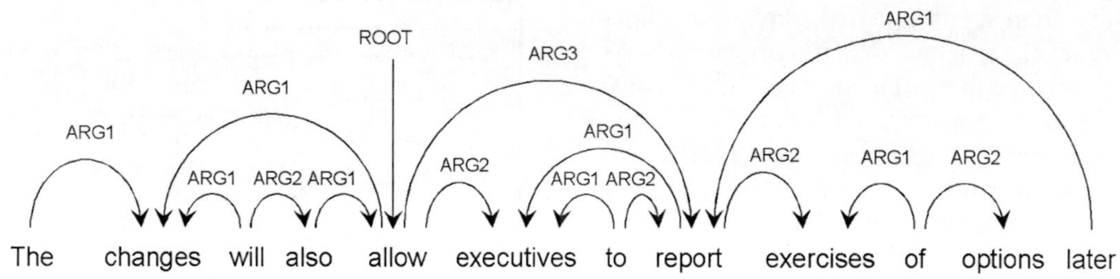

Figure 3: Predicate-argument dependency structure following the HPSG Treebank standard.

processing tasks with discriminative training. We add the syntactic clusters as features in a transition-based parser that uses a classifier to decide among shift/reduce parser actions based on the local context of the decision. This transition-based parsing approach has been found to be efficient and accurate in dependency parsing of surface syntactic dependencies (Yamada and Matsumoto, 2003; Nivre et al., 2004; Hall et al., 2007) and predicate-argument parsing (Henderson et al., 2008; Sagae and Tsujii, 2008).

Our experiments are based on an implementation of Sagae and Tsujii (2008)'s algorithm for basic shift-reduce parsing with multiple heads, which we use to identify predicate-argument dependencies extracted from the HPSG Treebank developed by Miyao et al. (2004). Using this data set allows for a comparison of our results with those obtained in previous work on data-driven HPSG predicate-argument analysis, while demonstrating the use of our clustering approach for cross-framework parser improvement, since the clusters were derived from syntactic trees in Penn Treebank format (as produced by the Charniak parser, without empty nodes, co-indexation or function tags), and used in the identification of HPSG Treebank predicate-argument dependencies. Figure 3 shows a predicate-argument dependency structure following the annotation standard of the HPSG Treebank, where arrows point from head to modifier. We note that unlike in the widely known PropBank (Palmer et al., 2005) predicate-argument structures, argument labels start from ARG1 (not ARG0), and predicate-argument relationships are annotated for all words. One difference between in our implementation is that, instead of maximum entropy classification used by Sagae and Tsujii, we perform parser action classification using the averaged perceptron (Freund and Schapire, 1999; Collins, 2002), which allows for the inclusion of all of Sagae and Tsujii's features, in addition to a set of cluster-based features, while retaining fast training times.

We now describe the parsing approach, starting with the dependency DAG parser that we use as a baseline, followed by how the syntactic cluster features were added to the baseline parser.

3.1 Arc-standard parsing for dependency DAGs

Sagae and Tsujii (2008) describe two algorithms for dependency parsing with words that have multiple heads. Each corresponds to extensions of Nivre (2004)'s arc-standard and arc-eager algorithms for dependency (tree) parsing. In our experiments, we used an implementation of the arc-standard extension.

Nivre's arc-standard dependency parsing algorithm uses a stack to process the input string one word at a time, from left to right, using two general types of parser action: *shift* (push the next input token onto the stack), and *reduce* (create a dependency arc between the top two items on the stack, and pop the item marked as the dependent). Reduce actions are subdivided into *reduce-right* and *reduce-left*, indicating which of the two items on the top of the stack is the head, and which is the dependent in the newly formed dependency arc. These two reduce actions can be further subdivided to reflect what type of dependency arc is created, in the case of labeled dependency parsing. The extension for allowing multiple heads per word consists of the addition a new type of parser action: *attach*, which creates a dependency arc without removing anything from the stack. As with reduce actions, there are two types of attach: *attach-left* which creates a dependency arc between the top two items on the stack such that the item on top is the head, and *right-attach*, which creates a dependency arc between the top two items on the stack such that the top item is the dependent, then pops it from the stack and unshifts it back into the input. Finally, this algorithm for unlabeled graphs can be extended to produce labeled dependencies in the same way as Nivre's algorithm, by replacing the reduce and attach actions with sets of actions that perform the reduce or attach operation and also name the label of the arc created. Sagae and Tsujii (2008) provide a more detailed description of the algorithm, including an example that illustrates the new attach actions.

This basic algorithm is only capable of producing labeled directed acyclic graphs where, if the nodes (which correspond to words) are placed on a left to right sequence on a horizontal line in the order in which the words appear in the input sentence, all arcs can be drawn above the nodes without crossing. This corresponds to the notion of projectivity that similarly limits the types of trees produced by Nivre's algorithm. Just as in dependency parsing with tree structures, a way to effectively remove this limitation is the use of pseudo-projective transformations (Nivre and Nilsson, 2005), where arcs that cross have their heads moved towards the root and have their labels edited to reflect this change, often making it reversible. Once crossing arcs have been "lifted" so that no crossing arcs remain, the "projectivized" structures are used to train a parsing model. Projective structures produced by this model can be "deprojectivized" through the use of the edits in the arc labels, in an attempt to produce structures that conform to the scheme in the original data. Sagae and Tsujii also propose a simple *arc reversal* transform, which simply reverses the direction of a dependency arc (editing the arc label to note this change). This transformation, which can be reversed trivially, makes it possible to remove cycles in dependency graphs.

3.2 Baseline features

To create output graph structures for an input sentence, the algorithm described in section 3.1 relies on an oracle that tells it what action to take at each parser state, where the state is the contents of the stack, remaining words in the input, and the dependency arcs formed so far. In grammar-based shift-reduce parsing, this oracle may take the form of a look-up table derived from grammar rules. In our data-driven setting, where the parser learns to choose actions based on examples of correctly parsed data, the (likely imperfect) substitute for the oracle is a classifier that takes features that represent the parser state as input, and produces a matching parser action as output. These features should represent aspects of the parser state that may be informative as to what the corresponding appropriate action is. Our baseline model uses the averaged perceptron with a core set of features derived from the following templates, where *S(n)* denotes the *n-th* item from the top of the stack (for example, *S(1)* is the item on top of the stack), and *I(n)* denotes the next *n-th* input token:

1. For the items *S(1)* and *S(2)*:
    a. the total number of dependents;
    b. the number of dependents to the right of the item;
    c. the number of dependents to the left of the item;
    d. the part-of-speech tag of the rightmost dependent of the item;
    e. the part-of-speech tag of the leftmost dependent of the item;
    f. the arc label of the rightmost dependent of the item;
    g. the arc label of the leftmost dependent of the item;
2. the words in items *S(1), S(2), S(3), I(1)* and *I(2)*;
3. the part-of-speech tags in items *S(1), S(2), S(3), I(1), I(2)* and *I(3)*;
4. the part-of-speech tag of the word i mmediaely to the right of *S(2)*;
5. the part-of-speech tag of the word immediately to the left of *S(1)*;
6. whether an arc exists between *S(1)* and *S(2)*;
7. whether an arc exists between *S(1)* and *I(1)*;
8. the direction of the arc between *S(1)* and *S(2)*, if any;
9. the label of the arc between *S(1)* and *S(2)*, if any;
10. the label of the arc between *S(1)* and *I(1)*, if any;
11. the distance, in linear sequence of words, between *S(1)* and *S(2)*;
12. the distance, in linear sequence of words, between *S(1)* and *I(1)*;

13. the previous parser action.

In addition to the core set of features, we also use features obtained by concatenating the part-of-speech tags in *S(1), S(2)* and *I(1)* with the features derived from templates 1-6, and additional features derived from selected concatenation of two or three core features.

3.3 Cluster-based features

To take advantage of the clusters that reflect syntactic similarity between words, we assign arbitrary unique labels to each of the hierarchical clusters obtained using the procedure described in section 2. These cluster labels are used to generate additional features that help the parser make its decisions base on the syntactic profile of words. As explained in section 2.4, each there may be several cluster labels (corresponding to clusters of different granularities) associated with each word. To select the set of cluster labels to be used to generate features, we first select a desired granularity for the clusters, and use the set of labels resulting from slicing the cluster tree at the appropriate level, as discussed in section 2.4. We experimented with several levels of cluster granularity using development data, and following Koo et al. (2008), we also experimented with using two sets of cluster labels with different levels of granularity at the same time. Given a specific level of granularity, the cluster-based features we used are:

14. the cluster labels for the words in items *S(1), S(2), S(3), I(1), I(2), I(3);*
15. the cluster labels for the words in the rightmost and leftmost dependents of *S(1)* and *S(2)*;
16. the concatenation of the cluster labels for the words in *S(1), S(2)* and *I(1),* and the features derived from feature templates 1-15.

In experiments where we used two sets of cluster labels corresponding to different levels of granularity, we added all the cluster-based features in 14 and 15 for both sets of labels, and the features in 16 only for the set corresponding to the coarser-grained clusters.

4 Experiments

Following previous experiments with Penn Treebank WSJ data, or annotations derived from it, we used sections 02-21 of the HPSG Treebank as training material, section 22 for development, and section 23 for testing. Only the predicate-argument dependencies were used, not the phrase structures or other information from the HPSG analyses. For all experiments described here, part-of-speech tagging was done separately using a CRF tagger with accuracy of 97.3% on sections 22-24. Our evaluation is based on labeled precision and recall of predicate-argument dependencies. Although accuracy is commonly used for evaluation of dependency parsers, in our task the parser is not restricted to output a fixed number of dependencies. Labeled precision and recall of predicate-argument pairs are also the standard evaluation metrics for data-driven HPSG and CCG parsers (although the predicate-argument pairs extracted from the HPSG Treebank and the CCGBank are specific to their formalisms and not quantitatively comparable).

We started by eliminating cycles from the dependency graphs extracted from the HPSG Treebank by using the arc reversal transform in the following way: for each cycle detected in the data, the shortest arc in the cycle was reversed until no cycles remained. We then applied pseudo-projective transformation to create data that can be used to train our parser, described in section 3. By detransforming the projective graphs generated from gold-standard dependencies, we obtain labeled precision of 98.1% and labeled recall of 97.7%, which is below the accuracy expected for detransformation of syntactic dependency trees. This is expected, since arc crossing occurs more frequently in predicate-argument graphs in the HPSG Treebank than in surface syntactic dependencies.

We first trained a parsing model without cluster-based features, using only the baseline set of features, which was the product of experimentation using the development set. On the test set, this baseline model has labeled precision and recall of 88.7 and 88.2, respectively, slightly below the precision and recall obtained by Sagae and Tsujii on the same data (89.0 precision and 88.5 recall).

We then used the development set to explore the effects of cluster sets with different levels of granularity. The baseline model has precision and recall of 88.6 and 88.0 on the development set. We found that by slicing the cluster tree relatively close to the root, resulting in a set of 50 to 100 distinct cluster labels (corresponding to relatively coarse clusters), we obtain small (0.3 to 0.4), but statistically significant ($p < 0.005$) improvements on precision and recall over the baseline model on the development set. By increasing the number of cluster labels (making the

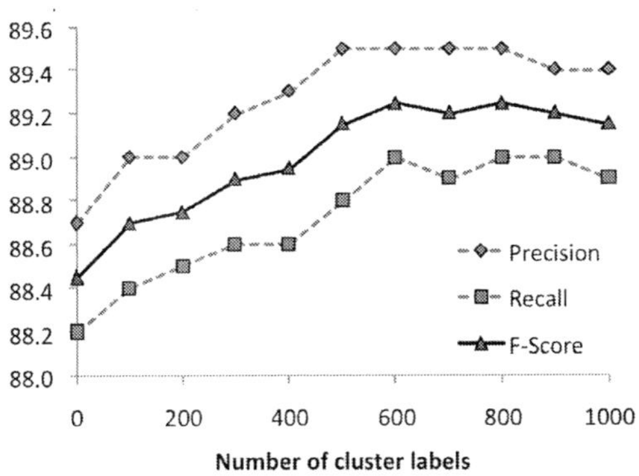

Figure 4: Effect of cluster granularity on labeled the precision and recall of predicate-argument pairs in the development set. The improvement in precision and recall between the baseline (zero cluster labels, where no cluster information is added) and 600 cluster labels is statistically significant ($p < 0.0005$).

distinctions among members of different clusters more fine-grained) in steps of 100, we observed improvements in precision and recall until the point where there were 600 distinct cluster labels. This set of 600 cluster labels produced the highest values of precision and recall (89.5 and 89.0) that we obtained for the development set using only one set of cluster labels. Figure 4 shows how precision, recall and F-score on the development set varied with the number of cluster labels used.

Following Koo et al. (2008), we also experimented with using two sets of cluster labels with different levels of granularity. We found that using the set of 600 labels and an additional set with fewer than 600 labels did not improve or hurt precision and recall. Finer grained clusters with more than 1,000 labels (combined with the set of 600 labels) improved results further. The highest precision and recall figures of 90.1 and 89.6 were obtained with the sets of 600 and 1,400 labels.

We parsed the test set using the best configuration of cluster-based features as determined using the development set (the sets with 600 and 1,400 cluster labels) and obtained 90.2 precision, 89.8 recall and 90.0 f-score, a 13.8% reduction in error over a strong baseline. Table 1 summarizes our results on the test set. For comparison, we also shows results published by Sagae and Tsujii (2008), to our knowledge the highest f-score reported for this test set, and Miyao and Tsujii (2005), who first reported results on this data set.

	Precision	Recall	F-score
Baseline	88.7	88.2	88.4
Clusters	**90.2**	**89.8**	**90.0**
S & T	89.9	88.5	88.7
Miyao et al.	85.0	84.3	84.6

Table 1: Results obtained on the test set using our baseline model and our best cluster-based features. The results in the bottom two rows are from Sagae and Tsujii (2008) and Miyao and Tsujii (2005).

4.1 Surface dependency parsing with cluster-based features

The parser used in our experiments with HPSG Treebank predicate-argument structures can assign more than one head for a single word, but when the parser is trained using only dependency trees, it behaves in exactly the same way as a parser based on Nivre's arc-standard algorithm, since it never sees examples of attach actions during training. To see whether our clusters can improve surface dependency parsing, and to allow for comparison of our results to a larger body of research on surface dependency parsing, we used dependency trees extracted from the Penn Treebank using the Yamada and Matsumoto (2003) version of the Penn Treebank head-percolation rules to train parsing models that produce dependency trees. However, no tuning of the features or metaparameters was performed; the parser was trained as-is on dependency trees.

We used the standard train, development and test sets splits to train two models, as in our experiments with predicate-argument dependencies: a baseline that uses no cluster information, and a model that uses two sets of clusters that were found to improve results in the development set. The unlabeled accuracy of our baseline model on the test set is 89.96%, which is considerably lower than the best current results. Koo et al. (2008) report 90.84% for a first-order edge-factored model, and 92.02% for a second-order model (and as high as 93.16% with a second-order model enriched with cluster features derived from plain text). Using two sets of clusters, one with 600 and one with 1,200 labels, accuracy improves by 1.32%, to reach 91.28% (a 13.15% reduction in error compared to our baseline). While still below the level of the strongest results for this dataset, it is interesting to see that the improvement in accuracy over the baseline observed for surface dependency trees is similar to the improvement observed for predicate-argument dependency graphs.

5 Related work

Many aspects of this research were inspired by the recent work of Koo et al. (2008), who reported impressive results on improving dependency parsing accuracy using a second order edge-factored model and word clusters derived from plain text using the Brown et al. (1992) algorithm. Our clustering approach is significantly different, focusing on the use of parsed data to produce strictly syntactic clusters. It is possible that using both types of clusters may be beneficial.

McClosky et al. (2006) used a large corpus of parsed text to obtain improved parsing results through self-training. A key difference in our general framework is that it allows for a parser with one type of syntactic representation to improve the accuracy of a different parser with a different type of formalism. In this regard, our work is related to that of Sagae et al. (2007), who used a stacking-like framework to allow a surface dependency parser to improve an HPSG parser. In that work, however, as in other work that combines different parsers through stacking (Martins et al., 2008; Nivre and McDonald, 2008) or voting (Henderson and Brill, 1999), multiple parsers need to process new text at run-time. In our approach for leveraging diverse parsers, one of the parsers is used only to create a parsed corpus from which we extract clusters of words that have similar syntactic behaviors, and only one parser is needed at run-time.

6 Conclusion

We have presented a novel approach for deriving word clusters based on syntactic similarity, and shown how these word clusters can be applied in a transition-based dependency parser.

Our experiments focused on predicate-argument structures extracted from the HPSG Treebank, which demonstrates that the syntactic clusters are effective in leveraging cross-framework parser representations to improve parsing accuracy. However, we expect that similar accuracy improvements can be obtained in parsing using other frameworks and formalisms, and possibly in other natural language processing tasks.

Acknowledgments

The project or effort described here has been sponsored by the U.S. Army Research, Development, and Engineering Command (RDECOM). Statements and opinions expressed do not necessarily reflect the position or the policy of the United States Government, and no official endorsement should be inferred.

References

Srinivas Bangalore and Aravind K. Joshi. 1999. Supertagging: an approach to almost parsing. *Computational Linguistics* 25, 2 (Jun. 1999), 237-265.

Peter F. Brown, Vincent J. Della Pietra, Peter V. deSouza, Jennifer C. Lai, and Robert L. Mercer. 1992. Class-Based n-gram Models of Natural Language. *Computational Linguistics*, 18(4):467–479.

Eugene Charniak. 2000. A maximum-entropy-inspired parser. In *Proceedings of the First Meeting of the North American Chapter of the Association for Computational Linguistics (NAACL)*, pages 132–139.

Charniak, E., Blaheta, D., Ge, N., Hall, K., Hale, J., and Johnson, M. (2000) *BLLIP 1987-89 WSJ Corpus Release 1*. Philadelphia, PA: Linguistic Data Consortium.

Michael Collins. 1999. *Head-Driven Statistical Models for Natural Language Parsing*. Ph.D. thesis, University of Pennsylvania.

Michael Collins. 2002. Discriminative Training Methods for Hidden Markov Models: Theory and Experiments with Perceptron Algorithms. In *Proceedings of EMNLP*, pages 1–8.

Yoav Freund and Robert E. Schapire. 1999. Large Margin Classification Using the Perceptron Algorithm. *Machine Learning*, 37(3):277–296.

Daniel Gildea and Daniel Jurafsky. 2002. Automatic Labeling of Semantic Roles. *Computational Linguistics* 28(3): 245-288.

Andrew Gordon and Reid Swanson. 2007. Generalizing semantic role annotations across syntactically similar verbs. *Proceedings of the 2007 meeting of the Association for Computational Linguistics (ACL-07)*, Prague, Czech Republic, June 23-30, 2007.

Johan Hall, Jens Nilsson, Joakim Nivre, Gulsen Eryigit, Beata Megyesi, Mattias Nilsson, and Markus Saers. 2007. Single malt or blended? A study in multilingual parser optimization. In *Proceedings of EMNLP-CoNLL*.

James Henderson, Paola Merlo, G. Musillo, and Ivan Titov. 2008. A latent variable model of synchronous parsing for syntactic and semantic dependencies. In *Proceedings of the Shared Task of the Conference on Computational Natural Language Learning (CoNLL)*, pages 178-182. Manchester, UK.

John Henderson and Eric Brill. 1999. Exploiting diversity in natural language processing: combining parsers. In *Proceedings of the Fourth Conference on Empirical Methods in Natural Language Processing (EMNLP).*

Terry Koo, Xavier Carreras and Michael Collins. 2008. Simple semi-supervised dependency parsing. In *Proceedings of the 46th Annual Meeting of the Association for Computational Linguistics: Human Language Technologies (ACL-08:HLT),* pages 595-603.

Dekang Lin. 1998. Automatic retrieval and clustering of similar words. In *Proceedings of the 17th international Conference on Computational Linguistics - Volume 2.* Montreal, Quebec, Canada.

Mitchell P. Marcus, Mary A. Marcinkiewicz, Beatrice Santorini. 1993. Building a large annotated corpus of English: The Penn Treebank, *Computational Linguistics*, 19(2), June 1993.

André F. T. Martins, Dipanjan Das, Noah A. Smith, and Eric P. Xing. 2008. Stacking Dependency Parsers. In *Proceedings of the Conference on Empirical Methods in Natural Language Processing, Waikiki*, HI.

David McClosky, Eugene Charniak, and Mark Johnson. 2006. Effective Self-Training for Parsing. In *Proceedings of HLT-NAACL*, pages 152–159.

Ryan McDonald, Koby Crammer, and Fernando Pereira. 2005. Online large-margin training of dependency parsers. In *Proceedings of ACL*, pages 91–98.

Scott Miller, Jethran Guinness and Alex Zamanian. 2004. Name Tagging withWord Clusters and Discriminative Training. In *Proceedings of HLT-NAACL*, pages 337–342.

Miyao, Yusuke, Takashi Ninomiya, and Jun'ichi Tsujii. 2004. Corpus-oriented grammar development for acquiring a Head-driven Phrase Structure Grammar from the Penn Treebank. In *Proceedings of the International Joint Conference on Natural Language Processing (IJCNLP).*

Miyao Yusuke and Jun'ichi Tsujii. 2005. Probabilistic disambiguation models for wide-coverage HPSG parsing. In *Proceedings of the 43rd Annual Meeting on Association for Computational Linguistics.*

Joakim Nivre.2004. Incrementality in Deterministic Dependency Parsing. In *Incremental Parsing: Bringing Engineering and Cognition Together (Workshop at ACL-2004).*

Joakim Nivre, Johan Hall, and Jens Nilsson. 2004. Memory-based dependency parsing. In Proceedings of CoNLL, pages 49–56.

Joakim Nivre. and Jens Nilsson. 2005. Pseudo-Projective Dependency Parsing. In *Proceedings of the 43rd Annual Meeting of the Association for Computational Linguistics (ACL)*, pp. 99-106.

Joakim Nivre, Johan Hall, Sandra Kubler, Ryan McDonald, Jens Nilsson, Sebastian Riedel, and Deniz Yuret. 2007. The CoNLL 2007 shared task on dependency parsing. In *Proceedings of EMNLP-CoNLL*, pages 915-932.

Nivre, J. and McDonald, R. (2008) Integrating Graph-Based and Transition-Based Dependency Parsers. In *Proceedings of the 46th Annual Meeting of the Association for Computational Linguistics: Human Language Technologies (ACL-08: HLT),* 950-958.

Martha Palmer, Dan Gildea and Paul Kingsbury. 2005. The Proposition Bank: A Corpus Annotated with Semantic Roles. *Computational Linguistics*, 31:1.

Kenji Sagae and Alon Lavie. 2006. Parser combination by reparsing. In *Proceedings of NAACL: Short Papers*, pages 129–132.

Kenji Sagae, Yusuke Miyao Jun'ichi and Tsujii. 2007. HPSG Parsing with shallow dependency constraints. In *Proceedings of the 44th Meeting of the Association for Computational Linguistics.*

Kenji Sagae and Jun'ichi Tsujii. 2008. Shift-reduce dependency DAG parsing. In *Proceedings of the International Conference on Computational Linguistics (COLING 2008).*

Hiroyasu Yamada and Y. Matsumoto. 2003. Statistical Dependency Analysis With Support Vector Machines. In *Proceedings of the Eighth International Workshop on Parsing Technologies (IWPT)*, pages 195–206.

The chunk as the period of the functions *length* and *frequency* of words on the syntagmatic axis

Jacques Vergne
GREYC - Université de Caen - France
Jacques.Vergne@info.unicaen.fr

Abstract

Chunking is segmenting a text into chunks, sub-sentential segments, that Abney approximately defined as stress groups. Chunking usually uses monolingual resources, most often exhaustive, sometimes partial : function words and punctuations, which often mark beginnings and ends of chunks. But, to extend this method to other languages, monolingual resources have to be multiplied. We present a new method : endogenous chunking, which uses no other resource than the text to be segmented itself. The idea of this method comes from Zipf : to make the least communication effort, speakers are driven to shorten frequent words. A chunk then can be characterized as the period of the periodic correlated functions length and frequency of words on the syntagmatic axis. This original method takes its advantage to be applied to a great number of languages of alphabetic script, with the same algorithm, without any resource.

Introduction

Chunking is a frequent segmentation step in many processing types : robust parsers, parsers of linear complexity (Vergne, 2000), computing stress groups and linking them in tts systems, to compute macro-prosody (Vannier et al., 1999), in automatic indexing, the chunk as another indexed grain above the word in the grain hierarchy, and in sub-sentential alignment, the chunk as an aligned grain.

The method we propose is based on the properties of the functions length and frequency of words on the syntagmatic axis. These two functions are correlated : integer, periodic, synchronous, in phase opposition, and their period allows to define the chunk. On a period, the length function is non-decreasing, and the frequency function is non-increasing. These concepts continue in Zipf's direction : minimizing the communication effort drives the speaker to shorten frequent words (Zipf, 1949). The length metrics defined by Zipf is not the number of letters, but the number of syllables or the number of phonemes of the written form (Zipf, 1935); the metrics of our method is also the number of syllables, or more precisely the number of vowel nuclei, computable from the written form; this metrics takes its root into the oral origin of the chunk. The word frequency is measured in the segmented text.

This method of segmentation into chunks is based on digital properties, and is valid on languages with alphabetic script. It is endogenous, as it computes on the text to be segmented and does not use any resource external to the parsed text.

1 Structure model of the chunk according to Abney and according to Déjean

The concept of chunk has been proposed by Steve Abney (1991). It has been based on properties of speech : Abney defined the chunk as a stress group. As speech is constrained by the vocal system, we can see the chunk as a generic concept on natural languages, a concept of language. Hervé Déjean (1998) has proposed a structure model for the chunk : beginnings and ends of chunk (words or morphemes) around a kernel (Déjean, 1998, page 117); our method uses this model.

For instance, the written form "Commission" has been found in the following chunks in the same text :

[Commission européenne]
[la Commission]
[la Commission européenne]
[dans la Commission]

And here is the synthesis :

[dans [la [Commission] européenne]
[beginnings [kernel] ends]

Proceedings of the 11th International Conference on Parsing Technologies (IWPT), pages 202–205,
Paris, October 2009.

2 Local deductions and their generalization at text level

Properties of the chunk are used locally at occurrence level : an occurrence of a written form is locally a beginning or an end of a chunk. An important question is to decide how to articulate local deductions at occurrence level and their global merging at text level.

We know that occurrences of the same written form may be occurrences of more than one word, in different contexts. For instance, "*on*" in English is the beginning of a chunk in "*on the contrary*", but it is the end of a chunk in "*it is going on*". These two occurrences correspond to two different words, which have different positions and different contexts, and their local deductions cannot be merged. So, we can merge local deductions for occurrences of the same word. In practice, we merge local deductions for occurrences of a written form if there is no beginning - end contradiction.

We tried full merging, as if all occurrences were of the same word. This solution remains valid for monofocused short texts (some thousands words). But, to be able to chunk longer texts, we have chosen now the solution of a partial generalization (see below in 4).

3 Two properties of a chunk

The algorithm exploits two properties of the chunk.

3.1 Property 1 : the chunk is a constituent of the virgulot

Hervé Déjean (1998) has defined the "entre-ponctuations" as a constituent delimited by two punctuations. Nadine Lucas (Lucas, 2001) has proposed the term "virgulot", that we will use now. We define the following constituent hierarchy : the text is constituted of virgulots, themselves constituted of chunks, themselves constituted of occurrences of written forms.

Property exploited by the algorithm :
- a written form attested at the beginning of a virgulot is a beginning of a chunk,
- a written form attested at the end of a virgulot is an end of a chunk.

Here are some instances of virgulots :

, ***in*** *denen Aale* ***leben*** ,
, ***bis*** *die Bewirtschaftungspläne* ***vorliegen*** .

. ***It*** *also intends to explore* ***measures*** ,
, ***before*** *migrating upstream to spend most of their* ***lives*** .

, ***en*** *las aguas centro-occidentales del Océano* ***Atlántico*** .
, ***donde*** *transcurre la mayor parte de su* ***vida*** .

. ***Lasciandosi*** *trasportare dalla corrente e* ***nuotando*** ,
, ***dove*** *si riproducono una sola volta e poi* ***muoiono*** .

First written forms of virgulots are beginnings of chunks (prepositions, pronouns, ...), and their last written forms are ends of chunks (nouns, verbs, adjectives, ...).

3.2 Property 2 : the chunk is the period of the correlated functions *length* and *frequency* of words on the syntagmatic axis

We define two integer functions of words on the syntagmatic axis (inside a virgulot) : their length, defined as their number of syllables, and their frequency in the text to be segmented.

Here is an instance of a virgulot :

	, *would*	*migrate*	*from*	*the*	*rivers*	*on*	*their*	*territories* ,
length:	1	3	1	1	2	1	1	4
frequ.:	10	3	6	65	2	6	4	1

On the length function, we have the following non-decreasing sequences : [1 3] [1 1 2] [1 1 4].

On the frequency function, we have the following non-increasing sequences : [10 3] [6] [65 2] [6 4 1].

For these two functions, a period corresponds to a sequence; in other words, these sequences give a way to segment; these 2 functions are synchronous : sequences of both functions (nearly) define the same periods; on a (synchronous) period, both functions are in phase opposition : on a period (which defines a chunk), the length function is non-decreasing, and the frequency function is non-increasing; the common properties of these two functions allow us to call them correlated; it is an other way to say that short words are frequent and that long words are rare.

We notice, following Zipf (1949) in "Human Behavior and the Principle of Least-Effort" that writing and speech are an optimal compression; it reminds the principles of file compression in computer science : frequent data are short coded, and rare data are long coded. Let us make an observation on the Zipf law, as it is known today : this law makes a relation between frequency and rows of words sorted by decreasing frequency; if we knew only this law, we would forget length of words; but Zipf proposed to consider length and frequency together, in a correlated way, as an optimization (the Least-Effort). As we use length and frequency together, in a correlated way, we go back to the origin of Zipf's concepts.

To compute word length from the written form, length is defined as the number of syllables, i.e. the number of vowel nuclei (a sequence of contiguous vowels corresponds to a vowel nucleus, and to a length equal to 1). This calculation needs as input the vowels of the alphabet (Latin or Greek). There is a particular case : is the *y* vowel or consonant. The *y* is vowel in "*system*" (length 2) and consonant in "*rayon*" (length 2); *y* is consonant by default; *y* is vowel at the beginning or the end of a word, or alone (*usually, by, y*); *y* is vowel between 2 consonants; these rules are enough to process all cases for the 20 natural languages of the corpus. Acronyms (sequences of uppercases) have a length equal to twice their numbers of letters (tendency to be in the end of chunk). A number (sequence of figures) has a length equal to 1, whatever its number of figures (tendency to be in the beginning of chunk).

4 An algorithm based on these properties

The frequency and the length of every written form are computed.

For the property 1, based on the virgulot, the text is processed, and occurrences of written forms at the beginning or end of virgulot are noted as beginning or end of chunk.

For the property 2, based on monotonous sequences, the text is processed, while noting borders between 2 monotonous sequences, that gives for each border an end and a beginning of chunk. A Boolean function "in the same sequence" returns whether 2 contiguous words are in the same monotonous sequence (i.e. in the same chunk). Four solutions are experimented : on length only, on frequency only, on length AND frequency (then shorter chunks), or on length OR frequency (then longer chunks). Results are very comparable, because both functions are strongly correlated[1]. For example, this function, in "length OR frequency" mode, on words i and i+1, to express the fact that these two words are in the same sequence, has the following form :

words i and i+1 are not separators of virgulot AND

(length(i+1) $\geq$ length(i) OR frequency(i+1) $\leq$ frequency(i))

[1] Using length alone allows, not using frequency, to get a method usable on a very short text, as a search engine query.

The generalization of local deductions is done the following way : for all occurrences of a written form, a synthesis of local deductions is done. There are 8 cases : 2 properties, 4 cases for each (2 Booleans : beginning, end). If all local deductions are compatible, they are merged, i.e. occurrences without any local deduction take the tag of occurrences with the same local deduction : either beginning or end of chunk.

Here is the trace of the process on our instance of virgulot :

virgul.	sequ.	general.	result			
b e	b e	b e	b e	len.	freq.	
[1,0]	[1,0]	[0,0]	[2,0]	1	10	*would*
[0,0]	[0,1]	[0,1]	[0,2]	3	3	*migrate*
[0,0]	[1,0]	[1,0]	[2,0]	1	6	*from*
[0,0]	[0,0]	[1,0]	[1,0]	1	65	*the*
[0,0]	[0,1]	[0,1]	[0,2]	2	2	*rivers*
[0,0]	[1,0]	[1,0]	[2,0]	1	6	*on*
[0,0]	[0,0]	[1,0]	[1,0]	1	4	*their*
[0,1]	[0,1]	[0,0]	[0,2]	4	1	*territories*

From the first property (the first column of Booleans), *would* is the beginning, and *territories* is the end of the virgulot, therefore beginning and end of a chunk ([marks a beginning of chunk,] marks an end of chunk) :

, [would migrate from the rivers on their territories],

The second property (the second column of Booleans) which exploits the monotonous sequences, here in "length OR frequency" mode, gives the following chunking :

, [would migrate] [from the rivers]
[on their territories] ,

The generalization of local deductions (the third column of Booleans) adds the fact that *the* and *their* are beginnings of a chunk elsewhere in this text.

Then these three sources of deduction are merged, and we obtain the following segmentation (the forth column) :

, [would migrate] [from [the rivers]
[on [their territories] ,

5 Some sentences segmented into chunks

The validation corpus of the method is composed of 12 press releases (about 1000 words each for one language), every release is written into 6 to 20 languages, and of the part 1 of the "Treaty establishing a Constitution for Europe" in 11 languages (about 10 000 words for one language), from the website of the European Union (http://europa.eu/).

The following sentences are extracted from the release IP/05/1018 of 2005 (and processed in "length OR frequency" mode) :

[Die Laichgründe] [der Aale] befinden] [sich [im Sargassosee] [im mittleren Westatlantik] .

[Eels spawn] [in [the Sargasso Sea [in [the western central Atlantic] Ocean] .

[Las anguilas] desovan] [en [el Mar [de [los Sargazos] , [en [las aguas] centro-occidentales] [del Océano Atlántico] .

[La zone [de frai] [de l'anguille] [se situe [en mer] [des Sargasses] , [dans [la partie centre-ouest] [de l'océan Atlantique] .

[Le anguille] [si riproducono] [nel mar [dei Sargassi] , [nell'Atlantico centro-occidentale] .

The following sentences are extracted from the part 1 of the "Treaty establishing a Constitution for Europe" (and processed in "length OR frequency" mode) :

[Die Union] steht allen europäischen] Staaten offen] , [die [ihre Werte] achten] [und [sich verpflichten] , [sie gemeinsam] [zu fördern] .

[The Union] [shall be open] [to [all [European States] [which respect] [its values] [and [are committed] [to promoting] them] together] .

[La Unión] [está abierta] [a todos] [los Estados] europeos] [que respeten] [sus valores] [y [se comprometan] [a promoverlos] [en común] .

[L'Union [est ouverte] [à [tous [les États] européens] [qui respectent] [ses valeurs] [et [qui s'engagent] [à [les promouvoir] [en commun] .

[L'Unione [è aperta] [a tutti] [gli Stati europei] [che rispettano] [i suoi valori] [e [si impegnano] [a promuoverli congiuntamente] .

Conclusion

While characterizing the chunk in a purely digital way, from properties of length et frequency functions of words on the syntagmatic axis, this original method consists in calculations on the text to segment; it has the advantage to be applied to a great number of languages, with the same algorithm, without any monolingual resource : languages with alphabetic script, with a written word which separates function words from content words (it is not the case in Finnish), and compatible with a structure model of the chunk where function words generally are before content words; the method is promising for the 22 languages of the European Community[2].

This method can be applied in automatic indexing, for search-engines (as Exalead does, to be able to output the most frequent terms associated to the documents of the answer), and in subsentential alignment, to constraint the statistical alignment (as in Similis, the alignment software of Lingua et Machina, but this software uses monolingual resources for every language). The interesting feature of this method is not to need any resource for a new language to process[3].

As it is independent from specificities of each language, this method is not "multilanguage", neither "multi-monolanguage", but as it exploits generic properties of natural languages, that is properties of language, as an abstraction of natural languages, we could perhaps simply call it a "linguistic" method.

References

Steven Abney. 1991. *Parsing By Chunks.* in Principle-Based Parsing, 257-278, Kluwer Academic Publishers.

Hervé Déjean. 1998. *Concepts et algorithmes pour la découverte des structures formelles des langues.* Thèse de doctorat de l'université de Caen, France.

Nadine Lucas. 2001. *Étude et modélisation de l'explication dans les textes.* Actes du Colloque "L'explication: enjeux cognitifs et communicationnels", Paris.

Gérald Vannier, Anne Lacheret-Dujour, Jacques Vergne. 1999. *Pauses location and duration calculated with syntactic dependencies and textual considerations for t.t.s. system.* ICPhS 1999, San Francisco, USA, August 1999.

Jacques Vergne. 2000. Tutorial : *Trends in Robust Parsing.* Coling 2000.

George K. Zipf. 1935. *The psychobiology of language : An introduction to dynamic philology.* Boston, Mass., Houghton-Mifflin.

George K. Zipf. 1949. *Human Behavior and the Principle of Least-Effort.* Addison-Wesley.

[2] See results on : http://www.info.unicaen.fr/~jvergne/chunking_multilingue_endogene/

[3] But a problem for this large scale multilingual method is to evaluate the results on so many languages : we need a speaker for every language. For the moment, it is done for German, English, Spanish, French and Italian.

Using a maximum entropy-based tagger to improve a very fast vine parser

Anders Søgaard
Center for Language Technology
University of Copenhagen
soegaard@hum.ku.dk

Jonas Kuhn
Dpt. of Linguistics
University of Potsdam
kuhn@ling.uni-potsdam.de

Abstract

In this short paper, an off-the-shelf maximum entropy-based POS-tagger is used as a partial parser to improve the accuracy of an extremely fast linear time dependency parser that provides state-of-the-art results in multilingual unlabeled POS sequence parsing.

1 Introduction

The dependency parsing literature has grown in all directions the past 10 years or so. Dependency parsing is used in a wide variety of applications, and many different parsing techniques have been proposed.

Two dependency parsers have become more popular than the rest, namely MSTParser (McDonald et al., 2005) and MaltParser (Nivre et al., 2007). MSTParser is slightly more accurate than MaltParser on most languages, especially when dependencies are long and non-projective, but MaltParser is theoretically more efficient as it runs in linear time. Both are relatively slow in terms of training (hours, sometimes days), and relatively big models are queried in parsing.

MSTParser and MaltParser can be optimized for speed in various ways,[1] but the many applications of dependency parsers today may turn model size into a serious problem. MSTParser typically takes about a minute to parse a small standard test suite, say 2–300 sentences; the stand-alone version of MaltParser may take 5–8 minutes. Such parsing times are problematic in, say, a machine translation system where for each sentence pair multiple target sentences are parsed (Charniak et al., 2003; Galley and Manning, 2009). Since training takes hours or days, researchers are also more reluctant to experiment with new features, and it is very likely that the features typically used in parsing are suboptimal in, say, machine translation.

Conceptually simpler dependency parsers are also easier to understand, which makes debugging, cross-domain adaption or cross-language adaptation a lot easier. Finally, state-of-the-art dependency parsers may in fact be outperformed by simpler systems on non-standard test languages with, say, richer morphology or more flexible word order.

Vine parsing is a parsing strategy that guarantees fast parsing and smaller models, but the accuracy of dependency-based vine parsers has been non-competitive (Eisner and Smith, 2005; Dreyer et al., 2006).

This paper shows how the accuracy of dependency-based vine parsers can be improved by 1–5% across six very different languages with a very small cost in training time and practically no cost in parsing time.

The main idea in our experiments is to use a maximum entropy-based part-of-speech (POS) tagger to identify roots and tokens whose heads are immediately left or right of them. These are tasks that a tagger can solve. You simply read off a tagged text from the training, resp. test, section of a treebank and replace all tags of roots, i.e. tokens whose syntactic head is an artificial root node, with a new tag ROOT. You then train on the training section and apply your tagger on the test section. The decisions made by the tagger are then, subsequently, used as hard constraints by your parser. When the parser then tries to find root nodes, for instance, it is forced to use the roots assigned by the tagger. This strategy is meaningful if the tagger has better precision for roots than the parser. If it has better recall than the parser, the

[1] Recent work has optimized MaltParser considerably for speed. Goldberg and Elhadad (2008) speed up the MaltParser by a factor of 30 by simplifying the decision function for the classifiers. Parsing is still considerably slower than with our vine parser, i.e. a test suite is parsed in about 15–20 seconds, whereas our vine parser parses a test suite in less than two seconds.

Proceedings of the 11th International Conference on Parsing Technologies (IWPT), pages 206–209,
Paris, October 2009.

parser may be forced to select roots only from the set of potential roots assigned by the tagger. In our experiments, only the first strategy was used (since the tagger's precision was typically better than its recall).

The dependency parser used in our experiments is very simple. It is based on the Chu-Liu-Edmonds algorithm (Edmonds, 1967), which is also used in the MSTParser (McDonald et al., 2005), but it is informed only by a simple MLE training procedure and omits cycle contraction in parsing. This means that it produces cyclic graphs. In the context of poor training, insisting on acyclic output graphs often compromises accuracy by $>$ 10%. On top of this parser, which is super fast but often does not even outperform a simple structural baseline, hard and soft constraints on dependency length are learned discriminatively. The speed of the parser allows us to repeatedly parse a tuning section to optimize these constraints. In particular, the tuning section (about 7500 tokens) is parsed a fixed number of times for each POS/CPOS tag to find the optimal dependency length constraint when that tag is the tag of the head or dependent word. In general, this discriminative training procedure takes about 10 minutes for an average-sized treebank. The parser only produces unlabeled dependency graphs and is still under development. While accuracy is below state-of-the-art results, our *improved* parser significantly outperforms a default version of the MaltParser that is restricted to POS tags only, on 5/6 languages ($p \leq 0.05$), and it significantly outperforms the baseline vine parser on all languages.

2 Data

Our languages are chosen from different language families. Arabic is a Semitic language, Czech is Slavic, Dutch is Germanic, Italian is Romance, Japanese is Japonic-Ryukyuan, and Turkish is Uralic. All treebanks, except Italian, were also used in the CONLL-X Shared Task (Buchholz and Marsi, 2006). The Italian treebank is the law section of the TUT Treebank used in the Evalita 2007 Dependency Parsing Challenge (Bosco et al., 2000).

3 Experiments

The Python/C++ implementation of the maximum entropy-based part-of-speech (POS) tagger first described in Ratnaparkhi (1998) that comes with the maximum entropy library in Zhang (2004) was used to identify arcs to the root node and to tokens immediately left or right of the dependent. This was done by first extracting a tagged text from each treebank with dependents of the root node assigned a special tag ROOT. Similarly, tagged texts were extracted in which dependents of their immediate left, resp. right neighbors, were assigned a special tag. Our tagger was trained on the texts extracted from the training sections of the treebanks and evaluated on the texts extracted from the test sections. The number of gold standard, resp. predicted, ROOT/LEFT/RIGHT tags are presented in Figure 1. Precision and f-score are also computed. Note that since our parser uses information from our tagger as hard constraints, i.e. it disregards arcs to the root node or immediate neighbors *not* predicted by our tagger, precision is really what is important, not f-score. Or more precisely, precision indicates *if* our tagger is of any help to us, and f-score tells us to what extent it may be of help.

4 Results

The results in Figure 2 show that using a maximum entropy-based POS tagger to identify roots (ROOT), tokens with immediate left heads (LEFT) and tokens with immediate (RIGHT) heads improves the accuracy of a baseline vine parser across the board for all languages measured in terms of unlabeled attachment score (ULA), or decreases are insignificant (Czech and Turkish). For all six languages, there is a combination of ROOT, LEFT and RIGHT that significantly outperforms the vine parser baseline. In 4/6 cases, absolute improvements are $\geq 2\%$. The score for Dutch is improved by $> 4\%$. The extended vine parser is also significantly better than the MaltParser restricted to POS tags on 5/6 languages. MaltParser is probably better than the vine parser wrt. Japanese because average sentence length in this treebank is *very* short (8.9); constraints on dependency length do not really limit the search space.

In spite of the fact that our parser only uses POS tags (except for the maximum entropy-based tagger which considers both words and tags), scores are now comparable to more mature dependency parsers: ULA excl. punctuation for Arabic is 70.74 for Vine+ROOT+LEFT+RIGHT which is better than six of the systems who participated in the CONLL-X Shared Task and who had access to *all* data in the treebank, i.e. tokens, lemmas, POS

Arabic	Gold	Predicted	Precision	F-score
ROOT	443	394	89.09	83.87
LEFT	3035	3180	84.28	86.24
RIGHT	313	196	82.14	63.26
Czech	Gold	Predicted	Precision	F-score
ROOT	737	649	85.36	79.94
LEFT	1485	1384	85.12	82.12
RIGHT	1288	1177	87.51	83.57
Dutch	Gold	Predicted	Precision	F-score
ROOT	522	360	74.44	60.77
LEFT	1734	1595	87.02	83.39
RIGHT	1300	1200	87.00	83.52
Italian	Gold	Predicted	Precision	F-score
ROOT	100	58	74.36	65.17
LEFT	1601	1640	90.30	91.39
RIGHT	192	129	84.87	74.14
Japanese	Gold	Predicted	Precision	F-score
ROOT	939	984	85.06	87.05
LEFT	1398	1382	97.76	97.19
RIGHT	2838	3016	92.27	95.08
Turkish	Gold	Predicted	Precision	F-score
ROOT	694	685	85.55	84.99
LEFT	750	699	91.70	88.47
RIGHT	3433	3416	84.19	83.98

Figure 1: Tag-specific evaluation of our tagger on the extracted texts.

	Arabic	Czech	Dutch	Italian	Japanese	Turkish
MaltParser	66.22	67.78	65.03	75.48	**89.13**	68.94
Vine	67.99	66.70	65.98	75.50	83.15	68.53
Vine+ROOT	68.68	66.65	66.21	78.06	83.82	68.45
Vine+ROOT+LEFT	69.68	68.14	68.05	77.14	84.64	68.37
Vine+RIGHT	68.50	67.38	68.18	**78.55**	84.17	**69.87**
Vine+ROOT+RIGHT	69.20	67.32	68.40	78.29	84.78	69.79
Vine+ROOT+LEFT+RIGHT	**70.28**	**68.70**	**70.06**	77.26	85.45	69.74

Figure 2: Labeled attachment scores (LASs) for MaltParser limited to POS tags, our baseline vine parser (Vine) and our extensions of Vine. Best scores bold-faced.

tags, features and dependency relations; not just the POS tags as in our case. In particular, our result is 2.28 better than Dreyer et al. (2006) who also use soft and hard constraints on dependency lengths. They extend the parsing algorithm in Eisner and Smith (2005) to labeled k-best parsing and use a reranker to find the best parse according to predefined global features. ULA excl. punctuation for Turkish is 67.06 which is better than six of the shared task participants, incl. Dreyer et al. (2006) (60.45).

The improvements come at an extremely low cost. The POS tagger simply stores its decisions in a very small table, typically 5–10 cells per sentence, that is queried in no time in parsing. Parsing a standard small test suite takes less than two seconds, and the cost of the additional look-up is too small to be measured. The training time of the maximum entropy-based tagger is typically a matter of seconds or half a minute. Even running it on the 1249k Prague Dependency Treebank (Czech) is only a matter of minutes.

5 Conclusion and future work

Vine parsers are motivated by efficiency and robustness (Dreyer et al., 2006), which has become more and more important over the last few years, but none of the systems introduced in the literature provide competitive results in terms of accuracy. Our experiments show how dependency-based vine parsers can be significantly improved by using a maximum entropy-based POS tagger for initial partial parsing with almost no cost in terms of training and parsing time.

Our choice of parser restricted us in a few respects. Most importantly, our results are below state-of-the-art results, and it is not clear if the strategy scales to more accurate parsers. The strategy of using a POS tagger to do partial parsing and subsequently forward high precision decisions to a parser only works on graph-based or constraint-based dependency parsers where previous decisions can be hardwired into candidate weight matrices by setting weights to 0. It would be difficult if at all possible to implement in history-based dependency parsers such as MaltParser. Experiments will be performed with the MSTParser soon.

Our parser also restricted us to considering unlabeled dependency graphs. A POS tagger, however, can also be used to identify grammatical functions (subjects, objects, ...), for example, which may be used to hardwire dependency relations into candidate weight matrices. POS taggers may also be used to identify other dependency relations or more fine-grained features that can improve the accuracy of dependency parsers.

References

Cristina Bosco, Vincenzo Lombardo, Daniela Vassallo, and Leonardo Lesmo. 2000. Building a treebank for Italian. In *LREC*, pages 99–105, Athens, Greece.

Sabine Buchholz and Erwin Marsi. 2006. CONLL-X shared task on multilingual dependency parsing. In *CONLL-X*, pages 149–164, New York City, NY.

Eugene Charniak, Kevin Knight, and Kenji Yamada. 2003. Syntax-based language models for statistical machine translation. In *MT Summit IX*, New Orleans, Louisiana.

Markus Dreyer, David A. Smith, and Noah A. Smith. 2006. Vine parsing and minimum risk reranking for speed and precision. In *CONLL-X*, pages 201–205, New York City, NY.

J. Edmonds. 1967. Optimum branchings. *Journal of Research of the National Bureau of Standards*, 71:233–240.

Jason Eisner and Noah A. Smith. 2005. Parsing with soft and hard constraints on dependency length. In *IWPT'05*, pages 30–41, Vancouver, Canada.

Michel Galley and Cristopher Manning. 2009. Quadratic time dependency parsing for machine translation. In *ACL'09*, Singapore, Singapore. To appear.

Yoav Goldberg and Michael Elhadad. 2008. splitSVM: fast, space-efficient, non-heuristic, polynomial kernel computation for NLP applications. In *ACL'08, Short Papers*, pages 237–240, Columbus, Ohio.

Ryan McDonald, Fernando Pereira, Kiril Ribarov, and Jan Hajič. 2005. Non-projective dependency parsing using spanning tree algorithms. In *HLT-EMNLP 2005*, pages 523–530, Vancouver, British Columbia.

Joakim Nivre, Johan Hall, Sandra Kübler, Ryan McDonald, Jens Nilsson, Sebastian Riedel, and Deniz Yuret. 2007. The CONLL 2007 shared task on dependency parsing. In *EMNLP-CONLL'07*, pages 915–932, Prague, Czech Republic.

Adwait Ratnaparkhi. 1998. *Maximum entropy models for natural language ambiguity resolution*. Ph.D. thesis, University of Pennsylvania.

Le Zhang. 2004. Maximum entropy modeling toolkit for Python and C++. University of Edinburgh. Available at homepages.inf.ed.ac.uk/lzhang10/maxent_toolkit.html.

HPSG Supertagging: A Sequence Labeling View

Yao-zhong Zhang [†] **Takuya Matsuzaki** [†] **Jun'ichi Tsujii**[†‡§]

† Department of Computer Science, University of Tokyo
‡ School of Computer Science, University of Manchester
§National Centre for Text Mining, UK
{yaozhong.zhang, matuzaki, tsujii}@is.s.u-tokyo.ac.jp

Abstract

Supertagging is a widely used speed-up technique for deep parsing. In another aspect, supertagging has been exploited in other NLP tasks than parsing for utilizing the rich syntactic information given by the supertags. However, the performance of supertagger is still a bottleneck for such applications. In this paper, we investigated the relationship between supertagging and parsing, not just to speed up the deep parser; We started from a sequence labeling view of HPSG supertagging, examining how well a supertagger can do when separated from parsing. Comparison of two types of supertagging model, point-wise model and sequential model, showed that the former model works competitively well despite its simplicity, which indicates the true dependency among supertag assignments is far more complex than the crude first-order approximation made in the sequential model. We then analyzed the limitation of separated supertagging by using a CFG-filter. The results showed that big gains could be acquired by resorting to a light-weight parser.

1 Introduction

Supertagging is an important part of lexicalized grammar parsing. A high performance supertagger greatly reduces the load of a parser and accelerates its speed. A supertag represents a linguistic word category, which encodes syntactic behavior of the word. The concept of supertagging was first proposed for lexicalized tree adjoining grammar (LTAG) (Bangalore and Joshi, 1999) and then extended to other lexicalized grammars, such as combinatory categorial grammar (CCG) (Clark, 2002) and Head-driven phrase structure grammar (HPSG) (Ninomiya et al., 2006). Recently, syntactic information in supertags has been exploited for NLP tasks besides parsing, such as NP chunking (Shen and Joshi, 2003), semantic role labeling (Chen and Rambow, 2003) and machine translation (Hassan et al., 2007). Supertagging serves there as an implicit and convenient way to incorporate rich syntactic information in those tasks.

Improving the performance of supertagging can thus benefit these two aspects: as a preprocessor for deep parsing and as an independent, alternative technique for "almost" parsing. However, supertags are derived from a grammar and thus have a strong connection to parsing. To further improve the supertagging accuracy, the relation between supertagging and parsing is crucial. With this motivation, we investigate how well a sequence labeling model can do when it is separated from a parser, and to what extent the ignorance of long distance dependencies in the sequence labeling formulation affects the supertagging results.

Specifically, we evaluated two different types of supertagging model, point-wise model and sequential model, for HPSG supertagging. CFG-filter was then used to empirically evaluate the effect of long distance dependencies in supertagging. The point-wise model achieved competitive result of 92.53% accuracy on WSJ-HPSG treebank with fast training speed, while the sequential model augmented with supertag edge features did not give much further improvement over the point-wise model. Big gains acquired by using CFG-filter indicates that further improvement may be achieved by resorting to a light-weight parser.

2 HPSG Supertags

HPSG (Pollard and Sag, 1994) is a kind of lexicalized grammar. In HPSG, many lexical entries are used to express word-specific characteristics,

Proceedings of the 11th International Conference on Parsing Technologies (IWPT), pages 210–213,
Paris, October 2009.

while only small amount of rule schemas are used to describe general constructions. A supertag in HPSG corresponds to a template of lexical entry. For example, one possible supertag for "big" is "[<ADJP>]N_lxm", which indicates that the syntactic category of "big" is adjective and it modifies a noun to its right. The number of supertags is generally much larger than the number of labels used in other sequence labeling tasks; Comparing to 45 POS tags used in PennTreebank, the HPSG grammar used in our experiments includes 2,308 supertags. Because of this, it is often very hard or even impossible to apply computationary demanding methods to HPSG supertagging.

3 Perceptron and Bayes Point Machine

Perceptron is an efficient online discriminative training method. We used perceptron with weight-averaging (Collins, 2002) as the basis of our supertagging model. We also use perceptron-based Bayes point machine (BPM) (Herbrich et al., 2001) in some of the experiments. In short, a BPM is an average of a number of averaged perceptrons' weights. We use average of 10 averaged perceptrons, each of which is trained on a different random permutation of the training data.

3.1 Formulation

Here we follow the definition of Collins' perceptron to learn a mapping from the input space $(w, p) \in W \times P$ to the supertag space $s \in S$. We use function **GEN(w,p)** to indicate all candidates given input (w, p). Feature function **f** maps a training sample $(w, p, s) \in W \times P \times S$ to a point in the feature space R^d. To get feature weights $\alpha \in R^d$ of feature function, we used the averaged perceptron training method described in (Collins, 2002), and the average of its 10 different runs (i.e., BPM). For decoding, given an input (w, p) and a vector of feature weights α, we want to find an output s which satisfies:

$$F(w, p) = \underset{s \in \mathbf{GEN(w,\ p)}}{argmax} \quad \alpha \cdot f(w, p, s)$$

For the input (w, p), we treat it in two fashions: one is (w, p) representing a single word and a POS tag. Another is (w, p) representing whole word and POS tags sequence. We call them point-wise model and sequential model respectively. Viterbi algorithm is used for decoding in sequential model.

template type	template
Word	w_i,w_{i-1},w_{i+1}, $w_{i-1}\&w_i$, $w_i\&w_{i+1}$
POS	p_i, p_{i-1}, p_{i-2}, p_{i+1}, p_{i+2}, $p_{i-1}\&p_i$, $p_{i-2}\&p_{i-1}$, $p_{i-1}\&p_{i+1}$, $p_i\&p_{i+1}$, $p_{i+1}\&p_{i+2}$
Word-POS	$p_{i-1}\&w_i$, $p_i\&w_i$, $p_{i+1}\&w_i$
Supertag†	s_{i-1} , $s_{i-2}\&s_{i-1}$
Substructure	$\{ss_{i,1}, ..., ss_{i,N}\}\times$ Word $\{ss_{i,1}, ..., ss_{i,N}\}\times$ POS $\{ss_{i,1}, ..., ss_{i,N}\}\times$ Word-POS $\{ss_{i-1,1}, ..., ss_{i-1,N}\}\times$ $\{ss_{i,1}, ..., ss_{i,N}\}^\dagger$

Table 1: Feature templates for point-wise model and sequential model. Templates with † are only used by sequential model. $ss_{i,j}$ represents j-th substructure of supertag at i. For briefness, s_i is omitted for each template. "$\times$" means set-product. e.g., {a,b}×{A,B}={a&A,a&B,b&A,b&B}

3.2 Features

Feature templates are listed in Table 1. To make the results comparable with previous work, we adopt the same feature templates as Matsuzaki et. al. (2007). For sequential model, supertag contexts are added to the features. Because of the large number of supertags, those supertag edge features could be very sparse. To alleviate this sparseness, we extracted sub-structures from the lexical template of each supertag, and use them for making generalized node/edge features as shown in Table 1. The sub-structures we used include subcategorization frames (e.g., subject=NP, object=NP_PP), direction and category of modifiee phrase (e.g., mod_left=VP), voice and tense of a verb (e.g., passive_past).

3.3 CFG-filter

Long distance dependencies are also encoded in supertags. For example, when a transitive verb gets assigned a supertag that specifies it has a PP-object, in most cases a preposition to its right must be assigned an argument (not adjunct) supertag, and vice versa. Such kind of long distance context information might be important for supertag disambiguation, but is not easy to incorporate into a sequence labeling model separated from a parser.

To examine the limitation of supertagging separated from a parser, we used CFG-filter as an ap-

Model Name	Acc%
PW-AP	92.29
SEQ-AP	92.53
PW-AP+CFG	**93.57**
SEQ-AP+CFG	**93.68**

Table 2: Averaged 10-cross validation of averaged perceptron on Section 02-21.

proximation of an HPSG parser. We firstly created a CFG that approximates the original HPSG grammar, using the iterative method by Kiefer and Krieger (2000). Given the supertags as preterminals, the approximating CFG was then used for finding a maximally scored sequence of supertags which satisfies most of the grammatical constraints in the original HPSG grammar (Matsuzaki et al., 2007). By comparing the supertagging results before and after CFG-filtering, we can quantify how many errors are caused by ignorance of the long-range dependencies in supertagger.

4 Experiments and Analysis

We conducted experiments on WSJ-HPSG treebank corpus (Miyao, 2006), which was semi-automatically converted from the WSJ portion of PennTreebank. The number of training iterations was set to 5 for all models. Gold-standard POS tags are used as input. The performance is evaluated by accuracy[1] and speed of supertagging on an AMD Opteron 2.4GHz server.

Table 2 shows the averaged results of 10-fold cross-validation of averaged perceptron (AP) models[2] on section 02-21. We can see the difference between point-wise AP model and sequential AP model is small (0.24%). It becomes even smaller after CFG-filtering (0.11%). Table 3 shows the supertagging accuracy on section 22 based on BPM. Although not statistically significantly different from previous ME model (Matsuzaki et al., 2007), point-wise model (PW-BPM) achieved competitive result 92.53% with faster training. In addition, 0.27% and 0.29% gains were brought by using BPM from PW-AP (92.26%) and PW-SEQ (92.54%) with P-values less than 0.05.

The improvement by using sequential models (PW-AP→SEQ-AP: 0.24%, PW-BPM→SEQ-BPM: 0.3%, statistically significantly different), compared to point-wise models, were not so large, but the training time was around 6 times longer. We think the reason is twofold. First, as previous research showed, POS sequence is very informative in supertagging (Clark, 2004). A large amount of local syntactic information can be captured in POS tags of surrounding words, although a few long-range dependencies are of course not. Second, the number of supertags is large and the supertag edge features used in sequential model are inevitably suffered from data sparseness. To alleviate this, we extracted sub-structure from lexical templates (i.e., lexical items corresponding to supertags) to augment the supertag edge features, but only got 0.16% improvement (SEQ-BPM+SUB). Furthermore, we also got 0.15% gains with P-value less than 0.05 by incorporating the sub-structure features into point-wise model (PW-BPM+SUB). We hence conclude that the contribution of the first-order edge features is not large in sequence modeling for HPSG supertagging.

Model Name	Acc%	Training/ Testing Time ‡
ME (Matsuzaki 07')	92.45	≈ 3h / 12s
PW-BPM	92.53	**285s / 10s**
SEQ-BPM	92.83	1721s / 13s
PW-BPM+SUB	92.68	1275s / 25s
SEQ-BPM+SUB	92.99	9468s / 107s
PW-BPM+CFG	**93.60**	**285s / 78s**
SEQ-BPM+CFG	**93.70**	1721s / 195s
PW-BPM+SUB+CFG	**93.72**	1275s / 170s
SEQ-BPM+SUB+CFG	**93.88**	9468s / 1011s

Table 3: Supertagging accuracy and training& testing speed on section 22. (‡) Test time was calculated on totally 1648 sentences.

As we explained in Section 3.3, sequence labeling models have inherent limitation in the ability to capture long distance dependencies between supertags. This kind of ambiguity could be easier to solve in a parser. To examine this, we added CFG-filter which works as an approximation of a full HPSG parser, after the sequence labeling model. As expected, there came big gains of 1.26% (from PW-AP to PW-AP+CFG) and 1.15% (from PW-BPM to PW-BPM+CFG). Even for the sequential model we also got 1.15% (from SEQ-AP to SEQ-AP+CFG) and 0.87% (from SEQ-BPM to SEQ-BPM+CFG) respectively. All these models were statistically significantly different from orig-

[1] "UNK" supertags are ignored in evaluation as previous.

[2] For time limitation, cross validation for BPM was not conducted.

inal ones.

We also gave error analysis on test results. Comparing SEQ-AP with SEQ-AP+CFG, one of the most frequent types of "correct supertag" by the CFG-filter was for word "and", wherein a supertag for NP-coordination ("NP and NP") was corrected to one for VP-coordination ("VP and VP" or "S and S"). It means the disambiguation between the two coordination type is difficult for supertaggers, presumably because they looks very similar with a limited length of context since the sequence of the NP-object of left conjunct, "and", the NP subject of right conjunct looks very similar to a NP coordination. The different assignments by SEQ-AP+CFG from SEQ-AP include 725 right corrections, while it changes 298 correct predictions by SEQ-AP to wrong assignments. One possible reason for some of "wrong correction" is related to the approximation of grammar. But this gives clue that for supertagging task: just using sequence labeling models is limited, and we can resort to use some light-weight parser to handle long distance dependencies.

Although some of the ambiguous supertags could be left for deep parsing, like multi-tagging technique (Clark, 2004), we also consider the tasks where supertags can be used while conducting deep parsing is too computationally costly. Alternatively, focusing on supertagging, we could treat it as a sequence labeling task, while a consequent light-weight parser is a disambiguator with long distance constraint.

5 Conclusions

In this paper, through treating HPSG supertagging in a sequence labeling way, we examined the relationship between supertagging and parsing from an angle. In experiment, even for sequential models, CFG-filter gave much larger improvement than one gained by switching from a point-wise model to a sequential model. The accuracy improvement given by the CFG-filter suggests that we could gain further improvement by combining a supertagger with a light-weight parser.

Acknowledgments

Thanks to the anonymous reviewers for valuable comments. The first author was partially supported by University of Tokyo Fellowship (UT-Fellowship). This work was partially supported by Grant-in-Aid for Specially Promoted Research and Special Coordination Funds for Promoting Science and Technology (MEXT, Japan).

References

Srinivas Bangalore and Aravind K. Joshi. 1999. Supertagging: An approach to almost parsing. *Computational Linguistics*, 25:237–265.

John Chen and Owen Rambow. 2003. Use of deep linguistic features for the recognition and labeling of semantic arguments. In *Proceedings of EMNLP-2003*, pages 41–48.

Stephen Clark. 2002. Supertagging for combinatory categorial grammar. In *Proceedings of the 6th International Workshop on Tree Adjoining Grammars and Related Frameworks (TAG+ 6)*, pages 19–24.

Stephen Clark. 2004. The importance of supertagging for wide-coverage ccg parsing. In *Proceedings of COLING-04*, pages 282–288.

Michael Collins. 2002. Discriminative training methods for hidden markov models: Theory and experiments with perceptron algorithms. pages 1–8.

Hany Hassan, Mary Hearne, and Andy Way. 2007. Supertagged phrase-based statistical machine translation. In *Proceedings of ACL 2007*, pages 288–295.

Ralf Herbrich, Thore Graepel, and Colin Campbell. 2001. Bayes point machines. *Journal of Machine Learning Research*, 1:245–279.

Bernd Kiefer and Hans-Ulrich Krieger. 2000. A context-free approximation of head-driven phrase structure grammar. In *Proceedings of IWPT-2000*, pages 135–146.

Takuya Matsuzaki, Yusuke Miyao, and Jun'ichi Tsujii. 2007. Efficient hpsg parsing with supertagging and cfg-filtering. In *Proceedings of IJCAI-07*, pages 1671–1676.

Yusuke Miyao. 2006. *From Linguistic Theory to Syntactic Analysis: Corpus-Oriented Grammar Development and Feature Forest Model*. Ph.D. Dissertation, The University of Tokyo.

Takashi Ninomiya, Yoshimasa Tsuruoka, Takuya Matsuzaki, and Yusuke Miyao. 2006. Extremely lexicalized models for accurate and fast hpsg parsing. In *Proceedings of EMNLP-2006*, pages 155–163.

Carl Pollard and Ivan A. Sag. 1994. *Head-driven Phrase Structure Grammar*. University of Chicago / CSLI.

Libin Shen and Aravind K. Joshi. 2003. A snow based supertagger with application to np chunking. In *Proceedings of ACL 2003*, pages 505–512.

Smoothing fine-grained PCFG lexicons

Tejaswini Deoskar
ILLC
University of Amsterdam
t.deoskar@uva.nl

Mats Rooth
Dept. of Linguistics and CIS
Cornell University
mr249@cornell.edu

Khalil Sima'an
ILLC
University of Amsterdam
k.simaan@uva.nl

Abstract

We present an approach for smoothing treebank-PCFG lexicons by interpolating treebank lexical parameter estimates with estimates obtained from unannotated data via the Inside-outside algorithm. The PCFG has complex lexical categories, making relative-frequency estimates from a treebank very sparse. This kind of smoothing for complex lexical categories results in improved parsing performance, with a particular advantage in identifying obligatory arguments subcategorized by verbs unseen in the treebank.

1 Introduction

Lexical scarcity is a problem faced by all statistical NLP applications that depend on annotated training data, including parsing. One way of alleviating this problem is to supplement supervised models with lexical information from unlabeled data. In this paper, we present an approach for smoothing the lexicon of a treebank PCFG with frequencies estimated from unannotated data with Inside-outside estimation (Lari and Young, 1990). The PCFG is an unlexicalised PCFG, but contains complex lexical categories (akin to *supertags* in LTAG (Bangalore and Joshi, 1999) or CCG (Clark and Curran, 2004)) encoding structural preferences of words, like subcategorization.

The idea behind unlexicalised parsing is that the syntax and lexicon of a language are largely independent, being mediated by "selectional" properties of open-class words. This is the intuition behind lexicalised formalisms like CCG: here lexical categories are fine-grained and syntactic in nature. Once a word is assigned a lexical category, the word itself is not taken into consideration further in the syntactic analysis. Fine-grained categories imply that lexicons estimated from treebanks will be extremely sparse, even for a language like English with a large treebank resource like the Penn Treebank (PTB) (Marcus et al., 1993). Smoothing a treebank lexicon with an external wide-coverage lexicon is problematic due to their respective representations being incompatible and without an obvious mapping, assuming that the external lexicon is probabilistic to begin with. In this paper, we start with a treebank PCFG with fine-grained lexical categories and *re-estimate* its parameters on a large corpus of unlabeled data. We then use re-estimates of lexical parameters (i.e. pre-terminal to terminal rule probabilities) to smooth the original treebank lexical parameters by interpolation between the two. Since the treebank PCFG itself is used to propose analyses of new data, the mapping problem is inherently taken care of. The smoothing procedure takes into account the fact that unsupervised estimation has benefits for unseen or low-frequency lexical items, but the treebank relative-frequency estimates are more reliable in the case of high-frequency items.

2 Treebank PCFG

In order to have fine-grained and linguistic lexical categories (like CCG) within a simple formalism with well-understood estimation methods, we first build a PCFG containing such categories from the PTB. The PCFG is unlexicalised (with limited lexicalization of certain function words, like in Klein and Manning (2003)). It is created by first transforming the PTB (Johnson, 1998) in an appropriate way and then extracting a PCFG from the transformed trees (Deoskar and Rooth, 2008). All functional tags in the PTB (such as NP-SBJ, PP-TMP, etc.) are maintained, as are all empty categories, making long-distance dependencies recoverable. The PCFG is trained on the standard training sections of the PTB and performs at the state-of-the-art level for unlexicalised PCFGs, giving 86.6% f-score on Sec. 23.

Proceedings of the 11th International Conference on Parsing Technologies (IWPT), pages 214–217,

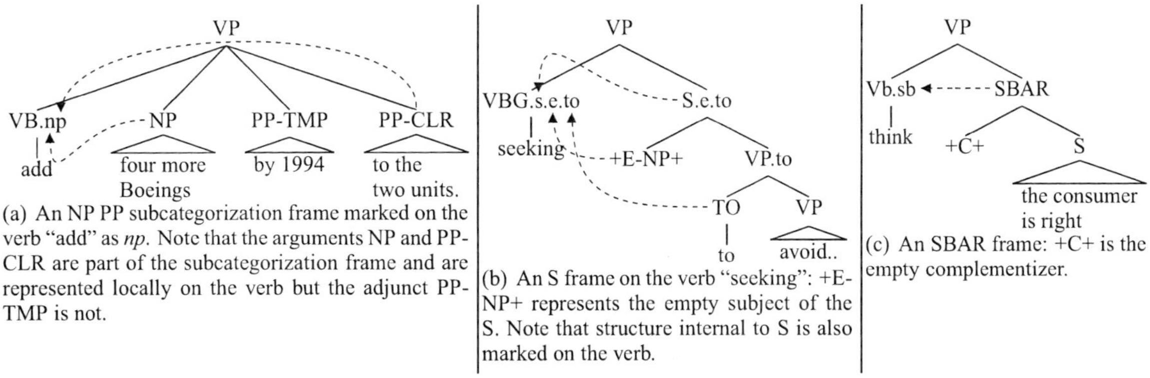

(a) An NP PP subcategorization frame marked on the verb "add" as *np*. Note that the arguments NP and PP-CLR are part of the subcategorization frame and are represented locally on the verb but the adjunct PP-TMP is not.

(b) An S frame on the verb "seeking": +E-NP+ represents the empty subject of the S. Note that structure internal to S is also marked on the verb.

(c) An SBAR frame: +C+ is the empty complementizer.

Figure 1: Subcategorized structures are marked as features on the verbal POS category.

An important feature of our PCFG is that pre-terminal categories for open-class items like verbs, nouns and adverbs are more complex than PTB POS tags. They encode information about the structure selected by the lexical item, in effect, its subcategorization frame. A pre-terminal in our PCFG consists of the standard PTB POS tag, followed by a sequence of features incorporated into it. Thus, each PTB POS tag can be considered to be divided into multiple finer-grained "supertags" by the incorporated features. These features encode the structure selected by the words. We focus on verbs in this paper, as they are important structural determiners. A sequence of one or more features forms the "subcategorization frame" of a verb: three examples are shown in Figure 1. The features are determined by a fully automated process based on PTB tree structure and node labels. There are 81 distinct subcategorization frames for verbal categories. The process can be repeated for other languages with a treebank annotated in the PTB style which marks arguments like the PTB.

3 Unsupervised Re-estimation

Inside-outside (henceforth I-O) (Lari and Young, 1990), an instance of EM, is an iterative estimation method for PCFGs that, given an initial model and a corpus of unannotated data, produces models that assign increasingly higher likelihood to the corpus at each iteration. I-O often leads to sub-optimal grammars, being subject to the well-known problem of local maxima, and dependence on initial conditions (de Marcken, 1995) (although there have been positive results using I-O as well, for e.g. Beil et al. (1999)). More recently, Deoskar (2008) re-estimated an unlexicalised PTB PCFG using unlabeled Wall Street Journal data. They compared models for which all PCFG parameters were re-estimated from raw data to models for which only lexical parameters were re-estimated, and found that the latter had better parsing results. While it is common to constrain EM either by good initial conditions or by heuristic constraints, their approach used syntactic parameters from a treebank model to constrain re-estimation of lexical parameters. Syntactic parameters are relatively well-estimated from a treebank, not being as sparse as lexical parameters. At each iteration, the re-estimated lexicon was interpolated with a treebank lexicon, ensuring that re-estimated lexicons did not drift away from the treebank lexicon.

We follow their methodology of constrained EM re-estimation. Using the PCFG with fine lexical categories (as described in §2) as the initial model, we re-estimate its parameters from an unannotated corpus. The lexical parameters of the re-estimated PCFG form its probabilistic "lexicon", containing the same fine-grained categories as the original treebank PCFG. We use this re-estimated "lexicon" to smooth the lexical probabilities in the treebank PCFG.

4 Smoothing based on a POS tagger : the initial model.

In order to use the treebank PCFG as an initial model for unsupervised estimation, new words from the unannotated training corpus must be included in it – if not, parameter values for new words will never be induced. Since the treebank model contains no information regarding correct feature sequences for unseen words, we assign all possible sequences that have occurred in the treebank model with the POS tag of the word. We assign all possible sequences to *seen* words as well – although the word is seen, the correct feature sequence for a structure in a training sentence might still be unseen with that word. This is done as follows: a standard POS-tagger (TreeTagger, (Schmid, 1994)) is used to tag the unlabeled corpus. A frequency table $c_{pos}(w, \tau)$ consisting of words and POS-tags is extracted from the resulting corpus, where w is the word and τ its POS tag. The frequency $c_{pos}(w, \tau)$ is split amongst all possible feature sequences ι for that POS tag in proportion to treebank marginals $t(\tau, \iota)$ and $t(\tau)$

$$c_{pos}(w, \tau, \iota) = \frac{t(\tau, \iota)}{t(\tau)} c_{pos}(w, \tau) \quad (1)$$

Then the treebank frequency $t(w, \tau, \iota)$ and the scaled corpus frequency are interpolated to get a smoothed model t_{pos}. We use λ=0.001, giving a small weight initially to the unlabeled corpus.

$$t_{pos}(w, \tau, \iota) = (1 - \lambda)t(w, \tau, \iota) + \lambda c_{pos}(w, \tau, \iota) \quad (2)$$

The first term will be zero for words unseen in the treebank: their distribution in the smoothed model will be the average treebank distribution over all possible feature sequences for a POS tag. For seen words, the treebank distribution over feature sequence is largely maintained, but a small frequency is assigned to unseen sequences.

5 Smoothing based on EM re-estimation

After each iteration i of I-O, the expected counts $c_{em_i}(w, \tau, \iota)$ under the model instance at iteration $(i - 1)$ are obtained. A smoothed treebank lexicon t_{em_i} is obtained by linearly interpolating the smoothed treebank lexicon $t_{pos}(w, \tau, \iota)$ and a scaled re-estimated lexicon $\bar{c}_{em_i}(w, \tau, \iota)$.

$$t_{em_i}(w, \tau, \iota) = (1-\lambda)t_{pos}(w, \tau, \iota) + \lambda\bar{c}_{em_i}(w, \tau, \iota) \quad (3)$$

where $0 < \lambda < 1$. The term $\bar{c}_{em_i}(w, \tau, \iota)$ is obtained by scaling the frequencies $c_{em_i}(w, \tau, \iota)$ obtained by I-O, ensuring that the treebank lexicon is not swamped with the large training corpus[1].

$$\bar{c}_{em_i}(w, \tau, \iota) = \frac{t(\tau, \iota)}{\sum_w c_{em_i}(w, \tau, \iota)} c_{em_i}(w, \tau, \iota) \quad (4)$$

λ determines the relative weights given to the treebank and re-estimated model for a word. Since parameters of high-frequency words are likely to be more accurate in the treebank model, we parametrize λ as λ_f according to the treebank frequency $f = t(w, \tau)$.

[1]Note that in Eq. 4, the ratio of the two terms involving c_{em_i} is the conditional, lexical probability $P_{em_i}(w|\tau, \iota)$.

6 Experiments

The treebank PCFG is trained on sections 0-22 of the PTB, with 5000 sentences held-out for evaluation. We conducted unsupervised estimation using Bitpar (Schmid, 2004) with unannotated Wall Street Journal data of 4, 8 and 12 million words, with sentence length <25 words. The treebank and re-estimated models are interpolated with $\lambda = 0.5$ (in Eq. 3). We also parametrize λ for treebank frequency of words – optimizing over a development set gives us the following values of λ_f for different ranges of treebank word frequencies.

$$\begin{array}{ll} \text{if}\, t(w, \tau) <= 5\,, & \lambda_f = 0.5 \\ \text{if}\, 5 < t(w, \tau) <= 15\,, & \lambda_f = 0.25 \\ \text{if}\, 15 < t(w, \tau) <= 50\,, & \lambda_f = 0.05 \\ \text{if}\, t(w, \tau) > 50\,, & \lambda_f = 0.005 \end{array} \quad (5)$$

Evaluations are on held-out data from the PTB by stripping all PTB annotation and obtaining Viterbi parses with the parser Bitpar. In addition to standard PARSEVAL measures, we also evaluate parses by another measure specific to subcategorization[2]: the POS-tag+feature sequence on verbs in the Viterbi parse is compared against the corresponding tag+feature sequence on the transformed PTB gold tree, and errors are counted. The tag-feature sequence correlates to the structure selected by the verb, as exemplified in Fig. 1.

7 Results

There is a statistically significant improvement[3] in labeled bracketing f-score on Sec. 23 when the treebank lexicon is smoothed with an EM-re-estimated lexicon. In Table 1, t_t refers to the baseline treebank model, smoothed using the POS-tag smoothing method (from §4) on the test data (Sec. 23) in order to incorporate new words from the test data[4]. t_{pos} refers to the initial model for re-estimation, obtained by smoothed the treebank model with the POS-tag smoothing method with the large unannotated corpus (4 million words). This model understandably does not improve over t_t for parsing Sec. 23. $t_{em_1,\lambda=0.5}$ is the model obtained by smoothing with an EM-re-estimated model with a constant interpolation factor $\lambda = 0.5$. This model gives a statistically significant improvement in f-score over both t_t and t_{pos}. The last model t_{em_1,λ_f} is obtained by smoothing with

[2]PARSEVAL measures are known to be insensitive to subcategorization (Carroll et al., 1998).

[3]A randomized version of a paired-sample t-test is used.

[4]This is always done before parsing test data.

	t_t	t_{pos}	$t_{em_1,\lambda=0.5}$	t_{em_1,λ_f}
Recall	86.48	86.48	86.72	87.44
Precision	86.61	86.63	86.95	87.15
f-score	86.55	86.56	*86.83	*87.29

Table 1: Labeled bracketing F-score on section 23.

an interpolation factor as in Eq. 5 : this is the best model with a statistically significant improvement in f-score over t_t, t_{pos} and $t_{em_1,\lambda=0.5}$.

Since we expect that smoothing will be advantageous for unseen or low-frequency words, we perform an evaluation targeted at identifying structures subcategorized by unseen verbs. Table 2 shows the error reduction in identifying subcat. frames in Viterbi parses, of unseen verbs and also of all verbs (seen and unseen) in the testset. A breakup of error by frame type for unseen verbs is also shown (here, only frames with >10 token occurrences in the *test* data are shown). In all cases (unseen verbs and all verbs) we see a substantial error reduction. The error reduction improves with larger amounts of unannotated training data.

Frame	# tokens (test)	%Error t_{pos}	%Error t_{em_1}	%Error Reduc.
All unseen (4M words)	1258	33.47	22.81	31.84
All unseen (8M words)	1258	33.47	22.26	33.49
All unseen (12M words)	1258	33.47	21.86	34.68
transitive	662	23.87	18.73	21.52
intransitive	115	38.26	33.91	11.36
NP PP-CLR	121	34.71	32.23	7.14
PP-CLR	73	27.4	20.55	25
SBAR	124	12.1	12.1	0
S	12	83.33	58.33	30
NP NP	10	90	80	11.11
PRT NP	21	38.1	33.33	12.5
s.e.to (see Fig.1b)	50	16	12	25
NP PP-DIR	11	63.64	54.55	14.28
All verbs (4M)	11710	18.5	16.84	8.97

Table 2: Subcat. error for verbs in Viterbi parses.

8 Discussion and Conclusions

We have shown that lexicons re-estimated with I-O can be used to smooth unlexicalised treebank PCFGs, with a significant increase in f-score even in the case of English with a large treebank resource. We expect this method to have more impact for languages with a smaller treebank or richer tag-set. An interesting aspect is the substantial reduction in subcategorization error for unseen verbs for which no word-specific information about subcategorization exists in the unsmoothed or POS-tag-smoothed lexicon. The error reduction in identifying subcat. frames implies that some constituents (such as PPs) are not only attached correctly but also identified correctly as arguments (such as PP-CLR) rather than as adjuncts.

There have been previous attempts to use POS-tagging technologies (such as HMM or maximum-entropy based taggers) to enhance treebank-trained grammars (Goldberg et al. (2009) for Hebrew, (Clark and Curran, 2004) for CCG). The re-estimation method we use builds full parse-trees, rather than use local features like taggers do, and hence might have a benefit over such methods. An interesting option would be to train a "supertagger" on fine-grained tags from the PTB and to supertag a large corpus to harvest lexical frequencies. This would form another (possibly higher) baseline for the I-O re-estimation approach presented here and is the focus of our future work.

References

S. Bangalore and A. K. Joshi. 1999. Supertagging: An Approach to Almost Parsing. *Computational Linguistics*, 25:237–265.

F. Beil, G. Carroll, D. Prescher, S. Riezler, and M. Rooth. 1999. Inside-outside estimation of a lexicalized PCFG for German. In *ACL 37*.

J. Carroll, G. Minnen, and E. Briscoe. 1998. Can subcategorization probabilities help parsing. In *6th ACL/SIGDAT Workshop on Very Large Corpora*.

S. Clark and J. R. Curran. 2004. The Importance of Supertagging for Wide-Coverage CCG Parsing. In *22nd COLING*.

Carl de Marcken. 1995. On the unsupervised induction of Phrase Structure grammars. In *Proceedings of the 3rd Workshop on Very Large Corpora*.

T. Deoskar. 2008. Re-estimation of Lexical Parameters for Treebank PCFGs. In *22nd COLING*.

Tejaswini Deoskar and Mats Rooth. 2008. Induction of Treebank-Aligned Lexical Resources. In *6th LREC*.

Y. Goldberg, R. Tsarfaty, M. Adler, and M. Elhadad. 2009. Enhancing Unlexicalized Parsing Performance using a Wide Coverage Lexicon, Fuzzy Tag-set Mapping, and EM-HMM-based Lexical Probabilities. In *EACL-09*.

M. Johnson. 1998. PCFG models of linguistic tree representations. *Computational Linguistics*, 24(4).

D. Klein and C. Manning. 2003. Accurate unlexicalized parsing. In *ACL 41*.

K. Lari and S. J. Young. 1990. The estimation of stochastic context-free grammars using the Inside-Outside algorithm. *Computer Speech and Language*, 4:35–56.

M. P. Marcus, B. Santorini, and M. A. Marcinkiewicz. 1993. Building a Large Annotated Corpus of English: The Penn Treebank. *Computational Linguistics*, 19(2):313–330.

H. Schmid. 1994. Probabilistic Part-of-Speech Tagging Using Decision Trees. In *International Conference on New Methods in Language Processing*.

H. Schmid. 2004. Efficient Parsing of Highly Ambiguous CFGs with Bit Vectors. In *20th COLING*.

Wide-coverage parsing of speech transcripts

Jeroen Geertzen
Research Centre for English & Applied Linguistics
University of Cambridge, UK
jg532@cam.ac.uk

Abstract

This paper discusses the performance difference of wide-coverage parsers on small-domain speech transcripts. Two parsers (C&C CCG and RASP) are tested on the speech transcripts of two different domains (parent-child language, and picture descriptions).

The performance difference between the domain-independent parsers and two domain-trained parsers (MSTParser and MEGRASP) is substantial, with a difference of at least 30 percent point in accuracy. Despite this gap, some of the grammatical relations can still be recovered reliably.

1 Introduction

Even though wide-coverage, domain-independent[1] parser systems may perform sufficiently well for the task at hand, obtaining highly accurate parses of sentences in a particular domain usually requires the parser to be domain-trained. Training a parser requires a sufficient amount of labelled data (a gold standard), something that is only available for very few domains. When accurate parses of sentences in a new domain are desired, there are several ways to proceed. Hand labelling all data in the new domain is a consideration, but is usually unfeasible as manual annotation is a costly activity. Another possibility is to minimise the amount of annotation effort required to achieve good performance by resorting to semi-automatic annotation or domain adaptation methods. In any case, dedicated effort is still required to obtain highly accurate parses, even with recent automated domain adaptation methods (Dredze et al., 2007).

Work that requires parsing in a new domain as basis of further study or as part of a larger natural language processing system usually involves a domain-independent parser with the expectation that parses are sufficiently accurate for the specific purpose.[2] For instance, Bos and Markert (2005) use a wide-coverage CCG-parser (Clark and Curran, 2007) to generate semantic representations for recognising textual entailment. Geertzen (2009) uses a HPSG-based dependency parser (Bouma et al., 2001) to obtain the semantic content of utterances. And in the study of child language acquisition, Buttery and Korhonen (2007) use RASP, a wide-coverage dependency parser (Briscoe et al., 2006), to look at lexical acquisition.

The goal of this paper is to give an indication of wide-coverage, domain-independent parser performance on specific domains. Additionally, the study gives insight into RASP's performance on CHILDES, allowing to factor in parsing performance in the syntax-based study of Buttery and Korhonen (2007).

2 Parsing speech transcripts

Parsing performance of two domain-independent parsers, C&C CCG en RASP, is evaluated on two speech domains. The first domain, CHILDES, involves parent-child interactions; the second domain, CCC, involves a picture description task.

2.1 Parsing systems

Two wide-coverage parser systems are used. RASP (Briscoe et al., 2006) is a parsing system for

[1]In this paper, the terms 'wide-coverage' and 'domain-independent' are used synonymously.

[2]Without gold standard there is no way of knowing how well the parser component performs with respect to a desired outcome of syntactic structure. This may not necessarily be a problem, as parsing in such cases is paramount, and application-based evaluation is preferable. Moreover, it may be that using linguistically most desired parses does not result in best application performance.

Proceedings of the 11th International Conference on Parsing Technologies (IWPT), pages 218–221,
Paris, October 2009.

English that utilises a manually-developed grammar and outputs grammatical dependency relations. The C&C CCG parser (Clark and Curran, 2007) is a parsing system that is based on an automatically extracted grammar from CCG-Bank and uses discriminative training. Both systems are able to output the exact set of dependency relations, and in a comparison on a 560-sentence test set used by Briscoe and Carroll (2006), Clark and Curran (2007) report a micro-averaged F-score of 81.14 for the CCG parser, and 76.29 for RASP. [3] Both parsing systems utilise the Grammatical Relations (GR) annotation scheme proposed by Carroll et al. (1998). This scheme is intended to cater for parser evaluation, and extends the dependency structure based method of evaluation proposed by Lin (1998). For the parent-child interaction domain both parsing systems are compared with two syntactic dependency parsers that were specifically trained for CHILDES transcripts: MEGRASP (Sagae et al., 2007) and MST-parser (McDonald et al., 2005).

2.2 Speech phenomena

As CCC and CHILDES transcripts are describing spoken language, they contain various markers that encode speech phenomena, particularly disfluencies (e.g. filled pauses, partial words, false starts, repetitions) and speech repairs (e.g. retractions and corrections). Prior to parser evaluation, such disfluencies have been deleted from the transcripts, which slightly improves parser performance for all systems mentioned. Similar performance improvements are also reported in studies that address the effect of deletion of repairs and fillers on parsing (e.g. Charniak and Johnson (2001); Lease and Johnson (2006)).

2.3 CHILDES data

The major part of the evaluation is based on the parsing of parent-child interactions from the CHILDES database (MacWhinney, 2000). A large portion of CHILDES transcripts was recently parsed with a domain-specific parser (Sagae et al., 2007), allowing more reliable systematic studies of syntactic development in child language acquisition. Sagae et al. also released their gold standard data, allowing others to train and evaluate other parser systems.

The gold standard data uses a GR scheme that is based on that of Carroll et al. (1998) but that differs in two respects: the scheme is extended to suit the specific need of the child language research community (cf. (Sagae et al., 2004)), and the scheme does not extensively and explicitly use the GR hierarchy.

To compare parsing performance, a mapping from RASP GRs to CHILDES GRs was manually constructed, containing 75 rules that involve the label and optional restrictions on the word or POS-tag of the head or dependent.

3 Parser evaluation

3.1 Measures

System performance is reported with accuracy measures for labelled and unlabelled dependencies resulting from 15-fold cross-validation.[4] The performance on each grammatical relation is expressed by precision, recall, and F_1-score. Punctuation has been excluded.

3.2 CHILDES

The gold-standard used for evaluation is based on 15 (out of 20) files in the Eve section of the Brown corpus. The annotations that are available were made with the CHILDES GR scheme, for which an inter-annotator percentage agreement of 96.5% ($N = 2$) has been reported by Sagae et al. (2004). From all manually annotated utterances initially available, duplicates, those with less than three tokens (about 30% of all), and those with missing or incomplete parses (1% of all) were removed, resulting in a set of 14.137 sentences, comprising 93,594 tokens with 4.5 tokens per utterance on average.

The performance scores that are obtained when the parsing systems are compared against the gold-standard are listed in the upper part of Table 1.

As can be seen from the accuracy scores, MEGRASP and the MSTParser perform with more than 30 percent point accuracy considerably better than the domain-independent parsers. However, the list of performance scores for each of the grammatical relations in Table 2 shows that some relations can be recovered with acceptable

[3] It should be remarked that such cross-formalism comparisons are difficult in nature. In this case, training data were different (RASP is not tuned to newspaper text), and CCG utilises a lexicalised parsing model where RASP does not.

[4] The exception being the MEGRASP, for which because of computation problems the full gold standard was used (7% larger than the other training sets), resulting in somewhat higher scores than expected with cross-validation.

Table 1: Parsing accuracy scores.

CHILDES	*labelled*	*unlabelled*
RASP	60.1	69.2
CCG parser	39.1	66.5
MSTParser	93.8	95.4
MEGRASP	90.7	93.5
CCC	*labelled*	*unlabelled*
RASP	66.7	72.3
CCG parser	60.2	68.5

F_1-scores, such as auxiliaries, determiners, subjects, and objects of prepositions.[5]

3.3 CCC

The Cambridge Cookie-theft Corpus (CCC, TO APPEAR, 2010) contains audio-recorded monologues of 196 subjects that were asked to fully describe a scene in a picture. As a result, the domain is small, but at the same time, sentence boundaries are difficult to indicate. From this corpus of 5,628 intonational phrases, a small evaluation set of 80 phrases has been manually annotated[6] with GRs. The performance scores for each of the parsers is listed in the lower part of Table 1. Accuracy scores are higher than those for CHILDES, and the difference in labelled accuracy between the domain-independent parsers is less than with CHILDES. Due to space restrictions it is not possible to present performance on individual GRs, but the GRs that are most reliably recovered are similar to those mentioned in Section 3.2.

4 Considerations

In the work reported here, performance of domain-independent parsers on narrow domains was calculated for two domains. The availability of more domain-specific datasets with manually supervised GR annotations would allow a better generalisation of parser performance. Unfortunately, datasets with manually verified annotations that use the same set of syntactic dependencies are rare.

The CHILDES figures show that the performance difference between domain-independent and domain-trained parsers is big. It should be noted that these results are obtained from speech, which is usually less syntactically well-formed than written language. For the speech data analysed, RASP performs better than the CCG parser, whereas Clark and Curran (2007) have shown that the CCG parser outperforms RASP on written text. To better explain this difference, it would be insightful to compare the confusion matrices of GR assignments. This would allow assessment on how the domain-independent parser errors compare to the domain-trained parser errors.

The mapping from RASP GRs to CHILDES GRs that was constructed is exhaustive, but there is still room for fine-tuning and more refined mappings, gaining up to about 2% accuracy by estimate.

5 Conclusions and future work

This paper has provided performance scores of wide-coverage parsers applied to narrow domain spoken language transcripts to assess the performance gap with domain-trained parsers. This gap appears to be considerable (more than 30 percent point for CHILDES), but a subset of GRs can still be recovered with fair accuracy.

We have not yet dealt with comparing domain-independent and domain-trained parser errors, which may provide additional insight into the strengths and weaknesses of wide-coverage parsers for narrow use.

Acknowledgements

This work is supported by UK EPSRC Grant EP/F030061/1.

References

Bos, J. and Markert, K. (2005). Recognising textual entailment with logical inference. In *Proceedings of the HLT and EMNLP conference*, pages 628–635.

Bouma, G., van Noord, G., and Malouf, R. (2001). Alpino: Wide-coverage computational analysis of dutch. In *Proceedings of the CLIN 2000*, pages 45–59.

Briscoe, T. and Carroll, J. (2006). Evaluating the accuracy of an unlexicalized statistical parser on the PARC depbank. In *Proceedings of the COLING/ACL on Main conference poster sessions*, pages 41–48.

[5] MSTParser scores did not fit in the table, but largely correspond in distributional characteristics, and are available upon request.

[6] Not with multiple coders yet, but percentage agreement for dependency annotation typically varies from 93-98%.

Table 2: Performance scores of the parsing systems for major GRs. Some of the relations could not be reliably be mapped, and are absent for the CCG parser.

	RASP			CCG parser			MEGRASP		
relation	*Prec*	*Rec*	F_1	*Prec*	*Rec*	F_1	*Prec*	*Rec*	F_1
aux	89.13	69.87	78.33	90.81	62.21	73.84	98.13	96.21	97.16
com	67.80	6.12	11.23	-	-	-	93.15	88.52	90.78
comp	22.73	64.18	33.57	24.53	53.66	33.67	80.00	84.72	82.29
coord	70.42	64.31	67.23	82.50	30.62	44.66	75.07	83.93	79.26
cpzr	74.67	20.97	32.75	-	-	-	90.16	85.77	87.91
det	90.34	89.38	89.86	60.88	82.54	70.07	96.38	97.27	96.82
jct	57.85	56.68	57.26	54.71	5.16	9.42	85.14	83.05	84.08
mod	63.04	76.93	69.29	16.89	47.43	24.91	90.00	90.63	90.32
obj	73.34	75.50	74.40	46.09	69.25	55.34	91.93	91.10	91.52
obj2	32.81	55.13	41.13	53.37	39.16	45.18	83.33	74.14	78.47
pobj	88.11	75.51	81.33	-	-	-	91.94	93.05	92.49
pred	54.77	48.94	51.69	64.60	15.55	25.07	90.21	91.08	90.65
quant	55.87	68.87	61.69	-	-	-	83.10	91.46	87.08
subj	74.53	67.58	70.89	66.94	66.11	66.52	94.68	95.01	94.84
xcomp	52.17	64.97	57.87	1.62	3.35	2.19	92.11	87.13	89.55
xmod	12.93	15.32	14.02	2.60	24.19	4.69	56.64	65.32	60.67

Briscoe, T., Carroll, J., and Watson, R. (2006). The second release of the RASP system. In *Proceedings of the COLING/ACL on Interactive presentation sessions*, pages 77–80.

Buttery, P. and Korhonen, A. (2007). I will shoot your shopping down and you can shoot all my tins—automatic lexical acquisition from the CHILDES database. In *Proceedings of the Workshop on Cognitive Aspects of Computational Language Acquisition*, pages 33–40.

Carroll, J., Briscoe, T., and Sanfilippo, A. (1998). Parser evaluation: a survey and a new proposal. In *Proceedings of the 1st LREC*, pages 447–454.

Charniak, E. and Johnson, M. (2001). Edit detection and parsing for transcribed speech. In *Proceedings of NAACL*, pages 118–126.

Clark, S. and Curran, J. R. (2007). Wide-coverage efficient statistical parsing with CCG and log-linear models. *Computational Linguistics*, 33(4):493–552.

Dredze, M., Blitzer, J., Pratim Talukdar, P., Ganchev, K., Graca, J. a., and Pereira, F. (2007). Frustratingly hard domain adaptation for dependency parsing. In *Proceedings of the CoNLL Shared Task Session of EMNLP-CoNLL 2007*, pages 1051–1055.

Geertzen, J. (2009). Semantic interpretation of Dutch spoken dialogue. In *Proceedings of the Eight IWCS*, pages 286–290.

Lease, M. and Johnson, M. (2006). Early deletion of fillers in processing conversational speech. In *Proceedings of the HLT-NAACL*, pages 73–76.

Lin, D. (1998). A dependency-based method for evaluating broad-coverage parsers. *Natural Language Engineering*, 4(2):97–114.

MacWhinney, B. (2000). *The CHILDES project: Tools for analyzing talk*. Lawrence Erlbaum Associates, Mahwah, NJ, USA, third edition.

McDonald, R., Crammer, K., and Pereira, F. (2005). Online large-margin training of dependency parsers. In *Proceedings of the 43rd Annual Meeting on ACL*, pages 91–98.

Sagae, K., Davis, E., Lavie, A., MacWhinney, B., and Wintner, S. (2007). High-accuracy annotation and parsing of CHILDES transcripts. In *Proceedings of the ACL-2007 workshop on Cognitive Aspects of Computational Language Acquisition*.

Sagae, K., MacWhinney, B., and Lavie, A. (2004). Adding syntactic annotations to transcripts of parent-child dialogs. In *In Proceedings of the Fourth LREC*, pages 1815–1818.

Interactive Predictive Parsing [1]

Ricardo Sánchez-Sáez, Joan-Andreu Sánchez and José-Miguel Benedí
Instituto Tecnológico de Informática
Universidad Politécnica de Valencia
Camí de Vera s/n, Valencia 46022 (Spain)
{rsanchez, jandreu, jbenedi}dsic.upv.es

Abstract

This paper introduces a formal framework that presents a novel Interactive Predictive Parsing schema which can be operated by a user, tightly integrated into the system, to obtain error free trees. This compares to the classical two-step schema of manually post-editing the erroneus constituents produced by the parsing system. We have simulated interaction and calculated evalaution metrics, which established that an IPP system results in a high amount of effort reduction for a manual annotator compared to a two-step system.

1 Introduction

The aim of parsing is to obtain the linguistic interpretation of sentences, that is, their underlying syntactic structure. This task is one of the fundamental pieces needed by a computer to unsderstand language as used by humans, and has many applications in Natural Language Processing (Lease et al., 2006).

A wide array of parsing methods exist, including those based on Probabilistic Context-Free Grammars (PCFGs). (Charniak, 2000; Collins, 2003; Johnson, 1998; Klein and Manning, 2003; Matsuzaki et al., 2005; Petrov and Klein, 2007). The most impressive results are achieved by subtree reranking systems, as shown in the semi-supervised method of (McClosky et al., 2006), or the forest reranking approximation of (Huang, 2008) in which packed parse forests (compact structures that contain many possible tree derivations) are used.

These state-of-the-art parsers provide trees of excelent quality. However, perfect results are virtually never achieved. If the need of one-hundred-percent error free trees arises, the supervision of a user that post-edits and corrects the errors is unavoidable.

Error free trees are needed in many tasks such as handwritten mathematical expressions recognition (Yamamoto et al., 2006), or creation of new gold standard treebanks (Delaclergerie et al., 2008)). For example, in the creation of the Penn Treebank grammar, a basic two-stage setup was employed: a rudimentary parsing system providad a skeletal syntactic representation, which then was manually corrected by human annotators (Marcus et al., 1993).

In this paper, we introduce a new formal framework that tightly integrates the user within the parsing system itself, rather than keeping him isolated from the automatic tools used in a classical two-step approach. This approach introduces the user into the parsing system, and we will call it "interactive predictive parsing", or simply IPP. An IPP system is interactive because the user is in continuous contact with the parsing process, sending and receiving feedback. An IPP system is also predictive because it reacts to the user corrections: it predicts and suggest new parse trees taking into account the new gold knowledge received from the user. Interactive predictive methods have been studied and successfully used in fields like Automatic Text Recognition (Toselli et al., 2008) and Statistical Machine Translation (Barrachina et al., 2009; Vidal et al., 2006) to ease the work of transcriptor and translators.

Assessment of the amount of effort saved by the IPP system will be measured by automatically calculated metrics.

2 Interactive Predictive Parsing

A tree t, associated to a string $x_{1|x|}$, is composed by substructures that are usually referred as constituents or edges. A constituent c_{ij}^A is a span de-

[1]Work supported by the MIPRCV "Consolider Ingenio 2010" (CSD2007-00018), iTransDoc (TIN2006-15694-CO2-01) and Prometeo (PROMETEO/2009/014) reserach projects, and the FPU fellowship AP2006-01363.

Proceedings of the 11th International Conference on Parsing Technologies (IWPT), pages 222–225,
Paris, October 2009.

fined by a nonterminal symbol (or syntactic tag) A that covers the substring x_{ij}.

Assume that using a given probabilistic context-free grammar G as the model, the parser analyzes the input sentence $\boldsymbol{x} = x_1 \ldots x_{|x|}$ and produces the parse tree $\hat{t}$

$$\hat{t} = \arg\max_{t \in \mathcal{T}} p_G(t|\boldsymbol{x}), \tag{1}$$

where $p_G(t|\boldsymbol{x})$ is the probability of parse tree t given the input string $\boldsymbol{x}$ using model G, and $\mathcal{T}$ is the set of all possible parse trees for $\boldsymbol{x}$.

In an interactive predictive scenario, after obtaining the (probably incorrect) best tree $\hat{t}$, the user is able to modify the edges c_{ij}^A that are incorrect. The system reacts to each of the corrections introduced by the human by proposing a new $\hat{t}'$ that takes into account the corrected edge. The order in which incorrect constituents are reviewed determines the amount of effort reduction given by the degree of correctness of the subsequent proposed trees.

There exist several ways in which a human analyzes a sentende. A top-to-bottom may be considered natural way of proceeding, and we follow this approach in this work. This way, when a higher level constituent is corrected, possible erroneous constituents at lower levels are expectedly automatically recalculated.

The introduced IPP interaction process is similar to the ones already established in Computer-Assisted Text Recognition and Computer-Assisted Translation [1].

Within the IPP framework, the user reviews the constituents contained in the tree to assess their correctness. When the user find an incorrect edge he modifies it, setting the correct label and span. This action implicitly validates a subtree that is composed by the corrected edge plus all its ancestor edges, which we will call the validated prefix tree t_p. When the user replaces the constituent c_{ij}^A with the correct one $c_{ij}'^A$, the validated prefix tree is:

$$t_p(c_{ij}'^A) = \{c_{mn}^B \ : m \le i,\ n \ge j \\ d(c_{mn}^B) \ge d(c_{ij}'^A)\} \tag{2}$$

with $d(c_{pq}^D)$ being the depth of constituent c_{pq}^D.

[1]In these fields, the user reads the sentence from left to right. When the user finds and corrects an erroneus word, he is implicitly validating the prefix sentence up to that word. The remaining suffix sentence is recalculated by the system taking into account the validated prefix sentece.

When a constituent correction is performed, the prefix tree $t_p(c_{ij}'^A)$ is fixed and a new tree $\hat{t}'$ that takes into account the prefix is proposed

$$\hat{t}' = \arg\max_{t \in \mathcal{T}} p_G(t|\boldsymbol{x}, t_p(c_{ij}'^A)). \tag{3}$$

Given that we are working with context-free grammars, the only subtree that effectively needs to be recalcuted is the one starting from the parent of the corrected edge. Let the corrected edge be $c_{ij}'^A$ and its parent c_{st}^D, then the following tree is proposed

$$\hat{t}' = \arg\max_{t \in \mathcal{T}} p_G(t|\boldsymbol{x}, t_p) = (\hat{t} \setminus \hat{t}_{st}^D) \cup \hat{t'}_{st}^D, \tag{4}$$

with

$$\hat{t'}_{st}^D = \arg\max_{t_{st}^D \in \mathcal{T}_{st}} p_G(t_{st}^D|\boldsymbol{x}_{mn}, c_{ij}'^A). \tag{5}$$

Expression (4) represents the newly proposed tree $\hat{t}'$, which consists of original proposed tree $\hat{t}$ minus the subpart of the original proposed tree $\hat{t}_{st}^D$ (whose root is the parent of the corrected edge c_{st}^D) plus the newly calculated subtree $\hat{t'}_{st}^D$ (whose root is also the parent of the corrected constituent c_{st}^D, but also takes into account the corrected one as shown in Expression (5)).

In Figure 1 we show an example that intends to clarify the interactive predictive process. First, the system provides a proposed parse tree (Fig. 1.a). Then the user, which has in his mind the correct reference tree, notices that it has two wrong constituents (c_{23}^X and c_{44}^Z) (Fig. 1.b), and choses to replace c_{23}^X by c_{22}^B (Fig. 1.c). Here, c_{22}^B corresponds to $c_{ij}'^A$ from expressions (3) and (5).

As the user does this correction, the system automatically validates the correct prefix: all the ancestors of the modified constituent (dashed line in the figure, $t_p(c_{ij}'^A)$ from expression (2)). The system also invalidates the subtrees related to the corrected constituent (dotted line line in the figure, $\hat{t}_{st}^D$ from expression (4)).

Finally, the system automatically predicts a new subtree ($\hat{t'}_{st}^D$ from expression (4)) (Fig. 1.d). Notice how c_{34}^Z changes its span and c_{44}^D is introduced which provides the correct reference parse.

Within the example shown in Figure 1, the user would obtain the gold tree with just one correction, rather than the three operations needed on a two-step system (one deletion, one substitution and one insertion).

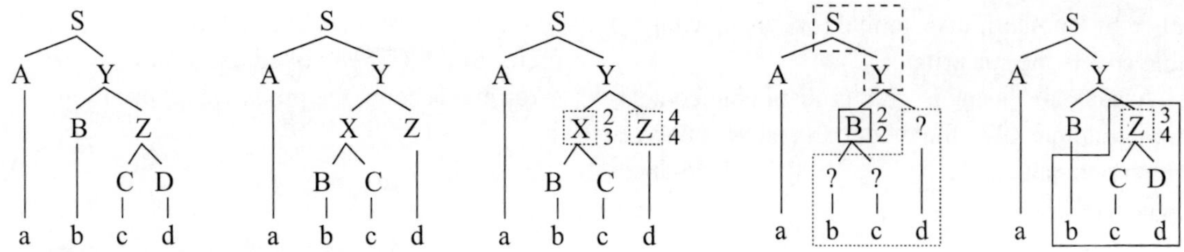

(a) Reference tree (b) Iteration 0: *Proposed output tree 1* (c) Iteration 0: *Erroneus constituents* (d) Iteration 1: *User corrected constituent* (e) Iteration 1: *Proposed output tree 2*

Figure 1: Synthetic example of user interaction with the IPP system.

3 IPP Evaluation

The objective of the experimentation presented here is to evaluate the amount of effort saved for the user using the IPP system, compared to the effort required to manually correct the trees without the use of an interactive system. In this section, we define a standard automatic evaluation protocol, akin to the ones used in Computer-Aided Translation and Computer Aided Text Recognition.

In the absence of testing of an interactive system with real users, the gold reference trees were used to simulate system interaction by a human corrector. In order to do this, the constituents in the proposed tree were automatically reviewed in a preorder manner [2]. In each step, the constituent in the proposed tree was compared to the corresponding one in the reference tree: if the constituent was equivalent no action was taken. When one incorrect constituent was found in the proposed tree, it was replaced by the correct one from the reference tree. This precise step simulated what a human supervisor would do, that is, to type the correct constituent in place of the erroneus one.

The system then performed the predictive step (i.e. recalculation of subtrees related to the corrected constituent). We kept a correction count, which was incremented by one after each predictive step.

3.1 Evaluation metrics

For evaluation, first we report a metric representing the amount of human correcting work needed to obtain the gold tree in a classical two-step process (i.e. the number of operations needed to post-edit the proposed tree in orther to obtain the gold one). We then compare this value to a metric that measures the amount of effort needed to obtain the gold tree with the human interacting within the presented IPP system.

Parsing quality is generally assessed by the classical evaluation metrics, precission, recall and F-measure. We defined the following metric that measures the amount of effort needed in order to post-edit a proposed tree and obtain the gold reference parse tree, akin to the Word Error Rate used in Statistical Machine Translation and related fields:

- *Tree Constituent Error Rate (TCER):* Minimum number of constituent substitution, deletion and insertion operations needed to convert the proposed parse tree into the corresponding gold reference tree, divided by the total number of constituents in the reference tree [3].

The TCER is in fact strongly related to the F-measure: the higher the F-measure is, the lower TCER will be.

Finally, the relevant evaluation metric that assessed the IPP system performance represents the amount effort that the operator would have to spend using the system in order to obtain the gold tree, and is directly comparable to the TCER:

- *Tree Constituent Action Rate (TCAC):* Number of constituent corrections performed using the IPP system to obtain the reference tree, divided by the total number of constituents in the reference tree.

4 Experimental results

An IPP system was implemented over the classical CYK-Viterbi algorithm. Experimentation was run

[2]Interaction in this ordered manner guaranteed that the evaluation protocol only needed to modify the label A and the end point j of a given edge c_{ij}^{A}, while i remained valid given the modifications of previous constituents.

[3]Edit distance is calcualted over the ordered set of tree constituents. This is an approximation of the edit distance between trees.

over the Penn Tree bank: sections 2 to 21 were used to obtain a vanilla Penn Treebank Grammar; test set was the whole section 23.

We obtained several binarized versions of the train grammar for use with the CYK. The Chomsky Normal Form (CNF) transformation method from the NLTK[4] was used to obtain several right-factored binary grammars of different sizes [5].

A basic schema was introduced for parsing sentences with out-of-vocabulary words: when an input word could not be derived by any of the preterminals in the vanilla treebank grammar, a very small probability for that word was uniformly added to all of the preterminals.

Results for the metrics discussed on section 3.1 for different markovizations of the train grammar can be seen in Table 1. We observe that the percetage of corrections needed using the IPP system is much lower than the rate of needed corrections just post-editing the proposed trees: from 42% to 46% in effort reduction by the human supervisor.

These results clearly show that an interactive predictive system can relieve manual annotators of a lot of burden in their task.

Note that the presented experiments were done using parsing models that perform far from the latest F_1 results; their intention was to assess the utility of the IPP schema. Expected relative reductions with IPP systems incorporating state-of-the-art parsers would not be so large.

PCFG	Baseline		IPP	RelRed
	F_1	TCER	TCAC	
h=0, v=1	0.67	0.40	0.22	45%
h=0, v=2	0.68	0.39	0.21	46%
h=0, v=3	0.70	0.38	0.22	42%

Table 1: Results for the test set: F_1 and TCER for the baseline system; TCAC for the IPP system; relative reduction beteween TCER and TCAC.

5 Conclusions

We have introduced a novel Interactive Predictive Parsing framewrok which can be operated by a user to obtain error free trees. We have simulated interaction with this system and calculated evaluation metrics, which established that an IPP system results in a high amount of effort reduction for a manual annotator compared to a two-step system.

Near term future work includes applying the IPP scenario to state-of-the-art reranking and parsing systems, as well as in the development of adaptative parsing systems

[4]http://nltk.sourceforge.net/

[5]This method implements the vertical (v value) and horizontal (h value) markovizations (Klein and Manning, 2003).

References

Barrachina, Sergio, Oliver Bender, Francisco Casacuberta, Jorge Civera, Elsa Cubel, Shahram Khadivi, Antonio Lagarda, Hermann Ney, Jess Toms, Enrique Vidal, Juan-Miguel Vilar. 2009. *Statistical approaches to computer-assisted translation*. In Computational Linguistics, 35(1) 3-28.

Charniak, Eugene. 2000. *A maximum-entropy-inspired parser*. In NAACL '00, 132-139.

Collins, Michael. 2003. *Head-driven statistical models for natural language parsing*. In Computational Linguistics, 29(4):589-637.

De la Clergerie, Éric, Olivier Hamon, Djamel Mostefa, Christelle Ayache, Patrick Paroubek and Anne Vilnat. 2008. *PASSAGE: from French Parser Evaluation to Large Sized Treebank*. In LREC'08.

Huang, Liang. 2008. *Forest reranking: discriminative parsing with non-local features*. In ACL '08.

Johnson, Mark. 1998. *PCFG models of linguistic tree representation*. In Computational Linguistics, 24:613-632.

Klein, Dan and Chistopher D. Manning. 2003. *Accurate Unlexicalized Parsing*. In ACL '03, 423-430.

Lease, Matthew, Eugene Charniak, Mark Johnson and David McClosky. 2006. *A look at parsing and its applications*. In National Conference on Artificial Intelligence, vol. 21-II, 1642-1645.

Marcus, Mitchell P., Mary Ann Marcinkiewicz and Beatrice Santorini. 1995. *Building a Large Annotated Corpus of English: The Penn Treebank*. Computational Linguistics 19(2), 313-330.

Matsuzaki, Takuya, Yasuke Miyao and Jun'ichi Tsujii. 2005. *Probabilistic CFG with latent annotations*. In ACL '05, 75-82.

McClosky, David, Eugene Charniak and Mark Johnson. 2006. *Effective self-training for parsing*. In HLT-NAACL '06

Petrov, Slav and Dan Klein. 2007. *Improved inference for unlexicalized parsing*. In NAACL-HLT '07.

Toselli, Alejandro, Verónica Romero and Enrique Vidal. 2008. *Computer Assisted Transcription of Text Images and Multimodal Interaction*. In MLMI '08.

Vidal, Enrique, Francisco Casacuberta, Luis Rodriguez, Jorge Civera and Carlos D. Martnez Hinarejos. 2006. *Computer-assisted translation using speech recognition*. In IEEE Trans. on Audio, Speech, and Language Processing, 14(3), 941-951.

Yamamoto, Ryo, Shinji Sako, Takuya Nishimoto and Shigeki Sagayama. 2006. *On-line recognition of handwritten mathematical expressions based on stroke-based stochastic context-free grammar*. In 10th International Workshop on Frontiers in Handwriting Recognition.

Using Treebanking Discriminants as Parse Disambiguation Features

Md. Faisal Mahbub Chowdhury[†] **and Yi Zhang**[‡] **and Valia Kordoni**[‡]
[†] Dept of Computational Linguistics, Saarland University
[‡] Dept of Computational Linguistics, Saarland University and DFKI GmbH, Germany
{chowd,yzhang,kordoni}@coli.uni-sb.de

Abstract

This paper presents a novel approach of incorporating fine-grained treebanking decisions made by human annotators as discriminative features for automatic parse disambiguation. To our best knowledge, this is the first work that exploits treebanking decisions for this task. The advantage of this approach is that use of human judgements is made. The paper presents comparative analyses of the performance of discriminative models built using treebanking decisions and state-of-the-art features. We also highlight how differently these features scale when these models are tested on out-of-domain data. We show that, features extracted using treebanking decisions are more efficient, informative and robust compared to traditional features.

1 Introduction

State-of-the-art parse disambiguation models are trained on treebanks, which are either fully hand-annotated or manually disambiguated from the parse forest produced by the parser. While most of the hand-annotated treebanks contain only gold trees, treebanks constructed from parser outputs include both preferred and non-preferred analyses. Some treebanking environments (such as the SRI Cambridge TreeBanker (Carter, 1997) or `[incr tsdb()]` (Oepen, 2001)) even record the treebanking decisions (see section 2) that the annotators take during manual annotation. These treebanking decisions are, usually, stored in the database/log files and used later for dynamic propagation if a newer version of the grammar on the same corpus is available (Oepen et al., 2002). But until now, to our best knowledge, no research has been reported on exploiting these decisions for building a parse disambiguation model.

Previous research has adopted two approaches to use treebanks for disambiguation models. One approach, known as generative, uses only the gold parse trees (Ersan and Charniak, 1995; Charniak, 2000). The other approach, known as discriminative, uses both preferred trees and non-preferred trees (Johnson et al., 1999; Toutanova et al., 2005). In this latter approach, features such as local configurations (i.e., local sub-trees), grandparents, n-grams, etc., are extracted from all the trees and are utilized to build the model. Neither of the approaches considers cognitive aspects of treebanking, i.e. the fine-grained decision-making process of the human annotators.

In this paper, we present our ongoing study of using treebanking decisions for building a parse disambiguation model. We present comparative analyses among the features extracted using treebanking decisions and the state-of-the-art feature types. We highlight how differently these features scale when they are tested on out-of-domain data. Our results demonstrate that features extracted using treebanking decisions are more efficient, informative and robust, despite the total number of these features being much less than that of the traditional feature types.

The rest of this paper is organised as follows — section 2 presents some motivation along with definition of treebanking decisions. Section 3 describes the feature extraction templates that have been used for treebanking decisions. Section 4 explains the experimental data, results and analyses. Section 5 concludes the paper with an outline of our future research.

2 Treebanking decisions

One of the defining characteristics of Redwoods-style treebanks[1] (Oepen et al., 2002) is that the candidate trees are constructed automatically by

[1] More details available in http://redwoods.stanford.edu.

Proceedings of the 11th International Conference on Parsing Technologies (IWPT), pages 226–229,
Paris, October 2009.

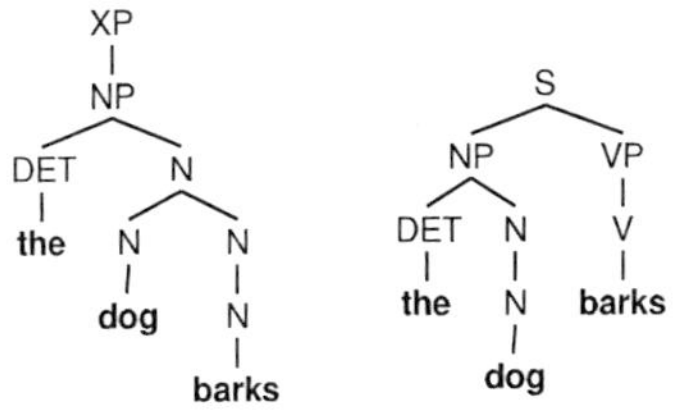

D1	SUBJH	the dog || barks
D2	HSPEC	the || dog barks
D3	FRAG_NP	the dog barks
D4	HSPEC	the || dog
D5	NOUN_N_CMPND	dog || barks
	...	...
D6	PLUR_NOUN_ORULE	barks
D7	*v_-_le*	barks
D8	*n_-_mc_le*	barks

Figure 1: Example forest and discriminants

the grammar, and then manually disambiguated by human annotators. In doing so, linguistically rich annotation is built efficiently with minimum manual labor. In order to further improve the manual disambiguation efficiency, systems like `[incr tsdb()]` computes the difference between candidate analyses. Instead of looking at the huge parse forest, the treebank annotators select or reject the features that distinguish between different parses, until only one parse remains. The number of decisions for each sentence is normally around $log_2(n)$ where n is the total number of candidate trees. For a sentence with 5000 candidate readings, only about 12 treebanking decisions are required for a complete disambiguation. A similar method was also proposed in (Carter, 1997).

Formally, a feature that distinguishes between different parses is called a *discriminant*. For Redwoods-style treebanks, this is usually extracted from the syntactic derivation tree of the Head-driven Phrase Structure Grammar (HPSG) analyses. Figure 1 shows a set of example discriminants based on the two candidate trees.

A choice (acceptance or rejection, either manually annotated or inferred by the system) made on a discriminant is called a *decision*. In the above example, suppose the annotator decides to accept the binary structure *the dog* || *barks* as a subject-head construction and assigns a value *yes* to discriminant *D1*, the remaining discriminants will also receive inferred values by deduction (*no* for *D2*, *no* for *D3*, *yes* for *D4*, etc). These decisions are stored and used for dynamic evolution of the treebank along with the grammar development.

Treebank decisions (especially those made by annotators) are of particular interest to our study of parse disambiguation. The decisions record the fine-grained human judgements in the manual disambiguation process. This is different from the traditional use of treebanks to build parse selection models, where a marked gold tree is picked from the parse forest without concerning detailed selection steps. Recent study on double annotated treebanks (Kordoni and Zhang, 2009) shows that annotators tend to start with the decisions with the most certainty, and delay the "hard" decisions as much as possible. As the decision process goes, many of the "hard" discriminants will receive an inferred value from the certain decisions. This greedy approach helps to guarantee high inter-annotator agreement. Concerning the statistical parse selection models, the discriminative nature of these treebanking decisions suggests that they are highly effective features, and if properly used, they will contribute to an efficient disambiguation model.

3 Treebanking Decisions as Discriminative Disambiguation Features

We use three types of feature templates for treebanking decisions for feature extraction. We refer to the features extracted using these templates as *TDF* (Treebanking Decision Feature) in the rest of this paper. The feature templates are

T1: *discriminant + lexical types of the yield*

T2: *discriminant + rule(left-child)*[2] *+ rule(right-child)*

T3: *instances of T2 + rule(parent) + rule(siblings)*

*TDF*s of T1, T2 and T3 in combination are referred to as *TDFC* or *TDF*s with context. For example in Figure 1, *instance of T1* for the discriminant *D4* is "HSPEC[3] + *le_type(the)*[4] + *le_type(dog)*"; *instance of T2* is "HSPEC + *rule(* DET*) + rule(*N*)* "; and *instance of T3* is "HSPEC + *rule(*DET *) + rule(*N*) + rule(*S*) + rule(*VP*)*".

A *TDF* represents partial information about the right parse tree (as most usual features). But in some way, it also indicates that it was a point of a decision (point of ambiguity with respect to the underlying pre-processing grammar), hence carrying some extra bit of information. *TDF*s allow to

[2] *rule(X)* represents the HPSG rule, applied on X, extracted from the corresponding derivation tree.

[3] HSPEC is the head-specifier rule in HPSG

[4] *le_type(X)* denotes the abstract lexical type of word *X* inside the grammar.

omit certain details inside the features by encoding useful purposes of relationships between lexical types of the words and their distant grandparents without considering nodes in the intermediate levels (allowing some kind of underspecification). In contrast, state-of-the-art feature types contain all the nodes in the corresponding branches of the tree. While they encode ancestor information (through grandparenting), but they ignore siblings. *TDF*s include siblings along with ancestor. Unlike traditional features, which are generated from all possible matches (which is huge) of feature types followed by some frequency cut-offs, the selection of *TDF*s is directly restricted by the small number of treebanking decisions themselves and exhaustive search is not needed. It should be noted that, we do not use treebanking decisions made for the parse forest of one sentence to extract features from the parse forest of another sentence. That is why, the number of *TDF*s is much smaller than that of traditional features. This also ensures that *TDF*s are highly correlated to the corresponding constructions and corresponding sentences from where they are extracted.

4 Experiment

4.1 Data

We use a collection of 8593 English sentences from the LOGON corpus (Oepen et al., 2004) for our experiment. 874 of them are kept as test items and the remaining 7719 items are used for training. The sentences have an average length of 14.68 and average number of 203.26 readings per sentence. The out-of-domain data are a set of 531 English Wikipedia sentences from WeScience corpus (Ytrestøl et al., 2009).

Previous studies (Toutanova et al., 2005; Osborne and Baldridge, 2004) have reported relatively high exact match accuracy with earlier versions of ERG (Flickinger, 2000) on datasets with very short sentences. With much higher structural ambiguities in LOGON and WeScience sentences, the overall disambiguation accuracy drops significantly.

4.2 Experimental setup and evaluation measures

The goal of our experiments is to compare various types of features (with TDF) in terms of efficiency, informativeness, and robustness. To compare among the feature types, we build log-linear training models (Johnson et al., 1999) for parse selection (which is standard for unification-based grammars) for TDFC, local configurations, n-grams and active edges[5]. For each model, we calculate the following evaluation metrics —

- *Exact (match) accuracy*: it is simply the percentage of times that the top-ranked analysis for each test sentences is identical with the gold analysis of the same sentence.
- *5-best (match) accuracy*: it is the percentage of times that the five top-ranked analyses for each of the sentences contain the gold analysis.
- *Feature Hit Count (FHC)*: it is the total number of occurrences of the features (of a particular feature type) inside all the syntactic analyses for all the test sentences. So, for example, if a feature (of a particular feature type) is observed 100 times, then these 100 occurrences are added to the total FHC.
- *Feature Type Hit Count (FTHC)*: it is the total number of *distinct* features (of the corresponding feature type) observed inside the syntactic analyses of all the test sentences.

While exact and 5-best match measures show relative informativeness and robustness of the feature types, *FHC* and *FTHC* provide a more comprehensive picture of relative efficiencies.

4.3 Results and discussion

As we can see in Table 1, local configurations achieve highest accuracy among the traditional feature types. They also use higher number of features (almost *2.7* millions). *TDFC* do better than both n-grams and active edges, even with a lower number of features. Though, local configurations gain more accuracy than *TDFC*, but they do so at a cost of *50* times higher number of features. This indicates that features extracted using treebanking decisions are more informative.

For out-of-domain data (Table 1), there is a big drop of accuracy for local configurations. Active edges and *TDFC* also have some accuracy drop. Surprisingly, n-grams do better with our out-of-domain data than in-domain, but still that accuracy is close to that of *TDFC*. Note that n-grams have *8* times higher number of features than *TDFC*. Hence, according to these results, *TDFC* are more robust, for out-of-domain data, than local configurations and active edges, and almost as good as n-grams.

[5] Active edges correspond to the branches (i.e. one daughter in turn) of the local sub-trees.

Feature template	Total features	5-best accuracy *(in-domain)*	5-best accuracy *(out-of-domain)*	Exact accuracy *(in-domain)*	Exact accuracy *(out-of-domain)*
n-gram	438,844	68.19%	62.71%	41.30%	42.37%
local configuration	2,735,486	75.51%	64.22%	50.69%	44.44%
active edges	89,807	68.99%	61.77%	41.88%	39.92%
TDFC	53,362	70.94%	62.71%	43.59%	41.05%

Table 1: Accuracies obtained on both in-domain and out-of-domain data using n-grams (n=4), local configurations (with grandparenting level 3), active edges and *TDFC*.

Feature template	FHC	FTHC	Active features
n-gram	18,245,558	32,425	7.39%
local config.	62,060,610	357,150	13.06%
active edges	22,902,404	27,540	30.67%
TDFC	21,719,698	17,818	33.39%

Table 2: *FHC* and *FTHC* calculated for in-domain data.

The most important aspect of *TDFC* is that they are more efficient than their traditional counterparts (Table 2). They have significantly higher number of active features ($\frac{FTHC}{TotalFeature\#}$) than n-grams and local configurations.

5 Future work

The results of the experiments described in this paper indicate a good prospect for utilizing treebanking decisions, although, we think that the types of feature templates that we are using for them are not yet fully conveying cognitive knowledge of the annotators, in which we are specifically interested in. For instance, we expect to model human disambiguation process more accurately by focusing only on human annotators' decisions (instead of only inferred decisions). Such a model will not only improve the performance of the parsing system at hand, but can also be applied interactively in treebanking projects to achieve better annotation speed (e.g., by ranking the promising discriminants higher to help annotators make correct decisions). Future experiments will also investigate whether any pattern of discriminant selection by the humans can be learnt from these decisions.

References

David Carter. 1997. The treebanker: A tool for supervised training of parsed corpora. In *Proceedings of the Workshop on Computational Environments for Grammar Development and Linguistic Engineering*, Madrid, Spain.

Eugene Charniak. 2000. A maximum entropy-based parser. In *Proceedings of the 1st Annual Meeting of the North American Chapter of Association for Computational Linguistics (NAACL 2000)*, pages 132–139, Seattle, USA.

Murat Ersan and Eugene Charniak. 1995. A statistical syntactic disambiguation program and what it learns. pages 146–159.

Dan Flickinger. 2000. On building a more efficient grammar by exploiting types. 6(1):15–28.

Mark Johnson, Stuart Geman, Stephen Canon, Zhiyi Chi, and Stefan Riezler. 1999. Estimators for stochastic unifcation-based grammars. In *Proceedings of the 37th Annual Meeting of the Association for Computational Linguistics (ACL 1999)*, pages 535–541, Maryland, USA.

Valia Kordoni and Yi Zhang. 2009. Annotating wall street journal texts using a hand-crafted deep linguistic grammar. In *Proceedings of The Third Linguistic Annotation Workshop (LAW III)*, Singapore.

Stephan Oepen, Kristina Toutanova, Stuart Shieber, Christopher Manning, Dan Flickinger, and Thorsten Brants. 2002. The LinGO Redwoods treebank: motivation and preliminary applications. In *Proceedings of COLING 2002: The 17th International Conference on Computational Linguistics: Project Notes*, Taipei, Taiwan.

Stephan Oepen, Helge Dyvik, Jan Tore Lønning, Erik Velldal, Dorothee Beermann, John Carroll, Dan Flickinger, Lars Hellan, Janne Bondi Johannessen, Paul Meurer, Torbjørn Nordgård, and Victoria Rosén. 2004. Som å kappete med trollet? towards mrs-based norwegian-english machine translation. In *Proceedings of the 10th International Conference on Theoretical and Methodological Issues in Machine Translation*, pages 11–20, MD, USA.

Stephan Oepen. 2001. [incr tsdb()] — competence and performance laboratory. User manual. Technical report, Computational Linguistics, Saarland University, Saarbrücken, Germany.

Miles Osborne and Jason Baldridge. 2004. Ensemble-based active learning for parse selection. In *HLT-NAACL 2004: Main Proceedings*, pages 89–96, Boston, USA.

Kristina Toutanova, Christoper D. Manning, Dan Flickinger, and Stephan Oepen. 2005. Stochastic HPSG parse selection using the Redwoods corpus. *Journal of Research on Language and Computation*, 3(1):83–105.

Gisle Ytrestøl, Stephan Oepen, and Daniel Flickinger. 2009. Extracting and annotating wikipedia sub-domains. In *Proceedings of the 7th International Workshop on Treebanks and Linguistic Theories*, pages 185–197, Groningen, the Netherlands.

Heuristic search in a cognitive model of human parsing

John T. Hale
Cornell University
217 Morrill Hall
Ithaca, New York 14853
jthale@cornell.edu

Abstract

We present a cognitive process model of human sentence comprehension based on generalized left-corner parsing. A search heuristic based upon previously-parsed corpora derives garden path effects, garden path paradoxes, and the local coherence effect.

1 Introduction

One of the most interesting applications of parsing technology has, for some researchers, been psycholinguistic models (Kay, 2005). Algorithmic models of language use have led in the past to a variety of cognitive insights (Kaplan, 1972; Marcus, 1980; Thibadeau et al., 1982; Pereira, 1985; Pulman, 1986; Johnson, 1989; Stabler, 1994). However they are challenged by a veritable tidal wave of new data collected during the 1990s and 2000s. Work during this later period reveals phenomena, such as the local coherence effect discussed in section 5, that have yet to be truly integrated into any particular theoretical framework.

This short paper presents a parsing system intended to serve as a model of the syntactic part of human sentence comprehension. Such a model helps make sense of sentence-difficulty data from self-paced reading, eye-tracking and other behavioral studies. It also sketches a relationship between calculations carried out in the course of automated syntactic analysis and the inferences about linguistic structure taking place in our minds during ordinary sentence-understanding.

Section 2 defines the model itself, highlighting its relationship to generalized left-corner parsing. Sections 3–5 apply this model to three controversial phenomena that are well-established in the psycholinguistics literature. Section 6 concludes.

2 Architecture of the model

2.1 Problem states and Operators

We model the human sentence comprehension mechanism as search within a problem space (Newell and Simon, 1972). We assume that all (incremental) parser states have a (partial) grammatical interpretation (Chomsky, 1965, 9). In this paper, the grammatical interpretation employs context-free grammar. An inventory of operators carries the model from one point in the problem space to another. In the interest of simplicity, we place no bound on the number of problem states the model can explore. However, we do acknowledge with Johnson-Laird (1983) and Resnik (1992) a pressure to minimize memory consumption internal to a problem state. The model's within-problem state memory usage should reflect human acceptability judgments with embedded sentences. These considerations motivate a generalized left-corner (GLC) parsing strategy (Demers, 1977) whose stack consumption is maximal on just the center-embedded examples that are so difficult for people to understand. To reflect the argument/adjunct distinction (Tutunjian and Boland, 2008) we adopt a mixed strategy that is bottom-up for optional postmodifiers but left-corner everywhere else. Leaving the arc-eager/arc-standard decision (Abney and Johnson, 1991) to the control policy allows four possible operators, schematized in Table 1.

2.2 Informed Search

Informed search differs from uninformed search procedures such as depth-first and breadth-first by making use of heuristic knowledge about the search domain. The strategy is to choose for expansion the node whose cost is lowest (Barr and Feigenbaum, 1981, 61). In A* search (Hart et al., 1968) this cost is divided up into a sum consisting of the known cost to reach a search node and an

Proceedings of the 11th International Conference on Parsing Technologies (IWPT), pages 230–233,
Paris, October 2009.

shift a word W	project a rule $LHS \rightarrow Trigger \underset{\substack{announce\\point}}{\uparrow} Rest$
scan the sought word W	project and match the sought parent LHS using the rule $LHS \rightarrow Trigger \underset{\substack{announce\\point}}{\uparrow} Rest$

Table 1: Four schema define the operators

stack	n	E[steps]	standard error
[VP] S [TOP]	55790	44.936	0.1572
S [TOP]	53991	10.542	0.0986
[NP] S [TOP]	43635	33.092	0.1633
NP [TOP]	38844	55.791	0.2126
NP [S] S [TOP]	34415	47.132	0.2122
[S] S [TOP]	33578	52.800	0.2195
[PP] S [TOP]	30693	34.454	0.1915
IN [PP] S [TOP]	27272	32.379	0.2031
DT [NP] S [TOP]	22375	34.478	0.2306
[AUX] [VP] S [TOP]	16447	46.536	0.2863
VBD [VP] S [TOP]	16224	43.057	0.2826
VB [VP] S [TOP]	13548	40.404	0.3074
the [NP] S [TOP]	12507	34.120	0.3046
NP [NP] S [TOP]	12092	43.821	0.3269
DT [TOP]	10440	66.452	0.3907

Table 2: Popular left-corner parser states. Stacks grow to the left. The categories are as described in Table 3 of Marcus et al. (1993).

estimate of the costs involved in finishing search from that node. In this work, rather than relying on the guarantee provided by the A* theorem, we examine the exploration pattern that results from an inadmissable completion cost estimator. The choice of estimator is Hypothesis 1.

Hypothesis 1 Search in parsing is informed by an estimate of the expected number of steps to completion, given previous experience.

Table 2 writes out the expected number of steps to completion (E[steps]) for a selection of problem states binned together according to their grammatical interpretation. Categories enclosed in square brackets are predicted top-down whereas unbracketed have been found bottom-up. These states are some of the most popular states visited during a simulation of parsing the Brown corpus (Kučera and Francis, 1967; Marcus et al., 1993) according to the mixed strategy introduced above in subsection 2.1. The quantity E[steps] serves in what follows as the completion cost estimate in A* search.

3 Garden pathing

Any model of human sentence comprehension should address the garden path effect. The contrast between 1a and 1b is an example of this phenomenon.

(1) a. while Mary was mending a sock fell on the floor
b. while Mary was mending, a sock fell on the floor

The control condition 1b includes a comma which, in spoken language, would be expressed as a prosodic break (Carroll and Slowiaczek, 1991; Speer et al., 1996).

Figure 1 shows the search space explored in the experimental condition 1a. In this picture, ovals represent problem states. The number inside the oval encodes the vistation order. Arcs between ovals represent operator applications. The path $(14, 22, 23, 24, 25, 29, 27)$ is the garden path which builds a grammatical interpretation where *a sock* is attached as a direct object of the verb *mend*. The grey line highlights the order in which A* search considers this path. At state 21 after shifting *sock*, experience with the Brown corpus suggests reconsidering the garden path.

Whereas the model examines 45 search nodes during the analysis of the temporarily ambiguous item 1a, it dispatches the unambiguous item 1b after only 40 nodes despite that sentence having an additional token (the comma). Garden paths, on this view, are sequences of parser states explored only in a temporarily ambiguous item.

4 Garden pathing counterexamples

Purely structural attachment preferences like Right Association (Kimball, 1973) and Minimal Attachment (Frazier and Fodor, 1978; Pereira, 1985) are threatened by paradoxical counterexamples such as 2 from Gibson (1991, 22) where no fixed principle yields correct predictions across both examples.

(2) a. I gave her earrings on her birthday .
b. I gave her earrings to another girl .

A parser guided by Hypothesis 1 interleaves the garden path attachment and the globally-correct attachment in both cases, resulting in a search that

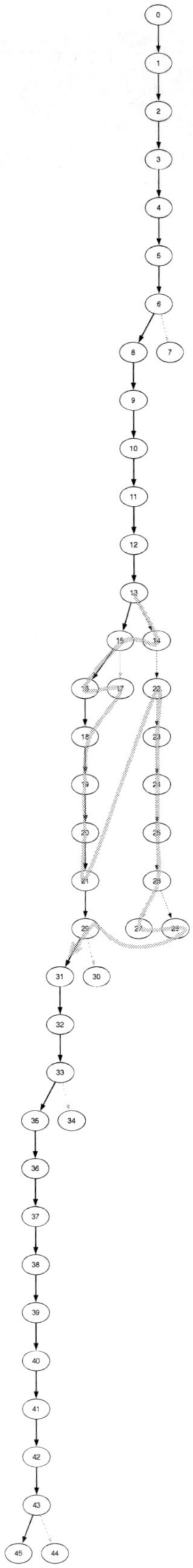

Figure 1: Heavy line is the globally-correct path

is strictly committed to neither analysis. In 2a, 32% of discovered states represent the globally-incorrect attachment of *her*. In 2b, 27% of states represent the globally-incorrect attachment of *her* to *give* as a one-word direct object. The paradox for purely structural attachment heuristics is dissolved by the observation that neither pathway fully achieves priority over the other.

5 Local Coherence

Tabor et al. (2004) discovered[1] a processing difficulty phenomenon called "local coherence." Among the stimuli they considered, the locally-coherent condition is 3a where the substring *the player tossed a frisbee* could be analyzed as a sentence, if considered in isolation.

(3) a. The coach smiled at the player tossed a frisbee by the opposing team.

b. The coach smiled at the player thrown a frisbee by the opposing team

c. The coach smiled at the player who was tossed a frisbee by the opposing team.

d. The coach smiled at the player who was thrown a frisbee by the opposing team.

Tabor and colleagues observe an interaction between the degree of morphological ambiguity of the embedded verb (*tossed* or *thrown*) and the presence or absence of the relative-clause initial words *who was*. These two factors are known as ±ambiguity and ±reduction, respectively. If the human parser were making full use of the grammar, its operation would reflect the impossibility of continuing *the coach smiled at...* with a sentence. The ungrammaticality of a sentence in this left context would preclude any analysis of *the player* as a subject of active voice *toss*. But greater reading times observed on the ambiguous *tossed* as compared to the unambiguous *thrown* suggest contrariwise that this grammatical deduction is not made uniformly based on the left context.

Table 3 shows how an informed parser's step counts, when guided by Hypothesis 1, derive Tabor et al.'s observed pattern. The cell predicted to be hardest is the local coherence, shaded gray. The degree of worsening due to relative clause reduction is greater in +ambiguous than in −ambiguous. This derives the observed interaction.

[1]Konieczny and Müller (2006) documents a closely related form of local coherence in German.

	+ambiguous	−ambiguous
+reduced	119	84
−reduced	67	53

Table 3: Count of states examined

6 Conclusion

When informed by experience with the Brown corpus, the parsing system described in this paper exhibits a pattern of "time-sharing" performance that corresponds to human behavioral difficulty in three controversial cases. The built-in elements — context-free grammar, generalized left-corner parsing and the A*-type cost function — are together adequate to address a range of comprehension difficulty phenomena without imposing an *a priori* memory limit. The contribution is an algorithmic-level account of the cognitive processes involved in perceiving syntactic structure.

References

Steven Abney and Mark Johnson. 1991. Memory requirements and local ambiguities of parsing strategies. *Journal of Psycholinguistic Research*, 20(3):233–249.

Avron Barr and Edward A. Feigenbaum, editors. 1981. *The Handbook of Artificial Intelligence*. William Kaufmann.

Patrick J. Carroll and Maria L. Slowiaczek. 1991. Modes and modules: multiple pathways to the language processor. In Jay L. Garfield, editor, *Modularity in Knowledge Representation and Natural Language Understanding*, pages 221–247. MIT Press.

Noam Chomsky. 1965. *Aspects of the Theory of Syntax*. MIT Press.

Alan J. Demers. 1977. Generalized left corner parsing. In *Conference Report of the 4th annual association for computing machinery symposium on Principles of Programming Languages*, pages 170–181.

Lyn Frazier and Janet Dean Fodor. 1978. The sausage machine: a new two-stage parsing model. *Cognition*, 6:291–325.

Edward Gibson. 1991. *A Computational Theory of Human Linguistic Processing: Memory Limitations and Processing Breakdown*. Ph.D. thesis, Carnegie Mellon University.

Peter E. Hart, Nils J. Nilsson, and Bertram Raphael. 1968. A formal basis for the heuristic determination of minimum cost paths. *IEEE Transactions of systems science and cybernetics*, ssc-4(2):100–107.

Philip N. Johnson-Laird. 1983. *Mental Models*. Cambridge University Press.

Mark Johnson. 1989. Parsing as deduction: the use of knowledge of language. *Journal of Psycholinguistic Research*, 18(1):105–128.

Ronald M. Kaplan. 1972. Augmented transition networks as psychological models of sentence comprehension. *Artificial Intelligence*, 3:77–100.

Martin Kay. 2005. A life of language. *Computational Linguistics*, 31(4):425–438.

John P. Kimball. 1973. Seven principles of surface structure parsing in natural language. *Cognition*, 2:15–48.

Lars Konieczny and Daniel Müller. 2006. Local coherences in sentence processing. CUNY Conference on Human Sentence Processing.

Henry Kučera and W. Nelson Francis. 1967. *Computational Analysis of Present-day American English*. Brown University Press.

Mitchell P. Marcus, Beatrice Santorini, and Mary Ann Marcinkiewicz. 1993. Building a large annotated corpus of English: the Penn Treebank. *Computational Linguistics*, 19.

Mitchell P. Marcus. 1980. *A theory of syntactic recognition for natural language*. MIT Press.

Allen Newell and Herbert A. Simon. 1972. *Human Problem Solving*. Prentice-Hall, Englewood Cliffs, New Jersey.

Fernando Pereira. 1985. A new characterization of attachment preference. In David Dowty, Lauri Karttunen, and Arnold Zwicky, editors, *Natural Language Parsing: Psychological, Computational and Theoretical Perspectives*, ACL Studies in Natural Language Processing, pages 307–319. Cambridge University Press.

Steven G. Pulman. 1986. Grammars, parsers, and memory limitations. *Language and Cognitive Processes*, 1(3):197–2256.

Philip Resnik. 1992. Left-corner parsing and psychological plausibility. In *Proceedings of the Fourteenth International Conference on Computational Linguistics*, Nantes, France.

Shari R. Speer, Margaret M. Kjelgaard, and Kathryn M. Dobroth. 1996. The influence of prosodic structure on the resolution of temporary syntactic closure ambiguities. *Journal of Psycholinguistic Research*, 25(2):249–271.

Edward Stabler. 1994. The finite connectivity of linguistic structure. In Charles Clifton, Lyn Frazier, and Keith Rayner, editors, *Perspectives on Sentence Processing*, pages 303–336. Lawrence Erlbaum.

Whitney Tabor, Bruno Galantuccia, and Daniel Richardson. 2004. Effects of merely local syntactic coherence on sentence processing. *Journal of Memory and Language*, 50(4):355–370.

Robert Thibadeau, Marcel A. Just, and Patricia Carpenter. 1982. A model of the time course and content of reading. *Cognitive Science*, 6:157–203.

D. Tutunjian and J.E. Boland. 2008. Do We Need a Distinction between Arguments and Adjuncts? Evidence from Psycholinguistic Studies of Comprehension. *Language and Linguistics Compass*, 2(4):631–646.

Dependency Parsing with Energy-based Reinforcement Learning

Lidan Zhang
Department of Computer Science
The University of Hong Kong
Pokfulam Road, Hong Kong
lzhang@cs.hku.hk

Kwok Ping Chan
Department of Computer Science
The University of Hong Kong
Pokfulam Road, Hong Kong
kpchan@cs.hku.hk

Abstract

We present a model which integrates dependency parsing with reinforcement learning based on Markov decision process. At each time step, a transition is picked up to construct the dependency tree in terms of the long-run reward. The optimal policy for choosing transitions can be found with the SARSA algorithm. In SARSA, an approximation of the state-action function can be obtained by calculating the negative free energies for the Restricted Boltzmann Machine. The experimental results on CoNLL-X multilingual data show that the proposed model achieves comparable results with the current state-of-the-art methods.

1 Introduction

Dependency parsing, an important task, can be used to facilitate some natural language applications. Given a sentence, dependency parsing is to find an acyclic labeled directed tree, projective or non-projective.The label of each edge gives the syntactic relationship between two words.

Data-driven dependency parsers can be categorized into graph-based and transition-based models. Both of these two models have their advantages as well as drawbacks. As discussed in (McDonald and Satta, 2007), transition-based models use local training and greedy inference algorithms, with a rich feature set, whereas they might lead to error propagation. In contrast, graph-based models are globally trained coupled with exact inference algorithms, whereas their features are restricted to a limited number of graph arcs. Nivre and McDonald (2008) presented a successful attempt to integrate these two models by exploiting their complementary strengths.

There are other researches on improving the individual model with a novel framework. For example, Daumé et al. (2006) applied a greedy search to transition-based model, which was adjusted by the resulting errors. Motivated by his work, our transition-based model is expected to overcome local dependencies by using a long-term desirability introduced by reinforcement learning (RL). We rely on a "global" policy to guide each action selection for a particular state during parsing. This policy considers not only the current configuration but also a few of look-ahead steps. Thus it yields an optimal action from the long-term goal. For example, an action might return a high value even if it produces a low immediate reward, because its following state-actions might yield high rewards. The reverse also holds true. Finally we formulate the parsing problem with the Markov Decision Process (MDP) for the dynamic settings.

The reminder of this paper is organized as follows: Section 2 describes the transition-based dependency parsing. Section 3 presents the proposed reinforcement learning model. Section 4 gives the experimental results. Finally, Section 5 concludes the paper.

2 Transition-based Dependency Parsing

In this paper, we focus on the transition-based dependency parsing in a shift-reduce framework (Kübler et al., 2009). Given a sentence $x = w_0, w_1, ..., w_n$, its dependency tree is constructed by a sequence of transitions. The data structures include a stack S to store partially processed words and a queue I to record the remaining input words and the partial labeled dependency structure constructed by the previous transitions. Four permissible transitions are considered: **Reduce**: pops word w_i from the stack; **Shift**: pushes the next input w_j onto the stack; **Left-Arc$_r$**: adds a labeled dependency arc r from the next input w_j to the top of the stack w_i, then pops word w_i from the stack; **Right-Arc$_r$**: adds a dependency arc r

Proceedings of the 11th International Conference on Parsing Technologies (IWPT), pages 234–237,
Paris, October 2009. ©2009 Association for Computational Linguistics

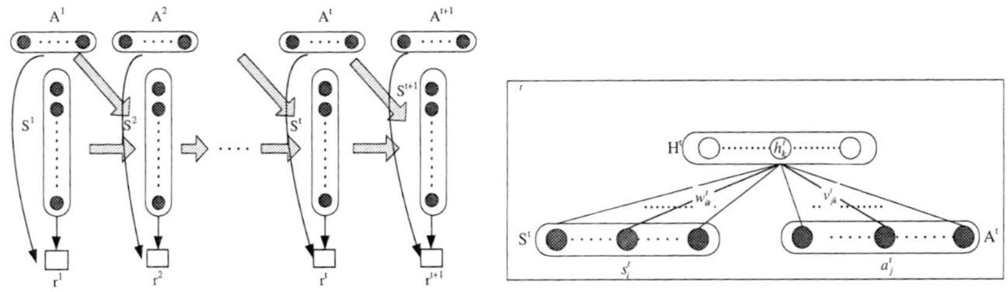

Figure 1: The MDP with factored states and actions. Left: The general network. Right: Detailed network with one hidden layer at time t. Visible variables (states and actions) are shaded. Clear circles represent hidden variables.

from the top of the stack w_i to the next input w_j, and pushes word w_j onto the stack.

Starting from the empty stack and initializing the queue I as the input words, the parser terminates when the queue I is empty. The optimal transition (or say, action/decision A) in each step is conditioned on the current configuration c of the parser. For non-projective cases, preprocessing and postprocessing are applied.

3 Reinforcement Learning

3.1 General Framework

We begin with looking at the general framework to integrate RL into the transition-based dependency model. In this paper, we reformulate the dependency parsing as Markov Decision Process (MDP, $(\mathcal{S}, \mathcal{A}, \mathcal{T}, r)$) where:

- $\mathcal{S}$ is the set of states.
- $\mathcal{A}$ is the set of possible actions.
- $\mathcal{T}$ is the transition function, $\mathcal{T} : \mathcal{S} \times \mathcal{A} \rightarrow \mathcal{S}$. we denote the transition probability $P_{ij}(a) = P(s^{t+1} = j | s^t = i, A^t = a)$.
- r is the reward function by executing action a in a certain state, which is denoted as $r_i(a)$.

As aforesaid, the key task of dependency parsing is to select the optimal action to be performed based on the current state. Given the expected immediate reward r, the optimal policy $(\pi : S \mapsto A)$ is to maximize the long-term expected reward as follows:

$$R_t = \sum_{k=0}^{\infty} \gamma^k r_{t+k} \tag{1}$$

Given a policy π, state-action function $Q^\pi(i, a)$ can be defined as the expected accumulative reward received by taking action a in state s. It takes the following form:

$$\begin{aligned} Q^\pi(i, a) &= E_\pi[\sum_{k=0}^{\infty} \gamma^k r_{t+k} | s^t = i, a^t = a] \\ &= \sum_j P_{ij}(a)[r_i(a) + \gamma \sum_b \pi(j, b) Q^\pi(j, b)] \end{aligned} \tag{2}$$

Here $\pi(j, b)$ is the probability of picking up action b in state j, $\gamma \in [0, 1]$ is a discount factor to control the involvement of further actions. According to the Bellman equation, the state-action function can be updated iteratively with equation(2).

Given the state-action function, a greedy policy can be found by maximizing over possible actions:

$$\pi' = \arg\max_a Q^\pi(i, a) \tag{3}$$

In the following, we will discuss how to compute the state-action function Q by investigating the free energy in RBM.

3.2 Restricted Boltzmann Machine

3.2.1 Free Energy

Figure 1 shows the general framework of our model. At each time step t, there is no connections between nodes within the same layer. In the network, "visible" variables include both states and actions ($V = S \cup A$). The visible layer is fully connected to a "hidden" layer, which can be regarded as a Restricted Boltzmann Machine (RBM).

In our model, both states and actions are factored. They are consisted of a sets of discrete variables (Sallans and Hinton, 2004). The stochastic energy of the network can be computed by the conductivities between visible and hidden variables.

$$E(s, a, h) = -\sum_{i,k} w_{ik} s_i h_k - \sum_{j,k} \mu_{jk} a_j h_k \tag{4}$$

The above energy determine their equilibrium probabilities via the Boltzmann distribution:

$$P(s,a,h) = \frac{exp(-E(s,a,h))}{\sum_{s',a',h'} exp(-E(s',a',h'))} \quad (5)$$

By marginalizing out the hidden variables, we can obtain the "equilibrium free energy" of s and a, which can be expressed as an expected energy minus an entropy:

$$\begin{aligned} F(s,a) = & -\sum_k (\sum_i (w_{ik} s_i \langle h_k \rangle) + \sum_j (\mu_{jk} a_j \langle h_k \rangle)) \\ & + \sum_k \langle h_k \rangle \log \langle h_k \rangle + (1-\langle h_k \rangle) \log(1-\langle h_k \rangle) \end{aligned} \quad (6)$$

where $\langle h_k \rangle$ is the expected value of variable h_k:

$$\langle h_k \rangle = \sigma(\sum_{i,k} w_{ik} s_i + \sum_{j,k} \mu_{jk} a_j) \quad (7)$$

where $\sigma = 1/(1+e^{-x})$ is a sigmoid function.

As is proved in (Sallans and Hinton, 2004), the value of a state-action function can be approximated by the negative free energy of the network:

$$Q(s,a) \approx -F(s,a) \quad (8)$$

3.2.2 Parameter Learning

The parameters of the network can be updated by the SARSA (State-Action-Reward-State-Action) algorithm. The inputs of the SARSA algorithm are the state-action pairs of the two neighboring slices. Then the error can be computed as:

$$\mathcal{E}(s^t, a^t) = [r^t + \gamma Q(s^{t+1}, t^{t+1})] - Q(s^t, a^t) \quad (9)$$

Suppose the state-action function is parameterized by θ. The update equation for the parameter is:

$$\triangle\theta \propto \mathcal{E}(s^t, a^t) \nabla_\theta Q(s^t, a^t) \quad (10)$$

Back to our model, the parameters $\theta = (w, u)$ are given by:

$$\begin{aligned} \Delta w_{ik} & \propto (r^t + \gamma Q(s^{t+1}, a^{t+1}) - Q(s^t, a^t)) s_i^t \langle h_k \rangle \\ \Delta u_{jk} & \propto (r^t + \gamma Q(s^{t+1}, a^{t+1}) - Q(s^t, a^t)) a_j^t \langle h_k \rangle \end{aligned} \quad (11)$$

Leemon (1993) showed that the above update rules can work well in practice even though there is no proof of convergence in theory. In addition, in dependency parsing task, the possible action number is small (=4). Our experimental results also showed that the learning rule can converge in practice.

3.3 Action Selection

After training, we use the *softmax* rules to select the optimal action for a given state. The probability of an action is given by Boltzmann distribution:

$$P(a|s) \approx \frac{e^{Q(s,a)/\tau}}{Z} \quad (12)$$

Here Z is an normalization factor. τ is a positive number called the *temperature*. High temperature means the actions are evenly distributed. Low temperature case a great variety in selection probability. In the limit as $\tau \rightarrow 0$, softmax action selection becomes greedy action selection.

4 Experiments

4.1 Settings

We use the CoNLL-X (Buchholz and Marsi, 2006) distribution data from seven different languages (Arabic, Bulgarian, Dutch, Portuguese, Slovene, Spanish and Swedish). These treebanks varied in sizes from 29,000 to 207,000 tokens. The cut-off frequency for training data is 20, which means we ignores any attribute (FORM, LEMMA, POS or FEATS) occurred less than 20. Furthermore we randomly selected 10 percent of training data to construct the validation set. Test sets are about equal for all languages. Since our algorithm only deals with projective cases, we use projectivization/deprojectivization method for training and testing data.

For fair comparison, we use the exactly same feature set as Nivre et al. (2006), which is comprised of a variety of features extracted from the stack, the queue and the partially built dependency graph.

In our experiment, the immediate reward value is defined as the Hamming Loss between partial tree and expected tree, which counts the number of places that the partial output $\hat{y}$ differs from the true output y: $\sum_{i=1}^{T} 1[y_i \neq \hat{y}_i]$.

As shown in Figure 1, we compute the state-action function using a feed-forward neural network with one hidden layer. The number of hidden variables is set to match the variable number in the visible layer (i.e. total number of state and action variables). The parameters of the network are modified by SARSA algorithm according to equation 2. Finally, 10-width beam search is employed for all languages, during testing.

There are other parameters in our experiments, which can be tuned using search. For simplicity,

		Ar	Bu	Du	Po	Sl	Sp	Sw
LAS	Our	63.24	88.89	79.06	87.54	72.44	82.79	87.20
	Nivre	66.71	87.41	78.59	87.60	70.30	81.29	84.58
UAS	Our	75.30	92.88	83.14	91.34	80.06	86.18	91.84
	Nivre	77.51	91.72	81.35	91.22	78.72	84.67	89.50

Table 1: Comparison of dependency accuracy with Nivre

the learning rate was exponentially decreased form 0.1 to 0.01 in the course of each epoch. In ideal cases, the discount factor should be set to 1. In our experiments, discount factor is fixed to 0.6 considering the computational burden in long sentence. The study of the this parameter is still left for future work. Finally, the inverse temperature linearly increased from 0 to 2.

4.2 Results

The performance of our model is evaluated by the official attachment score, including labeled (LAS=the percentage of tokens with the correct head and label) and unlabeled (UAS=the percentage of tokens with the correct head). Punctuation tokens were excluded from scoring.

The result comparison between our system and Nivre's transition-based system is shown in Table 1[1]. From the table, we can see that the proposed model outperformed the Nivre's score in all languages except Arabic. In Arabic, our results are worse than Nivre, with about 3.5% performance reduction in LAS measure and 2.2% in UAS. Most of our errors occur in POSTAGS with N (16% head errors and 31% dep errors) and P (47% head errors and 8% dep errors), which is probably due to the flexible usage of those two tags in Arabic. The best performance of our model happens in Swedish. The LAS improves from 84.58% to 87.20%, whereas UAS improves from 89.5% to 91.84%. The reason might be that the long dependent relationship is not popular in Swedish. Finally, we believe the performance will be further improved by carefully tuning parameters or broadening the beam search width.

5 Conclusions

In this paper we proposed a dependency parsing based on reinforcement learning. The parser uses a policy to select the optimal transition in each parsing stage. The policy is learned from RL in terms of the long-term reward. Tentative experimental evaluations show that the introduction of RL is feasible for some NLP applications. Finally, there are a lot of future work, including the hierarchical model and parameter selections.

[1]The performance of other systems can be accessed from http://nextens.uvt.nl/~conll

References

Sabine Buchholz and Erwin Marsi. 2006. Conll-x shared task on multilingual dependency parsing. In *Proceedings of the Tenth Conference on Computational Natural Language Learning (CoNLL-X)*, pages 149–164, New York City, June. Association for Computational Linguistics.

Hal Daumé III, John Langford, and Daniel Marcu. 2006. Searn in practice.

Leemon C. Baird III and A. Harry. Klopf. 1993. Reinforcement learning with high-dimensional, continuous actions. Technical Report WL–TR-93-1147, Wright-Patterson Air Force Base Ohio: Wright Laboratory.

Sandra Kübler, Ryan McDonald, and Joakim Nivre. 2009. *Dependency parsing*. Calif, Morgan & Claypool publishers, US.

Ryan McDonald and Giorgio Satta. 2007. On the complexity of non-projective data-driven dependency parsing. In *Proceedings of the Tenth International Conference on Parsing Technologies*, pages 121–132, Prague, Czech Republic, June. Association for Computational Linguistics.

Joakim Nivre and Ryan McDonald. 2008. Integrating graph-based and transition-based dependency parsers. In *Proceedings of ACL-08: HLT*, pages 950–958, Columbus, Ohio, June. Association for Computational Linguistics.

Joakim Nivre, Johan Hall, Jens Nilsson, Gülşen Eryiğit, and Svetoslav Marinov. 2006. Labeled pseudo-projective dependency parsing with support vector machines. In *Proceedings of the Tenth Conference on Computational Natural Language Learning (CoNLL-X)*, pages 221–225, New York City, June. Association for Computational Linguistics.

Brian Sallans and Geoffrey E. Hinton. 2004. Reinforcement learning with factored states and actions. *Journal of Machine Learning Research*, 5:1063–1088.

A generative re-ranking model for dependency parsing

Federico Sangati, Willem Zuidema and Rens Bod
Institute for Logic, Language and Computation
University of Amsterdam
Science Park 904, 1098 XH Amsterdam, The Netherlands
{f.sangati,zuidema,rens.bod}@uva.nl

Abstract

We propose a framework for dependency parsing based on a combination of discriminative and generative models. We use a discriminative model to obtain a k-best list of candidate parses, and subsequently rerank those candidates using a generative model. We show how this approach allows us to evaluate a variety of generative models, without needing different parser implementations. Moreover, we present empirical results that show a small improvement over state-of-the-art dependency parsing of English sentences.

1 Introduction

Probabilistic generative dependency models define probability distributions over all valid dependency structures, and thus provide a useful intermediate representation that can be used for many NLP tasks including parsing and language modeling. In recent evaluations of supervised dependency parsing, however, generative approaches are consistently outperformed by discriminative models (Buchholz et al., 2006; Nivre et al., 2007), which treat the task of assigning the correct structure to a given sentence as a classification task. In this category we include both transition based (Nivre and Hall , 2005) and graph based parsers (McDonald, 2006).

In this paper, we explore a reranking approach that combines a generative and a discrimative model and tries to retain the strengths of both. The idea of combining these two types of models through re-ranking is not new, although it has been mostly explored in constituency parsing (Collins et al., 2002). This earlier work, however, used the generative model in the first step, and trained the discriminative model over its k-best candidates. In this paper we reverse the usual order of the two models, by employing a generative model to re-score the k-best candidates provided by a discriminative model. Moreover, the generative model of the second phase uses frequency counts from the training set but is not trained on the k-best parses of the discriminative model.

The main motivation for our approach is that it allows for efficiently evaluating many generative models, differing from one another on (i) the choice of the linguistic units that are generated (words, pairs of words, word graphs), (ii) the generation process (Markov process, top-down, bottom-up), and (iii) the features that are considered to build the event space (postags/words, distance). Although efficient algorithms exist to calculate parse forests (Eisner, 1996a), each choice gives rise to different parser instantiations.

1.1 A generative model for re-ranking

In our re-ranking perspective, all the generative model has to do is to compute the probability of k pre-generated structures, and select the one with maximum probability. In a generative model, every structure can be decomposed into a series of independent events, each mapped to a corresponding conditioning event. As an example, if a generative model chooses D as the right dependent of a certain word H, conditioned uniquely on their relative position, we can define the event as *D is the right dependent of H*, and the conditioning event as *H has a right dependent.*

As a preprocessing step, every sentence structure in the training corpus is decomposed into a series of independent events, with their corresponding conditioning events. During this process, our model updates two tables containing the frequency of events and their conditioning counterparts.

In the re-ranking phase, a given candidate structure can be decomposed into independent events $(e_1, e_2, \ldots, e_n)$ and corresponding conditioning events $(c_1, c_2, \ldots, c_n)$ as in the training phase.

Proceedings of the 11th International Conference on Parsing Technologies (IWPT), pages 238–241,
Paris, October 2009. ©2009 Association for Computational Linguistics

The probability of the structure can then be calculated as

$$\prod_{i=1}^{n} \frac{f(e_i)}{f(c_i)} \quad (1)$$

where $f(x)$ returns the frequency of x previously stored in the tables.

It is important to stress the point that the only specificity each generative model introduces is in the way sentence structures are decomposed into events; provided a generic representation for the (conditioning) event space, both training phase and probability calculation of candidate structures can be implemented independently from the specific generative model, through the implementation of generic tables of (conditioning) events.

In this way the probabilities of candidate structures are exact probabilities, and do not suffer from possible approximation techniques that parsers often utilize (i.e., pruning). On the other hand the most probable parse is selected from the set of the *k* candidates generated by the discriminative model, and it will equal with the most probable parse among all possible structures, only for sufficiently high *k*.

2 MST discriminative model

In order to generate a set of k-candidate structures for every test sentence, we use a state-of-the-art discriminative model (McDonald, 2006). This model treats every dependency structure as a set of word-dependent relations, each described by a high dimensional feature representation. For instance, if in a certain sentence word i is the head of word j, $\mathbf{v}(i,j)$ is the vector describing all the features of such relation (i.e., labels of the two words, their postag, and other information including words in between them, and ancestral nodes). During the training phase the model learns a weight vector $\mathbf{w}$ which is then used to find the best dependency structure y for a given test sentence x. The score that needs to be maximized is defined as $\sum_{(i,j)\in y} \mathbf{w} \cdot \mathbf{v}(i,j)$, and the best candidate is called the maximum spanning tree (MST).

Assuming we have the weight vector and we only consider projective dependency structures, the search space can be efficiently computed by using a dynamic algorithm on a compact representation of the parse forest (Eisner, 1996a). The training phase is more complex; for details we refer to (McDonald, 2006). Roughly, the model employs a large-margin classifier which iterates over the structures of the training corpus, and updates the weight vector $\mathbf{w}$ trying to keep the score of the correct structure above the scores of the incorrect ones by an amount which is proportional to how much they differ in accuracy.

3 Generative model

3.1 Eisner model

As a generative framework we have chosen to use a variation of model C in (Eisner, 1996a). In this approach nodes are generated recursively in a top-down manner starting from the special symbol *EOS* (end of sentence). At any given node, left and right children are generated as two separate Markov sequences of nodes[1], each conditioned on ancestral and sibling information (which, for now, we will simply refer to as *context*).

One of the relevant variations with respect to the original model is that in our version the direction of the Markov chain sequence is strictly left to right, instead of the usual inside outwards.

More formally, given a dependency structure T, and any of its node N, the probability of generating the fragment $T(N)$ of the dependency structure rooted in N is defined as:

$$P(T(N)) = \prod_{l=1}^{L} P(N_{\lhd l})|context) \cdot P(T(N_{\lhd l})) \times \prod_{r=1}^{R} P(N_{\rhd r})|context) \cdot P(T(N_{\rhd r})) \quad (2)$$

where L and R are the number of left and right children of N in T $(L, R > 0)$, $N_{\lhd l}$ is the left daughter of N at position l in T (analogously for right daughters). The probability of the entire dependency structure T is computed as $P(T(\mathit{EOS}))$.

In order to illustrate how a dependency structure can be decomposed into events, we present in table 1 the list of events and the corresponding conditioning events extracted from the dependency structure illustrated in figure 1. In this simple example, each node is identified with its word, and the context is composed of the direction with respect to the head node, the head node, and the previously chosen daughter (or *NONE* if it is the first). While during the training phase the event tables are updated with these events, in the test phase they are looked-up to compute the structure probability, as in equation 1.

[1] Every sequence ends with the special symbol *EOC*.

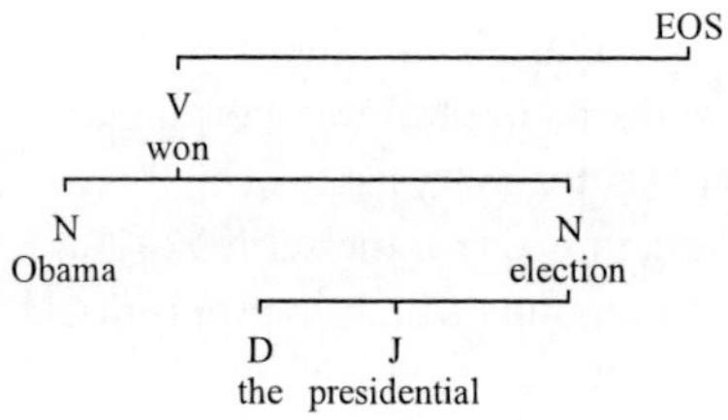

Figure 1: Dependency tree of the sentence *"Obama won the presidential election"*.

3.2 Model extension

In equation 2 we have generically defined the probability of choosing a daughter D based on specific features associated with D and the context in which it occurs. In our implementation, this probability is instantiated as in equation 3. The specific features associated with D are: the distance[2] $dist(H, D)$ between D and its head H, the flag $term(D)$ which specifies whether D has more dependents, and the lexical and postag representation of D. The context in which D occurs is defined by features of the head node H, the previously chosen sister S, the grandparent G, and the direction dir (left or right).

Equation 3 is factorized in four terms, each employing an appropriate backoff reduction list reported in descending priority[3].

$$
\begin{aligned}
&P(D|context) = \qquad (3)\\
&P(dist(H,D), term(D), word(D), tag(D)|H,S,G,dir) =\\
&P(tag(D)|H,S,G,dir)\\
&\text{reduction list: } \begin{array}{|c|}\hline wt(H), wt(S), wt(G), dir \\ \hline wt(H), wt(S), t(G), dir \\ \hline \left\{\begin{array}{l} wt(H), t(S), t(G), dir \\ t(H), wt(S), t(G), dir \end{array}\right. \\ \hline t(H), t(S), t(G), dir \\ \hline \end{array}\\
&\times P(word(D)|tag(D), H, S, G, dir)\\
&\text{reduction list: } \begin{array}{|c|}\hline wt(H), t(S), dir \\ \hline t(H), t(S), dir \\ \hline \end{array}\\
&\times P(term(D)|word(D), tag(D), H, S, G, dir)\\
&\text{reduction list: } \begin{array}{|c|}\hline tag(D), wt(H), t(S), dir \\ \hline tag(D), t(H), t(S), dir \\ \hline \end{array}\\
&\times P(dist(P,D)|term(D), word(D), tag(D), H, S, G, dir)\\
&\text{reduction list: } \begin{array}{|c|}\hline word(D), tag(D), t(H), t(S), dir \\ \hline tag(D), t(H), t(S), dir \\ \hline \end{array}
\end{aligned}
$$

[2]In our implementation distance values are grouped in 4 categories: $1, 2, 3-6, 7-\infty$.

[3]In the reduction lists, $wt(N)$ stands for the string incorporating both the postag and the word of N, and $t(N)$ stands for its postag. This second reduction is never applied to closed class words. All the notation and backoff parameters are identical to (Eisner, 1996b), and are not reported here for reasons of space.

[4]The counts are extracted from a two-sentence corpus which also includes "Obama lost the election."

Events	Freq.	Conditioning Events	Freq.
won L *EOS NONE*	1	L *EOS NONE*	2
EOC L *EOS* won	1	L *EOS* won	1
EOC R *EOS NONE*	2	R *EOS NONE*	2
Obama L won *NONE*	1	L won *NONE*	1
EOC L won Obama	1	L won Obama	1
election R won *NONE*	1	R won *NONE*	1
EOC R won election	1	R won election	1
EOC L Obama *NONE*	2	L Obama *NONE*	2
EOC R Obama *NONE*	2	R Obama *NONE*	2
the L election *NONE*	2	L election *NONE*	2
presidential L election the	1	L election the	2
EOC L election presidential	1	L election presidential	1
EOC R election *NONE*	2	R election *NONE*	2
EOC L the *NONE*	2	L the *NONE*	2
EOC R the *NONE*	2	R the *NONE*	2
EOC L presidential *NONE*	1	L presidential *NONE*	1
EOC R presidential *NONE*	1	R presidential *NONE*	1

Table 1: Events occurring when generating the dependency structure in figure 1, for the event space (dependent | direction, head, sister). According to the reported frequency counts[4], the structure has a associated probability of $1/4$.

4 Results

In our investigation, we have tested our model on the Wall Street Journal corpus (Marcus et al., 1993) with sentences up to 40 words in length, converted to dependency structures. Although several algorithms exist to perform such a conversion (Sangati and Zuidema, 2008), we have followed the scheme in (Collins, 1999). Section 2-21 was used as training, and section 22 as test set. The MST discriminative parser was provided with the correct postags of the words in the test set, and it was run in second-order[5] and projective mode. Results are reported in table 2, as unlabeled attachment score (UAS). The MST dependency parser obtains very high results when employed alone (92.58%), and generates a list of *k*-best-candidates which can potentially achieve much better results (an oracle would score above 95% when selecting from the first 5-best, and above 99% from the first 1000-best). The decrease in performance of the generative model, as the number of the candidate increases, suggests that its performance would be lower than a discriminative model if used alone. On the other hand, our generative model is able to select better candidates than the MST parser, when their number is limited to a few dozens, yielding a maximum accuracy for $k = 7$ where it improves accuracy on the discriminative model by a 0.51% (around 7% error reduction).

[5]The features of every dependency relation include information about the previously chosen sister of the dependent.

k-best	Oracle best	Oracle worst	Reranked
1	**92.58**	92.58	92.58
2	94.22	88.66	92.89
3	95.05	87.04	93.02
4	95.51	85.82	93.02
5	95.78	84.96	93.02
6	96.02	84.20	93.06
7	96.23	83.62	**93.09**
8	96.40	83.06	93.02
9	96.54	82.57	92.97
10	96.64	82.21	92.96
100	98.48	73.30	92.32
1000	99.34	64.86	91.47

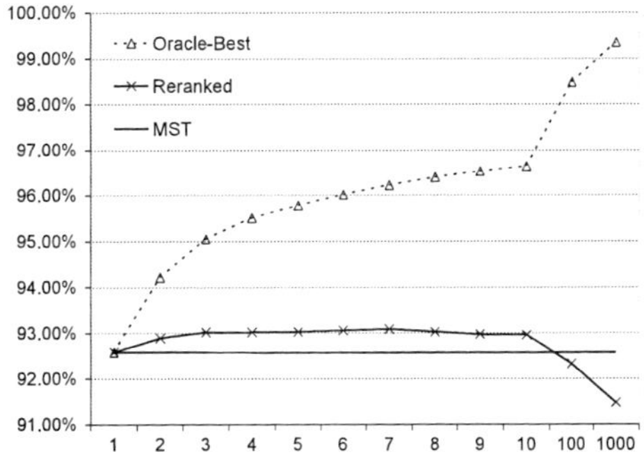

Figure 2: UAS accuracy of the MST discriminative and re-ranking parser on section 22 of the WSJ. *Oracle best*: always choosing the best result in the *k*-best, *Oracle worst*: always choosing the worst, *Reranked*: choosing the most probable candidate according to the generative model.

5 Conclusions

We have presented a general framework for dependency parsing based on a combination of discriminative and generative models. We have used this framework to evaluate and compare several generative models, including those of Eisner (1996) and some of their variations. Consistently with earlier results, none of these models performs better than the discriminative baseline when used alone. We have presented an instantiation of this framework in which our newly defined generative model leads to an improvement of the state-of-the-art parsing results, when provided with a limited number of best candidates. This result suggests that discriminative and generative model are complementary: the discriminative model is very accurate to filter out "bad" candidates, while the generative model is able to further refine the selection among the few best candidates. In our set-up it is now possible to efficiently evaluate many other generative models and identify the most promising ones for further investigation. And even though we currently still need the input from a discriminative model, our promising results show that pessimism about the prospects of probabilistic generative dependency models is premature.

Acknowledgments We gratefully acknowledge funding by the Netherlands Organization for Scientific Research (NWO): FS and RB are funded through a Vici-grant "Integrating Cognition" (277.70.006) to RB, and WZ through a Veni-grant "Discovering Grammar" (639.021.612) of NWO. We also thank 3 anonymous reviewers for useful comments.

References

S. Buchholz, and E. Marsi. 2006. CoNLL-X Shared Task on Multilingual Dependency Parsing. In *Proc. of the 10th CoNLL Conference*, pp. 149–164.

M. Collins. 1999. *Head-Driven Statistical Models for Natural Language Parsing*. Ph.D. thesis, University of Pennsylvania.

M. Collins, N. Duffy, and F. Park. 2002. New Ranking Algorithms for Parsing and Tagging: Kernels over Discrete Structures, and the Voted Perceptron. In *In Proceedings of the ACL 2002*, pp. 263–270.

J. Eisner. 1996a. Three New Probabilistic Models for Dependency Parsing: An Exploration. In *Proc. of the 16th International Conference on Computational Linguistics (COLING-96)*, pp. 340–345.

J. Eisner. 1996b. An Empirical Comparison of Probability Models for Dependency Grammar. *Technical Report number IRCS-96-11*, Univ. of Pennsylvania.

M.P. Marcus, B. Santorini, and M.A. Marcinkiewicz. 1993. Building a large annotated corpus of English: The Penn Treebank. In *Computational Linguistics*, 19(2), pp. 313–330.

R. McDonald. 2006. Discriminative Learning and Spanning Tree Algorithms for Dependency Parsing. Ph.D. thesis, University of Pennsylvania.

J. Nivre and J. Hall. 2005. MaltParser: A Language-Independent System for Data-Driven Dependency Parsing. In *Proc. of the Fourth Workshop on Treebanks and Linguistic Theories*, pp. 137–148.

J. Nivre, J. Hall, S. Kübler, R. McDonald, J. Nilsson,S. Riedel, and D. Yuret. 2007. The CONLL 2007 shared task on dependency parsing. In *Proc. of the CoNLL 2007 Shared Task Session*, pp. 915–932.

F. Sangati and W. Zuidema. 2008. Unsupervised Methods for Head Assignments. In *Proc. of the EACL 2009 Conference*, pp. 701–709.

Dependency Constraints for Lexical Disambiguation

Guillaume Bonfante
LORIA INPL
guillaume.bonfante@loria.fr

Bruno Guillaume
LORIA INRIA
bruno.guillaume@loria.fr

Mathieu Morey
LORIA Nancy-Université
mathieu.morey@loria.fr

Abstract

We propose a generic method to perform lexical disambiguation in lexicalized grammatical formalisms. It relies on dependency constraints between words. The soundness of the method is due to invariant properties of the parsing in a given grammar that can be computed statically from the grammar.

1 Introduction

In this work, we propose a method of lexical disambiguation based on the notion of dependencies.

In modern linguistics, Lucien Tesnière developed a formal and sophisticated theory with dependencies (Tesnière, 1959). Nowadays, many current grammatical formalisms rely more or less explicitly on the notion of dependencies between words. The most straightforward examples are formalisms in the Dependency Grammars family but it is also true of the phrase structure based formalisms which consider that words introduce incomplete syntactic structures which must be completed by other words. This idea is at the core of Categorial Grammars (CG) (Lambek, 1958) and all its trends such as Abstract Categorial Grammars (ACG) (de Groote, 2001) or Combinatory Categorial Grammars (CCG) (Steedman, 2000), being mostly encoded in their type system. Dependencies in CG were studied in (Moortgat and Morrill, 1991) and for CCG in (Clark et al., 2002; Koller and Kuhlmann, 2009). Other formalisms can be viewed as modeling and using dependencies, such as Tree Adjoining Grammars (TAG) (Joshi, 1987) with their substitution and adjunction operations. Dependencies for TAG were studied in (Joshi and Rambow, 2003). More recently, Marchand et al. (2009) showed that it is also possible to extract a dependency structure from a syntactic analysis in Interaction Grammars (IG) (Guillaume and Perrier, 2008).

Another much more recent concept of polarity can be used in grammatical formalisms to express that words introduce incomplete syntactic structures. IG directly use polarities to describe these structures but it is also possible to use polarities in other formalisms in order to make explicit the more or less implicit notion of incomplete structures: for instance, in CG (Lamarche, 2008) or in TAG (Kahane, 2006; Bonfante et al., 2004; Gardent and Kow, 2005). On this regard, Marchand et al. (2009) exhibited a direct link between polarities and dependencies. This encourages us to say that in many respects dependencies and polarities are two sides of the same coin.

The aim of this paper is to show that dependencies can be used to express constraints on the taggings of a sentence and hence these dependency constraints can be used to partially disambiguate the words of a sentence. We will see that, in practice, using the link between dependencies and polarities, these dependency constraints can be computed directly from polarized structures.

Exploiting the dependencies encoded in lexical entries to perform disambiguation is the intuition behind supertagging (Bangalore and Joshi, 1999), a method introduced for LTAG and successfully applied since then to CCG (Clark and Curran, 2004) and HPSG (Ninomiya et al., 2006). These approaches select the most likely lexical entry (entries) for each word, based on Hidden Markov Models or Maximum Entropy Models. Like the work done by Boullier (2003), our method is not based on statistics nor heuristics, but on a necessary condition of the deep parsing. Consequently, we accept to have more than one lexical tagging for a sentence, as long as we can ensure to have the good ones (when they exist!). This property is particulary useful to ensure that the deep parsing will not fail because of an error at the disambiguation step.

In wide-coverage lexicalized grammars, a word

Proceedings of the 11th International Conference on Parsing Technologies (IWPT), pages 242–253,
Paris, October 2009.

typically has about 10 corresponding lexical descriptions, which implies that for a short sentence of 10 words, we get 10^{10} possible taggings. It is not reasonable to treat them individually. To avoid this, it is convenient to use an automaton to represent the set of all paths. This automaton has linear size with regard to the initial lexical ambiguity. The idea of using automata is not new. In particular, methods based on Hidden Markov Models (HMM) use such a technique for part-of-speech tagging (Kupiec, 1992; Merialdo, 1994). Using automata, we benefit from dynamic programming procedures, and consequently from an exponential temporal and space speed up.

2 Abstract Grammatical Framework

Our filtering method is applicable to any lexicalized grammatical formalism which exhibits some basic properties. In this section we establish these properties and define from them the notion of Abstract Grammatical Framework (AGF).

Formally, an **Abstract Grammatical Framework** is an n-tuple $(\mathcal{V}, \mathcal{S}, \mathcal{G}, \mathbf{anc}, \mathcal{F}, \mathbf{p}, \mathbf{dep})$ where:

- $\mathcal{V}$ is the **vocabulary**: a finite set of words of the modeled natural language;
- $\mathcal{S}$ is the set of **syntactic structures** used by the formalism;
- $\mathcal{G} \subset \mathcal{S}$ is the **grammar**: the finite set of initial syntactic structures; a finite list $[t_1, \ldots, t_n]$ of elements of $\mathcal{G}$ is called a **lexical tagging**;
- $\mathbf{anc} : \mathcal{G} \to \mathcal{V}$ maps initial syntactic structures to their anchors;
- $\mathcal{F} \subset \mathcal{S}$ is the set of final syntactic structures that the parsing process builds (for instance trees);
- $\mathbf{p}$ is the **parsing function** from lexical taggings to finite subsets of $\mathcal{F}$;
- $\mathbf{dep}$ is the **dependency function** which maps a couple composed of a lexical tagging and a final syntactic structure to dependency structures.

Note that the $\mathbf{anc}$ function implies that the grammar is lexicalized: each initial structure in $\mathcal{G}$ is associated to an element of $\mathcal{V}$. Note also that no particular property is required on the dependency structures that are obtained with the $\mathbf{dep}$ function, they can be non-projective for instance.

We call **lexicon** the function (written ℓ) from $\mathcal{V}$ to subsets of $\mathcal{G}$ defined by:

$$\ell(w) = \{t \in \mathcal{G} \mid \mathbf{anc}(t) = w\}.$$

We will say that a lexical tagging $L = [t_1, \ldots, t_n]$ is a lexical tagging of the sentence $[\mathbf{anc}(t_1), \ldots, \mathbf{anc}(t_n)]$.

The final structures in $\mathbf{p}\,(L) \subset \mathcal{F}$ are called the **parsing solutions** of L.

Henceforth, in our examples, we will consider the ambiguous French sentence (1).

(1) *"La belle ferme la porte"*

Example 1 *We consider the following toy AGF, suited for parsing our sentence:*

- $\mathcal{V}$ = { "la", "belle", "ferme", "porte" }*;*
- *the grammar $\mathcal{G}$ is given in the table below: each $\times$ corresponds to an element in $\mathcal{G}$, written with the category and the French word as subscript. For instance, the French word* "porte" *can be either a common noun ("door") or a transitive verb ("hangs"); hence $\mathcal{G}$ contains the 2 elements $\mathtt{CN}_{porte}$ and $\mathtt{TrV}_{porte}$.*

	la	*belle*	*ferme*	*porte*
Det	×			
LAdj		×	×	
RAdj		×	×	
CN	×	×	×	×
Clit	×			
TrV			×	×
IntrV			×	

In our example, categories stand for, respectively: determiner, left adjective, right adjective, common noun, clitic pronoun, transitive verb and intransitive verb.

With respect to our lexicon, for sentence (1), there are $3 \times 3 \times 5 \times 3 \times 2 = 270$ lexical taggings.

The parsing function $\mathbf{p}$ is such that 3 lexical taggings have one solution and the 267 remaining ones have no solution; we do not need to precise the final structures, so we only give the English translation as the result of the parsing function:

- $\mathbf{p}([\mathtt{Det}_{la}, \mathtt{CN}_{belle}, \mathtt{TrV}_{ferme}, \mathtt{Det}_{la}, \mathtt{CN}_{porte}]) =$
{*"The nice girl closes the door"*}
- $\mathbf{p}([\mathtt{Det}_{la}, \mathtt{LAdj}_{belle}, \mathtt{CN}_{ferme}, \mathtt{Clit}_{la}, \mathtt{TrV}_{porte}]) =$
{*"The nice farm hangs it"*}
- $\mathbf{p}([\mathtt{Det}_{la}, \mathtt{CN}_{belle}, \mathtt{RAdj}_{ferme}, \mathtt{Clit}_{la}, \mathtt{TrV}_{porte}]) =$
{*"The firm nice girl hangs it"*}

3 The Companionship Principle

We have stated in the previous section the framework and the definitions required to describe our principle.

3.1 Potential Companion

We say that $u \in \mathcal{G}$ is a **companion** of $t \in \mathcal{G}$ if $\mathbf{anc}(t)$ and $\mathbf{anc}(u)$ are linked by a dependency in $\mathbf{dep}(L, m)$ for some lexical tagging L which contains t and u and some $m \in \mathbf{p}(L)$. The subset of elements of $\mathcal{G}$ that are companions of t is called the **potential companion set** of t.

The Companionship Principle says that if a lexical tagging contains some t but no potential companion of t, then it can be removed.

In what follows, we will generalize a bit this idea in two ways. First, the same t can be implied in more than one kind of dependency and hence it can have several different companion sets with respect to the different kinds of dependencies. Secondly, it can be the case that some companion t has to be on the right (resp. on the left) to fulfill its duty. These generalizations are done through the notion of atomic constraints defined below.

3.2 Atomic constraints

We say that a pair $(\mathcal{L}, \mathcal{R})$ of subsets of $\mathcal{G}$ is an **atomic constraint** for an initial structure $t \in \mathcal{G}$ if for each lexical tagging $L = [t_1, \ldots, t_n]$ such that $\mathbf{p}(L) \neq \emptyset$ and $t = t_i$ for some i then:

- either there is some $j < i$ such that $t_j \in \mathcal{L}$,
- or there is some $j > i$ such that $t_j \in \mathcal{R}$.

In other words, $(\mathcal{L}, \mathcal{R})$ lists the potential companions of t, respectively on the left and on the right.

A **system of constraints** for a grammar $\mathcal{G}$ is a function $\mathcal{C}$ which associates a finite set of atomic constraints to each element of $\mathcal{G}$.

The Companionship Principle is an immediate consequence of the definition of atomic constraints. It can be stated as the necessary condition:

The Companionship Principle
If a lexical tagging $[t_1, \ldots, t_n]$ has a solution then for all i and for all atomic constraints $(\mathcal{L}, \mathcal{R}) \in \mathcal{C}(t_i)$

- $\{t_1, \ldots, t_{i-1}\} \cap \mathcal{L} \neq \emptyset$
- or $\{t_{i+1}, \ldots, t_n\} \cap \mathcal{R} \neq \emptyset$.

Example 2 *Often, constraints can be expressed independently of the anchors. In our example, we use the category to refer to the subset of $\mathcal{G}$ of structures defined with this category:* LAdj *for instance refers to the subset* $\{\mathtt{LAdj}_{belle}, \mathtt{LAdj}_{ferme}\}$.

We complete the example of the previous section with the following constraints[1]*:*

❶ $t \in \mathtt{CN} \Rightarrow (\mathtt{Det}, \emptyset) \in \mathcal{C}(t)$
❷ $t \in \mathtt{LAdj} \Rightarrow (\emptyset, \mathtt{CN}) \in \mathcal{C}(t)$
❸ $t \in \mathtt{RAdj} \Rightarrow (\mathtt{CN}, \emptyset) \in \mathcal{C}(t)$
❹ $t \in \mathtt{Det} \Rightarrow (\emptyset, \mathtt{CN}) \in \mathcal{C}(t)$
❺ $t \in \mathtt{Det} \Rightarrow (\mathtt{TrV}, \mathtt{TrV} \cup \mathtt{IntrV}) \in \mathcal{C}(t)$
❻ $t \in \mathtt{TrV} \Rightarrow (\mathtt{Clit}, \mathtt{Det}) \in \mathcal{C}(t)$
❼ $t \in \mathtt{TrV} \Rightarrow (\mathtt{Det}, \emptyset) \in \mathcal{C}(t)$
❽ $t \in \mathtt{IntrV} \Rightarrow (\mathtt{Det}, \emptyset) \in \mathcal{C}(t)$
❾ $t \in \mathtt{Clit} \Rightarrow (\emptyset, \mathtt{TrV}) \in \mathcal{C}(t)$

The two constraints ❹ and ❺ for instance express that every determiner is implied in two dependencies. First, it must find a common noun on its right to build a noun phrase. Second, the noun phrase has to be used in a verbal construction.

Now, let us consider the lexical tagging: $[\mathtt{Det}_{la}, \mathtt{LAdj}_{belle}, \mathtt{TrV}_{ferme}, \mathtt{Clit}_{la}, \mathtt{CN}_{porte}]$ *and the constraint ❾ (a clitic is waiting for a transitive verb on its right). This constraint is not fulfilled by the tagging so this tagging has no solution.*

3.3 The "Companionship Principle" language

Actually, a lexical tagging is an element of the formal language $\mathcal{G}^*$ and we can consider the following three languages. First, $\mathcal{G}^*$ itself. Second, the set $C \subseteq \mathcal{G}^*$ corresponds to the lexical taggings which can be parsed. The aim of lexical disambiguation is then to exhibit for each sentence $[w_1, \ldots, w_n]$ all the lexical taggings that are within C. Third, the Companionship Principle defines the language P of lexical taggings which verify this Principle. P squeezes between the two lat-

[1]These constraints are relative to our toy grammar and are not linguistically valid in a larger context.

ter sets $C \subseteq P \subseteq \mathcal{G}^*$. Remarkably, the language P can be described as a regular language. Since C is presumably not a regular language (at least for natural languages!), P is a better regular approximation than the trivial $\mathcal{G}^*$.

Let us consider one lexical entry t and an atomic constraint $(\mathcal{L}, \mathcal{R}) \in \mathcal{C}(t)$. Then, the set of lexical taggings verifying this constraint can be described as

$$L_{t:(\mathcal{L},\mathcal{R})} = \complement((\complement\mathcal{L})^* t (\complement\mathcal{R})^*)$$

where $\complement$ denotes the complement of a set.

Since P is defined as the lexical taggings verifying all constraints, P is a regular language defined by :

$$P = \bigcap_{(\mathcal{L},\mathcal{R}) \in \mathcal{C}(t)} L_{t:(\mathcal{L},\mathcal{R})}$$

From the Companionship Principle, we derive a lexical disambiguation Principle which simply tests tagging candidates with P. Notice that P can be statically computed (at least, in theory) from the grammar itself.

Example 3 *For instance, for our example grammar, this automaton is given in the figure 1 where c=Clit, n=CN, d=Det, i=IntrV, l=LAdj, r=RAdj and t=TrV.*

A rough approximation of the size of the automaton corresponding to P can be easily computed. Since each automaton $L_{t:(\mathcal{L},\mathcal{R})}$ has 4 states, P has at most 4^m states where m is the number of atomic constraints. For instance, the grammar used in the experiments contains more than one atomic constraint for each lexical entry, and $m > |\mathcal{G}| > 10^6$. Computing P by brute-force is then intractable.

4 Implementation of the Companionship Principle with automata

In this section we show how to use the Companionship Principle for disambiguation. Actually, we propose two implementations based on the principle, an exact one and an approximate one. The latter is really fast and can be used as a first step before applying the first one.

4.1 Automaton to represent sets of lexical taggings

The number of lexical taggings grows exponentially with the length of sentences. To avoid that, we represent sets of lexical taggings as the sets of paths of some acyclic automata where transitions are labeled by elements of $\mathcal{G}$. We call such an automaton a **lexical taggings automaton** (LTA). Generally speaking, such automata save a lot of space. For instance, given a sentence $[w_1, \ldots, w_n]$ the number of lexical taggings to consider at the beginning of the parsing process is $\Pi_{1 \leq i \leq n} |\ell(w_i)|$. This set of taggings can be efficiently represented as the set of paths of the automaton with $n+1$ states $s_0, \ldots, s_n$ and with a transition from s_{i-1} to s_i with the label t for each $t \in \ell(w_i)$. This automaton has $\sum_{1 \leq i \leq n} |\ell(w_i)|$ transitions.

Example 4 *With the data of the previous examples, we have the initial automaton:*

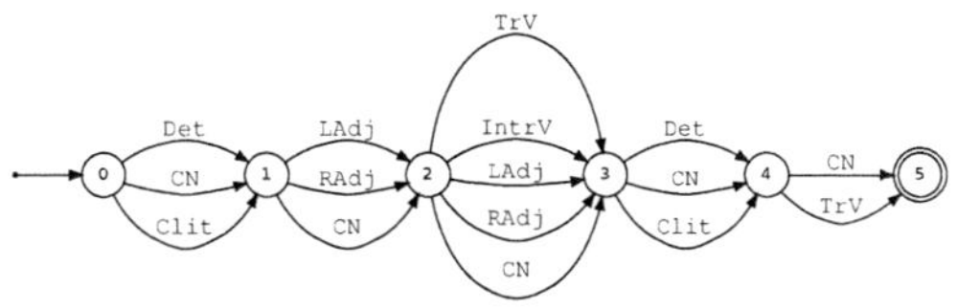

To improve readability, only the categories are given on the edges, while the French words can be inferred from the position in the automaton.

4.2 Exact Companionship Principle (ECP)

Suppose we have a LTA $\mathcal{A}$ for a sentence $[w_1, \ldots, w_n]$. For each transition t and for each atomic constraint in $(\mathcal{L}, \mathcal{R}) \in \mathcal{C}(t)$, we construct an automaton $\mathcal{A}_{t,\mathcal{L},\mathcal{R}}$ in the following way.

Each state s of $\mathcal{A}_{t,\mathcal{L},\mathcal{R}}$ is labeled with a triple composed of a state of the automaton $\mathcal{A}$ and two booleans. The intended meaning of the first boolean is to say that each path reaching this state passes through the transition t. The second boolean means that the atomic constraint $(\mathcal{L}, \mathcal{R})$ is necessarily fulfilled.

The initial state is labeled $(s_0, \mathtt{F}, \mathtt{F})$ where s_0 is the initial state of $\mathcal{A}$ and other states are labeled as follows: if $s \xrightarrow{u} s'$ in $\mathcal{A}$ then, in $\mathcal{A}_{t,\mathcal{L},\mathcal{R}}$, we have:

1. $(s, \mathtt{F}, b) \xrightarrow{u} (s', \mathtt{T}, b)$ if $u = t$
2. $(s, \mathtt{F}, b) \xrightarrow{u} (s', \mathtt{F}, \mathtt{T})$ if $u \in \mathcal{L}$
3. $(s, \mathtt{F}, b) \xrightarrow{u} (s', \mathtt{F}, b)$ if $u \notin \mathcal{L}$
4. $(s, \mathtt{T}, b) \xrightarrow{u} (s', \mathtt{T}, \mathtt{T})$ if $u \in \mathcal{R}$
5. $(s, \mathtt{T}, b) \xrightarrow{u} (s', \mathtt{T}, b)$ if $u \notin \mathcal{R}$

where $b \in \{\mathtt{T}, \mathtt{F}\}$.

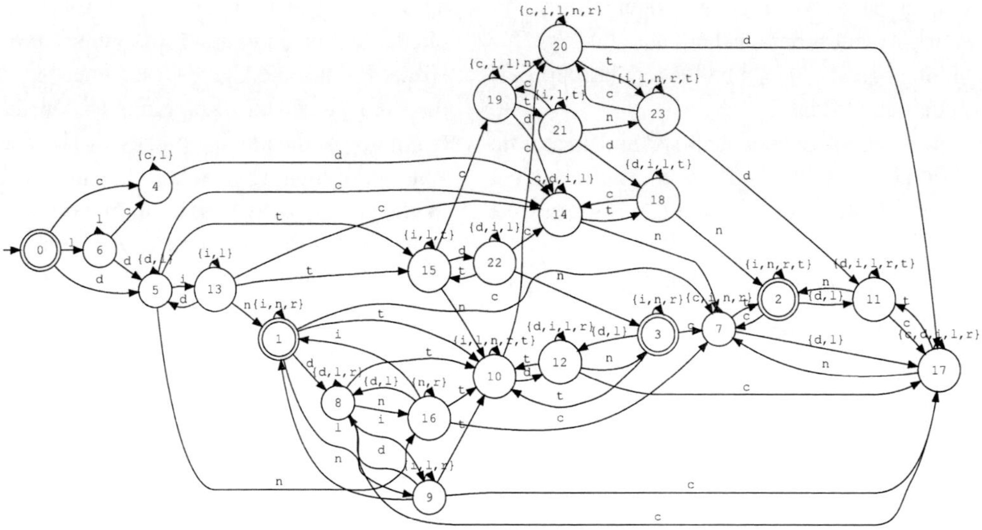

Figure 1: The P language for $\mathcal{G}$

It is then routine to show that, for each state labeled (s, b_1, b_2):

- b_1 is $\mathtt{T}$ iff all paths from the initial state to s contain the transition t;
- b_2 is $\mathtt{T}$ iff for all paths p reaching this state, either there is some $u \in \mathcal{L}$ or p goes through t and there is some $u \in \mathcal{R}$. In other words, the constraint is fulfilled.

In conclusion, a path ending with $(s_f, \mathtt{T}, \mathtt{F})$ with s_f a final state of $\mathcal{A}$ is built with transitions 1, 3 and 5 only and hence contains t but no transition able to fulfill the constraint. The final states are:

- $(s_f, \mathtt{F}, b)$: each path ending here does not contain the edge t and thus the constraint does not apply here,
- $(s_f, \mathtt{T}, \mathtt{T})$ each path ending here contains the edge t but it contains also either a transition 2 or 4, so the constraint is fulfilled by these paths.

The size of these automata is easily bounded by $4n$ where n is the size of A. Using a slightly more intricated presentation, we built automata of size $2n$.

Example 5 *We give below the automaton $\mathcal{A}$ for the atomic constraint* ❽ *(an intransitive verb is waiting for a determiner on its left):*

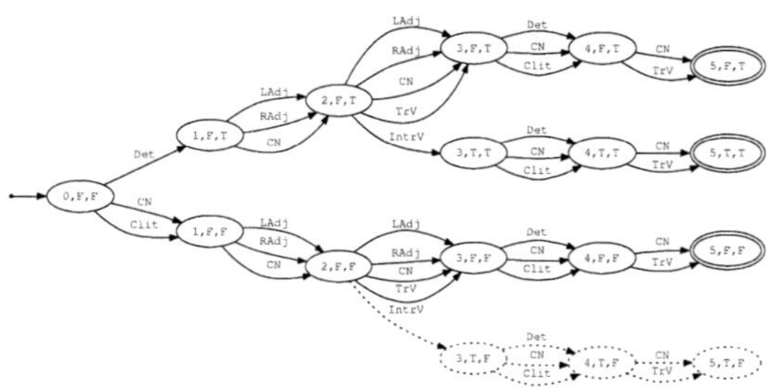

The dotted part of the graph corresponds to the part of the automaton that can be safely removed. After minimization, we finally obtain:

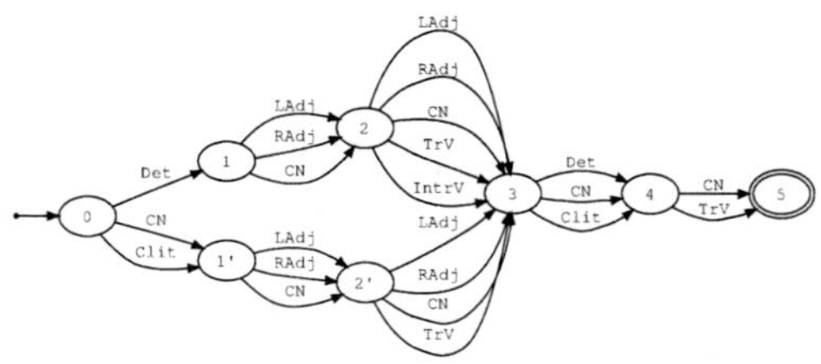

This automaton contains 234 paths (36 lexical taggings are removed by this constraint).

For each transition t of the lexical taggings automaton and for each constraint $(\mathcal{L}, \mathcal{R}) \in \mathcal{C}(t)$, we construct the atomic constraint automaton $\mathcal{A}_{t,\mathcal{L},\mathcal{R}}$. The intersection of these automata represents all the possible lexical taggings of the sentence which respect the Companionship Principle.

That is, we output :

$$\mathcal{A}_{CP} = \bigcap_{1 \leq i \leq n,\ t \in \mathcal{A}; (\mathcal{L}, \mathcal{R}) \in \mathcal{C}(t)} \mathcal{A}_{t, \mathcal{L}, \mathcal{R}}$$

It can be shown that the automaton is the same as the one obtained by intersection with the automaton of the language defined in 3.3:

$$\mathcal{A}_{CP} = \mathcal{A} \cap P$$

Example 6 *In our example, the intersection of the 9 automata built for the atomic constraints is given below:*

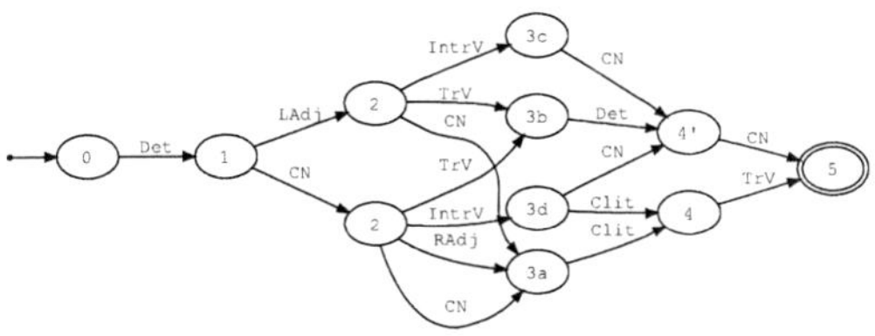

This automaton has 8 paths: there are 8 lexical taggings which fulfill every constraint.

4.3 Approximation: the Quick Companionship Principle (QCP)

The issue with the previous algorithm is that it involves a large number of automata (actually $O(n)$) where n is the size of the input sentence. Each of these automata has size $O(n)$. The theoretical complexity of the intersection is then $O(n^n)$. Sometimes, we face the exponential. So, let us provide an algorithm which approximates the Principle. The idea is to consider at the same time all the paths that contain some transition.

We consider a LTA $\mathcal{A}$. We write $\prec_{\mathcal{A}}$ the precedence relation on transitions in an automaton $\mathcal{A}$. We define $l_{\mathcal{A}}(t) = \{u \in \mathcal{G}, u \prec_{\mathcal{A}} t\}$ and $r_{\mathcal{A}}(t) = \{u \in \mathcal{G}, t \prec_{\mathcal{A}} u\}$.

For each transition $s \xrightarrow{t} s'$ and each constraint $(\mathcal{L}, \mathcal{R}) \in \mathcal{C}(t)$, if $l_{\mathcal{A}}(t) \cap \mathcal{L} = \emptyset$ and $r_{\mathcal{A}}(t) \cap \mathcal{R} = \emptyset$, then none of the lexical taggings which use the transition t has a solution and the transition t can be safely removed from the automaton.

This can be computed by a double-for loop: for each atomic constraint of each transition, verify that either the left context or the right context of the transition contains some structure to solve the constraint. Observe that the cost of this algorithm is $O(n^2)$, where n is the size of the input automaton.

Note that one must iterate this algorithm until a fixpoint is reached. Indeed, removing a transition which serves as a potential companion breaks the verification. Nevertheless, since for each step before the fixpoint is reached, we remove at least one transition, we iterate the double-for at most $O(n)$ times. The complexity of the whole algorithm is then $O(n^3)$. In practice, we have observed that the complexity is closer to $O(n^2)$: only 2 or 3 loops are enough to reach the fixpoint.

Example 7 *If we apply the QCP to the automaton of Example 4, in the first step, only the transition* $0 \xrightarrow{\texttt{CN}} 1$ *is removed by applying the atomic constraint* ❶*. In the next step, the transition* $1 \xrightarrow{\texttt{RAdj}} 2$ *is removed by applying the atomic constraint* ❸*. The fixpoint is reached and the output automaton (with 120 paths) is:*

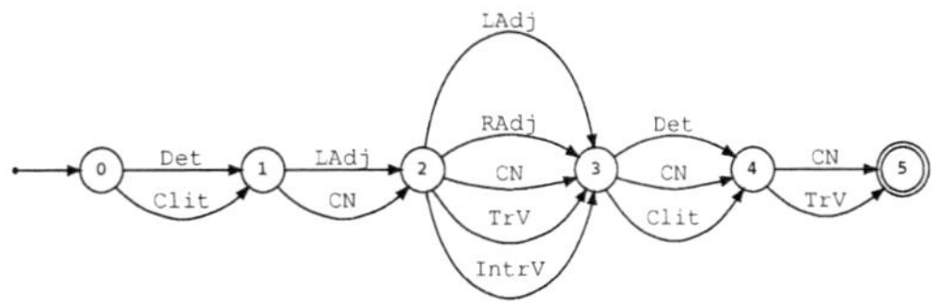

5 The Generalized Companionship Principle

In practice, of course, we have to face the problem of the computation of the constraints. In a large coverage grammar, the size of $\mathcal{G}$ is too big to compute all the constraints in advance. However, as we have seen in example 2 we can identify subsets of $\mathcal{G}$ that have the same constraints; the same way, we can use these subsets to give a more concise presentation of the $\mathcal{L}$ and $\mathcal{R}$ sets of the atomic constraints. This motivates us to define a Generalized Principle which is stated on a quotient set of $\mathcal{G}$.

5.1 Generalized atomic constraints

Let $\mathcal{U}$ be a set of subsets of $\mathcal{G}$ that are a partition of $\mathcal{G}$. For $t \in \mathcal{G}$, we write $\bar{t}$ the subset of $\mathcal{U}$ which contains t.

We say that a pair $(\mathcal{L}, \mathcal{R})$ of subsets of $\mathcal{U}$ is a **generalized atomic constraint** for $u \in \mathcal{U}$ if for each lexical tagging $L = [t_1, \ldots, t_n]$ such that $\mathrm{p}(L) \neq \emptyset$ and $u = \overline{t_i}$ for some i then:

- either there is some $j < i$ such that $\overline{t_j} \in \mathcal{L}$,
- or there is some $j > i$ such that $\overline{t_j} \in \mathcal{R}$.

A **system of generalized constraints** for a partition $\mathcal{U}$ of a grammar $\mathcal{G}$ is a function $\mathcal{C}$ which associates a finite set of generalized atomic constraints to each element of $\mathcal{U}$.

5.2 The Generalized Principle

The Generalized Companionship Principle is then an immediate consequence of the previous definition and can be stated as the necessary condition:

> **The Generalized Companionship Principle**
> If a lexical tagging $[t_1, \ldots, t_n]$ has a solution then for all i and for all generalized atomic constraints $(\mathcal{L}, \mathcal{R}) \in \mathcal{C}(\overline{t_i})$
>
> - $\{\overline{t_1}, \ldots, \overline{t_{i-1}}\} \cap \mathcal{L} \neq \emptyset$
> - or $\{\overline{t_{i+1}}, \ldots, \overline{t_n}\} \cap \mathcal{R} \neq \emptyset$.

Example 8 *The constraints given in example 2 are in fact generalized atomic constraints on the set (recall that we write* $\texttt{LAdj}$ *for the 2 elements set* $\{\texttt{LAdj}_{belle}, \texttt{LAdj}_{ferme}\}$*):*

$$\mathcal{U} = \{\texttt{Det}, \texttt{LAdj}, \texttt{RAdj}, \texttt{CN}, \texttt{Clit}, \texttt{TrV}, \texttt{IntrV}\}.$$

Then the constraints are expressed on $|\mathcal{U}| = 7$ *elements and not on* $|\mathcal{G}| = 13$.

A generalized atomic constraint on $\mathcal{U}$ can, of course, be expressed as a set of atomic constraints on $\mathcal{G}$: let $u \in \mathcal{U}$ and $t \in \mathcal{G}$ such that $\overline{t} = u$

$$(\mathcal{L}, \mathcal{R}) \in \mathcal{C}(u) \Longrightarrow \left(\bigcup_{L \in \mathcal{L}} L, \bigcup_{R \in \mathcal{R}} R\right) \in \mathcal{C}(t)$$

5.3 Implementation of lexicalized grammars

In implementations of large coverage linguistic resources, it is very common to have, first, the description of the set of "different" structures needed to describe the modeled natural language and then an anchoring mechanism that explains how words of the lexicon are linked to these structures. We call **unanchored grammar** the set $\mathcal{U}$ of different structures (not yet related to words) that are needed to describe the grammar. In this context, the lexicon is split in two parts:

- a function $\overline{\ell}$ from $\mathcal{V}$ to subsets of $\mathcal{U}$,
- an anchoring function α which builds the grammar elements from a word $w \in \mathcal{V}$ and an unanchored structure $u \in \overline{\ell}(w)$; we suppose that α verifies that $\mathbf{anc}(\alpha(w, u)) = w$.

In applications, we suppose that $\mathcal{U}$, $\overline{\ell}$ and α are given. In this context, we define the grammar as the codomain of the anchoring function:

$$\mathcal{G} = \bigcup_{w \in \mathcal{V}, u \in \overline{\ell}(w)} \alpha(w, u)$$

Now, we can define generalized constraints on the unanchored grammar, which are independent of the lexicon and can be computed statically for a given unanchored grammar.

6 Application to Interaction Grammars

In this section, we apply the Companionship Principle to the Interaction Grammars formalism. We first give a short and simplified description of IG and an example to illustrate them at work; we refer the reader to (Guillaume and Perrier, 2008) for a complete and detailed presentation.

6.1 Interaction Grammars

We illustrate some of the important features on the French sentence (2). In this sentence, *"la"* is an object clitic pronoun which is placed before the verb whereas the canonical place for the (non-clitic) object is on the right of the verb.

(2) *"Jean la demande."* [John asks for it]

The set $\mathcal{F}$ of final structures, used as output of the parsing process, contains ordered trees called **parse trees** (PT). An example of a PT for the sentence (2) is given in Figure 2. A PT for a sentence contains the words of the sentence or the empty word ϵ in its leaves (the left-right order of the tree leaves follows the left-right order of words in the input sentence). The internal nodes of a PT represent the constituents of the sentence. The morpho-syntactic properties of these constituents are described with feature structures (only the category is shown in the figure).

As IG use the Model-Theoretic Syntax (MTS) framework, a PT is defined as the model of a set of constraints. Constraints are defined at the word level: words are associated to a set of constraints formally described as a **polarized tree description** (PTD). A PTD is a set of nodes provided with relations between these nodes. The three PTDs used to build the model above are given in Figure 3. The relations used in the PTDs are: immediate dominance (lines) and immediate sisterhood (arrows). Nodes represent syntactic constituents

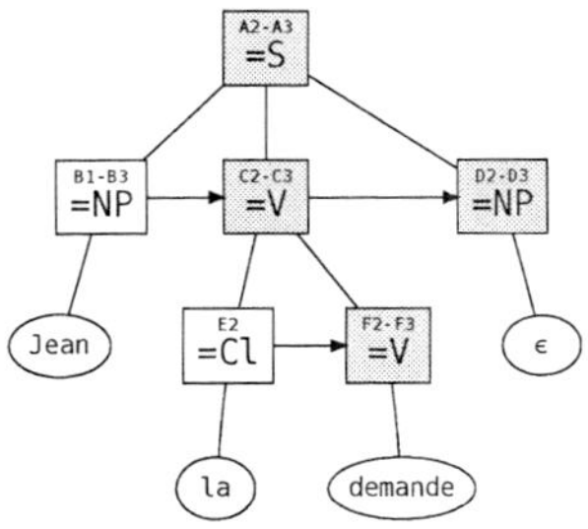

Figure 2: The PT of sentence (2)

and relations express structural dependencies between these constituents.

Moreover, nodes carry a polarity: the set of polarities is $\{+, -, =, \sim\}$. A $+$ (resp.$-$) polarity represents an available (resp. needed) resource, a $\sim$ polarity describes a node which is unsaturated. Each $+$ must be associated to exactly one $-$ (and vice versa) and each $\sim$ must be associated to at least another polarity.

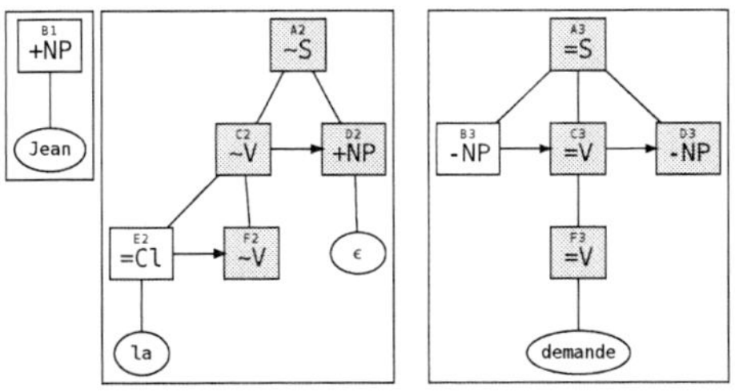

Figure 3: PTDs for the sentence (2)

Now, we define a PT to be a **model** of a set of PTDs if there is a surjective function $\mathcal{I}$ from nodes of the PTDs to nodes of the PT such that:

- relations in the PTDs are realized in the PT: if M is a daughter (resp. immediate sister) of N in some PTD then $\mathcal{I}(M)$ is a daughter (resp. immediate sister) of $\mathcal{I}(N)$;
- each node N in the PT is saturated: the composition of the polarities of the nodes in $\mathcal{I}^{-1}(N)$ with the associative and commutative rule given in Table 4 is $=$;
- the feature structure of a node N in the PT is the unification of the feature structures of the nodes in $\mathcal{I}^{-1}(N)$.

One of the strong points of IG is the flexibility given by the MTS approach: PTDs can be partially superposed to produce the final tree (whereas superposition is limited in usual CG or in TAG for instance). In our example, the four grey nodes in the PTD which contains *"la"* are superposed to the four grey nodes in the PTD which contains *"demande"* to produce the four grey nodes in the model.

	$\sim$	$-$	$+$	$=$
$\sim$	$\sim$	$-$	$+$	$=$
$-$	$-$		$=$	
$+$	$+$	$=$		
$=$	$=$			

Figure 4: Polarity composition

In order to give an idea of the full IG system, we briefly give here the main differences between our presentation and the full system.

- Dominance relations can be underspecified: for instance a PTD can impose a node to be an ancestor of another one without constraining the length of the path in the model. This is mainly used to model unbounded extraction.
- Sisterhood relations can also be underspecified: when the order on subconstituents is not total, it can be modeled without using several PTDs.
- Polarities are attached to features rather than nodes: it sometimes gives more freedom to the grammar writer when the same constituent plays a role in different constructions.
- Feature values can be shared between several nodes: once again, this is a way to factorize the unanchored grammar.

The application of the Companionship Principle is described on the reduced IG but it can be straightforwardly extended to full IG with unessential technical details.

Following the notation given in 5.3, an IG is made of:

- A finite set $\mathcal{V}$ of words;
- A finite set $\mathcal{U}$ of unanchored PTDs (without any word attached to them);
- A lexicon function $\bar{\ell}$ from $\mathcal{V}$ to subsets of $\mathcal{U}$.

When $t \in \overline{\ell}(w)$, we can construct the anchored PTD $\alpha(w, u)$. Technically, in each unanchored PTD u, a place is marked to be the anchor, i.e. to be replaced by the word during the anchoring process. Moreover, the anchoring process can also be used to refine some features. The fact that the feature can be refined gives more flexibility and more compactness to the unanchored grammar construction. In the French IG grammar, the same unanchored PTD can be used for masculine or feminine common nouns and the gender is specified during the anchoring to produce distinct anchored PTDs for masculine and feminine nouns. $\mathcal{G}$ is defined by:

$$\mathcal{G} = \bigcup_{w \in \mathcal{V}, u \in \overline{\ell}(w)} \alpha(w, u)$$

The parsing solutions of a lexical tagging is the set of PTs that are models of the list of PTDs described by the lexical tagging:

$$\mathrm{p}(L) = \{m \in \mathcal{F} \mid m \text{ is a model of } L\}$$

With the definitions of this section, an IG is a special case of AGF as defined in section 2.

6.2 Companionship Principle for IG

In order to apply the Companionship Principle, we have to explain how the generalized atomic constraints are built for a given grammar. One way is to look at dependency structures but in IG polarities are built in and then we can read the dependency information we need directly on polarities. A requirement to build a model is the saturation of all the polarities. This requirement can be expressed using atomic constraints. Each time a PTD contains an unsaturated polarity $+$, $-$ or $\sim$, we have to find some other compatible dual polarity somewhere else in the grammar to saturate it.

From the general MTS definition of IG above, we can define a step by step process to build models of a lexical tagging. The idea is to build incrementally the interpretation function $\mathcal{I}$ with the atomic operation of **node merging**. In this atomic operation, we choose two nodes and make the hypothesis that they have the same image through $\mathcal{I}$ and hence that they can be identified.

Now, suppose that the unanchored PTD u contains some unsaturated polarity p. We can use the atomic operation of node merging to test if the unanchored PTD u' can be used to saturate the polarity p. Let $\mathcal{L}$ (resp $\mathcal{R}$) be the set of PTDs that can be used on the left (resp. on the right) of u to saturate p, then $(\mathcal{L}, \mathcal{R})$ is a generalized atomic constraint in $\mathcal{C}(u)$.

7 Companionship Principle for other formalisms

As we said in the introduction, many current grammatical formalisms can more or less directly be used to generate dependency structures and hence are candidate for disambiguation with the Companionship Principle. With IG, we have seen that dependencies are strongly related to polarities: dependency constraints in IG are built with the polarity system.

We give below two short examples of polarity use to define atomic constraints on TAG and on CG. We use, as for IG, the polarity view of dependencies to describe how the constraints are built.

7.1 Tree Adjoining Grammars

Feature-based Tree Adjoining Grammars (hereafter FTAG) (Joshi, 1987) are a unification based version of Tree Adjoining Grammars. An FTAG consists of a set of elementary trees and of two tree composition operations: substitution and adjunction. There are two kinds of trees: auxiliary and initial. Substitution inserts a tree t with root r onto a leaf node l of another tree t' under the condition that l is marked as a place for substitution and l and r have compatible feature structures. Adjunction inserts an auxiliary tree t into a tree t' by splitting a node n of t' under the condition that the feature structures of the root and foot nodes of t are compatible with the *t*op and *b*ottom ones of n.

Getting the generalized atomic constraints and the model building procedure for lexical tagging is extremely similar to what was previously described for IG if we extend the polarization procedure which was described in (Gardent and Kow, 2005) to do polarity based filtering in FTAG. The idea is that for each initial tree t, its root of category C is marked as having the polarity $+C$, and its substitution nodes of category S are marked as having the polarity $-S$. A first constraint set contains trees t' whose root is polarized $+S$ and such that feature structures are unifiable. A second constraint set contains trees t'' which have a leaf that is polarized $-C$. We can extend this procedure to auxiliary trees: each auxiliary tree t of category A needs to be inserted in a node of category A of another tree t'. This gives us a constraint in the spirit of the $\sim$ polarity in IG: $\mathcal{C}(t)$ contains all the trees t' in which t could be inserted[2].

7.2 Categorial Grammars

In their type system, Categorial Grammars encode linearity constraints and dependencies between constituents. For example, a transitive verb is typed $NP\backslash S/NP$, meaning that it waits for a subject NP on its left and an object NP on its right. This type can be straightforwardly decomposed as two $-NP$ and one $+S$ polarities. Then again, getting the generalized atomic constraints is immediate and in the same spirit as what was described for IG.

7.3 Non-lexicalized formalisms

The lexicalization condition stated in section 2 excludes non-lexicalized formalisms like LFG or HPSG. Nothing actually prevents our method from being applied to these, but adding non-lexicalized combinators requires to complexify the formal account of the method. Adapting our method to HPSG would result in a generalization and unification of some of the techniques described in (Kiefer et al., 1999).

8 Experimental results

8.1 Setup

The experiments are performed using a French IG grammar on a set of 31 000 sentences taken from the newspaper *Le Monde*.

The French grammar we consider (Perrier, 2007) contains $|\mathcal{U}| = 2\,088$ unanchored trees. It covers 88% of the grammatical sentences and rejects 85% of the ungrammatical ones on the TSNLP (Lehmann et al., 1996) corpus.

The constraints have been computed on the unanchored grammar as explained in section 5: each tree contains several polarities and therefore several atomic constraints. Overall, the grammar contains 20 627 atomic constraints. It takes 2 days to compute the set of constraints and the results can be stored in a constraints file of 10MB. Of course, an atomic constraint is more interesting when the sizes of $\mathcal{L}$ and $\mathcal{R}$ are small. In our grammar, 50% of the constraints set (either $\mathcal{R}$ or $\mathcal{L}$) contain at most 40 elements and 80% of these sets contain at most 200 elements over 2 088.

We give in figure 5 the number of sentences of each length in the corpus we consider.

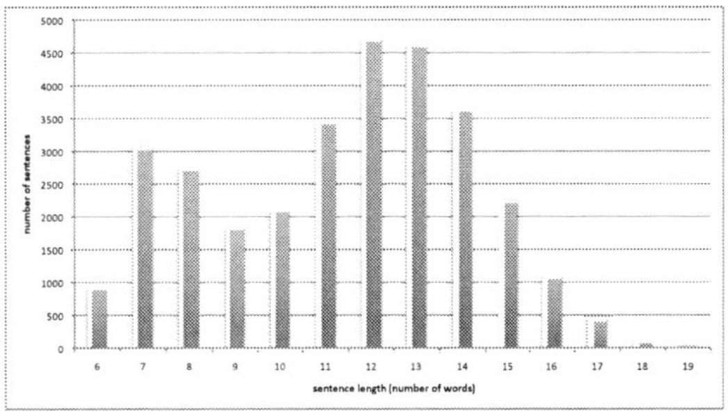

Figure 5: number of sentences of each length

8.2 Results

Two preliminary comments need to be made on the treatment of the results.

First, as we observed above, the number n of lexical taggings is a priori exponential in the length of the sentence. We thus consider its log. Moreover, because we use a raw corpus, some sentences are considered as ungrammatical by the grammar; in this case it may happen that the disambiguation method removes all taggings. In order to avoid undefined values when $n = 0$, we in fact consider $\log_{10}(1 + n)$.

Second, as expected, the ECP method is more time consuming and for some sentences the time and/or memory required is problematic. To be able to apply the ECP to a large number of sentences, we have used it after another filtering method based on polarities and described in (Bonfante et al., 2004).

Thus, for each sentence we have computed 3 different filters, each one finer than the previous:

- **QCP** the Quick Companionship Principle;
- **QCP+POL** QCP followed by a filtering technique based on polarity counting;
- **QCP+POL+ECP** the Exact Companionship Principle applied to the previous filter.

Figure 6 displays the mean computation time for each length: it confirms that the ECP is more time consuming and goes up to 5s for our long sentences.

[2]Note that in the adjunction case, the constraint is not oriented and then $\mathcal{L} = \mathcal{R}$.

Finally, we report the number of lexical taggings that each method returns. Figure 7 displays the mean value of $\log_{10}(1+n)$ where n is either the initial number of lexical taggings or the number of lexical taggings left by the filter.

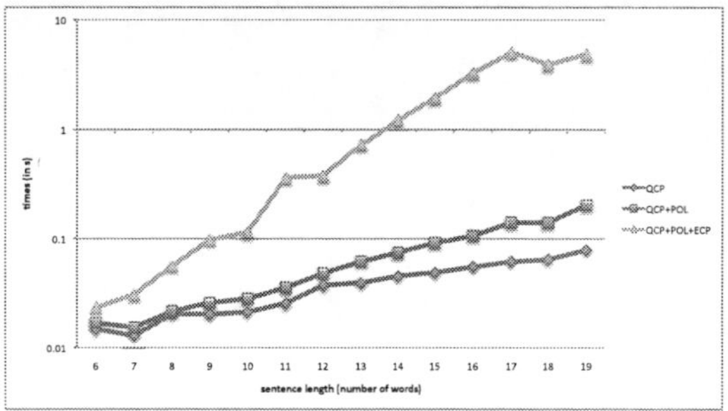

Figure 6: mean execution time (in s)

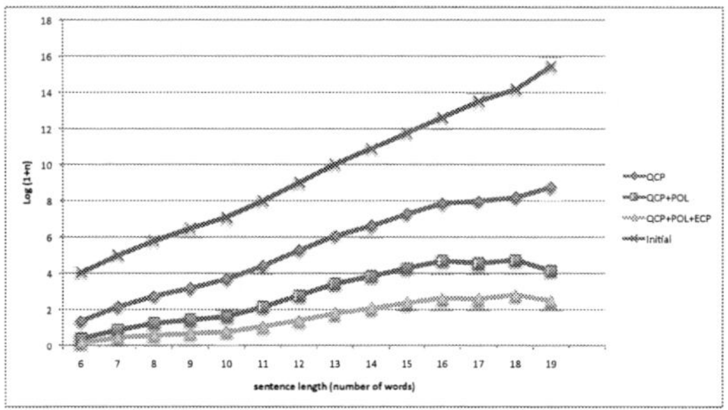

Figure 7: number of taggings (initial and after the 3 disambiguation methods)

We can observe that the slope of the lines corresponds to the mean word ambiguity: if the mean ambiguity is a then the number of taggings for a sentence of length n is about a^n and then $log(a^n) = n \cdot log(a)$. As a consequence, the mean ambiguity can be read as 10^s where s is the slope in the last figure.

An illustration is given in figure 8 which exhibits the mean word ambiguity for sentences of length 16.

init	QCP	QCP+POL	QCP+POL+ECP
6.13	3.41	1.93	1.41

Figure 8: mean word ambiguity for sentences of length 16

9 Conclusion

We have presented a disambiguation method based on dependency constraints which allows to filter out many wrong lexical taggings before entering the deep parsing. As this method relies on the computation of static constraints on the linguistic data and not on a statistical model, we can be sure that we will never remove any correct lexical tagging. Moreover, we manage to apply our methods to an interesting set of data and prove that it is efficient for a large coverage grammar and not only for a toy grammar.

These results are also an encouragement to develop further this kind of disambiguation methods. In the near future, we would like to explore some improvements.

First, we have seen that our principle cannot be computed on the whole grammar and that in its implementation we consider unanchored structures. We would like to explore the possibility of computing finer constraints (relative to the full grammar) on the fly for each sentence. We believe that this can eliminate some more taggings before entering the deep parsing.

Concerning the ECP, as we have seen, there is a kind of interplay between the efficiency of the filtering and the time of the computation. We would like to explore the possibility to define some intermediate way between QCP and ECP either by using approximate automata or using the ECP but only on a subset of elements where it is known to be efficient.

Another challenging method we would like to investigate is to use the Companionship Principle not only as a disambiguation method but as a guide for the deep parsing. Actually, we have observed for at least 20% of the words that dependencies are completely determined by the filtering methods. If deep parsing can be adapted to use this observation (this is the case for IG), this can be of great help.

Finally, we can improve the filtering using both worlds: the Companionship Principle and the polarity counting method. Two different constraints cannot be fulfilled by the same potential companion: this may allow to discover some more lexical taggings that can be safely removed.

Acknowledgments

We would like to thank the anonymous reviewers for their helpful comments and suggestions.

References

Srinivas Bangalore and Aravind K. Joshi. 1999. Supertagging: an approach to almost parsing. *Comput. Linguist.*, 25(2):237–265.

G. Bonfante, B. Guillaume, and G. Perrier. 2004. Polarization and abstraction of grammatical formalisms as methods for lexical disambiguation. In *CoLing 2004*, pages 303–309, Genève, Switzerland.

P. Boullier. 2003. Supertagging : A non-statistical parsing-based approach. In *Pro- ceedings of the 8th International Workshop on Parsing Technologies (IWPT 03)*, pages 55–65, Nancy, France.

Stephen Clark and James R. Curran. 2004. The importance of supertagging for wide-coverage CCG parsing. In *COLING '04: Proceedings of the 20th international conference on Computational Linguistics*, page 282, Morristown, NJ, USA. Association for Computational Linguistics.

S. Clark, J. Hockenmaier, and M. Steedman. 2002. Building Deep Dependency Structures with a Wide-Coverage CCG Parser. In *Proceedings of ACL'02*, pages 327–334, Philadephia, PA.

Ph. de Groote. 2001. Towards abstract categorial grammars. In *Association for Computational Linguistics, 39th Annual Meeting and 10th Conference of the European Chapter, Proceedings of the Conference*, pages 148–155.

C. Gardent and E. Kow. 2005. Generating and selecting grammatical paraphrases. *Proceedings of the ENLG*, Aug.

B. Guillaume and G. Perrier. 2008. Interaction Grammars. Research Report RR-6621, INRIA.

A. Joshi and O. Rambow. 2003. A Formalism for Dependency Grammar Based on Tree Adjoining Grammar. In *Proceedings of the Conference on Meaning-Text Theory*.

A. Joshi. 1987. An Introduction to Tree Adjoining Grammars. *Mathematics of Language*.

S. Kahane. 2006. Polarized unification grammar. In *Proceedings of Coling-ACL'02*, Sydney.

Bernd Kiefer, Hans-Ulrich Krieger, John Carroll, and Rob Malouf. 1999. A bag of useful techniques for efficient and robust parsing. In *Proceedings of the 37th annual meeting of the Association for Computational Linguistics on Computational Linguistics*, pages 473–480, Morristown, NJ, USA. Association for Computational Linguistics.

A. Koller and M. Kuhlmann. 2009. Dependency trees and the strong generative capacity of CCG. In *EACL' 2009*, Athens, Greece.

J. Kupiec. 1992. Robust Part-of-Speech Tagging Using a Hidden Markov Model. *Computer Speech and Language*, 6(3):225–242.

F. Lamarche. 2008. Proof Nets for Intuitionistic Linear Logic: Essential Nets. Technical report, INRIA.

J. Lambek. 1958. The mathematics of sentence structure. *American mathematical monthly*, pages 154–170.

S. Lehmann, S. Oepen, S. Regnier-Prost, K. Netter, V. Lux, J. Klein, K. Falkedal, F. Fouvry, D. Estival, E. Dauphin, H. Compagnion, J. Baur, L. Balkan, and D. Arnold. 1996. TSNLP: Test Suites for Natural Language Processing. In *Proceedings of the 16th conference on Computational linguistics*, pages 711–716.

J. Marchand, B. Guillaume, and G. Perrier. 2009. Analyse en dépendances à l'aide des grammaires d'interaction. In *Actes de TALN 09*, Senlis, France.

B. Merialdo. 1994. Tagging English Text with a Probabilistic Model. *Computational linguistics*, 20:155–157.

M. Moortgat and G. Morrill. 1991. Heads and phrases. Type calculus for dependency and constituent structure. In *Journal of Language, Logic and Information*.

Takashi Ninomiya, Takuya Matsuzaki, Yoshimasa Tsuruoka, Yusuke Miyao, and Jun'ichi Tsujii. 2006. Extremely lexicalized models for accurate and fast HPSG parsing. In *Proceedings of the 2006 Conference on Empirical Methods in Natural Language Processing*, pages 155–163, Sydney, Australia, July. Association for Computational Linguistics.

G. Perrier. 2007. A French Interaction Grammar. In *RANLP 2007*, pages 463–467, Borovets Bulgarie.

M. Steedman. 2000. *The Syntactic Process*. MIT Press.

L. Tesnière. 1959. *Éléments de syntaxe structurale*. Klinksieck.

Parsing Directed Acyclic Graphs with Range Concatenation Grammars

Pierre Boullier and Benoît Sagot
Alpage, INRIA Paris-Rocquencourt & Université Paris 7
Domaine de Voluceau — Rocquencourt, BP 105 — 78153 Le Chesnay Cedex, France
{Pierre.Boullier,Benoit.Sagot}@inria.fr

Abstract

Range Concatenation Grammars (RCGs) are a syntactic formalism which possesses many attractive properties. It is more powerful than Linear Context-Free Rewriting Systems, though this power is not reached to the detriment of efficiency since its sentences can always be parsed in polynomial time. If the input, instead of a string, is a Directed Acyclic Graph (DAG), only *simple* RCGs can still be parsed in polynomial time. For non-linear RCGs, this polynomial parsing time cannot be guaranteed anymore. In this paper, we show how the standard parsing algorithm can be adapted for parsing DAGs with RCGs, both in the linear (simple) and in the non-linear case.

1 Introduction

The Range Concatenation Grammar (RCG) formalism has been introduced by Boullier ten years ago. A complete definition can be found in (Boullier, 2004), together with some of its formal properties and a parsing algorithm (qualified here of *standard*) which runs in polynomial time. In this paper we shall only consider the positive version of RCGs which will be abbreviated as PRCG.[1] PRCGs are very attractive since they are more powerful than the Linear Context-Free Rewriting Systems (LCFRSs) by (Vijay-Shanker et al., 1987). In fact LCFRSs are equivalent to simple PRCGs which are a subclass of PRCGs. Many Mildly Context-Sensitive (MCS) formalisms, including Tree Adjoining Grammars (TAGs) and various kinds of Multi-Component TAGs, have already been translated into their simple PRCG counterpart in order to get an efficient parser for free (see for example (Barthélemy et al., 2001)).

However, in many Natural Language Processing applications, the most suitable input for a parser is not a sequence of words (forms, terminal symbols), but a more complex representation, usually defined as a Direct Acyclic Graph (DAG), which correspond to finite regular languages, for taking into account various kinds of ambiguities. Such ambiguities may come, among others, from the output of speech recognition systems, from lexical ambiguities (and in particular from tokenization ambiguities), or from a non-deterministic spelling correction module.

Yet, it has been shown by (Bertsch and Nederhof, 2001) that parsing of regular languages (and therefore of DAGs) using simple PRCGs is polynomial. In the same paper, it is also proven that parsing of finite regular languages (the DAG case) using arbitrary RCGs is NP-complete.

This papers aims at showing how these complexity results can be made concrete in a parser, by extending a standard RCG parsing algorithm so as to handle input DAGs. We will first recall both some basic definitions and their notations. Afterwards we will see, with a slight modification of the notion of ranges, how it is possible to use the standard PRCG parsing algorithm to get in polynomial time a parse forest with a DAG as input.[2] However, the resulting parse forest is valid only for simple PRCGs. In the non-linear case, and consistently with the complexity results mentioned above, we show that the resulting parse forest needs further processing for filtering out inconsistent parses, which may need an exponential time. The proposed filtering algorithm allows for parsing DAGs in practice with any PRCG, including non-linear ones.

[1]Negative RCGs do not add formal power since both versions exactly cover the class *PTIME* of languages recognizable in deterministic polynomial time (see (Boullier, 2004) for an indirect proof and (Bertsch and Nederhof, 2001) for a direct proof).

[2]The notion of parse forest is reminiscent of the work of (Lang, 1994).

Proceedings of the 11th International Conference on Parsing Technologies (IWPT), pages 254–265,
Paris, October 2009.

2 Basic notions and notations

2.1 Positive Range Concatenation Grammars

A *positive range concatenation grammar* (PRCG) $G = (N, T, V, P, S)$ is a 5-tuple in which:

- T and V are disjoint alphabets of *terminal symbols* and *variable symbols* respectively.

- N is a non-empty finite set of *predicates* of fixed *arity* (also called *fan-out*). We write $k = arity(A)$ if the arity of the predicate A is k. A predicate A with its *arguments* is noted $A(\vec{\alpha})$ with a vector notation such that $|\vec{\alpha}| = k$ and $\vec{\alpha}[j]$ is its jth argument. An argument is a string in $(V \cup T)^*$.

- S is a distinguished predicate called the *start predicate* (or *axiom*) of arity 1.

- P is a finite set of *clauses*. A clause c is a rewriting rule of the form $A_0(\vec{\alpha_0}) \rightarrow A_1(\vec{\alpha_1}) \dots A_r(\vec{\alpha_r})$ where r, $r \geq 0$ is its *rank*, $A_0(\vec{\alpha_0})$ is its *left-hand side* or *LHS*, and $A_1(\vec{\alpha_1}) \dots A_r(\vec{\alpha_r})$ its *right-hand side* or *RHS*. By definition $c[i] = A_i(\vec{\alpha_i})$, $0 \leq i \leq r$ where A_i is a predicate and $\vec{\alpha_i}$ its arguments; we note $c[i][j]$ its jth argument; $c[i][j]$ is of the form $X_1 \dots X_{n_{ij}}$ (the X_k's are terminal or variable symbols), while $c[i][j][k]$, $0 \leq k \leq n_{ij}$ is a *position* within $c[i][j]$.

For a given clause c, and one of its predicates $c[i]$ a *subargument* is defined as a substring of an argument $c[i][j]$ of the predicate $c[i]$. It is denoted by a pair of positions $(c[i][j][k], c[i][j][k'])$, with $k \leq k'$.

Let $w = a_1 \dots a_n$ be an input string in T^*, each occurrence of a substring $a_{l+1} \dots a_u$ is a pair of positions $(w[l], w[u])$ s.t. $0 \leq l \leq u \leq n$ called a *range* and noted $\langle l..u \rangle_w$ or $\langle l..u \rangle$ when w is implicit. In the range $\langle l..u \rangle$, l is its *lower bound* while u is its *upper bound*. If $l = u$, the range $\langle l..u \rangle$ is an *empty* range, it spans an empty substring. If $\rho_1 = \langle l_1..u_1 \rangle$, $\dots$ and $\rho_m = \langle l_m..u_m \rangle$ are ranges, the *concatenation* of $\rho_1, \dots, \rho_m$ noted $\rho_1 \dots \rho_m$ is the range $\rho = \langle l..u \rangle$ if and only if we have $u_i = l_{i+1}$, $1 \leq i < m$, $l = l_1$ and $u = u_m$.

If $c = A_0(\vec{\alpha_0}) \rightarrow A_1(\vec{\alpha_1}) \dots A_r(\vec{\alpha_r})$ is a clause, each of its subarguments $(c[i][j][k], c[i][j][k'])$ may take a range $\rho = \langle l..u \rangle$ as value: we say that it is *instantiated* by ρ. However, the instantiation of a subargument is subjected to the following constraints.

- If the subargument is the empty string (i.e., $k = k'$), ρ is an empty range.

- If the subargument is a terminal symbol (i.e., $k + 1 = k'$ and $X_{k'} \in T$), ρ is such that $l + 1 = u$ and $a_u = X_{k'}$. Note that several occurrences of the same terminal symbol may be instantiated by different ranges.

- If the subargument is a variable symbol (i.e., $k + 1 = k'$ and $X_{k'} \in V$), any occurrence $(c[i'][j'][m], c[i'][j'][m'])$ of $X_{k'}$ is instantiated by ρ. Thus, each occurrence of the same variable symbol must be instantiated by the same range.

- If the subargument is the string $X_{k+1} \dots X_{k'}$, ρ is its instantiation if and only if we have $\rho = \rho_{k+1} \dots \rho_{k'}$ in which $\rho_{k+1}, \dots, \rho_{k'}$ are respectively the instantiations of $X_{k+1}, \dots, X_{k'}$.

If in c we replace each argument by its instantiation, we get an *instantiated clause* noted $A_0(\vec{\rho_0}) \rightarrow A_1(\vec{\rho_1}) \dots A_r(\vec{\rho_r})$ in which each $A_i(\vec{\rho_i})$ is an *instantiated predicate*.

A binary relation called *derive* and noted $\underset{G,w}{\Rightarrow}$ is defined on strings of instantiated predicates. If Γ_1 and Γ_2 are strings of instantiated predicates, we have

$$\Gamma_1\, A_0(\vec{\rho_0})\, \Gamma_2 \underset{G,w}{\Rightarrow} \Gamma_1\, A_1(\vec{\rho_1}) \dots A_m(\vec{\rho_m})\, \Gamma_2$$

if and only if $A_0(\vec{\rho_0}) \rightarrow A_1(\vec{\rho_1}) \dots A_m(\vec{\rho_m})$ is an instantiated clause.

The *(string) language* of a PRCG G is the set $\mathcal{L}(G) = \{w \mid S(\langle 0..|w| \rangle_w) \overset{+}{\underset{G,w}{\Rightarrow}} \varepsilon\}$. In other words, an input string $w \in T^*$, $|w| = n$ is a *sentence* of G if and only there exists a *complete derivation* which starts from $S(\langle 0..n \rangle)$ (the instantiation of the start predicate on the whole input text) and leads to the empty string (of instantiated predicates). The *parse forest* of w is the CFG whose axiom is $S(\langle 0..n \rangle)$ and whose productions are the instantiated clauses used in all complete derivations.[3]

We say that the arity of a PRCG is k, and we call it a k-PRCG, if and only if k is the maximum

[3]Note that this parse forest has no terminal symbols (its language is the empty string).

arity of its predicates ($k = \max_{A \in N} arity(A)$). We say that a k-PRCG is *simple*, we have a simple k-PRCG, if and only if each of its clause is

- *non-combinatorial*: the arguments of its RHS predicates are single variables;
- *non-erasing*: each variable which occur in its LHS (resp. RHS) also occurs in its RHS (resp. LHS);
- *linear*: there are no variables which occur more than once in its LHS and in its RHS.

The subclass of simple PRCGs is of importance since it is MCS and is the one equivalent to LCFRSs.

2.2 Finite Automata

A *non-deterministic finite automaton* (NFA) is the 5-tuple $A = (Q, \Sigma, \delta, q_0, F)$ where Q is a non empty finite set of *states*, Σ is a finite set of *terminal symbols*, δ is the ternary *transition relation* $\delta = \{(q_i, t, q_j) | q_i, q_j \in Q \wedge t \in \Sigma \cup \{\varepsilon\}\}$, q_0 is a distinguished element of Q called the *initial state* and F is a subset of Q whose elements are called *final states*. The size of A, noted $|A|$, is its number of states ($|A| = |Q|$).

We define the ternary relation δ^* on $Q \times \Sigma^* \times Q$ as the smallest set s.t. $\delta^* = \{(q, \varepsilon, q) \mid q \in Q\} \cup \{(q_1, xt, q_3) \mid (q_1, x, q_2) \in \delta^* \wedge (q_2, t, q_3) \in \delta\}$. If $(q, x, q') \in \delta^*$, we say that x is a *path* between q and q'. If $q = q_0$ and $q' \in F$, x is a *complete path*.

The *language* $\mathcal{L}(A)$ *defined* (*generated*, *recognized*, *accepted*) by the NFA A is the set of all its complete paths.

We say that a NFA is *empty* if and only if its language is empty. Two NFAs are *equivalent* if and only if they define the same language. A NFA is ε*-free* if and only if its transition relation does not contain a transition of the form (q_1, ε, q_2). Every NFA can be transformed into an equivalent ε-free NFA (this classical result and those recalled below can be found, e.g., in (Hopcroft and Ullman, 1979)).

As usual, a NFA is drawn with the following conventions: a transition (q_1, t, q_2) is an arrow labelled t from state q_1 to state q_2 which are printed with a surrounded circle. Final states are doubly circled while the initial state has a single unconnected, unlabelled input arrow.

A *deterministic finite automaton* (DFA) is a NFA in which the transition relation δ is a *transition function*, $\delta : Q \times \Sigma \rightarrow Q$. In other words, there are no ε-transitions and if $(q_1, t, q_2) \in \delta$, $t = \varepsilon$ and $\nexists (q_1, t, q_2') \in \delta$ with $q_2' = q_2$. Each NFA can be transformed by the *subset construction* into an equivalent DFA. Moreover, each DFA can be transformed by a *minimization algorithm* into an equivalent DFA which is *minimal* (i.e., there is no other equivalent DFA with fewer states).

2.3 Directed acyclic graphs

Formally, a directed acyclic graph (DAG) $D = (Q, \Sigma, \delta, q_0, F)$ is an NFA for which there exists a strict order relation $<$ on Q such that $(p, t, q) \in \delta \Rightarrow p < q$. Without loss of generality we may assume that $<$ is a total order.

Of course, as NFAs, DAGs can be transformed into equivalent deterministic or minimal DAGs.

3 DAGs and PRCGs

A DAG D is *recognized* (*accepted*) by a PRCG G if and only if $\mathcal{L}(D) \cap \mathcal{L}(G) = \emptyset$. A trivial way to solve this recognition (or parsing) problem is to extract the complete paths of $\mathcal{L}(D)$ (which are in finite number) one by one and to parse each such string with a standard PRCG parser, the (complete) parse forest for D being the union of each individual forest.[4] However since DAGs may define an exponential number of strings w.r.t. its own size,[5] the previous operation would take an exponential time in the size of D, and the parse forest would also have an exponential size.

The purpose of this paper is to show that it is possible to directly parse a DAG (without any unfolding) by sharing identical computations. This sharing may lead to a polynomial parse time for an exponential number of sentences, but, in some cases, the parse time remains exponential.

3.1 DAGs and Ranges

In many NLP applications the source text cannot be considered as a sequence of terminal symbols, but rather as a finite set of finite strings. As

[4]These forests do not share any production (instantiated clause) since ranges in a particular forest are all related to the corresponding source string w (i.e., are all of the form $\langle i..j \rangle_w$). To be more precise the union operation on individual forests must be completed in adding productions which connect the new (super) axiom (say S') with each root and which are, for each w of the form $S' \rightarrow S(\langle 0..|w| \rangle_w)$.

[5]For example the language $(a|b)^n$, $n > 0$ which contains 2^n strings can be defined by a minimal DAG whose size is $n + 1$.

mentioned in th introduction, this non-unique string could be used to encode not-yet-solved ambiguities in the input. DAGs are a convenient way to represent these finite sets of strings by factorizing their common parts (thanks to the minimization algorithm).

In order to use DAGs as inputs for PRCG parsing we will perform two generalizations.

The first one follows. Let $w = t_1 \dots t_n$ be a string in some alphabet Σ and let $Q = \{q_i \mid 0 \leq i \leq n\}$ be a set of $n+1$ *bounds* with a total order relation $<$, we have $q_0 < q_1 < \dots < q_n$. The sequence $\pi = q_0 t_1 q_1 t_2 q_2 \dots t_n q_n \in Q \times (\Sigma \times Q)^n$ is called a *bounded string* which *spells* w. A range is a pair of bounds (q_i, q_j) with $q_i < q_j$ noted $\langle p_i..p_j \rangle_\pi$ and any triple of the form $(q_{i-1} t_i q_i)$ is called a *transition*. All the notions around PRCGs defined in Section 2.1 easily generalize from strings to bounded strings. It is also the case for the standard parsing algorithm of (Boullier, 2004).

Now the next step is to move from bounded strings to DAGs. Let $D = (Q, \Sigma, \delta, q_0, F)$ be a DAG. A string $x \in \Sigma^*$ s.t. we have $(q_1, x, q_2) \in \delta^*$ is called a *path* between q_1 and q_2 and a string $\pi = q t_1 q_1 \dots t_p q_p \in Q \times (\Sigma \cup \{\varepsilon\} \times Q)^*$ is a *bounded path* and we say that π *spells* $t_1 t_2 \dots t_p$. A path x from q_0 to $f \in F$ is a *complete path* and a bounded path of the form $q_0 t_1 \dots t_n f$ with $f \in F$ is a *complete bounded path*. In the context of a DAG D, a range is a pair of states (q_i, q_j) with $q_i < q_j$ noted $\langle q_i..q_j \rangle_D$. A range $\langle q_i..q_j \rangle_D$ is *valid* if and only if there exists a path from q_i to q_j in D. Of course, any range $\langle p..q \rangle_D$ defines its associated sub-DAG $D_{\langle p..q \rangle} = (Q_{\langle p..q \rangle}, \Sigma_{\langle p..q \rangle}, \delta_{\langle p..q \rangle}, p, \{q\})$ as follows. Its transition relation is $\delta_{\langle p..q \rangle} = \{(r,t,s) \mid (r,t,s) \in \delta \wedge (p, x', r), (s, x'', q) \in \delta^*\}$. If $\delta_{\langle p..q \rangle} = \emptyset$ (i.e., there is no path between p and q), $D_{\langle p..q \rangle}$ is the empty DAG, otherwise $Q_{\langle p..q \rangle}$ (resp. $\Sigma_{\langle p..q \rangle}$) are the states (resp. terminal symbols) of the transitions of $\delta_{\langle p..q \rangle}$. With this new definition of ranges, the notions of instantiation and derivation easily generalize from bounded strings to DAGs.

The language of a PRCG G for a DAG D is defined by $\overset{\bullet}{\mathcal{L}}(G, D) = \bigcup_{f \in F} \{x \mid S(\langle q_0..f \rangle_D) \overset{+}{\underset{G,D}{\Rightarrow}} \varepsilon\}$. Let $x \in \mathcal{L}(D)$, it is not very difficult to show that if $x \in \mathcal{L}(G)$ then we have $x \in \overset{\bullet}{\mathcal{L}}(G, D)$. However, the converse is not true (see Example 1), a sentence of $\mathcal{L}(D) \cap \overset{\bullet}{\mathcal{L}}(G, D)$ may not be in $\mathcal{L}(G)$. To put it differently, if we use the standard RCG parser, with the ranges of a DAG, we produce the shared parse-forest for the language $\overset{\bullet}{\mathcal{L}}(G, D)$ which is a superset of $\mathcal{L}(D) \cap \mathcal{L}(G)$.

However, if G is a simple PRCG, we have the equality $\mathcal{L}(G) = \bigcup_{D \text{ is a DAG}} \overset{\bullet}{\mathcal{L}}(G, D)$. Note that the subclass of simple PRCGs is of importance since it is MCS and it is the one equivalent to LCFRSs. The informal reason of the equality is the following. If an instantiated predicate $A_i(\vec{\rho_i})$ succeeds in some RHS, this means that each of its ranges $\vec{\rho_i}[j] = \langle k..l \rangle_D$ has been recognized as being a component of A_i, more precisely their exists a path from k to l in D which is a component of A_i. The range $\langle k..l \rangle_D$ selects in D a set $\delta_{\langle k..l \rangle_D}$ of transitions (the transitions used in the bounded paths from k to l). Because of the linearity of G, there is no other range in that RHS which selects a transition in $\delta_{\langle k..l \rangle_D}$. Thus the bounded paths selected by all the ranges of that RHS are disjoints. In other words, any occurrence of a valid instantiated range $\langle i..j \rangle_D$ selects a set of paths which is a subset of $\mathcal{L}(D_{\langle i..j \rangle})$.

Now, if we consider a non-linear PRCG, in some of its clauses, there is a variable, say X, which has several occurrences in its RHS (if we consider a top-down non-linearity). Now assume that for some input DAG D, an instantiation of that clause is a component of some complete derivation. Let $\langle p..q \rangle_D$ be the instantiation of X in that instantiated clause. The fact that a predicate in which X occurs succeeds means that there exist paths from p to q in $D_{\langle p..q \rangle}$. The same thing stands for all the other occurrences of X but nothing force these paths to be identical or not.

Example 1.

Let us take an example which will be used throughout the paper. It is a non-linear 1-PRCG which defines the language $a^n b^n c^n$, $n \geq 0$ as the intersection of the two languages $a^* b^n c^n$ and $a^n b^n c^*$. Each of these languages is respectively defined by the predicates $a^* b^n c^n$ and $a^n b^n c^*$; the start predicate is $a^n b^n c^n$.

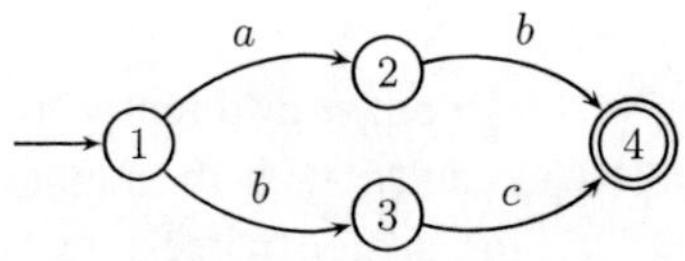

Figure 1: Input DAG associated with $ab|bc$.

$$
\begin{array}{lcl}
a^n b^n c^n(X) & \rightarrow & a^* b^n c^n(X)\ a^n b^n c^*(X) \\
\\
a^* b^n c^n(aX) & \rightarrow & a^* b^n c^n(X) \\
a^* b^n c^n(X) & \rightarrow & b^n c^n(X) \\
b^n c^n(bXc) & \rightarrow & b^n c^n(X) \\
b^n c^n(\varepsilon) & \rightarrow & \varepsilon \\
\\
a^n b^n c^*(Xc) & \rightarrow & a^n b^n c^*(X) \\
a^n b^n c^*(X) & \rightarrow & a^n b^n(X) \\
a^n b^n(aXb) & \rightarrow & a^n b^n(X) \\
a^n b^n(\varepsilon) & \rightarrow & \varepsilon
\end{array}
$$

If we use this PRCG to parse the DAG of Figure 1 which defines the language $\{ab, bc\}$, *we (erroneously) get the non-empty parse forest of Figure 2 though neither* ab *nor* bc *is in* $a^n b^n c^n$.[6] *It is not difficult to see that the problem comes from the non-linear instantiated variable* $X_{\langle 1..4\rangle}$ *in the start node, and more precisely from the actual (wrong) meaning of the three different occurrences of* $X_{\langle 1..4\rangle}$ *in* $a^n b^n c^n(X_{\langle 1..4\rangle}) \rightarrow a^* b^n c^n(X_{\langle 1..4\rangle})\ a^n b^n c^*(X_{\langle 1..4\rangle})$. *The first occurrence in its RHS says that there exists a path in the input DAG from state* 1 *to state* 4 *which is an* $a^* b^n c^n$. *The second occurrence says that there exists a path from state* 1 *to state* 4 *which is an* $a^n b^n c^*$. *While the LHS occurrence (wrongly) says that there exists a path from state* 1 *to state* 4 *which is an* $a^n b^n c^n$. *However, if the two* $X_{\langle 1..4\rangle}$*'s in the RHS had selected common paths (this is not possible here) between* 1 *and* 4, *a valid interpretation could have been proposed.*

With this example, we see that the difficulty of DAG parsing only arises with non-linear PRCGs.

If we consider linear PRCGs, the sub-class of the PRCGs which is equivalent to LCFRSs, the standard algorithm works perfectly well with input DAGs, since a valid instantiation of an argument of a predicate in a clause by some range $\langle p..q\rangle$ means that there exists (at least) one path between p and q which is recognized.

The paper will now concentrate on non-linear PRCGs, and will present a new valid parsing algorithm and study its complexities (in space and time).

In order to simplify the presentation we introduce this algorithm as a post-processing pass which will work on the shared parse-forest output by the (slightly modified) standard algorithm which accepts DAGs as input.

3.2 Parsing DAGs with non-linear PRCGs

The standard parsing algorithm of (Boullier, 2004) working on a string w can be sketched as follows. It uses a single memoized boolean function *predicate*$(A, \vec{\rho})$ where A is a predicate and $\vec{\rho}$ is a vector of ranges whose dimension is *arity*(A). The initial call to that function has the form *predicate* $(S, \langle 0..|w|\rangle)$. Its purpose is, for each A_0-clause, to instantiate each of its symbols in a consistant way. For example if we assume that the ith argument of the LHS of the current A_0-clause is $\alpha'_i XaY\alpha''_i$ and that the ith component of $\vec{\rho_0}$ is the range $\langle p_i..q_i\rangle$ an instantiation of X, a an Y by the ranges $\langle p_X..q_X\rangle$, $\langle p_a..q_a\rangle$ and $\langle p_Y..q_Y\rangle$ is such that we have $p_i \leq p_X \leq q_X = p_a < q_a = p_a + 1 = p_Y \leq q_Y \leq q_i$ and $w = w'aw''$ with $|w'| = p_a$. Since the PRCG is non bottom-up erasing, the instantiation of all the LHS symbols implies that all the arguments of the RHS predicates A_i are also instantiated and gathered into the vector of ranges $\vec{\rho_i}$. Now, for each i $(1 \leq i \leq |RHS|)$, we can call *predicate* $(A_i, \vec{\rho_i})$. If all these calls succeed, the instantiated clause can be stored as a component of the shared parse forest.[7]

In the case of a DAG $D = (Q, \Sigma, \delta, q_0, F)$ as input, there are two slight modifications, the initial call is changed by the conjunctive call *predicate*$(S, \langle q_0..f_1\rangle) \vee \ldots \vee$ *predicate* $(S, \langle q_0..f_{|F|}\rangle)$ with $f_i \in F$[8] and the terminal symbol a can be instantiated by the range $\langle p_a..q_a\rangle_D$ only if (p_a, a, q_a)

[6] In this forest oval nodes denote different instantiated predicates, while its associated instantiated clauses are presented as its daughter(s) and are denoted by square nodes. The LHS of each instantiated clause shows the instantiation of its LHS symbols. The RHS is the corresponding sequence of instantiated predicates. The number of daughters of each square node is the number of its RHS instantiated predicates.

[7] Note that such an instantiated clause could be unreachable from the (future) instantiated start symbol which will be the axiom of the shared forest considered as a CFG.

[8] Technically, each of these calls produces a forest. These individual forests may share subparts but their roots are all different. In order to have a true forest, we introduce a new root, the *super-root* whose daughters are the individual forests.

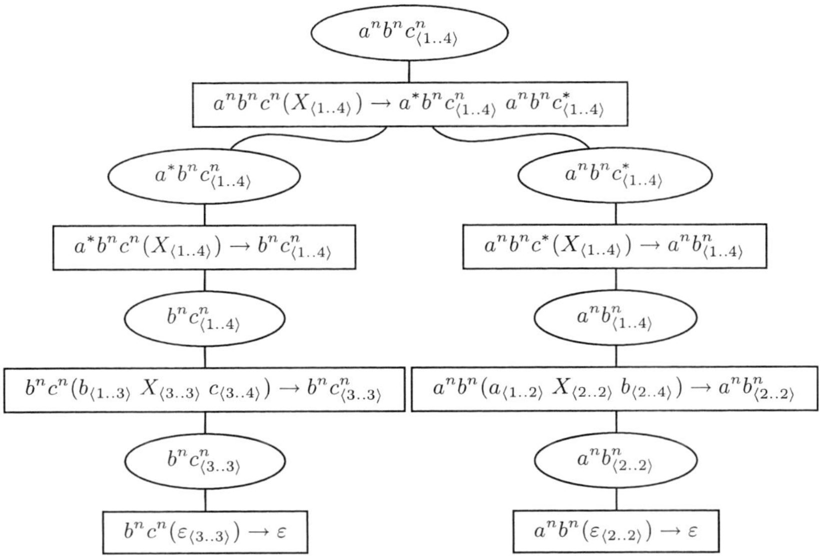

Figure 2: Parse forest for the input DAG $ab|bc$.

is a transition in δ. The variable symbol X can be instantiated by the range $\langle p_X..q_X\rangle_D$ only if $\langle p_X..q_X\rangle_D$ is valid.

3.3 Forest Filtering

We assume here that for a given PRCG G we have built the parse forest of an input DAG D as explained above and that each instantiated clause of that forest contains the range $\langle p_X..q_X\rangle_D$ of each of its instantiated symbols X. We have seen in Example 1 that this parse forest is valid if G is linear but may well be unvalid if G is non-linear. In that latter case, this happens because the range $\langle p_X..q_X\rangle_D$ of each instantiation of the non-linear variable X selects the whole sub-DAG $D_{\langle p_X..q_X\rangle}$ while each instantiation should only select a sub-language of $\mathcal{L}(D_{\langle p_X..q_X\rangle})$. For each occurrence of X in the LHS or RHS of a non-linear clause, its sub-languages could of course be different from the others. In fact, we are interested in their intersections: If their intersections are non empty, this is the language which will be associated with $\langle p_X..q_X\rangle_D$, otherwise, if their intersections are empty, then the instantiation of the considered clause fails and must thus be removed from the forest. Of course, we will consider that the language (a finite number of strings) associated with each occurrence of each instantiated symbol is represented by a DAG.

The idea of the forest filtering algorithm is to first compute the DAGs associated with each argument of each instantiated predicate during a bottom-up walk. These DAGs are called *decorations*. This processing will perform DAG compositions (including intersections, as suggested above), and will erase clauses in which empty intersections occur. If the DAG associated with the single argument of the super-root is empty, then parsing failed.

Otherwise, a top-down walk is launched (see below), which may also erase non-valid instantiated clauses. If necessary, the algorithm is completed by a classical CFG algorithm which erase non productive and unreachable symbols leaving a *reduced* grammar/forest.

In order to simplify our presentation we will assume that the PRCGs are non-combinatorial and bottom-up non-erasing. However, we can note that the following algorithm can be generalized in order to handle combinatorial PRCGs and in particular with overlapping arguments.[9] Moreover, we will assume that the forest is non cyclic (or equivalently that all cycles have previously been removed).[10]

[9]For example the non-linear combinatorial clause $A(XYZ) \rightarrow B(XY)\ B(YZ)$ has overlapping arguments.

[10]By a classical algorithm from the CFG technology.

3.3.1 The Bottom-Up Walk

For this principle algorithm, we assume that for each instantiated clause in the forest, a DAG will be associated with each occurrence of each instantiated symbol. More precisely, for a given instantiated A_0-clause, the DAGs associated with the RHS symbol occurrences are composed (see below) to build up DAGs which will be associated with each argument of its LHS predicate. For each LHS argument, this composition is directed by the sequence of symbols in the argument itself.

The forest is walked bottom-up starting from its leaves. The constraint being that an instantiated clause is visited if and only if all its RHS instantiated predicates have already all been visited (computed). This constraint can be satisfied for any non-cyclic forest.

To be more precise, consider an instantiation $c_\rho = A_0(\vec{\rho_0}) \rightarrow A_1(\vec{\rho_1}) \ldots A_p(\vec{\rho_p})$ of the clause $c = A_0(\vec{\alpha_0}) \rightarrow A_1(\vec{\alpha_1}) \ldots A_m(\vec{\alpha_m})$, we perform the following sequence:

1. If the clause is not top-down linear (i.e., there exist multiple occurrences of the same variables in its RHS arguments), for such variable X let the range $\langle p_X..q_X \rangle$ be its instantiation (by definition, all occurrences are instantiated by the same range), we perform the intersection of the DAGs associated with each instantiated predicate argument X. If one intersection results in an empty DAG, the instantiated clause is removed from the forest. Otherwise, we perform the following steps.

2. If a RHS variable Y is linear, it occurs once in the jth argument of predicate A_i. We perform a brand new copy of the DAG associated with the jth argument of the instantiation of A_i.

3. At that moment, all instantiated variables which occur in c_ρ are associated with a DAG. For each occurrence of a terminal symbol t in the LHS arguments we associate a (new) DAG whose only transition is (p, t, q) where p and q are brand new states with, of course, $p < q$.

4. Here, all symbols (terminals or variables) are associated with disjoints DAGs. For each LHS argument $\vec{\alpha_0}[i] = X^i_1 \ldots X^i_j \ldots X^i_{p_i}$, we associate a new DAG which is the concatenation of the DAGs associated with the symbols $X^i_1, \ldots, X^i_j, \ldots$ and $X^i_{p_i}$.

5. Here each LHS argument of c_ρ is associated with a non empty DAG, we then report the individual contribution of c_ρ into the (already computed) DAGs associated with the arguments of its LHS $A_0(\vec{\rho_0})$. The DAG associated with the ith argument of $A_0(\vec{\rho_0})$ is the union (or a copy if it is the first time) of its previous DAG value with the DAG associated with the ith argument of the LHS of c_ρ.

This bottom-up walk ends on the super-root with a final decoration say R. In fact, during this bottom-up walk, we have computed the intersection of the languages defined by the input DAG and by the PRCG (i.e., we have $\mathcal{L}(R) = \mathcal{L}(D) \cap \mathcal{L}(G)$).

Example 2.

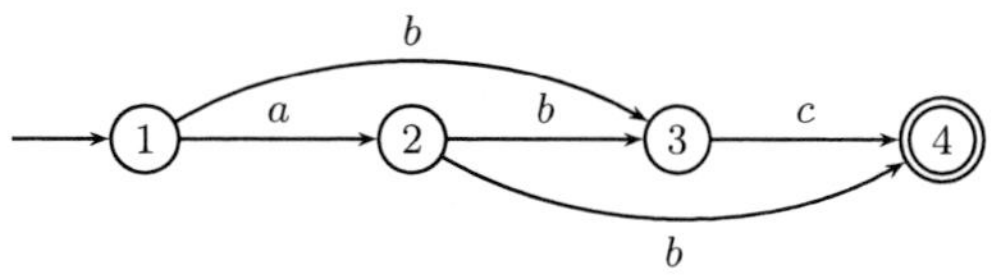

Figure 3: Input DAG associated with $abc|ab|bc$.

With the PRCG of Example 1 and the input DAG of Figure 3, we get the parse forest of Figure 4 whose transitions are decorated by the DAGs computed by the bottom-up algorithm.[11]
The crucial point to note here is the intersection which
is performed between $\{abc, bc\}$ *and* $\{abc, ab\}$ *on* $a^nb^nc^n(X_{\langle 1..4\rangle}) \rightarrow a^*b^nc^n_{\langle 1..4\rangle}\ a^nb^nc^*_{\langle 1..4\rangle}$. *The non-empty set* $\{abc\}$ *is the final result assigned to the instantiated start symbol. Since this result is non empty, it shows that the input DAG D is recognized by G. More precisely, this shows that the sub-language of D which is recognized by G is* $\{abc\}$.

However, as shown in the previous example, the (undecorated) parse forest is not the forest built for the DAG $\mathcal{L}(D) \cap \mathcal{L}(G)$ since it may contain non-valid parts (e.g., the transitions labelled $\{bc\}$ or $\{ab\}$ in our example). In order to get the

[11]For readability reasons these DAGs are represented by their languages (i.e., set of strings). Bottom-up transitions from instantiated clauses to instantiated predicates reflects the computations performed by that instantiated clause while bottom-up transitions from instantiated predicates to instantiated clauses are the union of the DAGs entering that instantiated predicate.

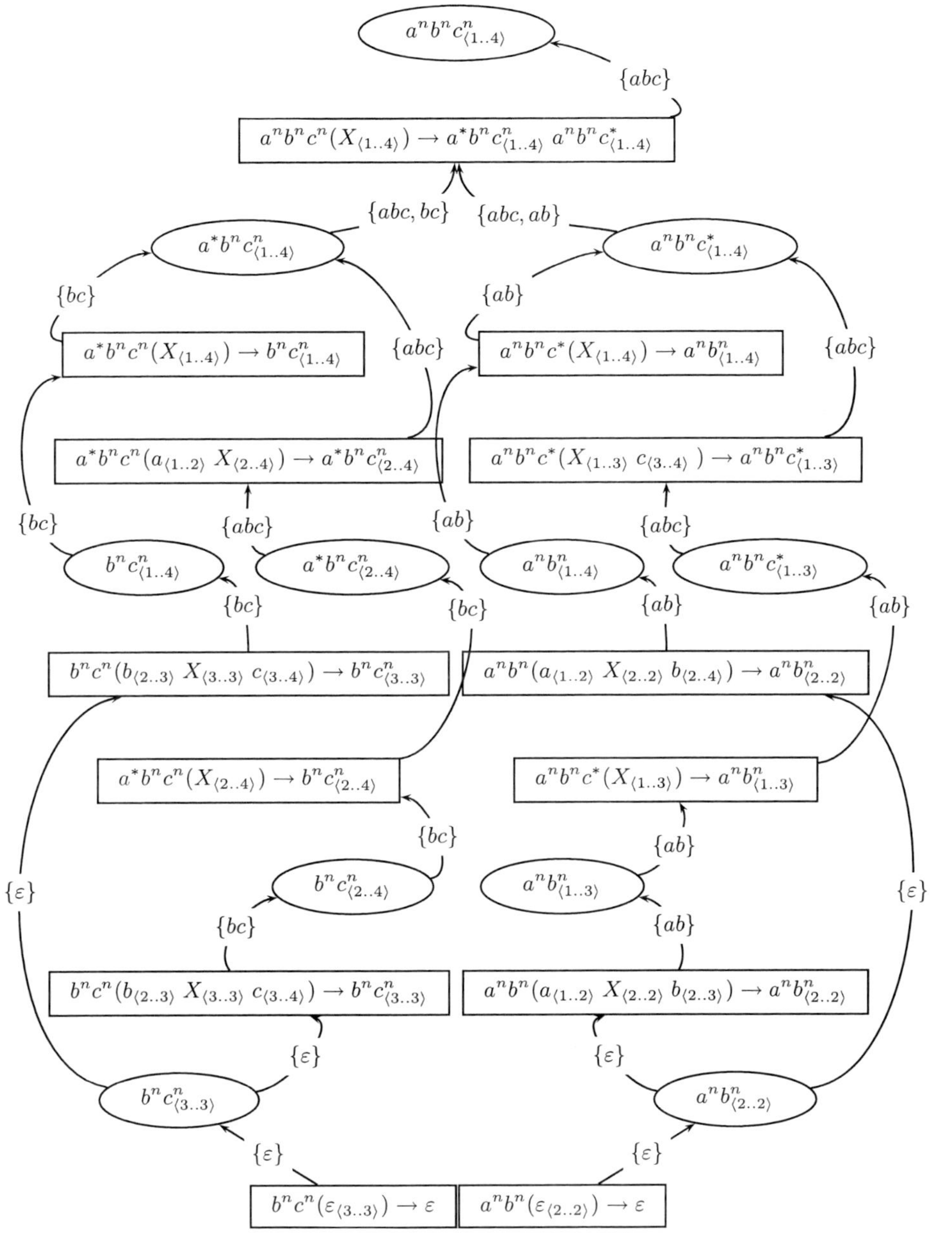

Figure 4: Bottom-up decorated parse forest for the input DAG $abc|ab|bc$.

right forest (i.e., to get a PRCG parser — not a recognizer — which accepts a DAG as input) we need to perform another walk on the previous decorated forest.

3.3.2 The Top-Down Walk

The idea of the top-down walk on the parse forest decorated by the bottom-up walk is to (re)compute all the previous decorations starting from the bottom-up decoration associated with the instantiated start predicate. It is to be noted that (the language defined by) each top-down decoration is a subset of its bottom-up counterpart. However, when a top-down decoration becomes empty, the corresponding subtree must be erased from the forest. If the bottom-up walk succeeds, we are sure that the top-down walk will not result in an empty forest. Moreover, if we perform a new bottom-up walk on this reduced forest, the new bottom-up decorations will denote the same language as their top-down decorations counterpart.

The forest is walked top-down starting from the super-root. The constraint being that an instantiated $A(\vec{\rho})$-clause is visited if and only if all the occurrences of $A(\vec{\rho})$ occurring in the RHS of instantiated clauses have all already been visited. This constraint can be satisfied for any non-cyclic forest.

Initially, we assume that each argument of each instantiated predicate has an empty decoration, except for the argument of the super-root which is decorated by the DAG R computed by the bottom-up pass.

Now, assume that a top-down decoration has been (fully) computed for each argument of the instantiated predicate $A_0(\vec{\rho_0})$. For each instantiated clause of the form $c_\rho = A_0(\vec{\rho_0}) \rightarrow A_1(\vec{\rho_1}) \ldots A_i(\vec{\rho_i}) \ldots A_m(\vec{\rho_m})$, we perform the following sequence:[12]

1. We perform the intersection of the top-down decoration of each argument of $A_0(\vec{\rho_0})$ with the decoration computed by the bottom-up pass for the same argument of the LHS predicate of c_ρ. If the result is empty, c_ρ is erased from the forest.

2. For each LHS argument, the previous results are dispatched over the symbols of this argument.[13] Thus, each instantiated LHS symbol occurrence is decorated by its own DAG. If the considered clause has several occurrences of the same variable in the LHS arguments (i.e., is bottom-up non-linear), we perform the intersection of these DAGs in order to leave a single decoration per instantiated variable. If an intersection results in an empty DAG, the current clause is erased from the forest.

3. The LHS instantiated variable decorations are propagated to the RHS arguments. This propagation may result in DAG concatenations when a RHS argument is made up of several variables (i.e., is combinatorial).

4. At last, we associate to each argument of $A_i(\vec{\rho_i})$ a new decoration which is computed as the union of its previous top-down decoration with the decoration just computed.

Example 3. *When we apply the previous algorithm to the bottom-up parse forest of Example 2, we get the top-down parse forest of Figure 5. In this parse forest, erased parts are laid out in light gray. The more noticable points w.r.t. the bottom-up forest are the decorations between* $\boxed{a^nb^nc^n(X_{\langle 1..4\rangle}) \rightarrow a^*b^nc^n_{\langle 1..4\rangle}\ a^nb^nc^*_{\langle 1..4\rangle}}$ *and its RHS predicates* ($a^*b^nc^n_{\langle 1..4\rangle}$) *and* ($a^nb^nc^*_{\langle 1..4\rangle}$) *which are changed both to* $\{abc\}$ *instead of* $\{abc, bc\}$ *and* $\{abc, ab\}$*. These two changes induce the indicated erasings.*

[12]The decoration of each argument of $A_i(\vec{\rho_i})$ is either initially empty or has already been partially computed.

[13]Assume that $\vec{\rho_0}[k] = \langle p..q\rangle_D$, that the decoration DAG associated with the kth argument of $A_0(\vec{\rho_0})$ is $D'_{\langle p..q\rangle} = (Q'_{\langle p..q\rangle}, \Sigma_{\langle p..q\rangle}, \delta'_{\langle p..q\rangle}, p', F'_{\langle p..q\rangle})$ (we have $\mathcal{L}(D'_{\langle p..q\rangle}) \subseteq \mathcal{L}(D_{\langle p..q\rangle})$) and that $\vec{\alpha_0}[k] = \alpha^1_k X \alpha^2_k$ and that $\langle i..j\rangle_D$ is the instantiation of the symbol X in c_ρ. Our goal is to extract from $D'_{\langle p..q\rangle}$ the decoration DAG $D'_{\langle i..j\rangle}$ associated with that instantiated occurrence of X. This computation can be helped if we maintain, associated with each decoration DAG a function, say d, which maps each state of the decoration DAG to a set of states (bounds) of the input DAG D. If, as we have assumed, D is minimal, each set of states is a singleton, we can write $d(p') = p$, $d(f') = q$ for all $f' \in F'_{\langle p..q\rangle}$ and more generally $d(i') \in Q$ if $i' \in Q'$. Let $I' = \{i' \mid i' \in Q'_{\langle p..q\rangle} \wedge d(i') = i\}$ and $J' = \{j' \mid j' \in Q'_{\langle p..q\rangle} \wedge d(j') = j\}$. The decoration DAG $D'_{\langle i..j\rangle}$ is such that $\mathcal{L}(D'_{\langle i..j\rangle}) = \bigcup_{i' \in I', j' \in J'} \{x \mid x \text{ is a path from } i' \text{ to } j'\}$. Of course, together with the construction of $D'_{\langle i..j\rangle}$, its associated function d must also be built.

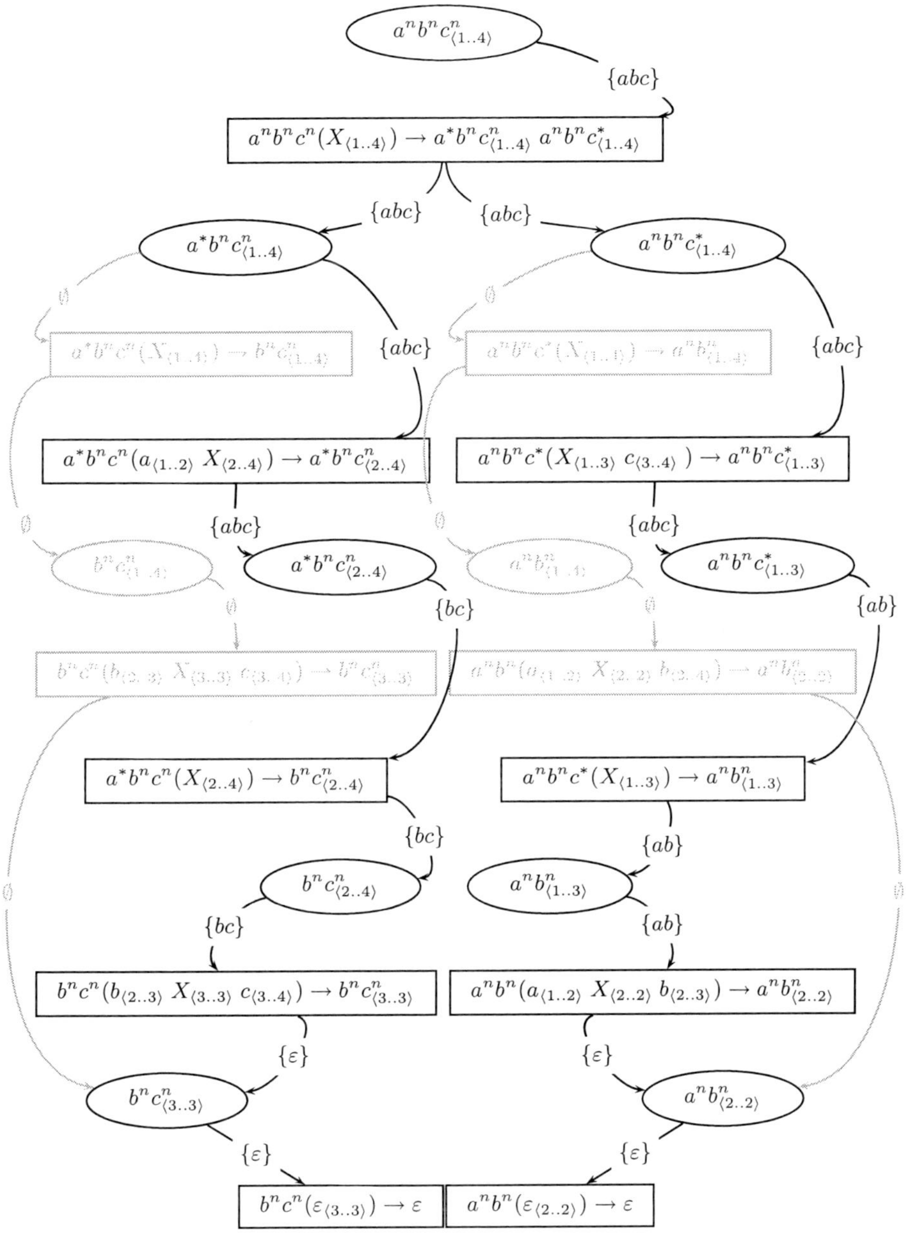

Figure 5: Top-down decorated parse forest for the input DAG $abc|ab|bc$.

3.4 Time and Space Complexities

In this Section we study the time and size complexities of the forest filtering algorithm.

Let us consider the sub-DAG $D_{\langle p..q \rangle}$ of the minimal input DAG D and consider any (finite) regular language $L \subseteq \mathcal{L}(D_{\langle p..q \rangle})$, and let D_L be the minimal DAG s.t. $\mathcal{L}(D_L) = L$. We show, on an example, that $|D_L|$ may be an exponential w.r.t. $|D_{\langle p..q \rangle}|$.

Consider, for a given $h > 0$, the language $(a|b)^h$. We know that this language can be represented by the minimal DAG with $h+1$ states of Figure 6.

Assume that $h = 2k$ and consider the sub-language L_{2k} of $(a|b)^{2k}$ (nested well-parenthesized strings) which is defined by

1. $L_2 = \{aa, bb\}$;

2. $k > 1$, $L_{2k} = \{axa, bxb \mid x \in L_{2k-2}\}$,

It is not difficult to see that the DAG in Figure 7 defines L_{2k} and is minimal, but its size $2^{k+2} - 2$ is an exponential in the size $2k+1$ of the minimal DAG for the language $(a|b)^{2k}$.

This results shows that, there exist cases in which some minimal DAGs D' that define sub-languages of minimal DAGs D may have a exponential size (i.e., $|D'| = \mathcal{O}(2^{|D|})$. In other words, when, during the bottom-up or top-down walk, we compute union of DAGs, we may fall on these pathologic DAGs that will induce a combinatorial explosion in both time and space.

3.5 Implementation Issues

Of course, many improvements may be brought to the previous principle algorithms in practical implementations. Let us cite two of them. First it is possible to restrict the number of DAG copies: a DAG copy is not useful if it is the last reference to that DAG.

We shall here devel the second point on a little more: if an argument of a predicate is never *used* in ant non-linearity, it is only a waste of time to compute its decoration. We say that A^k, the kth argument of the predicate A is a *non-linear predicate argument* if there exists a clause c in which A occurs in the RHS and whose k^{th} argument has at least one common variable another argument B^h of some predicate B of the RHS (if $B = A$, then of course k and h must be different). It is clear that B^h is then non-linear as well. It is not difficult to see that decorations needs only to be computed if they are associated with a non-linear predicate argument. It is possible to compute those non-linear predicate arguments statically (when building the parser) when the PRCG is defined within a single module. However, if the PRCG is given in several modules, this full static computation is no longer possible. The non-linear predicate arguments must thus be identified at parse time, when the whole grammar is available. This rather trivial algorithm will not be described here, but it should be noted that it is worth doing since in practice it prevents decoration computations which can take an exponential time.

4 Conclusion

In this paper we have shown how PRCGs can handle DAGs as an input. If we consider the linear PRCG, the one equivalent to LCFRS, the parsing time remains polynomial. Moreover, input DAGs necessitate only rather cosmetic modifications in the standard parser.

In the non-linear case, the standard parser may produce illegal parses in its output shared parse forest. It may even produce a (non-empty) shared parse forest though no sentences of the input DAG are in the language defined by our non-linear PRCG. We have proposed a method which uses the (slightly modified) standard parser but prunes, within extra passes, its output forest and leaves all and only valid parses. During these extra bottom-up and top-down walks, this pruning involves the computation of finite languages by means of concatenation, union and intersection operations. The sentences of these finite languages are always substrings of the words of the input DAG D. We choose to represent these intermediate finite languages by DAGs instead of sets of strings because the size of a DAG is, at worst, of the same order as the size of a set of strings but it could, in some cases, be exponentially smaller.

However, the time taken by this extra pruning pass cannot be guaranteed to be polynomial, as expected from previously known complexity results (Bertsch and Nederhof, 2001). We have shown an example in which pruning takes an exponential time and space in the size of D. The deep reason comes from the fact that if L is a finite (regular) language defined by some minimal DAG D, there are cases where a sub-language of

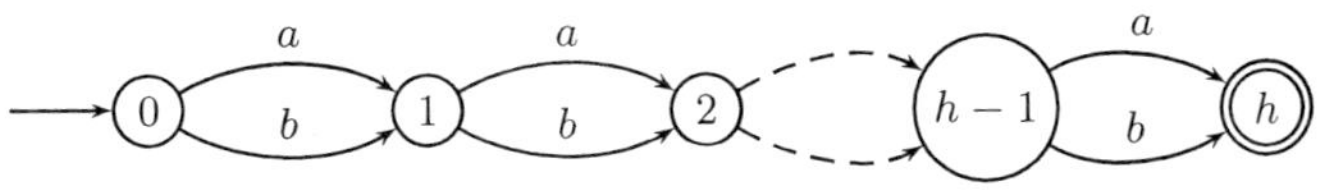

Figure 6: Input DAG associated with the language $(a|b)^h$, $h > 0$.

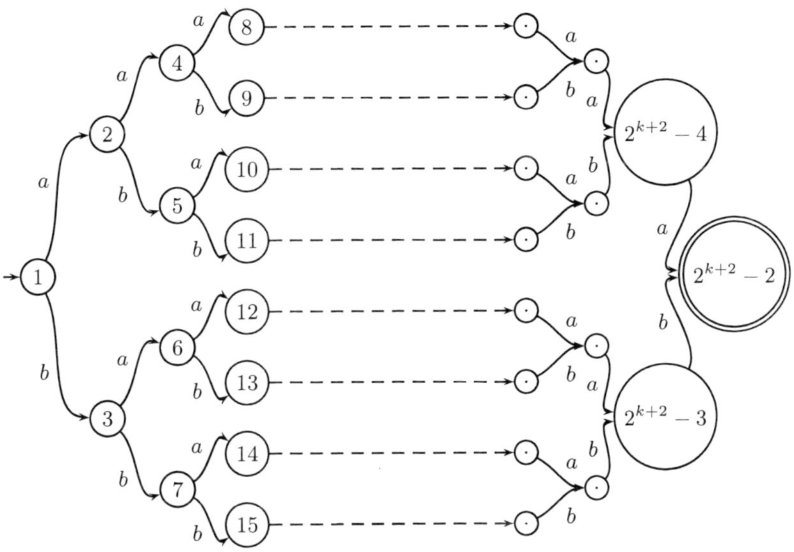

Figure 7: DAG associated with the language of nested well-parenthesized strings of length $2k$.

L may require to be defined by a DAG whose size is an exponential in the size of D. Of course this combinatorial explosion is not a fatality, and we may wonder whether, in the particular case of NLP it will practically occur?

References

Franois Barthélemy, Pierre Boullier, Philippe Deschamp, and Éric de la Clergerie. 2001. Guided parsing of range concatenation languages. In *Proceedings of the 39th Annual Meeting of the Association for Comput. Linguist. (ACL'01)*, pages 42–49, University of Toulouse, France.

Eberhard Bertsch and Mark-Jan Nederhof. 2001. On the complexity of some extensions of rcg parsing. In *Proceedings of IWPT'01*, Beijing, China.

Pierre Boullier, 2004. *New Developments in Parsing Technology*, volume 23 of *Text, Speech and Language Technology*, chapter Range Concatenation Grammars, pages 269–289. Kluwer Academic Publishers, H. Bunt, J. Carroll, and G. Satta edition.

Jeffrey D. Hopcroft and John E. Ullman. 1979. *Introduction to Automata Theory, Languages, and Computation*. Addison-Wesley, Reading, Mass.

Bernard Lang. 1994. Recognition can be harder than parsing. *Computational Intelligence*, 10(4):486–494.

K. Vijay-Shanker, David Weir, and Aravind K. Joshi. 1987. Characterizing structural descriptions produced by various grammatical formalisms. In *Proceedings of the 25th Meeting of the Association for Comput. Linguist. (ACL'87)*, pages 104–111, Stanford University, CA.

Author Index

Association for Computational Linguistics
209 N. Eighth Street
Stroudsburg, Pennsylvania 18360

CURRAN ASSOCIATES INC
proceedings.com

4th International Conference on the "Hydrology of the Great Rivers of Africa"

Hydrology of Large River Basins of Africa

Proceedings of the International Association of Hydrological Sciences (PIAHS) Volume 384, 2021

Cotonou, Benin
16 – 20 November 2021

IAHS AISH